Mexico's Hope

To Susan

MEXICO'S HOPE
An Encounter with Politics and History

James D. Cockcroft

Monthly Review Press
New York

Library of Congress Cataloging-in-Publication Data

Cockcroft, James D.
    Mexico's hope : an encounter with politics and history / James D. Cockcroft.
       p.   cm.
    Includes bibliographic references and index.
    ISBN 0-85345-926-6 (cloth). — ISBN 0-85345-925-8 (pbk.)
    1. Mexico—Economic conditions. 2. Mexico—Social conditions.
    3. Social conflict—Mexico—History. 4. Mexico—History.
    I. Title.
    HC133.C62   1998
    330.972—dc21   98-46777
                                            CIP

Maps courtesy of Cambridge University Press

Illustrations by Rini Templeton

Monthly Review Press
122 West 27th Street
New York NY 10001

Manufactured in the United States of America

10 9 8 7 6 5 4 3 2 1

CONTENTS

MAPS AND TABLES

ACKNOWLEDGMENTS

This book represents many years of research, during which so many workers, peasants, students, and scholars of Mexico have assisted me that it would be impossible to list them all. I especially want to thank my Mexican colleagues Alejandro Alvarez Béjar, Enrique Semo, Sergio de la Peña, and Edur Velasco Arregui for their intellectual help in my work over the years, and Edgard Sánchez Ramírez for his similar assistance in 1997-1998. Edur Velasco Arregui's preparation of the statistical tables and his commentary on them added greatly to the value of this book. A very special thanks goes to another valuable Mexico City colleague, Heather Dashner Monk, and to longtime friend Ross Gandy of Cuernavaca, both of whom provided me important insights into Mexico.

Many colleagues in the United States and Europe have also been generous with their critical suggestions. In the notes I acknowledge them and their works. I especially want to thank historians John M. Hart and Friedrich Katz for their consulting with me over the years on U.S. archival materials concerning U.S. acts of intervention in the Mexican Revolution. I also wish to thank historian and labor analyst Dan La Botz for his helpful suggestions and insights given me in both Mexico and the United States, 1997-1998.

My work has been aided by several research projects I conducted in Mexico in the early 1980s and again in 1997. My 1980s work was assisted by a Fulbright-Hays Research Grant on migration and border problems and a Visiting Professorship, Departamento de Sociologia, Universidad Autónoma Metropolitana (UAM-Azcapotzalco), Mexico City, 1980-1981.

Some of this book's seminal ideas appeared in earlier forms in the following works of mine: *Intellectual Precursors of the Mexican Revolution, 1900-19!3* (Austin: University of Texas Press, 1968; paperback ed. with "Note to Chicano Readers," 1976); chapter on Mexico in Ronald Chilcote and Joel Edelstein, eds., *Latin America: The Struggle with Dependency and Beyond* (Cambridge, MA: Schenkman, 1974); *El imperialismo, la lucha de clases y el estado en Mexico* (Mexico City: Nuestro Tiempo, 1979); "Subordinated Technological Development: The Case of Mexico," in *Research in Social Movements, Conflicts and Change*, vol. 4, ed. Louis Kriesberg, (Greenwich, CT: JAI Press, Inc., 1981); (with UAM-Azcapotzalco Migration Research Team) *Trabajadores de Michoacán: Historia de un pueblo migrante* (Mexico City: imisac, Ediciones Contraste,

1982); "Immiseration, Not Marginalization: The Case of Mexico," in Nora Hamilton and Timothy F. Harding (eds.), *Modern Mexico: State, Economy, and Social Conflict* (Beverly Hills: Sage, 1986); *Mexico: Class Formation, Capital Accumulation, and the State* (New York: Monthly Review Press, 1983, 1990); and *Latin America: History, Politics, and U.S. Policy* (Chicago: Nelson-Hall Publishers, 1996).

Special thanks go to indexer Elliot Linzer; to Cambridge University Press for the maps; and to editor Ethan Young and the entire staff of Monthly Review Press. I also want to extend a special memory of thanks to graphic artist and good friend Rini Templeton (d. 1986); to my late best friend Hedda Garza (d. 1995); and to another late friend, that dynamo of Monthly Review Press, Judy Ruben (d. 1997). All three of these individuals inspired countless people with their selfless lives of commitment to the cause of social justice and also helped me personally in analyzing political and historical events in Mexico and elsewhere.

Most of all, I want to thank my colleague Susan Caldwell for her keen insights into issues of gender, race, and class, and for her many helpful suggestions that hopefully have made this book both theoretically precise and an easy, enjoyable read. Her theoretical acumen has assisted me immensely.

Friends Lake, Chestertown, N.Y.
September 15, 1998

INTRODUCTION

Modern Mexico's Encounter with History

MEXICO REACHES THE NEW MILLENNIUM wracked with political crisis and economic uncertainty. As the United States' second largest trading partner after Canada, it is moving to the world's center stage.

Nearly 4,000 increasingly high-tech assembly plants (*maquiladoras*) exploit a largely female workforce at miserable wages. U.S. companies draw profit rates from these plants nearly double those in the rest of Latin America. A strike at one of the *maquiladoras* could trigger layoffs of thousands of U.S. workers who are dependent on parts assembled there, while a strike at a plant in the United States could lead to a shutdown and a move to Mexico.

Economists call it the "silent integration" of the two nations' economies. U.S. trade-union activists excoriate it as shameless exploitation of labor. Corporate executives laud it as "good sensible business." U.S. State Department analysts call it "mutual dependence." But because so much more wealth flows out of Mexico than into it, a lot of Mexicans and even some U.S. scholars call it "imperialism."

Mexico's semi-industrialized capitalist economy is rife with paradoxes. An agrarian nation imports its tortillas: one-fifth of the corn eaten in corn-growing Mexico comes from the United States. Mexico's stores brim with goods made by transnational corporations. For example, supermarkets regularly display shelves of toilet paper in different brands, textures, colors, and prices, but few Mexicans can afford any of them: most use newspaper or, in the countryside, a smooth stone. The many models of automobiles that choke Mexico City's streets, exhaling a veil of smog that envelopes the central plateau, are owned by 13 percent of the residents; everyone else spends four hours a day going to and from work on overloaded buses and subways.

Mexico has a home market that potentially could build on economies of scale based on abundant resources, starting with its hard-working people. Mexico's estimated population in 1998 was 95 million people, increasing by 1.94 percent a year, with nearly 90 percent of the adult workforce able to read and write. Besides its immense oil and natural gas reserves, Mexico is well-endowed with natural resources like coal, coke, copper, fluorspar, gold, graphite, iron, lead, manganese, mercury, rubber, silver, sulfur, uranium, and zinc. Its steel industry ranks among the world's top fifteen, just behind Canada. Its

1

factories provide all sorts of consumer goods, but for the most part they do so as assembly operations—importing, mainly from the United States, 90 percent of the needed capital and intermediate goods (machinery, materials, and spare parts). Mexico is a major producer of crude oil, automobiles, and agricultural products, but mainly for export to the United States.

Mexico also exports workers to the United States, boosting both nations' economies. U.S. labor unions and jobless Americans complain about "millions" of Mexicans crossing into their territory. These migrants find temporary or longer term work and take home to Mexico what is left of their wages—after they pay their living expenses and pay off the traffickers and loan sharks who "help" in their migration. The immigrant flow provides cheap nonunion labor to U.S. agribusinesses, hotels, restaurants, automotive plants, electronics factories, and garment producers who increasingly rely on such labor. Despite new harsh laws against immigrants, the U.S. government allows the Mexican immigrants to go on cleaning toilets in Houston, packing meat in Chicago, picking crops in California's Imperial Valley, and assembling parts in Los Angeles and other cities in exchange for easier and cheaper U.S. access to Mexican oil and natural gas—and because capitalists like to blame the immigrants for economic problems such as unemployment or sagging real wages for U.S. workers. Employers bolster their sagging rates of profit through exploiting Mexican and other immigrants.

U.S. and other foreign investors have billions of dollars invested in Mexico, where their profit rates surpass the world average because of abundant cheap labor. Two-thirds of foreign investment is in the hands of U.S.-based transnational corporations. After the North American Free Trade Agreement (NAFTA) went into effect, foreign investment rose to $8 billion or more a year. Some of it went into manufacturing, but most of it fueled Mexico's world-scale stock market. A third of the stock market's transactions went through U.S. markets, where Mexican firms account for 11 percent of foreign stocks traded. The upper 5 percent of Mexicans grew richer (the number of Mexican billionaires rose from two to twenty-four), while most of the rest of the population received a dwindling share of national income.

Then, in the twelfth month of NAFTA, the financial bubble burst, investors pulled out, and in 1995 Mexico's economy sank to rock bottom. The "recovery" that followed was as unstable as the "NAFTA miracle" had been. More than ever before, Mexico's economy "petrolized" and "maquiladorized."

Meanwhile, some 40 million rag-clad Mexicans wander across the volcanic landscape of mountainous escarpments, eroded hillsides, drought-plagued valleys, arid deserts, and overcrowded cities, following the harvest trail or searching for a day's work. They are the struggling families, landless peasants, migrant workers, urban jobless, single mothers, sierra Indians, abandoned children, homeless beggars, and occasional bandits. Many of these immiserated have no identity papers; they are "undocumented aliens" in their own country. Three million are street vendors in the teeming capital, Mexico City—the world's most populous urban center (22 million), veiled in smog generated by industrial smokestacks and snarled automobile traffic. Less than 40 percent of the workforce is regularly employed, and only one-third of those earn the minimum wage, sufficient for less than half of what a family of five needs to maintain itself.

Nearly one-fifth of all Mexicans receive incomes lower than those in Haiti and Nicaragua, Latin America's poorest countries. Mexico's handful of rich people live in luxurious homes protected by extensive security patrols and two-story-high walls topped with jagged glass. The bottom half of the population, including 90 percent of all preschool children, suffers from malnutrition and goes barefoot. They have no plumbing, no safe drinking water, no electricity. Their income is seldom more than twenty-five cents (U.S.) per person per day.

"Today is like yesterday," wails a Mexican popular song, "in a world without tomorrow. How sad the rain beats on the tin roofs of the cardboard houses."

How long will the majority of Mexicans put up with being exploited on both sides of the Mexican-U.S. border? Why doesn't all that oil and natural gas benefit the poor? Why doesn't the money pay for medical care, housing, and education? Why instead are government bureaucrats, domestic and foreign capitalists, and narcotraffickers free to invest it largely outside of Mexico or stash it in secret bank accounts? How can capital investment in Mexico increase or profits be maintained at their traditional levels without a low wage scale, and how can low wages be guaranteed unless unemployment and underemployment in turn guarantee a "reserve army of the unemployed"? This is the dilemma of Mexico's capitalist economy.

Why is Mexico's labor so cheap? Why has Mexico become the central pivot of U.S. relations with Latin America? What is the debt crisis all about? What factors lie behind the sudden rise in drug trafficking and the sudden interest in creating NAFTA? Could a military coup happen in "stable" Mexico? To answer these questions we need to review Mexico's amazing history, much as Mexicans themselves are doing.

In this book I attempt a comprehensive analysis of the Mexican political economy and the current state crisis, by tracing their historical roots in the process of class struggle, capital accumulation, and the emergence of the modern authoritarian-technocratic state. I examine the interweaving of interests of domestic elites with those of stronger foreign powers, from Spanish colonialism to U.S. imperialism. I also analyze the periodic conflicts between such interests. The origins of the economic system and the state crisis are traced to a long, uneven historical process of state formation, changes in the

organization of economic production, accumulation by ruling groups of
the wealth produced by Mexico's workers, and internal and international
conflict.

The book is divided into two parts. Part I traces the process of capital
accumulation and state and class formation from the time of the earliest
Mexican states, through the colonial period of Spanish rule, to the birth of the
independent nation. It is written in the belief that to understand modern
Mexico we must delve into the history of its diverse peoples—each with unique
customs and heritage—and their struggles to define and control the state and
the economy through their repeated uprisings against domestic and foreign
oppressors. Part I goes on to analyze Mexico's post-Independence civil and
foreign wars and the rise of the "liberal" dictatorship of Porfirio Díaz, toppled
by the Revolution of 1910 to 1920. Recently uncovered archival materials help
document U.S. intervention that helped defeat the Revolution. More important, however, in causing the Revolution's defeat were the internal class splits
in the peoples' revolutionary ranks and the gender and racial biases of most of
the revolutionary leadership. Part I concludes by examining the consolidation
of the roots of the modern capitalist corporatist state during the social
upheavals of the 1930s.

Part II examines the development of monopoly capitalism after 1940 and
the class structure of contemporary Mexico, with particular emphasis on how
both were affected by state policies and the impact of immense U.S. investments
and cultural influences. Part II takes up themes like the "new international
division of labor";[1] the relative decapitalization of Mexico caused by foreign
capital and its alliance with domestic elites and the state; the role of the
intermediate ("middle") classes, and of students and intellectuals; the immiseration of the majority of Mexicans and yet their centrality to capital accumulation and their rising political activism; the central role of women and Indians
in class struggle to change Mexico; and new waves of labor militancy among
the nation's industrial and rural proletariats.

The final chapters examine economic neoliberalism and privatization,[2]
NAFTA, the "free trade wars," and what all this meant for Mexico. I analyze
here the roles of Mexico's elections and "political reform" (projecting to the
year 2000); the new Zapatistas and other guerrillas; the national security forces;
the narcotraffickers and the "narco-state alliance"; the Church; the mass media;
U.S.-Mexican relations; and the "border wars" accompanying the migratory
flow of Mexican workers to the United States.

Each chapter in this book includes, where appropriate, explanations of
concepts or terms being introduced. Further theoretical elaboration may be
found in the notes. A glossary of frequently used abbreviations and Spanish
terms is included at the end of the book. Concerning the statistics and research
offered here, historical and contemporary statistics must be treated with a

certain caution. The tables and figures presented cannot pretend to some ideal level of exactitude; there are too many controversies to permit that. They do, however, reflect a consensus among scholars or, in case of doubt, the more modest of the estimates available. The main purpose is to show proportions, not to give exact figures. In the case of the factual record of events, personalities, and the historical course of social change, only in cases of new research or of sufficient doubt or controversy are points amplified in the text or notes. There exists an abundant literature on Mexico (more than that on any other Latin American country), and numerous examples are included in the notes and referred to in the bibliographical commentary.

Throughout the book I emphasize the structural forces underlying Mexico's incomplete industrialization, as well as the many instances of popular resistance to oppression, and of peoples' struggles to change Mexico for the better. The final chapters and conclusion build off this approach to outline possible alternative scenarios to neoliberalism and NAFTA, and to document how in the mid-1990s some of these scenarios actually began gaining practical support from growing numbers of working women and men of all three NAFTA countries.

The stability and legitimacy of the world's longest lasting ruling party, Mexico's PRI, is no longer taken for granted. Why? Despite frequent setbacks, over several decades wave after wave of popular resistance to Mexico's one-party, corporatist state and to the domestic and foreign bourgeoisies it was servicing had swelled into a veritable tide. The state made various adjustments to this challenge, growing more sophisticated in its mixture of repression, concessions, revolutionary rhetoric, and acknowledgment of its failures. Some Mexicans grew cynical and despaired of ever changing "the system" that kept them down. Others, however, developed a stubborn hope that their struggles would not be in vain.

Their hope became Mexico's hope, and that hope is the *leitmotif* of this book. In the final analysis, their hope was based on modern Mexico's encounter with history. In the words of a February 1994 communiqué "from the mountains of the Mexican Southeast" sent by the Zapatista guerrillas to their supporters throughout Mexico:

> For years and years we harvested the death of our people. . . . The oldest of the old of our peoples spoke words to us...about when our voice was silenced. And [in] the truth . . . came hope for our history. And in their word appeared the image of one like us: Emiliano Zapata. And in it we saw the place toward which our feet should walk in order to be true, and our history of struggle returned to our blood. . . . Our strength had to break down those [bad government] walls in order to enter our history again, the history they had snatched away from us, along with the dignity and reason of our peoples. In that first blow to the deaf walls of those who have everything, the blood of our people, our blood, ran generously to wash away injustice. To live, we die. Our dead once again walked

the way of truth. Our hope was fertilized with mud and blood. But the oldest of
the old of our peoples didn't stop. It spoke the truth, saying that our feet couldn't
walk alone, that our history of pain and shame was repeated and multiplied in
the flesh and blood of the brothers and sisters of other lands and skies . . . walking
in step with you and with all the good people of this world, we will have to grow
and finally find the place that our dignity and our history deserve.[3]

PART I

A Troubled History

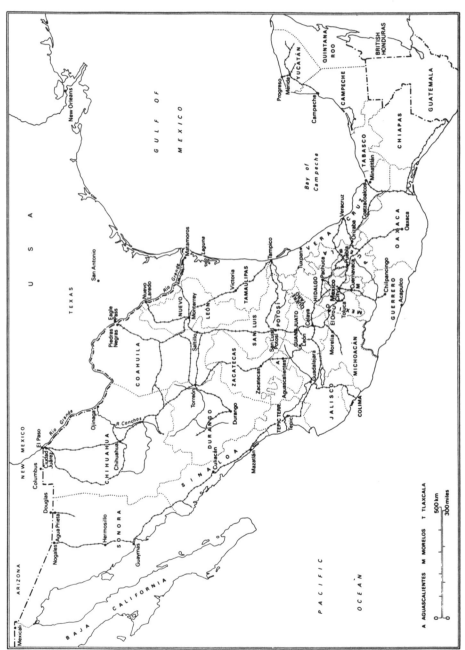

Revolutionary Mexico

CHAPTER I

Invasion, Colonization, and the Beginnings of Mexican Capitalism

I come for gold, not to till the land like a peasant.

—Hernán Cortés

THE PRECOLONIAL AND COLONIAL CONDITIONS in Mexico set the basis for its state and class formation and for the subsequent development of a capitalist economy sharply divided between rich and poor. In colonial times, Mexico was known as "New Spain," an area then encompassing today's Central America and the U.S. Southwest (including Texas and California).

This chapter has a multiple approach. First, it documents the deep colonial roots of Mexico's current economic problems in the history of Mexico's uneven economic development. Second, it looks at matters from the different points of view of the Mexican people, in terms of a social histroy marked by race, gender, and class. Specifically, these groupings include the darker-skinned laboring masses; the lighter-skinned, usually white elites; the Spanish invaders (*conquistadores*) and their descendants, who often had interests different from not only those of the masses but also those of the colonial authorities of the monarchy governing Spain; and finally, the representatives of the colonial state. Third, the chapter lays out the history of popular resistance to oppression by the lower classes, including the important roles played by women. Finally, the chapter relates earlier events to later ones, occasionally moving across entire centuries at a single bound. It is important for the reader to know from the outset the *socioeconomic* (rather than political) periodization of Mexican history adopted here.

The precolonial period incorporates the creation of Mexico's great indigenous civilizations prior to the arrival of the Spaniards in 1519. In pre-colonial times, strong centralized states emerged, resulting in the establishment of the Aztec empire.

The early-to-late colonial period (1519-1770) witnessed the Spanish overthrow of the Aztecs and the emergence of an embryonic dependent capitalism stimulated by merchant capital and under the tutelage of a powerful colonial state. Colonial times saw mass impoverishment for most of Mexico's original inhabitants and limited or blocked upward mobility for those who worked the land. These conditions triggered repeated popular uprisings (often called *tumultos*, or riots) that ultimately threatened Mexico's ties to the Spanish "mother country" and, more importantly, challenged the power of the colony's traditional elites and nascent bourgeoisie.

The late colonial and early postcolonial period (1770-1880) was an ongoing but often disrupted process of uneven capitalist development. It started at a time of radical changes in Europe and North America, when Spain undertook a series of reforms in its colonial policies. For Mexico, the result of these changes was an era of dynamic economic growth, accompanied by even harsher suffering for the agrarian population.

This fostered an intensification of class conflict between Mexico's rich and poor that erupted in a series of three disruptive political moments: from 1810 to 1822, Mexicans won national independence; from 1846 to 1848, the United States militarily seized nearly half of the new republic's territory, including most of today's U.S. Southwest and California; and from 1854 to 1867, Mexico's elites squabbled in a civil war over the nature of the state and its relations with the Catholic Church. During the latter period, France invaded and occupied Mexico in 1861. A national liberation movement freed the country from the French in 1867 and set up a bourgeois-democratic state that soon gave way to an oligarchic-dictatorial one. Both states were committed to replacing the already dissolving mercantilist-capitalist mode of accumulation of the previous period with a more purely capitalist mode, one capable of industrializing Mexico and generating capitalist accumulation on an extended scale. This process gained momentum during subsequent decades.

The main laborers in the process of economic change transforming Mexico after the Spanish invasion were the indigenous peoples, known in Mexico as "Indians" (even though each indigenous group had its own name and its own language or dialect)—and, later, the various racial mixes of people that emerged after widespread raping of women by Spanish settlers and intermarriages. Mexico's rigid colonial system of race, class, and gender hierarchies had a built-in social pecking order defined by the power of the *conquistadores* and of the monarchy and Church they represented. Spaniards were at the top of the social pyramid, followed by successful *criollos* (whites born in Mexico), mestizos (of mixed Spanish/Indian descent), mulattos (of mixed black and white descent), *negros* (Africans), and, at the bottom, Indians. The mixing of all the different races created what were known as the *castas*—mestizos, mulattos, *zambos* (Afro-Indians), Afromestizos, etc.—or, in the eyes of the Spaniards and those *criollos* making it into the upper class, "the unwashed rabble" that launched the *tumultos*. Although in time Mexico's racism became less severe than what developed in the United States, it functioned in the colonial period to place people in rigid economic niches that limited geographical mobility and discouraged economic dynamism.

In class terms, Mexico's social pyramid was built upon a mass base of peasants and wage-workers. At the apex were a small number of government, religious, and military authorities and privileged families in commerce, mining, agriculture, and nascent manufacturing. Some of these elites, whether Spanish or *criollo*, eventually evolved into an early productive bourgeoisie, but the process was a limited and uneven one.

As is well known, the European colonization of the original peoples of Mexico and Latin America was a violent affair and, for some, an extraordinarily profitable one. Precious metals produced by different types of highly exploited labor fueled a vast accumulation of wealth in Europe. New Spain provided Europe with gold, silver, and a number of other valuable primary products, including cochineal dye and medicinal plants important in the development of European textile manufacturing and medicine.

Globally, mercantilist trade aided by powerful states, a growing division of labor, and outright plunder characterized this period of what Marx called "the original accumulation of capital," the necessary condition for the development of capitalism. It was a time when there grew in northern Europe an economic surplus sufficient to initiate the reproduction of a surplus on an extended basis, "the rosy dawn for the era of capitalist production."[1]

Elements of division of labor and original accumulation of capital directed by strong states existed in the advanced indigenous civilizations of pre-Spanish Mexico as well. The Spaniards made relatively good, if opportunistic, use of these legacies. In the course of time, the economic changes that they fomented laid the groundwork for the emergence of a new kind of system: an unevenly developed capitalism with a strong state heavily influenced by outside forces.

Mexico's post-colonial process of capital accumulation was largely defined in colonial times by the habitual tendency of the country's elites to ignore the "home market" by sending their mining and agricultural surpluses abroad. New Spain's wealthy landowners, miners, and merchants paid the work force that produced these surpluses at below the value of a worker's labor power— that is, below the amount needed by the worker to maintain minimal support for self and/or family. (This "superexploitation" is examined in more detail in Chapter 5.) Consequently, there was rarely any surplus left over among New Spain's working families with which to expand consumption of goods, further limiting the size of the home market.

With cheap labor so readily at hand, Mexico's colonial elites displayed little interest in modernizing the forces of production with the new technologies being applied in European or North American transportation and industry. Mexico's subsequent unequal exchange of products with foreign powers derived from this early colonial shaping of the character of capital accumulation and its correspondingly low level of productivity.

The nature of Mexico's economy was strongly influenced by the colonial state and church. By imposing a medley of surcharges on all economic transactions, including the recruitment of labor at a royal labor exchange called the *repartimiento*, the state made it difficult for anyone to engage in any economic activity other than one directly related to production for the "mother country." The Crown routinely collected its "royal fifth" *(quinto real)* of all colonial trade revenues, including a fifth of the value of Mexico's exported precious metals. State institutions had little interest in investing in public works or much economic infrastructure.

For its part, the Catholic Church collected its 10 percent tithe (a tax called "*diezmo*") from owners of huge estates (*haciendas*), as well as peasants, artisans, and other small producers. The *diezmo*, collected in some rural areas even today, reduced economic surplus in Mexico while increasing it in European Church coffers.

As the Church grew wealthy in colonial Mexico, it also reinforced patriarchy and *machismo* (the ideology and practice of male supremacy with its corresponding emphasis on bravery, virility, women's intellectual "inferiority," women's assigned role to care for the family, etc.), expressions of which were already present in some of Mexico's Indian cultures. These customs were greatly expanded by Spanish and Catholic practices, with the result that the female half of the population experienced greater hardships and a restricted role in the colonial market economy, although women became a key part of the underpaid workforce in several areas (*e.g.,* tobacco, textiles, and production of the ceremonial drink *pulque*).

Women were viewed not only as sexual objects to be seized by force if necessary, but also as brood mares, expected to produce as many future laborers as possible—for without workers, economic surplus could not be generated. In the absence of generational production of labor power—that is, women having and raising babies who grow up to become workers generation after generation—no economy can exist for long. Women's unpaid family "duties" and household labor, as well as subsistence and handicraft production, added directly to the generation of economic surplus. Indeed, women's daily production of labor power at no cost to employers (family feeding, clothing, and educating; maintenance of community cohesion, etc.), then as now, made a huge contribution to the generation of wealth that to this day does not appear in statistics.[2]

Several modern-day customs in Mexico date from colonial times. One is *personalismo*, or defining social relations as "personal." Colonial state regulations protecting royal monopolies led to personal favors and graft in order to cut through red tape. The minuscule but growing intermediate classes of military junior officers, regular clergy, professionals, and intellectuals often depended on bribes for their advancement. This set an early precedent for Mexico's famous "*mordida*" (literally, "little bite," or bribe) and often proved both efficient and corrupt.

As Mexico experienced economic change, semi-enslaved Indians initially supplied the labor, generated some of the capital, and provided much of the necessary technology and social organization for the production of goods, especially in mining and agriculture. Eventually, Indians, Africans, the *castas*, and the majority of whites (losing the description "*criollos*") became subjugated as, in main part, "free" wage labor, that is, separated from the means of production, one of the fundamental preconditions for the emergence of the capitalist mode of production.

Throughout the colonial period, Indians and others from the lower classes launched revolts, with women often playing important and even leading roles. These rebellions were ruthlessly crushed. Meanwhile, the fruits of people's long days and nights of labor continued to be largely appropriated by the economic elites or their state allies, the royal bureaucrats.

Mexico's increased economic growth and the continued development of a home market in the eighteenth century—an embryonic capitalism stimulated by merchant capital in control of much of the appropriated mineral wealth— contributed to social change. Together with events in Europe triggered by the transition there from mercantile capitalism to early industrial capitalism, such internal economic growth helped to disarticulate older forms of production (communal, slave, petty-commodity, etc.) and to create the conditions for a renewed and more explosive outbreak of class conflict in "New Spain" that was about to occur.

First Peoples

Who the original peoples of Mexico were remains a subject of inquiry, but the radiocarbon (C-14) method of dating and other innovative methods have given rise to some areas of tentative agreement. The evidence suggests that humans have existed in America for at least 50,000 years and probably longer.[4]

The common view is that the first peoples originated in Asia, using the Bering Strait between Siberia and Alaska as a crossing place. Archaeological excavation in Mesoamerica (a region comprising considerable parts of present-day Mexico and the Central American states) has unearthed small wheeled objects, considered to be toys or cult objects. The early inhabitants of Mexico, then, were familiar with the principle of the wheel—although neither the wheel nor the plow were used, since there were no draught animals.

Agriculture developed early in Mesoamerica. Maize (corn) was the prevalent crop; beans, sapots (a kind of plum), squash, pumpkins, chile peppers, avocado pears, and tuber plants were also harvested. Some excavated agrarian villages in central Mexico date back at least 3,500 years. Archeologists have uncovered thousands of clay female heads and figures in these villages, implying that women had either temporal power or religious significance or both; the figures might be fertility gods.[5]

Many agricultural communities throughout Mexico conducted communal farming. Productive technology consisted of highly finished implements of stone, obsidian, and jade, as well as the wooden digging stick, or *coa*, still in use today.

The evolution of early impressive class-stratified "civilizations" such as those of the Olmecs, Monte Albán, the Maya, or Teotihuacán are the focus of much controversy. There is general agreement that the scientific, artistic, architectural, irrigation, and state-building achievements of these pre-Columbian societies could not have occurred without the production of an economic surplus (freeing portions of the population from direct food production), a significant division of labor, and a degree of political centralization in the form of a state representing the interests of a ruling elite.[6] Various pieces of research from diverse viewpoints have shown that social stratification, class conflict, and state systems of complex social organization had developed and flourished in Mexico long before the arrival of the Europeans.

All these early societies exhibited high levels of organizing labor and production; a growth in long-distance trade; and sometimes the development of cities much larger than any in Europe. The sheer size and the fine art of the monumental architecture, wall paintings, pottery, and sculpture suggest something less simple and egalitarian than either "primitive communism" or scattered "democratic city-states."

Noted for the highest intellectual achievements of pre-Columbian America, the Maya (Classic Period, A.D. 325-925) extended from the highlands of today's Guatemala and El Salvador to the semi-arid frontier zones of the Yucatán in Mexico. Trading with places as distant as South America's Pacific Coast, the Maya were ahead of the world's other peoples in astronomy, mathematics, architectural sculpture, graphology, mural art, and painting.[7]

Mayan social organization revolved around small agricultural villages of twenty to forty households, although some of their ceremonial centers were cities housing as many as 80,000 residents. Land was owned in common by lineage groups whose members were not permitted to marry within their own group. Each household farmed a plot of communal land. It is estimated that the Maya agricultural household could produce twice the food it needed in four months, leaving ample time to labor on public works, temples, and other services for the benefit of the upper classes. Despite their being exploited by those above them, "commoners" had a fairly comfortable standard of living in some regions.[8]

The absence of signs of large war fortifications has led many scholars to view Mayan societies as peaceful theocracies: independent city-states governed by a priesthood. Other scholars have concluded, however, that the Maya were ruled by "warrior kings." Egon Z. Vogt has hypothesized that the Maya had a democratic social organization, with religious and administrative functions distributed and rotated according to a complex system of time periods, services rendered, wealth, and social prestige. In other words, there was not a single professional group as such, and the nobility was not hereditary.

How the Mayan and other earlier civilizations disappeared remains unclear. A hiatus of detailed knowledge exists for the period between the end of the Classic pre-Columbian civilizations, *ca.* A.D. 1000, and the rise of the more secular, complex, class-divided societies encountered by the Spaniards, such as the Aztec empire (A.D. 1327-1519). Frequent explanations for the end of the earlier civilizations include natural catastrophes, famines, or epidemics (which of course were caused in part by leaders, since inadequate steps were taken to forestall their consequences), population growth exceeding food supplies (related to failures by ruling groups to distribute food fairly), class warfare, and warfare with other peoples. Conditions in early civilizations could become unbearable during times of inadequate food supplies, especially for women, as is reflected by lack of growth in physical stature over time and growing gaps between men and women in their heights, documented through examination of uncovered human remains.

Many scholars have concluded that expanding groups from Mexico's north swept down over the central plateau and on south, destroying the earlier civilizations. Rival states from other directions (e.g., that of the Mixtecans in the southeast) expanded as well.

From A.D. 900 to 1300, the Toltecs moved southward and gradually incorporated other peoples of central Mexico into a tribute system, extending their influence at least as far as Oaxaca and the Guatemalan highlands, either through conquest or alliance-building. Trade with Andean cultures apparently took place, explaining perhaps the appearance of metallurgy and related Peruvian techniques. The Toltecs mismanaged their affairs, however, suffering famines and falling victim to another invasion from the north—by the peoples known as the Chichimeca.

The Chichimeca extended their influence over the vast network of lakes that then constituted the Valley of Mexico, site of today's Mexico City. But they engaged in warfare among themselves. Consequently, many of them sought to consolidate their local societies into small tight-knit city-states. Then, in the fifteenth century, the Aztecs began to assert their power.

By the time of the Aztecs, new inventions in metallurgy, expanded irrigation works, more centralized social organization, greater contact between peoples, a higher degree of state centralization, and the supremacy of a military elite and secular nobility (rather than a priesthood) were all in evidence. Economically, the Aztecs accumulated surplus through conquest and tribute exacted from other states and peoples. The Aztecs also appropriated some of the producers from these other societies, forcing them to work on the construction of Tenochtitlán's irrigation and drainage system, to build the houses of the nobility, or to fight in further Aztec wars of expansion. A vastly expanded and improved system of irrigation, including the *chinampa* system (later misnamed "floating gardens"), together with increased division of labor, artisan production, and trade (which characterized other states as well, such as those of the Mixtecs and Zapotecs), generated a sizable economic surplus distributed among the Aztec elite of military officers, state bureaucrats, priests, and nobles.

Socially, the Aztecs' expanded material base of production enabled increased class differentiation. There was opportunity to improve one's station in life, even for slaves who could buy their freedom with war booty.

Politically, at the heart of the Aztec state were the *calpulli*. Translated literally, *calpulli* means "large house," an institution that antedated the Aztecs and was a community endowed with inalienable land that each member was obliged to work. Under the Aztecs, the *calpulli* became economic, religious, military, and (by the middle of the fifteenth century) administrative units. The *calpullec,* or head of the *calpulli,* was elected by community members. He was always from the same family, so that there developed a hereditary nobility. A council of elders supported the *calpullec.* The Aztec priesthood enjoyed economic independence, ran the *calpulli* schools, and brought other religions into its domain, smashing idols or, more commonly, incorporating other deities—much as the Spaniards later would do.[9]

In 1376 the Aztecs initiated the rank of "Chief Speaker," who, with his descendants, enjoyed the highest authority and exceptional rights, including polygamy. These descendants *(pipiltin)* added numbers to the nobility. In addition there existed a meritorious nobility, consisting largely of warriors who distinguished themselves in battle. Organized into military orders, they were awarded shares of tribute moneys and conquered lands, as well as high state offices. This military aristocracy became the authority that decided on the succession to the Chief Speaker, thereby removing this power from representatives of the *calpulli.* All nobles had the right to private land ownership; their estates were farmed by slaves and bondsmen.

Beneath the ruling elites were the merchants, artisans, and laboring classes. The merchants, some of whom shared the privileges of the nobility, helped the Aztecs in their expansion of wealth and power, often bringing back from their travels messages and useful military or political information. Wielding significant power, they had their own judiciary, but they always remained under the ultimate control of the ruling class. The merchants brought from the tropical lowlands raw materials for the artisans and took back the plateau's textile, pottery, and metal products. Yet they encountered limits to their ability to accumulate great wealth. Because of the *calpulli* system they had little chance to accumulate land, and they were not permitted to break into the tight guild structure of the artisans.

In Tenochtitlán's neighboring city Tlatelolco, the main marketplace, merchants enjoyed an economic autonomy that was rapidly moving an otherwise state-dominated system toward a free-market economy in commodities (though not in land and labor).[10] The *conquistador* Hernán Cortés reported 60,000 people gathering every day at Tlatelolco "to buy and sell every imaginable kind of merchandise." His aide, Captain Bernal Díaz del Castillo, marveled at the quantities of gold and silver products. He wrote: "Gazing on such wonderful sights we did not know what to say or whether what appeared before us was real." But Cortés knew it was real. He told the Aztecs, "We Spaniards are troubled by a disease of the heart for which the specific remedy is gold."[11]

The position of artisans in Aztec society was quite inferior to that of the merchants but above the rest of the working population. Artisans were permitted a voice in the city councils, and the more successful ones had sizable labor crews at their beck and call.

The working masses in Aztec society consisted of three groups: the freemen (*i.e.*, members of the *calpulli* who held most of the land in the Valley of Mexico and constituted more than half the Valley's population); the bondsmen, or *mayeques,* who composed a third of the Valley's population; and the so-called slaves, or *tlacotin,* who constituted about 5 percent of the population. (This does not include the numerous conquered peoples.)

In addition to these major groups in Aztec society there plied their trades various thieves, murderers, prostitutes, and so on. These miscellaneous elements grew in number as more traditional disciplines and loyalties began to disintegrate before the inexorable march of Aztec conquest and state centralization.

By 1500, the Aztec state ruled over a population of diverse peoples across Mesoamerica estimated at from 5 to 35 million.[12] Since the Aztecs were also known as the "Mexica," their rulers called their empire "Mexica" (in Spanish, Mexico). Yet they did not conquer, integrate, or administer all of Mesoamerica. Trade and military forays served to assert their hegemony. Aztec colonization was far less complete than the Spanish version that replaced it.

In their empire-building, the Aztecs sacrificed their prisoners to the gods—a likely reason for the remarkable "stability" of their rule. (Earlier ruling groups had also used human sacrifice as an instrument of statecraft.) Aztec religion asserted that sacrifice was necessary to keep the sun in movement through the sacrificial deaths, first of the gods and later of human beings. "Periods" of the sun ended in catastrophe, and the fifth period, coming to a close at the time of the Spanish invasion, had benefited the faithful with a new material basis for life: maize.[13]

In the last years of Aztec rule, human sacrifices notably increased—as did internal dissension within the Aztecs' domains, especially from other Indian societies, which revolted in various parts of Mexica. The Aztec system contained the seeds of its own internal unraveling: a diversified network of forced labor, tied labor, tribute, specialized producers and distributors, and an increasingly free exchange of commodities. Struggle and revolt came mainly from the toiling masses but, after a devastating famine in 1505, better-off elements also rebelled. Thus, increased human sacrifices paralleled the state's need to maintain fear, and thereby stability. Yet the number of those sacrificed was paltry compared with the number of Indians who would perish at the hands of the Spaniards, or the number of European women who were burned at the stake as "witches" in medieval Europe during the Inquisition.

The Tlaxcala and Tarascan Indians, fiercely independent peoples who survive today, proved particularly unyielding when the Aztecs tried to conquer them in the late fifteenth century. Then, after the 1505 famine, the emperor Moctezuma faced rising tensions within the Valley of Mexico, from allied cities, and even from groups inside Tenochtitlán. His response was to massacre opponents, dismiss all high state officials who were not nobles, crack down on aspiring merchants, and deify himself so that all loyalty had to go not to the ruler and the state—as in the past—but to the god-emperor, Moctezuma.

Invasion and Colonization

When the Spaniards arrived in 1519, warfare broke out between Cortés's soldiers and the Indians. Once subdued, however, the Otomí and Tlaxcala, resentful of Aztec domination, opened negotiations with the Spaniards, and were recruited by Cortés to march on Tenochtitlán. En route, Cortés sought to strengthen his hand by massacring the unarmed residents of the Aztec-controlled city of Cholollan (Cholula).

Duly intimidated, Moctezuma sought to prevent a similar fate for Tenochtitlán by plying Cortés with gifts of gold, silver, and headfeathers. Cortés accepted the gifts and made Moctezuma his prisoner. Then, while Cortés was making a return trip to the port city of Veracruz to meet with a new landing of Spaniards sent by his superior, the Governor of Cuba, who earlier had ordered him not to advance to Tenochtitlán, Cortés's second-in-command, Pedro de Alvarado, led a gruesome massacre of the capital's residents, who were armed only with wooden staves.

Thus, after winning over the newly arrived Spanish soldiers in Veracruz, Cortés returned to an agitated Tenochtitlán, where he met an aroused and angry people. United under the leadership of Moctezuma's brother Cuitlahuac, the Aztecs used their superior numbers and familiarity with the bridge and canal system to isolate and almost decimate Cortés's army. Cortés sought to retrieve the situation by presenting Moctezuma to the people as a peace gesture, but the disgraced emperor was promptly stoned to death by his former subjects. In what Western history books call the "Noche Triste" (Sad Night), Cortés and the remnants of his army slipped out of Tenochtitlán under cover of darkness.

The Aztecs' victory was short-lived, however. Cortés regrouped his remaining forces, buttressing them with soldiers from Tlaxcala anxious to end Aztec tyranny. With this immense army of Indians and the superior Spanish technology of firearms, swords, plated armor, and horses, he then re-invaded Tenochtitlán in 1521. An epidemic of smallpox, a disease unknown in Mesoamerica, debilitated the Aztec forces and took the life of Cuitlahuac. His nephew Cuauhtémoc assumed leadership.

In a prolonged siege, during which the canals ran red with blood and the stench of the dead made Cortés ill, the Spaniards had to destroy Tenochtitlán in order to capture it. They wrecked the intricate irrigation system and slaughtered the citizenry; Cortés estimated they killed 100,000. They took Cuauhtémoc prisoner, and later executed him. On August 13, 1521, the Aztecs capitulated, bringing to an end their already unstable reign.

In today's Mexico, one looks in vain for a statue of Cortés or of his much maligned mistress, Malinche (from whose name derives the idiomatic word for treason, *malinchismo*). Malinche, from an anti-Aztec group of Indians, served as Cortés's translator and, after birthing him a son, is reputed to have been either strangled to death by the ungrateful wretch or to have died of an unknown disease while still less than thirty years of age. Statues of Cuauhtémoc, on the other hand, appear in prominent places. Parents often name their male children after him. For example, the first popularly elected mayor of Mexico City (1997), a mestizo like most Mexicans, is named Cuauhtémoc Cárdenas.

With the original Cuauhtémoc out of the way, the *conquistadores*, aided by the Catholic clergy, set about their immediate business: to harness the wealth, land, and labor power of the Indians, the better to enrich themselves and the Crown. In the words of Cortés, "I come for gold, not to till the land like a peasant," to which Bishop Alonso de la Mota y Escobar added, "Where there is no silver, the gospel does not enter . . . where there are no Indians, there is no silver." [14]

The Spanish invasion destroyed the economic and political autonomy of the Indian states, restructuring those parts that the Crown, Church, and colonists could use for their own aggrandizement. Thus, the heterogeneous Indian societies gradually became reduced to a more homogeneous, tribute-paying population—and eventually a disciplined labor force.

Death became the Indians' daily companion. Killings, floggings, overwork, malnutrition, poor hygiene, starvation, and disease caused more than 90 percent of the Indian population to be wiped out by 1650. Many perished from diseases imported by the Spaniards or on slave ships, especially smallpox, but also typhoid, measles, malaria, yellow fever, diphtheria, and mumps.

The Indians' agrarian communities—though permitted to continue because of their stabilizing influence and provision of labor power—were reduced or damaged by Spanish importation of sheep and plows and production of wheat for the whites. (Sheep destroyed lands with their root-killing grazing, while plows required more cultivable land per unit of food produced.) The Spaniards drained the lake that supported *chinampa* agriculture and monopolized sources of water, thereby furthering malnutrition and starvation among the Indians. Table 1, based on the very low demographic estimates of Charles Gibson, shows the marked decimation and partial recovery of the Indian population in the Valley of Mexico between 1520 and 1800, as well as the years of extreme epidemics.

This population decline heightened Indian suffering as the whites competed for increasingly scarce labor power. The whip, gibbet, and stock, imprisonment, torture, rape, and occasional killing became standard weapons for enforcing labor discipline.

An occasional cleric like Bishop Bartolomé de Las Casas, known as the "Protector General of the Indians," defended Indian human rights. Assisted by a few other priests, Las Casas forced a papal bull in 1537 that declared the Indians "free." In 1542 the Crown promulgated the New Laws, forbidding further allocation of Indian lands to the colonists. Local officials evaded the New Laws with the famed dodge of "Obedezco pero no cumplo" (I obey but do not comply). They and Franciscan and Dominican friars persuaded the Crown that strict enforcement was impossible, leading to revocation of the New Laws in 1545. Five years later the Crown ordered further expeditions of conquest to cease until the government could decide if they were "just." Finally, in 1573, the Standard Law resolved much of the Crown-colonist tension by replacing the word "conquest" with "pacification" and merely urging the colonists to moderate their use of force.[15]

Despite biological holocaust, cultural disruption, and unprecedented economic exploitation, some Indians managed to adjust to their new situation. The Catholic Church's lavish, exotic rituals and orderly hierarchy contained forms already familiar to them, and they transferred much of their old religious identity to the new doctrine imposed in place of their smashed (and obviously unsuccessful) idols. A village's Catholic patron saint day was celebrated with much joy and dancing that harked back to the devotional tributes offered the old gods and goddesses. Bonds of reciprocity between Indian communities and the Church's authorities were established, obligating the Church to support—or at least appear to support—the community's demands for fairer treatment.

Table 1
Indian Population and Extreme Epidemics, Valley of Mexico

Est. population	Year	Extreme epidemics
1.5 million	1520	1521
300,000	1570	1545-1548, 1576-1579
70,000	1650	1629-1634
120,000	1742	1736-1739, 1761-1762
275,000	1800	1784-1787

Source: Charles Gibson, The Aztecs under Spanish Rule (Stanford, CA: Stanford University Press, 1964).

In 1531 a humble Indian named Juan Diego claimed to have seen an image of the "Virgin of Guadalupe" (mother of the gods, or "Earth Mother") miraculously coming to bless and heal her suffering people. The Virgin quickly became a symbol of salvation for the oppressed. Rebels in all of Mexico's revolutions and social movements ever since have carried her banner into their battles and demonstrations.

Church officials in Rome, however, resisted incorporating the Earth Mother Virgin of Guadalupe into Catholic doctrine until 1648. The original church of the Madonna of Guadalupe was built by the Spaniards with Indian labor upon the site of what once was a temple to Coatlicue (Aztec earth goddess and mother of the gods). Many Aztec deities represented the forces of nature, so critical in the agricultural production and trade, which—with the booty of conquest—had formed the material basis of the Aztec empire. After overcoming their doubts, the Catholic authorities simply adapted the Aztec Earth Mother Virgin of Guadalupe into their standard liturgy. The celebration of the Virgin of Guadalupe continued uninterrupted right to the present. On each December 12, known as Guadalupe Day, tens of thousands of pilgrims trek to the Basilica of Guadalupe outside Mexico City to pay her homage. In honoring the (virgin) mother of Jesus Christ, Indians honor the ancient mother of the gods. Some Aztec prayers continue to be expressed in Catholic ceremonies for today's Indians. Even so, Indians and mestizos continue to feel ambivalent about the clergy, often viewing them as oppressors.

More important than the Indians' religious incorporation in colonial times, however, was the integration of many of their social practices into the Spanish system of exploitation. For example, the Maya had practiced a system of compadrazgo (literally, co-fatherhood), which readily became amalgamated with the European "godfather" system. Compadrazgo served as a patriarchical form of harnessing Indian labor and fortifying class hierarchy. It provided a patron-client form of exchange that remains common today. A better-off *compadre* was expected to assist his "godchild" with gifts on birthdays—keeping his eye on the activities of the peasant or worker family at the same time to make sure there were no signs of rebellion.[16]

Though exempted from taxes and tithes, Indians had to pay a yearly head-tax, called tribute. Men, women, and children were herded into mines and *obrajes* (textile workshops, mills, or factories), sacrificed, in anthropologist Eric Wolf's words, "to the production of objects intended to serve no end beyond the maximization of profit and glory for the individual conqueror."[17] Describing the laborers as "pitilessly exploited," one researcher noted that some "*obraje* owners locked their Indians up at night in guarded dormitories."[18]

The Spanish colonists at first sought to maintain remnants of the old ruling classes to assist them in exacting tribute and organizing and disciplining the labor force. After initial resistance (such as the repressed Mixton Rebellion of 1541), most of the former Indian nobles and high bureaucrats cooperated, retaining their domineering ways under new conditions. They became known as *caciques* (bosses). Some of them in turn became "governors," elected by the Indian communities they administered. In addition to male *caciques*, there were female ones, known as *cacicas*.[19]

Each community had its own *cabildo* (town council), to which it elected five to ten councilors from the old ruling class. The governor and councilors maintained "law and order." They supervised communal lands and the local market; collected tribute on behalf of the *corregidores* (local Spanish officials in charge of districts and tribute collection); enforced Church attendance; and organized labor for the colonists. In exchange, they were allowed to own land and pass it on to their children (entail), engage in trade, own slaves, and pretend to Spanish ways. Some became landowners and traders on a significant scale (with slaves and mulatto servants) and lorded it over the commoners. In performing their tasks, the *caciques* delegated authority to an intermediate class of lesser officers, who were also exempted from labor for the colonists. To this day Mexicans still use the term *cacique* to refer to powerful labor leaders, usually rural ones, or local officials.

Initially, the Spanish invaders divided up the Indians for their own use—as concubines, slaves, and sources of new generations of desperately needed labor power. Crown approval was taken for granted, since earlier practices in the Spanish Caribbean had included such labor-recruitment devices as *repartimiento* and *encomienda*. Under the *repartimiento* system, colonists had to hire Indian labor at a royal labor exchange at predetermined wages for set periods of time. The *encomienda* derived from a Crown decree giving Christopher Columbus access to Indians and their labor—but not their land—"in trust" *(en encomienda)*. In return the *conquistadores* were to Christianize the indigenous peoples. By 1542, some thirty *encomiendas* incorporated an estimated 180,000 Indian laborers, whose production went to the *encomenderos*.

The zeal of the Catholic clergy in helping to subdue and discipline the Indians became legendary. A Franciscan father, Juan de Zumárraga, boasted in 1531 of the destruction of over 20,000 idols. Missionaries frowned on Indian practices of polygamy and homosexuality, which they suppressed. They forced the occasionally bare-breasted women to cover themselves with the typical Indian blouse, the *huipil.* They had men in loincloths cover their legs with white trousers, standard peasant dress for centuries to come.

Shortly after the Spanish invasion, the papacy conferred on the Castillian monarchy complete supervision of the ecclesiastical establishment in the Americas, in return for the conversion of Indians and economic maintenance of the Church. In 1536 this church-state alliance introduced into New Spain the Inquisition, by means of which terms like "heresy," "misbehavior," and "treason" became almost synonymous. The clergy meted out harsh punishments.[20]

Supported by tithes, religious fees, and income from food produced by Indian labor on immense tracts of Church land, the curates also financed and administered schools, hospitals, and charity, while indoctrinating the populace in the new faith. Benefiting from state privileges and the powerful tool of the Inquisition, the Church emerged as a dynamizing, productive economic force, calculating its varied enterprises along rational, profit-oriented lines. By investing its revenues in mortgage loans and other credits to private enterprises in mining, trade, and agriculture at interest rates lower than the market rate, the Church became the major credit institution in Mexico. Its rural "banks," for instance, greased the entire agrarian economy. By 1700, income from Church funds in the Americas was maintaining the ecclesiastical establishment not only in Spain and Portugal but also in Italy. In brief, the Church was simultaneously landlord, banker, and capitalist.

Crown Policies

Spain's earlier history shaped its colonial policies in the Americas more in the direction of free enterprise than feudalism. In 1492 the "Catholic Monarchs" of the reunified kingdoms of Castile and Aragon ordered the expulsion of the Muslims and Jews, collecting considerable wealth from the deportees' properties. Since the days of the Islamic rule of Spain (711 to 1031), the Muslims and Jews had proven quite tolerant of one another and of the Christians. They had helped shape Spanish culture in many lasting ways. Linguistically, for example, Arabic terms infused everyday Spanish—e.g., "ojalá" ("would to Allah") became "would it were so."

In the course of the Catholic Crusades and the expulsion of the Muslims and Jews (in Spanish history known as the Reconquest, 1031 to 1492), Spain had established a centralized state, administered by a bureaucracy of *letrados* (university-trained lawyers) and dependent on the export of primary products (more than manufactured goods) to other parts of Europe. Since the Spanish textile industry could not compete with cheaper woolens and silks from France, Holland, or England, the privately controlled livestock monopoly (*mesta*) found it more profitable to export raw wool than Castilian cloth.

Spain's lifeline was based on a thriving mercantile system of production guilds, private monopolies, shipping companies, and state-protected merchant monopolies. Consequently, with the recent advances in long-distance shipping possibilities, Spain's ruling elites naturally feasted their eyes on new riches abroad.

During the Reconquest much of the military and political power of Spain's feudal nobility had been broken. New values and institutions had emerged: strong authority vested in a monarchical state; a militant Catholicism; rewards for military prowess and individual enterprise; use of family ties and connections to the court (*personalismo*) for garnering wealth or prestige; a focus on trade, guild production, or direct seizure of land or wealth rather than on new manufacturing production techniques; and a corresponding emphasis on individual exploits for obtaining grandeur. Given these new values and the immense distances and risks involved in overseas trade, the Crown found it practical to let state-sponsored free enterprise conduct the overseas explorations.

Private individuals or groups paid their own way. State-backed merchants helped finance overseas expeditions to find maritime trade routes to the Indies and the precious embroidered fabrics, exotic spices, and other wealth reputed to be there. The militaristic tradition of the Reconquest provided many a willing explorer, accustomed to acting boldly and greedily.

To the surprise and delight of the merchants, explorers, and would-be conquerors, a midway point was encountered—the Americas. A better helmsman than geographer, Columbus thought he had discovered the Indies and so named America's inhabitants "Indians." Mexico and Peru (then including today's Bolivia) proved to be the biggest prizes, pregnant with unanticipated wealth: gold, silver, and local workforces accustomed to paying tribute, whether in products or labor. Wealth garnered in earlier invasions (e.g., by Cortés in Cuba) financed further ones (Mexico, and then Peru).

Cortés was representative of the new "free-enterprise" spirit. He started gold placer-mining in southern Mexico, opened the first silver mines at Taxco, and established himself in a wide range of business activities besides agriculture. By 1569, his 25,000-square-mile *hacienda* in Oaxaca was netting his son a fabulous annual tribute in gold pesos. The Cortés *hacienda* included a nascent silk industry based on the mulberry tree, two sugar mills, wheat, fruit, horses, cattle, sheep, pigs, and corrals for the mules bred in Tehuántepec to service the mines to the north. In Mexico, the successful *conquistador* or colonist became a mining entrepreneur, a rancher, a merchant, and a producer of commercial crops on *haciendas* and textiles in *obrajes* (workshops, mills, or factories).

While encouraging free enterprise, the Crown made sure it retained the upper hand. It signed a *capitulación*, or contract, with the head of every overseas expedition, assigning him an area for conquest and granting him certain titles should the venture succeed. The *capitulación* obliged the explorer to pay the Crown tribute on the wealth he obtained abroad. Those adventurers who conquered territory without first having signed such a contract usually signed later, to protect themselves against competitors in the marketplace of conquest. Bitter feuds among the colonists became legend, with rivals even killing one another. Such strife made it easier for the Crown to maintain its authority, although the *conquistadores* by no means welcomed the Crown's restrictions.

No sooner had the invasion of Mexico been completed than the Crown began to undermine the authority of the *conquistadores*, reducing their status to that of ordinary royal governors and in some cases repealing earlier *capitulaciones* and replacing them with royal appointees. In 1523 the monarchy prohibited *encomiendas*, placing most of the largest *encomiendas* under royal jurisdiction (incorporated by the Crown). It exempted Cortés's estates.

The Crown declared all Spanish colonists, their descendants, and Indians vassals of the king. It sent viceroys and other officials to enforce royal discipline on the unruly settlers. The colonists chafed at the bit, and in 1566 a conspiracy by Alonso de Avila (son of a prominent *conquistador*) to make Cortés's son king of Mexico was nipped in the bud. Avila and his brother were decapitated and their heads publicly displayed on pikes as grim warnings against future conspiracies against the Crown.

By 1575, the largest *encomiendas* (not counting Cortés's), producing 75 percent of New Spain's tribute, had been incorporated by the Crown. This assured the monarchy and Spanish merchant monopolies of huge revenues from such leading exports as sugar and hides, as well as cochineal (a red dye from insects) and indigo (a blue dye from a shrub-like plant) essential to Europe's expanding textile industry.

Since Spain gained its relative prosperity through international trade, vastly enriched by the Crown's "royal fifth" *(quinto real)* of the Americas' precious metals and of colonial trade revenues, the monarchy and Spanish merchants jealously guarded their monopolistic powers, epitomized by the authority vested in the Casa de Contratación (Board of Trade) and the Consulado (merchant guild) of Seville, and after 1717, Cádiz. State regulation and the power of wealthy import merchants prevented manufacturing in New Spain (Mexico) from reaching a point where it might challenge or supersede the import of luxury and manufactured goods from Europe. Economic conflicts between the powerful Mexican merchants' Consulado in Mexico City and the merchant oligarchy of Seville were common.[21]

The Crown periodically outlawed the production of olive oil, wine, certain textiles, and other goods that might compete with Spain's major items of trade.

Consequently, most *obrajes* and successful artisan workshops clustered around mines, *haciendas*, and urban centers, although a few sold to national and international markets. Not even producers of agricultural commodities were permitted to develop too large-scale a production if the Crown became convinced by Spanish merchants in Mexico's eastern port city of Veracruz that a competitive colonial elite might emerge.

After its 1523 decree against the use of the *encomienda* system and its prohibition against settlers using unpaid labor (except for African slaves), the Crown implemented alternative methods of labor recruitment. It introduced the *repartimiento* (royal labor exchange), regulated by its *corregidores*. This pitted the colonists in fierce competition with one another for the same precious surplus-producing commodity: labor power. The fabulous silver discoveries of 1546 and the corresponding high wages and *partidos* (minority shares of ore mined) offered to workers attracted large numbers of Indians to the northern mines.

After the 1576 to 1579 epidemic, labor shortages grew even more severe, and the Crown permitted the *repartimiento* system to give way to one of "free" labor hired in an open market with no regulations. By 1602, the *repartimiento* was all but finished. There remained only 140 Indian communities in privately held *encomiendas* (compared with 480 in 1560). "Free" (wage) labor prevailed at most mines and on a majority of *haciendas*.

In New Spain's largest silver-producing area, Zacatecas, by 1598 there were no *repartimiento* Indians at all and only 130 African slaves, compared with 1,014 free laborers. Wage labor also became common in the textile *obrajes*, in other workshops, in transport, and in trade, as well as among artisans, servants, haulers, sweepers, and the work crews engaged in Mexico City's public drainage operations (*desague*). Few of the colonists—least of all merchants, miners, *hacendados* (owners of *haciendas*), and manufacturers—complained when the Crown decreed an official end to the *repartimiento* in 1632.

Thus, by the early seventeenth century, free (wage) labor and different forms of debt-labor had become a common practice. There existed regional variations, of course. These included instances of slavery in some coastal areas and parts of the northeast; use of the *encomienda* and labor drafts in Yucatán and Chiapas; and a late-eighteenth-century shift toward debt-peonage on *haciendas*.[22]

Moreover, free labor often amounted to paid forced labor, debt-labor, or payment in kind, only rarely alleviating the intense exploitation suffered by Indians. Many Indians ostensibly hired for a wage became entrapped in a web of debts for their purchases of basic necessities—the first steps in the long process that led to the nineteenth-century institutionalization of "company stores" (*tiendas de raya*). In addition, they had to pay Church and brotherhood fees and (relatively low) royal taxes. Also, they had tasks to perform in their communities, under the surveillance of the *caciques* and lesser officers.

Given the low wage structure and the large amounts of unpaid household labor and subsistence production engaged in by women and children, the production costs of Indian labor power were borne largely by the Indians themselves. Peasant producers usually had their surpluses appropriated by others, forcing them to resort to unpaid family labor in subsistence farming and household handicraft production simply to stay alive. These practices reinforced the larger system of exploitation of low-wage "free" labor.

The most affluent colonists—given their reliance on cheap labor and use of means of production less capitalized than those of foreign competitors—were rarely able to develop New Spain's home market more than regionally. To grow wealthy, most of them transferred to the international market their mining and agricultural surpluses, which they obtained on the basis of superexploitation. Thus, for the toiling masses, noncapitalist forms of economic activity like petty trade, domestic handicraft, and small-parcel subsistence farming became absolutely necessary and, in a contradictory fashion, functional for the elites' original accumulation of capital.

To sum up: in the early colonial period, the Crown's encouragement of free enterprise and a free wage labor system, together with its decrees to make most of the American territories royal provinces instead of proprietary domains for enterprising individuals, served its interests well. All political and economic rights were circumscribed by the Crown, which legally owned all the land and controlled the main source of wealth, the labor power of Indians. These policies also served the interests of Spain's merchant oligarchy and of nascent capitalist groups in northern Europe. The monarchy allowed some colonists enough opportunity to accumulate handsome surpluses. The Crown had thus taken sufficient steps—for the moment, at least—to prohibit the formation in New Spain of a rival group of miners, merchants, manufacturers, or landowners able to seriously threaten its hegemony, while at the same time facilitating the elites' accumulation of capital in New Spain.

Intercolonial Rivalries and Unequal Exchange

Spain proved less successful in dealing with its mercantilist colonial rivals in Europe. The Spanish Armada was defeated in the mid-1580s. Consolidation of British naval supremacy and Dutch commercial supremacy soon followed, accompanied by British and Dutch penetration of Spanish America. Piracy, smuggling, slave-running, and pillage dominated the next two centuries.

In Marx's words, "The treasures captured outside Europe by undisguised looting, enslavement, and murder floated back" to Holland, England, and other European powers to be "turned into capital."[23] Mexican silver and gold flowed through Spain to pay for north-European manufactured goods or the costs of war and empire, ending more often than not in the hands of Genoese, Dutch, and German bankers or England's nascent industrialists. In effect, the Spanish

merchant guild (Consulado) became a front and funnel for the capital of
north-European merchants and early manufacturers.

Spanish merchants settling in Mexico established commercial monopolies,
conducting their trade through the Atlantic and Pacific ports of Veracruz and
Acapulco. They and their descendants resided for the most part in Mexico City,
itself a growing commercial center. At times, more than half of Spain's shipping
to the Americas was bound for Mexico. From Acapulco ships carried Mexican
and Peruvian silver to the East Indies in exchange for the silks and spices coveted
by Europeans. In the words of Adam Smith:

> In China and Indostan, the value of the precious metals . . . was much higher
> than in Europe and it still continues to be so. . . . The silver of the new continent
> seems in this manner to be one of the principal commodities by which the
> commerce between the two extremities of the old one (Europe and Asia) is
> carried on, and it is by means of it, in great measure, that these distant parts of
> the world are connected to one another.[24]

Spanish merchants found themselves transferring their profits to banking
and insurance operations on which they depended. As Tomás de Mercado, a
Dominican theologian in New Spain writing about Seville's merchants, observed: "To all the Indies they ship great cargoes of every kind of merchandise,
and return with gold, silver, pearls, cochineal, and hides in vast quantities . . .
to insure their cargoes (which are worth millions) they have to take out
insurances in Lisbon, Burgos, Lyons, and Flanders, because so vast are their
shipments that neither the merchants of Seville nor of twenty cities like Seville
are capable of insuring them."[25] Meanwhile, manufacturing development in
Spain was further inhibited by the inflationary impact of silver from the
colonies.

The monopoly structure of this expanded worldwide trade facilitated draining enormous surpluses from Mexico. Some estimates available for the early
1700s put the value ratio of New Spain's exports to its imports at five to one.
Adding direct tribute collection, we can appreciate Mexico's loss to the
"mother" country. With so much focus on global trade, little was left for
development of a dynamic home market for Mexico.[26]

If mining was the motor of Mexico's colonial economy, merchant capital
was its grease. Merchants had the initial capital with which to take advantage
of the discovery of fabulous new silver mines in 1546 and the introduction of
the patio process in 1557, by means of which silver is extracted from ore
through its amalgamation with mercury, permitting profitable exploitation of
low-grade ores. Merchant monopolies and the Crown predominated in the
valuable trade of silver and gold.

After the big silver finds, there was a rapid expansion of economic activity
in such mountainous northern mining centers as Guanajuato, San Luis Potosí,
Pachuca, and, above all, Zacatecas. Mining expansion generated vastly augmented

internal and external trade, related productive activities, and the invasion and development of Santa Fe (in today's New Mexico) and Nuevo León (today's Monterrey). By 1609 some 65 percent of New Spain's exports were silver.

Yet, while great fortunes were being made in mining, it was a risky business, as its decline in the mid-seventeenth century illustrated. Mining depended heavily on the scarce resource of labor, as many workers died in the mineshafts or revolted against working conditions. Mining was also dependent on credit, on mercury supplies, on royal bureaucratic decrees, and on machinery, transport, and marketing channels. There were small mining ventures as well as large ones, and competition was intense. Moreover, financial control over mining profits was in significant part exerted by intermediaries: miners had to accept the prices offered by the *aviadores,* the agents of the big silver merchants in Mexico City.

In 1634 Spain decided to ship its mercury to Peru instead of New Spain and to collect the debt owed on the mercury and salt sent to New Spain. The subsequent decline in Mexico's mining production was not as serious as often supposed, since Mexico City's *criollo* merchants infused new credits into the mining sector, new discoveries were made, and local smelting of silver increased. Then, with the renewed availability of mercury from Spain in the late 1660s and the aid of local capital, mining recovered, exceeding in the 1675-1690 period Zacatecas's peak production of the 1620s. After 1700, the total annual value of minted silver and gold (mostly silver) rose gradually—from 3 million pesos to 13 million by 1775.[27]

From 1770 to 1820, the mining industry was organized as a guild, the Cuerpo de Minería, which was headed by a Tribunal General and led mainly by *criollos.* The tribunal stimulated a late eighteenth-century boom by cutting mercury prices, creating credit "banks" involving local capital, and permitting foreigners to invest in mining. Mine workers continued to strike and rebel, however, and new silver discoveries accomplished more than all the tribunal's reforms combined. The minted value of silver and gold jumped to more than 27 million pesos a year by 1805, when more than 3,000 mines were employing an estimated 35,000 laborers. An additional number of workers, refiners, artisans, carriers, street peddlers, shopkeepers, speculators, prostitutes, and so on, gravitated around the mines, a few making their fortunes, most not. Technical problems like flooding, combined with growing labor unrest, led to a severe slump at the end of the colonial period. Mintage value dropped to less than 4 million pesos in 1810.

Mexicans who made their wealth from the mines were unable to retain control of the whole process. No Mexican miner, for example, was able to finance the importation of special pumping machines from Europe, even when in 1803 the Crown issued a decree permitting such importation.[28]

New Spain's rich merchants not only financed the mines but also exerted influence in agriculture, manufacturing, and a medley of speculative activities. Seventeenth-century merchants in Mexico City, though mostly of European origin, included a number of *criollos* who augmented their capital by cultivating good relations with top state and Church officials, and entering into creditor and partnership arrangements with lower-level bureaucrats. By taking bribes, loans, or promised shares of profits, bureaucrats became, in effect, the merchants' "employees."

Corruption was so widespread that every *criollo* entrepreneur was likely to have a contact in the state bureaucracy. The merchants colluded with the bureaucrats to outwit the Crown on taxes, trade, and manufacturing prohibitions. Alliances, partnerships, and intermarriages cemented the common economic and social interests of wealthy *criollos* and the *peninsulares* (as the Spaniards were called) involved in commerce, mining, agriculture, or manufacturing.[29]

By 1604 merchant capital had helped finance some twenty-five textile mills *(obrajes)* in Mexico City alone, and many others in Cuernavaca, Puebla, Texcoco, Tlaxcala, and Querétero. One of the largest employed 120 workers, while others employed from 50 to 100—sizable figures for any manufacturing enterprise at the time.

Producing mainly cotton and woolen textiles—silk manufacturing prospered for a century but gave way to competition from Asia—the *obrajes* concentrated laborers in sweatshop conditions. Some *obrajes* used the "putting out" system, permitting nearby Indian villagers to do the initial spinning. The tendency in most places was toward the concentration of production under one roof (manufacturing) and toward centralized control by *obraje* owners or the merchant bourgeoisie, often one and the same. The technology of spinning wheel, reel, horizontal loom, and water-driven machinery, however, often remained primitive. The typical owner of an *obraje* was a Spanish settler (or his descendants) who had other economic interests, usually as a merchant (*mercader*) but increasingly in other areas as well.

For an occasional immigrant, *obraje* ownership was a means of upward mobility, opening doors to the principal elite groups of New Spain. A few of the tens of thousands of new Spanish settlers who poured into Mexico in the sixteenth century actually did quite well in select parts of manufacturing industry, as well as in the less-developed cottage industries relating to leather goods, spurs, pottery, and textiles. The Spanish guild system was introduced early (iron guild, 1524; hatmakers, 1561; silk production, 1584; woolen products, 1592; gold-thread sewing, 1599; etc.), and many immigrants worked as artisans, while others engaged in petty commerce as shopkeepers, served as overseers of laborers, or joined the ranks of the commoners.

The merchants, though never gaining complete control from other owners over the textile productive process, dominated it from start to finish. In cotton textiles, for instance, they provided the raw materials (cotton from the lowlands, sometimes from merchant-owned farms), transportation, credit, productive instruments, and final sales outlets. Merchant and other owners of *obrajes* increasingly hired artisans on a wage basis. In woolen textiles, Spanish and *criollo* merchants dominated the productive and distribution process to an even greater extent, at first enslaving Indians and eventually relying on a form of wage labor that sometimes bound the workers through a system of debts.

Artisans and others underwent a process of gradual, though incomplete, proletarianization, losing control of much of both their means of production and the sale of their final products. The colonial legal system caught up with these realities in 1790 and 1810, when the regulations assuring guild input into textile production were largely lifted in order to extend to the merchant bourgeoisie further control over the textile industry and labor.

Nationally, the *obrajes* came to employ thousands, forming in some instances the economic hub of major population centers—for example, Puebla, with its 20,000 cotton-textile workers and population of 70,000 in 1810. Moreover, regions dominated by such manufacturing centers thrived on commerce. In Puebla, thirty *obrajes* at the start of the seventeenth century stimulated a lively trade linking the city to Veracruz, Havana, Caracas, and Lima, as well as to its own regional market in agriculture and manufactured and artisan-produced goods. This partial but vigorous growth in the home market is the reason recent scholarship has viewed the seventeenth century not as one of depression but as one of transition toward capitalism, economic diversification, and the development of strong regional economies.

Nevertheless, with the ups and downs of the market and of the supply of capital (credits from merchants or the Church, provision of raw materials, etc.), there was frequent turnover in *obraje* ownership, which discouraged the development of a cohesive manufacturing class. Periodic economic hard times led to massive layoffs of workers and a recurring problem of urban unemployment, which grew worse during the last fifty years of the colonial period.

Moreover, centuries of colonialism generated what sociologist Peter Singelmann has called a "disarticulation" of markets for the production and circulation of commodities.[30] One market, the more profitable one, was international, involving the trade of primary commodities for European luxury and capital goods imported by the upper classes. The other market was national or regional, including the distribution of food, clothing, and some instruments of production among the general population for its survival and reproduction. Although both markets counted heavily on cheap labor, the export sector and the home market were not well synchronized, and the realization of surpluses in the former remained independent of the size of the latter. The elites continuously reinforced the ties to Europe by sending their money back to Spain, or reinvesting it in production for export, or importing capital goods for the same end, or purchasing imported items for their own consumption.

Wages in most sectors of the economy remained fairly stable from 1650 to the end of colonial times, and the level of exploitation of those incorporated into the work force did not noticeably change. Whether in state monopolies, like tobacco production, or in the private sector, workers continued to labor from twelve to fifteen hours a day at miserable wages. On such a basis, for example, the Royal Tobacco Factory of Querétero employed 3,000 workers, 60 percent of them women, and made a regular profit of well over 100 percent a year.[31]

There was thus little incentive for either the state or New Spain's elites to increase production through mechanization—at least at the pace European manufacturers were setting. The corresponding greater productivity of European capital furthered a process of unequal exchange between New Spain and Europe.

As economic historian Jeffrey Bortz has pointed out:

> European exports derived from a special productivity greater than that of the colonies, allowing the sending (to the colonies) of manufactured goods and the tools of production. Mexican exports derived from the fruits of nature and the low costs of labor power, allowing the sending abroad of goods complementary to European accumulation (and making Mexico dependent) in the sense that its economic reproduction was based upon the development of productivity in the metropolitan countries.[32]

Commercial Agriculture and Popular Resistance

As mining flourished and more people moved to the mining areas, the demand for agricultural goods increased, as did the need for labor. Both led to a reduction of Indian lands. Landowners sought to enlarge the pool of landless labor by forcibly dispossessing the Indians, which also served to eliminate the competition of Indian producers in what were becoming ever larger internal and external markets.

To service the booming mining centers, agriculture was put on a more commercial basis: breeding mules and horses to transfer the wealth; cultivation of sugar and maize to feed the labor force that produced it; and establishment of immense wheat fields, grinding mills, and sugar mills (or *ingenios*—literally, engines) on *haciendas* that spread throughout much of New Spain. In the words of German geographer and man of letters Alexander von Humboldt:

> Trips through the mountainous part of Mexico offer the most obvious examples of the beneficent influence of the mines on agriculture. . . . The foundation of a city follows immediately after the discovery of a large mine. . . . *Haciendas* are established nearby; the scarcity of foodstuffs and the high prices caused by consumer competition favors agricultural products. . . . In this way, arising only out of the desire for profit . . . a mine . . . is very quickly linked up with lands long under cultivation.[33]

Hacendados and merchants made fabulous fortunes in the course of agriculture's commercialization. New Spain's agricultural goods—cochineal, indigo, silk, cotton, hides, tallow, leather products, sugar—were increasingly traded for European manufactured goods, including Spanish arms, paper, fine cloth, books, wine, olive oil, and soap. Even regions removed from the main locations of mineral or agricultural production for export developed farming for profit. Indeed, during declines in mining production, as in the mid-seventeenth century or between 1805 and 1810, agricultural production for the internal market tended to overtake mining in total value. (One observer estimated the value of agrarian production at almost four times that of mining in 1810.) *Hacendados* often purchased mid-size farms, especially in Mexico's so-called "bread basket," the Bajío (greater Guanajuato area).[34]

Shifting their investments according to market opportunities, in hard times temporarily parceling out their lands for needed cash, many *hacendados* also participated in mining or commerce. As social historian Doris M. Ladd has observed, rich *hacendados* were

> very active in the processing industries in New Spain. Miners invested great sums of money in refining *haciendas* to process the ores from their mines. . . . In Mexico, when great wealth was involved, "the merchant," "the miner," "the financier," "the *hacendado*" turned out to be, more often than not, the same person.[35]

Smallholders (*rancheros*), tenant farmers, and sharecroppers also existed, with the largest number of prosperous *rancheros* establishing themselves in the Bajío region. While most small producers experienced miserable conditions, those producing goods that required close supervision or highly motivated workers (garden products, cochineal, small animals, eggs, and even sometimes cotton, tobacco, or wine) were sometimes able to compete with the *hacendados*.

Land-tenure patterns and agrarian practices varied. In the southeast there were few *haciendas* and many Indian villages. In Chiapas and Yucatán, technologically primitive *haciendas* exploited subsistence Indian communities. In central Mexico, there were more *haciendas*, though they were still outnumbered by Indian villages. In the north, *haciendas* barely outnumbered Indian villages, and there were even more *ranchos* (small estates or homestead farms, owned or rented).

As the eighteenth century progressed, increasing numbers of Indians joined the ranks of the free labor force to work in the new mines and on the expanding commercial *haciendas* or the few successful small and medium-size agrarian parcels. Free laborers could sometimes get the support of colonial authorities if the *hacendados* forebade them from leaving the *haciendas*. This slowed the growth of debt-peonage, although many peasants remained dependent on better-off landowners during epidemics or economic hard times. Also, in the mid-1770s it became legal for landowners to transmit their workers with their land in cases of property sales.

The *hacendados* followed the Spanish tradition of organizing their estates to function as self-contained units. A typical *hacienda* incorporated farming activities, artisanry, commerce, and even occasional *obrajes* within its far-flung borders. Besides wage laborers, *hacendados* used tenants, sharecroppers, and peasants from neighboring Indian communities—all of whom they treated with patriarchical condescension, and frequently violence, especially in the manhandling of women.

Constituting an emergent but unevenly developed agrarian bourgeoisie, the better-off *hacendados* overlapped with the most prosperous mining, commercial, and manufacturing families. The richest *hacendados* were often absentee landlords. The middle ranks of the emergent agrarian bourgeoisie consisted of *mayordomos* (administrators who received a minority share of profits), *arrendatarios capitalistas* (who paid the *hacendados* rent and retained the profits from production), and prosperous *rancheros*. Some of these elements also developed their own business enterprises on the side (e.g., *ingenios*, urban real estate, sugar trade, etc.).[36]

Women, including those who owned property or were not economically hurting, faced many difficulties under colonialism's heavy-handed patriarchy. An occasional strong voice against patriarchy as a system spoke out, only to be silenced. For example, the seventeenth-century nun and poet Sor Juana Inés de la Cruz wrote highly rational lines exposing men's hypocrisy and foolishness, condemning patriarchy, and championing women's wisdom. Sor Juana pointed out that marriage subjugated women to misery and abuse. At age forty-two, she was deprived of her library, musical instruments, pen, and ink. Some say Sor Juana wrote in blood after that. She died a year later (1695).[37]

Steve Stern has noted that although women could not overthrow the patriarchical system of dominance they certainly knew how to challenge and modify its practices. Women resisted their husbands' violent acts against them, which ranged from routine beatings to outright murder, by appealing to influential kin and forming female friendship networks for protection or retribution. In this and other ways they were often able to force men to compromise the seemingly unquestionable male authority in home and community. Some women also used their spiritual and medicinal practices to advantage. More than a few learned how to approach non-kin patriarchical figures such as *hacendados*, Inquisition judges, or colonial secular authorities with success. As a result, an abusive husband or male relative could face public whippings—a form of punishment that discouraged excessive violence against women but also reinforced the power of upper-class male authorities over lower-class men. The Inquisition, a quintessential patriarchical institution, frequently punished female "witches," yet it also occasionally brought male abusers to justice.[38]

Whether Indian, African, *casta*, or poor white, New Spain's lower classes (and later, some emergent intermediate-class[39] elements as well) did not accept their subjugation or abuse passively. Many authors on Mexico's colonial period, using the language and perspective that permeates their primary sources, equate "lower classes" with "nonwhite" or "Indian" groups, thereby blurring the important role that *class* position played in defining how a person acted or was stereotyped. Accepting many of their sources' stereotypes, some writers portray the Indians as having behaved "passively" and "obediently," while declining into "alcoholism" or "laziness"; or, alternatively, as having found in Christianity a solace preferable to the exploitation they suffered before the arrival of the Spaniards.[38]

That in fact Indians actively engaged in rebellion after the Spanish invasion has been well documented, and Indian revolts probably occurred more frequently than the written evidence indicates. In the face of the Spanish expansion across the Mexican landscape, many Indians who did not actively rebel abandoned their communities or took refuge in the mountains instead. Some committed collective suicide rather than be enslaved, and some women refused to continue procreating. In addition, as under any system of exploitation, Indians resisted covertly and on a daily basis—slowing up their labor, doing less careful work, and so on.

The Huasteca Indians along the Pánuco River (in today's states of Veracruz, Hidalgo, and San Luis Potosí) bitterly fought the Spaniards. Thousands were burned alive. Others were captured and sent to the Caribbean as slaves. Still others held out and conducted guerrilla actions for more than two centuries. In fact, as late as the mid-nineteenth century some of the Huasteca were secure in their own communities, practicing a self-declared anarchism. Serious Indian revolts occurred in the Huasteca region during the last two decades of the dictatorship of Porfirio Díaz (1876-1911), and these Indians helped launch the Mexican Revolution of 1910. Many of them were still actively resisting oppression in the 1990s.

Maya communities in the Yucatán also held off the Spaniards for many years. Francisco de Montejo, and later his descendants, finally subdued them only after burning chieftains alive, cutting off the arms and legs of male prisoners, and hanging or drowning the women. More than 500 Spaniards perished in these early battles. Then, in 1761, the Maya rose up under the leadership of Jacinto Cano, protesting excessive tribute. In 1846-1848 they waged a bloody revolution against the predominantly white upper classes, the so-called "Caste War of Yucatán."

The Yopes in coastal Guerrero joined with some of their former enemies in 1531 to combat the greater threat of Spanish rule. The massive and sanguinary

Mixton Rebellion of 1541 in the Zacatecas-Jalisco area of western Mexico resulted in the death of the *conquistador* Alvarado and led to a prolonged period of guerrilla warfare. Churches and monasteries were prime targets. (This, like a few other early Indian revolts, involved the participation of *caciques* seeking autonomy from the Spaniards in order to establish independent control over Indian labor power.)

Also in the west, Tepic miners revolted in 1598 and again under Mariano in 1801. As late as the Díaz dictatorship, the Indians of this region took refuge in the Sierra de Nayarit, from where they launched forays against *hacendados*.

The Chichimeca, as the northern groups of hunters and foodgatherers were called (Otomí, Zacatecos, etc.), fought the advancing Spaniards and their Indian auxiliaries with extreme ferocity in the silver-mining triangle between Guadalajara, Saltillo, and Querétero. With their raids along the Zacatecas-Mexico City road and elsewhere, they inflicted more losses in lives and property than in any previous Spanish-Indian conflict. By 1570 the entire frontier was aflame with rebellion, and the Chichimeca advanced on Guadalajara and to within sixty miles of Mexico City.

The Spaniards responded by organizing the first regular Spanish army in New Spain (made up mostly of *criollos*) and a network of armed garrisons *(presidios)* to carry out a war policy of "fire and death." They also enslaved frontier Indians. Final Spanish and *criollo* victory (in the 1600s) occurred only by means of superior firepower combined with a "pacification" program that included recruitment of captured Chichimeca into the army; awarding them special privileges (including titles of nobility), money, food, and clothing; and assimilating them into a new religion (Catholicism). Even then, the peaceful Pueblo Indians of today's New Mexico actually reversed the Spanish advance by secretly organizing an armed revolt that chased the newcomers out in 1680 and kept them out for twelve years.

In the northwest, the Yaquis of Sonora held off much of the whites' advance until the twentieth century. Their revolts threatened the Díaz regime and were brutally repressed. Captured Yaqui warriors were sent as slaves to harvest tobacco in Oaxaca.

In the south, Oaxaca's Indians jealously guarded their nearly autonomous communities throughout the colonial period, rising up repeatedly against abuses by *corregidores* or priests. For example, in 1660 more than twenty Oaxacan towns revolted, protesting the *repartimiento;* peasants killed royal officials and looted royal coffers. In the next year or two, some 200 communities in Tehuantepec revolted and took control of much of the Isthmus for more than a year. In the mid-1990s, their descendants mobilized against plans to create a new "Panama Canal" across the Isthmus.

Throughout New Spain there occurred dozens of indigenous millenarian movements harking back to earlier gods and goddesses. Indians in Chiapas periodically mounted insurrections against outside domination, and in 1712 the Tzetzal revolt created a confederation based on a mythical avenging virgin. Chiapas Indians took up arms again in 1994 under the secular banner of the Zapatistas.

Almost all of the Indian resistance focused on retaining or repossessing land, or opposing forced labor. Issues were defined regionally rather than nationally (although not in the case of the 1994 Zapatistas). The fight to retain communal roots or identity was an important part of the struggle. Women often played leading roles. William B. Taylor has noted that Mexico's women led the attacks in at least one-fourth of the 142 *tumultos* ("riots" or rebellions) he studied. Stern has described how women developed "a gendered etiquette for revolt," in which they distinguished between responsible and irresponsible father figures in the patriarchical power structure: "Women drew on their own gendered sensibilities of moral right—as outraged wives, mothers, and widows—to justify physical intimidation or attack against abusive or extortionary authorities." In this way women were able simultaneously to protect their own interests and to arouse entire communities to take action, as in Mexico City's so-called corn riot of 1692.

Often colonial officials, in an effort to avoid military defeat or the spread of insurrection, as well as to maintain a steady source of out-migrating labor, negotiated truces and compromises with the rebellious communities—and then executed or imprisoned local leaders. Where negotiations failed, the state response was always one of brute force—a lesson of history that the 1994 Zapatistas in Chiapas noted.

Thus, Indian resistance to exploitation was active and sometimes armed, not merely passive or cultural. By 1810, Indians still constituted a majority of the population—about 60 percent of an estimated 6 million. *Caciques* and lesser officers made up about 7 percent of the Indian population in the early seventeenth century, but they increasingly migrated to the cities, along with occasional skilled rural worker migrants. From this new urban sector emerged a new type of Mexican: the Spanish-speaking Indian or rural emigrant who imitated the manners of the urban whites and mestizos.

Africans, first brought to New Spain on a regular basis in the late sixteenth century to help fill the void left by the precipitous demographic decline among Indians, also resisted subjugation. The first slaves arrived in Mexico in small numbers with Cortés, one of whose faithful lieutenants was a black Catholic named Juan Garrido who became a *conquistador* in his own right.[39]

More slaves arrived in the following two decades, and the first "black scare" in Mexico dates from 1537, when a slave uprising was brutally crushed. The peak of slave importation (never conducted on a massive scale) was during the mining boom of 1580-1635—a time when larger numbers of Spanish immigrants arrived as well.

In general, the Crown discouraged slavery as a means of labor exploitation, particularly after the end of the mining boom. The *tlacotin* and *mayeques* of Aztec times were initially resettled in Indian communities, where they had the rights of commoners and joined them in laboring for or paying tribute to the whites. Thus, only blacks were slaves in the colonial period.

By the mid-seventeenth century, mulattos outnumbered blacks almost four to one, the combined total being estimated at 165,000. Many blacks were free, having been able to purchase their freedom. Others had run away and formed "maroon" bands. While some worked the mines, by 1650 those still enslaved were limited largely to the sugar-growing areas of Oaxaca or the coasts of New Spain. The Spaniards (known as *peninsulares*) and the *criollos* often used slaves in specialized capacities—as servants, as overseers of Indian labor, and as mistresses and concubines.

Resistance came from maroons and slaves alike. The maroon bands fought off *peninsular* and *criollo* attempts to reconquer them along both coasts and in the interior of New Spain from 1607 to 1611. They raided major transportation routes, like the one linking Puebla to Veracruz. One leader, an ex-African chieftain named Yanga, finally agreed to compromise with colonial authorities, and his followers were granted their own autonomous town in exchange for a promise to return future runaway slaves. There followed more maroon upris-ings, in 1617-1618, which were put down by force and compromise. More rebels were permitted to establish a community in the sierra near Córdoba, Veracruz, which received the name of San Lorenzo de los Negros. And in 1646 momentary fighting between mulatto and white soldiers broke out at the Veracruz garrison.

Black and mulatto revolts erupted periodically throughout colonial times.[40] Blacks and mulattos in general opposed the royal bureaucracy and sought out the freer, less-regulated urban atmosphere of the *criollos* and mestizos, among whom they had a better chance of creating their own opportunities. By 1810, there remained fewer than 10,000 black slaves—and their rebellious spirit infused the Wars of Independence (1810-1822).

A small number of other peoples entered Mexico during the colonial period: Jews, Arabs, Europeans from countries other than Spain. Some Asians, mainly Filipinos and a smattering of Chinese, arrived on the Manila galleons. The Asians engaged in petty trading, usually as peddlers, and like other minorities tended to assume Spanish names.

The mixing of all the different races created social strata known as the *castas*. Members of the *castas* were generally poor; only a few gained positions that exploited Indians or Africans. Mulattos, *zambos*, and Afro-mestizos suffered racist degradation more than did mestizos, who, to a degree, shared white racists' disdain for Indians and blacks. This was in part because of the sliding color scale of racism and the social emphasis placed by the ruling elites on light skin (or as they called it, "purity of blood"). Although most mestizos had Indian features, some were lighter-complected than others.

The *castas* numbered about 6 percent of the population in 1700 and 19 percent in 1810, roughly equal to the number of whites—although in fact most demographic estimates supposedly based on phenotype actually took class positions into account. For example, immigrant white Europeans who sank into the lower classes were described and known as *castas*, "vagabonds," or any category other than white. Especially in the north, but also in the center and to a lesser degree in the southeast of the country, the vast majority of *castas*, including poor whites, worked alongside Indians, acting as direct competitors for land and for wages. It was these people who, after the Indians and blacks, suffered from racism the most. In the prejudiced words of the Consulado of Mexico merchants writing to the Spanish Cortes (parliament) in 1811:

> The *castas*, whose lazy hands are employed in peonage, domestic service, trades, artifacts and the army, are of the same condition, the same character, the same temperament and the same negligence as the Indian . . . drunken, incontinent, lazy, without honor, gratitude, or fidelity. . . .The whites who call themselves American Spaniards *(criollos)* show their superiority over the . . . Indians and *castas* . . . by their inherited wealth, their career, their love of luxury, their manners and the refinement of their vices.[41]

Because of their oppression, the *castas* were quick to join the numerous underdog revolts in New Spain's cities known as *tumultos*, or, in the eyes of the white elites, "rioting of the rabble." Even some *criollos*, though terrorized by these wild uprisings, would occasionally join, use, or attempt to lead them in order to threaten the *gachupines* (a derogatory term for Spaniards, or *peninsulares),* their rivals for power in control of commerce and the bureaucracy. In almost every *tumulto* the masses moved against the symbols of wealth and state power by looting stores and destroying government offices, the gibbet, and the stock.

Tumultos, then, constituted the gravest and most recurrent threat to Spanish colonial power and to the hegemony of the white elites. They were a profoundly class phenomenon, with undertones of anticolonial nationalism.[42]

The particularly violent *tumulto* of 1624, provoked by Archbishop Juan Pérez de la Serna, a *criollo*, and Spanish Viceroy Marqués de Gelves, his rival, ravaged Mexico City. Afterward, the *visitador* (Crown-appointed inspector) Martín de Carrillo y Alderete sent the king a description of the conditions that provoked it:

> The *tumulto* shows three facts of great importance to the Spanish Government: first, the conspiracy was organized, directed, and led by the clergy, that is to say, by the class believed at court to be the principal and most firm support of the government of the mother country; second, if the matter were followed through, it would be found that all, or almost all, the populace were accomplices; third,

the hatred of the mother country's domination is deeply rooted in all classes of society, especially among the Spaniards who come to establish themselves in Mexico City (criollos), and was one of the principal means used to excite the populace to action.[43]

Food shortages and skyrocketing food prices provoked the devastating Mexico City "corn riot" in 1692. Women led the way, as people burned down the viceregal palace, city hall, and offices of the Audiencia (royal court), and ransacked 280 shops and stalls. As in 1624, there were cries of "Death to the gachupines!" Church property went untouched. Order was restored when the viceroy's soldiers opened fire on the people.

The principal class division in colonial society was that separating a small bureaucratic, religious, mining, landed, manufacturing (obraje), and urban commercial set of elites from an immense peasantry and working class that produced the marketable wealth; the elites, however, were not always united. They often found themselves in competition for scarce labor power, quarreling over the spoils of colonialism, disagreeing about Crown policies, and feuding over the question of status and power associated with "pure" Spanish blood (gachupines versus criollos). Within the clergy, the friars tended to ally with the Crown, its bureaucracy, and the Indian caciques, while the secular bishops and priests (who increasingly were criollo) lined up with the colonist landholders, miners, obraje owners, and merchants (also increasingly criollo). Consequently, when Viceroy Gelves arrived in New Spain in 1621 to crack down on smuggling and the general unruliness of the colonists, he also sought to discipline the secular priests, who responded by closing the churches.

Secular clergy in the churches (the only arena of relatively free speech) became the chief spokesmen against the colonial bureaucracy and Crown authority. Some Inquisition officials and peninsular bishops went along with the secular clergy. In 1642 Viceroy Juan de Palafox y Mendoza conceded to the criollos some posts in the militia and bureaucracy and granted hacendados some of their claims to Indian labor and positions in the new trade fleet; over the next few years he attempted to reduce the wealth and power of the Jesuit order. (The Jesuits were later scapegoated and expelled, as explained in the next chapter.)

Concessions to the criollos were offset by the Crown's increased taxes to finance the fleet and a general crackdown on those economic activities of the colonists that posed a threat to the royal monopolies, as well as by the Crown's appointing a majority of high Church officials from among the Spanish-born. Tensions between the viceroys and secular clergy simmered off and on right up to the Wars of Independence.

Food riots, caused by poor harvests and price speculation, sometimes leading to full-scale tumultos, became a leading form of revolt in the eighteenth century, much of which was marked by crop failures and poor economic conditions for the masses. Population recovery and periodic economic down-turns led to a labor surplus, to Indian migrations in quest of employment, and to a significant amount of vagabondage and banditry. Anger fermented.

In sum, Mexico's early-to-late colonial period witnessed the gradual establishment of an embryonic dependent capitalism under the tutelage of a powerful state but it also generated mass impoverishment and limited or blocked upward mobility. These conditions triggered repeated mass upris-ings (tumultos) that ultimately had the potential to break Mexico's ties to the "mother" country and even challenge the power of "New Spain's" traditional elites and emergent bourgeoisie.

CHAPTER 2

Independence and Civil War, 1770-1880

We say one thing only to you and the venerable saintly priests. Why didn't you remember or take notice when the Governor began killing us?

—Reply of Indian captains to the Bishop of Yucatán, 1848[1]

Laboring citizens are condemned to be mere passive instruments of production for the exclusive profit of the capitalist.

—Ponciano Arriaga to the 1856-1857 constitutional convention[2]

THE DRIVING FORCE of Mexico's late-colonial economy was an embryonic capitalism, stimulated by merchant capital in control of most of the appropriated mineral wealth and much of the country's manufacturing production. The forms this capitalism was taking in Mexico[3] were varied, reflecting the socio-economic materials out of which it was growing. These included both Indian communal traditions and those of the Spanish nobility; invasion, enslavement, pillage, and "original accumulation of capital"; the separation of laborers and artisans from the means of production, and their development into free wage labor for the accumulation of capital on an extended scale; production for an external market, and production for a suddenly fast-growing home market. Labor recruitment occurred in a free and open market, and capitalists—*hacendados*, merchants, mine owners, and manufacturers—profited from the masses' frequent bouts of starvation, unemployment, and debt obligations by being able to hire at exceedingly low wages. Elite families grew fat as poor ones grew thin. Use of child labor was widespread.

The forces of early capitalism gained momentum from intensified inter-colonial rivalries among the great powers. Spain's introduction of the "Bourbon Reforms" and expulsion of the Jesuits sped Mexico's transition from the earlier mercantile forms of capital accumulation to capitalist ones. Class conflicts soon took on new, more complex and intense forms, adding a stronger political dimension to the traditional *tumultos*. These developments generated an aborted social revolution in the 1810s and, at the same time, Mexico's winning of national independence in 1822 (a kind of counter-revolution sponsored by the *criollo* elites).

The class conflicts that gave rise to the independence movement continued to shape the new nation's state and patterns of capital accumulation for decades to come. After independence, Mexico's economy underwent a gradual dissolution of the mercantilist-capitalist mode of accumulation and its replacement by more purely capitalist ones.

The 1770-1880 period as a whole, then, can best be viewed as a continuous economic process having three disruptive political moments: 1810-1822; 1846-1848, when the United States militarily seized nearly half of Mexico's territory, including most of today's U.S. Southwest and California; and 1854-1867, starting as a liberal-conservative civil war and ending with a war of national liberation against French military occupation. The first political moment established national sovereignty; the second tore the nation apart; and the third created a stable nation-state for the purposes of capitalist accumulation on an extended scale.[4]

European Competition and Bourbon Reforms

In the late eighteenth century, Spain's European competitors flooded colonial markets and undermined the prosperity of the monopolistic Cádiz-America trade network. In 1762 the British seized Havana and Manila and threatened to occupy Mexico's key port of Veracruz. English, French, Dutch, and (after 1776) U.S. contrabanders increasingly penetrated Spain's colonial trade network and raked off growing portions of Mexico's economic surplus.

In an effort to cope with these challenges, Spain implemented a series of policy changes known as "the Bourbon Reforms," after the Bourbon dynasty, which had replaced the Hapsburgs in 1701. Most of the reforms occurred during the reign of Charles III (1759-1788). The reforms introduced the French-style *intendencia* administrative system and further centralized Spain's political control over Mexico. At the same time, the reforms made economic and occasional political concessions to Mexico's *criollo* elite, such as more positions in the bureaucracy. They also abolished juridical differences based on ethnicity and placed limits on the economic monopolies of the Church.

To defend against European rivals, the Bourbon Reforms decreed formation of an army and a militia. The lower classes soon complained about the forced troop levies. This grievance, added to others, triggered a series of popular revolts in major population centers like Puebla, San Luis Potosí, Guanajuato, Morelia, and Pátzcuaro. So, in actuality, the army was used to control Mexico's restless masses, especially the Indians.

Foremost among the Bourbon Reforms was the series of Free-Trade Acts that commenced in 1765 and gradually liberalized trade over the next few decades. The acts reduced and equalized duties for Veracruz, Buenos Aires, and other major ports. The aim was to reduce contraband by opening limited channels through which foreign traders could legitimately operate, and by means of which Mexican traders could, for the first time, trade with other parts of Latin America and (in the case of grains) with the Spanish islands of the Caribbean.

Since the intent was to augment the export of Spanish goods to the colonies, the Acts permitted no re-export of European imports. Nonetheless, the steady expansion of the Free-Trade Acts in the last third of the century helped create a golden age for all European and Mexican commerce. Free trade, then as now, favored economically powerful nations against weaker ones that did not have sufficient strength to compete. Even so, free trade did stimulate economic expansion in Mexico, which became Spain's most important colony and the only one that housed several millionaires. The fortunate few were heads of big trading houses in Mexico or owners of large mining, agricultural, or manufacturing interests, usually the same individuals.

From 1779 to 1803, mining production in Mexico almost doubled. Agricultural and industrial production also rose sharply. By the late 1700s, Mexico's manufacturing production was valued at 72 million pesos a year, with 25 percent being the preparation of foodstuffs for shipment, 15 percent textiles, and 20 percent candles and soap. Table 2 reveals the rising volume of the area's exports during the colonial era's final years, as well as the expanding home market for agricultural and manufactured goods.

Such growth in domestic production, together with the Cádiz monopoly's preference for sustaining its old ties with European manufacturers, contributed to the Bourbon administration's recognition that more efficient management techniques and economic reforms in the colonies might sustain the empire better than the most dedicated efforts at fulfilling unrealistic dreams of a sudden capitalist transformation of Spain. To finance its wars with France and England, Spain sought to increase revenues from the colonies from public funds remitted to Spain, and from taxes on the trade with the Americas.

The Crown's income from Mexico's economic activities *quadrupled* from 1763 to 1792. The value of the colony's exports jumped more than 50 percent in the 1780s as compared with the 1770s—in spite of a severe drought, an epidemic, and a consequent reduction in production from 1784 to 1787. Mining continued to account for the bulk of exports. An approximate doubling of grain, food, and livestock prices between 1779 and 1803 benefited *hacienda* agriculture, which vastly increased production on the backs of terribly exploited peasants.

A rise in *diezmos* (the one-tenth of produce delivered to the Church by peasants, artisans, and other small producers), similar to a hike in food prices, drove most rural Mexicans to the edges of survival and furthered land concentration in the hands of a few. By 1800, the number of *haciendas* (large and medium-size) in the Valley of Mexico was 150. Some 50 of these provided all the maize consumed in Mexico City, whose population had grown to 137,000

Table 2

Estimates of Mexico's Economic Product, ca. 1791-1809

(expressed as annual market in pesos)

Sector	Domestic market	Export market	Total	Percent
Agriculture	133,782,625	4,844,685	138,627,310	62
Industry	54,744,047	257,264	55,001,311	25
Mining	924,259	27,026,741	27,951,000	13
	189,450,931	32,128,690	221,579,621	100
percent	86	14	100	

Sources: These estimates are based on consumer market estimates made by José María Quirós, *Memoria de estatuto* (Veracruz, 1817), as elaborated by Doris M. Ladd, *The Mexican Nobility at Independence, 1780-1826* (Austin: University of Texas Press, 1976), 26, and David A. Brading, *Miners and Merchants in Bourbon Mexico, 1763-1810* (Cambridge: Cambridge University Press, 1971), 18. They involve some speculation as to average annual consumption. In a long note Ladd explains the details of these compilations, drawing critical support from the calculations of economist Fernando Rosenzweig Hernández, "La economía novohispana al comenzar el siglo XIX," *Ciéncias Políticas y Sociales* 9, no. 33 (July-September 1963): 45-94.

(still far below the population of the Aztecs' Tenochtitlán). Most of the sales occurred in a free marketplace rather than through state markets and warehouses.

Frightened by the French Revolution, the Crown severed its ties with republican France in 1793 and temporarily joined forces with England against the French revolutionary upsurge. In 1795, the Crown issued decrees creating new Consulados (merchant guilds) in Veracruz and Guadalajara. By then, Crown revenues had become very dependent on the activities of Spanish and *criollo* merchants operating in Mexico. The new Consulados represented one more instance of legal and administrative changes catching up with material reality. In effect, their creation recognized the end of the monopoly of the Mexico City Consulado. Veracruz merchants took over control from the merchants in Mexico City of the Oaxaca cochineal and other regional trade networks. Native-born merchants gaining their wealth from the growth in Mexico's home market found their ambitions and expectations furthered.

England sought control over the lucrative colonial trade with the American colonies, leading to a renewal of war between England and Spain in 1796. Needing its fleet for the war, Spain authorized the right of *criollos* to ship their goods in their own vessels to Spain and back. In practice, neutral nations were also allowed to engage in this shipping, so that by the first half of 1799, of thirty foreign ships landing at Veracruz, twenty-five were of U.S. registry. Thirteen years earlier, Thomas Jefferson had expressed the expansionist goals of the emergent republic to the north: "Our confederacy must be viewed as the nest, from which all America, North and South, is to be peopled."[5]

Economically, a lot was at stake. U.S. merchants appointed agents at Veracruz, and leading trading houses in Mexico did likewise in U.S. cities. Foreign agents also engaged in military adventures and conspiracies to try to "free Mexico" from Spanish domination. These included Wilkinson's "Mexican Association," 1805, with U.S. government support; the British agent Williams, sent in 1808; the increase in French Bonapartist agents, 1809; and U.S. armed expeditions into Texas.

Revolt from Below

In the course of the Bourbon Reforms, Spain's many wars, and the masses' increased hardships, the Crown decided to scapegoat the independent, well organized religious order of the Jesuits for the problems it faced in its colonies. Latin America's Jesuits were well known for their high intellectual training, valuable property holdings, and tendency to favor Indians' human rights. The Crown's expulsion of over 400 Jesuits from Mexico in 1766-1767 was ostensibly an effort to prove it was still "in control," while trying to free the monarchy from excessive clerical influence by choosing the most vulnerable group to attack. In fact, it served to enrich the elites, who grew fat off Jesuit lands and properties.

Ironically, the expulsion order provided a good pretext for political protest against the "arbitrariness" of Spanish colonialism. Masses of rioting peasants, workers, and unemployed persons seized towns, stormed jails, and insulted local authorities. The Crown's emissary, *visitador* José de Gálvez, was appalled. Described by historians as a "mild" ruler compared with his predecessors, he ordered the hanging of 85 persons, the lashing of 73 into bloody ribbons, the jailing of 674 others, and the banishing of 117. All the victims of his "mild" rule were either Indian or *casta.*

Nineteen years later, in 1786, the people were rebelling again. Mexico City's lower classes sacked and burned the granaries of *hacendados.* The following year, *tumultos* erupted in Acayucan and Papantla near the Gulf Coast. Indians took over both towns and held them until troops were dispatched from Veracruz. Once again, women played important roles in the "revolt from below."

For the masses, famine, epidemic, death, migration, and family disintegration accompanied the concentration of land and wealth, particularly after 1795. Recurrent outbreaks of drought or frost, normally followed by bad harvests and epidemics, plagued Mexico. Economic historian Enrique Florescano has summarized the consequences: dying off of livestock; layoff of *hacienda* workers; ruin of small and medium farmers; ravenous hunger; strikes in mines and *obrajes;* declines in commerce; massive emigration of hundreds of unemployed families toward zones less hit by scarcity and hunger; stagnation in rural salaries and those of urban day-workers; continuous rise in prices; more and more landless peasants and discontent in the countryside; and rising social tension in the cities.[6] The economic elites shrewdly utilized the periodic bad harvests to increase their own wealth and power through price speculation and land monopolization.

Spain's turn-of-the-century wars curtailed its trade and contributed to a decline in royal incomes. From 1793 to 1807, remissions from the Indies' trade dropped from 20 percent of royal income to 9 percent. Spain tried to keep the commerce alive by allowing neutral trade (1797-1799), by assigning warships to carry merchandise, and by permitting the colonies to trade with non-belligerents. When these efforts failed and war again broke out with Britain, the Crown implemented the "Act of Consolidation of Royal Revenues" (1805) which called for the redemption of mortgages belonging to chantries and pious foundations. Mexico's wealthy elites had willed these mortgages to the Church. Over the next three years the Crown collected one-quarter of the mortgages.

This angered the clergy and some of Mexico's elites—although the very rich withstood the crisis and some merchants and moneylenders gained an advantage through the relative weakening of the Church credit system. The upper clergy, which lived off tithes, was not hurt, but the lower clergy, which depended heavily on the chantries, was. Even a relatively well-off Mexican *criollo* priest like Miguel Hidalgo y Costilla (reputed "father" of Mexican Independence), who was the son of a *hacienda* manager, had one of his three farms embargoed when he could not redeem his debt. Spanish and *criollo* nobles grumbled. They depended heavily on the credit system to finance their economic affairs and lavish fiestas, to pay royal taxes, to gain royal permissions for entails (special property inheritance rights), and to maintain the primogeniture system allowing a noble to pass his wealth on to the oldest son in perpetuity. Hardest hit were small and medium-size producers, who suffered from the resultant credit pinch and rising interest rates.

Most of Mexico's elites were caught up in the cycle of increased investments and profits in productive enterprises for both the internal and external markets. Profit ultimately ruled over prestige in their minds, as when, toward the end of the colonial period, the nobility agreed to give up the institution of entail (special property inheritance rights). Prohibited by Spain earlier, entail had become so encumbered by liens as to be no longer economical.

In the midst of all these changes, there soon occurred audible murmurs about "bad government" around which Mexicans of any class or race could rally. As one well-off landholder said, "This continuous extraction (by the Crown) is why our colonies have been maintained in a state of infancy; agriculture kept behind.... Well, if in such a state we are to suffer the extraction of the pious funds, who will be able to doubt our total ruin?"[7]

European and U.S. suppliers, traders, and smugglers—especially the British—easily broke through the old Spanish merchant monopoly. Mexico-based
merchant guilds, which had controlled Havana, La Guaira, Maracaibo, and
Campeche (important inter-colonial ports of trade), also lost their dominance
to European traders, as many European commodities circumvented Veracruz.
On the other hand, some Veracruz merchants became commercial agents for
the foreign traders.

Much of Spain's traditional imperial and intercolonial trade fell into the
hands of multinational commercial interests, which accounted for almost half
of Mexico's imports by the end of the colonial period. Spain's efforts at political
and economic renewal, thus undermined, were brought to a humiliating end
in 1808 by the military invasion and takeover of Spain by the French troops of
Napoleon advocating bourgeois-republican ideals.

The Nascent Bourgeoisie

During the early 1800s, *criollo* merchants greedily eyed the expanding
markets offered by Britain. Parts of the Caribbean were already effectively
under British economic control. By 1810, British traders were solidifying
commercial relations with all of "Spanish" America. South American *criollo*
advocates of national independence like Francisco de Miranda and Simón
Bolívar were counting on British and U.S. funds and guns. Industrialists,
merchants, slave traders, and arms dealers throughout Europe and in the
United States anticipated vast new markets in Latin America if the independence movements succeeded.

The "liberal" tie that was uniting British and *criollo*-elite commercial and
political interests was not the political liberalism of the Jacobin ideologues of
the French Revolution of 1789. Nor was it the revolutionary liberalism of the
dark-skinned slave and proletarian insurgents who smashed the British and
French armies in Santo Domingo and Haiti in several years of fighting, creating
Latin America's first independent nation, Haiti, in 1804. Rather, the liberal tie
was *economic liberalism*. This liberalism championed "free trade"—the key
doctrine in the transition from mercantilism to capitalism worldwide, as well
as the banner of present-day neoliberalism.

Within Mexico's nascent commercial and productive bourgeoisie, an ascendant group of *criollo* (and mestizo, considered "*criollo*") landowners, manufacturers, miners, and merchants wished to consolidate and extend their newly
gained wealth. They considered themselves "Spanish" in prestige but "*criollo*"
in deprivation. If the opportunity presented itself, they were more than willing to
seize political power. Landlords, especially those expanding their wealth rapidly,
began asserting their class interests politically. So did other prominent *criollos*.

The main tension among elites was between the Spanish bureaucratic-
commercial colonial oligarchy (including high clergy and military), many of

whom were connected to the Mexico City Consulado, and the emergent Mexican bourgeoisie, including the merchants of the Veracruz and Guadalajara Consulados, who eagerly endorsed the slogan of "free trade."

The nascent Mexican bourgeoisie's goal of profit maximization, however, was tempered by its historical formation in the context of Spanish traditionalism. For centuries, all of the colony's elites—including, technically, the Indian nobles—had called themselves Spaniards and pretended to the values of European nobility. Titles had easily been purchased. Both the clergy and the military enjoyed special privileges, known as *fueros,* such as juridical immunity. Colonial bureaucrats, including *criollos,* also enjoyed special status—a lawyer in the bureaucracy often had as many rights as a wealthy merchant.

The elites championed the values of progress and piety, innovative entrepreneurship, class unity, and kinship loyalty. Their favorite reading ranged from works on the newest technological innovations to religious stories of miracles. As Ladd has observed, "Great wealth was so organized as to maximize family relations and minimize Creole and Peninsular distinctions. It was focused on Mexican resources, and it was produced by Mexican labor, Mexican technology, and Mexican capital . . . wealthy entrepreneurs were capitalist in the Hispanic tradition."[8]

Even when draped in the liberal, rationalist, or radical rhetoric of the Enlightenment or the French and American revolutions, the demands of Mexico's elites were limited in practice to modest reformism. Resenting the monopoly of political power held by the Spanish "*gachupines*," the native-born wealthy looked for ways to eliminate colonial restrictions on trade and circumvent regional marketing taxes *(acabalas)* and royal and Church taxes that were slowing their economic advance. They objected to having to pay for Spain's defenses in its endless wars with rival European powers. As Fray Servando Teresa de Mier complained: "Since Spain is unable to protect her commerce and unwilling to allow others to export our products and us to import theirs, and has deprived us of factories and industries, the European war is more cruel for us than for her, and is ultimately waged with our money."[9] In his newspaper *Diario de México* in 1806, future insurgent Carlos María de Bustamante lambasted the viceroy for his support of "a reduced number of cruel monopolists who in years of scarcity augment their fortune at the cost of the blood of the destitute."[10] Some clergy talked of reducing the large estates. Michoacán's bishop bemoaned the "wretched, vile" conditions of the poor. Even an occasional viceroy denounced landlord greed.

Landowners had long objected to the "protection" the Crown had offered Indians and Indian village lands, wanting instead to extend their *haciendas* in a free and open market. Many *hacendados* and expanding middle-size landlords began thinking seriously of political autonomy for Mexico.

For all its fascination with the new bourgeois ideals emanating from abroad and its resentment of colonial despotism, Mexico's nascent bourgeoisie was still constrained by the contours of its colonial past. Rarely was it economically autonomous, and its political and cultural domination by an exterior state further limited its ability to think and act independently. It had grown accustomed to relying on state favors.

Yet it was far from "underdeveloped" in the normal economic skills or traits of early capitalist bourgeoisies—indeed, its greed and contentment in exploiting others, judging from its own historical records (deeds, accounting books, proclamations, etc.), equaled or exceeded those of its European counterparts. It was, however, still relatively weak in the larger social context in which it operated—and, therefore, *incompletely developed as a self-conscious, self-perpetuating socioeconomic class.*

Thus the early Mexican bourgeoisie looked to the state and foreign allies among stronger bourgeoisies for support, especially against the threat of mass rebellion. They were torn by their need for profit and terror of the impoverished masses. This helps explain why they welcomed the Crown's expansion of the colonial army to some 40,000 by 1810. They needed the army to control the volcano of discontent erupting from below. A *tumulto* shook the key port city of Veracruz in 1808. Moreover, half of the army was non-Spanish and some of its officers were *criollo.*[11]

More and more peasants were being forced to surrender their lands to the expanding *hacienda* system; more and more unemployed or day laborers (*jornaleros*) were crowding into the already strife-torn cities. In the early 1800s, the German scientist Alexander von Humboldt toured Mexico, in part to send reports back to British and other north-European industrialists and traders. He was struck by the depth of the colony's problems and predicted an "explosion of social conflict."[12]

A crisis in agricultural production from 1808 to 1810 crippled Mexico's economy and generated further unemployment. With the spread of epidemics and hunger, an immense floating population of restless, desperate workers stalked the land. Even *hacendados* faced a crisis. They owed immense sums to the Church and to merchants for loans. They had to pay most wages in cash and needed further credit to expand. Competition in regional markets had driven many to increase their scale of production, forcing new cash outlays and further indebtedness.

The Intermediate Classes and the Working Poor

Adding to the conditions in Mexico that led von Humboldt to foresee an "explosion of social conflict" were the rising aspirations of the intermediate classes—small in number but, like the masses, experiencing rapid social change and racial or social discrimination. Theoretical confusion abounds about the concept "intermediate classes." Some writers on Mexican history equate mestizos with "middle class," thereby mixing race and class. But class determined race much more than the other way around. Many people calling themselves Spanish were mestizo; many mestizos and *castas* in general were workers or peasants, as were a number of *criollos*; and some Indians, above all *caciques*, were considered mestizo. Other authors lump clergy, lawyers, and intellectuals together with small producers (or the "traditional petty bourgeoisie" in European thought) as "middle class," thereby overlooking the fact that the petty bourgeoisie owns, or at least possesses, its own means of production and employs others. Intellectuals and professionals, with some exceptions of course, rarely own more than their labor power and personal possessions and are either self-employed or employed by others.

"Intermediate classes" (plural) is a more accurate concept than "middle class" (singular), because various groups compose the category. They are "intermediate" not because of supposedly "middle" levels of income, property, or power, but because *they are situated in an intermediate position between major social classes that either own the means of production or apply their labor power to activate them*. In other words, intermediate classes do not constitute a major pole of a bipolar class contradiction—such as landlord-serf, bourgeoisie-proletariat, and so forth. They are "caught in the middle," now siding with one pole, now with another, and almost always dividing among themselves, always "intermediate" to the central class conflict of the society in question.

Accompanying the economic expansion of the Bourbon Reform era had been an increased role for small and medium-size merchants and middle-level transport workers. They had prospered despite the primitive nature of their distribution system, which depended on Indian carriers *(tamemes)*, other "beasts of burden" (mules, etc.), and difficult mountain trails and roads. Adding to their numbers the better paid mineworkers, successful artisans, small-scale miners, and occasionally prosperous Indian and *casta* property holders, formation of ever darker colored intermediate classes with rising expectations had been underway for decades.

In the early 1800s, the intermediate classes could count among their number the owners of their own means of production, whether traditional peasant owners of small land parcels *(rancheros)*, artisans engaged in simple commodity production, or occasional incipient capitalists. Guild masters, scattered *rancheros*, owners of workshops (*talleres*), and artisans all employed others and constituted Mexico's "traditional petty bourgeoisie."

Their simple-commodity form of production, however, was under great pressure. Merchant capital's financial power over the petty bourgeoisie had generated a growing separation of craft producers from their means of production. Merchant capital was also weakening the control of guild organizations over guild members and over the labor force employed by artisan masters. The merchants were introducing early-capitalist manufactories, distribution of whose products they controlled through a system of regional, national, and international monopolies. While an occasional small producer was able to accumulate capital, expand sales or trade, and begin to organize production on a capitalistic basis, more often it was a section of the existing merchant class that began to take possession directly of production.[13]

More powerful and influential than traditional petty commodity producers, certain other petty-bourgeois elements were enjoying success in agriculture and commerce. The rural petty bourgeoisie, whose most successful members rose into the ranks of the agrarian bourgeoisie, included prosperous *rancheros,* renters of small *haciendas* or Church estates, and some *mayordomos* who established cattle, sugarmill, or other enterprises of their own. In northern Mexico, including today's southwestern United States, the *vaquero* (cowboy) was becoming a colorful, independent-minded fixture. The *vaquero* owned his own horse and arms, and was free to transmit the patriarchal authority of the *hacendado* down to those "beneath" him or even to challenge the *hacendado* should occasion merit it. An occasional cowboy climbed into the ranks of the rural petty bourgeoisie. Even though the rural petty bourgeoisie employed others, it generally had a difficult time competing with the agrarian bourgeoisie and merchant monopolies.

The commercial petty bourgeoisie included a wide variety of people, ranging from street peddlers to small and medium-size traders and merchants, smugglers, muleteers and middle-level transport operators, and small shopkeepers. Some of its members—particularly successful smugglers and muleteers—accumulated tidy piles of capital, but most, like the majority of Mexico's intermediate-class people, lived austere lives of hard work.

Those few who were able to sustain and expand their capital accumulation were admitted into the ranks of the upper classes, and some even bought titles. Recent regional case studies by Mexican and foreign scholars have revealed a remarkable flexibility in access to upper-class status, something that probably provided a safety valve for putting off revolution in the colonial period for many years.

Various groups within the intermediate classes did not own any means of production or form part of the petty bourgeoisies just discussed. Nor were they peasants, workers, land owners, or capitalists. They were professionals, *letrados* in the bureaucracy, intellectuals, priests, or military officers. During the eighteenth century, lawyers, journalists, teachers, parish priests, minor officials, and other professionals emerged as intermediate groups spawned by the flourishing universities and schools. The rapidly expanding economy at the end of the century increased some of their expectations, as well as those of occasional better-paid mine workers or successful artisans, *rancheros,* or small-scale merchants and mine owners.

The race factor played a role in the intermediate classes' struggle for social definition. For most literate members of the *castas,* government patronage or enlistment in the army were the only means of achieving wealth. Many aspired to the upper-class values associated with wealth and with white skin in colonial Mexico. Their supposed "middle-class" ideology was strongly marked by the values of the nascent bourgeoisie and the titular nobility. They looked down on manual labor—not from the heights of a class fully "superior" to it, but from alongside the workbenches and cultivated furrows to which they might find themselves consigned any day.

Mexico's intermediate classes, then, lacked cohesiveness and a class ideology of their own. Neither the petty bourgeoisie nor the intelligentsia and professional groups were socially or psychologically united around a common class or ideological program. Usually adhering to upper-class values, most of their members were blocked from even a middle level of income or prestige. Constantly being pressured down into the ranks of the working class, peasantry, or lowest echelons of the state, religious, or merchant establishments, the intermediate classes—especially the intelligentsia and professionals—were experiencing rising, yet blocked, economic and political expectations.

In the end, many of them became the voices of an anticolonial movement for independence. Readily they would cry out "Death to the *gachupines!*" Feeling themselves victimized by race and class, they easily gave expression to what in fact were mass demands for an end to slavery, tribute collection, and racism in all its forms (regardless of their own exclusion of "Indians" from their circles). Economically pinched, the intermediate classes welcomed an end to royal and Church taxes. Agrarian and other reforms could only benefit them.

Behind the embrace by some elites of bourgeois revolutionary ideas reaching Mexico from abroad were definite economic interests with which the intermediate classes could identify but not yet enjoy. Unable to assert power on their own, the intermediate classes shared one particular "class interest" with the nascent bourgeoisie: fear of the toiling masses. While from their ranks there might emerge an occasional revolutionary leader able to identify with the poor, most of them could assert leadership in an anticolonial struggle only by pooling their efforts with those bourgeois elements that shared their resentment of Spain. Together, the intermediate classes and bourgeoisie might achieve what neither could accomplish alone.

The poverty, desperation, and restlessness engulfing the general population were not undifferentiated. While many lost, some profited. Middle-size landlords, *arrendatarios capitalistas,* and a few *rancheros* found in the reduction of the peasantry an opportunity to enlarge their holdings and profits. Obtaining more field hands by advancing into the Indian *ejidos* (communal or village lands), they also achieved, as Marx would observe in describing early capitalist transformation of rural areas in general, "more efficient cultivation (by making) use of the hired services of their poor neighbors."[14]

On the eve of Mexico's independence, large numbers of the populace were becoming pauperized and were surviving by begging, engaging in day labor, farming on a tenant or sharecropping basis, or tilling subsistence parcels granted them by *hacendados,* whom they served as debt-peons. Those attaching themselves to the *haciendas* were sometimes better off than their "free" job-seeking counterparts.

Most Mexicans were peasants, field hands, miners, carriers, *obraje* employees, apprentices, workers of various kinds (including occasional slaves)—proletarians in the broad sense, yet by no means a modern industrial proletariat (even by early nineteenth-century standards). Exploited for centuries, these laboring masses had periodically fought in vain to overthrow the forces holding them down. And they were more than willing to fight again.

The one common enemy that existed, making possible national independence and some degree of cross-class and cross-race unity among Mexicans, was the colonial state itself and the *peninsulares* who constituted its voices of political command and also held considerable economic power. It was against this colonialism and these "*gachupines*" that many Mexicans, though by no means all, could agree, finally, to fight.

Late at night, idealistic individuals from the intermediate and upper classes met in their homes to discuss political change. Outside looking in were the dark faces of the huddled hungry. How long before they would launch a bigger *tumulto* that would lead to devastating social upheaval?

Class Wars for Independence

Mexico's Wars of Independence (1810-1822) were profoundly anticolonial, inter-class struggles that succeeded in establishing national sovereignty but failed to achieve a social revolution. No single class or class fraction was able to assert or maintain hegemony over the tide of rebellion that swept the land.

Politically, the foremost precondition for the movement of independence was the steady erosion of Spain's traditional system of control over the American colonies, which climaxed in 1808 when Napoleon's army occupied Spain and seized Charles IV. At that time, even Mexico's viceroy sided with dissatisfied *criollos* against the disintegrating colonial system. Secret societies like the Literary and Social Club of Querétaro and the Freemasons plotted to throw out the colonial bureaucrats. (Freemasonry was a secret fraternal social organization influential in the European, U.S., and Latin American bourgeois social ferment of the eighteenth and nineteenth centuries.)

Then, in 1810, the explosion occurred—not coincidentally, in that part of Mexico with the most capitalist-oriented economic activity and the most intense social differentiation: the north-central region known as the Bajío, rich in mining, manufacturing, and agriculture. A parish priest, Father Hidalgo, after receiving a message that the plot to revolt had been discovered by Spanish officials, called people to mass in Dolores, Guanajuato, where he issued his historic "Grito de Dolores" (Cry of Dolores) on September 16, 1810: "My children, will you make the effort to recover the lands stolen 300 years ago from your forefathers by the hated Spaniards? . . . Long live our most Holy Mother of Guadalupe! Long live (Latin) America! Death to bad government! Death to the *gachupines!*"[15]

Taking Hidalgo's words literally, the parishioners grabbed their machetes and stormed Guanajuato's *alhóndiga* granary, a fortress filled with royal treasure where Spanish troops and wealthy *criollos* had taken refuge. They set fire to Spanish forts and homes. Soon they were an 80,000-strong army, sweeping through towns and pushing fleeing Spanish and *criollo* soldiers southward. Here, in the greater Bajío region, were bred the mixed traditions of armed class struggle and religious idolatry, symbolized by the Indians' carrying the banner of the Virgin of Guadalupe into the front lines of battle.

Other groups of peasants rose up. To the south, the dark-skinned, mostly Indian "mestizo" priest Father José María Morelos organized a guerrilla band that soon grew into an army. A passionate antiracist, Morelos forbade the use of the term "mestizo." Peasants and the impoverished rallied to Morelos's condemnation of "all the rich, *criollos* and *gachupines*" and his plan to distribute half of all seized wealth to the poor. Morelos's 1813 Congress of Chilpancingo resolved to end slavery and all caste distinctions; initiate an income tax; abolish state monopolies, sales taxes, and tributes; guarantee rights of private property; and introduce higher wages for the poor. When Spanish bishops excommunicated him as an "atheist and materialist," Morelos excommunicated the bishops as traitors to Christ.

The military successes of Hidalgo's and Morelos's rapidly growing popular armies forced the wealthy *criollos* to ask Spain for help. However, when the *criollos* later realized that the explosive class threat from below could not be contained even with Spanish aid, many of them opted for independence. As the *criollo* "Liberator" of South America, Simón Bolívar, put it in his famous 1815 "Letter from Jamaica," the *criollos*' main grievance was Spain's not giving the elites sufficient authority to maintain "respect" among the aroused Indians and *castas*. These commoners, Bolívar said, threatened to disrupt all America with revolution. "We have been deprived of an active tyranny, since we have not been permitted to exercise its functions," he complained. In other words, ascendant economic groups had been kept from the highest offices of government in Spanish America and thereby deprived from exercising the class dictatorship so necessary to avoid the disruption and chaos of revolution from below. On September 15, 1821, the Guatemalan Act of Independence openly proclaimed independence "in order to prevent the consequences that would be fearful in the event that the people should proclaim it."[16]

During the 1810s, most of Mexico's elites and some of the intermediate classes pragmatically hedged their bets by spreading their financial backing and ideological support among all political groups, from the most royalist through those seeking autonomy or even independence. As the insurgent Carlos María de Bustamante would later recall, "If we were to punish all those who failed at their duties in this revolution, now making war on us unashamedly, now doing a balancing act so as to land on their feet, now staying home like hearth cats while their brothers knifed each other in battle, it would be necessary to execute two-thirds of our population." To which liberal ideologue José María Luis Mora, who lost a brother in the insurgent cause, was to add:

> Many people would have powerfully supported the revolution with their influence and wealth were it not for the fact that they were profoundly afraid of losing everything in the general disorder; this is how . . . men who truly loved and were committed to their native land not only abandoned Hidalgo's cause but actually took arms against it.[17]

In late 1810, Hidalgo's army arrived at the outskirts of Mexico City when, for reasons unknown, Hidalgo chose not to attack the metropolis but instead led his troops westward and seized Guadalajara. Then, in January 1811, royalist soldiers won a victory that demoralized and scattered thousands of Hidalgo's troops. In July, Hidalgo himself was captured, tried by the Inquisition, defrocked, and executed.

In 1813, General Félix Calleja, a Spaniard, and his largely *criollo* army attacked and eventually overwhelmed Morelos's well disciplined army that threatened Mexico City. Two years later, Morelos too was defrocked and executed. Rebel actions continued for the next five years, but mainly along regional and guerrilla lines, with victories won in the mountains and forested regions south of Mexico City. One of the main leaders was Juan Alvarez, an Afro-Indian peasant.

In 1820, a military *coup d'état* in Spain overthrew Ferdinand VII and led to the reintroduction of the liberal Cádiz Constitution of 1812. It included laws protecting Indians and Indian lands and thereby threatened the *criollos'* shaky rural hegemony. The Spanish parliament (Cortes) also re-evoked the Act of Consolidation, which again threatened the elites' source of internal credit. The Cortes vowed to limit the right of the Church to acquire property and to abolish ecclesiastical and military *fueros* (special privileges). Rich *criollos* naturally saw loyalty to Spain under these new conditions as imprudent, and looked for a leader other than Calleja, one from among their own ranks.

They found their man in *hacendado* Augustín de Iturbide, son of a wealthy Spanish (Basque) merchant and a *criolla* mother, who earlier had fought against Hidalgo, Morelos, and Alvarez. Iturbide succeeded in persuading the viceroy to name him commander of the Spanish army in the south. He then met with Vicente Guerrero, a key southern Indian guerrilla leader, and convinced him to form an alliance to free Mexico from Spanish rule.

Pro-Iturbide officers agreed to give up the *fuero militar,* while those liberals joining Iturbide forced him to agree to the abolition of slavery and the provision of full citizenship for blacks, "Orientals," and Europeans residing in Mexico. Iturbide also curried favor among royalists, gradually winning them over to his "Army of the Three Guarantees." These guarantees were: "Unity," among *criollos* and Spaniards; "Religion," to reassure the Church; and "Independence," meaning only autonomy from Spain.

On September 27, 1821, Iturbide's army seized Mexico City. Iturbide received communion at the Cathedral and installed a coalition parliament—in effect establishing home rule. The new nation's tricolor flag was unfurled: white for religion, green for independence, and red for the blood of union. A year later, in September 1822, Iturbide abolished racial definitions on citizenship documents and censuses.

In spite of Iturbide's having agreed to honor the Cádiz Constitution and the Cortes laws of 1820 to 1821, in February 1822 the Cortes rejected home rule for Mexico. This hardened the political position of the *criollo* elites and their new-found *gachupín* allies, who had already begun to experience some economic benefits from their having proclaimed home rule, particularly after the new government further opened Mexican ports to world trade.

Duties were reduced from 16 to 6 percent. Muleteers were allowed free trade overland to the northern frontiers. War taxes on *pulque* marketing and mining were reduced. Import duties were lifted on mercury and on machinery for use in mining, crafts, and farming. Mexican farm produce and manufactured goods could now be exported duty free. The tobacco and cotton-textile industries, which had entered a wartime boom in production for the sizable popular armies, received from the new home government protective tariffs restricting imports.

Criollos in the merchant, mining, and agrarian sectors, in order to protect their commerce, had named their sons commanders of regional armies. While these military "protectors of commerce" occasionally became radical anticolonial *caudillos* (military strongmen), most formed themselves into regional networks of *caudillos* and *caciques* and became influential in the series of coups and countercoups that followed independence when the elites fell to squabbling among themselves.

Iturbide was unsympathetic to liberal republican ideas. In May 1822 he rejected autonomy for Mexico and proclaimed himself Emperor Augustín I of "independent" Mexico. Five months later he dissolved parliament. In the eyes of his republic-minded critics whom he had thrown in jail—many of them from the intermediate classes—the "emperor" had no clothes. Iturbide trusted no one, including his commander in the port of Veracruz, Antonio López de Santa Anna, an *hacendado* and former royalist officer whom Iturbide tried to recall to Mexico City.

Sensing a rising republican tide of revolt against Iturbide, Santa Anna seized control of Veracruz, proclaimed a republic, and called for the restoration of the 1821 parliament. Groups in other regions joined the revolt in the name of republican federalism and began to march on Mexico City. Rather than face a humiliating military defeat, in February 1823 Iturbide abdicated and went into exile. (He returned in July 1824, in an attempt to reassume political power, only to be captured and executed as a traitor.)

Thus, Iturbide's experiment with autonomy from Spain under a constitutional monarch failed, in large part because of Spain's refusal to recognize home rule and Iturbide's own heavy-handed treatment of his opponents. It was the forces of republican liberalism (which Santa Anna opportunely claimed to represent) that consummated Mexico's winning of independence.

Struggles at the Top

From 1822 to 1857, the young nation experienced over fifty separate governments, ranging from monarchy or dictatorship to constitutional republicanism. Meanwhile, Mexico's elites scrambled for power while simultaneously seeking to hold back the demands of the masses. Inter-elite rivalries were heightened by the multiplication and fragmentation of markets, competing regional power blocs, and the economic leverage of foreign capitalists and states, whose financial support the elites welcomed but whose military intervention many feared.

Rancheros, blacksmiths, lawyers, artisan manufacturers, and other intermediate-class elements that had proven influential in the radical wing of the anticolonial insurgent forces now sought new opportunities for economic well-being. The post-1821 expansion of international trade led to an upsurge in petty bourgeois commerce, production, and paperwork. Although some intermediate-class leaders of the anticolonial revolution achieved government positions after independence, they were unable to gain either economic (class) power or political (state) hegemony. The intermediate classes were far too weak, fragmented, and confused to accomplish that.

There instead began an era in which local oligarchs and regional *caudillos,* many with their own armies, gained control over peasants, workers, and the unemployed. The control was institutionalized through a complex chain of command extending from *caudillo* through local *cacique,* priest, mayor, *hacienda* owner or *mayordomo,* factory or workshop owner or foreman, and block "captain" (often a labor contractor). People were tied into the system through a dependence on personalized patronage, involving elaborate networks of payoffs and favors. The colonial legacy of *personalismo* and corruption deepened.

It is often assumed that the Wars of Independence shattered Mexico's economy, but there is considerable evidence that this was true only in selected areas, particularly Guanajuato and Michoacán. Most mines were unaffected by war damage, and the slowness of mining's recovery from the flooding problems of 1805-1821 had more to do with the loss of assured supplies of lower priced Spanish mercury than with actual war-caused destruction. Mining did not recover its 1805 level of production until 1850. Textile and tobacco production boomed, and in the 1820s Mexican exports doubled. Wily officers carved out parts of the cochineal trade for themselves or took to contraband, as a new class of speculators emerged—what Ladd has called the "merchant military" and Arguello the "armies of commerce."[18]

The new nation's economy was based on regional markets dominated by local oligarchs. Most successful merchants and capitalists had strong links to foreign capital, and at least one (Béistegui) had the majority of his investments in Europe. Many relied on land rent (rural and urban), state favors, commerce, moneylending, and speculative financial ventures for their initial accumulation of capital.

Despite regional growth and individual success stories, the post-independence economic recovery of Mexico as a whole was slow and uneven for many decades. There were a number of obstacles besides political instability. During the Wars of Independence more than half a million people had been killed. In the absence of that raw labor power, capital accumulation had to proceed more slowly than was the case among the expanding U.S. and European populations. Additional deaths resulting from Mexico's subsequent internal and international wars, high infant mortality, and shortened life spans caused by malnutrition, disease, or overwork further limited the labor supply. The population barely grew at all—from about 6 million in 1810 to 8.7 million in 1874—and Mexico did not achieve the 1800 U.S. literacy level of 80 percent until the 1980s.

There were other obstacles to economic growth. Mexico's mountainous geography and primitive transportation system posed big problems. The new nation lacked economic surplus, which was drained first by the forces of colonialism and then by the "flight of capital" during the Wars for Independence. The withdrawal (or expulsion) of Spanish capital left a dearth of funds. Add to these the mounting foreign debt; unequal exchange patterns in trade with Europe and the United States; and loss of more than half the nation's territory to the United States after 1848 (including the lucrative gold veins of California). Last but not least, Mexico suffered from inefficient economic organization—exemplified by parts of *hacienda* agriculture or the Church's *diezmo,* as well as by the maze of official permits and fiscal or customs regulations inherited from colonial times and maintained for many decades.[19]

Here, desperate people reverted to production of handicrafts or subsistence farming, strengthening "domestic economies" of petty-commodity production; there, a new textile factory, paper mill, or export crop was introduced for production by wage or piecework labor on a mass scale. Everywhere class revolt and military conflict threatened to boil over.

Foreign powers hovered along the coasts with gunships and troops, ever ready to recolonize a vulnerable land rich in natural resources. The viewpoint of the industrializing and colonizing British bourgeoisie in 1824 was summed up by Foreign Minister George Canning: "The nail is driven, Spanish America is free, and if we do not mismanage our affairs badly, she is English."[20] For the British bourgeoisie, particularly the owners of large merchant houses, banks, and industries, consolidation and extension of British power on a global basis depended on preventing autonomous Latin American industrial development, while opening up the world's markets through free trade, where they held a competitive advantage. Foreign capitalists in general saw the advantages of free trade and so sided with Mexico's *hacendados,* miners, and exporters against emergent Mexican industrial interests.

Mexico's new governments owed European citizens and governments—Great Britain in particular—more than 76 million pesos, including moneys advanced for the purchase of arms for the pro-independence insurgents. Private British banking firms loaned an additional 16 million pesos in 1824. (Mexico defaulted on these in 1827, but granted the British a favorable trade treaty as part of the settlement.) Successive Mexican governments exempted Spanish investors from expulsion orders if they made loans to the state. In this way, some Spaniards retained their status as leading members of Mexico's bourgeoisie.

Through free trade, British manufactured goods flooded the Mexican market. As early as 1824 cotton textiles constituted 30 percent of imported manufactured goods through Veracruz, thereby undermining Mexico's textile industry, which accounted for about a quarter of Mexican manufacturing enterprises.

Yet in the first two post-independence decades Mexico did not fall under the control of another nation. Discouraged by the chaotic internal situation, foreign capitalists preferred to operate in the spheres of public debt, credits, and trade more than in new direct investments or military conquest. Until 1850, only the Spaniards held large investments in Mexican manufacturing; French, German, British, and U.S. citizens held lesser amounts.

The one area in which foreign capitalists, especially from Britain, maintained an active interest was mining. They continued to invest in rehabilitating the mines and received the greatest part of the profits from the increased production that followed. Mexico depended more than ever on silver and gold for its export earnings (86 percent in 1872), while hides, sisal, and ixtle (a cactus fiber used in making binding twine) led the way in agricultural exports, followed by coffee.

By 1870, England and the United States accounted for about 70 percent of Mexico's trade. Until 1884, when dictator Porfirio Díaz renegotiated the foreign debt and courted foreign investments, early industrialization attempts were largely a domestic matter. However, nationally based industrial development schemes were blocked by free-trade *practices* (including the smuggling into Mexico of foreign manufactured goods that evaded state tariffs) and by foreign bondholders' pressures on the government to repay them.

Given Mexico's foreign debts and budgetary and balance-of-payments deficits (which got worse the more "free" trade became), it was an easy matter for foreigners to continue the process of financing Mexican "economic development" for their own benefit. Foreign loans were followed by the collection of debts and the acquisition of property as payment, thereby augmenting the flow of capital out of Mexico. Mariano Otero was among a handful of Mexicans who bothered to complain, observing in 1842 that "trade is no more than the passive instrument of foreign industry and commerce . . . and today those cabinets, in everything submissive to the mercantile spirit, are profoundly interested in keeping us in a state of misery or backwardness from which foreign commerce draws all the advantages."[21]

By 1867, the state's foreign debt had soared to 375 million pesos and its domestic debt to 79 million pesos—while public income had still not reached 20 million pesos. Currency devaluations and inflation, then as today, benefited merchants and large-scale property owners at the expense of those whose labor produced the wealth—robbing artisans, workers, and peasants not only of their real income but also of much of their property.

Agiotistas, Liberals, and Conservatives

Other than foreign loans, where could Mexico's governments obtain much-needed capital? The army, the Church, and the *hacendados* were obvious possibilities. But if scarce capital were to be saved, it would mean cutting back the payroll of the 18,000 officers and 5,000 soldiers, who drained over half the federal budget, or confiscating Church property, or taxing the *criollo* bourgeoisie. They would hardly tolerate this, and the government would fall.

So successive governments turned to another source: the *agiotistas,* moneylenders who emerged as a powerful fraction of Mexico's commercial bourgeoisie.

Far from acting like old-fashioned usurers, the *agiotistas* constituted a nascent banking community interested in gaining monopolistic control over diverse productive activities. Their influence over the state, desperate for funds, aided them in investing in manufacturing, commerce, mining, and agriculture.

The profits the *agiotistas* made from lending to the government—the state paid them the cream off the customs duties collected at the ports—were often plowed back into productive enterprises.

The state's debt structure, as well as its sources of income like customs duties and its trade policies and practices, ultimately contributed to an original accumulation of capital by both national and foreign capitalists. A series of financial agreements made with the government by national and foreign entrepreneurs gave them not only state support but a steady stream of payments with which to increase their economic interests. Britain, France, and Spain settled both public and private debts by diplomatic convention—and no Mexican diplomat was free of the fear of foreign military intervention should the state not pay up or grant alternative economic concessions. As economic historian Barbara Tenenbaum has shown, the *agiotistas,* through their many deals with foreign capitalists, sometimes made use of the diplomatic conventions in order to improve their own chances at recovering their investments. Other members of the commercial bourgeoisie, like the Martínez del Río brothers, also increased their capital in this way, transforming themselves later into an industrial bourgeoisie. Foreign capital was augmented by capital generated internally by the *agiotistas,* who in turn built alliances with foreign capitalists.[22]

Although the most successful *agiotistas* diversified their investments into textiles and other home industries, internal production of many items was not sufficient to supply a fully developed home market. For example, not enough cotton was produced for the home clothing industry, and so Mexico imported raw cotton from the United States, processing it in Mexico. Because the pressures of the foreign debt and free trade kept mounting, protective tariffs, strong through a good part of the 1820s and 1830s, existed only on finished goods by the 1840s.

For the first years after independence, agiotista-merchant-landlords were hegemonic within the bourgeoisie. Together with the Church credit system, *agiotista* capital tended to merge with landed capital in a stepped-up process of dispossessing the peasantry. *Agiotistas* bought up *haciendas* ruined by the 1808-1810 economic crisis or unable to meet debt payments, and organized them on a sound economic basis. The number of *haciendas* doubled between 1810 and 1854, with one-fifth belonging to the Church. In addition, the *agiotistas* grew fat off Mexico's internal wars—each new triumphant general had first to settle up with them.

For most of Mexico's richest families, independence meant the elimination of rival commercial intermediaries and Spanish monopolists and a strengthening of trade relations with Britain, in which Mexico produced and exported mineral and agricultural products in exchange for English manufactured goods. Inter-elite struggles for political power were more between families than between class fractions based on distinct capitals, since family monopolies usually extended into every major economic activity. In their rush to build up or consolidate monopolies in competition with one another, Mexico's wealthy families only occasionally advocated alternative emphases for national economic development. These emphases sometimes overlapped with political-ideological conflicts between the philosophies of "liberalism" and "conservatism" (which eventually became the banners of diverse contending class forces in the civil war of 1854-1867).

After independence, in the absence of political parties, the social network of Freemasonry became a convenient arena for political combat. Liberals, stronger in the provinces than in Mexico City and most involved in agriculture and mining, advocated a U.S.-style federation. Aided by the first U.S. ambassador to Mexico, Joel Robert Poinsett, a notorious meddler in Mexico's internal affairs who viewed Mexicans as "ignorant and debauched,"[23] the liberals organized Freemason lodges of the York Rite.

Tied to the export of minerals and agricultural products in exchange for imported manufactured and luxury goods, liberal oligarchs sought to maintain the free-trade-based export economy. Measures like tariffs to protect nascent industries held little attraction for them.

Whenever they achieved state power, liberals attacked the Church, often for economic reasons. For instance, the Church-owned Juzgado was Mexico's principal banking institution, and since it normally had its loans secured by real estate, the Church exercised considerable control over land. To favor their own landed interests, the liberals repeatedly sought to eliminate the Church's tax on agricultural production. But special privileges, or *fueros,* excused clergymen from normal civil and juridical procedures, which made it difficult for a liberal government to curtail Church power.

The conservatives, on the other hand, had close ties to the Church and advocated a strong central government. Many belonged to the Scottish Rite of Freemasonry and had been sympathetic to Spain. They saw tariffs as a way to protect the local textile industry, fortify manufacturing, and move toward industrialization via control over the customs houses, which might prohibit free entry of European imports. Since there were frequent changes in government, each one in need of revenue, tariffs were used by the state to raise revenues although they also served from time to time to finance an industrialization program. Conservative leaders included large-scale landholders less interested in capitalist agriculture than the liberal *hacendados,* as well as some fabulously wealthy merchants and early industrialists.

Like the liberals, the conservatives wished to reactivate the mines—but usually for the purpose of developing the home market. They sometimes found support among middle-level merchants in the interior who were integrated with the home market and wished to invest their surplus in manufacturing production, mining, or commercial agriculture.

In practice, liberal-conservative differences among the elites on issues of economic policy were minor, so much did their economic interests overlap. Both liberals and conservatives among the bourgeoisie grew rich off the state, switched sides at moments of political change at the state level, and used the state to control or repress peasant revolts, strikes, or other forms of labor protest. In terms of industrial development, the liberal Estevan de Antuñano and the conservative Lucas Alamán each tried to launch a modern textile manufacturing industry.

Much of the liberal-conservative struggle for state power reflected competing interests within classes or groups other than the bourgeoisie. For example, some of the urban intermediate classes (professionals, bureaucrats, and liberal intellectuals) opposed the military and clergy. The military officer corps was split between liberals and conservatives, but united in its determination to maintain its *fueros*. The military retained the power of arms, as well as its new commercial interests. It, along with the *agiotistas,* was a potent arbiter in the nation's internal affairs. Landlords who survived the credit crunch often built alliances with the army and the Church in order to control peasant unrest and assure sources of credit. Much Mexican mining capital went into landed property, as did some merchant capital. Still other landlords sided with the liberals in their anticlericalism, foreseeing the day when Church properties would be confiscated and (presumably) added to their own.

Manuel Escandón and other *agiotistas* put in Alamán as head of the state's General Directorate of Industry in 1842, in part to oversee development of the home market. State decrees favored domestic industry, along with educational and technological advances in agriculture. Industrialists organized themselves into manufacturing assemblies, which were given a veto power in the 1843 constitution on tariff questions. British diplomatic correspondence reveals that foreign bondholders frowned on these industrialization plans and pressured for continuing the pattern of export of agricultural and mineral products and import of manufactured goods. Their pressures largely succeeded. Alamán's job in the end became one of facilitating trade rather than domestic manufacturing, by compiling statistics and screening for new market opportunities in order to expand Mexico's internal and external trade.

The state, rather than industrialize Mexico, continued to help the *agiotistas* and related interest groups find the best markets, keep abreast of financial and related matters, and garner additional federal contracts for transport or other public construction projects. The state deferred to its foreign creditors, whom the *agiotistas* also served. It remained an unstable state, weakened by the liberal-conservative quarreling among contending politicians, competition between regional *caudillos*, insurrection from below, and foreign invasions.

Invasions, Revolts, and War

Whenever popular rebellions interrupted the flow of dividends, foreign military intervention occurred. Between 1823 and 1861, Mexico suffered an average of one invasion every six years. In 1829, the Spanish briefly occupied Tampico. In 1838, during the so-called Pastry War, the French invaded Veracruz, leaving only when Mexico guaranteed payment of a 600,000-peso debt.

The United States was the most successful aggressor. Having gained its independence almost half a century earlier than Mexico, the northern republic had long coveted Latin American lands. In 1823, President James Monroe had enunciated the Monroe Doctrine, ineffectually warning European powers to stay out of the Americas. Ambassador Poinsett was then instructed to explore the possibility of incorporating northeastern Mexico (today's Texas).

By 1820, thousands of U.S. settlers fleeing the 1819 economic depression had moved with their slaves to northeastern Mexico. Presidents John Quincy Adams and Andrew Jackson offered Mexico millions of dollars to buy the territory. The Mexicans were uninterested, instead abolishing slavery in 1829 and prohibiting further U.S. immigration into what is today's Texas. Mexico offered safe haven for runaway slaves. White U.S. settlers in "Texas," outnumbering Mexicans by six to one, viewed the Mexicans as pro-black and therefore "inferior."

In 1835-1836, the settlers (and a few "inferior" Mexican friends) led a bloody fight for secession of the Texas settlement from Mexico. They eventually defeated and captured Mexico's General Santa Anna, who signed the territory away, leading to the formation of the Lone Star Republic with Sam Houston as its president. Declared Houston: "The Anglo-Saxon race must pervade the whole southern extremity of this vast continent. . . . The Mexicans are no better than the Indians and I see no reason why we should not . . . take their land."[24] In 1845 the United States annexed the Republic as the state of Texas. In early 1846 U.S. military personnel helped seize California and proclaim the Bear Flag Republic. Mexicans driven from their homes later mounted a revolt in Los Angeles and liberated "their" city in the fall of 1846 only to lose it a few months later.

Not surprisingly, Mexicans felt that war had been declared upon them. When U.S. and Mexican patrols clashed in April 1846, President James K. Polk, who, like President Andrew Jackson before him, had been seeking an excuse to seize not only California and Texas but other parts of northern Mexico as well, claimed American blood had been shed on U.S. soil. Congressman Abraham Lincoln asked Polk to indicate precisely where this had occurred, but to no avail. The battle had in fact taken place well inside Mexican territory, near the Río Grande, about 150 miles south of the Texas-Mexico border (the Nueces River). Polk used the incident as a pretext for declaring war and invaded Mexico.

The racist doctrine of Manifest Destiny had just become fashionable. It proclaimed that it was the "destiny" of the United States to occupy the entire North American continent. By 1847, the *Congressional Globe* was reporting the takeover of Mexico as "the destiny of the white race . . . the destiny of the Anglo-Saxon race."[25] Patriotic fervor was whipped up, and soon the United States had 70,000 troops and volunteer militia in Mexico, easily outnumbering and out-gunning the Mexicans.

In the face of the "Yankee" onslaught, Mexico's elites were little more courageous than Santa Anna had been. They and their political representatives took care to prevent popular resistance from getting out of hand by delegating all military authority to the regular army, which they could control. They had their hands full attempting to crush a peasant revolt of 300,000 Maya in Yucatán and a series of uprisings against their class rule by peasants, workers, and squatters in central Mexico. A massive peasant uprising in Oaxaca, Guerrero, and Michoacán between 1842 and 1844, followed by one led by Luciano Velázquez in the Huasteca region of Veracruz from 1845 to 1849, had generated among Mexico's masses new calls for breaking up *haciendas* and giving back "land to the tiller." Agrarian movements ranging from social banditry and anarcho-communalism to Catholic and Indian millenarianism spread across Mexico.

The peasants directed their anger not only at landlords, merchants, and industrialists, but also at the Church hierarchy. For example, replying to the Bishop of Yucatán, who had asked them to lay down their arms, a group of Indian captains leading the Maya revolt wrote (through a scribe) in 1848:

> We say one thing only to you and the venerable saintly priests. Why didn't you remember or take notice when the Governor began killing us? Why didn't you stand up or take interest in us when the whites were slaughtering us so much? Why didn't you do it when a certain Father Herrera did whatever he liked with impoverished Indians? This priest tossed his saddle on a poor Indian, mounted him, and began to whip him, lacerating his belly with lashes. Why didn't you have any concern when that happened? And now you remember, now you know there is a true God? . . . If the whites' houses and *haciendas* are burning, it's because earlier they had burned the town of Tepich and all the hamlets where poor Indians dwelled, and the whites ate all their cattle.[26]

Hoping to stem such peasant rebellions, many prominent families collaborated with the U.S. invaders, thereby hastening the defeat of a Mexican officer corps reluctant to fight and thousands of aroused peasants and workers who genuinely defended the nation's honor.

Meanwhile, U.S. citizens launched a peace movement. Senator Daniel Webster called the war against Mexico "unconstitutional." The prominent African-American leader of the abolitionist movement against slavery Frederick Douglass called it a "disgraceful, cruel" war that was making Mexico "a doomed victim to Anglo Saxon . . . love of dominion." Famed writer and naturalist Henry David Thoreau refused to pay taxes for the war. Clapped in jail, he was visited by his equally famous friend, the writer Ralph Waldo Emerson.

"Henry David," asked Ralph, "what are you doing in there?"

"Ralph Waldo," Thoreau replied, "what are you doing out there?"

Future U.S. President Ulysses S. Grant, an army lieutenant, described "a great many murders" and other atrocities committed by U.S. troops, noting "how much they (Texans) seem to enjoy acts of violence." Concluded Grant: "We have no moral right to go into Mexico. . . . I am bitterly opposed to this war, one of the most unjust ever waged by a stronger against a weaker nation." Later, Grant wrote, "I had a horror of the Mexican War . . . only I had not moral courage enough to resign."

General Zachary Taylor, who headed the initial invasion, reported "shameful atrocities" by the Texas Rangers, who left Monterrey's streets, in the words of one officer, "slippery with . . . foam and blood." General Winfield Scott, who commanded the taking of Mexico City, acknowledged that "murder, robbery, and rape of mothers and daughters in the presence of tied-up males of the families have been common." A soldier wrote a book called *My Confessions* that described scenes like his entering a cave where U.S. volunteers were busily scalping and butchering Mexican women and children.[27]

The United States' sixth president, Congressman John Quincy Adams, saw the annexation of Texas as a shameless act of aggression to expand the South's "slavocracy." He publicly urged military officers to resign and soldiers to desert. Some 5,331 enlisted men, 13 percent of the regular army, deserted, as did thousands more of draftees. It was the highest desertion rate in U.S. history— more than double the rate of the equally unpopular and unjust Vietnam War over a century later. Mutinies also occurred, but officers did not punish the mutineers for fear of even more desertions.

Several recent Irish Catholic immigrants, who had fled the potato famine and British colonialism only to be drafted into the U.S. Army, initiated the desertions by deciding to form the "Saint Patrick's Battalion" and fight on the side of their Mexican Catholic "brothers," similar victims of a big power. They were joined by at least four slaves in their encampment and, later, by more than a thousand other draftees. One-fifth of the *San Patricios*, as the Mexicans affectionately called them, were U.S. native-born citizens. The rest were European immigrants (half of them Irish).

General Zachary Taylor wrote that he was afraid of "seeing our ranks thinned daily." He stepped up discipline through torture, leading to the song most frequently sung by U.S. soldiers during the war:

Sergeant, buck him and gag him, our officers cry,
For each trifling offense which they happen to spy,

Till with bucking and gagging of Dick, Pat and Bill,
Faith, the Mexican's ranks they have helped to fill.[28]

Mexico City was captured on September 14, 1847. General Santa Anna fled, but young military cadets *(los niños héroes)* vainly defended Chapultepec Castle, some reportedly wrapping themselves in Mexican flags and leaping from the cliffs while shouting "Viva México!" School children still recite their names. Most members of the "Saint Patrick's Battalion" were killed in earlier battles or captured during the attack on Mexico City and put before a firing squad, despite Mexicans' pleas to spare them. Annual ceremonies honor them both in Ireland and in Mexico City's San Jacinto Plaza, which sports a marble plaque with their names. Several Irish Americans in San Francisco and other U.S. cities carry the flag of the Saint Patrick's Battalion in the annual Saint Patrick's Day parades, usually as a way to call for the defense of immigrants' rights.

The U.S. war against Mexico dragged on until the signing of the 1848 Treaty of Guadalupe Hidalgo, through which the United States obtained nearly half of Mexico's territory. Chief U.S. negotiator Nicholas Trist later recalled that when he signed the treaty he felt "shame as an American. . . .That was a thing for every right-minded American to be ashamed of."[29] Mexico's elites welcomed the $15 million war indemnities allotted Mexico under the treaty's terms, hoping it would fill up the state's drained treasury and help reestablish a semblance of social order. They used the money to snuff out most of the Maya revolt.

Agrarian revolts then erupted elsewhere. In 1849 Eleuterio Quirós led a thousand peasants in the takeover of Río Verde, San Luis Potosí, a revolt that quickly spread to Guanajuato and Querétaro and engulfed the Sierra Gorda. Liberal spokesman José María Luis Mora called for total suppression of all Indian revolts shaking the nation.

In 1854, the United States paid Mexico 10 million pesos in the Gadsden Purchase of more territory (now part of southern Arizona). The Mexican government was once again led by Santa Anna, who had proven to be a genius at adapting to new political situations. By then an absolute monarch except in name, President Santa Anna used the Gadsden funds to repress peasant revolts and finance his own pageantry.

From its conquest of Mexico, the United States obtained wealthy territory soon to be the scene of the fabulous California Gold Rush. Mexico, on the other hand, lost an estimated 50,000 lives. In addition, some 100,000 Mexicans in the conquered territories became labor power for U.S. capital.

U.S. railroad and mine owners, industrialists, ranchers, farmers, and land tycoons immediately began violating provisions of the Treaty of Guadalupe Hidalgo guaranteeing the property and civil rights of those Mexicans remaining at their homesites in today's southwestern United States. In the following few decades, U.S. citizens of Mexican descent lost some 20 million acres. The treaty's clause guaranteeing respect for the Mexicans' culture and language (an often overlooked legal basis for twentieth-century experiments in bilingual education) was systematically violated. Poor whites were similarly pillaged or abused, although not subjected to the widespread lynchings suffered by Mexicans and Indians.[30]

Civil War and the 1857 Constitution

Most popular resistance in Mexico against repeated foreign invasions was conducted with guerrilla tactics on the part of regional armies. Many radicals and liberals from the intermediate classes reasserted their voice in national affairs, and in some cases lent leadership to the popular uprisings. Many of these same leaders went into exile when conservatives periodically wielded dictatorial powers in the 1840s and 1850s. When they returned they brought with them the ideas of Fourier, Proudhon, Owen, Saint-Simon, and Marx, and infused the mass struggle with such new terms as "socialism," "anarchism," and "brotherhood." European exiles from the defeated revolutions of 1848 also brought these ideas to Mexican soil.

Until the late 1840s, the elites' interfamilial squabbles had rarely cost the life of one of their own. Each attempt to establish hegemony in the disputes over free trade and protectionism, federalism and centralism, limited Church activities and expanded ones, had called on the armies of the poor, while elite leaders had negotiated compromises or even switched sides according to the balance of forces and the availability of opportunities for their own financial aggrandizement.

After the U.S. invasion, however, political and social issues became much more sharply defined. The lower classes escalated their demands for economic justice as their revolts spread and they experienced the power of guerrilla warfare. Many petty-bourgeois leadership types and commercial *hacendados* increased their demands for confiscating Church wealth. Pro-capitalist and anti-capitalist ideas filled the air.

Much of the bourgeoisie recognized the need to consolidate a constitutional republic, with a strong enough executive to further their economic interests and divert or contain the surging unrest from below. Some of the elites rallied behind a popular leader named Benito Juárez, a self-made lawyer of Zapotec Indian stock.

Orphaned at age three, Juárez had been raised by a rural uncle who had beaten him. At age twelve, he had fled the cruel uncle to become a servant boy in the "big city" of Oaxaca. He later studied at a Catholic seminary. Rejecting a chance to become a priest because of the way he had seen the Church mistreat Indians, Juárez instead studied physics and law at a new "liberal" institute in Oaxaca. To pay his way, he waited table for the richer students. He served as a lieutenant in the Oaxaca militia. At age twenty-seven, he was elected to the provincial congress. He became a lawyer and defended poor Indians. He then became a judge, married Margarita Mazza, a blond, blue-eyed daughter of a wealthy Italian immigrant family, and was elected governor of Oaxaca (1847 to 1852). In the eyes of the elites, Juárez had become more or less acceptable. He seemed intelligent and reliable. Deeply religious, he believed in God and human decency. As governor, he had been honest and responsible. He had built many schools and encouraged girls to go to school (an uncommmon thing in those days). On the other hand, pro-Church conservatives saw his liberal ideas as dangerous. But for much of the bourgeoisie, the short, stocky Juárez had a commanding presence that combined liberalism with religiosity, popularity with upright social reserve—in a word, "balance."[31]

By 1854, Santa Anna and his clerical and military allies had established a repressive regime that jailed, executed, or exiled its opponents on a massive scale. Juárez himself was arrested and sent to the damp, dark dungeons of the military fortress island prison of San Juan de Ulúa. Actions like these had the effect of unifying warring factions among the liberals, known as the "purists" (puros) and "moderates" (moderados). The purists drew their main support from the urban petty bourgeoisie, rancheros, and an occasional hacendado like firebrand anticlerical ideologue Melchor Ocampo. Together with vocal urban or town-based liberal artisans, intellectuals, and lawyers, they advocated small and middle-size farms as an alternative to the "inefficient" system of huge rural estates enslaving peasants in debt-peonage. Artisans, facing continued proletarianization, also championed anticlericalism and the ideology of small family enterprises. Purists were directed by men like Juárez, Ocampo, and Ponciano Arriaga.

The moderate liberals, on the other hand, drew their support from the commercial bourgeoisie, some big industrialists, most hacendados, and many ex-government ministers and functionaries purged by the conservative dictatorship. Moderates were led by men like Ignacio Comonfort and the brothers Miguel and Sebastián Lerdo de Tejada.

In 1854, after being imprisoned for several months, Juárez joined Ocampo and Arriaga in exile in New Orleans, Louisiana, where he made a living rolling cigars. Margarita Juárez Mazza stayed behind raising their several children, selling off everything she owned, and taking up weaving to make a living.

The exiled liberal leaders decided to support an antigovernment rebellion in Guerrero, led by the old and by-now wealthy Afro-Indian guerrilla fighter Juan Alvarez. They sent him a statement of principles, many of which became incorporated into Alvarez's "Plan of Ayutla." Juárez sailed to the Guerrero port city of Acapulco and joined Alvarez's army, which marched on to Mexico City. Santa Anna was unable to stop the spread of this revolt and, when he heard that peasants to the north and west were rallying behind it, he sailed into exile.

In mid-1855 Alvarez's army triumphantly entered the nation's capital. The liberals installed Comonfort as president and introduced what became known as the Liberal Reform. Comonfort's moderate administration was soon challenged by enraged conservatives, who, distressed at its legal decrees affecting their vested interests, set up an alternative government backed by segments of the army. By 1857, civil war was sweeping across Mexico.

The problem for the Comonfort government was once again an empty treasury. So it passed the Ley Juárez in 1855, abolishing clerical and military *fueros* (special privileges), and the Ley Lerdo in 1856, forbidding any "corporation" from owning property. Both the Ley Juárez and the Ley Lerdo were then expanded into Articles 26 and 27 of the 1857 Constitution. "Corporately held property" included not just Church lands but also peasant *ejidos*. Under protection of the new Constitution, the moderates' *hacendado* backers—as well as liberal bureaucrats, ambitious merchants and moneylenders, some *rancheros,* and various land speculators—were legally able to purchase or confiscate huge quantities of Indian communal land. Workers were granted the constitutional right to "associate," but artisan guilds were defined as "corporately held property."

To make sure some funds would enter the treasury immediately, the Comonfort government promised that the Church would be paid for confiscated lands, with the government receiving a part of the transfer price and a 5 percent sales tax. This strategy raised some moneys in the short run, but only delayed the attempt to capture the most attractive financial prize (other than Indian lands) promised by the Liberal Reform, the legendary wealth of the Church.

By the time the liberals finally unified their various disentailment decrees in 1859, much of the Church's wealth had dissipated, fled, or been exaggerated in the first place. Both conservative and liberal governments and armies had used it to pay for conducting the civil war of 1857 to 1859. Some of it had been rescued by Church agents through subterfuge; some was plundered and consumed by the liberal forces; and some was converted by speculators into paper—leading to rapid depreciation in the value of the peso. Finally, foreign interests obtained some of the Church wealth by calling in complicated loan arrangements made with previous governments.

Of 16 million pesos worth of nationalized properties sold in Mexico City in 1861 to help finance the newly elected Juárez government, only 1 million was received, the rest going to pay off credits, promissory notes, and bonds. To run a government or make occasional concessions to the peasantry or labor, more money was needed. Juárez suspended payment on the foreign debt for two years and ordered confiscation of any remaining Church wealth.

"People's War"

The conservatives launched a powerful comeback through the assistance brought them by direct European military intervention. In 1861, with the United States bogged down in its own civil war, Britain, France, and Spain signed a tripartite agreement that divided Mexico among them. Spanish troops landed at Veracruz that same year, but did not remain long. The French took over the military operation, invading Mexico in 1862 and occupying it until 1867 to protect Mexico's most famous "emperor" since Iturbide, Archduke Maximilian of Austria.

In a letter to one of his generals, Napoleon III revealed France's motives behind this bold, but risky, undertaking: "If a stable government is established there with the help of France . . . we will have established our beneficent influence in the center of America, and such influence, upon creating immediate avenues for our commerce, will procure for us indispensable primary materials for our industry."[32] France had already taken over Algeria in northern Africa and invaded Vietnam in Asia. Mexico would presumably open the doors to a French empire in Latin America.

To overcome the conservatives and the French, Mexico's liberals had to win the support of the hungry masses. Responding both to peasant demands and to rising agrarian-export and land prices, the liberals implemented an agrarian reform. As in the confiscation of Church wealth, the reform served only to accelerate the very economic processes that had stimulated it in the first place. The 5 percent *alcabala,* or marketing tax, made it impossible for most peasants to compete against the land sharks who descended on them to legally break up "corporately held property."

Land monopolization was also furthered by the "vacant lands" *(baldíos)* decrees issued by Juárez in 1863 to raise funds for fighting the French invaders. In four years, some 4.5 million acres of prime land, much of it belonging to Indians who allegedly could not prove title, passed into the hands of *latifundistas* (big landholders) at about $.025 an acre. Similar *baldío* laws in 1883 and 1894 accentuated the process. *Criollo* (and some mestizo) landowners were thus able to achieve what not even the colonial elites had been able to do: take over the vast majority of Indian land!

An occasional purist liberal voice cried out against the deception of the agrarian reform legislation and its underlying capitalist motivation. For example, Arriaga prophetically had told delegates to the 1856-1857 constitutional convention that Article 27 would inevitably produce "monopolistic capitalism." His proposal to break up the *latifundia* had been unanimously rejected by the delegates, whose votes reflected the class interests they represented. Arriaga correctly perceived that under Article 27, "laboring citizens are condemned to be mere passive instruments of production for the exclusive profit of the capitalist."[33]

Ideologically, the liberals waved the flag of antifeudalism to combat such voices of reason, but other Mexicans, including many of the constitutional delegates, had long since recognized that Mexico had never been feudal. As Mariano Otero stated in 1842:

> When it has been said to us very seriously that we have an aristocracy, when we have been exhorted to bring it up to date and we have been told of the European nobility and the feudal clergy, no one has known what he was talking about; words have miserably been mistaken for things, and an error in language has brought about one in politics . . . the Mexican aristocracy was not at all similar to the European: it was . . . a parody . . . and the individuals that composed it . . . . lived indolently upon capital, enjoying their profits.[34]

In fact, the liberals had a credo that extended beyond their sanctimonious antifeudalism and incorporated the very ingredients of their own class interests: free wage labor, foreign immigration, free non-corporate land, private property, private industry, freedom of religion, free secular education, and free trade and investment (which furthered the bourgeoisie's embrace of foreign capital). Here too Arriaga had voiced a realistic warning:

> Upon decreeing freedom of trade, industry, and other franchises, great concessions are made to foreigners, scarcely reflecting upon the impossibility of our industry and crafts competing with the foreigners, given three centuries of delay, monopoly, and servitude that have weighed upon the Mexican people.[35]

The cloaking of the new onslaught on Indian land in the liberal rhetoric of agrarian reform and "family farming" suggests the extent to which the peasants' class struggle against *latifundismo* had become a serious threat to Mexico's landed elites. "Land to the tiller" movements had spread. Moreover, radical priests, former military officers, and leftist agitators had penetrated the ranks of the peasant rebellions and lent them a degree of ideological coherence, many radical ideas, and occasional leadership.

Yet, during the civil war years, the peasants, like other social classes, were far from unified, much less allied in an organized fashion with other groups. Only rarely were they able to win legislative victories—for example, the Querétaro state legislature passed a minimum-wage law for rural *jornaleros* (day workers) and the San Luis Potosí legislature confiscated a few *haciendas*, delivering them to the peasants.

An immense urban subproletariat of street vendors, beggars, migrants, vagabonds, semiemployed and unemployed—colloquially called by the elites the *léperos*—constituted, with seasonal rural workers, a majority of the labor force. They had been recruited by both liberals and conservatives to fight the civil war. Many, like the peasants, were economically and spiritually tied to the Church, which had an elaborate system of siphoning off much of their paltry earnings and then doling out charity.

Some subproletarians became highway robbers, who did a lucrative business during the war years, adding to the lack of stability needed for capitalist development. They often protected humble muleteers or artisan produce, while directing their blows against foreigners and the rich.

Doubly challenged by their own civil war and the social turbulence of the lower classes, Mexico's elites had been more than willing to seek outside economic and military support. Conservative oligarchs played a key role in inviting and supporting the French military occupation of 1862-1867. A former pro-slavery commander of the Confederacy, General John B. Magruder, lent his services to the French. In 1858, Juárez offered to cede the United States lands for possible canal construction to facilitate inter-oceanic trade and passage through Tehuántepec and Baja California (the McLane-Ocampo Treaty), in exchange for recognition of his government. Then, in 1865-1866, Juárez's anti-French army recruited some 3,000 Union veterans of the U.S. Civil War with offers of good pay and land bonuses.

Even as the nation's elites had learned well the colonial lesson that to govern is to pillage, so their embrace of foreign aid and manners was part of their colonial heritage. Ever since the days of the Bourbons, and even more so during the French occupation, many members of the upper class were known as *los afrancesados,* or "the Frenchified," because of their adoption of French customs and putting on of airs. These customs were now briefly reinforced.

The French occupation marked history's first modern experiment in what emergent imperialist powers would later develop into a fine art—"counterinsurgency warfare." An elite troop of French soldiers was trained and equipped to put down the Mexicans' guerrilla war of resistance being conducted by peasants and workers. French strategy included all the modern counterinsurgency techniques of terrorism combined with political appeal to the people through pseudo-agrarian reform, democratic proclamations, and cultural changes in education and science.

French troops burned entire villages and put men, women, and children before firing squads. As a French officer said in a verse:

> *We come, we kill, we loot, we pass and unflinching*
> *Leave behind us a land scorched and stenching,*
> *And the things that we do in blood and flame*
> *Are glorious, or they would be our shame.*[36]

The crowning irony for Mexico's conservatives was that the French, practicing counterinsurgency, carried out what amounted to the liberals' program insofar as education, land, property, and freedom of press and commerce were concerned. The French validated the confiscation and sale of Church property. They promised the restoration of Indian *ejidos*—to the horror of *hacendados.* They even began construction of the nation's first railroad.

Since liberals led the anti-French national liberation movement, the liberals' cause became equated with Mexico's national independence and honor. This, and France's counterinsurgency programs, left conservatives worse off than they had been before inviting the French takeover. The first victorious "people's war" against imperialism and its counterinsurgency techniques occurred not in the second half of the twentieth century in Algeria, Cuba, or Vietnam, but in Mexico in the second half of the nineteenth century. It was won by mostly illiterate peasants and workers using guerrilla hit-and-run tactics, a *"guerra de guerrillas"* ("war of little wars").[37]

Most peasants were fighting not just a nationalist war against foreign invaders but a *class* war, a "people's war." They could not be "pacified" either by the techniques of French counterinsurgency or by the anti-peasant policies of scorched earth and deportation practiced by occasional liberal army officers. Wherever feasible, Juárez assigned regular army officers to lead the peasant-worker war of national liberation—men like Brigadier General Porfirio Díaz, who gained his liberal and "nationalist" credentials through his leading role in the Mexicans' first major victory, the Battle of Puebla, May 5, 1862, now a national holiday celebrated by Mexicans and their descendants all over the world (especially in U.S. cities). In this battle, Díaz took advantage of a sudden rain shower that made the slopes of the fort he was defending slippery with mud. As advancing French soldiers slid downhill, Díaz attacked them and put them to rout. The unexpected victory rallied many Mexicans to the liberals' nationalist cause.

It also probably saved the United States, since at the time the slave south was winning the U.S. Civil War and a French victory at Puebla would have led to Napoleon III's recognition of the Confederacy. England likely would have followed suit and the non-slave north's economic blockade of the Confederacy would have been broken.[38] Little wonder that the government of Abraham Lincoln extended diplomatic recognition to the Juárez government in Mexico and later supplied it with arms.

To help finance the war, Juárez decreed the confiscation of the property of those Mexicans supporting the French, on the grounds that they were "traitors to the fatherland." At least 200 leading bourgeois families suffered expropriation, reducing the strength of the conservative wing of the *criollo* bourgeoisie and increasing that of the liberal wing. Landlords, *rancheros,* industrialists, and petty-bourgeois radicals also gained from these and related measures of the *Juarista* state. Bourgeois families who accepted state authority had their properties protected. Many big merchants and some industrialists conformed to the *Juarista* movement only at the last moment—under the double pressure of people's liberation war and threatened expropriation.

Although it cost 50,000 Mexican lives, the people's war against 40,000 French soldiers finally triumphed in early 1867, at least in its nationalist garb.

Maximilian surrendered, was tried by court martial, and on June 19 was executed by a firing squad. (His wife Carlotta, a Belgian princess, had by then lost her mind.) Juárez had rejected international pleas for clemency for Maximilian's life, noting that the "emperor" had decreed and implemented the death penalty for all captured *Juarista* soldiers or sympathizers.

Twentieth-century Mexican murals show a stern dark Indian (Juárez) facing a tall blond Nordic (Maximilian), the tips of guerrillas' rifles spitting fire at the emperor's head: a rare symbol of Indoamerica's revenge on imperialist Europe. Statues of Juárez appear everywhere in Latin America today, and he is remembered world-wide for his famous statement upon entering Mexico City, July 15, 1867: "Between individuals as between nations, respect for the rights of others is peace."

At last victorious, Juárez was rejoined by his wife Margarita, who had rallied U.S. support while residing in Washington, D.C., where two of their sons had died, one of dysentery, the other of cholera. Juárez once characterized Margarita as a person "of titanic force," saying "I owe what little I am to her."[39] His political and military success, however, he ultimately owed to the Mexican lower classes. Exhausted, Margarita died in 1871, and Juárez died of a heart attack a year later.

A National and Capitalist State

The guerrilla victory over the French left the most reactionary segments of Mexico's bourgeoisie politically isolated. Most of the clergy and military officer corps, together with some more traditional-minded *hacendados* and entrepreneurs tied to them, found themselves on the losing side against an insurmountable liberal tide. Eager to guide Mexico's finally independent state were a handful of military officers and a massive number of landholders, small and medium-size manufacturers, artisans, professionals, aging peasant guerrilla heroes, and various big moneylenders, merchants, miners, and industrialists.

After the French military withdrawal, the Juarista state continued to be based on an alliance of many classes—but it was the agro-export fraction of the bourgeoisie that tended to dominate. Commercial *hacendados*, manufacturers, miners, and much of banking-merchant capital held hegemonic class power. All these forces favored modern capitalist development and were anxious to associate themselves with the trade and foreign capital of the more industrialized countries, their "natural" allies.

The many years of internal and international war thus ended in the establishment of a well-defined nation-state, victorious in war and firmly committed to "freedom"—that is, freedom for unchecked capitalist development. The Liberal Reform was more than an aggression by parts of the landlord-merchant-industrial bourgeoisie against Church properties and traditions (tithes, *diezmo*, etc.). It also delivered a telling blow to artisan corporations (guilds), accelerating the separation of artisans from their means of production and their incorporation into the textile industry's wage-labor force. Most significantly, the Reform laid the legal basis for the final reduction of the peasantry that would dispossess them of their lands and convert them into "free" wage laborers or debt-peons. The Reform thus laid the foundations in both urban and rural areas for a speedier development of capitalist forms of production.

Much of the success of the Juarista movement against the clergy and the French derived from its building class alliances and offering possibilities of advance for elements of nonelite groups—small farmers, artisans, workers, mestizos, professionals, and so forth—at least in the arena of democratic rights and the chance to organize. Many professionals (mostly lawyers) took sides not out of conviction but out of job hunger (empleomanía) and a devotion to the benefits of the corrupt system of political payoffs. Artisans, on the other hand, had organized into "mutual aid" societies in 1853-1855, and in 1861 they consolidated their Gran Familia Artística, which, with members' dues, guaranteed medical care. Tailors, small-scale merchants, carpenters, typesetters, hatmakers, seamstresses, bricklayers, stonecutters, silversmiths, and others formed similar organizations in the 1860s. Workers' banks and credit unions were organized.

Producers' co-ops shared the capitalist ethos of private property but opposed the big bourgeoisie, which stood in the way of the creation of a society of small and equal producers. The co-ops rallied to the mine pickmen's strike at Real del Monte in 1872 and the hatmakers' and textile workers' strikes of 1875. By 1880, there existed one hundred such "mutual-aid societies" in Mexico City; most members, known as mutualistas, were artisans, whose families constituted a sixth of the capital's population of 300,000 (at last, equal to that of Tenochtitlán).

As industrial and mining production and transportation works expanded during the second half of the nineteenth century, so did the proletariat. The cotton textile industry doubled its installed capacity between 1854 and 1879. A rough estimate of the economically active population in 1861 showed 61 percent to be jornaleros (day workers) in agriculture and mining and another 2.5 percent to be stably employed in factories or artisanal workshops. By 1877, similarly rough estimates showed the regularly employed proletariat to include approximately 100,000 mine workers, 100,000 muleteers, 25,000 textile and tobacco workers, 60,000 urban artisans, 12,000 railway workers, and thousands of other wage and piecework laborers in industry or construction—a total of about 9 percent of the adult work force.

In spite of such expansion in wage labor, much of the proletariat still experienced preindustrial or semi-industrial forms of exploitation. Many resided in miserable barracks provided by capitalist employers and were tied by debts to the company store *(tienda de raya)*. All were subject to sudden layoffs and replacement by an immense reserve army of labor queuing up at factory gates, mineshafts, or other labor recruitment centers for a day's work. Sons and daughters of peasants increasingly migrated to the cities in desperate quest for a means of survival. Up to a third of urban women were employed as domestic servants. Unemployment still hovered around 50 percent. Almost all the proletariat were superexploited. Worst off were the thousands of women and children employed in industry (over a third of the textile labor force) or mining.

The slowly expanding proletariat, working long days at low wages in mining, transport, and construction, or in the textile, paper, glass, sugar, liquor, wheat, tobacco, soap, rope, and other factories and mills, gradually began to organize at the local level with the help of the artisans. Between 1872 and 1880, various local workers' organizations united nationally into the Great Circle of Workers, the Great Confederation of Workers, the Workers' Congress, and similar organizations incorporating thousands of members. These organizations espoused mutual aid, workers' defense, and a variety of radical ideologies (Christian humanism, liberalism, utopian socialism, workers' internationalism, and anarchism) that were gaining adherents in industrializing countries, plus a few conservative ones, although in their practice they were generally reformist.

Working-class struggle throughout the nineteenth century was sparked by artisans, miners, railway workers, and textile workers. But it suffered the contradictions of the petty-bourgeois consciousness of many of its artisan leaders, who also organized against manufactured imports, a demand shared by those textile industrialists whose modernizing factories were contributing to the inviability of artisan workshops and the proletarianization of the artisans themselves. Further, many of the workers' demands were aimed at eliminating such backward conditions as the company store, fines, night work, fifteen-hour workdays, or child labor, while advocating public secular education as the road to proletarian advancement.

In their early years, some workers' organizations received donations from the liberal state, as part of a political trade-off for their having backed the liberals against the conservatives and the French. Others remained independent of the state and, in elections made possible by the Liberal Reform's introduction of male universal suffrage, gained political positions and even hegemony in the local governments of various municipalities. The Great Circle of Workers often acted as mediator between the state and protesting workers.

An evolution toward what became more class-conscious, revolutionary programs and militant strikes on the eve of the Mexican Revolution of 1910 took shape in debates that filled the pages of artisan, anarchist, and worker radical tabloid newspapers: *The Workers' Voice, The International, The Socialist,*

The International Worker, The Child of Labor, and so forth. Dozens of these papers began circulating in the 1860s and 1870s, often with abbreviated life spans, or underground because of the stepped-up repression suffered by the nascent proletarian movement. Most advocated autonomy for municipal governments, workers' control, free peasant villages, women's rights, and one or another form of a universal social republic.[40]

The modern Mexican capitalist state dates from this period of the liberal-conservative civil war, the war of national liberation against the French, and their immediate aftermath. The state-expropriation policy of Juárez against the Church and uncooperative bourgeois property holders was the forerunner of the strong state interventionism of President Lázaro Cárdenas in the 1930s. Similarly, precedents for the modern state's constitutional "protection" and regulation of the activities of peasants and workers were written into the 1857 Constitution. The modern state as a national entity constitutionally enshrined above the interests of traditional corporations or privileged oligarchies (the *ancien régime*) and supposedly oriented toward the "public good" rather than toward any special-interest group (or class) was ideologically conceived and juridically consolidated by the Liberal Reform and anti-French war of national liberation.

In Mexico, this capitalist ideological definition of the state reflected the class hegemony of the bourgeoisie's triumphant fractions. Because the establishment of this state was rooted in internal class war against reactionary segments of the elites and certain traditional noncapitalist forms of appropriation of wealth (Church, artisan guilds, and Indian communities) and external war against foreign invaders, Mexico's new state had some popular legitimacy. Therefore, it had more options for controlling the rebelliousness of the masses, advancing capitalist accumulation, and consolidating the triumphant liberal bourgeoisie's "natural" alliance with foreign capitalists—at the expense of the lower classes and the Church and to the joint profit of domestic and foreign (increasingly U.S.) capital.

Now firmly established, the Mexican state was to assume both bourgeois-democratic and oligarchic-dictatorial forms, depending on the conditions of the class struggle which ultimately defines the forms assumed by any state. From 1867 to 1880, bourgeois freedoms flourished, as urban citizens enjoyed an unprecedented range of free expression. But they were increasingly to lose this privilege as both the modernizing bourgeoisie and the traditional *hacendados* found it necessary to call on stronger state repression to contain the class struggle.

Final resolution of Mexico's civil war and defeat of the French army by no means put an end to worker or peasant resistance. Examples of the continuing radicalization of the class struggle in the countryside included the following:

• From 1836 to 1910, the state of Veracruz was the scene of almost constant peasant revolt.

• Between 1857 and 1881, an agrarian rebellion led by Manuel Lozada (the "tiger of Alica") in Nayarit spread to Jalisco and engulfed both states.

• After 1868, Julio López's Chalco revolt spread to peasant communities in the states of Hidalgo, Tlaxcala, México, and Puebla before Benito Juárez had López executed in 1869. López's final words were reportedly, "Long live socialism!"[41]

• In 1869, to the south, a messianic movement of Chamula Indians in Chiapas erupted.

• Between 1877 and 1881, the Sierra Gorda peasant movement was renewed, incorporating a detailed program of agrarian socialism.

• Between 1877 and 1883, the Cuidad del Maíz region of San Luis Potosí experienced peasant revolt.

• In 1879, a rebellion led by socialist Alberto Santa Fé in San Martín Texmelucan, Puebla, proclaimed a "Law of the People" inspired by utopian socialism, provoking further agrarian revolts in Morelos, Guerrero, and San Luis Potosí.

In the face of this type of social unrest, in which radical ideologies were gaining influence, only a ruthless dictatorship could sustain the class rule of Mexico's bourgeoisie. Unlike the first half of the nineteenth century, the last two decades would be marked by the stability of a clearly defined state serving the interests of the agro-mineral export and industrial-financial fractions of the bourgeoisie, together with foreign capital. Commercial capital's role in stimulating expanded production and a transition toward modern capitalism would continue, but with changes in the forces and relations of production permitting more than mere "original accumulation of capital." An era of domestic and foreign monopolistic enterprises exploiting cheap wage labor for capital accumulation on an extended scale was getting underway.

Yet far from being a uniform process, Mexican capitalist development would continue in an uneven manner, combining various forms of labor exploitation and production. This process would reflect itself in both the state and the class struggle that followed. In a sense, Mexico's internal and external wars were just beginning.

CHAPTER 3

From Dictatorship to Revolution, 1880-1920

De los campos los burgueses se adueñaron
Explotando los veneros que en el subsuelo encontraron
Mientras tanto los millones de pesos al extranjero
Se llevaban los patrones con escarnio verdadero.

(The bourgeoisie helped themselves to the fields
Exploiting the rich veins they found below
While millions of pesos went to foreigners
Taken out by bosses who couldn't care less.)

—Mexican revolutionary song

It is better to die on one's feet than to live on one's knees.

—Saying attributed to Emiliano Zapata on eve of 1910-1920
Revolution

WEAKENED BY WAR DEBTS AND FEUDING among the liberals, Mexico's bourgeois-democratic state gave way to an oligarchic-dictatorial one, led by the part-Indian war hero General Porfirio Díaz. Díaz ran the country like a capitalist preserve for his Mexican and foreign friends. His thirty-five year dictatorship (1876-1911, the "Porfiriato") developed communications, energy, transportation, industry, and commercial agriculture through concessions to foreign and domestic business interests and the use of wage and forced labor. A special rural police force, the *"Rurales"* patrolled the countryside, while a strong army crushed strikes. Censorship and prison dungeons silenced dissenters.

A significant industrial proletariat with a growing class consciousness developed by the end of the Porfiriato. Dozens of industrial, mining, and rail strikes occurred from 1906 to 1908. Most involved both men and women, and almost all were sparked by the illegal Partido Liberal Mexicano (PLM), whose revolutionary goals included equal rights for women. Although put down at great cost of human life, the strikes undermined the Díaz regime's claims to legitimacy. In addition, in 1906-1908 the PLM launched armed revolts in several states. Seasoned fighters from those unsuccessful armed actions played a major role in the military victories that drove Díaz from power in 1910-1911.[1]

In Morelos, a small landholder named Emiliano Zapata, whose lands had been taken by the rich, echoed the PLM war cry: *"¡Tierra y Libertad!"* (Land and Liberty).

A thousand miles north, a distant counterpoint: *"¡Viva Villa!"*

In just a few years, Zapata found himself sitting beside a large mestizo cowboy known as Francisco "Pancho" Villa (real name Doroteo Arango) in Mexico City's presidential palace. Mexico would never be the same again.

From generation to generation the word was passed along, in song, verse, and storytelling. Mexicans recalled their Revolution even more passionately than they did the U.S. invasion of 1846-1848. Today, an occasional old peasant says he can still see Zapata riding a white horse across the escarpments overlooking the once again stolen *ejidos*. At official celebrations or after raucous drinking bouts, the visitor to Morelos can still hear the emotional shout of "Viva Zapata!" New revolutionary political movements like the mid-1990s Zapatistas of Chiapas echo the old war cry.

By 1910-1911, when the Mexican Revolution exploded onto the scene, 96.6 percent of the nation's rural households held no land whatsoever. High government officials described farming as "capitalist agriculture based on labor's cheapness . . . worked by a rural proletariat."

Of Mexico's land surface, foreigners owned between 14 and 20 percent. U.S. investors owned more industries than Mexicans, dominated rails and mining, and, with the British, controlled Mexican oil—almost one fourth of world production by 1921.

Illiteracy plagued 84 percent of the populace. The gap between the rich and the poor had grown wider than ever, although a handful of industrial workers fared better than their rural brethren, and more intermediate-class people competed for jobs in the state bureaucracy.

The driving social force of the revolutionary upheaval of the 1910s was the rural peasantry and proletariat. They divided, however, in 1915, leading to some of the Revolution's most deadly battles. By the time the triumphant bourgeois revolutionary faction voted on the 1917 Constitution, nearly 2 million Mexicans had perished (12 percent of the population). Zapata refused to surrender but was tricked into attending a "peace conference" in 1919 and was assassinated.

The results of the Revolution's bloodshed were: a defeated peasantry; a crippled labor movement dependent on state favors; a wounded, divided, but victorious set of elites led by industrialists, *hacendados,* and enterprising entrepreneurs and regional *caudillos*; and a paper triumph, the 1917 Constitution, a very progressive document for its time.

The outstanding characteristics of the Revolution of 1910-1920 were, first, its initial explosive class confrontation pitting peasants and proletarians, on the one hand, against big landholders and capitalists, on the other; and second, its heavy anti-foreign and anti-imperialist overtones (nationalism). Although the bourgeoisie was divided, with the more "modern" industrial-financial fractions trying to assert hegemony over the more oligarchic, traditional ones, this intra-class conflict was secondary to the need on the part of both bourgeois fractions to fight off the peasants and workers and prevent the lower classes from defeating the upper classes in their entirety. In this sense, there was no social revolution, only a political one, and even the political one was less complete than often claimed.

The "revolutionary" capitalist state that superseded the old oligarchic capitalist state would need time to consolidate itself. Many were the contestants for state power. But most of them proved quite adept at manipulating revolutionary rhetoric for capitalist ends.

Díaz in Power

The liberals' bourgeois-democratic state soon divided and gave way to an oligarchic-dictatorial one. In 1871, the liberals split into three camps, with Juárez gaining a fourth term as president by congressional vote after no single candidate won a majority of popular votes. On July 19, 1872, President Juárez died, and a special presidential election in October became a two-man contest in which Sebastián Lerdo de Tejada defeated Porfirio Díaz. In 1876, Lerdo decided to seek reelection, but the liberals underwent further internal divisions, providing the military with an opportunity to assert its leverage. Proclaiming the slogan "No Reelection" and rallying dissident officers, Díaz seized power in November 1876.

There followed a period of political crisis during which no single fraction of the bourgeoisie was able to achieve hegemony. The United States withheld recognition of the new government until it obtained a number of concessions in 1877, including indemnities for damages incurred by U.S. property owners during Mexico's recent wars and the right for U.S. citizens to own property in Mexico. Free trade was extended along the 2,000-mile U.S.-Mexico border all the way from Tamaulipas in the east (where its practice had been legalized since 1861) to Baja California in the west. Díaz also granted the United States permission to send its troops across the border in pursuit of hostile Indians such as the Apache.

Before leaving office to allow Secretary of War Manuel González to become president (1880-1884), Díaz persuaded the Mexican congress to authorize exceptionally lucrative contracts for U.S. companies to build the main rail lines from Mexico City to the border towns of Ciudad Juárez and Nuevo Laredo. González, unable to meet the fiscal challenges faced by the still heavily indebted state, stopped payment on the salaries of many government bureaucrats; cries for his removal became deafening. Díaz handily won the 1884 election and had the Constitution reformed to permit his reelection in 1888.

Díaz immediately set about patching up old wounds among the nation's elites, granting state favors to big landowners, merchants, and industrialists regardless of their past positions in the liberal-conservative civil war. (In his personal life, he had begun this process in 1881 when he married the daughter of a prominent pro-Lerdo statesman.) This set the stage for the economy's start of a continuous accumulation of capital on an extended scale: full blown capitalism. The economic transformation was made possible in great part by unprecedented political stability, peacetime population growth, and an oligarchic-dictatorial state's encouragement of local and foreign capitalists.[2]

In a pattern that would be somewhat repeated a century later in the name of "neoliberalism," the Díaz dictatorship institutionalized a repressive apparatus and an ideological system emphasizing political stability, science, technology, and material progress as alternatives to the preceding years of "chaos and idealism." The administration's slogans *"Poca política y mucha administración" (Little politics and much administration)* and *"Orden y progreso" (Order and progress)* expressed the new ideology. The goal was to "modernize" Mexico.

A group of businessmen and technocrats known as the *"Científicos"* (scientific ones) became Díaz's brain trust. They were positivists and social Darwinists who argued that everything in politics and economics had to be done according to the rules of "science" rather than those of "metaphysics" or "religion." Inspired by Charles Darwin's ideas of evolutionary progress and "survival of the fittest" made popular by sociologist Auguste Comte and historian Herbert Spencer, the Científicos had gained wealth and status from the Liberal Reform measures taken against the Church and the *ejidos*. They were enamored of the supposed virtues of foreign capital and culture. They discouraged or excluded those intellectuals and professionals who did not accept their way of thinking.

Education, which was for the elite, emphasized teaching English because, in the words of educator Ezequiel Chávez, "it was believed necessary . . . given the growing union between the Anglo-American people and our people."[3] Justo Sierra, minister of education, encouraged the "saxonization" of Mexico—including more U.S. and European immigration—to develop the nation's culture and economy. A national normal school was created in 1887, and from then until 1919 almost all Mexican textbooks became the private business of Appleton Publishing Company of New York and were written by U.S. authors.

Many Científicos had ties to French capital, which, of all foreign capital, was the most involved in the development of the home market. French capitalists helped establish a central bank, the Banco de México, which in turn helped start up the private banking groups of Puebla and Monterrey.

Initially, the Díaz administration facilitated loans and used protective tariffs to assist Mexican industrialists in such areas as textiles, cement, steel manufacturing, beer brewing, and leather goods. Mexico's bourgeoisie welcomed the strong state support it received, although some individuals eventually resented Díaz's picking of "favorites." A couple of dozen merchant families, many of them foreign in origin, came to dominate domestic industry.

The greatest advances in production and trade occurred in the 1890s and early 1900s. Industrial wages improved slightly, the intermediate classes grew, and there was an increase in production for the home market. Even so, the low wages of most Mexicans prevented their becoming mass market consumers. For investors, production for export was more profitable than investing in the home market. For awhile, almost all of Mexico's bourgeois and large-land-holder interests prospered: merchants, new bankers and industrialists, mine owners, liberal military and civilian politicians (most of whom had become rich during the Liberal Reform period), *hacendados* employing wage or debt-peon labor, former "conservative" opponents of the Reform, and even the Catholic Church, which reasserted much of its economic and social influence over daily life.

In terms of total production, foreign investors led by U.S. interests took over much of the economy. By 1911 foreigners owned most of the eighty largest commercial and industrial establishments. Of these eighty, twenty-one were U.S. and twenty-three British; only six were Mexican. The rest were French, German, Spanish, Canadian, or a combination (including sixteen with Mexican participation). Some 90 percent of all fixed investment in mining was foreign, 80 percent of it U.S. As early as 1890, a former treasury minister of the bourgeois-democratic state expressed his satisfaction to the Chamber of Deputies "on seeing foreigners as owners of high finance, of credit institutions, of the electric power plants, of the telegraphs, of the railroads, and of all those things which signify culture and the progress of Mexico."[4]

The United States predominated. By 1897, U.S. investments in Mexico totaled more than $200 million and exceeded U.S. investment in the rest of Latin America, in Canada, in Europe, or in Asia. In the next fourteen years, this figure *quintupled*, and by 1911 U.S. investments were estimated to be greater than those of the Mexican bourgeoisie and double those of all other foreign investors. Eighty-three percent of U.S. investment was in rails and mining, with Anaconda, Phelps Dodge, and U.S. Mining, Smelting, and Refining in the lead. In oil, an American named Edward L. Doheny, aided by loans from Mexican banking and commercial interests, created the Mexican Petroleum Company, which was later absorbed by the Rockefellers' Standard Oil. By 1911 the United States was receiving 74 percent of all Mexico's exports. British interests were second to those of the United States in mining and metallurgy.[5]

The Díaz administration introduced a medley of economic measures to "modernize" Mexico. First, it renegotiated the foreign debt. Then it introduced a new commercial code (1884) that began eliminating protective tariffs and expanding the banking system. Between 1887 and 1892, it introduced new mining codes that permitted private capital subsoil rights. Its elimination of the local marketing taxes *(alcabalas)*, which had favored regional oligarchies, facilitated the growth and unification of the home market, as well as the centralization of economic and political power in Mexico City. *Caciques* were still encouraged to function, but now in greater coordination with the federal government. By 1894, Mexico had its first balanced budget.

The construction of some 19,000 kilometers of railway reduced the cost of transport more than fifteen times by 1900. The rail grid connected regional markets and helped consolidate a national home market. Built by Indian wage labor and owned by foreign capital, it linked the rich mining areas of northern and central Mexico to key gulf ports, Texas border towns, and industrial centers like Chicago and Pittsburgh. This facilitated the export of raw materials and of labor power in the form of Mexican emigrating workers, whose dollar remittances, then as today, kept the bottom from falling out of several village and family economies.

Better able to monopolize markets, control job and wage conditions, and assure rapid economic expansion, large-scale units of production soon put small-scale producers, individual artisans, traders, the peasantry, and the proletariat in a precarious position. Despite impressive economic growth during the Porfiriato, real wages dropped from forty-two to thirty-six centavos a day, a pittance; malnutrition continued; the average life expectancy stayed at about thirty years.

Because of these harsh living conditions and the absence of war, the population nearly doubled—from an estimated 8.7 million in 1874 to 15 million in 1910—a rate of increase not to be reached again until after the Second World War, when the next major period of economic growth would commence. Here at last, almost a century later than in the United States, was the sizable labor force needed for the long sought accumulation of capital on an extended scale.

In northern Mexico, large U.S. investments in mining, iron, steel, and agriculture stimulated wage-price inflation and mass migration from Mexico's interior to better-paid work places further north and in the United States. Masses of wage-oriented peasants began moving from harvest to harvest and from farm to factory over huge expanses of territory. In the United States they increasingly replaced Chinese (excluded in 1882) and Japanese (excluded in 1907) immigrants, and became a principal labor force in mining, railroads, parts of industry, and, above all, agriculture. The number of Mexicans residing in the United States tripled between 1880 and 1910. In perhaps the world's largest movement of a people ever recorded in history, an estimated one-eighth of Mexico's population would end up moving permanently to the United States between 1890 and 1933, most of it recruited by U.S. employers and their Mexican agents.

On the basis of transportation improvement, imported modern machinery, and cheap labor, Mexico's industrial production almost tripled during the Porfiriato, while agricultural and livestock production nearly doubled. The textile and beverage industries were modernized. New industries, such as iron and steel, began to develop. In the mines, steam power was replaced by electricity; air compression drilling and the cyanide and electrolysis processes were introduced; and manganese largely replaced mercury as the transforming agent for silver. Immense piles of tailings could now be tapped for additional silver. Huge quantities of the mineral could be processed in a single day. Much of the labor force could be laid off, particularly from among the 40 percent employed as carriers and the 25 percent employed as pickmen—obviously a great saving in wages.

Mine profit rates shot up by 200 percent between 1876 and 1911. Mineral and metallurgical production increased tenfold. Mexico became the second largest producer of silver in the world. (Mexican silver remained the chief medium of trade with Asia even after the introduction of the gold standard in 1905.) Other mineral production in Mexico also expanded, and by 1910 copper, iron, and zinc had replaced silver in tonnage produced.

Throughout the Porfiriato, the value of all exports increased an average of 6 percent a year, and mining's share of export value eventually tapered off—from two-thirds in 1889 to less than half by 1911. Part of mining's lower percentage derived from a drop in silver prices caused by the 1905 switch to the gold standard, which in turn provoked a serious balance-of-payments problem because of the heightened transfer of value out of Mexico in silver exports and higher costs for imports, as well as credit constrictions—all contributing to an economic crisis on the eve of the Mexican Revolution of 1910-1920.

During the Porfiriato, hydraulic pumps, electric motors, reapers, tractors, and combines dotted Mexico's countryside. Cotton production increased to meet the needs of the expanding textile industry. In sugar, new electric motors and metal (instead of wood) grinders and improved irrigation works more than quadrupled production. The labor force was paid in money wages, or sometimes in "chits" (coupons) accepted for workers' purchases at the company store. Morelos in particular—the home state of Zapata—became one vast monopolized network of rural sugar factories, and, after Hawaii and Puerto Rico, the most productive sugarcane region in the world. By 1908, the seventeen owners of Morelos's twenty-four modern sugar factories and thirty-six sugar-producing *haciendas* owned more than 25 percent of the state's land area.[6]

U.S. wheat interests, which needed "binder twine," and producers of agricultural machinery such as International Harvester converted the Yucatán economy into one based on the production of sisal, or henequen, a fiber from the agave plant. Trading firms like the Olegano Molina Company signed

long-term contracts with International Harvester stabilizing the price of henequen and assuring mutual market access. Yucatán's booming economy of the
time was called "wage-debt slavery" because Indians, *hacienda* peons, and small
peasants were housed on, or hired by, the plantation-*haciendas* and tied to a
company store. Debt peonage or "wage-debt slavery" existed elsewhere in
Mexico as well (such as Oaxaca's Valle Nacional), but in most areas "free wage
labor" prevailed. Villagers and peasants, forced off their land by encroaching
hacienda and agribusiness interests, had to sell their labor power on a temporary or seasonal basis. Many displaced peasants moved to the cities, where they
became members of the new industrial proletariat.

Estimates of the size of the industrial proletariat (including miners) by 1900
ranged from 8 to 15 percent of the adult labor force. Using Díaz government
statistics, Colegio de México researchers and labor historian Jorge Basurto
calculated that there were 107,000 mine and 624,000 manufacturing workers.
The new century dawned in Mexico, then, with free wage labor for the purposes
of capital accumulation on an extended scale firmly in place.[7]

Throughout the nineteenth century such new commercial crops as chiles,
coffee, chicle, maguey, tomatoes, and chickpeas *(garbanzos)* had been introduced, converting many local economies into agro-export areas and the labor
force into a wage labor one. According to the 1910 census, 80 percent of the
population depended on agricultural wages and worked for 20,000 landholders.

Hacendados and land speculators benefited from state policies. For example,
between 1881 and 1906, as a result of *baldío* (vacant-land) legislation, nearly a
quarter of the nation was surveyed by private companies, which received up to
a third of the land surveyed in payment; they often profited by selling it to the
hacendados. In addition, a federal waters act increased the number of waterways
classified as state property, and the state then leased or sold "use rights" to
hacendados—further dispossessing peasants and Indians, who were also refused access to water or pasture lands for their animals.

Thus Mexico saw generalized capitalist monopolization of the means of
production and the consequent conversion of most peasants into a wage-earning or unemployed proletariat. At the same time, rural Mexico was characterized by regional variations and complex internal social stratification
involving "capitanes" (labor contractors), field foremen, transport workers,
rancheros, sharecroppers, and full-and part-time wage laborers, including hundreds of thousands of *jornaleros* (day laborers). *Rancheros*—small and medium-scale landholders infused with a peasant culture—constituted a rural
petty bourgeoisie sympathetic to the ideology of agrarian reform, with its talk
of "middle-size" and "family" farms.[8] Sharecroppers and allotment-holding
workers on *haciendas* farmed minuscule plots of land allotted them by *hacendados* and sometimes hired wage labor from the ranks of other dispossessed
peasants. They were also generally wage workers themselves, since they could

not survive on their own production alone and had to raise the capital necessary to make their allotments productive.

Díaz and his advisers were well aware of what was happening and saw it in capitalist terms. Minister of Agriculture Lauro Viadas summed the matter up:

> Agriculture is, before and above all else, a business, and in every business the amount and safety of the profits are what determine the character of the enterprise. . . . Large-scale agriculture asserts itself and excludes small-scale family agriculture; it takes possession of the land, attracted, and I would say strongly attracted, by economic advantages that spring from the two following causes: (1) The high price of the means of livelihood. . . . The high price of these goods leads first to a high profit for the growers and subsequently, a high price for arable land, which places it within the reach only of capitalist entrepreneurs. (2) The cheapness of labor, which reduces, relatively if not absolutely, the cost of production and produces, thereby, the above-mentioned effect of raising agricultural profits.[9]

Cheaper even than male laborers were females, who generally earned only half of what men earned and may have numbered up to a fifth of the nation's waged labor force (not counting domestic servants). When an investigative U.S. reporter in 1908 asked the mayor of Oaxaca's Valle Nacional why planters did not use inexpensive mills to grind corn, he was told: "Women are cheaper than machines."[10] To help maintain their families in the face of widespread peasant dispossession, more and more women entered the labor market or engaged in handicraft production and commerce. Large numbers were recruited into the burgeoning "sexual services" industries of Mexico's expanding oil, mining, and industrial centers.

Popular uprisings were ruthlessly crushed. Massacres, rapes, whippings, starvation, and even forced deportations were the vicious "order and progress" championed by Mexico's ideologues of modern capitalism. A strong army, streamlined from a sprawling, officer-heavy, ill-equipped mass of 100,000 in 1875 into a well-equipped and more disciplined force of 40,000 in 1910, guaranteed political stability. To forestall possible military revolts and suppress uprisings among peasants and miners, Díaz also created an elite rural police corps ("Rurales"), which became a veritable praetorian guard for private capital and the state.

For example, rebellious Yaqui Indians in Sonora and Chihuahua were militarily subdued in the early 1890s. Their protests put at risk the rapidly expanding farms producing *garbanzos* (chickpeas) and other vegetables for export to the U.S. market. Many of the Yaquis were forcibly deported to the henequen plantations of the Yucatán or the tobacco fields of Valle Nacional, where they worked as virtual slaves in what one U.S. diplomat described as "penal colonies from whence but few return."[11] The Yaquis' most famous female leader, Teresa Urrea (1873-1905), was deported in 1892 to Arizona. She later worked closely with Partido Liberal Mexicano (PLM) labor organizers in the U.S. southwest. Because of her immense popularity among workers and her skills in the healing arts of folk medicine (which became internationally famous), people in both countries called her "Saint Teresa of Cabora."[12]

Rapid income growth for some Mexicans and impoverization for others was producing a nation of stark contrasts, but these were not the result of "feudalism" or "traditionalism," as some writers have assumed. On the contrary, they were the result of the development of modern capitalist forms of production combined with dictatorial social and political forms of control over a restive population. The countryside, mines, and oilfields were not characterized by supposed "feudalism" but by real turn-of-the-century capitalism. Mexico as a country was less an independent nation than it was a company country—that is, a capitalist one where foreign investors heavily influenced economic decisionmaking.

It might seem that Díaz, and the policies that he advocated and instituted, were well entrenched by the early 1900s. But seeds of discord were evident at all levels: in conflicts within the bourgeoisie over the advantages of ties to foreign capital as opposed to greater independence; in tensions between the agro-export and industrial-financial fractions of the bourgeoisie; in restiveness on the part of petty-bourgeois traders and producers ruined or blocked by the forces of monopoly capital; in resentment among intellectuals and professionals left out of power by an authoritarian cliquish regime; in bitterness among lower-level bureaucrats at being blocked from entering the upper ranks; in seething discontent among peasants, Indians, and women over physical abuses and loss of lands and communal rights; and in increasing unrest among urban proletarians over miserable working conditions and wages. Moreover, there was an underground opposition political party that was slowly building a base of support, especially among workers: the PLM.

The Precursor Movement

The first two decades of the Porfiriato had been marked by a division in the urban workers' movement into two sections. Most artisan "masters" and better-paid workers, backed by moderate intellectuals, wanted to work out a *modus vivendi* with the Díaz dictatorship. The more radical section included members of the industrial proletariat and employees in artisan workshops, supported by radical intellectuals, who began to seek more revolutionary and proletarian solutions. During the first decade of the twentieth century, when stepped-up production in the textile, beverage, cement, brick, mine, printing, and cigarette and cigar industries was dealing the final blow to all but a minority of independent artisans, the reduced artisanry together with growing numbers of the industrial proletariat began to assert revolutionary demands. Several strikes broke out, usually led by the PLM. Throughout the Porfiriato there were 250 strikes, mainly in textiles, tobacco, railways, mining, and bakeries.

Officially organized in 1905, the PLM had its roots in the hundreds of "Liberal Clubs" launched at the beginning of the century by disgruntled bourgeois liberals and intellectuals from the intermediate classes upset by the regime's authoritarianism and concessions to the clergy.[13] PLM leaders, like the anarchists Ricardo and Enrique Flores Magón and Antonio Díaz Soto y Gama (later to be a major political spokesman and ideologue for Zapata), radicalized the pro-democracy anticlericalism of these clubs and moved their demands in a more class-based peasant-proletarian direction. This lost them some bourgeois members and speeded up the pace of their suppression by the government, but it also attracted increasing numbers of workers and peasants. The PLM became known as the Magonistas, after the three Flores Magón brothers, Ricardo, Enrique, and Jesús.

The PLM widely circulated its reformist program, a significant part of which was to be incorporated into the 1917 Constitution. It called for an eight-hour day, a minimum wage, an end to child labor, an end to *latifundismo,* "land to the tiller," protection of the human rights of Mexican migrants in the United States, an end to U.S. interference in Mexican affairs, and only one term for the president.

The PLM's underground newspaper, *Regeneración,* financed mainly by worker donations, reached most areas of the country and achieved a circulation of 30,000 as early as 1906. It was a particular target of the Díaz security forces, which had its editors jailed, exiled, even killed, and the presses shut down—but the newspaper's backers always found the means to continue publication.

In 1906 the PLM led a strike against an Anaconda subsidiary at the Cananea mine in Sonora near the U.S. border. Strike leaders demanded equal pay for Mexican workers with U.S. workers and the promotion of Mexicans to some of the positions held by U.S. citizens. Some 275 armed U.S. volunteers under the command of six Arizona Rangers temporarily occupied Cananea, before being replaced by 2,000 Mexican soldiers who crushed the strike. Nearly one hundred workers were killed. As miners' protests continued off and on during the next few years, U.S. Cavalry troops mobilized along the Sonora-Arizona border.

In 1906 the PLM turned itself into a political-military organization and proclaimed a revolutionary ideology opposed to imperialism and in favor of workers, peasants, and progressive elements of the intermediate classes and bourgeoisie. Tens of thousands rallied to its cause.

From 1906 to 1907 and again in 1908, the PLM launched a series of armed revolts in several northern states and elsewhere, along with a nationwide strike wave. All of these revolts and strikes were militarily crushed, most violently in the Río Blanco-Orizaba area of Veracruz, where two successive massacres of striking textile workers occurred (the textile strike was nationwide). The second massacre occurred January 8, 1907, when workers' families were approaching

Río Blanco to collect the bodies of those killed in the first massacre. Federal troops killed up to 1,000 of the approaching families—men, women, and children—the single bloodiest slaughter of the Porfiriato.

In 1906, the PLM-dominated railroad workers' 10,000-strong Gran Liga de Empleados de Ferrocarril launched what one newspaper called "one of the most serious strikes ever registered in our country."[14] The rail workers struck again in 1908, bringing rail traffic to a grinding halt for six days. Their leaders called off the strike when they were shown a telegram from Díaz reminding them of what had happened to the strikers at Río Blanco. The striking rail workers were later fired.

After the failure of their initial armed uprisings, the PLM claimed to have several guerrilla units operating throughout Mexico. The United States beefed up its troops along the U.S.-Mexico border from 1908 to 1910. In August 1910 another PLM armed uprising occurred in San Luis Potosí's Huasteca region.

Though few in number, women in the anti-Díaz struggle—especially journalists—moved to its front ranks. They included schoolteacher Juana B. Gutiérrez de Mendoza and Elisa Acuña y Rosete of the newspaper *Vesper* (1901), the cofounders of the 1907 Mexico City group "Mexican Socialists." Often arrested, they were joined in jail by other anti-Díaz women, such as poet Dolores Jiménez y Muro. Those three activists were forced to flee to the United States. They founded a pro-labor feminist group, Hijas de Cuauhtémoc. Gutiérrez de Mendoza and Acuña y Rosete later joined Zapata's army, the former becoming a commander of troops.

"The worker is the arm, the heart of the world," wrote schoolteacher, poet, and labor organizer Sara Estela Ramírez of the newspaper *La Corregidora*. A major PLM spokesperson, she died in 1910 at age twenty-nine.[15] Women workers, particularly in the textile and cigarette and cigar industries, were militant participants in the PLM strikes.

The PLM encouraged women to join its ranks as full-fledged members. Its most well known and most frequently jailed leader Ricardo Flores Magón wrote in *Regeneración*:

> Women work more than men, they are paid less, and misery, mistreatment and insult are today as yesterday the bitter harvest for a whole existence of sacrifice. ... Bondage does not recognize sex; the infamy [capitalism] that degrades men equally degrades you.[16]

Ricardo Flores Magón's "companion" María Talavera (the PLM was critical of marriages performed by either the Church or the Díaz government) was described by the *Los Angeles Times* as "a brilliant and bold woman anarchist who dared more than any of the men."[17] Like Ricardo, she was often arrested by U.S. authorities and imprisoned. The *New York Times* observed in early 1911 that "women have taken a spectacular part in the revolution."[18] Many of these revolutionary women came from, or were inspired by, the PLM, the backbone of what became known as the "Precursor Movement" of the Mexican Revolution.

From their U.S. exile in the early 1900s, PLM leaders organized Mexican migrant workers, who had long been active in the U.S. southwest, where the word "huelga" was heard before its English equivalent "strike." The U.S. government and Pinkerton detectives hounded the Magonista labor organizers, beating and jailing them or keeping them on the run as "illegal immigrants," as well as opening their mail and coordinating intelligence operations with the Díaz dictatorship. Archival records show that the Mexican and U.S. governments coordinated repressive actions against the PLM on both sides of the border.

Ricardo Flores Magón, who would eventually die under mysterious circumstances at Fort Leavenworth Prison in 1922, and other Mexican political exiles received considerable support from the rapidly growing Mexican communities of Los Angeles and the U.S. southwest. U.S. and Mexican migrant workers in the insurgent anarchist and socialist movements, led by people like Emma Goldman and Eugene V. Debs, rallied to defense campaigns for PLM leaders whenever they were incarcerated. The PLM's internationalist cooperation with U.S. trade-unionist radicals like the Industrial Workers of the World (IWW, founded 1905) led to spurious accusations by the Díaz government that the PLM was "anti-Mexican." The government attacked the PLM's role in the 1906 to 1908 armed revolts, subsequent military actions in Chihuahua, Coahuila, San Luis Potosí, and Veracruz, and armed liberation of northern Baja California in early 1911, by calling the rebels U.S.-sponsored "filibusterers."

The PLM lost some of its members after declaring in June 1908 its total commitment to an anarchist ideology. (Unlike socialists, anarchists called for abolition of the state.) Some prominent PLM leaders who opposed the tilt to anarchism stayed in the organization until 1911 or even later, but the ideological differences of opinion caused major problems after 1908. Debs and many U.S. socialists ended their support of the PLM in early 1911 when they decided to back the revolutionary movement of the 1910 anti-Díaz presidential candidate Francisco I. Madero, a prominent bourgeois political figure. Meanwhile, pro-PLM Mexicans in the United States struggled on. At the peak of IWW organizing more than half of the total annual dues of the union came from Mexican immigrant workers, and half of the victims of the famous 1914 Ludlow Massacre at John D. Rockefeller's mines in Colorado were Mexicans, mostly women and children.[19]

After the onset of a major economic depression in 1907, triggered by a Wall Street panic, the fabric of unity among Mexico's bourgeoisie became frayed. Bankers were suddenly weakened. Some Mexican capitalists responded by shifting their investments into domestic manufacturing, which strengthened the growing industrial fraction of the bourgeoisie in comparison with the financial and mining fractions. The industrial fraction also bought up smaller factories that could not survive the crisis.

The Díaz government, already rattled by the PLM armed revolts, now took a series of desperate steps that satisfied no one. Trying to stop a run on the banks in 1908, Finance Minister José Yves Limantour started calling in loans from *hacendados,* thereby alienating many in the Porfiriato's political network of landlords and *caciques.* Banks were overextended, more loans were called in, mineral production plummeted, industries began to close, and unemployment quickly surpassed the 50 percent mark. Food shortages caused by crop blights and the Porfiriato's emphasis on agricultural exports deepened the crisis.

The government sought to stop the economic hemorrhaging by granting the most valuable petroleum concessions to a British firm, El Aguila; by buying from U.S. owners majority shares in the railroads; and by canceling the railroads' contracts with Doheny's Mexican Petroleum Company. The U.S. government did not see these steps as even-handed. After all, Mexican oil production was increasing—it *quadrupled* in 1910. Fearing the British were getting the inside track with Díaz, U.S. officials began reconsidering its approach to the Díaz government. Díaz himself told U.S. journalist James Creelman in early 1908 that he would not run for reelection in 1910, when he would be eighty years old. The scramble for succession was on.

Within the bourgeoisie, northern financiers, industrialists, and landholders were the most disgruntled. They blamed the deteriorating economic situation on Limantour and the Científicos, as well as the senile, ingrown character of the dictator and the old men around him. Future presidents Madero, Venustiano Carranza, Alvaro Obregón, and Plutarco Elías Calles all hailed from the north. They and others like them realized that a political change to increase their voice in government could improve their enterprises vis-à-vis foreign monopolies (even if often in alliance with them) and expand the home market by bringing the peasantry into the consumer economy. Throughout his reign Díaz had been forced to grant greater autonomy to governors in the northern states, where the elites moved increasingly into industrial production and financial and political power, often benefiting from alliances with U.S. capitalists, who had 22 percent of their Mexican investments in just three northern states (Sonora, Chihuahua, and Coahuila).[20]

The financial fraction of the bourgeoisie had strength in the north's largest city, Monterrey, a burgeoning industrial center. Entire northern states were practically "owned" by a few bourgeois families, the most notorious case being that of Chihuahua, where the "liberal" Terrazas-Creel clique owned most of the state's cultivable land and had large investments in livestock, cotton, banking, textiles, and other manufacturing industries. Northern agricultural production as well, particularly in the northwest, had been profitably commercialized and was based on wage labor.

Much of the northern bourgeoisie got behind the Democratic Party movement of 1908 to 1909, which called for the presidential candidacy of General Bernardo Reyes. His early backers included future presidents Madero (1911-1913) and Carranza (1917-1920), as well as some Científicos. Díaz was torn between throwing his support to Reyes and the industrial-financial bourgeoisie or to vice-president Ramón Corral, who represented the dictatorship's underlying political network of landlords-*caciques*. He finally decided to send Reyes on a military study assignment to Europe and to accept the nomination for president himself.[21]

At that point, most of the urban bourgeoisie, particularly the industrialists, and the "modern" landlords of the commercialized countryside, threw their support to the northerner Madero. Although he was a personal friend of both Díaz and Limantour, Madero had been an early financial backer of the PLM's *Regeneración*. This made it easier for him to represent discontented intermediate-class people and the petty bourgeoisie and also to appeal for support from the only active revolutionary force on the scene, the PLM.

Indeed, Madero was an ideal representative for the bourgeoisie in its hour of need. Madero's family was highly respected. It had interests in commerce, banking, ranching, cotton production, wine distilleries, mining, refining, iron and steel, and the guayule (rubber) and textile industries. It was also reputed to be 8 million pesos in debt to Mexican banks in 1910. Madero himself epitomized the ingenuity and idealism of the bourgeois-democratic vision that saw civilian rule, civil law, and civil behavior—backed by adequate military force when necessary—as key components of the orderly process of "democratic" politics. He made this view clear in his widely circulating book *La sucesión presidencial en 1910*, which called for modernization of the political system.

Madero had important friends inside and outside of government, at home and abroad. Like Díaz, he was a high-ranking Freemason. Madero's year of studying agricultural technology at the University of California at Berkeley and his brother Gustavo's ownership of stock shares in Standard Oil (which reportedly helped finance Madero's election campaign in 1910) suggested a leaning toward cooperation with the United States that might forestall further U.S. intervention. The United States eventually did support Madero behind the scenes, and Madero later rewarded Standard Oil with what one historian has characterized as "one of the most one-sided business concessions imaginable."[22]

Ironically, Madero's 1910 presidential campaign was based on Díaz's original slogan, "Effective Suffrage and No Re-election." In the few campaign speeches he was allowed to make, Madero opposed the Liberal Reform laws on the grounds that they violated political freedom and that religious interests were no longer a threat. He made only vague promises to the peasants, while informing workers that there would be no reductions in work hours or increases in wages but "only freedom, because freedom will let you conquer bread ... the people do not ask for bread, they ask for freedom."[23]

The PLM considered Madero's electoral politics "a crime, because the malady that afflicts the Mexican people cannot be cured by removing Díaz and putting in his place another man. . . . Our electoral ballots will be bullets from our guns."[24] Díaz too opposed Madero's electoral dream—and had him jailed in San Luis Potosí. But on October 5, 1910, Madero escaped the prison and fled to exile in the United States, from where he issued his call for armed insurrection known as the "Plan of San Luis Potosí." He set the date of November 20 for a national uprising. He was well aware that his call might unleash a revolutionary tide that would topple not only the Porfiristas but the entire bourgeois state apparatus and introduce a revolutionary peasant-worker system of class-based redistribution of wealth. The PLM, the only experienced anti-Díaz political-military apparatus on the scene, was advocating precisely that.

Indeed, the mass response to Madero's call for an armed uprising was instantaneous. In the numerous armed battles launched against the dictatorship, the most significant military forces in the north came from the ranks of the PLM and the armed groups led by Chihuahua's Pascual Orozco, Jr., and (to a lesser extent) by Villa, while those in the south came from the peasant army led by Zapata in Morelos. Madero was a leader without his own army, sitting things out across the border. Meanwhile, PLM troops won a major battle at Casas Grandes, Chihuahua (December), and went on to capture Mexicali, Baja California (January), and Guadalupe, Chihuahua (February).

Sorely in need of a military victory, Madero reentered Mexico to claim leadership of revolutionary forces moving against Zaragoza, Chihuahua. About to be defeated, Madero and others retreated to the PLM stronghold of Guadalupe, where the local commander Prisciliano G. Silva welcomed them. Fresh PLM reinforcements arrived from across the border under the command of Lázaro Gutiérrez de Lara, a member of the PLM's minority socialist wing. The PLM majority led by Flores Magón had kept its military plans to revolt secret from the socialist wing, leading to internal resentments. Madero and Gutiérrez de Lara privately struck a deal to combine their forces and "arrest" the unsuspecting Silva, a Flores Magón loyalist. On February 14, 1911, they took Silva prisoner.[25] Not surprisingly, ideological splits and internal personal conflicts deepened after that, in both the PLM and the Mexican Revolution.

Still seeking a military victory, Madero went with his armed followers to engage in battle at Casas Grandes, Chihuahua, where he was defeated (March 6). The decisive battle against Díaz's army was conducted in early May at the border city of Ciudad Juárez, Chihuahua, and was won by Orozco's troops, many of whom had fought side by side with PLM soldiers in the earlier engagements.

Díaz's military losses, made possible in significant part by PLM fighters, forced the dictator to arrange a compromise with Madero, enshrined in the Ciudad Juárez peace treaties of May 17-21, 1911. The treaties allowed Díaz to go into exile, named an interim president, and provided for new presidential elections in October. But Madero's election that year did not bring peace, bread, or freedom. The Mexican Revolution of 1910-1920 was just beginning.

Revolution I: 1910-1913

Prior to his election, Madero ordered the various revolutionary guerrilla bands and armies, including his own, to turn in their weapons. Many fighters, trusting his assurances that the national army would return to the barracks now that "democratic elections" had been scheduled, obeyed his order. Zapata met with Madero and explained that his peasant troops could not lay down their arms without assurances of an agrarian reform. Madero assured him that once the arms were turned in, an agrarian reform could begin. In August 1911, the army's General Victoriano Huerta was sent to Morelos to oversee the Zapatistas' delivery of arms. After most of the peasants tossed their weapons into a pile, Huerta ordered his troops to open fire on them.

Three months later, Zapata issued his "Plan de Ayala," calling for continuation of the revolution until land was returned to the peasants and a regime of social justice introduced. The Zapatistas rearmed, and a class war of armed peasants and workers against the bourgeoisie was unleashed in all its fury. Through brilliant guerrilla tactics, Zapata's forces seized major centers of sugar production, commerce, communications, and government administration, running them like communes based on village traditions of self-government— "the commune of Morelos."[26]

In the north, the PLM had already established its commune. It had taken over northern Baja California and governed it largely on anarchist principles of egalitarianism and direct local democracy from January to June 1911. However, its success in Baja weakened the PLM elsewhere since it had to bring key cadre from the interior of Mexico to defend its liberated territory. This and internal ideological and personal leadership splits, like Gutiérrez de Lara's betrayal of Silva, caused the PLM to lose momentum in the rest of the nation.

Moreover, larger mass movements were emerging to challenge Madero and the bourgeoisie. For example, in March 1912 Orozco declared his revolutionary opposition to Madero with a program incorporating many of the PLM's class demands. (The Terrazas-Creel clique opportunistically backed Orozco.) And there were other class-based uprisings throughout the nation. As historian John M. Hart has documented, U.S. properties became favorite targets of Mexico's aroused masses.[27]

To many a dispossessed peasant, small *ranchero*, Indian *comunero*, or rural proletarian, the solution appeared obvious: take back the land and water, seize the mills, provide for self, family, and community rather than for the boss or the foreigner. And this is what thousands of *jornaleros* (day laborers) and peasants began doing. Their actions sparked a prairie fire of revolt, as peasant armies, federal troops (the *federales* that became so maligned in the popular *corridos*, or folk ballads, of this period), and even *cacique*-led bands spread across Mexico in armed combat.

The most active revolutionaries among the peasantry were the landless wage-labor workers and *jornaleros*. As agrarian-reform advocate Luis Cabrera told the Chamber of Deputies in late 1912: "The rural population . . . not having *ejidos* is forced to live six months off day wages and the other six it takes up the rifle and becomes Zapatista."[28] Meanwhile, sharecroppers, tenant farmers, and allotment-holding farmers were often too busy trying to feed themselves and their families to take up arms. Some of those most under an *hacendado*'s authority (the so-called *acasillados*) did not even hear of the events shaking Mexico.[29]

Women revolutionary *soldaderas*, some calling themselves *"generalas"* (generals), played an important part in the Mexican Revolution. Many children also took up the gun. It was a time of fierce loyalties, mixed with much abuse of women, in which a curious combination of license and respect emerged for Mexico's "women in arms." An ex-tortilla maker named "La China" led an entire combat unit of Zapata's army. Socialist schoolteacher Juana B. Gutiérrez de Mendoza became a Zapatista colonel. Women were also numerous in the "Red Battalions," composed of urban workers who joined the civil-war battles after the revolutionary forces divided in 1915. Later, many of these real-life revolutionary heroines were mythologically transformed by Mexico's patriarchical culture into either prostitutes or brave camp followers patting tortillas for their sweethearts.[30]

While class war raged, Madero's "parliamentary democracy" drifted. General Huerta became increasingly impatient with the socially unproductive debating of the Congress and the army's inability to stabilize the situation. In 1913, he and some pro-Díaz generals decided to mount a military coup. The coup generated artillery battles in Mexico City that lasted ten days and killed countless civilians, remembered as *la decena trágica*.

The plot to make Huerta president was hatched in the American Embassy (the "Pact of the Embassy"). The coup resulted in the assassination of President Madero and his vice-president, although it was not clear who ordered the murders. Based on his archival research, historian Friedrich Katz concluded that the German ambassador to Mexico believed that Madero had dissatisfied his earlier backers in Standard Oil by not granting them enough oil concessions, causing the U.S. government to cease backing Madero.[31]

It was not the first or last time that the United States intervened in Mexico. Mexico's foreign policy doctrine of nonintervention in other nations' internal affairs was a result of public reaction to experiences like these.

Revolution II: 1913-1914

The Mexican public now perceived Huerta and the Díaz supporters around him as "usurpers" and "counterrevolutionaries." Peasants and workers rushed to join Zapata in the south or Villa in the north. For the next three years, popular regional armies fought federal troops across the breadth of Mexico in a veritable dance of bullets.

The revolutionaries eventually split into two broad warring camps, a "radical" one led by Zapata and Villa and a "moderate" one led by northern landholder-capitalist Venustiano Carranza, an ex-governor under Díaz, and Carranza's talented military field marshal, Alvaro Obregón, a sixth-grade graduate, ex-mechanic, and successful chickpea farmer from the northern state of Sonora. Carranza decreed the death penalty for prisoners, adding to the carnage.

The Carranza-Obregón forces became known as the Constitutionalists, in symbolic representation of their leaders' supposed defense of constitutional norms and democratic legitimacy. They included many intermediate-class professionals and prosperous farmers, *rancheros*, and even landlords who shared the class background and goals of the leadership. Many proletarian and peasant foot soldiers also joined their ranks, believing such propagandistic promises as the one Carranza made before a rally in Sonora on September 23, 1913: "Once the armed conflict . . . is over, the formidable and majestic social struggle will have to begin, the class war, whether we ourselves want it or not."[32]

Obregón realized the strategic importance of being open to the left and rallied around him many left-leaning intellectuals and nationalists with strong "Jacobin" (meaning radical) tendencies. Carranza took Obregón's advice and decreed progressive labor and agrarian reform laws in late 1914 and early 1915, which helped attract further popular support. He did not, however, wish to form an open alliance with the working class.

Obregón, on the other hand, understood that such an alliance was necessary to win the civil war and implement the political project of the modernizing industrial-financial fraction of the bourgeoisie. The socialist and anarcho-syndicalist ideas of the urban workers' Casa del Obrero Mundial (House of the World's Workers)—which was closed down by Huerta in May 1914—boded no evil for him. He believed that "The principal purpose of socialism is to extend a hand to the downtrodden in order to establish a greater equilibrium between capital and labor."[33] In other words, socialism could be coopted to serve capitalism's purposes.

Another Constitutionalist radical of the time was Salvador Alvarado, a former owner of a small business in Sonora who introduced socialistic measures as governor of Yucatán from 1915 to 1917. A statement he made in 1919 further illuminated the bourgeois character of the Constitutionalists' "socialism":

> Today there is a formula for the collective good, namely, the socialization of the state . . . [under a socialized state] the capitalist will be able to dedicate himself to business in peace, without the anxieties that today disorder his hours. Capital, which is only accumulated labor, will be in perfect accord with real and effective labor, because each needs the other as an unquestionable basis for the good of all.[34]

In Yucatán, Alvarado was backed by 7,000 troops, peons whose debts were pardoned, workers who were allowed to organize, and second-level *hacendados* who were appointed to administer the state agency that regulated the henequen market and prospered from the threefold increase in world henequen prices stimulated by the outbreak of the First World War. Money from henequen contracts with International Harvester helped finance the Constitutionalists' war chest, as did funds from rubber contracts with U.S. firms in the neighboring state of Campeche.

The Zapatistas and Villistas, even though allied, had different class compositions. The Zapatistas were mostly peasants and rural proletarians, and their demands were "Land and Liberty." They fought for the restitution of stolen lands and water and pasture rights and the restoration of grassroots village democracy.

The supporters of Villa, on the other hand, came from various social classes. Villa himself was a large, roughhewn working man, who neither smoke nor drank but reputedly could out-dance anyone. He had a very strong sense of justice. He had been a fanatical admirer of Madero ever since the martyred president had helped save his life in 1912 when General Huerta had almost had him executed. So Villa welcomed anyone into his camp who could claim Maderista credentials, and his army and staff absorbed much of the Madero government bureaucracy. (Martin Luis Guzmán, later a famous novelist, served as a secretary in Villa's camp.)

The top ranks of Villa's followers included more cowboy caudillos (*vaqueros* or *charros*), *rancheros*, and petty bourgeois storekeepers than it did communal peasant farmers; the foot soldiers were usually cowboys, fieldhands, peasant *jornaleros* (day laborers), migrant farmworkers who had lost their lands, miners, railway workers, and the unemployed. The aims of the Villistas were thus more worker-oriented and petty bourgeois than they were pro-peasant, although several Villistas put forward serious land claims. Villista *caudillos*, as foremen of large estates, *rancheros, vaqueros*, or independent ranchers, had commanded peasants, but few of them had personally experienced land hunger. Workers among the Villistas, unlike the landless peasants, were more interested in gainful employment than in farming for themselves.

Lands seized by Villa's army were often held by the state, not necessarily given to the peasants. Land and agrarian reform were nonetheless demanded by more Villistas than is usually recognized.[35] Villa expropriated many of the landholdings of the Terrazas-Creel clique, but the clique's other industrial-financial interests survived. The Terrazas-Creel dynasty was able to reassert its power after 1920, when it recognized the new "revolutionary" state, and its members intermarried with some of the "new revolutionaries." (Today, the Creels are a leading industrial group.) Further, most U.S. properties in Villista areas paid taxes to Villa (including American Smelting and Refining and those owned by William Randolph Hearst) and were thus protected from the peasants. Villa depended on the United States for guns and ammunition, obtained in exchange for cattle and cash.

Huerta turned to the British for aid. Lord Cowdray, chairman of the oil firm El Aguila, floated him a loan that helped keep him in power. Huerta was leery of the new U.S. president, Woodrow Wilson. He rejected a special envoy sent by Wilson to try to buy him out. President Wilson saw Huerta as an anti-democrat. What was really at stake, of course, was not the competing imperialist powers' investments in democracy—their long support for Díaz belied that—but their desire to control all of Mexican oil. Mexican reserves were large and production was increasing. The United States controlled 70 percent, Great Britain, 27 percent.

President Wilson proceeded to withhold recognition from the Huerta regime and to establish a financial blockade and an arms embargo against Mexico. Secretary of State William Jennings Bryan cabled U.S. representatives in Mexico on November 24, 1913, that U.S. policy on Huerta was "to cut him off from foreign sympathy and . . . to force him out," resorting, if necessary, to "less peaceful means to put him out."[36]

The Constitutionalists readily obtained financial and military aid from the U.S. government and U.S. oil interests. President Wilson worried that Huerta's occasional social reforms, which outnumbered those of the Madero administration, might prolong his stay in power. Therefore, Wilson lifted the arms embargo on February 3, 1914, in order to rush in military aid for the anti-Huerta forces, particularly the Constitutionalists. At the same time, U.S. oil tycoon Edward L. Doheny and other U.S. investors provided Carranza's Constitutionalists with millions of dollars in credit and military equipment and refused to pay taxes to Huerta.

In April 1914, claiming that it had to prevent a German "munitions ship" from landing and delivering cargo to Huerta, the United States sent Marines and bluejackets (sailors) to occupy Veracruz. Actually, the arms and munitions on the German ship were U.S.-made, purchased in the United States by Huerta agents, and shipped via Europe to decoy U.S. federal authorities. The fact that they finally ended on a German steamer of the American-Hamburg line was coincidental and not originally planned. No matter—Wilson needed a pretext for asserting U.S. power in determining the course of events inside Mexico.[37]

Hundreds of Mexican civilians perished during the bombardment and invasion of Veracruz. Latin American attempts to mediate the U.S.-Mexican conflict caused President Wilson to tell his diplomats that should the attempts fail to reach a pro-democracy solution, "then the settlement must come by arms, either ours or those of the Constitutionalists."[38]

The U.S. occupation of Veracruz had grave economic consequences for Huerta. Edith O'Shaughnessy, married to the U.S. chargé d'affaires in Mexico City, noted at the time, "With the taking of Veracruz, through whose customs a full fourth of the total imports come, Huerta is out a million pesos a month, more or less. We are certainly isolating and weakening him at a great rate. 'Might is right.' We can begin to teach it in the schools."[39]

In the United States, Samuel Gompers and some other leaders of the American Federation of Labor (AFL) supported the invasion of Mexico, while more leftist labor leaders vigorously protested it. Left-wing mineworkers leader William D. Haywood, still smarting from the Ludlow massacre, told those who accused him of lack of patriotism that "it is better to be a traitor to a country than to be a traitor to your class."[40]

Huerta's enemies soon began converging on Mexico City, with Zapata and Obregón in a race to see who could get there first. Huerta transferred troops from the north of Mexico City to the east, in anticipation of a possible U.S. military advance on the capital from Veracruz. In this way, the U.S. invasion of Veracruz had the effect of allowing Obregón easier access to Mexico City from the north and to win the race against Zapata. Blaming President Wilson for his troubles, Huerta resigned on July 8, 1914.

The U.S. invasion redounded to the advantage of the Constitutionalist camp in other ways. When Carranza pulled his forces out of the October 1914 Aguascalientes Convention of anti-Huerta forces because of the radical voices prevailing there, he found a sanctuary for them in the U.S.-occupied Veracruz area. There too he could control the lucrative customs houses. At the same time, Carranza publicly spoke of "throwing out the Yankee invaders" and "saving national sovereignty." In this way he was able to claim credit for the U.S. troop withdrawal that promptly followed his arrival in Veracruz.

The Aguascalientes Convention itself proved a tumultuous affair. Villista and Zapatista soldiers lined the packed convention hall with guns at the ready. Debaters from all camps outlined positions that well reflected the Constitutionalists' bourgeois biases and the Zapatistas' and Villistas' identification with the downtrodden. At one point, former PLM militant Antonio Díaz Soto y Gama, a radical lawyer high up in Zapata's group of advisers, threw the convention into wild confusion by crumpling the Mexican flag in his fist and asserting that it symbolized "the lie of history" since "our independence was

Table 3

U.S. Interventions in Mexico, 1906-1920

1906
Some 275 armed U.S. volunteers led by Arizona Rangers temporarily occupied Cananea, Sonora, to help put down a PLM-led strike against a U.S. copper company. Nearly one hundred workers were later killed by Mexican soldiers.

1907-1916
U.S. Cavalry and regular Army troops repeatedly mobilized in the Sonora-Arizona border area and other areas along the U.S.-Mexico border to crush labor strikes in the U.S. southwest and "contain" the Mexican Revolution.

1912-1913
"Pact of the [U.S.] Embassy" made General Huerta president in a military coup against democratically elected president Madero.

1914-1915
U.S. troops seized Veracruz, with hundreds of civilians killed during the invasion, in an attempt to isolate Huerta, who had sided with British oil interests; Washington blocked arms shipments to Villa and Zapata and extended diplomatic recognition, loans, and arms to *hacendado* Carranza, "First Chief" of the anti-Villa, anti-Zapata moderate wing of the revolution.

1916-1917
General John J. Pershing led a 6,000-man invasion of Mexico's north but failed to capture Pancho Villa or to defeat his army.

1919-1920
U.S. military planners drew up a secret 8-inch-thick "Special Plan Green" for an invasion of Mexico "and replacement of U.S. troops by a native Mexican constabulary" in the event of problems in oil fields or along border. The special planning for an invasion was maintained until 1942, when Mexico became a U.S. ally in the Second World War.

no independence for the native race, but for the *criollos* alone," a sensational challenge that brought leveled pistols before his chest.[41]

The class lines separating the Zapata-Villa forces from the Constitutionalists remained foremost in the minds of the "Centaur of the North," as Villa had been called by the bourgeois press, and the "Attila of the South," as Zapata had been described. In December 1914 the two men met for the first time, on the southern outskirts of Mexico City. Observers recalled how nervous and laconic each man seemed. But mention of some of the Constitutionalist leaders triggered this sudden outburst:

> Villa: "They are men who have always slept on soft pillows."
> Zapata: "Those *cabrones*! As soon as they see a little chance, well, they want to take advantage of it to line their own pockets! Well, to hell with them!"[42]

Zapata and Villa agreed to fight the class enemy—represented in their eyes by the Constitutionalists. Each returned to his respective stronghold to prepare for the assault that was to follow.

Revolution III: 1915-1920

The Constitutionalists' Obregón and Carranza were similarly mobilizing for civil war. Realizing the need to split off urban workers from their previous allies, the peasants, Obregón finally convinced Carranza of the need to accept worker support. The key was the 50,000-strong Casa del Obrero Mundial, based in Mexico City but with regional affiliates spreading throughout the nation. The Casa had unionized industrial workers in shoe factories, print shops, breweries, smelters, mills, and various small and medium-size industries, and it had led strikes in urban areas. It had gradually moved from its anarchist ideology into a medley of ideas combining anarcho-syndicalism (which sought to replace the state with a national industrial union) with the many strands of socialism then being espoused in Mexico.

In early 1915, Obregón gave the Casa material aid in exchange for its organizing union members into "Red Battalions" to help defeat Villa's and Zapata's armies. The Obregón-Casa deal split the ranks of workers and peasants and led to military victory for Carranza.

The Casa's decision to back the Constitutionalists was the turning point in the Mexican Revolution. It sealed the doom of the nascent peasant-worker war against the bourgeoisie. Besides being in desperate need for food and other supplies, Casa members had cultural differences separating them from peasants. They were not favorably impressed by the Zapatistas' seeming religiosity, their carrying the banner of the Virgin of Guadalupe through Mexico City's streets, or by some of the Villistas ransacking of homes. In later explaining his own role in opting for the "Red Battalions," which he helped organize and lead, Casa member Rosendo Salazar pointed out that in difficult conditions bordering on starvation, the Casa had allowed itself to be "bought out" by Obregón,[43] thereby undermining its previous autonomy and leading to its eventual suppression in August 1916.

But in the short run the alliance between the urban working class and the bourgeoisie gave urban workers a new opportunity to spread their movement and consolidate their position. The Casa's six Red Battalions numbered 7,000 workers and played a key role in the string of Constitutionalist military victories that followed. Women factory workers in greater Mexico City organized the 1,500-strong ácratas (those opposed to all authority) to serve with the Red Battalions.[44] The Red Battalions helped push Villa back to northern Chihauhua, near the U.S. border, where his army, reduced in size, was isolated. A wedge was driven between the Villistas and the Zapatistas, who were unable to help Villa from their Morelos stronghold hundreds of miles to the south. In addition, some of the Red Battalions moved against the Zapatistas, helping to keep them restricted to the south.

Up to this point, the thrust of the Revolution reflected the relative unity of workers and peasants. This unity was broken by the alliance between the urban working class, with its leftist ideas and record of militant strikes against capital, and the enlightened bourgeoisie as represented by Obregón, with its willingness to make concessions to the proletariat when necessary. From 1915 on, organized labor in Mexico remained closely associated with the state. The state put forward a rhetoric and inconsistent practice of what political scientist Arnaldo Córdova called the "politics of masses."[45]

The government granted most of the workers' demands in the May 1916 general strike sponsored by the Casa, which had grown to 90,000 members. One signer of the agreement was Luis Morones, who in 1918 founded the Confederación Regional Obrera Mexicana (CROM), a pillar of support for the bourgeois governments of the 1920s. On the other hand, in February 1916 the government closed down Casa's headquarters and jailed its regional directors. Then it ordered out the army to crush the general strike of July 31 to August 2. "First Chief" Carranza himself dusted off an 1862 Juárez statute that decreed the death penalty for anyone "disturbing the public order." The "politics of masses" was obviously one of an iron fist in a velvet glove.

Meanwhile, the United States provided Carranza's faction with arms and, in October 1915, granted its government diplomatic recognition. As U.S. Secretary of State Robert Lansing wrote in his private notes, Carranza was the least of the evils and could be won over with dollar diplomacy, whereas Zapata and Villa might be more intransigent: "The real problem Carranza will have to face is financial. He has no credit; his paper money is worthless; his source of revenue uncertain; and his soldiers without pay. We can help him in this."[46]

Mexico had been in default on its bonds since 1913. The U.S. State Department huddled with Thomas W. Lamont, senior partner of the investment bankers J. P. Morgan and Company, and worked out a plan for an international bankers' committee to handle the negotiations with Mexico that would reschedule debt payments and work out future loan guarantees. The bankers' committee was, in the State Department's words, "under the leadership of American bankers and the policy of the United States Government regarding Mexico [shall] be the dominating influence in the operations of this group." As Leon J. Canova of the State Department's division of Mexican affairs put it, "We hold the whip handle at the present time. We are the bankers of the world."[47] President Wilson, noting that "the masters of the government of the U.S. are the combined capitalists and manufacturers of the U.S.," was more blunt in recognizing U.S. emergence as a world imperialist power:

> Do you know the significance of this single fact that within the last year or two we have . . . ceased to be a debtor nation and have become a creditor nation? . . . We

have got to finance the world in some important degree, and those who finance
the world must understand it and rule it with their spirits and with their minds.[48]

The United States cut off arms to Villa. In response, he launched a punitive
attack on the border town of Columbus, New Mexico, March 9, 1916. The
United States then ordered General John J. Pershing to invade Mexico with
6,000 troops and seize Villa. Villa's guerrilla tactics ran circles around the
frustrated general, and the Pershing expedition pulled out of Mexico in January
1917. But even if it failed in its main mission, the expedition did accomplish
one thing that smoothed Carranza's path to victory: it kept Villa fighting on
two fronts and made real the threat that another U.S. invasion might be
launched against Zapata. Accordingly, some of the Zapatistas laid down their
arms and sought amnesty from Carranza.[49]

Villa's military defeats in 1915-1916 and Zapata's increasing isolation in the
south made it possible for the triumphant Constitutionalist moderate wing of
the Revolution to convene the Constitutional Convention of Querétaro in late
1916. The 1917 Constitution finally approved by the delegates was a triumph
for the liberal wing of bourgeois democracy. The "Jacobin" forces loyal to
Obregón were able to win many, though by no means all, of the debates. Besides
guarantees for private property and effective [male] suffrage, the Constitution
included the following articles: Article 3, severely limiting the powers of the
Church; Article 27, providing for agrarian reform and the nation's ownership
of all minerals and sub-soils, including oil; and Article 123, granting labor the
right to form trade unions and to conduct "legal" strikes, with arbitration
boards having equal representation from workers, employers, and government.

Even so, the 1917 Constitution still vested ultimate authority in the "nation,"
whose only representative was the executive power of the state—the president.
Thus the strong executive of the days of Juárez and Díaz became the law of the
land, legitimizing the capitalist state's power to govern and control the country.

Carranza wisely signed the Constitution, even though he opposed much of
it. Not to sign it would have meant renewed civil war. As constitutionally elected
president from 1917 to 1920, he ignored the Constitution's progressive articles
and ruled with a firm hand. He approved fewer funds for social measures than
either Madero or Huerta had done, so that the long years of class war produced
only token gains for peasants and workers, not a successful social revolution.

Meanwhile, Zapata and Villa continued fighting a guerrilla war to make real
the social revolution. A pro-Carranza agent infiltrated Zapatista ranks and
lured Zapata into a "peace conference." When approaching the conference site
on April 10, 1919, Zapata was ambushed and assassinated. This left the
Zapatista movement divided and without a leader.

Ironically, Carranza suffered a similar fate in May 1920 when, after he tried
to keep Obregón out of power by naming his own successor, a pro-Obregón
member of his personal guard assassinated him. Villa, after five years of

guerrilla warfare, accepted a peace offer and settled on a *hacienda* given him by the government. He was assassinated in 1923. New archival evidence uncovered by historian Friedrich Katz suggests that the U.S. and Mexican governments played significant roles in Villa's murder. The man convicted of Villa's murder was released after serving a small part of a long sentence and was received by President Obregón. According to a report by the U.S. Bureau of Investigation (forerunner of the FBI), a letter from Obregón's successor, Calles, noted that the final condition laid down by the U.S. government for recognition of the Obregón government had been met by Villa's assassination.[50]

Lessons of the Revolution

The toll in human suffering during the Mexican Revolution was staggering. Nearly 2 million Mexicans perished (12 percent of the population); many others were wounded. A large number of deaths resulted from inadequate medical care or sanitation, as well as from generals' invoking the death penalty for captured soldiers, a precedent established in 1913 by Carranza.

The split of workers and peasants into warring factions made the bourgeoisie's task easier. Nevertheless, the combined struggle of workers and peasants, however much beaten back and ultimately divided, did undermine the oligarchic-capitalist state and win for working people rights they had long been denied. Their struggle made possible the limited democratic concessions and social reforms that characterized the Mexican Revolution. And it was their struggle, through its repeated attacks on foreign bourgeois overlords dating from the PLM's Cananea strike, that gave real strength to the Revolution's nationalism and anti-imperialism.

The peasants' and workers' struggles also were responsible for the bourgeoisie's willingness to share power in the new post-Díaz state with a number of military *caudillos*, regional *caciques*, labor leaders, small business owners, intellectuals, and bureaucrats—the intermediate classes and petty bourgeoisie. Unfortunately, these elements proved easily corrupted. Their reception of state favors, administrative posts, and the chance to forge policies favorable to large-scale capitalists reinforced traditions of corruption in high places and of circumventing announced reforms (agrarian reform, labor agreements, etc.). Since these intermediate-class people gained status, wealth, and power by thus cooperating with, and benefiting from, the new state, a growing convergence of class interests began to occur, increasingly tying leading members of the top and middle ranks of the petty bourgeoisie and intermediate classes to the bourgeoisie proper.

Ironically, the ideology that would legitimize the bourgeoisie's hegemonic project was that of the "glorious Mexican Revolution," particularly as embodied in Carranza's anti-imperialist statements, in the rhetoric of agrarian reform, and in the call for all Mexicans to unite and avoid renewed bloodshed. Just as liberalism became the ideology of the bourgeoisie in the nineteenth century, so "the Revolution" now became the ideological banner legitimizing bourgeois class rule in the twentieth.

In terms of the key interests of peasants and workers, the Revolution did not succeed; nor was it aborted or "interrupted."[51] It was *defeated*. But since the revolutionary project of the urban and rural proletariat was a historic one, preceding 1910 as well as following 1920, we cannot say that the workers and peasants lost the war. They lost a battle, but the war continued, here peacefully, there violently, in the decades ahead.

This is not how the Mexican Revolution is always seen, however. Some authors characterize the Mexican Revolution as a true social revolution, or as one that overthrew feudalism. Others explain the defeat of the peasants and workers as a product of their political underdevelopment. Still others see the problem as lack of leadership in the form of a vanguard party. Each of these three interpretations is flawed.

For the first, there is no doubt that some bourgeois elements wished to cleanse the landscape of *haciendas* and debt-peonage in order to advance capitalist agriculture and "middle-size" farms, even as a few had sought to do half a century earlier. But the notion of a "bourgeois revolution against feudalism" oversimplifies a much more complex reality, including the actual dominance of the capitalist mode of production prior to 1900. Nor can the Revolution be reduced to the aim of replacing "original accumulation" of capital with "accumulation of capital on an extended scale," since the latter had already commenced. The Revolution simply helped eliminate obstacles to its continuation and advancement.

For the second of the flawed interpretations, to say that the proletariat was "underdeveloped" as a class is both condescending and distorted. Perhaps the massive penetration of foreign monopoly capital affected the so-called underdevelopment of the Mexican bourgeoisie, but it had a contrary impact insofar as the working class was concerned. It concentrated and centralized thousands upon thousands of workers in factories, mines, railyards, and mills, thereby objectively forming a modern (for its time) proletariat—not an underdeveloped one.

Subjectively, this growing proletariat expressed itself, however erratically, in a militant way and with typically proletarian ideologies (anarchism, anarcho-syndicalism, socialism, etc.). Its massive strike activities in Cananea, Río Blanco, Puebla, San Luis Potosí, Veracruz, and elsewhere hardly reflected its underdevelopment as a class. Indeed, precisely because of its *development*, its members were often massacred, as they were when strikers were put down in Río Blanco, Orizaba, and Cananea in 1906-1907. This same *development* of the proletariat helps explain the ferocity of the class war that became so bloody during the Revolution. Among the proletariats of the world at the start of the twentieth century, Mexico's was one of the most militant and advanced in its class outlook.

Yet there were many peasants and workers whose class consciousness remained unstable and confused. In the rural areas, the mixed consciousness of the stratified peasantry reflected the fact that many forms of economic production were combined—from large-scale capitalist agriculture with modern machinery to traditional subsistence farming. Peasants who acted to seize the means of production might thus also yearn for the restoration of their land rights.

For the third flawed interpretation, Mexico in fact had a vanguard political-military organization—first in the PLM (until 1911) and then in the Zapatista "army of the south." Even as the Paris Commune foreshadowed the possible future of proletarian power in Europe toward the end of the nineteenth century, so the "commune of Morelos" embodied the possible future of peasant-worker power in Latin America at the beginning of the twentieth century.

Other factors, including the limited character of the vanguard organizations, caused the defeat of the peasant-worker uprising. These were the peasant-worker split of 1915; geographical regionalism; personal and ideological leadership rivalries; U.S. intervention; and, not least of all, the failure of the Morelos "commune" to reach out beyond its liberated zones and offer a concrete revolutionary program that would recognize *all* workers' and peasants' demands and invite class alliances. A spread of such a program with the "Morelos commune" model to back it up might have contributed to greater lower-class and intermediate-class unity capable of transforming the entire social structure of Mexico.

Likewise, the short-lived Aguascalientes Convention government of late 1914 and early 1915, which briefly united the Villista and Zapatista forces, lacked a clear and specific multiclass revolutionary program. The question that arises, of course, is what would have happened during the 1911-1915 phase of the Revolution had class-conscious peasant and worker leaders actually organized either a coalition of social movements or a vanguard party espousing a national revolutionary program unmarred by the anti-state and anti-organizational tenets of anarchism. For then, as anti-capitalist revolutions elsewhere in the world later confirmed, the bourgeoisie might well have been defeated in its effort to divide and control the revolutionary forces.

Finally, if all the aforementioned formulaic explanations of the Revolution and its results are misleading, so too is the romantic belief that the class struggle today is the same as that of yesterday—the notion that the Mexican Revolution is "permanent." Without denying the historical roots of contemporary class struggle, we must recognize that Mexico changed considerably after 1910—and even more after 1940 and after 1968. Moreover, all these changes were directly related to the 1910-1920 Revolution and the consequent alteration and intensification of the anti-imperialist class war during the 1920s and 1930s.

In brief, the class struggle of peasants, workers, and progressive intermediate-class elements became complicated by the confused legacies of the "Mexican Revolution in power." After 1940, the "Revolution in power" was increasingly exposed as a social counterrevolution and a political one-party dictatorship.

Thus the Mexican Revolution was assuredly not permanent. Yet the class struggle continued, necessarily adjusting itself to new conditions and learning from the lessons of the past. Perhaps the three most important historical lessons of the Revolution of were: (1) the danger of turning in one's arms prematurely and trusting peace offers (the Zapatistas in Morelos in 1910); (2) the pitfall of allowing an antagonistic division to occur between the urban working class and the rural proletariat and peasantry (the Casa del Obrero Mundial's Red Battalions in 1915); and (3) the need to recognize and incorporate the special demands and needs of the oppressed, especially women and Indians.

CHAPTER 4

Corporatism and Cárdenas: 1920-1940

Cárdenas es como el sol:
Brilla sobre todo
Pero calienta a nadie.

(Cárdenas is like the sun:
He shines upon everyone
But warms no one.)

—Mexican saying

THE MEXICAN REVOLUTION had dismantled an old oligarchic state. Now a new one was to be constructed. Starting in 1917, the triumphant segments of the bourgeoisie, led by the industrial-financial bourgeoisie of the north (the so-called Northern Dynasty, still influential today), undertook their political project of reconsolidating Mexico's capitalist state along new lines.

Any state, as we have seen, develops in the general interests of its society's ruling class, or combination of dominant classes or class fractions. It serves to reproduce and reinforce the prevalent economic conditions of life. So it was that Mexico's state remained a capitalist state.

The state in any society performs a variety of functions and can take many different forms. But it is always the organizer of society in the interests of the class structure taken as a whole. While the state is rooted in the economic infrastructure from which it springs and which it in turn affects, it always retains a certain degree of autonomy from the infrastructure.[1]

In the immediate post-Revolution situation in Mexico during the 1920s, no major social class or class fraction could assert total or clear-cut hegemony. It was the type of situation that Italian Marxist Antonio Gramsci theorized as "catastrophic equilibrium."[2] Mexico's victorious modernizing bourgeoisie was still a weak one, facing the more powerful U.S. bourgeoisie with its huge economic investments in key sectors of the Mexican economy. Moreover, Mexico's bourgeoisie had to fight off rivals within its own class and within the Church who were seeking to restore the old oligarchic order. It also faced challenges from peasants, workers, and intermediate-class radicals who were

111

demanding implementation of reforms promised by the Revolution and the 1917 Constitution.

Because of continued economic chaos and renewed power struggles among rival political figures and military *caudillos*, state policy until 1934 was inconsistent, at one moment economically nationalist, at yet another subservient to foreign economic interests. This complicated the building of the new "modern" state, which would take more stable shape only after the founding of a national political party in 1929 and sufficient social and nationalistic reforms in the mid-1930s to alleviate the pressures of continuing agitation from below.

To assuage lower-class unrest and consolidate itself, the new one-party capitalist state had to adopt *corporatist*[3] features that tied mass organizations of workers and peasants to its tutelage. Each interest group—business, labor, peasantry, teachers, and so on—was encouraged to form organizations with which the state would work. By 1940, the state was able to regulate the worker, peasant, and intermediate-class organizations in the interest of a more stable capitalist development.

The "catastrophic equilibrium," the uncertain economic situation, and Mexico's personalist traditions of corruption boosted the influence of national and regional military *caudillos*, who directed much of the state apparatus, starting with the presidencies of "First Chief" Carranza and General Obregón (1917-1924). The *caudillos* were soon able to convert themselves—and many of the petty bourgeois lawyers, intellectuals, and labor racketeers who joined their governments—into powerful political bureaucrats waxing fat from state favors to big capitalists, domestic and foreign.

The capitalist structure of the economy conditioned state policies, with the result that decisions were taken that facilitated capitalist economic development—and the corresponding enrichment of bureaucrats and *caudillos*, who were often able to join the ranks of the bourgeoisie on leaving government. Eventually, this informal state/bourgeoisie alliance gave rise to a new political elite that became known as "the revolutionary family."[4] Historian Jean Meyer characterized the process as "public money going to private companies by means of the State, or better said, the men who are the State."[5] Political scientist Francisco Valdés Ugalde has put it this way: "politicians made into businessmen thanks to the private appropriation of public money."[6]

Several "revolutionaries" became big capitalists during the 1920s. Typical of the pattern was Aarón Sáenz, pioneer of the influential "Sáenz group." Holding several cabinet posts in the governments of the 1920s, Sáenz, a former staff member of Obregón's army, expanded his construction-company interests with state aid into sugar refining, tourism, pulp and paper, food products, steel, and banking, achieving by 1970 a business empire worth $150 million.[7]

Employing a revolutionary rhetoric to co-opt the majority, and state repression to smash the most militant or leftist elements, the new state of the 1920s and 1930s proved increasingly able to introduce "modernizing" measures that encouraged the growth of monopoly capital. These steps included state financing of the economic infrastructure; termination of unproductive *haciendas*; a readjustment to, or modification of, foreign capital's dominance, especially in petroleum; corporatist control over peasant and worker movements; and subjugation of the reactionary wing of the Church. This task was at first made difficult by Mexico's high level of class conflict and by intra-class tensions. For example, there were 1,289 strikes between 1920 and 1924, before the "social pact" between the urban workers' CROM (Regional Mexican Worker Confederation) and President Obregón finally guaranteed labor peace.

The split and defeat of the peasant-worker challenge of 1910 to 1915 and the subsequent state tutelage of labor and support for capitalism eventually provided enough opportunity for various leading bourgeois elements of the Díaz period (bankers, industrialists, landlords, etc.) to recover and expand their economic strength. Indeed, such subsequent economic powerhouses as the Monterrey group and the private Banco Nacional de México group, whose roots went back to the Porfiriato, benefited from the situation. The most reactionary members of the Monterrey group, the Garza and Sada families, diversified their brewery and glass industries into banking and commerce and by 1936 had consolidated into the VISA and FICA holding companies. To combat labor unions at a national level, Luis G. Sada spearheaded the 1929 founding of the business organization COPARMEX (Employers Confederation of the Mexican Republic). The Banco Nacional de México group, headed by the Legorreta family, was less reactionary, tolerating or supporting social-reform measures. It helped negotiate Mexico's huge foreign debt, and in later decades helped place Mexican bonds in U.S. and European markets.

Yet the Mexican bourgeoisie failed to achieve its own class hegemony. One reason was that foreign capital still dominated the Mexican economy, which depended on the United States for 69 percent of its imports and 60 percent of its exports (mainly raw materials, minerals, and agricultural products). Until the 1938 nationalization of oil, foreign companies heavily dominated the oil industry, mining, metallurgy, the textile industry, and major areas of commerce.

Another reason Mexico's bourgeoisie remained relatively weak was that the class struggle periodically intensified, thereby checking its potential power. Additional reasons, of course, were the economic crises that plagued Mexico, such as those of 1929 and the 1930s.

Both state and economy develop on the basis of contending classes. Under capitalism, the state plays an active role in class formation and even class creation, as well as in the accumulation of capital or economic surplus. When emergent, vital bourgeois fractions are pushing the development of capitalism forward and seeking both economic and political hegemony, they often confront the resistance of older ruling-class fractions, including indolent large landowners, some of the merchant bourgeoisie, certain bankers tied to outside interests, and so on. Simultaneously, all these dominant economic interests may be threatened in common by ferment from below, especially from those being proletarianized by capitalism's relentless advance: e.g., peasants and workers as during Mexico's revolution. Short of revolutionary transformation of both the economy and the polity in their own interests, the next best solution in such situations, from the point of view of those benefiting from the overall exploitative structure, is to delegate (or *accept*) sufficient power on the state's part (relative autonomy) to, in Engels's words, meet "the economic necessities of the national situation."[8]

In effect, this is what much of Mexico's weak bourgeoisie did in the mid-1930s, although by no means willingly. It was then that the corporatist roots of Mexico's modern state were finally established.

Foreign Interference and Renewed Class Struggle

After Carranza's assassination in May 1920, the armies of Sonora led by Obregón, Plutarco Elías Calles, and Adolfo de la Huerta, and supported by armed workers of CROM, were able to stabilize the situation sufficiently to permit the election of Obregón. Several big capitalists distrusted President Obregón. Agricultural interests of the American Association of Mexico, among others, encouraged disruptive actions to destabilize his government.[9]

The United States refused to grant Obregón diplomatic recognition, fearing the expropriation of its oil interests under Article 27 of the Constitution. From 1919 to the Second World War, the United States regularly drafted contingency plans for unilateral military intervention to secure access to oil resources. One version of the "Special Plan Green" (for Mexico) was more than eight inches thick and, in language perhaps relevant for years to come, called for "protection of U.S. citizens and interests along the border; seizure of the Tampico oil and coal fields south of Eagle Pass; blockade of principal Mexican ports; advance on Mexico City from Veracruz; advances south from the border along railway lines; and occupation and replacement of U.S. troops by a native Mexican constabulary under U.S. leadership and control."[10]

Obregón assured the United States that Article 27 was not retroactive and therefore would not affect properties already granted to foreign oil interests, but Washington wanted the guarantee in writing. Thomas W. Lamont of J. P. Morgan and Company negotiated an agreement with the Obregón government concerning Mexico's external debt, estimated to be three times what it had been in 1911 (not counting an additional $1 billion in private foreign claims). Finally, in 1923, the two countries signed the Bucareli Agreements, which reaffirmed the nonretroactive clause Obregón had applied to Article 27 and obliged Mexico to pay compensation for damage to U.S. property incurred during the Revolution. This, and the assassination of Pancho Villa, led to the United States finally granting Obregón's government diplomatic recognition.

U.S. recognition came at a most opportune moment for Obregón, whose power was being threatened by rebellious generals incensed at his cost-saving cuts in the army's budget who were nominally led by his former treasury minister, Adolfo de la Huerta. What triggered the revolt was Obregón's choice of Calles, his minister of the interior, to run for president in the 1924 elections. (The Constitution barred Obregón from succeeding himself.) Like Obregón, Calles was a Sonoran Constitutionalist, and fear of his possible radicalism led many conservatives, *hacendados,* and Catholic leaders to take de la Huerta's side. So did some intermediate-class democrats shocked at the personalist and arbitrary character of the presidential succession.

A number of nationalists critical of the Bucareli Agreements and some independent labor organizations unattached to the Obregón-CROM alliance also joined the de la Huerta revolt. Workers were growing resentful of the strong-arm tactics of CROM's corrupt labor boss Luis Morones, who routinely ordered the assassination of rival labor leaders, particularly those of the anarchist-oriented CGT (General Confederation of Workers, which earlier in the 1920s had about as many members as the CROM). The American Federation of Labor (AFL) supported CROM, and AFL president Samuel Gompers proclaimed in mid-1924 his satisfaction at seeing what he called a "rapid departure from the teachings of the European anarchist and syndicalist authorities who were in previous times so readily accepted."[11] Sporting glitzy diamond rings, one or another chorus girl on his arm, and traveling in a bullet-proof Cadillac, Morones (himself a former anarchist electrical worker) was the archtypical gangster union boss.

For a few months during the de la Huerta uprising, battles raged between rival military forces, costing the lives of 7,000 Mexicans. Three things tipped the military balance to Obregón and saved his government: U.S.-supplied war materiel; the support of militant peasants, whose interests were represented in parliament by the Partido Nacional Agrarista, led by people like former Zapata brain-truster Díaz Soto y Gama; and the support of CROM, which mounted peasant and worker brigades to help crush the revolt. The United States further intervened on Obregón's side by sending a cruiser to blockade the oil port of Tampico and to prevent the anti-Obregón forces from receiving arms from unnamed external sources. On June 12, 1925, Secretary of State Frank B. Kellogg made clear what the price for all this support was:

> It must remain very clear that this Government will continue maintaining the present government in Mexico only so long as it protects American lives and the rights of Americans and lives up to its international agreements and obligations. The Mexican government now stands in judgment before the world.[12]

Calles was elected in 1924 and proceeded to try to legitimize his power by appealing to Mexicans' sense of nationalism. He ordered oilfield owners to exchange their titles for fifty-year leases, dating from the time of acquisition—a clear violation of the Bucareli Agreements. The oil magnates clamored for U.S. military intervention. But U.S. public opinion was lukewarm. U.S. citizens still remembered the military humiliation Villa had dealt Pershing. After the blood-shed of the First World War, they were not interested in embarking on another military involvement. Worse yet, the Teapot Dome scandals that rocked Washington in the early 1920s had given a bad name to such leading U.S. oil figures in Mexico as Doheny and Albert B. Fall.

In 1927, President Calvin Coolidge dispatched a new and clever ambassador to Mexico, Dwight Morrow, like Thomas W. Lamont a partner of J. P. Morgan and Company. Morrow was an astute diplomat. He outfitted his home in Cuernavaca with Mexican handicrafts and commissioned the prominent muralist Diego Rivera to paint a fresco in the local town hall, thereby appealing to Mexican national pride. In this he was taking a page from the Mexican government's own book. In the early 1920s, Minister of Education José Vasconcelos had subsidized a breathtaking mural, sculpting, and literary renaissance that helped legitimize the new state and its nationalist, pro-Indian rhetoric, even while successive governments failed to grant Indians genuine equal rights or to implement more than token agrarian reform.

Morrow and Lamont made an effective team. Finance Minister Alberto Pani had set up the Banco de México in 1925 and encouraged talk of controls on foreign capital. Pani explained that this represented no "utopian socialistic leveling" but was rather intended to stimulate private enterprise and the "formation and encouragement of an autonomous middle class."[13] The Lamont-Pani Agreement of 1925 created a climate for renewed U.S.-Mexican cooperation in the capitalist development of Mexico. Foreign bankers accepted the new state bank, while Mexico promised to return the railways, partially nationalized in the final years of the Díaz dictatorship, to private management—a clear signal that the state bank was supportive of private enterprise.

Ambassador Morrow huddled frequently with President Calles to work out friendlier relations. In 1927 the Mexican Supreme Court declared the fifty-year-oil-lease legislation unconstitutional. It ruled that foreigners who had acquired subsoil rights before 1917 were entitled to perpetual concessions. In 1928-1929 Mexico's foreign debt was renegotiated on amicable terms. Morrow and Calles clearly agreed that cooperation between U.S. and Mexican capital represented the key to Mexico's future prosperity. Calles publicly stated that Mexico's interests "can be satisfied only within the limits set up by the present so-called capitalist system" and promised "to safeguard the interests of foreign capitalists."[14]

Table 4

U.S. Interventions in Mexico, 1920-1941

1920-1941
U.S. "Special Plan Green" for a possible invasion of Mexico to secure access to oil resources, maintained until 1942 when Mexico became a U.S. ally in the Second World War.

1920-1923
United States refused to recognize elected government of Obregón until it signed "Bucareli Agreements" protecting U.S. oil interests and the murder of Villa was accomplished.

1924
During an anti-government revolt, the U.S. supplied war material for Obregón and sent a cruiser to protect the oil port of Tampico.

1932-1933
United States deported more than 300,000 Mexican immigrants, aggravating unemployment in Mexico.

1938-1941
After Mexico nationalized oil, the United States terminated its silver-purchase program and withheld loans.

Meanwhile, throughout the 1920s and early 1930s, the class struggle continued. CROM organized the Mexican Labor Party and assured workers that it would be transformed into a "class party." Yet in 1925 CROM proposed legislation—which eventually became incorporated into the Labor Law of 1931 still largely in effect in the mid–1990s—that gave the state a deciding vote on the labor-conflict arbitration boards. This granted the state the power to permit or deny a strike request and to oversee, as CROM's proposal put it, "an equilibrium between the diverse factors of production, which harmonizes the rights of workers and employers." It marked an important subordination of CROM to the state, as important union leaders, anticipating state favors for labor, now no longer took seriously the idea of forming a class party. Through its "social pact" with the state, CROM created not a class party but class collaboration.

In return for its agreement to put the brakes on strikes, CROM leaders were allowed to participate in Calles' cabinets and received government license for their unionizing activities. CROM sometimes assisted the government in its repression of independent labor actions, such as the 1926 strike of railroad workers, among whom communists were strong. The number of officially recognized strikes declined precipitously, from 300 a year in the early 1920s to 71 in 1925 to only 12 in 1928, not passing 60 until 1934 (when there were 202).

In the countryside, class war raged. Peasants and workers organized themselves into agrarian leagues and unions, constantly pressuring the state for
agrarian reform and for arms to defend themselves against the *hacendados'*
hired gunmen. Obregón and Calles sought to bring peasants under their
tutelage by granting the demands of some of the more militant villages and by
tying them into a system of state credits for seeds, fertilizers, and tools. On the
other hand, they launched repeated attacks on more independent peasant
groups led by socialists, communists, and anarcho-syndicalists, such as the
League of Agrarian Communities in Veracruz.

The state supported the development of an agrarian and commercial bourgeoisie by protecting from agrarian-reform legislation commercial *hacendados,*
particularly those producing for export. It also favored them with state loans.
In 1926, the state established an agrarian credit bank, an ejidal credit bank, and
an irrigation commission. All of these favored private landholders, large and
small, and encouraged the growth of the agrarian bourgeoisie—augmented by
former army officers or civil servants rewarded for their services with state-dis-
tributed lands. To move militant peasants away from big capitalist farms, the
state encouraged "colonization"—the establishment of new small and medium-size farms in previously uncultivated areas. Occasionally a nonproduc-
tive *hacienda* was broken up, the peasant beneficiaries usually being less class
combative as a result.

Many peasants recognized they were being manipulated and deceived.
Those in the Bajío region west and north of Mexico City grew particularly
resentful. The Church, long opposed to agrarian reform of any kind, stirred
them up against the "communists" in government. Many became soldiers in
the "Cristero Revolt" of 1926-1929, led by enraged clerics dissatisfied with
Calles's enforcement of anticlerical provisions of the Constitution, especially
obligatory secular education (Article 3). Other peasants took up arms to help
the government put down the revolt, which was not ended until Ambassador
Morrow intervened to negotiate a settlement easing the enforcement of the
anticlerical measures.[15]

In 1928, shortly after being elected president, Obregón was assassinated by
an obscure Catholic fanatic. By now, Calles was one of the nation's largest
landowners and the major figure of Mexico's polity. Congress appointed a
Calles supporter, lawyer Emilio Portes Gil, former governor of the northern
state of Tamaulipas, to the presidency until new elections could be called in 1929.

To further stabilize the situation, Calles and his backers organized early in
1929 the National Revolutionary Party (PNR—today's PRI), the first national
political party. Claiming to represent the Revolution and all social forces and
factions, the PNR was able to draw together most rival parties, military
officers, and *caudillos*—to give cohesion to the political, civilian, and military
bureaucracies.

For generations to come, the "official" political party of Mexico would control all national elections and run the federal and local governments. The 1929 election results made this clear. An obscure PNR party functionary named Pascual Ortiz Rubio handily won the presidency against the more experienced and much better known José Vasconcelos, who ran under the rubric of the National Anti-Re-electionist Party. The fraudulent and incredible vote spread was 1,948,848 to 110,979.

Ortiz Rubio governed until 1932, when he dared to disagree with Calles on minor policy questions and was forced to resign. He was succeeded by millionaire banker Abelardo Rodríguez (1932-1934), a more faithful Calles puppet. Indeed, the entire 1928-1934 period, during which the PNR political machine moved into high gear, was known as the "Maximato" after Calles's unofficial title of "Jefe Máximo."

But the state, despite its increasing power, still faced problems with workers and peasants. In 1926, Calles had warned militant independent unions to fall into line with the new reality of "official" labor unions under state tutelage. But in 1928 CROM, seeking to make up for its reputation of class collaborationism and to win back disillusioned members who were departing in droves, withdrew from its pact with the government.

In 1929, the state retaliated by cutting CROM's funds and briefly throwing support to some of the revolutionary-left unions. Armed battles erupted between these and CROM. The government, satisfied at seeing CROM's strength reduced, now acted as Carranza had done in 1916, turning against the leftist unions in a ruthless campaign of goon-squad attacks and repression. Communist and anarcho-syndicalist leaders were murdered. Thus, although unionization was growing and the onset of the worldwide economic depression was placing workers in ever more difficult conditions leading to increased radicalization, the stepped-up state repression meant that few strikes were officially recognized.

Within CROM, which still accounted for a majority of the unions, a "radical" wing emerged under the leadership of Vicente Lombardo Toledano, who had been active in the teachers' strikes of the 1920s. While opposing the Communist Party (founded in 1919) for introducing "politics" into the "apolitical" labor-organizing drive, Lombardo Toledano claimed to be a "Marxist." He advocated an eventual "socialist transformation of the bourgeois regime." But, he advised his followers in 1932, "We cannot proclaim or praise the dictatorship of the proletariat . . . because we are living during a period of organized capitalism."[16]

CROM boss Morones attacked Lombardo Toledano, who reluctantly resigned from CROM, taking many militants with him. In October,1933, Lombardo Toledano's dissidents met in a national labor convention to found the General Confederation of Workers and Peasants of Mexico (CGOCM).

Communists, other leftists, and Lombardo Toledano's CGOCM (which by 1934 included over half of the nation's organized workers) showed particular strength in such basic heavy industries as mining, petroleum, electricity, textiles, and railroads. Even as Morones earlier had emerged as the new "revolutionary" state's alternative to the radicals of the Casa del Obrero Mundial, so Lombardo Toledano now began to emerge as a potential state ally and alternative to the renewed labor militancy of the early 1930s—in which he himself had played an outstanding role.

The rural proletariat, Mexico's most numerous class, also stepped up its demands for reform. The suffering of the peasants and workers intensified after 1931, when Mexico went off the gold standard and the value of the peso declined, to the advantage of U.S. capitalists.

All this was happening at a time when Calles and Morrow were seeking to cut back social welfare expenditures in order to reduce the budget deficit. In 1932-1933, the Communist-influenced League of Agrarian Communities in Veracruz was severely attacked; its peasant militia was disarmed. By 1934, peasants and workers almost everywhere in Mexico were at a boiling point.

Cárdenas

The worldwide depression started in 1929. Once the effects of the sudden slowdown in U.S. economic activity reached Mexico, the number of Mexican unemployed (mostly laid-off workers) skyrocketed, tripling by 1933. For those who were lucky enough to work, the minimum wage did not cover even a third of the average family's basic necessities.

In addition, the U.S. government scapegoated Mexican migrant workers for the high unemployment plaguing the U.S. work force, rounding up and deporting more than 300,000 workers and their families, many of them U.S. citizens, thereby aggravating Mexico's unemployment and social unrest. U.S. organized labor backed the deportations, even though Mexican workers played leading roles in several important strikes, such as the 1933 cotton strike in California. The virus of anti-Mexican racism had spread during the previous two decades and could not be stopped. Samuel Gompers, president of the American Federation of Labor (AFL), repeatedly emphasized the Mexicans' alleged inferior productive capacity. The eugenics movement, which called for a "biological housecleaning" aimed at people of color, spread its virulent ideas into schools and the mass media. A popular pseudoscientific writer affirmed that the Mexican migrant was "inferior" because he was "born communist." Books and newspaper articles called Mexicans a "eugenic menace" and tried to demonstrate "scientifically" that Mexicans are racially inferior. Eugenics-based sterilization laws spread across the United States, remaining on the books in twenty-six states as late as 1980. The attacks on Mexican immigrants and U.S. citizens of Mexican descent became so severe that in 1932 the head of the U.S.

Department of Agriculture had to rush to the aid of U.S. employers in agriculture, mining, and industry by publicly declaring, "We have depended upon these people; they are not a social burden but honest men and workers who have helped so much to develop this country."[17]

At its party convention in December 1933, the ruling PNR entertained suggestions for social and economic reform advanced by younger party leaders eager to rise in the ranks. These "young Turks" rewrote the Six-Year Plan which Calles had submitted. They recommended reducing Mexico's dependence on foreign markets and mineral and agricultural exports. They called for the promotion of agrarian reform and small and medium-size industry. They wrote into the Plan state assistance for Mexican enterprises rather than foreign ones and a pledge for development of a national oil company.

Outgoing President Rodríguez, a tool of Calles's political machine, found it expedient to implement some of the progressive parts of the rewritten Six-Year Plan before leaving office. He approved a minimum-wage bill and engineered a constitutional reform making public education "socialistic." In Spanish and Latin American thought at that time, socialistic education meant "rational and secular," as distinguished from "religious and clerical."

Following Calles's advice, the convention delegates nominated for the presidency a respected and socially progressive candidate, General Lázaro Cárdenas, a brigadier general during the Revolution and governor of Michoacán from 1928 to 1932. Calles had little doubt that he could control the forty-year-old Cárdenas the way he had controlled previous presidents. As minister of war in early 1933 Cárdenas had done his bidding in ordering the disarming of Veracruz's peasant militia; in doing so, Cárdenas practically assured his nomination for president, since his chief rival's social base was among Veracruz's militant peasants.

In his presidential campaign, Cárdenas went out among the people. He advocated collective bargaining, an increase in the minimum wage, and other welfare measures commonly recommended in more industrialized capitalist countries at the time. In calling for agrarian reform, Cárdenas emphasized the protection of private property and favored small private landholdings over communal ones. He also acknowledged the existence of the class struggle—"an essential within the capitalist regime"—and promised support for the working class.

Calles had obviously accepted the idea of reform. Moreover, a reformist government had taken power in the United States under President Franklin D. Roosevelt, whose ambassador to Mexico, Josephus Daniels, arrived before Cárdenas took office and talked of social reform, education, the welfare of the masses, and Mexico's indisputable right to develop an ideology of social revolution. The 1934 silver purchase program, which enabled the United States to buy huge quantities of Mexican silver, helped Cárdenas finance his economic development plans.

So Cárdenas did not expect U.S. hostility. "The United States will not intervene in our internal affairs," he said in December 1935, "first, because of its Good Neighbor Policy and second, because it is profoundly concerned with meeting the problems that have arisen within its own territory."[18]

If Cárdenas was to become, in modern parlance, "his own man" or "captain of his own team," he would have to challenge the powerful Calles machine, with its control of the national political party and its connections to big business, the old-guard labor leadership (CROM), the foreign investment community, and the army (although here General Cárdenas also had some support). So Cárdenas started his administration by making sweeping changes in the PNR, the government bureaucracy, and the military. He raised military salaries and benefits, improved army education, courted and won rank-and-file soldier support, promoted junior officers, and gradually maneuvered the generals into a position of neutrality. He then set about healing the long rift between the government and the Catholic Church. In his second cabinet, he appointed the pro-Catholic General Saturnino Cedillo minister of agriculture and declared the "era of Church persecution" at an end.

Historically, new leaders had turned to organized labor—Obregón to the Casa del Obrero Mundial in 1915 and to CROM in 1920, and Calles to CROM as well. As it happened, Lombardo Toledano's rapidly growing CGOCM was available to Cárdenas.

CROM had lost many of its major unions (printers, iron and metalworkers, and textile workers), as rank-and-file workers had become disillusioned with the corruption of its leadership and the failure of Calles to pay off in social-welfare benefits. In the first year of the Cárdenas presidency (1934-1935), a rash of strikes broke out against such companies as the Mexican Tramways Company (Canadian owned), Huasteca Petroleum Company (Standard Oil), San Rafael Paper Company (Spanish-French capital), and the Mexican Telephone and Telegraph Company (American Telephone and Telegraph's allied company, in which Calles held a large number of shares). These strikes were in the tradition of continuing labor militancy against foreign capital, which dated back to the eruption of anti-imperialist strikes under Porfino Díaz and showed once again that the Mexican proletariat was not underdeveloped when compared with Mexico's weak bourgeoisie.

In July 1934, the CGOCM launched a nationwide general strike to protest the state's siding with employers in the decisions of the labor arbitration and conciliation boards. The CGOCM's moral example and fighting spirit in leading the struggle for more jobs and decent wages resulted in its incorporating more than half of all Mexico's organized workers by the end of the year. According to official figures, the number of strikes rose from 13 in 1933 to 642 in 1935—one unofficial estimate put the number at more than 1,000 for the first half of 1935 alone. In the Laguna district in north-central Mexico, where half the nation's cotton was produced, unionizing farmworkers launched 104 strikes in 1935.

Mexico's Labor Code, a federal labor law passed in 1931, had affirmed workers' rights to unionize and strike, but laid the basis for state regulation of labor by granting the state the right to declare strikes legal or nonexistent and to recognize or ignore the elections and directorates of all labor unions. The capitalist state was thus in a good position to carry out its class role of being an organ of one class (the bourgeoisie) over another (the proletariat), of being responsible for "law and order" that legalizes and facilitates class domination, and of creating the appropriate agencies for the amelioration or resolution of confrontations between classes. Under these circumstances, the labor movement did not rush to embrace Cárdenas. On the contrary, it launched a series of strikes.

Thus, Cárdenas, intent on carrying out a program of social reform and economic recovery, found himself faced with a complex set of problems. First, the Mexican variant of corporatism heavily favored the presidency, leaving much of the old Calles machine in control of the ruling political party, of CROM, and of numerous government agencies. Second, big business was pressuring Cárdenas to proceed cautiously with his program of social reform or even abandon it. Third, there was a heightened class threat from below that both challenged the state and yet gave Cárdenas an opportunity to use it for his own ends. And this is what Cárdenas did in order to out-maneuver the Calles forces. He threw his support to the main organizing force behind the labor unrest, the CGOCM.

By recognizing labor's right to strike and by abetting the development of the CGOCM (with government assistance and juridical decisions against recalcitrant private corporations), the Cárdenas administration extended the state-labor alliance begun by Obregón and Calles. In February 1936, the CGOCM, with Cárdenas's support, became the officially recognized national labor movement and was renamed the Confederation of Mexican Workers (CTM). Under its general secretary Lombardo Toledano, CTM joined together some 3,000 unions and 600,000 workers.

Yet Cárdenas's handling of labor was highly complex, assisting here, restraining there—and in the long run continuing the state's role of controlling labor. Committed to the reform of capitalism rather than its destruction, Cárdenas could not side completely with labor without risking such a shift in class power that the capitalist system itself might be called into question. Similarly, rank-and-file workers might take advantage of unlimited presidential support to marshal a full-scale attack against the bourgeoisie and for state power, regardless of the alliance of their leaders with government. On the other hand, if Cárdenas sided too completely with the owning classes against labor, labor's leaders might defect from their alliance with the government, also aggravating the danger of a direct proletarian attack on the bourgeoisie and the state. Cárdenas chose to steer a middle course and avoid a bloody class war.

Cárdenas's actions throughout his regime ranged from approvals of socialism to denials that he sought it; from outright support of workers on strike to declaring strikes illegal; from appearing at worker demonstrations to sending troops to quell them. This constituted political entrepreneurship, with Cárdenas employing a policy of carrot-and-stick toward labor in order to consolidate a state-regulated and state-supported capitalism.

Cárdenas's "socialistic" education measures reflected his intent to develop a better-trained work force. As the president stated in a circular dated June 30, 1934, "It is necessary to stimulate utilitarian and collectivist teaching which prepares pupils for production, which foments the love of work as a social obligation."[19] An increase in the education budget helped reduce illiteracy, raising literacy rates to 50 percent of males and 42 percent of females by 1940. Government documents from this period clearly conceived socialistic education as "education to community responsibility." Socialist rhetoric in education, as in other areas, was intended to win over the most radical revolutionaries then active in strategic parts of the society, including the schools, where teachers had a long tradition of labor militancy and social concern. The one consistent ideological theme of the Cárdenas administration was the creation not of a socialist regime but of a government that would be "liberal, democratic, and nationalist."

Cárdenas was aided in his approach by the political line taken by organized labor's most popular leader, Lombardo Toledano, who argued that if capitalism were to be abolished it would happen only in a distant future after the break with "feudalism" and "imperialism" necessary to establish Mexico's economic and political freedom. This line was even more influential when it became part of the Popular Front tactics pushed by the Communist International in its opposition to the rise of fascism. (In Mexico, organized forces of the extreme right known as "Sinarquistas" and their paramilitary appendage, the "Gold Shirts," posed a growing threat.

Thus, prevailing conditions in Mexico were such that no single class or class fraction was in a position to get its way easily. Even though many rural oligarchs had interlocking urban investments, the bourgeoisie had conflicting landed and industrial interests. It also included numerous *comprador* elements whose interests were closely tied to those of foreigners, and these were in conflict with the more independent-minded "nationalist" industrialists.

With the misnamed "national" bourgeoisie weak and divided, other classes seemingly had a good chance to eliminate once and for all its partial hegemony. But these too were weak. They included a relatively directionless petty bourgeoisie and many confused intermediate-class people. The coopted workers and peasants depended on the state, a fact which undercut the autonomy of their threat. In such a situation, with no class or class fraction able to assert clear-cut hegemony, the state emerged as a natural arbiter and central power in Mexico's class war.

This increased role for the state was in fact welcomed by modernizing fractions of the bourgeoisie, whose members had been engaged in their own "hegemonic project"[20] of reconsolidating the capitalist state on a new basis since 1917. As historian Steven Haber has pointed out, Cárdenas's use of state funding for public works, highway construction, and other projects, like his budgeting of assistance for small and medium businesses, worked to the advantage of Mexico's larger investors.[21] These elements needed to allow some of the demands of the masses and the petty bourgeoisie to be met through state-directed social reforms in order to avoid a revolutionary challenge from below potentially as serious as that of 1910-1915. Many industrialists and bankers welcomed increased state intervention, and even social reforms, if such measures would control the class struggle and if the bourgeoisie would gain an ally (the state) in its hegemonic project to maintain capitalism and achieve stable political power.

As in Gramsci's theory, so in Mexico's reality: any group's hegemonic project was not necessarily clear or well-articulated, since it was confused by different contestants' formations of new alliances of class and social forces—new "power blocs" (such as Morones's CROM alliance with Obregón and, briefly, Calles, both of whom in turn were busy expanding their capitalist interests in chickpeas and construction, respectively). Moreover, hegemonic projects were risky since the ideas that accompanied their propaganda implied a change in basic social relations and the dominant ideology, with corresponding instability (such as the Cárdenas period and the appeals to "socialism"). There was no guarantee that the contest would not lead to the common ruin of the contesting forces, or that the doors would not be opened to a more revolutionary (or counterrevolutionary) transformation of society. Yet whenever circumstances of crisis and heightened class antagonism prevailed in the past, they usually did lead to one or another form of hegemonic project built on new class alliances. History was full of such experiences.

In Mexico's case, modernizing elements in the bourgeoisie could break, or at least discipline, any bourgeois fraction opposed to them by calling on the support of the developmentalist and reformist currents within the state bureaucracy and national political party—at least so long as the worker and peasant movements remained vibrant. But this use of the state as the key power resource, rather than the use of a single, united class (either the proletariat or the bourgeoisie), meant that there could be neither an independent "nationalist-bourgeois" industrialization program for autonomous economic development from above nor a thoroughgoing revolution from below. The state could only introduce sufficient reforms to keep the class war under control. Moreover, both the state and the contending bourgeois fractions were structurally constrained by the dependence of the Mexican economy on external conditions— accumulated foreign debt, agreements with foreign bondholders, and the worldwide economic depression.

Cárdenas's administration set about supporting the most modern and patriotic segments of the bourgeoisie, those most rooted in nationally controlled areas of production, at the expense of *comprador* and imperialist groups. It also developed good relations with several powerful Mexican financial groups. Not unlike the Roosevelt administration in the United States, it sought increased state regulation of the economy so that the economic depression might be eased and private ownership preserved. It fomented private enterprise by allowing the government's major development corporation, the Nacional Financiera (founded in 1934), to borrow additional funds from the Banco de México to underwrite private investments and to provide initial capital for industrial enterprises.

Moreover, by doubling the amount of federal expenditure going to economic development between 1934 and 1937, the Cárdenas administration did indeed pull the country out of its economic slump. Between 1929 and 1933, the Gross National Product (GNP) had dropped an average of 2.7 percent a year, but from 1934 to 1940 it increased at an annual average rate of 4.5 percent. In the words of historian James Wilkie, "The basis for rapid industrialization was firmly established when Cárdenas left office. In fact, the volume of manufacturing production increased about as fast during the Cárdenas era as it did during the [succeeding Manuel] Avila Camacho epoch."[22]

In responding to the demands of the workers, Cárdenas at first hedged on the right of workers or the state to take over factories, whether those with idle productive machinery or those in which owners disobeyed labor laws or court decisions. Militant elements in the working class grew impatient and in 1934-1935 stepped up the pace of strikes and mass mobilizations, forcing Cárdenas to form, for a time at least, an "anti-imperialist" alliance with the proletariat, the peasantry, and the *anti-comprador* segment of the bourgeoisie and to encourage mass mobilizations in order to counterbalance the forces of the rest of the bourgeoisie, including Calles loyalists and the resurgent political right.

In the midst of this heightened social and political unrest, on June 11, 1935, Calles reentered the political arena to denounce all strikers as engaging in unpatriotic behavior equivalent to treason. He red-baited union leaders, especially Lombardo Toledano. He then challenged Cárdenas to restore order or suffer the consequences. Cárdenas responded on June 13 with a statement midway between labor's demands and Calles's adamant opposition. Cárdenas viewed many of labor's demands as reasonable and claimed that by meeting some of them the economic situation might be made more stable, assuming that concessions to labor were granted "within the economic possibilities of the capitalist sector." To reassure business, Cárdenas warned that "in no case will the President of the Republic permit excesses of any kind or acts that involve transgressions of the law or unnecessary agitations."[23]

The working class—led by the strikers, independent unions like those of railway workers and electricians, and new leaders like Lombardo Toledano—responded to Calles's attacks by threatening another general strike, branding Calles a traitor to the Revolution, and forming the National Committee for Proletarian Defense (which was soon to be reconstituted as the CTM). This new labor coalition applauded Cárdenas's June 13 statement, and from that moment on "the labor movement was wedded to Cárdenas, and he, in turn, to the labor movement . . . but the government kept, always, the upper hand."[24]

Meanwhile, among the bourgeoisie were many who opposed Cárdenas's reforms. Organized workers faced factory lockouts, and armed goon squads were used against land-grabbing peasants or state bureaucrats seeking to implement agrarian reform. The focus of the nationwide class warfare became Monterrey, the nation's largest industrial center and a veritable hotbed of bourgeois reaction. In February 1936, when striking workers immobilized the city, Cárdenas took the occasion to issue his famous "Fourteen Points"—the statement that best reflects his populist and corporatist strategy. It was a broad populist appeal to almost all social classes and groups, particularly those with any kind of real or potential power, in order to bring them under state regulation.

Cárdenas's Fourteen Points encouraged workers to form a "united front," which the government would deal with "to the exclusion of minority groups which might choose to continue" (e.g., CROM). He warned industrialists that should they cease production in the factories "because of the demands of the unions," the factories could rightfully be turned over "to their laborers or the government" (a warning against the employers' use of the shutdown and lockout). On the other hand, he also encouraged employers "to associate in a united front"—which many of them rapidly did, forming chambers of commerce and industry in cities across the country. Cárdenas applauded the further growth of industry, since the government "depends upon its prosperity for its income through taxation." And he urged capitalists "not to continue provoking agitations," because "this would bring on civil warfare."[25]

All of this reflected the corporatist part of Cárdenas's strategy to divert the class struggle into safe channels under state regulation. While encouraging a multitude of organizations—workers, peasants, bureaucrats, big business executives, owners of small enterprises, teachers, and so forth—to bargain with the state and (where feasible) affiliate with the national political party, at the same time he was keeping them separate from each other, while granting them state recognition as legal entities. Thus Cárdenas was able to lay the groundwork for a stable new capitalist state that had been the political project of the wounded but triumphant bourgeoisie since 1917.

Throughout 1936, Cárdenas continued to reassure the big capitalists (mainly those in Monterrey) that he had no intention of nationalizing industry. Occasionally Cárdenas spoke of the need to "socialize the means of production" but by this he meant only the regulation of privately owned productive property, as was being introduced in several more industrialized capitalist countries during the Great Depression of the 1930s.[26]

Throughout the class turbulence of 1935 and early 1936, many political figures previously loyal to Calles noted the changes in the army and the favors being offered pro-Cárdenas *politicos* by the state. They grew increasingly awed by the sight of tens of thousands of workers marching in the streets, threatening a general strike in support of Cárdenas. They understood the shift in the political balance when they saw the president arming 100,000 peasants and lesser numbers of workers to form peasant and worker militias in the name of resisting armed reactionaries and "imperialist threats." They knew that such militias were under the control of the ministry of defense and could be used to check any attempted army revolt. So, pragmatically, they shifted their support from Calles to Cárdenas.

Calles and CROM's Morones were overcome by the newly fashioned labor-government alliance and the deterioration in their own ranks. Few protested when they were deported in April 1936.

Once again, a new political leadership had met the rising demands of the workers part way, and in so doing had replaced the older, more recalcitrant leadership (as Obregón and Calles had done against the Carrancistas in 1919-1924). Once again it was the actions of the working class, through large-scale strikes and demonstrations, that had precipitated the change. And once again the new government moved in to help meet some of labor's demands and to bend the labor movement back—in Cárdenas's words—"within the economic possibilities of the capitalist sector."

Among the changes Cárdenas introduced during this tumultuous time were federal price controls and the appointment of federal agents to manage some of the enterprises resisting worker demands or disrupted by strikes—for example, the railroads, electrical installations, and selected factories and farms. Cárdenas gradually nationalized the railroads and established the Federal Electricity Commission (CFE), which became a powerful state force in the electrical industry. All these measures meant an increase in the influence of workers and peasants on key economic institutions.

Such proletarian influence naturally raised concern among the bourgeoisie that the workers and peasants might eventually gain political hegemony. This was unlikely, however, since Cárdenas was also increasing state regulation of the proletarian movement. True, he introduced reforms in agriculture and industry that sometimes permitted workers' increased involvement in the management of select enterprises. But this involvement was short-lived, since he also took care to appoint state bureaucrats to manage and control the reforms, in order that workers might be disciplined and their production increased. Once labor unrest ended, business could resume as usual.

Cárdenas's agrarian reform policies, which laid the basis for state-supported capitalist agriculture, typified the populism and corporatism of his administration. In the late 1920s and early 1930s, much of the countryside had become engulfed in violence, with peasants engaged in a fierce war against the "white armies" of the *latifundistas*. Often the peasants' only allies in demanding implementation of agrarian reform both before and after Cárdenas's assumption of the presidency were rural schoolteachers, more than 200 of whom were shot down by the large landholders' hired *pistoleros*. Women teachers and peasant women played a pivotal role in defense of community lands and family parcels. Cárdenas was sensitive to the peasants' problems. His administration distributed more than 20 million hectares of land, more than twice the amount distributed by all previous post-1917 regimes combined. It also responded, if only partly, to the demands of women, granting them the right to vote for the Chamber of Deputies and to run for office. It provided maternity leave for state employees.

Ironically, as historian Mary Kay Vaughn has pointed out, the agrarian reform and the literacy campaigns that accompanied it sometimes reinforced patriarchy by emphasizing female domesticity and stable peasant households as goals. Most rural women were conservative and religious in social outlook and could not easily relate to the intermediate-class feminist movements that were surfacing around issues of suffrage or divorce. Urban literacy instructors pushed "socialistic education" and other newfangled ideas, causing many peasant women to resent the pressures put on them to change their ways. Rural women's demands were related to family and community preservation and restoration rather than gender empowerment or the latest fads to come out of the big cities. Yet in subtle ways the revolutionary upheavals and women's own tenacity and creativity, as well as women's increased exposure to new ideas and opportunities to improve their lives, undermined or subverted patriarchy. Technological changes accompanying the agrarian reform began to benefit women. Examples included the increased use of the home sewing machine and the *molino de nixtamal* (mill for grinding maize soaked in lime and water, the mixture for making tortillas) that reduced by several hours a woman's daily toil spent in traditional activities, not to mention her exhaustion. The number of molinos multiplied sixfold during the Cárdenas presidency. Most peasants appreciated Cárdenas's efforts and affectionately started calling their new president "Tata" (Nahuatl for father), as some today now call his son, Mexico

City mayor and presidential aspirant Cuauhtémoc Cárdenas—a curious Mexican blend of patriarchy, *personalismo,* and presidentialism.[33]

Based on Article 27 of the Constitution (which protected private property and *ejidos),* Cárdenas's land program provided for state credits and aid to small private farms and to productive *ejidos. Ejidatarios* increased their irrigated holdings fourfold, or half their allotments. The agrarian reform facilitated the expropriation of many of the *latifundistas'* unproductive or idle lands, although here the government had to tread lightly. Even though some of the nation's *hacendados* had been killed during the Revolutionary civil war or had gone into exile, many had survived to rebuild or expand their estates, their ranks swelled by the "revolutionary landlords"—military officers and politicians who, with state encouragement, had amassed immense amounts of land for themselves.

Cárdenas allowed large landowners to keep 150 irrigated hectares or the equivalent and to retain the upper hand in matters of credit, technical inputs, wages, and marketing. Not untypically, when distributing land to rural proletarians—as in the case of the prolonged worker-employer conflict in the prosperous sugar-growing area of Los Mochis, Sinaloa (northwestern Mexico) in 1938—Cárdenas left the properties of the principal producers (in this case the United Sugar Company) untouched and refused to concede any wage increases to the workers. On the other hand, he did not hesitate to send in federal troops when regional *caciques,* allied with conservative and foreign oil interests, tried to stop his allegedly "atheistic, Bolshevik reforms," as in the case of the swiftly repressed revolt of mid-1938 led by General Saturnino Cedillo in San Luis Potosí.

Similarly, in the areas of the most radical land distribution, where labor unrest was intense, many of the largest landholdings and productive installations were protected from expropriation. In the Yucatán, for example, Cárdenas left the henequen-processing plants in the hands of the second-level *hacendados* established by Alvarado in 1915 as managers of the henequen trade, and they were thereby able to retain control of most of the area's peasants.

Cárdenas used agrarian reform to avoid impending agricultural paralysis and peasant disruption, not only in the Yucatán and Sinaloa but also in the troubled Laguna region of northern Mexico, which was selected for an ambitious state-sponsored project of collective production on *ejido* lands. (Nationally, less than 10 percent of all *ejido* farmers worked on a collective basis; most farmed individual small parcels within an *ejido.)* Cárdenas left the most productive Laguna land in the hands of twelve corporations, 70 percent of which were foreign-owned. In fact, the best one-third of the Laguna lands, with more than two-thirds of the artesian wells, remained untouched by his agrarian reform. The reforms paid off, as the Laguna, Yucatán, and northwestern and northern Mexico, where *ejidos* received the strongest state support, experienced increased production for export. This contributed to a subsequent boom in capitalist agriculture.

Elsewhere in rural Mexico, there remained widespread unemployment, partially caused by ongoing mechanization of production and the corporate capitalists' near monopoly on fertile land, water, credit, and technology, forcing the *ejidatarios* to hire themselves out as peons and even to rent their land out to the private farmers and then work it for them. Despite the entrance of the state-sponsored ejidal bank, meant to help alleviate their economic plight, many *ejidatarios* continued to obtain credit from private corporate farmers or moneylenders, however exploitative and usurious their rates of interest might be. The ejidal bank's employees often had worked for the old private banks or were in sympathy with the *latifundistas;* in addition, the ejidal bank was widely known for its corruption.

Consistent with his corporatist-style politics of maintaining different mass organizations separate from one another, Cárdenas took care to prevent peasant organizations—which he initially had helped develop by political appointments at every level—from affiliating with the official labor organization CTM. He also kept the bank employees' unions, the public employees' unions, and the teachers' unions out of the CTM. As historian Lyle Brown has pointed out:

> There was no doubt that Cárdenas desired separately organized labor and peasant confederations that would look to him for support and over which he could exercise such control as might be necessary to keep them functioning in harmony with the objectives of his administration. . . . Both the Communists and Lombardo Toledano spoke of the importance of uniting peasant and labor groups in a great proletarian organization, but Cárdenas was too shrewd a politician to allow such a development.[27]

The largest agrarian organization was the Mexican Peasant Confederation (CCM), formed initially to support Cárdenas's presidential candidacy. Incorporating most of the peasant leagues, it was renamed the National Peasant Confederation (CNC) in 1938, by which time it claimed to represent 3 million peasants and rural workers. Some of its militants fought the iron-fisted control of *caciques* and government bureaucrats and sought to create an independent movement, but the influential Communists chose to go along with Cárdenas by "boring from within" the CNC.

Cárdenas's agrarian reform was curtailed in 1936-1937, when the combined turmoil in the countryside and cities contributed to a decline in food production and a sharp rise in food prices. By then, however, the reform had won Cárdenas the adoration of hundreds of thousands of rural Mexicans and granted the peasant a dignity not felt since the days of Zapata.

As we have seen, the agrarian reform served primarily to preserve and stimulate the private system of farming for commercial profit. In May 1938, the government opened the Office of Small Property, which issued certificates of exemption from seizure. Between 1930 and 1940, the number of privately owned farms increased by 44 percent. Some 800,000 people were still living on *haciendas* in 1940, when the government acknowledged that Mexico continued to be fundamentally a country of great estates. More than half the cultivable land consisted of estates of more than 5,000 hectares in size. More than 60 percent of the peasants eligible to receive land had either inadequate parcels or no land at all.

It is no coincidence then that *neolatifundismo* soon emerged as the dominant form of capitalist agriculture in Mexico. It flourished in precisely the most prominent areas of Cárdenas's much-disputed agrarian reform. Ultimately, civil war and disruption were avoided by agrarian reform, while capitalist production increased manyfold.

The Cárdenas administration's failure to maintain the pace of land distribution after 1937, together with runaway inflation and organized labor's questioning of corruption among bureaucrats, placed the government in a difficult political situation. Cárdenas's own increasingly ambivalent policy toward strikes added to the problem. The Sinarquistas' fascist ideology began making inroads among those peasants relatively unaffected by agrarian reform, among intermediate-class people suffering inflation, and among ultrareactionary clerical and business figures. By 1940 the Sinarquistas numbered nearly half a million, some of them organized into paramilitary units.

A long-term intermittent strike by oil workers from 1936 to 1938 once more pitted organized labor against foreign capital. Talk of "imperialist intervention" filled the pages of the newspapers. The striking oil workers were demanding that the government annul all previous contracts and insist on the companies' providing a higher wage scale. By early 1938, they were calling for a nationwide general strike to force nationalization. Many observers wondered if Cárdenas might not have to terminate his populist program altogether or else face a power play by conservative army generals.

The time was thus ripe for a bold government action against a long-time common enemy, the foreign oil interests. According to noted Mexican historian and economist Jesus Silva Herzog, a close presidential aide at the time, "Had General Cárdenas not carried out [oil] nationalization, his government would not have been able to stay in power."[28]

For the most part, the oil companies had stopped exploring for new wells and worked out the old ones. Production had peaked in 1921, and by 1937 Mexican oil accounted for only 3 percent of Standard Oil of New Jersey's world production. The companies' prime concern was the example nationalization might set in more critical oil areas of the world and in other investment sectors in Mexico itself. Cárdenas, who accepted the oil companies' final wage proposals to the striking workers, was insulted by their insistence that it be put in writing and by their refusal to accept a guaranteed partial share of Mexico's oil output. Apparently the companies wanted all or nothing. So, on March 18, 1938, Cárdenas expropriated the foreign-controlled oilfields.

The companies retaliated with a "blockade" of oil sales to the United States, England, and France. England broke off diplomatic relations, and the Roosevelt administration terminated the silver agreement. Immediate indemnity was demanded, and foreign loans were withheld or delayed. These and other economic pressures forced Cárdenas to devalue the peso and turn to the Axis powers as an outlet for Mexican oil. In 1941, the oil boycott was lifted, after negotiations on an indemnity agreement were completed. (Mexico eventually paid more than $200 million to the companies.)

There took place a massive outpouring of public support for Cárdenas's act of economic independence, including approval by the Church. Millions of people contributed whatever they could to a national indemnity fund that had been created to pay off the oil firms.

Cárdenas seized this time of national unity to further consolidate a corporatist model of social and political organization. The national political party was renamed the Party of the Mexican Revolution (PRM—today's PRI). It incorporated the major mass organizations, grouped into four "sectors": labor (CTM), peasant (CNC), "popular," and military. The popular sector consisted of teacher and state employee unions excluded from CTM, small farmers outside CNC, professionals and other groups outside CTM or CNC, youth and women's organizations, and so forth. In 1940, the military sector merged with the popular sector.

Retreat from Radicalism

Cárdenas quickly assured foreign investors that the oil case was exceptional and that their investments would be protected as long as they served the national interest and conformed to Mexican law. Cárdenas had no intention of going any further than necessary in resolving these crises, or of undermining long-run developmentalist goals "within the economic possibilities of the capitalist sector," as was swiftly proven by his antilabor actions following the expropriation. A mineworkers' sit-down strike, directed mainly against the Anaconda Copper Company, was broken, and the mining companies were assured that further expropriations would not occur. The distribution of land to the peasants, as noted, ground to a halt.

Despite Cárdenas's "anti-imperialist" and economic reforms, by 1940 Mexico depended more than ever on foreign trade, particularly with the United States, which accounted for 87 percent of its foreign commerce. The number of workers involved in strikes had declined drastically, from 145,000 in 1935 and 113,885 in 1936 to 61,732 in 1937, 13,435 in 1938, 14,486 in 1939, and 19,784 in 1940. In 1940 the oil and railway workers were still on strike, however. Cárdenas responded by refusing their demands and expounding on "the necessity of ending extreme situations which would endanger the collective interest."[29] The oil workers, objecting to Cárdenas's plan to reorganize the industry's work force along state-controlled corporatist lines, then pulled out of CTM. Cárdenas sent federal troops to break a strike at the Azcapotzalco refinery. This broke the back of the strike movement but not the militancy of the workers.

Cárdenas, like Calles, could not run again for the presidency. In 1939 he selected the moderate General Manuel Avila Camacho, his minister of defense, to run in 1940, counting on him to carry out the next decade's industrial development program—or, as he put it in his last major public address, the task of "unification, peace, and work." Incoming presidents echoed these themes every six years.

The selection of Cárdenas's successor, however, was not without conflict. Conservatives, most state governors, much of the military, and powerful capitalists favored Avila Camacho, but various labor unions and peasant leagues backed General Francisco Múgica, who had gained a reputation as a radical in the Cárdenas administration for his defense of labor's causes and advocacy of petroleum expropriation. Nevertheless, the CTM and CNC leadership came out for Avila Camacho in early 1939, and their preference was imposed on the membership. The PRM likewise imposed party discipline on its dissidents and carried out a well-financed nationwide campaign to make sure Avila Camacho would win. The retreat from radicalism was consolidated when the billowing clouds of war in Europe and Asia led to an ideological shift by most progressive groups away from an emphasis on continuing the reform process and maintaining the anti-imperialist posture to one of urging "national unity" among all democratic forces against fascism—and, therefore, support for the PRM's Avila Camacho. The CTM replaced its "class struggle" slogan with one of "national unity."

Nonetheless, the difficult economic conditions caused a sizable number of Mexicans from all walks of life to rally behind an opposition candidate, General Juan Andréu Almazán, one of the new "revolutionary millionaires." Almazán initially drew support from Monterrey capitalists and the recently formed (1939) conservative National Action Party (PAN). But he also had the backing of old Calles loyalists, including former CROM boss Morones, and many workers fed up with the state's corporatist management of their lives.

Fearful that Almazán's candidacy might unleash unpredictable lower-class forces, the Monterrey capitalists considered shifting their support to Avila Camacho, who assured them that economic development relying on private enterprise would be the focus of his administration. They were also promised that they would be able to appoint their own state governor and municipal president. In effect, this "consulting" between the private sector and the state served to have private economic interests recognized as "official" rights. Also, future president Miguel Alemán arranged a deal with the Sinarquistas not to run candidates in the election in exchange for *ejido* lands. Although some national and foreign business groups helped finance the campaigns of both Almazán and Avila Camacho, U.S. interests tilted toward the latter, apparently, like the Monterrey group, preferring political continuity and stability to the probable social unrest an Almazán presidency might provoke.

Both candidates campaigned on similar platforms: protection for Mexican and foreign investment; class conciliation; law and order; and support for private enterprise, including small family farms in preference to *ejidos*. After a campaign marred by violence and claims of fraud, Avila Camacho predictably emerged the victor by the little-believed count of 2,476,641 votes to 151,101.

As Part II of this book examines in detail, the 1940 election in the final analysis represented a victory for the combined interests of the domestic and foreign bourgeoisies. In political scientist Nora Hamilton's words, "The conservative alliance again controlled the state, with the difference being that the state itself had been strengthened through its control, via the new government party, of the working class and peasantry, and through the revolutionary legitimacy given the state by the Cárdenas government."[30]

Even Cárdenas's historic anti-imperialist act against the oil companies in 1938 did not seriously jeopardize the overall pattern of capitalist development, with its heavy dependence on foreign capital. Indeed, it sufficiently rallied peasants and workers around the government so as to permit the finishing of the political project of the modernizing fraction of the bourgeoisie: the consolidation of the national political party; the final steps of the corporatist practice of organizing separate constituencies tied to the party and dependent on the state (CTM, CNC, etc.); the limiting of populist reforms and periodic declaration of their "end"; and the establishment of a strong state to facilitate capitalist development in collaboration with foreign capital in the name of nationalism and the Revolution.

While unduly harsh on Cárdenas, who evoked tremendous affection from millions of peasants and workers, the bitter statement of a railway brakeman in Mariano Azuela's novel *La nueva burguesía* undoubtedly reflected the feeling of many Mexicans, then as today: "Isn't it true, Campillo, that the only thing that Mexico has to thank Cárdenas for is that the cost of living is five times higher than it was when he came into power? . . . and how many thousands are dying of hunger because there is no work?"[31]

State and Accumulation

It is useful to end the first part of this book with a brief observation about historical continuity in the development and evolution of Mexico's state, class struggle, and patterns of capital accumulation. The entire 1880-1940 period of capitalist economic development was structurally the same, based on agro-mineral exports and a strong insertion into the relations of world capitalism. In 1940 Mexico's population was only 19.6 million, 70 percent of it still rural and two-thirds of it still illiterate. The estimated number of *haciendas* was 11,470, perhaps more than in 1910, while the portion of national territory controlled by large-scale landholders was 42 percent, down from 60 percent in 1910. And although political alliances had undergone changes and massive revolutionary upheavals had occurred—in 1910-1920 and again in the 1930s—none of the political forces managing the different governments doubted the validity of the pro-capitalist role of the state, established in the 1857 Constitution and strengthened in the 1917 Constitution.

The decades after 1940 witnessed changes in the forces of production and strong state support of capitalist development that helped make Mexico a semi-industrialized country. But it remained a capitalist country of a special kind. Dependence on foreign capital, domestic capital's reliance on cheap labor, and other forces already noted, contributed to the great divisions between rich and poor that came to characterize contemporary Mexico. Equally, the corporatist state, which had its origin in the pre-1940 period, was a critical factor in Mexico's subsequent uneven and oppressive pattern of industrial development.

It is useful, then, to summarize here the nature of this corporatist state, which came to play such a crucial role in the post-1940 period. In Mexican corporatism, political actors were not so much individuals or members of organizations as they were the ruling political party and mass organizations, which functioned from the top down. For the purposes of politics and state decisionmaking, what existed were organized entities; anything not organized did not, in that sense, exist. Because the official party held a monopoly of power within the mass organizations, no other political party, old or new, had any significant political effect, at least within the electoral system, unless "the rules of the game" were changed (as happened in the 1990s).

Even though Mexican anarchists, socialists, communists, and other leftists had played a pivotal role in organizing peasants and workers since the final decades of the nineteenth century, the corporatist state and its party defined them as "subversive," thus keeping them in a continuous minority status. The corporatist system was one in which class-based organizations obtained periodic concessions from the state or capital on the one hand, and the state was an instrument of political control over the toiling masses on the other.

In the eyes of many Mexican political dissidents, therefore, the fight against state-supported corporate capitalism and imperialism necessarily became one for a genuine labor unionism representative of workers' or peasants' interests. It became a struggle to establish a mass organized base for an urban and rural proletarian social movement capable of democratizing the state and transforming the economic structure. An arduous task in any circumstance, this was made more difficult by the ease with which a strong state could divert it from its ultimate goals through cooptation and repression, and the practices of "presidentialism" and "populism."

Presidentialism, or centralized power in the hands of the president making other branches of government strictly secondary, had a long tradition in Mexico. It dated directly back to nineteenth-century *caudillos* and presidents and indirectly back to colonial viceroys. It was enshrined in the 1917 Constitution and carried out by all the presidents of the post-1917 state.

Populism in Mexico, as elsewhere, was a program and movement advocating pro-people and relatively classless egalitarian demands, a "something for everyone" approach. Most writings on populism, however, tend to confuse three overlapping areas: (1) ideology; (2) class alliances; and (3) social movement (i.e., ideological and political practice of a class or of a class alliance). In any of these three areas, populism tends to prevail only under certain historical conditions. In capitalist societies, populism has generally emerged as the program of an ascendant fraction of the bourgeoisie in its battle against class rivals from within and without. In Mexico's case, these class rivals for hegemony were the landed oligarchy, the *comprador* fraction of the bourgeoisie, intermediate-class radicals, and workers and peasants. As the events in the 1920-1940 period of Mexican history—and particularly the Cárdenas reforms—so clearly revealed, the modernizing fraction of the bourgeoisie was able to achieve its goal of growth and prosperity only with the assistance of a populist movement based on class alliances, and a strong state taking a populist ideological stance.

Any class or class fraction may use populism as a program, for the use of populism is always geared toward specific class ends. The proletariat uses it to win reforms; the ascendant bourgeois fraction uses it to gain hegemony and to limit proletarian class demands to reforms instead of revolution.

As we saw in earlier chapters, populism *as an ideology* has existed in Mexico for a long time, first under the ideological rubric of Independence, then under the rubric of Liberal Reform and finally under that of the Mexican Revolution. Sociological theorist Ernesto Laclau has written that contemporary forms of populism in Mexico emerged with the collapse of the Madero regime and prevailed in the subsequent "long process of the Mexican Revolution."[32] By this logic, modern populism existed since at least 1913 and would continue until the Revolution was completed. In other words, the Revolution is seen by Laclau as "permanent" in Mexico. In a rhetorical or propaganda sense, of course, this is so, but when populism is perceived in such a narrow ideological sense, the concept loses its specific aspects of class allinces and social movement.

It is more useful to view Mexican populism as a specific phenomenon prevailing only at certain historical moments—in this case, the Cárdenas period, where it clearly took center stage in Mexican political reality. The historical conjuncture helps explain why. Imperialism was weakened and distracted by problems at home; globally, inter-imperialist rivalries were heightened; class agitation from below was rising rapidly; and the Mexican bourgeoisie was divided. Whoever the president is—and no Mexican president has ever failed to utilize populist *ideological* appeals—the degree of populism varies directly with the state of the class struggle and the relative strength of imperialism.

As we shall see, the economic structure of Mexico underwent radical changes after 1940, changes that had a direct impact on the character of the class structure and class struggle. Yet a historical continuity remained at the state and ideological levels. That continuity was embodied in the capitalist state's practices of cooptation and repression, corporatism, presidentialism, and populism, which helped make intelligible the apparent "political stability" of Mexico for the next half century or more.

PART II

The Era Of Monopoly Capitalism

Contemporary Mexico

U S A

Gulf of Mexico

New Orleans

San Antonio

Nuevo Laredo

Matamoros

Tampico

Tijuana

BAJA CALIFORNIA

PACIFIC OCEAN

El Paso
Ciudad Juaréz

SONORA

Hermosillo

CHIHUAHUA

Chihuahua

COAHUILA

Monterrey
Saltillo

NUEVO LEÓN

Torreón

DURANGO

Durango

SINALOA

NAYARIT

ZACATECAS

Zacatecas

SAN LUIS POTOSÍ

San Luis Potosí

TAMAULIPAS

A

León

GUANA-
JUATO

JALISCO

Guadalajara

COLIMA

MICHOACÁN

Morelia

QUERÉTARO

HIDALGO

CO

Mexico City

MEX

M

T

Puebla

Acapulco

GUERRERO

OAXACA

Oaxaca

Veracruz

V E R A C R U Z

Bay of Campeche

Campeche

CAMPECHE

TABASCO

CHIAPAS

Mérida

YUCATAN

QUINTANA ROO

Cozumel

(BR. HONDURAS (BELIZE)

GUATEMALA

A AGUASCALIENTES
M MORELOS
T TLAXCALA

500 km

300 miles

0

0

CHAPTER 5

The State, Foreign Capital, and Monopoly Capitalism

Nationalism is a phenomenon that exists throughout the world. As for the nationalism of Mexico, that nation opens its doors to foreigners, as it always has done in the past. So nationalism is no problem in Mexico.

—Henry Ford II, December 2, 1970

But is there any other country in the world where the working class . . . took a hit in their purchasing power of in excess of 50 percent over an eight-year period and you didn't have a social revolution?

—Nicholas Scheele, head of Ford Motor Company in Mexico, 1991

The state and private enterprise are, at bottom, the same thing.

—Agustín F. Legorreta, director of the private Banco Nacional de México (Banamex)

I imagine that Mexico's problems come from people with money stashing it in foreign banks and that is why we are so poor here in Mexico. That money could be setting up factories and industries here.

—Michoacán migrant farm worker[1]

BECAUSE OF THE MORE SOLID SOCIAL FOUNDATIONS provided by the Cárdenas reforms of the 1930s, capital accumulation on an extended scale after 1940 proceeded for several years in an atmosphere of unusual political stability. By the late 1950s, economists were hailing Mexico's relatively strong GNP (Gross National Product) growth rates as an "economic miracle." Mexico was rapidly being transformed into a semi-industrialized, highly urbanized economic giant, destined to be the United States' second largest trading partner after Canada. (It was third until 1997, when it passed Japan.)

Yet an unbalanced class structure and uneven income distribution (still today more unequal than that in India or Puerto Rico), together with the existing demand structure and the character of the bourgeoisie and state, resulted in Mexico's state and bourgeoisie concentrating on the production of

141

what Marx theorized as "Department II" goods (consumer goods), mainly for the nation's affluent minority, as opposed to "Department I" goods (capital and intermediate goods, the means of production). For its part, foreign capital increasingly shifted its activities into heavy and intermediate industry (including technology sales), agribusiness, tourism, and the financial and export sectors of the economy, with the result that it came to play a preponderant role in the character of the nation's economic growth and the state's economic decisionmaking. As in the past, foreign loans and Mexico's foreign debt became bargaining chips for foreign capitalists' influence.[2]

In terms of economic programs, the ideas of "modernization" and "economic development" held center stage. Development was measured in terms of GNP growth rates with little regard for environmental or human consequences. A shrinking number of powerful groups of monopoly capitalists and transnational corporations (TNCs)[3] commanded the labor of ever more millions of intermediate-class people, proletarians, peasants, and immiserated subproletarians. For the masses, there was no significant "trickle-down effect" of the billions of dollars being poured into the "development" of the Mexican economy. By 1998, monopoly capitalism was firmly in the saddle, and Mexico was as sharply divided between rich and poor as it had been in 1910.

In the early 1900s, the word *imperialism* was commonly used to characterize the export of capital by wealthy, industrialized countries to less industrially developed areas of the world, in order to resolve capitalism's periodic crises of overproduction and to obtain much-needed natural resources for the maintenance and expansion of production (without which no capitalist economy can prosper). These early imperialist industrialized countries, including the United States, were experiencing the ascendance of monopoly capital. Often the term *imperialism* was applied as well to the military invasion and occupation of foreign lands, as in the U.S. colonization of Puerto Rico or French colonization of Vietnam and Algeria.

After the Second World War, when so many of the world's colonized nations broke the bonds of colonialism to become independent nations (notably in Asia and Africa), the term "neocolonialism" came into fashion to characterize their continued economic domination by imperialism (that is, monopoly capital and the export of capital to resolve overproduction crises, while scouring the world for natural resources). These former colonies, together with Latin America, became known as the *third world* (distinct from both the major capitalist powers and the Soviet camp). However, economic imperialism, as defined here, continues to operate as one—but by no means the only—determinant agent in the "misdevelopment" of Mexico's economy and politics.

Starting in the 1940s, the "Green Revolution" increased yields of several crops but worsened the lot of the peasantry in Mexico's countryside. Rural Mexicans served as the source of cheap food and cheap labor for Mexico's industrialization. A process of proletarianization of the peasantry and increased migration to Mexican and U.S. cities occurred. Mexico's "economic development" was built on the backs of not just workers but, above all, of the "superexploited"—Indians, peasants, migrants, women, and the "working poor" (or "immiserated").

Workers are "superexploited" when they receive a wage (or often no wage in the case of women) for their labor power *below* its minimal value, or what it takes for a worker to maintain minimal support for self and/or family. The superexploiting employers' *rates* of profit, of course, correspondingly rise, although the total sum of profits from sales inside Mexico were sometimes diminished by the consequent inability of the underpaid workers to become steady consumers of goods produced.

Depending on prevailing economic circumstances, Mexico's state gave its "modernization" and "development programs" different rhetorical spins, such as "import substitution" (1940 to 1955, to favor domestic production of consumer goods) and "stabilizing development" (1956 to 1970, to continue industrialization while reducing inflation). In 1965, Mexico added to its industrialization policy a border area program of foreign-owned *maquiladoras* (assembly plants).

A political crisis in 1968 coincided with the first signs of what later became major economic crises. Consequently, in the 1970s the state offered two new "spins" to its "development" policies. First, it sought to increase production of capital goods (Department I), and then, announcing fabulous new oil discoveries, it shifted to "oil-export-based development" (1977 to 1982). To finance these programs, the state took out copious loans. It also ratcheted up its nationalistic rhetoric, even though making further concessions to foreign capital.

Finally, when in late 1982 Mexico could no longer meet the interest payments on its foreign debt, the state announced its "bankruptcy" and an "economic readjustment" based on its creditors' dictates. This in turn led to Mexico's joining the General Agreement on Tariffs and Trade (GATT) in 1986 and the North American Free Trade Agreement (NAFTA) in 1994 and a "restructuring of the economy" under the banner of "neoliberalism."

Under neoliberalism, "development" was to be based on a market-driven, private-sector led, export-based strategy that would open up the country even more to foreign capital, similar to what the Díaz dictatorship had tried a century earlier. Privatization of state sectors of the economy, reduced social spending, and "opening up" Mexico's economy to foreign investment became the hallmarks of state policy. Neoliberalism served both as ideology and policy practice. This post-1982 neoliberal phase greatly accelerated the "petrolization" and "maquiladorization" of the economy and generated an even worse economic crisis.

In the post-Second World War era, Mexico's state became increasingly an authoritarian-technocratic one. U.S.-educated Ivy League graduates known as technocrats gradually took over those government ministries most concerned with the economy, and in the 1980s and 1990s they occupied the presidency itself. These changes—together with deepening economic crises, private capital's increased pressures on the state, the mass media's exposures of state links to drug trafficking, peoples' protest movements, and localized armed uprisings—led eventually to a "crisis of the one-party state" examined in later chapters. This chapter offers an initial basis for understanding *the economic roots of Mexico's political crisis.*

The Authoritarian-Technocratic State

After Cárdenas's reforms, an authoritarian and increasingly technocratic state enforced "political stability." As if to symbolize the state's commitment to stability and the socialization of the public to the ideals of social harmony and national unity, Cárdenas's successor, General Manuel Avila Camacho (1940-1946), started his administration by repealing the "socialistic" reform of education and becoming the first president since Díaz to declare himself a believer in the Catholic faith. In 1941, the business organizations Cárdenas had made obligatory were declared "public interest entities for consulting with the State." A "Law of Social Dissolution," which established long jail sentences for anyone attempting to "dissolve" society, was passed by the governing party's rubber-stamp congress, presumably to defend the nation against any "subversive" endeavors by fascism. In reality, the Law of Social Dissolution lasted for three decades and was repeatedly invoked to intimidate or repress left-wing reformist and revolutionary dissidents. Among opposition groups, only the fascistic Unión Nacional Sinarquista grew noticeably during the war years, claiming a membership of 800,000 by 1946.

During the Second World War, Avila Camacho had the Labor Code revised to restrict the right of public employees to strike and to make it easier to fire workers. To symbolize the end, or "institutionalization," of the Mexican Revolution, the official ruling party was renamed in 1946 the PRI—Institutional Revolutionary Party. Avila Camacho's successor, President Miguel Alemán, outlawed the Communist Party and then denied registration to the Sinarquista political party.

The state played a central role in Mexico's economic "modernization." It masked its often anti-Indian, anti-woman, anti-peasant, anti-worker, and anti-democracy policies behind the ideological banners of "revolutionary nationalism" and "directed democracy." It presented itself as the defender of the "revolutionary nationalist" ideals for which peasants, workers, students, and others had made great sacrifices and achieved at least some advances. These ideals included national ownership of natural resources; agrarian reform;

"effective suffrage and no re-election"; "autonomous" state universities and preparatory schools; "Indianism" *(indigenismo)*, and, long after women won the right to vote in 1953, "women's equal rights." Every government spokesperson and every PRI leader, right down to the local precinct, claimed to represent "the poor" *(los pobres)* and "the humble ones" *(los humildes)*.

By invoking the figures of Hidalgo, Morelos, Juárez, Madero, Villa, Zapata, Carranza, Obregón, and Cárdenas, the state was always able to accuse its opponents of being unpatriotic or "against the nation." After violently crushing the student pro-democracy demonstrations of 1968 under this demagogic rationale, the government decided to place one of the students' inspirations, the incendiary anarchist revolutionary Ricardo Flores Magón, in the pantheon of national heroes, in spite of the bourgeoisie's previous denunciations of Flores Magón's proletarian internationalism as "anti-Mexican." Meanwhile, the very state behind the assassinations of peasant leaders like Rubén Jaramillo of Morelos, a veteran of Zapata's army killed in 1962 by federal troops, erected busts of their heads in village plazas.

The revolutionary heritage of peasants and workers' struggles that gave rise to this misnamed "revolutionary" state was taught at every level of society—not just in the schools (average grade completed by 1997: seventh for males, a bit less for females), but also in the "free" (indirectly state-controlled) press, as well as in political and social organizations and block clubs, workshops, and *ejidos*. Everywhere, working Mexicans were told about *their* contribution to the creation of a strong "independent" nation. At the same time, the state emphasized the bloodshed and violence that their contribution had entailed, leaving people with the conviction that another outbreak of civil war must be avoided at all costs. Citizens were assured that, however gradually, the earlier popular goals were still being sought and that they would be attained if people worked hard and did not cause trouble.

For decades the state spent immense sums propagandizing this normative model of "revolutionary nationalism," along with the political model of a "directed democracy." Neither of these models ever again even approximated their fairly credible levels under Cárdenas. The "directed democracy" was institutionalized in the corporativist three-sector makeup of the PRI. For nearly three decades many peasants, workers, and people of the intermediate classes (plus segments of the poor) felt that they had at least token political representation in "their" sectors of the party (rural labor's CNC, urban labor's CTM, and the "popular" sector, respectively). Actual power rested with the party's twelve-member national executive committee and the nation's constitutionally strong presidency.

A key technique used by the state to maintain social peace was to channel divisions among people, wherever possible, into organized "competing constituencies" along corporatist lines. Workers, peasants, Indians, women, students, and immiserated groups were kept as separate as possible, while class and racial divisions were blurred by the ideologies of populism, national unity, and class harmony. In this way, Mexico's era of relative political stability lasted until 1968. (Some would say it lasted until 1988, when the PRI's candidate lost the presidential election but, by the slimmest of margins, was declared the winner by the PRI-dominated elections board.)

"Those Most Easily Exploitable"

As observed in Part I, throughout Mexican history the extreme exploitation of Indians and their participation in the class struggle were paralleled by what was happening with Mexico's working women. Consequently, the post-1940 authoritarian-technocratic state paid particular lip service to these constituencies even while doing nothing to alter the basic *structure* of their oppression. In fact, the state added to their oppression in many ways, first by strengthening the capitalist structure of the economy, and second by cynically promoting the ideologies of *indigenismo* and, later, "women's equal rights" to present an illusion of progress.

Indigenismo consisted of an officially proclaimed respect for the nation's Indian heritage—one of the few, though contradictory, accomplishments of the Revolution, as exemplified in the murals of Rivera, Siqueiros, Orozco, and others. In fact, *indigenismo* served the purpose of undermining Indian culture and integrating Mexico's Indians into the national and international economy. As an ideology and practice of integration, *indigenismo* became institutionalized in 1936 with the creation of the Department of Indian Affairs, which in 1948 was incorporated into the low-budget National Indian Institute (INI). This agency tried to tie Indians more closely to the national economy. In effect, it either masked or legitimized the exploiting and cheating of Indians routinely carried out by *caciques,* big landholders, merchants, moneylenders, migrant-labor recruiters, agribusiness henchmen, and farm, factory, or workshop owners. Anthropologist and historian Marcela Lagarde pointed out that INI programs were "directed and planned by anthropologists who proclaim themselves to be for the Indian, but whose end is that he cease to be one." Anthropologists Ricardo Pozas and Isabel H. de Pozas observed that the "true content" of *indigenismo* was "expediting the exploitation of those human conglomerates most easily exploitable."[4]

The same might be said of working women, because of the capitalist structure of the economy. On another level, because of patriarchy, it might even be said to some degree of *all* women. The pre-colonial and post-colonial legacy of *machismo* was deep set in Mexican culture—as were patriarchy and *machismo* throughout most of the contemporary world.[5] In Mexico, these patriarchical values elevated women to one or another pedestal, usually that of virtuous wife and/or mother, while successfully keeping them "in their place."

Granting women the right to vote in 1953, like granting Indians token recognition through the ideology of *indigenismo*, amounted to a perfectly manageable concession in a political system where the ruling party always officially won (until 1997).

In Mexico, as anywhere else, women had long held different class positions, and distinct political or other convictions. Because of patriarchy and sexism, however, they continued to have a double relationship to the capitalist mode of production: first, as workers, depending on what they did (nonwage housework and subsistence labor; farm or factory work; teacher; clerk; etc.); and second, per the system of patriarchical values, through their families or menfolk, whose activities and attitudes reinforced their subordination as unwaged workers.

In this new and important conceptualization, *the production of labor power is realized on a daily as well as generational basis, organized through the family in a patriarchical framework.* Its importance is manifested by capital's resistance to socializing costs of this form of production through the provision of public community services, free pre-natal care, day-care centers, paid maternity and paternity leaves, free laundry and cafeteria services, free education to all levels, and the like. Without this form of production, production as a whole—whether capital and intermediate goods or consumer goods—would be impossible, since without activated labor power there can be no production.

Production of labor power *did not have to be feminized or unwaged.* It happened to evolve that way under patriarchical capitalism, much to the advantage of others, especially employers who laid out nary a penny for the costs of raising generations of workers. Costs of labor power production could be picked up by society as a whole, but socialization of these expenses normally occurred only to the degree that social movements demanded it. The global spread of corporate giants like McDonald's reflected the capitalization, not socialization, of labor power production.

While paid wages were easy to measure, it was difficult to measure the monetary value of the huge sum of misnamed "man hours" provided to capitalists free of charge in labor power production. A clear sign of its importance and magnitude, however, was the resistance offered by most employers and their political representatives to all attempts to socialize the costs of labor power production.

It should be noted that Mexico's women, in producing society's labor power that was the ultimate source of all wealth, shared labor power's production to a small degree with other groups—for example, unwaged subsistence farmers and family artisans, some of whom happened to be male. Under capitalism, women's "socially assigned family role" in labor power's daily reproduction—feeding, clothing, nurturing, educating to society's values, and taking care of family and community members—was constantly being reinforced by a

ırchical and *macho* value system because employers, in their competitive
to accumulate, needed to minimize the costs of labor power and its
maintenance. In other words, it was in the capitalists' interest to keep women
in a non-paid position of family work or in low-wage jobs—or both!

Women were, in fact, "superexploited"—not only in labor power production, but also in the more traditionally recognized forms. There, thanks to the
prevailing patriarchical value system, the mere fact of being born female was
used to superexploit them. This occurred first through the ideology of supposed female inferiority and propensity to pregnancy, which was used to justify
their being paid lower wages (or, when they were pregnant, to justify their
dismissal). Secondly, it occurred through the almost daily practice of on-the-
job sexual harassment which drove many women to quit, or more often, to be
fired because of their refusal to perform sexual acts expected of them. This
forced rotation of jobs held by women in turn made them look as if they were
unable to "hold a job" and were therefore "unreliable" and "less qualified" for
a decent wage.

Succinctly put, *patriarchy structured (i.e., maintained and exaggerated)
women's superexploitation.* That was why any class analysis had to be a *gendered*
one if it were to reflect reality.[6]

Labor power production relations affected all social classes in diverse ways.
For example, men's salaries were socially expected to be enough to fund
supplies for family maintenance, whether they were in fact sufficient or not
(patriarchy's value system of "the men bring home the bacon"). Because of the
gendered nature of class, power relationships were more complex than mere
"owner-worker" class conflict. An example *within a class* was when a husband
joined his fellow employees in a strike. He was acting in his own class interest.
But, in the short run at least, this ran counter to the needs of his wife, since his
loss of wages reduced her ability to buy the supplies needed for performing her
daily "duties" (unwaged labor) of feeding and clothing the family.

Strictly speaking, then, while we can correctly say that men who earned
substandard wages were superexploited, we must also note that superexploited
women were doubly or triply so. Their work in labor power production was
not just *under*paid. It was *un*paid—a double superexploitation right there. And,
for those women who also worked outside the home, or brought home outside
contracted work as so many seamstresses did (so-called "homework" in the
"informal" economy), their "double day" was by then, in terms of superexploitation, a "triple day."

Indeed, if we could measure the magnitude of this triple superexploitation
of women, it would come out to more than triple, since in the salaried
workforce women earned not just substandard wages but considerably less
than what a man received for the equivalent expenditure of labor power.
Moreover, in the case of Mexico, women were undercounted as part of the

workforce in the formal sector of the economy—where they were more than a third in late 1998, according to the Mexican National Institute of Statistics (INEGI). Those doing subcontracted "home work" usually went uncounted, as did millions more in the informal sector of the economy.

According to the statistical calculations of the United Nations Development Program report of 1995, women's economic contributions globally were undervalued to the tune of $11 trillion. Just the unpaid housework of women was estimated at the market equivalent of 15 to 30 percent of Gross Domestic Product (GDP). UN and other global estimates showed women providing two thirds of the world's hours of work, earning one tenth of the world's income, and possessing less than one hundredth of the world's wealth.[7]

The exaggerated degree of superexploitation of women was why the struggle for improvement of the working class as a whole involved gendered issues like the struggles for women's equal rights and the socialization of labor power production. Yet patriarchy's values so thoroughly permeated the largely male leadership ranks of organized labor in Mexico that only in the 1980s and 1990s did some—and then only a few—male leaders catch on to the actual meaning of women's triple oppression for the working class as a whole. Most male union leaders paid lip service to women's struggles without taking concrete steps to alter organized labor's overall strategy—or, for that matter, the underrepresentation of women in union leadership.

Yet by the 1980s and 1990s women were playing a central role in the workforce that was generating Mexico's exports and foreign exchange earnings and were also speaking out for their rights as workers. Women were the bulk of the *maquiladora* and textiles workforce and key producers of agricultural goods and foodstuffs. Moreover, considering tourism as an export because of its often bringing in more foreign exchange than any other export except petroleum, women were critical to the tourism industry, not only in hotel and restaurant services but often through the provision of "sexual services," although more "sales" were made to Mexican males.

Over the decades, to keep women in their "triply superexploited" situation, the authoritarian-technocratic Mexican state helped organize and reinforce the value system of patriarchy and *machismo* and its practices (*e.g.*, woman beating), while simultaneously converting women into commodities for the capitalist marketplace as underpaid wage laborers and as sex commodities for Mexican males and the booming tourist industry developed in great part with state funding and promotion. After the end of the Second World War, imperialism exported to Mexico the accouterments of sexism and the corresponding ideological message packaged in television programs, comic books, cheap romances, and other cultural wrappings. The double message consisted of women as beautiful objects—active and passionate "Latin American spitfires"—yet passive and all accepting of their superexploited situations. They were also propagandized to be good consumers (called by some "the feminization of consumption"). The contradictory messages were only heightened by the simultaneous celebration of women's "equal rights" and women's superlative performances as mothers, lovers, homemakers, churchgoers, and upholders of "clean homes" and "the wholesomeness of family life"—all the while they were being superexploited as unwaged or cheap wage labor and falling into the ranks of the very poor (called by some "the feminization of poverty").

While hardly unique to Mexico, *machismo* became particularly institutionalized there. Until the 1970s, few women dared to confront it head-on, and many internalized its value system. The sexual double standard was applied in all social classes. Indeed, the nation's president was honored for the number of female lovers he could claim.

Obviously unaware of problems faced by U.S. women, a male Mexican migrant worker who had recently returned from California once told me that "there the woman beats the man instead of the man beating the woman!" Hearing this, his wife looked skeptical. A Mexican male wage laborer's socially condoned license to completely dominate his *mujer* (woman or wife) served, in effect, as a kind of perverse "compensation" for the exploitation he suffered at work—while seriously undermining his own integrity and sense of self-worth. This reinforced the ability of capitalists to dominate both male and female labor.

Illustrative of the obstacles to women's equality among the intermediate classes—besides the structural ones thrown up by the active forces of capital—were the "women's rights" or "feminist" manipulations of the state. The government sent its male attorney general to head the Mexican delegation to the International Women's Congress convened in Mexico City in 1975 ("International Women's Year"). It also passed an equal rights amendment for women that year, which it proceeded to ignore: most waged working women were still paid far less than men for equivalent exertion of physical or mental labor. In the 1997 off-year elections, every political party ran at least one female candidate. A lesbian was elected to Congress. In sum, the appearance was one of progress for "minorities" while the reality was that the structural obstacles to their equality remained largely in place.

Generally speaking, women from the affluent minority of the intermediate classes and from the upper class, most of whom exploited other women (as servants, child caretakers, etc.) and expended little energy producing the commodity labor power, helped the bourgeoisie to maintain a patriarchical system. Expected to be "good wives" and attractive adornments of the men's homes, few of them were admitted into the ranks of high political office or the professions. When women did reach prestigious professional positions they sometimes received equal pay and status with men (although the sexual stereotypes were not broken). This was because of their *class status*. It was not uncommon, for instance, for a woman professor to chair or participate in a high-powered intellectual panel and have her views attended to—typically with a male colleague's reference to his "beautiful and charming colleague's" contribution.

Despite all this, for several decades large numbers of Mexicans saw through the ideological manipulations of the state. So, whenever they began to surmount their divisions and create even a semblance of popular unity, whether for reformist or revolutionary change, the state responded with violent repression and the corresponding ideological justification of "defending the Revolution and the nation against foreign plots, communists, terrorists, etc." Women and men as workers on strike or peasants seizing lands were accused of being unpatriotic or disruptive of the "harmony between business and labor." Massacres of unarmed peasants, male and female, occurred all too frequently. In this, women achieved equity. The state's massacre of peacefully marching students and others in 1968, however, marked a critical turning point that, as we shall see in later chapters, ultimately backfired and led to a successful challenge to the one-party system.

The State Role in the Economy

Prior to the era of neoliberalism, the Mexican state's central role in the economy derived from three things: the relative weakness of the bourgeoisie; the corresponding relative strength of workers and peasants in the class struggle (even if the official party kept most of them in separate corporativist organizations); and the illegitimate character of imperialism's power over Mexico. The state presented itself as the guarantor of the interests of "the nation," pretending to be "above" the contending social classes or regions. This way the state more easily played its corporatist role of ultimate arbiter.

Since the nature of any state corresponds to the nature of the class forces dominating the system of economic production, Mexico's state remained a capitalist one. Therefore, the state negotiated directly with the bourgeoisie, with foreign capital, and with the imperialist states, usually taking their advice and applying it to overall economic policy. Each successive government sought to reduce private capital's costs and to increase sales and profit margins. The state played an activist role of assisting, stimulating, and complementing private capital. Since private capital, even in the most industrialized countries, finds it difficult to afford the large investments demanded by the modern scientific and technological revolution, the Mexican state budgeted money for research and development (R & D) and the production of improved technologies—although not nearly on the scale of its importation of foreign machinery and "know-how." In the R & D and technology areas, as elsewhere, the state's investments facilitated capital accumulation in the private sector but only rarely focused on servicing the daily needs of the rest of the citizenry.[6]

Prior to the post-1982 era of neoliberalism's "restructuring and privatization" of the economy, the state contributed 40 percent or more of total investment in every decade (except the 1950s). State investments were mainly in economic infrastructure or other areas useful for private capital (energy, irrigation, transportation, utilities, financial services, etc.). Favored by this type of state subsidization and maintenance of relative political stability, Mexico's capitalist economy experienced a 120 percent jump in industrial production and a 100 percent increase in agricultural output from 1940 to 1960. Propagandists called it the "Mexican economic miracle." Stimulated initially by increased U.S. demands for food and raw materials during the Second World War and the Korean War, and aided by an abundant labor supply made possible by rapid population growth—from 19.6 million people in 1940 to 35 million in 1960 (72 million in 1982, an estimated 100 million in 2000)—the Mexican economy showed substantial GNP growth rates between 1950 and 1970, when 6 percent a year was not uncommon.

The outbreak of the Second World War distracted the major imperialist powers from paying much attention to Mexico's internal affairs and permitted Mexico to undertake the first steps of its industrialization program on its own. With its northern neighbor unable to export the usual quantity of manufactured goods, Mexico increased protective tariffs to shield its own manufactured goods and engaged in import substitution. Industrial production jumped 35 percent. Meanwhile, Mexico's exports doubled during the war, as the United States, to help finance its war production, purchased copious amounts of Mexican silver, minerals, and foodstuffs. The United States also advanced loans for Mexico's industrialization program. In addition, a number of U.S. investors, fleeing wartime price regulations and high taxes, invested in Mexico.[7]

Immediately after the war, U.S. capitalists increased their investments and began purchasing many of Mexico's new industries. New direct foreign investments in Mexico started to rise sharply in 1946; doubled in the 1950s; tripled in the 1960s; quadrupled in the 1970s; almost doubled in what the UN called Latin America's economically depressed "lost development decade" of the 1980s; and more than doubled in the first half of the 1990s. By 1996, total direct foreign investment in Mexico totaled $67,708.3 million, a sum greater than many nations' GDPs. More than half of foreign capital was located in manufacturing, and more than a third in financial services (banking, insurance, etc.—see Table 11).

The large amount of foreign and state investment made possible the installation of ever newer technologies and their products in agriculture and industry—tractors, reapers, fertilizers, hybrid seeds, machine tools—all of which sped Mexico's economic growth. Industry and agriculture experienced an unprecedented degree of concentration as scattered productive units, artisans, workers, and peasants were moved into modern factories and onto large farms. The resultant productivity gains and higher level of profits facilitated centralization of capital (monopoly) in the hands of the big bourgeoisie and foreign capitalists. Assembly-line production of automobiles and various durable and nondurable consumer goods sharpened class cleavages between workers and owners. Dispossessed peasants trekked to the cities, and by 1960 Mexico was 50 percent urban (defining "urban" as communities of more than 2,500 inhabitants).[8] By the 1990s, it was 75 percent urban—one of the most urbanized countries of the world.

Until the late 1960s, when signs of economic crisis and social unrest became unmistakable, Mexico's industrialization program was dubbed one of "stabilizing development." While economic growth did occur, it was far from stabilizing; it did, however, make Mexico more industrialized than most other Latin American countries.[9]

The postwar administration of Miguel Alemán (1946 to 1952), the nation's first full-term civilian president since Juárez, typified the new spirit of collaboration with foreign capital that Mexico's bourgeoisie and its partners in the state were undertaking. The longstanding unwritten rule that those in top government posts may filch public money without risk of serious reprisal was reaffirmed in blatant ways. Where before bureaucrats on the lower rungs had at least to pretend to be careful, under Alemán everyone used the same excuse: "President Alemán leads and I follow."

Alemán himself, having made a fortune from graft and deals with U.S. capitalists, including partnerships with hotel magnate Conrad Hilton, left office in 1952 a millionaire—but only after placing a thirty-foot statue of himself at the entrance to the Universidad Nacional. (A generation later, indignant students toppled it.) Alemán went on to serve for decades as the major official in the nation's tourism industry, so critical in obtaining foreign exchange needed to help offset Mexico's trade deficits. Alemán's successors to the presidency upheld this colonial and postcolonial tradition of corruption, although none did so as sensationally as Alemán did until the arrival of neoliberalism's and NAFTA's champion, the subsequently disgraced President Carlos Salinas de Gortari (1988 to 1994).

Under Alemán, state corruption and collaboration with private capital reached new heights in the countryside. His administration reinstated the so-called law of *amparo* (a kind of writ of appeal) to protect all private landholders from undue confiscation. Alemán extended the legal size of landholdings to a range of from 100 to 300 irrigated hectares, or up to 50,000 hectares of arid grazing land. His government enforced the parcelization and privatization of *ejido* lands, while offering private farmers state subsidies and incentives for improving their technology and productivity. It dispatched federal troops and the traditional "white guards" (private armies) of the *latifundistas* to disband progressive peasant organizations.

Ironically, the preservation or creation of small landholdings and highly parcelized *ejidos* served to maintain an illusion of an ongoing agrarian reform and to deflect the rural class struggle into reformist channels. The function of the *ejido* and *minifundium* (a small subsistence parcel) became, in sociologist Roger Bartra's words, to act as a "shock absorber" for the social violence inherent in the rapid expansion of capitalist agriculture.[10] A network of the old *ejido* bureaucracy and *caciques* (local leaders), commercial intermediaries, and state technocrats became mediating forces that effectively allowed the banking, agrarian, and industrial bourgeoisies (Mexican and foreign) to expand their economic power and define the nation's economic future without total revolt in the countryside. A Mexican book published in 1968 highlighted the role of peasant labor, foreign investment, and land monopolization in this process:

> After 1940 when, during the war, American demand for Mexican agricultural products increases again: (1) Agricultural development depends more an external forces (demand and supply of inputs) than on the domestic market; (2) the best lands, the irrigated ones, and other resources like capital, labor, credit and physical inputs, become concentrated in certain regions and in the hands of a few owners; (3) growth opens the doors to foreign capital, which begins the process of control of national agriculture . . . the *minifundium* really constitutes 86 percent of the units of production. . . . In 1960, 2 percent of the farms accounted for 70.1 percent of all sales. . . . In the United States 10 percent of the farms generate 40 percent of sales, and it is said that this already constitutes a high degree of concentration. This means that [Mexican] agriculture is a wonderful business for a very few people, while the vast majority of the working population lives under extremely poor conditions . . . *neolatifundismo* is simply the natural result of the present power structure, that is, of the class structure.[11]

The state further stimulated and guided the process of capitalist expansion by maintaining one of the lowest corporate tax rates in Latin America. It procured international loans and offered state credits and tax incentives to private industry, while allowing relatively free remittance of profits abroad for foreign investors. The state also invested heavily in economic infrastructure, effecting a $3 billion state subsidization of private companies from 1953 to 1972 through lower prices offered them by the Federal Electricity Commission (CFE) and the state petroleum company, Petróleos Mexicanos (PEMEX). In public education, it halved the illiteracy rate between 1940 and 1970 and created high schools and universities for the intermediate and upper classes.

The most important role of the state in capital accumulation for private interests, however, was its enforcement of strict labor discipline and a low wage scale. From 1939 to 1946, the manufacturing worker's real wage dropped 50 percent; it did not recover its 1939 purchasing power (back then already *very low* because of runaway inflation) until 1968. A 1963 survey revealed that

Table 5

Purchasing Power of the Legal Minimum Wage, 1980-1997

Year	Minimum Wage*	Consumer price index	Purchasing power**
1980	163	100	163
1981	210	126	166.7
1982	294	202.8	144.9
1983	489	386.2	126.6
1984	748	614.5	121.7
1985	1,155	963.2	119.9
1986	1,961.3	1679.5	116.8
1987	4,131.5	4020.6	102.8
1988	7,749.9	8040.4	96.4
1989	8,732.7	10156.6	85.9
1990	10,034	13180.4	76.1
1991(1)	11,777.5	16070.7	73.3
1992	12,975.5	18427.4	70.4
1993	14,023.5	20608.1	68.1
1994	14,864.9	22050.7	67.4
1995	16,261	29767.5	54.6
1996	20,180	40,000	51.5
1997(est.)	24,300	48,800	49.8

* current pesos
**constant 1980 pesos
(1) Mexico's monetary system was changed in 1991 with the elimination of three zeros from the value of the currency. Thus, 1,000 pesos became one new peso. To make comparisons easier, in this table the minimum wage for all the years has been expressed in "old pesos."
Sources: Leopoldo Solís, *La Crisis Económica Financiera 1994-1995* (1996); INEGI, *Cuadernos de Información Oportuna*, 1994-1997

65 percent of average expenses for an urban family and 84 percent for a rural family went for basic food supplies, in either case an indication of grinding poverty. The state turned a blind eye to illegal work conditions, maintained a low level of social security, and offered no unemployment compensation. Two-thirds of the population received no share of the benefits of the economic growth their labor helped generate.[12]

As Tables 5 and 6 illustrate, the situation grew even worse under neoliberalism. Table 5 shows the purchasing power of the minimum wage experiencing a kind of free-fall in the 1980s and 1990s.

In 1997, a worker earning the minimum wage could buy less than a third of what the same pesos might have bought in 1980. The purchasing power of the legal minimum wage, having fallen almost 75 percent, sufficed to purchase less than a fifth of what a family of five needed to maintain itself. Worse yet, fewer than 40 percent of the "economically active population" received the minimum wage. (The "economically active population" was composed of some 38.1 million people in late 1997, of whom only 14 million worked in the formal sector, most of them covered by social security, the other 24 million travailing in the so-called underground or informal sector.) The purchasing power of "contractual salaries" of unionized industrial workers also plummeted (60 percent), *as in 1996 it fell below the minimum wage of 1976.*

Moreover, Mexico's workers in the 1990s had to confront attempts to have them fund the privatization of the social security system (pensions, health care, workers disability)—eventually losing the battle against the privatization of their pensions and having to buy private retirement plans. In Mexico City, malnutrition increased 600 percent in 1995, a year when neoliberal policies helped throw nearly two million Mexicans out of work (rivaling the rates of malnutrition in Ethiopia).[13]

Table 6 illustrates the unequal distribution of family income in Mexico. From 1958 to 1977, when Mexico's economy experienced its best GNP growth rates, income for the wealthiest 5 percent of Mexicans skyrocketed from 22 to 47 times the income of the poorest 10 percent. The intermediate classes grew in number, although few of their families improved their lot. Only in one decade, the 1970s when the oil boom began, did a significant percentage (nearly half) of Mexican families increase their share of national income—and then just barely.

Under neoliberalism in the 1980s and 1990s, the situation grew much worse. Almost all families except the upper ten percent received *lesser* portions of the nation's family income than what they had received before—and they had to work harder to get it! According to the World Bank, this left Mexico with one of the world's most severe cases of maldistribution of income. In 1996, the country's richest ten percent of families accounted for an estimated 42.8 percent of income, while the poorest twenty percent of families received only 4.5 percent. Mexico ranked fourth in the world for the number of billionaires (in dollars). *Fortune* magazine included fifteen of them on its 1996 list of the world's 447 richest individuals. The wealth of Mexico's 24 billionaires was equal to what the nation's 24 million poorest persons had.[14]

Labor Discipline

The unionized industrial proletariat often rebelled against these worsening conditions. But they faced an uphill battle against class-collaborationist leaders of urban labor's CTM and rural labor's CNC, who lined up with the PRI and became "men of the state."[15] Most CTM unions deducted a sum from membership fees as a "contribution" to the PRI; those funds not invested in the party or simply stolen by corrupt union leaders were often invested in state and

Table 6

Distribution of Family Income, 1950-1996 (by percent)

Deciles (10% of families)	1950 b.d.	1950 cumul.	1970 b.d.	1970 cumul.	1977 b.d.	1977 cumul.	1984 b.d.	1984 cumul.	1994 b.d.	1994 cumul.	1996 (e) b.d.	1996 (e) cumul.
I	2.43	2.43	1.42	1.42	1.08	1.08	1.70	1.70	1.59	1.59	1.59	1.59
II	3.17	5.60	2.34	3.76	2.21	3.29	3.11	4.81	2.76	4.35	2.90	4.49
III	3.18	8.78	3.49	7.25	3.23	6.52	4.20	9.01	3.67	8.02	3.81	8.30
IV	4.29	13.07	4.54	11.79	4.42	10.94	5.32	14.33	4.64	12.66	3.98	12.28
V	4.93	18.00	5.46	17.25	5.73	16.67	6.41	20.74	5.67	18.33	5.01	17.29
VI	5.96	23.96	8.24	25.49	7.15	23.82	7.85	28.59	7.06	25.39	6.40	23.69
VII	7.04	31.00	8.24	33.73	9.11	32.93	9.71	38.30	8.74	34.13	7.42	31.11
VIII	9.63	40.63	10.94	44.17	11.98	44.91	12.16	50.46	11.34	45.47	10.02	41.13
IX	13.89	54.52	16.62	60.79	17.09	62.00	16.75	67.21	16.11	65.58	16.11	57.24
X	45.48	100.00	39.21	100.00	38.00	100.00	32.79	100.00	38.42	100.00	42.76	100.00

b.d. = by decile   cumu. = cumulative   (e) = estimated

Sources: INEGI, *Estadísticas Históricas de México* (1978), Vol. I, and *Encuesta Nacional de Ingresos y Gastos 94*; Banco de México, *Indicadores Económicos*.

private industry. The state in turn heavily subsidized these official labor organizations and, when necessary, sent troops to repress independent or left-leaning labor unionists or strikers. For example, on September 23, 1941, the Union of Workers in War Industry marched to President Avila Camacho's luxurious home in Chapultepec Heights demanding to be heard. Federal troops killed nine and wounded eleven. Then, in 1943 and 1944, spontaneous strikes spread across the nation to protest the wartime slash in wages, a 300 percent rise in prices, and corresponding superprofits piling up for big business. They too were repressed, even more violently.

In spite of this, some leftists and antifascists remained influential among certain key industrial trade unions after the war. Consequently, President Alemán completed a withering purge of progressives from organized labor in the spirit of the Cold War and McCarthyism then spreading on both sides of the U.S.-Mexican border. Helping to spearhead the witch hunt was a corrupt CTM boss named Fidel Velázquez, who had replaced Lombardo Toledano in 1941. As a young man in the 1920s, Velázquez had admired the CROM's ostentatious gangster boss, Luis Morones.

Repelled by Velázquez's crackdown on free thought and militant labor, Lombardo Toledano left the PRI in 1947 to found the People's Party (since 1960 the PPS, or Socialist People's Party, which ironically later became a decoy for the PRI within the opposition). Velázquez and the CTM executive committee expelled Lombardo Toledano and three of his followers from the committee and the CTM.

In 1948, Velázquez worked with the state to crush the militant National Railway Workers Union. He imposed the leadership of Jesús Díaz de León, alias "El charro" ("cowboy" or "dude," because of his fondness for fancy *charro* clothes). Díaz de León's alias swiftly spread throughout the labor movement, spawning the term *"charrismo,"* common parlance for violence, corruption, anticommunism, and antidemocracy on the part of state-sponsored union leadership.

Yet workers did not willingly submit to *charrismo*. Between 1958 and 1962 they launched a strike wave of up to 60,000 strikes a year, ignited by the railway strike of 1958 to 959, which sparked strikes in petroleum, communications, education, and agriculture. Members of the railworkers' union voted to disaffiliate from the PRI, and for eight months the union experienced genuine internal democracy. The government broke the strike with troops and jailed its Communist leaders. Renowned Communist muralist David Siqueiros was thrown into prison for four years; strike leaders Valentín Campa and Demetrio Vallejo were imprisoned for more than a decade. Telephone, oil, educational, and other workers or peasants who attempted to back the rail strikers or to assert democratic demands of their own were attacked and arrested.

Two decades later David Vargas Bravo, a key ally in Velázquez's and Díaz de León's installation of *charrismo* in the railworkers' union, publicly detailed the authoritarian and unconstitutional steps taken by the administration of President Adolfo López Mateos to quell this labor unrest—as well as similar state practices since (the 1964-1965 doctors' and nurses' strikes, the 1968 student strike, etc.). The heroic legacy of the 1958-1962 strike wave helped inspire growing labor agitation in the 1970s and early 1980s, which in turn helped gain the release of the imprisoned leaders.

Fidel Velázquez, or "Don Fidel" as he became known, ruled labor with an iron fist for almost fifty-six years, dying in 1997 at age ninety-seven. He typified Mexico's official anti-left and anti-democratic union leadership that solidified after the postwar witch hunt. It tied itself to state favors, class collaborationism, and upper-class aspirations and values. In exchange for sending hired thugs to murder or maim labor dissidents and for guaranteeing labor "peace," labor leaders received personal luxuries that elevated them into the living rooms of the bourgeoisie. In addition, they periodically obtained institutional payoffs for their organizations, being sure to pocket the bulk for themselves. For example, a 1962 profit-sharing law was passed to cool out rising labor unrest; after union leaders took their cut, few of the shared profits actually ever reached rank-and-file workers.

With Velázquez at the helm, the CTM bolted the Confederation of Latin American Workers (CTAL, an organization inspired by Lombardo Toledano) and the pro-Soviet World Federation of Trade Unions (WFTU). It joined the notoriously anticommunist Inter-American Regional Organization of Workers (ORIT, founded 1951) and the International Confederation of Free Trade Unions (ICFTU). The ORIT's use of "dirty tricks" to help U.S. business interests topple pro-labor governments in Latin America soon became legend.

After ORIT became discredited, the AFL-CIO's anticommunist leadership got together with TNC executives and the U.S. government to found (in Mexico in 1962) the American Institute for Free Labor Development, or AIFLD. Funded largely by the U.S. government's Agency for International Development (AID), but also by transnational corporations and AFL-CIO membership dues, AIFLD worked closely with the U.S. Central Intelligence Agency against progressive governments and labor unions throughout Latin America, protecting foreign capital in the region.

State tutelage of organized labor left little room for Mexico's working classes to act on their own. Whether to obtain and keep a job, to enjoy the few social benefits written into a union contract, or simply to get on a waiting list for seasonal or part-time work, a worker routinely became entangled in a web of *mordidas* (bribes) and fees to *charros* and their lackeys, often other workers. This humiliated and separated workers, enriched the widespread, deeply rooted *charro* network, and discouraged protest. Since the unions played a major role in the job market and were the workers' only legally recognized representatives, few could afford not to pay their union dues and follow orders. Ritualistically, CTM and CNC memberships "approved" the leaderships imposed from above by the self-reproducing labor and political bureaucracy. Rarely did they democratically choose their own leaders, make their own decisions, or conduct the class struggle on an independent basis. When they did, they faced severe repression, including murder.

In labor-capital relations, labor discipline on behalf of employers was guaranteed by the union itself, the supposed protector of labor's interests. Velázquez became famous for his use of "protection contracts" (to protect employers from union militancy) and "ghost unions" (known to employers and the state but not the workers). Labor contracts were renewed every one or two years, and official union leaders did little more than arrange these—usually demanding just enough to keep union members quiet but rarely obtaining economic gains sufficient to improve people's lives.

Laws governing labor's conduct were heavily weighted in capital's favor. For example, the conciliation and arbitration boards could make one of three rulings on strikes: the action was "legal," "illegal," or "nonexistent." Since the last two resulted in state intervention and also prohibited restitution of pay for days lost in the action, and since the boards could delay deciding for months, dissatisfied workers often postponed action or settled matters peaceably. If they did decide to strike, they frequently obtained government approval—sometimes tacit, sometimes explicit—before acting.

As a result of deliberate state and *charro* policy, most unions were limited to a single plant. Consequently, the number of unions grew much more rapidly than did union membership, furthering the atomization of organized labor. By 1970, about 42 percent of all employed industrial workers were concentrated in the Federal District (greater Mexico City), and the CTM accounted for at least 75 percent of those unionized. Puppet or "satellite" union confederations of the PRI accounted for most of the rest. By the 1990s, industry was not as concentrated in the Federal District as in the past, and on a national level the CTM controlled a lesser percentage of unionized workers while the "satellite" unions controlled almost an equal amount.

With increased industrialization and migration to the cities, the size of the urban proletariat grew considerably. The percentage of salaried workers (with or without steady employment) jumped from 46 percent of the economically active population in 1950 to an estimated 75 percent in 1982, and the percentage employed in manufacturing reached 19 percent as early as 1960 and 23.2 percent by 1995 (see Tables 7 and 8). Compared with most of the rest of Latin America, Mexico's industrial proletariat was large. About half of it was unionized in 1997, according to Francisco Hernández Juárez, head of the telephone

Table 7
Economically Active Population by Sector, 1940-1995 (percent)

	1940	1960	1970	1990	1995
Total workforce (in millions)	5.86	11.27	13.18	30.71	37.91
Agriculture	65	54	35.3	17.3	15.7
Industry	15	19	19.8	21.2	23.2
Mining / petroleum	2	1	0.9	0.9	nd
Manufacturing	11	14	15	14.6	——
Construction	2	4	3.6	5.2	nd
Electricity	0.4	0.4	0.3	0.5	nd
Services	19	27	29.5	35.1	34.1
Trade and Tourism	8	10	8.1	10.1	nd
Transport / Communication	3.1	3	2.7	3.4	nd
Other Services	9	13	18.7	21.6	nd
Unemployed workers or migrants in the United States	nd	nd	9.2	2 6.4	27.0
Not specified	——	——	6	——	——

nd = no data available

Sources: INEGI, *Censos de Población y Vivienda* (1940-1990) and *Conteo de población y Vivienda* (1995); US Bureau of Census, *US Statistical Abstract*

workers union, although other estimates went as low as 14 percent. Moreover, half of the unionized were covered by pro-employer "protection contracts."

As Table 8 shows, the best paid workers ended up in large, monopolized industries, many of them dominated by foreign capital. By the mid-1980s, these biggest firms accounted for some 1.8 million manufacturing workers (nearly 57 percent of total industrial employment) and paid out 67 percent of all Mexico's industrial wages. By contrast, small or medium firms hired the remaining 43 percent of the industrial workforce that received 33 percent of the wages. According to the Industrial Census of 1975, the hundred largest companies accounted for half of industrial production and nearly a third of Mexico's GDP. In 1991, a prominent Mexican business magazine reported that a mere ten large conglomerates accounted for 56 percent of sales, 61 percent of assets, and 53.7 percent of employment in Mexico. A year later, economist Carlos Morera concluded that 150 families controlled about one-fourth of Mexico's GDP.[16]

Table 8
Distribution of Industry by Size, Number of Employees, and Wages Paid, 1985-1993

	Small Industry			Medium Industry			Large Industry		
	1985	1988	1993	1985	1988	1993	1985	1988	1993
No. of firms	125,940	133,188	255,851	6,905	6,254	7,291	2,230	2,004	2,285
Percent	93.3	94.2	96.4	5.1	4.0	2.8	1.7	1.4	0.8
No. of workers	666,742	677,502	1,037,633	751,860	679,994	790,854	1,850,748	1,348,200	1,417,555
Percent	20.4	25.0	32.0	23.0	25.1	24.0	56.6	49.8	44.0
Wages paid (millions of new pesos)	429	2,402	9,242	687	4,896	17,845	2,296	14,677	43,118
Percent	12.6	10.9	13.2	20.1	22.3	25.4	67.3	66.8	61.4
Avg. annual wage per worker (current pesos)	643	3,598	8,907	914	7,201	22,564	1,241	10,886	30,417
Avg. annual wage per worker (1993 pesos)	14,061	8,507	8,907	19,980	17,018	22,564	27,122	25,730	30,417

Source: *Industrial Census* (1986,1989, and 1994).

Interlocking through holding companies and mergers with other firms in commerce, banking, and services, the biggest industrial firms in turn became part of powerful "private capital groups." By 1980, of the fifty largest "private capital groups," seventeen had foreign capital participation. Foreign corporations accounted for 40 percent of Mexico's industrial production. In 1997, under neoliberalism's stimulus to the further monopolization of Mexican exports, 2.7 percent of export companies accounted for 80 percent of exports. The export sector employed a tenth of Mexico's workforce. All these figures reflected the concentration and centralization of capital (and workers) under the control of a small number of private capital groups and manufacturing, banking, and exporting firms—in short, the development of monopoly capitalism in Mexico.

Despite CTM's iron hand, there occurred periodic rank-and-file labor protests that by 1997 contributed to a serious split in the CTM. Employers in the monopoly sectors of production, whether state-dominated firms or private ones, reacted to labor unrest by moving their investments or plants elsewhere. For example, because of the 1959 railworkers' rebellion, investments in railroad equipment dropped, while those in the automotive and air transport sectors skyrocketed. By 1980 Mexico had the world's fifth largest infrastructure in air transportation (airports, etc.) and a giant automotive industry. In turn, automotive workers' demands for decent wages eventually caused that industry to shift most of its production from central to northern Mexico, where the installation of "company unions" with lower entry wages was an easy matter.

By the mid-1970s, Mexico's largely U.S.-dominated car and truck industry had become the nation's fastest growing industrial branch (13 percent annually). In the early 1980s it was employing 140,000 mostly unionized workers who produced yearly half a million vehicles for the home market and 2 million car engines for export to the United States. Chrysler, Ford, and General Motors (GM)—in that order—accounted for 60 percent of sales. The reason for U.S. companies shifting production from Detroit to Mexico in the first place was obvious: a U.S. autoworker earned an average of $14 an hour, while a Mexican one made $3.90 an hour (1979).

Mexican auto and electrical workers ignited rank-and-file labor's revolt of the mid-1970s and early 1980s in much the same manner as railroad workers had done in the 1950s. In response, the auto companies fled the Federal District the way they had abandoned Detroit. They converted northern Mexico into the newest zone of automotive "development." Wages at GM's new plant in Ramos Arizpe were one-fourth to one-fifth of those in the Federal District, and "white" company unions were standard practice in the north. By the mid-1990s, Mexico's newest auto plants were perhaps the world's most modern and had shifted to the Japanese-style "team" production with its emphasis on speed-up and fewer workers. Those workers were highly educated, very low-paid and overworked, and frequently dismissed from work. Earning as little as $1.25 an hour, they had mostly worthless unions or no unions at all.

In part to rationalize the organization of labor and in part to check the recurrent signs of rank-and-file insurgency, the CTM and the state repeatedly sought to centralize all industrial workers' organizations into a so-called unity bloc. In 1955 they organized the Bloc of Worker Unity (BUO); in 1960 they founded the National Central of Workers (CNT); and in 1966 they merged these two organizations with some of the unions nominally outside their control to form the umbrella Congress of Labor (CT). In effect an arm of the PRI, the CT brought together leaders from some thirty-two labor-union confederations of unions. It was dominated by labor boss Velázquez until his death, after which it split.

Superexploitation

All the developments described in the section above, along with the rise of the largely union-free or "company union," very low-wage *maquiladora* industrial sector—where three-fourths of the workers were female—helped make Mexicans among the lowest paid industrial workers of the world. The many decades of superexploitation of the industrial proletariat contributed to the inability of Mexico to complete its industrialization on a stable and steadily expanding basis. Superexploitation, or the reduction of wages below the value of labor power (the costs necessary for workers to maintain themselves and their families), as Marx pointed out, "transforms, within certain limits, the laborer's necessary consumption fund into a fund for the accumulation of capital."[17]

The fundamental forms of superexploitation are: increase in the intensity of work, extension of the working day, and, above all, payment for labor power below its value. Mexico experienced all three. Total wages became less than the bare minimum necessary to meet the daily costs of the ongoing production of labor power on a daily and generational basis (feeding, housing, clothing, etc.), and as the bourgeoisie and the state refused to assume these costs, they had to be met by the larger wage and nonwage working class in its entirety. Women as workers and sole family heads (about a third of Mexican households in 1998 were headed by women) bore the brunt of these costs. Workers and their families could survive only by having all, or almost all, family members seek some form of money income. Children and the elderly increasingly had to work, at least part-time. Dollar remittances from family members working in the United States helped immensely.

As working-class families adopted a multiple wage-earning "family strategy," more women entered the labor force. Employers welcomed them, since they were easier to exploit, easier to lay off (e.g., on the grounds of pregnancy), and more difficult to organize on a traditional class or trade-union basis. By

1982, women made up one-fourth of the labor force in the economy's formal sector; by 1997, they were more than one-third. More than 2 million women were employed in industry, principally textiles, food processing, electronics, and the *maquiladoras*.

Consistent with the working class family strategy (and patriarchical tradition), a woman wage earner, even if heading a household, often distributed her earnings to the "responsible" male authority: a father, an uncle, an unemployed husband, even a brother. Money for her own necessities or diversion she frequently pocketed on the sly. Moreover, at her workplace she was routinely bullied into working harder and faster, while often being expected to provide sexual services to her male superiors during breaks or after hours. Because of, and in spite of, such abuses, the women *maquiladora* employees began forming labor unions in the 1970s, encountering such strong repression that, when not losing their struggles completely, they had to allow CTM locals or "satellite" unions of the PRI to incorporate them. One union managed to stay independent but collapsed when the San Diego-based parent company shut down the *maquiladora*.

Subsequent experiences showed that *maquila* women continued to be, rather than the "docile" and "accepting" employees plant managers had expected, painfully aware of their unfair treatment and ready to resist, although unsure as to how best to improve their situations. In the cases of married women, or single women who were primary breadwinners for families, there often appeared to be no choice but to put up with harsh conditions, since blatant disobedience could lead to loss of employment and starvation for children and other dependent family members.[18]

Capital accumulation in any country depends on a dynamically expanding home market and the fact that adequately paid workers make better consumers—an important factor in the realization and expansion of production. Mexico's "miracle" of industrial growth was a poor example of a self-sustaining, ever-expanding cycle of capital accumulation: only 35 percent of GNP went to wages in 1970, about half the figure for the United States and less than that for many other Latin American countries. Since wages included salaries paid to corporate managers, state bureaucrats, and the intermediate classes, the actual share of GNP going to those who ultimately generated it—the workers and peasants—was far less.

Furthermore, as noted earlier, the purchasing power of wages declined over the years, perpetuating the low-wage basis of capital accumulation. As it had done since its inception in colonial times, Mexico's bourgeoisie continued to choose maximizing profits based on low wages and an external market for a few select items over raising wages and ultimately expanding both the home and external markets. The availability of a large, low-wage labor force also discouraged attempts at developing an indigenous technology capacity.

Mexico's failure to maximize labor utilization and remuneration for the purposes of expanded social production and consumption was reflected by the fact that in the early 1980s only 27 percent of the population was described by census takers as "economically active," compared with 39 percent at the start of the century—the figure rose to 35 percent in the mid-1990s. These figures were lower than those for many other Latin American countries. Mexico never tried to absorb its available labor force since the bourgeoisie always preferred to maintain a large reserve army of unemployed and underemployed in order to keep wages low.

According to the Ministry of Labor in 1981 there existed 8.5 million underemployed persons. CTM boss Velázquez claimed there were more than 2 million unemployed by the government's own testimony. In other words, some 10.5 million Mexicans or 52.5 percent of the work force lacked sufficient employment. Just to keep unemployment from rising, 800,000 new jobs a year had to be created. The 1980 census showed 42.6 percent of the population to be under fifteen years of age. Millions of these youngsters later entered the job market, where the state and employers, practicing the "downsizing" and "economic austerity for the masses" of neoliberalism, failed them almost entirely. More than a million new jobs a year had to be created in the crisis year of 1995, a year when nearly two million Mexicans were thrown out of work. Estimates of those living off the underground or "informal" economy ranged up to 70 percent of the population, and the number of those reduced to poverty reached an estimated 80 percent. The chickens of Mexico's "economic misdevelopment" began to come home to roost.

The "Suction Pump Effect"

Under neoliberalism, U.S. and other foreign capitalists greatly accelerated their penetration of the Mexican economy. Foreign investment shot up eight-fold, zipping past the $67 billion level in 1996, from less than $8.5 billion in 1980 (see Table 11). Foreign investors picked up state enterprises at bargain basement prices and placed huge sums in the ballooning Mexican stock market.

The basis for the prevailing U.S. influence on Mexico's economy had long since been laid, when the United States had emerged from the Second World War as the undisputed leader of the capitalist world. From 1945 to 1978, U.S. companies and banks had invested an estimated $150 billion abroad, creating an overseas commercial empire that by 1980 generated half a trillion dollars in sales, $20 billion in profits per year, and one-quarter of the world's GNP. Mexico's share of this investment had grown to about 4 percent, most of it in the manufacturing and financial sectors. The 18.3 percent rate of return on investment in Mexico was the highest in all Latin America.

Foreign capital concentrated in the fastest growing and most technologically advanced areas of Mexico's economy, particularly the capital goods and basic intermediate goods industries. This was increasingly the case of much overseas investment by the rich nations of the world. By 1997, U.S. companies reportedly had $3.72 trillion worth of investments overseas. The world's richest seven nations accounted for more than 70 percent of global GDP.[19]

"Mexicanization" legislation, a series of laws passed prior to the neoliberalism of the 1980s and 1990s, permitted 51 percent Mexican control of any industry and required it in such strategic areas as mining. This legislation was largely eliminated in 1989. But even in its heyday, it rarely discouraged foreign investors, who often dominated "Mexicanized" enterprises by concentrating stock ownership in their own hands and encouraging the dispersal of Mexican participation among a larger number of very junior partners.[20] Moreover, "Mexicanization" was not applied very often, and many firms remained 100 percent foreign-owned—General Motors, Ford, Chrysler, Volkswagen, General Electric, Kodak, Sears, Anderson-Clayton, Dow Chemical, and several other U.S. firms from the top ranks of the top 500 U.S. manufacturing concerns ranked by sales, known as the *Fortune* 500.

By investing in joint enterprises, foreign capitalists often found it easier to borrow from Mexican public and private lending institutions and to diversify into other lines of business. U.S. corporations financed 71 percent of their direct investments in Mexico by means of the Mexican state or private Mexican capital. A 1967 Harvard Business School survey discovered that a full half of the Mexican ventures of the 187 U.S.-based TNCs most heavily involved in foreign direct manufacturing investment worldwide were either acquisitions or branches of other previously established enterprises. By the early 1970s, three-fourths of all new foreign investments were acquisitions of existing companies. Later, neoliberalism's "privatization" and "free trade" schemes furthered this trend.

U.S. capitalists took full advantage of the opportunities offered them in Mexico. Of the *Fortune* 500 corporations, 277, or 55 percent, had Mexican operations by 1977. Of the top 100 U.S. companies, 71 percent had Mexican manufacturing investments. As early as 1970, U.S.-based TNCs had at least 47 percent and usually more control of such key sectors of Mexico's economy as mining and metallurgy, copper and aluminum, petroleum products and coke, industrial chemicals, electrical and non-electrical machinery, transportation equipment, automotive, rubber, food and beverages, and commerce. They controlled tobacco 100 percent, computers and office equipment 88 percent, and chemicals and pharmaceuticals 86.4 percent. U.S. firms dominated television programming, tourist hotels, and related services. The areas of most rapid growth in U.S. investment were petroleum, petrochemicals, transport equipment, and machinery.

Significantly, TNCs were located in those sectors of industrial production having the highest levels of capital concentration. According to economists

Fernando Fajnzylber and Trinidad Martínez Tarrago, by the early 1970s almost two-thirds of TNC investments, compared with less than one-third of Mexican investments, were located in sectors with more than 50 percent concentration—the four largest firms in the sector accounted for more than half the sector's total production. These monopoly sectors also tended to be the most dynamic ones, veritable engines of capital accumulation. Since they also tended to be capital-intensive, they aggravated Mexico's unemployment problem by reducing the number of labor hours required for maintaining production and by further elevating the amount of capital needed for the creation of new jobs.

Consequently, when in 1964 the United States terminated the *bracero* program, which had legally contracted up to 450,000 Mexican workers a year for seasonal farm labor in California, Texas, and other states since 1942, Mexico tried to provide more jobs through its Border Industrialization Program of labor-intensive assembly plants (*maquiladoras*). The Mexican government allowed the *maquiladoras* to import parts duty-free, while the U.S. government allowed the return of assembled products in like manner. One Mexican minister of industry and commerce said that the goal was "to offer an alternative to Hong Kong, Japan, and Puerto Rico for free enterprise."[21] By 1972, nearly a third of the value of all U.S. components sent abroad for assembly went to Mexico, and by 1977 more than $1 billion worth of *maquiladora*-assembled products was being returned to the United States every year. This was *before* NAFTA and the greatly accelerated maquiladorization of the economy under neoliberalism!

Mexican workers received wages far less than those paid U.S. workers in the same industries, worked longer days, and produced more per hour at greater risk to their health. For example, women performing electronic assembly operations with the naked eye produced 25 percent more than their U.S. counterparts using microscopes. Of those employed by the 500 border-area plants established between 1965 and 1975, most (85 percent) were poorly paid single women between sixteen and twenty-three years of age. Besides traditional U.S. manufacturers like GM, Dupont, Dow Chemical, and so on, such diversified concerns as Transitron Electronic Corp., Litton Industries, Fairchild Camera, Hughes Aircraft Co., and Lockheed Aircraft, most of them among the top twenty subsidized clients of the Pentagon, moved into Mexico.

The *maquiladora* program proved particularly profitable for U.S. interests. A TNC paid wages according to Mexican norms but sold the finished products in the United States according to much higher U.S. price norms. Moreover, sizable portions of the wages earned by *maquiladora* employees were spent on the U.S. side of the border.

Prior to the state's adoption of neoliberal policies, Mexico permitted the establishment of foreign *maquiladoras* in the interior of the country as well. By 1982, U.S. companies owned some 700 of Mexico's *maquiladoras*. By late 1998, Mexico sported nearly 4,000 *maquiladoras*, most of which still superexploited young women. Japan and South Korea had established several *maquiladoras*. Almost every time there occurred labor unrest or a recession, *maquiladoras* routinely dismissed personnel, closed down, or moved to another part of Mexico. Each new locale of such plants experienced a small economic boom until the next economic downturn.

Consequently, far from being reduced, unemployment rates in those cities penetrated by the *maquiladoras* rose, boosted by the arrival of thousands of persons from other regions of the country in quest of work. From 1965 to 1982, fewer than 140,000 jobs were provided by the *maquiladoras*. Under neoliberalism, especially after NAFTA took effect in 1994, the economy "maquiladorized," raising the number of *maquiladora* jobs to a million in 1998.

The unemployment pattern persisted in most *maquila* zones. The one possible exception was the incredibly booming Ciudad Juárez on the southwestern Texas border, which had its own special problems, including well publicized contrasts of wealth and poverty, a population doubling in a decade to 1.6 million (1998), a housing shortage of 70,000 units, serial killings of women, drug-related disappearances, and pollution. Ciudad Juárez's government had long banned unions for the city's 200,000 *maquiladora* workers, 65 percent of them female, most of whom earned $3.25 for a ten-hour day and worked six days a week.

The Mexican state had repeatedly tried to justify its generosity to foreign investors on the grounds that they furnished jobs and helped Mexico industrialize by providing infusions of much needed capital and machinery. Tables 9, 10, and 11 present a profile of direct foreign investment in Mexico between 1960 and 1996 that suggests otherwise. For the years 1960-1984, foreign investors took out of Mexico more than twice the new sums they invested. This became known as foreign investment's "suction pump effect," *draining Mexico of capital.*[22]

Then, when Mexico introduced neoliberal policies to open up the economy even more to foreigners, conditions became so lucrative that new foreign investments skyrocketed fivefold in just one decade (1985 to 1995). Foreigners tripled their manufacturing investments and increased more than twelvefold their stake in services (real estate, insurance, banking, investment firms for the Mexican stock market, etc.). They no longer took out of Mexico more money than they invested per year, but their profits on new investments ranged from 35 to 85 percent per year and *the sums of their income more than doubled.* Much of the new foreign investment was

Table 9

Foreign Direct Investment and Income, 1960-1996
(Millions of U.S. dollars)

Year	New foreign direct investment	Net earnings on foreign investment
1960-79	4,288	8,687
1980	1,623	1,473
1981	1,701	2,120
1982	627	2,645
1983	684	1,785
1984	1,430	2,030
1985	1,729	1,793
1986	2,424	1,631
1987	3,877	1,727
1988	3,157	1,644
1989	2,500	1,714
1990	3,722	2,541
1991	3,565	2,561
1992	3,600	2,913
1993	4,901	3,391
1994	8,026	4,571
1995	9,773	3,556
1996	7,535	4,193

Sources: Poder Ejecutivo Federal de los Estados Unidos Mexicanos, *Sexto Informe de Gobierno* (1994) and Banco de México, *Indicadores del Sector Externo* (1997)

Table 10

Profits from Foreign Direct Investments
plus Interest Payments on Foreign Debt 1980-1996
(In Billions of U.S. dollars)

Year	Profits
1980	7.8
1985	11.3
1990	11.9
1993	13.6
1994	16.4
1995	17.2
1996	17.7

Sources: Poder Ejecutivo Federal, *Informes de Gobierno*; Banco de México, *Indicadores Económicos*

Table 11

Foreign Direct Investment, 1980-1996 (in Millions of U.S. dollars)

year	total	agriculture	mining & metallurgy	manu-facturing	commerce	services
1980	8, 458.8	8.4	419.6	6,559.8	745.5	716.5
1985	14,628.9	6.2	276.0	11,379.1	1,125.4	1,842.2
1988	24,087.4	9.6	380.5	16,718.5	1,502.2	5,476.6
1989	26,587.1	28.9	390.0	17,700.9	1,888.5	6,578.8
1990	30,309.5	90.0	483.9	18,893.8	2,059.9	8,781.9
1991	33,874.5	134.9	514.9	19,857.4	2,447.4	10,919.9
1992	37,474.1	174.2	523.5	20,958.2	3,198.3	12,619.9
1993	42,374.1	208.7	578.6	23,278.7	3,958.2	14,350.6
1994	50,401.0	216.7	590.6	26,482.7	4,593.9	18,517.1
1995	60,173.6	226.5	660.9	32,024.2	5,605.6	21,658.4
1996	67,708.3	226.5	668.3	36,771.5	6,010.8	24,031.2

Sources: Instituto Nacional de Estadística Geografía e Información, *Anuario estadístico* (1995) and Banco de México, *Indicadores de sector externo* (Enero de 1997)

speculative and subject to sudden flight, as happened just before and during the 1994-1995 collapse of the peso. Consequently, the much ballyhooed "infusion of capital from abroad" was, at best, unstable and unreliable.[23]

Technology "Transfer Pricing" and Cultural Imperialism

Part of the U.S. TNCs' power in Mexico derived from the head start they enjoyed in technology and capital reserves when compared with Mexico. Although in the 1980s and 1990s the United States' technological supremacy was challenged by Japan and Western Europe, as late as the decade of the 1960s the United States still accounted for more than two-thirds of all receipts based on patents and licenses accruing to the six capitalist nations most active in patent activity.[24] By 1970, research-and-development (R & D) funding in the United States, more than half of it paid for by taxpayers' moneys (even though most of its products remained within TNC hands), approached $40 billion a year, an amount far greater than most countries' GNPs and 2.5 times more than that spent on R & D by all the West European nations combined.[25] Of course, quantity did not entail quality, as any U.S. consumer could verify. U.S. corporate activity in technology was monopolistic or oligopolistic, with the advantages quantitatively measurable but qualitatively insecure.

Classically, when dealing with weaker countries, TNCs used technology sales to help "denationalize" strategic economic sectors, such as oil, mainly through the capitalization of technological inputs. Whether through joint-venture deals or pure licensing agreements, a TNC stipulated that part or all of the technology furnished had to be paid through "equity participation," together with a lump-sum payment or a running royalty, usually calculated as a percentage of net sales. Later renegotiations of technological agreements often included the demand for equity participation. Sometimes the terms of payment for technology implied an increase of the debt/equity ratio that could lead to some sort of equity "sale" or "transfer" to the supplier of the technology.

While Mexican industrial output increased 5 times between 1940 and 1965, imports of foreign (mainly U.S.) industrial or capital goods and replacement parts increased 12.5 times. This not only added directly to capital accumulation for U.S. corporations but also provided them with critical leverage for increasing their investments in related areas of Mexico's economy. U.S. companies "tied" their sales of technology to further sales and expansion possibilities, using a panoply of means, including patents, licenses, and know-how agreements. Yet, as economists Fajnzylber and Martínez Tarrago pointed out, most of the technology that Mexico imported was inappropriate both in terms of cost and labor utilization. They concluded that "fewer and fewer productive jobs" were created "per unit of capital invested" and that capital was increasingly remunerated "at the expense of workers' incomes."[26]

Starting in the 1950s, most U.S. TNCs became interested in exporting investment capital, technology, and capital goods rather than merely manufactured items, seeking abroad an outlet for their own overproduction of capital goods and access to pools of cheap labor in order to achieve rates of profit superior to those at home. Products then manufactured in a country like Mexico were in turn sold there or, more commonly, exported at handsome profits.

To assure ongoing reproduction of these superprofits and to fend off potential nationalization or "Mexicanization," TNCs used their technological supremacy as a lever. Many retained full control over factories; some opted for joint ventures; yet others preferred direct technology sales to state enterprises since they could fetch high prices. In 1970, Business International Corporation, a consulting firm for TNCs, suggested that "a new era of international investments has dawned, in which the predominant characteristic is the exploitation of technology. . . . If licensed technology and management contracts can afford sufficient income and control without equity ownership, all the better in terms of [the threat of] economic nationalism."[27] A 1972 U.S. Agency for International Development (AID) report made its central point the need for "steadily increasing foreign sales of U.S. capital goods and technologically intensive products."[28]

Consequently, U.S. Secretary of State Henry Kissinger made so-called "technology transfers" (actually sales) a key agenda item at the 1976 meeting of the Organization of American States. By the 1980s, the TNCs' insistence on finding global guarantees for "their" technology and other *intellectual property rights* (IPRs) moved into high gear. IPRs became the major focus of all international trade discussions, as a means of securing protection for capital investment worldwide. GATT and NAFTA enshrined IPRs. The GATT called them TRIPs (for Trade Related Intellectual Property Rights).

As physicist and technology researcher Vandana Shiva acerbically suggested, the TRIPs agreement in the GATT, negotiated by a handful of TNC representatives behind closed doors, amounted to "bioimperialism—the belief that only the knowledge and production of Western [and Japanese] corporations needs protection [but the knowledge of Third World farmers and forest dwellers does not]." IPRs, according to Shiva, "protect neither people nor knowledge systems" and "are recognized only when knowledge and innovation generate profits, not when they meet social needs. . . . By reducing human knowledge to the status of private property, intellectual property rights shrink the human potential to innovate and create; they transform the free exchange of ideas into theft and piracy"—including the piracy of third world farmers' and forest dwellers' knowledge of local plants, trees, and seeds, of great interest to the suddenly "environmentally conscious" pharmaceutical companies.[29]

Technology sales helped increase foreign domination of Mexico's economy and enabled TNCs to evade nationalist laws ostensibly aimed at regulating foreign investment. As the manager of one U.S. affiliate in Mexico was reported in 1975 to have stated, "The use of payments for technology is the easiest legal way to transfer profits out of the country."[30] TNCs in the Mexican pharmaceutical industry, for instance, by using various tricks of internal bookkeeping, particularly "transfer pricing" whereby they underpriced exports and overpriced technology imports (sometimes using a fictitious third-party "dummy office" as an intermediary), were reported as making up to $400 million a year on transfer pricing alone.[31]

Transfer pricing and disguising profits as costs for technology imports enabled TNCs to increase their capital accumulation in Mexico. By raising their declared "costs" they reduced whatever profits they declared and had to pay taxes on. They further reduced their declared profits and taxes owed by declaring low prices for exports (underpricing) of the goods produced in Mexico by the "expensive" imported technology. Transfer pricing thus had the effect of partially *decapitalizing* Mexico in the name of capitalizing it! Such disguised parts of imperialist capital accumulation never appeared in the statistics on foreign profits, such as those in Table 10. By 1970, so-called technology transfers, through the tricks of transfer pricing, were remitting to the United States from Mexico almost twice as much money as officially declared profits.[32] Later, under neoliberalism, most state regulations on foreign remittances of profits were eliminated.

Although the Mexican government periodically paid lip service to the idea of independent technological development, it never spent more than 0.6 percent of GNP on R & D. Its research aims were oriented toward reproducing

U.S. technology. Research for meeting the needs of the masses remained practically nonexistent. "Comparative-cost tables" were drawn up and a decision then made whether it was more economical and conducive to economic growth to import foreign know-how and entire productive installations or to invest in developing an indigenous science and technology—and the former usually won out. Yet Mexico usually could not import a piece of machinery without importing the entire technology-and-science package insisted on by the TNCs, including "know-how," thereby making its economic development decisions inseparable from its approaches to such cultural questions as the production of knowledge, that is, education.

Much of the success of imperialism's historic expansion and survival derived not only from its maximization and maintenance of advantages in technology but also from technology's intellectual sources: science and education. In the 1940 to 1970 period, the Rockefeller and Ford Foundations spent millions of dollars on Mexican educational projects, much of it going to scholarships and professional training. U.S. public and private "aid" flowed heavily into Mexican private universities and technical or business administration schools. Trained Mexican professionals often limited their services to the wealthy elite, the state, or private (often foreign) corporations; or they emigrated (the so-called "brain drain" typical of so many third world nations).

Similarly, when the Mexican state launched the National Council on Science and Technology (CONACYT) in the 1970s (the nation's modestly funded but most ambitious effort ever to develop a more autonomous science and technology), the majority of graduate students sent abroad by CONACYT never returned. Then, with the state's switch to neoliberalism and its emphasis on privatization and guarantees for foreign capital's intellectual property rights, the Mexican state dismantled its earlier modest efforts at a more independent production of knowledge and slashed public investments (including funding for domestic capital goods production) to the bone. It substituted an authoritarian approach to research compatible with the focused goals of neoliberalism. The centerpiece of the new approach was the National System of Researchers (SNI), an elitist, neoliberal club founded in 1985 to hike salaries for a few thousand carefully screened researchers. In the process, the state politicized knowledge by firing or demoting scores of prominent intellectuals in both the physical and social sciences for their refusal to buy into neoliberalism.

Several of Mexico's most prominent research institutes were privatized or closed down, including the Institute for the Research of Biotic Resources, founded in 1975 and famed for its field research on heavy metals and pesticide poisoning. Other casualties of neoliberalism's authoritarian approach to knowledge were Mexico City's prestigious Center for Ecodevelopment and the Colegio de México's programs in Energy Studies, Environmental Studies, and Women's Studies. CONACYT's original project collapsed. Its budget, augmented by World Bank loans, now focused on industrial research for private firms. The projects and budgetary outlays of its "research centers" were declared proprietary information. Beneficiaries of the new CONACYT policies included such TNCs as IBM, Nestlé, and Ericsson. As one well researched study concluded: "the interactions of Mexican with global or transnational forces . . . and the decomposition of the Mexican political system have progressively undermined indigenous capabilities for science and inquiry."[33]

Capitalism tended to reproduce itself wherever it asserted its dominance as a mode of production, and this reproduction, however uneven in practice, occurred also in the superstructural areas of science and culture. Anyone who experienced the spread of the English language and U.S. cultural norms abroad, along with the export of Coca Cola, Disneyland characters, and U.S. technology, readily appreciated the validity of the concept "cultural imperialism." By 1960, *Selecciones del Reader's Digest* had the largest circulation of any magazine in Mexico, and U.S.-style goods and fashions, including the latest model cars or rock and pop music, were being mimicked by Mexico's bourgeoisie and affluent segments of the intermediate classes as devotedly as ever they imitated the French. U.S. tourists, magazines, films, and television programs began flooding Mexico. In spite of their own nationalism and bountiful culture, many Mexicans found themselves imitating and aspiring to the values and goals of the historically hated "gringo."

In the end, technology sales contributed not only to capital accumulation for the seller but also to a culturally deformed and economically subordinated capitalist development for the buyer. Both the Mexican and the non-Mexican bourgeoisies, directly or indirectly, managed to accumulate capital as a result of "technology transfers" at the expense of the working class, which ultimately operationalized the technology. But the non-Mexican bourgeoisies, being the technology sellers, accumulated far more capital and at faster rates.

In spite of its "miracle" of economic growth, Mexico experienced a deepening pattern of *relative decapitalization*, manifested in the outflow of declared (and, in the case of transfer pricing, undeclared) remitted profits, payments on technology patents, licenses, royalties, and "know-how packages," debt amortization, trade imbalances, "brain drain," and the like. Because of dependence on foreign loans, capital, and technology, because of large-scale state participation in productive and infrastrcture investments, and because of domination by domestic and foreign private capitalist monopolies, Mexico's economic system became a dependent state monopoly-capitalism by the 1970s. U.S. capital did not control the economy in its entirety, but it wielded sufficient influence to make a critical difference—and therein lay Mexico's structural economic dependence.

Later, under neoliberalism in the 1980s and 1990s, the Mexican state continued to play a significant role in the economy. However, it did so no longer as a major investor but as an agent for the privatization of state enterprises and the opening of the doors to unrestrained foreign investment and remittance of profits abroad. Mexico's economic system became dependent monopoly capitalism, pure and simple, openly integrated into the "global" (mainly U.S.) economy.

The "Green Revolution"

Hand in hand with Mexico's industrialization programs went a transformation of Mexico's countryside, at great costs to the majority of peasants. Introduced to the world for the first time by the Rockefeller Foundation and Mexico's Ministry of Agriculture in 1943, the "Green Revolution" increased yields through the implementation of a "package of inputs" (hybrid seeds, chemical fertilizers, insecticides, systematic regulation of water, provision of credits favoring agro-exports). This and related state policies effectively replaced many acres of traditional foodstuffs with specialized commodities for export, ranging from fruits and vegetables to cattle and animal feed. The food processing industry was also developed for export. Mexican agricultural production multiplied sixfold.

By the early 1970s, livestock-raising and the animal-feed industry had become the chief arena for capital accumulation in rural Mexico. One-third of reusable land was kept idle in the interest of cattlemen, and 64 percent of Mexico's agricultural land actually in use was devoted to cattle. The number of head of cattle and acreage for grazing in Chiapas doubled between 1967 and 1976, reducing the corn and bean fields of the peasantry. Huge areas of trees were felled for the timber export industry and for the World Bank-supported hydroelectric projects that soon harnessed the rivers of Chiapas to generate 60 percent of Mexico's electricity. Peasants found themselves having to import basic forestry items for cooking and heating. All this led to eighty-six major protests by village Indians and peasants deprived of their lands, and a heightened level of violence against the peasantry by the hired goons of ranchers and the Mexican army and police.

Nationally, production of sorghum (used to fatten cattle for export) doubled. Mexico began importing large amounts of corn to feed its people, most of whom hardly ever ate meat. By the 1980s, TNCs had gained control of Mexico's food imports and Continental Grain had begun exporting Mexican corn to the Soviet Union. *Animals and foreign consumers were eating more basic foodstuffs produced in Mexico than were the Mexican people themselves.*

Bank credits from the Mexican state's Banco Rural (Banrural) and the two largest private banks, Banco de Comercio and Banco Nacional de México, financed sorghum production by *ejidatarios,* smallholders, and large-scale farmers. The Carrétero family of Tamaulipas, the northeastern state accounting for a quarter of the nation's sorghum crop, handled 40 percent of sorghum's commercialization through direct sales contracts to the U.S.-based TNC Ralston Purina. Another 40 percent was accounted for by the multimillion-dollar Mexican state food agency CONASUPO, which in turn sold directly to Ralston Purina, Anderson Clayton, International Multifoods, Malta, or the state-private joint venture Alimentos Balanceados Mexicanos (Albamex). In "the Bajío" (as the traditional heartland of Mexico's domestic food production in the greater Guanajuato area of central Mexico is known), one-fourth of sorghum production was absorbed by Ralston Purina—which, together with Anderson Clayton, removed 3 million tons of corn and 6 million tons of sorghum a year from human consumption for the animal-feed industry.

Hunger and the threat of starvation made some peasants rebellious, in Chiapas and elsewhere. Mexico's National Center of Agrarian Research repeatedly told the nation's presidents of the rising winds of rural revolt, but the government, complicitous in the "modernization" trends in agriculture, looked the other way. Meanwhile, state price guarantees on agricultural commodities worked to the advantage of large-scale mechanized units of production with high labor productivity, further reducing the prospects of peasant producers. CONASUPO—supposedly engaged in providing low-cost food for the masses—set fairly decent prices for crops only to routinely cheat the peasants. At the same time, CONASUPO paid for many of the imported inputs of agricultural industries and for most of the nation's corn imports. Food prices eventually went up, not down.

For several years, food imports approximated one-fifth of Mexico's balance-of-trade deficit. Together with shortages in locally produced food staples caused by the state's and the Green Revolution's emphasis on mass mechanized production for export, these imports helped fuel Mexico's rising rate of inflation. Then, under neoliberalism, the emphasis on large-scale mechanized agriculture for export reached its apogee. A 1992 constitutional amendment removed legal protections for *ejidos*, as agribusiness moved to absorb those communal and village lands it had not already reduced or indirectly tied to its global chain of command.

According to the Chiapas Zapatista declaration of war against the Mexican state, the 1992 constitutional amendment was the "root cause" of the insurrection, since it threatened the only means of cultural and economic survival left for the largely Indian peasantry of the region—the *ejido*. The "final cause" of the Zapatista rebellion was NAFTA which, by reducing tariffs on corn imports, threatened to flood the Mexican market with cheaper U.S. corn and deprive peasants of income they were counting on from sales of their corn surpluses. In brief, the end of the *ejido* system and the implementation of NAFTA spelled death for Chiapas's peasantry.

A 1997 report by the UN Economic Commission for Latin America and the Caribbean described the situation in Mexico's countryside as "an authentic crisis." It concluded that neoliberalism and NAFTA had led to the expansion of fruit and vegetable production for export, the elimination of CONASUPO's price supports for farmers' products, and Banrural's sevenfold reduction in the amount of land its credits serviced that was being dedicated to feeding Mexico's populace. Banrural, facing privatization, was dealing almost exclusively with the one third of Mexico's 1.1 million farmers who had "productive potential for export."[34]

The Green Revolution, which initiated these trends a half century earlier, was incubated in Mexico and soon spread to the rest of the third world. It was like a dream come true for modern agribusiness. Continental joined Cargill, Cook Industries, Burge Corp., Luis Dreyfus Corp., and Garnac in obtaining control of more than 80 percent of the world's grain trade. (Cook later receded, as Japanese firms began playing a larger role.)

Modern agribusiness tied Mexican peasant producers to its interests through the provision of credits and technical inputs. Del Monte developed the largest agricultural machinery complex in "the Bajío." John Deere and Ford also established thriving tractor factories there. Many TNCs engaged in "contract farming" in Mexico, providing large growers with financial advances for everything from seeds to workers' wages, and then collecting these advances on the basis of delivered produce. This helped cement the alliance between Mexico's rural bourgeoisie and foreign capital. Large firms —especially TNCs whose diversified investment portfolios permitted them to pay better wages and to obtain higher rates of productivity than Mexican companies—further controlled rural producers by becoming the "pacesetters" in wages, prices, product selection (by arbitrarily rejecting part of a harvest), marketing, and the ultimate use and distribution of agricultural products.

In 1950, Mexican farmers were utilizing only 3,500 tons of fertilizer a year. In 1980, they used more than a million tons. Only 3.5 percent of farms absorbed more than two-thirds of modern inputs, including irrigation and total agrarian capital investment. By 1982, some 85 percent of agricultural credit went to the top 0.5 percent of landowners. Unable to compete with these state-favored sharks, the lesser fish of the agrarian sea were steadily gobbled up. *Neolatifundistas*, many of them allied with TNCs, accumulated huge grids of landholdings as they reduced peasants to conditions of virtual servitude.

Official credit unions, energy co-ops, and fertilizer plants swiftly turned any remaining small-scale landholders into a captive market for supplies, charging them higher rates than those offered to large-scale landholders, whose professional organizations carried more clout with officialdom. As early as 1965, four-fifths of the peasants and Indians who had received land parcels earlier under agrarian reform in the Yaqui Valley of Sonora had lost their lands.

Commenting on the credit mechanisms of peasant dispossession, agrarian analyst John W. Barchfield observed:

The more common association of the *ejidatario* with private capital owners involves one of a series of arrangements that is tantamount to rental. The *ejidatario* is paid a fee for the use of his parcel . . . and, if he is fortunate, permitted to participate as a *peon* on his own land. . . . In both cases [of the state's Banco Rural and private creditors], however, there occurs a humiliating juxtaposition in which the *ejidatario* is deprived of his autonomy and subjected to the decisions of irresistible bureaucratic or commercial interests . . . which channel . . . the *ejido's* surplus . . . to the support of domestic and international [agro-] industrial capital.[35]

Most costs and risks of actual production in the field were thus passed on to peasants with small or medium-sized landholdings. Peasant labor was regularly undervalued and often not even remunerated. For instance, the work of children or poor kin, often women, went unpaid. Crops were taken to cover interest payments (of 18 to 100 percent). There occurred a multitude of swindles. These, plus the low prices paid peasant producers by commercial intermediaries, represented a constant transfer of value (estimated at $300 million between 1942 and 1961 and in the thousands of millions after that) from the peasantry to the more favored elements of society. Of the price paid for food by an urban consumer, precious little remained in the hands of the peasant producer.

Peasants with small or medium-sized landholdings received the Green Revolution's new technological inputs on credit. Failure to pay on time resulted in default and the loss of land or water rights, or in their having to rent or sell their parcels outright. Various agrarian-reform laws allowed the leasing of *ejido* parcels. "Rent parcels?" groaned one Sonora peasant in 1963. "Why here entire *ejidos* are rented out."[36] By 1970, some 70 percent of Sonora's *ejidos* were rented; in other areas of high-profit capitalist agriculture, like the Zamora Valley of Michoacán, famed for its U.S.-controlled strawberry industry and for the provision of cheap migrant labor for Texas and California, the figure for rented *ejidos* approximated 80 percent.

Such "modern agricultural development" entailed substantial investment from the very outset. Since only 7 percent of Mexico's cultivable land could produce good harvests without irrigation, the government dedicated 15 percent of *all* its investments between 1941 and 1946 to irrigation projects. After the war, additional funding for the Green Revolution came from the Ford Foundation, U.S. AID, European Economic Community aid programs, and the World Bank. The state further participated by channeling funds, limiting land distribution, rewriting agrarian laws, regulating certain agricultural prices, and subsidizing the social costs of production and infrastructure (roads, electrification, fuel, warehousing) in a manner favorable to the rural bourgeoisie and modern agribusiness.

Based on the biased assumption that large-scale landholders were more receptive to technological change than "mere" peasants, and on the recognition that only *latifundistas* could afford new expensive inputs, the Rockefeller Foundation and Mexico's Ministry of Agriculture focused postwar agricultural development aid on select regions, especially the northern states, which had a high degree of land concentration in the hands of former Porfiristas and new "revolutionary" landlords. By the 1980s, the North Pacific region had 53 percent of the nation's irrigated surface, compared with only 1.7 percent for the south. Yet the southern, largely Indian, state of Chiapas—Mexico's poorest—contained more than one-fourth of the nation's potential hydraulic resources.

Although most incoming presidents claimed there was no more land to be distributed, the state responded to peasant protest movements by periodically breaking up a few estates, distributing new land, or settling old land claims. For example, during the peak of the peasant revolt in Morelos led by Rubén Jaramillo, the regime of Adolfo López Mateos (1958-1964) decreed that 12 million hectares be distributed, more than the combined total of the previous three presidents. Only 25 percent was actually delivered, however. On the other hand, a tiny minority of state-favored *ejidos* achieved agribusiness size, contributing to a sixfold increase in *ejidos'* hiring of wage labor (often other *ejidatarios*) in the 1960s. Land reform was pretty much dead by the time of neoliberalism, which officially buried it.

Since the onset of the Green Revolution, agribusiness hired the bulk of agrarian labor, but it also absorbed less labor per unit of production every year due to ongoing mechanization. Because of the opportunity to exploit women at lower wages, most male labor employed by the food-processing industry was replaced with female labor, and male unemployment correspondingly increased.

Unemployment, induced by mechanization and peasant dispossession, became widespread in agrarian communities—and with it, alcoholism, factionalism, violence, and out-migration. The average number of workdays for the rural proletariat and day laborers declined from 190 a year in 1950 to 65 in 1980. In the 1960s the average annual wage of day laborers dropped, and 3 million rural inhabitants migrated to the cities. Many of the earliest migrants were young women from thirteen to sixteen years of age seeking ways to support their impoverished families. Movement to the cities or the United States escalated after that.

Despite all these hardships, those dispossessed peasants reduced to farming marginal lands still generated 40 percent of Mexico's corn production, often on steep slopes. They were forced to rent their good lands out to agribusiness interests, for whom they became wage or piecework laborers.

Some 5 million displaced peasants had signed up with the Mexico-U.S. *bracero* program during its twenty-two-year existence (1942-1964). Up to four times that many, known as "illegals," had attempted to "pass" as *braceros*.

(*Bracero* in Spanish means "field hand," from *brazo*, or arm.) The *bracero* agreement had been initiated as an emergency wartime measure to solve the U.S. labor shortage in agriculture, railroads, and other sectors, and to combat militant labor unionism in the United States. It was periodically reenacted and increasingly came under the direct control of modern agribusiness or its agents, leading to widespread complaints in both countries about the abuse of the *braceros* and the "illegals."

The U.S. Labor Department executive who oversaw the *bracero* program during its last five years later called it "legalized slavery."[37] The program helped to create modern U.S. agribusiness and to keep the wages of other workers down. It also widened the gap between rich and poor in Mexico's countryside, since holders of small and medium-sized land parcels who emigrated often had to rent or even surrender their lands. Braceros and "illegals" alike were scammed at every point of their journey. For example, one Michoacán old-timer related:

> Here in Mexico they formed a bank that we had to deposit a certain percentage of our dollars in, and that bank grew rich off us *braceros*. In the end the bank disappeared and all the *bracero* savings were lost.[38]

Eventually, organized labor in the United States and other interests brought about the *bracero* program's termination, but the migratory flow continued, as did the abuses—of men and women alike. Leonel Castillo, commissioner of the Immigration and Naturalization Service (INS, the migrants' hated "*migra*") resigned in 1979, telling the press that INS policy was a "disgraceful black mark" and that Mexican immigrants were like "indentured workers."

Many peasants who did not leave Mexico migrated internally, and not just to the cities. The 1970 census showed 1.2 million migratory farmworkers, representing more than 20 percent of the rural population, following the harvests from one part of Mexico to another.

As ever larger numbers of desperate peasants were driven into urban slums in the late 1960s and early 1970s, the actual farming population in Mexico declined in absolute numbers despite an annual national population growth rate of more than 3 percent. The waves of rural migration to the cities served to maintain a surplus labor force for industrialization, commerce, and services; to keep wages depressed; and to provide "scabs" for breaking strikes. Those who found steady jobs in the cities abandoned their small rural parcels, while those who did not sometimes returned to the countryside to engage in subsistence farming in little-noticed spurts of "reverse migration."

Meanwhile, Mexico's low rural wage structure attracted agribusiness TNCs in quest of higher profit rates than those available in their home countries. Wage differentials between Mexican and California farmworkers revealed the basis for agribusiness superprofits in Mexico. In his famous book on "strawberry imperialism," UN agronomist Ernest Feder calculated a $95 million

annual difference in strawberry agribusiness profits based *only* on the fact that
Mexican farmworkers earned one-tenth the wages paid California farmworkers. Similar calculations could be produced for other cash crops. Del Monte, to
escape the militant unionizing inspired by Cesar Chavez's United Farm Workers (UFW) movement in California, moved its entire white-asparagus production to Mexico in 1975, making over $8 million a year on it through exports
worldwide. A similar threat to move to Mexico faced California's remaining
30,000 strawberry industry workers (many of them Mexicans) trying to join
the UFW in 1997.[39]

During the heyday of the Green Revolution and then under NAFTA, TNCs
set the trends in land allocation through their impact on yields, profitability,
and global market demand. By the late 1970s, fruits and vegetables accounted
for almost a third of Mexico's agricultural production and one-half of the
nation's agricultural exports (for the U.S. winter and spring markets). Freezing,
canning, jarring, and the preparation of soups and sauces, which made up 90
percent of Mexico's industrial food processing, became TNC-dominated.
TNCs, often in joint ventures with Mexicans, appropriated a third or more of
the Mexican food industry's total gross product and profits.

Foreign agribusinesses were glad to share their dominance with Mexico's
neolatifundistas, select *caciques,* and powerful private or public merchant and
banking interests, because these were the ones best able to impose the required
production, credit, and marketing systems on the rural labor force. These
"locals" arranged for the renting of *ejidos* and parcels, and for labor contracts.
They spared the TNCs the need to tie up capital in land or take on the problems
endemic to agricultural production, including not only bad weather but also
the risk of nationalization or peasant land grabs.

Utilizing such methods, United Brands (formerly United Fruit) and an array
of small and medium TNCs known as *brokercapitalists* introduced the huge
strawberry industry, which, after ruining Irapuato's human and natural
ecology in the state of Guanajuato, moved across the state line to Zamora,
Michoacán. U.S. investors generally were able to amortize their entire investment in this industry in one year. Similarly, together with Mexican investors,
Ralston Purina and International Multifoods came to control the poultry
industry.

Condensed, evaporated, and powdered milk became a Nestlé operation. Yet
by the 1980s, 35 percent of Mexicans never drank milk. This was because the
food-processing industry consumed 30 percent of Mexican milk production
for export and many agrarian capitalists raised cattle for meat export rather
than for domestic milk sales. On the other hand, the average Mexican downed
five bottles of soft drinks a week, 45 times his or her milk consumption. Coca
Cola alone accounted for 42 percent of soft-drink sales, which increased 31
percent from 1976 to 1979 (compared with less than 10 percent for milk).

High-powered advertising campaigns selling infant formula as a "modern" substitute for breast-feeding in Mexico (and in similar countries with impure water and little refrigeration) contributed to increased infant malnutrition, disease, and death.

Anderson Clayton, which ranked second in sales among companies in Mexico in 1967, dominated the cotton business. In 1975, it decided to stop financing Mexican cotton cultivation. Production dropped more than 50 percent and nearly half a million Mexican farmworkers were thrown out of work. The Mexican government took over the financing, but Anderson Clayton still controlled processing. At the same time, Anderson Clayton expanded its investments into production of cattle feed, chocolate, planting seeds, edible oils, chickens, and insecticides, a diversification model followed by such other TNCs as Heinz, John Deere, and Ralston Purina. In this way, Mexico's agriculture came to be dominated by foreigners—from the production and sale of machinery and fertilizers to the processing and merchandising of agricultural goods.

The predictable result of the Green Revolution was land concentration on the scale of the final days of the Porfiriato. By 1970, half of Mexico's farms were so minuscule as to represent not so much landholders as landless farmers with access to subsistence plots for supplementing whatever income they could obtain from selling their labor power to others. From 1967 to 1976, a period of high economic growth, the average caloric intake per Mexican declined 10 percent. Malnutrition worsened after that.

Disease spread, as agribusiness in Mexico doused fields (and sometimes the peasants working them) with pesticides like DDT and dozens of other agro-chemicals banned in the United States or listed by the United Nations as extremely hazardous. Environmental damage became widespread, drinking water unsafe. Cases of cholera began being reported in Mexico in 1991.

By 1997, the United Nations Children's Fund (UNICEF) was reporting that two million Mexican children were "at risk" because of their living in extreme poverty; 70,000 of them were living on city streets permanently. Child labor was on the rise. A million minors (below age fourteen) were working in agriculture, and more than 100,000 minors were working in major cities. Child prostitution was becoming a major problem.

Meanwhile, foreign corporations stepped up their demands for "patent protection" in agriculture in an effort to convert Mexican farmers into cost-free seed providers for the new hybrid seeds being developed, and into cost-paying consumers of the new "more productive" seeds. Later, foreign agribusiness and pharmaceutical companies used the intellectual property rights clauses of GATT and NAFTA to secure much of the protection they had already begun obtaining under the Green Revolution, including a stranglehold on the $43 billion world market in medicinal plants.[40]

The Green Revolution had helped convert Mexico into the world's ninth largest food producer by 1980, when Mexico had to import 25 percent of its food from the United States. Mexico ranked sixtieth in life expectancy and food consumption per person. An agro-export giant, hungry Mexico *imported* $3 billion worth of corn, grains, frijoles (beans), sugar, and edible fats and oils in 1981, a sum more than the total value of its agricultural exports. By the early 1990s, Mexico had become "the third largest customer for U.S. agricultural goods"[41]—*before* NAFTA opened the doors to the Mexican market even wider.

UN researcher Cynthia Hewitt de Alcántara concluded her widely acclaimed study of the Green Revolution in Mexico by calling it

> waste: waste of natural resources . . . ; of manufactured agricultural inputs (and the foreign exchange needed to acquire many of them) . . . ; waste of profits generated by rapid technological change, that went into conspicuous consumption or speculative investment . . . ; above all, waste of human skills possessed by the landless workers, *ejidatarios,* and *colonos* [private possessors of state lands in agrarian colonies] whose control over their own land was taken away in the course of agrarian technification.[42]

But it was not wasteful in the eyes and pockets of the domestic and foreign bourgeoisies profiting from it. For them, the Green Revolution and the state policies integrated with it established four cornerstones for their capital accumulation on an extended scale. First, it provided relatively low-cost food—until 1965 at least—for the urban population, thereby holding down the production costs of labor power and the level of industrial wages. Second, it generated a relative surplus population of displaced peasants who served as labor power for industrialization and as a reserve army of unemployed, thereby helping sustain a low wage base and limiting organized labor's ability to strike or increase its social benefits (while also having a somewhat similar impact in its immigrant form in the United States). Third, it supplied inexpensive raw materials (cotton, tobacco, hemp, etc.) for industry. Finally, through its stimulation of agricultural exports, it became a principal source of foreign exchange, then used for the importation of capital goods for industrial production and of items for luxury consumption. The Green Revolution and agricultural "modernization" thus proved to be a basic *condition* for the "economic miracle" of industrialization and its corresponding immiseration of millions of Mexicans.

Industrialization and Decapitalization

The billions of dollars' worth of capital that foreign investors poured into Mexico after the Second World War penetrated the commanding heights of the economy. As already noted, they included joint ventures with Mexican private and state enterprises. This created a structural connection that united foreign

Table 12

Type of Manufacturing Activity 1960-1994

(percent, at constant 1980 prices)*

	1960	1975	1980	1985	1990	1994
Nondurable consumer goods	61.1	47.0	46.2	41.6	39.4	38.7
Intermediate goods	27.6	33.5	30.6	37.0	38.1	37.0
Durable consumer & capital goods	9.1	17.5	21.4	19.7	20.7	22.4
Other Industries	2.2	2.0	1.8	1.7	1.8	1.9
Total	100.0	100.0	100.0	100.0	100.0	100.0

* Except for 1960, which is at constant 1960 prices

Sources: UNIDO, Desarrollo Industrial, Informe Mundial (1996, Mexico Section); for 1960, Banco de México, Annual Report

Table 13

Gross Domestic Product (GDP) by Economic Activity, 1970-1996

(percent, at constant 1993 prices)

Year	GDP*	Agriculture	Industry Total	Industry manu-facture	Construction	W&R** trade	T&C***	other ser-vices
1970	486,744	12.2	32.7	23.7	5.3	25.9	4.8	24.4
1980	922,338	8.2	32.7	22.1	6.4	30.0	6.4	24.6
1985	1,005,190	8.5	31.7	21.3	5.4	26.6	6.2	27.0
1990	1,087,822	7.8	33.0	22.8	5.0	25.7	6.6	27.0
1994	1,206,674	6.0	27.0	19.0	5.0	22.3	9.7	35.0
1995	1,131,889	6.5	26.5	19.2	4.0	20.0	9.8	37.2
1996	1,189,537	6.2	27.8	20.3	4.2	19.8	10.2	36.0

* In millions, 1993 pesos
**Wholesale and retail
***Transport and communications

Sources: INEGI, Sistema de Cuentas Nacionales (1980-1995); Banco de México, Annual Reports (1980-1996)

capital with Mexican monopoly capital, the political bureaucracy, and the class-collaborationist trade-union leaders. The authoritarian-technocratic state that evolved did not separate public from private capital in a "mixed" economy, but rather practiced *a capitalism backed by the state.*

The state, claiming to act on behalf of "national" capital and "the nation," subsidized private monopoly capital, both domestic and foreign. State-produced energy, fertilizers, paper products, and air, rail, and truck transport were offered to capitalists at prices well below the international norm; the state also subcontracted lucrative public works projects to private firms. The federal budget allotted ever greater sums ($5 billion in 1980) for the *importing* of capital goods and spare parts, from whose use private capital profited the most. The state also invested in activities considered by private capital to be too unprofitable or risky, and, during recessions, engaged in "pump-priming" the economy to stimulate recovery.

Prior to their political offensive leading up to the introduction of neoliberalism, Mexico's large-scale capitalists were the first to acknowledge that their businesses could not prosper and social stability could not be maintained were it not for the state's role in the economy. Paraphrasing a Mexican banker, economist Alonso Aguilar felicitously described the state's role: "It is the duty of the state humbly to set the table, and the job of private enterprise to eat what it finds there."[43] Agustín F. Legorreta, director of the private Banco Nacional de México, was more blunt: "The state and private enterprise are, at bottom, the same thing."[44] State expenditures soared from only 8 percent of Gross Domestic Product (GDP) in the 1930s to 25 percent in the 1960s, 45 percent or more in the 1970s, and, with the expansion in oil production, more than 50 percent in the early 1980s, dropping back to 21 percent by 1990.

Tables 12 and 13 reveal the character of Mexico's semi-industrialization. Table 12 shows the distribution of manufacturing activity in 1960 and the slow changes beginning to appear by the early 1970s as efforts were made to confront the underdeveloped nature of capital and intermediate goods. By 1968, capital goods represented 50 percent of Mexican imports while raw materials for industrial production (intermediate goods) accounted for another 32 percent. Import substitution had thus turned out to be import-intensive. Further, those enterprises producing capital goods were dominated by foreign capital, which in 1970 received 70 percent of the income from capital goods production: 20 percent went to state firms and 10 percent to private Mexican companies.[45]

The administration of President Luis Echeverría Alvarez (1970-1976) attempted to correct the problem by supplementing import-substitution industrialization with the development of heavy industry. Mexico's technology development plans coincided, consciously or not, with those of U.S. imperialism. TNCs were committed to a new export drive euphemistically called "technology transfers" (i.e., technology sales) as a means of solving their cash liquidity crisis—since most technology sales were paid for promptly with cash transfers through international credit institutions. Because of rising production costs and overproduction at home, TNCs were also committed to a strategy of selling more industrial installations abroad, particularly to low-wage areas and expanding home markets like those in Mexico. Such technology commercialization and capital export constituted the fastest growing means of capital accumulation for U.S.-based TNCs and had become crucial for their survival and growth. Moreover, U.S. imperialism was momentarily on the defensive after the Vietnam setback; the dollar was no longer hegemonic on the international money market; the terms of trade had stiffened due to the activities of OPEC (Organization of Petroleum Exporting Countries) and similar cartels; there was a recession in the United States plus "stagflation" (high unemployment with inflation); there were intensified inter-imperialist rivalries and the rise of revolutionary governments and liberation movements throughout the world. Thus, Mexico was one of the first test cases for U.S. imperialism's strategy to displace part of its own crisis onto the backs of the working classes in the third world.

President Echeverría's advisers claimed that the 1972 Law on Registration of Technology Transfers, implemented through CONACYT, would provide government oversight and forestall TNCs from "ripping off" Mexico through the tricks of transfer pricing. Yet they conceded there was no adequate way to discipline the TNCs short of opening their accounting books, which would require a revolution. Three years later, CONACYT publicly acknowledged the failure of the 1972 law on technology transfers—and the previous thirty years' development strategy in general. The savings derived from registering technology sales had been insignificant. The registering had been irregular and only after contracts had already been negotiated.

Yet the Mexican state, wedded as it was to the interests of private monopoly capital, stuck to its strategy, and from 1976 to 1980 the importation of production goods tripled—despite state development plans that demagogically called for Mexico's becoming a capital goods exporter.[46] In 1980, durable consumer and capital goods peaked at 21.4 percent of Mexico's manufacturing activity, sliding slightly backwards under neoliberalism and not passing the 1980s mark until 1994 (and then by only a percentage point). Under neoliberalism, intermediate goods production shot forward at first, then stagnated (see Table 12). In other words, the underlying trend of weak or incomplete development of capital and intermediate goods continued unabated. Moreover, as noted earlier, any pretense to an even relative technological independence disappeared altogether.

Of capital goods developed in the 1970s, for example, more than 80 percent were imported. The state cooperated with foreign capital by offering such incentives as the elimination of all *ad valorem* import duties on raw materials and components and of 75 percent of them on machinery, 75 percent cuts in sales taxes, 15-20 percent cuts in income taxes, and increased depreciation allowances. It was estimated that for every $1.00 of new foreign investment entering the country, there left some $2.50 to $3.00 in profits, royalties, other payments, and tricks of transfer pricing on technology imports—a structural basis of the economy's "dollarization" and relative decapitalization (the "suction pump" effect of foreign investment). Further concessions were made to foreign capital under neoliberalism, which increased the percentage of imported capital goods to 90 and, as we have seen, accelerated Mexico's maquiladorization and relative decapitalization.

Table 13 shows the stagnation and falling off of manufacturing activity as a percentage of Mexico's GDP between 1970 and 1996. The GDP shares of agriculture and wholesale and retail trade also declined. The gainers in GDP shares were transport and communications (doubling to 10.2 percent) and "other services" (up from one-fourth to more than a third of GDP, as foreign capital rushed into the Mexican banking, insurance, real estate, and financial services under the green lights offered by GATT and NAFTA). Since manufacturing's share had peaked in 1970, it was obvious that Mexico never more than semi-industrialized. More importantly, Table 13 illustrates how neoliberal policies proved to be deadly for Mexico's industrialization dreams, the very opposite of what its defenders promised.

Moreover, Mexico's manufacturing activity became increasingly foreign-dominated and export-oriented. The portion of all foreign investment dedicated to manufacturing advanced to 76 percent by the year 1976, before shifting more sums to financial services. Most of foreign-dominated manufacturing was export-oriented. According to the annual reports of the Banco de México, the share of manufactured goods in total exports moved from 11 percent in 1960 to 22.5 percent in 1968 to more than 35 percent in 1978-1979. Then, as Mexico began emphasizing petroleum production for export as the new "salvation" for its sagging "economic miracle," manufactured goods' share of exports dropped back to an estimated 15 percent in 1981 (in the face of petroleum's 72 percent share, up from 21 percent in 1977).

Most of the manufactured exports were generated in significant part by foreign capital, including those produced by the U.S. *maquiladora* plants first established in the northern border's free-trade zone in the 1960s. Prior to the boom-and-bust cycles established there, however, U.S. investors had already begun exporting to Mexico manufacturing technologies—as in the 1950s when they sent obsolete, overpriced machinery to "help" Mexico begin developing a wasteful, expensive, and irrational system of producing automobiles, later to be replaced by a system of direct U.S.-owned and managed production with the latest technologies inside Mexico. By 1994, Mexico's foreign-dominated auto industry (Ford, GM, Volkswagen, Nissan, etc.) accounted for one-tenth of GNP and more than a third of manufacturing exports (or 18 percent of total exports). GM was Mexico's largest private employer. The facilities of the automotive industry were on a par with most of those in Japan and the United States. A highly skilled workforce, earning one-eighth of what U.S. autoworkers were paid, showed quality and productivity levels equal to or higher than U.S. levels. Similar trends of highly skilled and productive low-wage, high-tech production were visible in the foreign-owned electronics and computer *maquiladoras* of Mexico.[47]

The automotive and electronics experience soon became generalized, as U.S. investors insisted on newer technologies and on increasing the number of original production or assembly plants inside Mexico. Using reinvested profits or Mexican capital and highly productive low-wage Mexican labor, they produced and sold finished goods for both the domestic and foreign markets. The United States simultaneously maintained and even augmented export profits and favorable trade balances with Mexico by replacing the export of finished goods with that of capital goods needed in Mexico's industrial firms. Additional profits were garnered by the export of products manufactured in Mexico to other Latin American countries grouped in regional common markets.

Under NAFTA and its presumed successor, a single hemispheric common market, this pattern of U.S. investment and trade became even more marked. Mexico had the potential to become not only a center of low-wage, high-tech production but also a U.S. launching pad for trade with the rest of Latin America and other parts of the world (much as Japan used parts of Southeast Asia).

Meanwhile, Mexican capitalists traditionally focused their investments in light industry, commerce, banking, agriculture, services, and tourism. The most successful Mexican industrialists centralized their ownership in areas using advanced technology, clustering with other capitalists into "private capital groups" and often employing unionized workers disciplined by CTM unions. They obtained better productivity that way. This process was accompanied by a dispersal of other workers, usually non-unionized, in numerous smaller, less technologically advanced industries that produced far fewer profits and doled out lower wages (see Table 8).

Skewed distribution of wages was only one result of the continued development of monopoly capitalism in Mexico (also called "uneven" development, "subordinated" development, or "misdevelopment," of the Mexican economy). Other results were a sharp imbalance in the distribution of labor internally and the radical increase in the export of surplus labor to the United States. Tables 7 and 13 reflect the neglect of the subsistence sector of agriculture and the growing importance of industry and services, which by 1995 absorbed more than 57 percent of the labor force (compared with only 34 percent in 1940 and 49 percent in 1970). Meanwhile, the combined number of "officially" unemployed workers in Mexico and migrant Mexicans in the United States jumped from 9.4 percent of the economically active population in 1970 to 27 percent in 1995.

Despite the heavy emigration, a comparison of Tables 7 and 13 shows that almost 16 percent of the work force remained in agriculture, even though agriculture accounted for little more than 6 percent of GDP. In other words, manufacturing industry, which generated 27 percent of GDP with only 23 percent of the labor force, was not absorbing workers rapidly enough to uplift the rural poor or their migrant kinfolk, who constituted the majority of Mexico's unemployed and underemployed—estimated at 40 percent in the 1950s and early 1960s and *well over 50 percent in 1998*. Allowing for a shift in production from mining to manufacturing between 1910 and 1998, the picture of unbalanced and unequal distribution of labor and income in 1998 resembled in its proportions that of 1910.[48]

Mortgaging Mexico's Future

Discussion of the growth of monopolies is incomplete without examining the incredible monopolization process in banking. By the early 1970s, seven private banking groups controlled an estimated 85 percent of all capital, while the two largest private banks, Banco Nacional de México (Banamex) and Banco de Comercio (Bancomer), controlled almost half of all the nation's banking resources. This powerful financial bourgeoisie retained close links to the state—as well as to other banks, insurance companies, investment houses (*financieras*), industries, and foreign corporations.

A series of interlocks and overlaps developed among a handful of leading private banks and the largest national and foreign industrial firms, all favored by the state. These behemoth conglomerates in turn maintained close relationships to the state banking sector, which, through its rapidly increasing capitalization from oil revenues and foreign loans and its diversification into the "mixed" (public and private) banking and industrial sectors, came to account for almost half of all credit resources in Mexico by the end of the 1970s. The state's credit and banking system increasingly served to grease the entire production system. It was tied to the major international lending markets, headed by the International Monetary Fund (IMF) and the World Bank. Mexico's industrialization was furthered by international loans, mostly from U.S. and Japanese banks for PEMEX (oil) and CFE (electricity) infrastructure expansion.

By mid-1982 Mexico owed U.S. banks more money than any other country in the world. It was the world's most indebted nation ($85 billion at the time). Fifteen years later that debt had doubled to $170 billion, despite several renegotiations of the debt *downward* and three major IMF/U.S. bailouts in exchange for neoliberal "restructuring" of Mexico's economy and Mexico's agreement to guarantee debt payments from state oil revenues (see Chapters 7 and 8).

The use of such debts by foreign powers has already been illustrated in Part I. The role played by a developing country's debt structure in foreign capitalists' accumulation goes beyond interest payments or the opening up of new investment opportunities. Labor ultimately produces the economic surplus used to meet the payments on the foreign debt. Capital accumulation for foreign monopoly capital, while originating in the sphere of Mexican production, takes place in the sphere of *international money circulation* as well (especially through the debt structure). This circulation taps into Mexico's economic surplus and siphons it increasingly into the hands of financial institutions outside of Mexico—further decapitalizing Mexico. Equally important, imperialism uses a nation's debt structure to intervene in the shaping of critical national decisions, such as the use to which oil revenues will be put.

But it was not just through its joint ventures and financial services to the private sector that the Mexican state played such a pivotal role in the monopolies' accumulation of capital during the 1940-1982 period. The state itself helped gather the necessary resources by directly exploiting labor, including peasant labor indebted through its lending agencies. By 1982, the state employed at least 1 million workers in its industries and banks, plus another 4 million in joint ventures and subcontracted operations. In addition, the state employed 1.1 million people in federal government administration, and another 1.5 million or so in the public education system, the social security system, the military and police forces, local government, and the like.

Thus, in launching Mexico on the road to rapid but incomplete industrialization dominated by domestic and foreign monopoly capital, the state came to exploit labor on a double scale: directly as the employer of a large labor force, including important parts of the unionized industrial proletariat; and indirectly, through its development of a vast, unproductive state bureaucracy, which implemented and enforced labor discipline and political conformity through a complex series of institutions reaching into the remotest rural communities and most degraded urban slums. No worker, no peasant, no small businessperson, state office employee, street vendor, or aspiring student was immune from one part or another of this multiple exploitation at the hands of the chief agent of private monopoly capital, the state.

In the end, as we now know, the Mexican "economic miracle" became a real-life disaster. In 1982 the debt crisis led to Mexico's state declaring bankruptcy and the government's nationalization of private Mexican banks, later to be re-privatized. A huge U.S. and international economic bailout was conditioned on Mexico's privatizing its relatively strong state sector and introducing neoliberalism. Centralization of capital in a few private groups' hands rapidly accelerated. In 1988, when the entire commercial banking sector was privatized, there remained only eighteen commercial banks. By 1992, some 234 investors effectively controlled Mexican banks. As economic historian Carlos Marichal noted:

> By 1994, according to official reports of the Mexico City stock exchange, a group of 183,000 individuals—0.2% of the population—held capital equivalent to 51% of total GNP. The profits of these capitalists during the banner year 1993—the year NAFTA was signed—were greater than the sum of expenditures by the Mexican government on education, health, urban programs, ecology and water programs, and all public social investments.[49]

In 1994-1995, the 1982 scenario of economic crisis was repeated on a far larger scale. Mexico devalued the peso and fell into a massive economic depression. Once again, capital centralized, leaving only thirteen commercial banks. And once again, a predominantly IMF/U.S. bailout of Mexico's floundering economy left the largest banking monopolies intact. Even so, *after* the international economic bailout, more than half of Mexico's banks went into default. In 1996, the Mexican government had to bail out these banks. This reportedly cost Mexico 8.6 percent of its GNP. Mexico's dreamed miracle had become a living nightmare, except for a fortunate few.

Foreign bankers used these repeated crises to acquire huge chunks of Mexican banks at bargain basement prices. For example, the Bank of Nova Scotia in Canada took control of 50 percent of Grupo Inverlat, the banking complex managed by Agustín Legorreta, one of Mexico's most powerful capitalists. Spain's largest banking group, the Santander Financial Group, gained majority control of the Banco de México. Banamex fell under the control of a few wealthy Mexican elites from all sectors of the economy who had formed alliances with such powerful foreign concerns as Kimberley Clark. Bancomer's largest stockholder became Bank of Montreal. New York's Citibank agreed to buy Banca Confía for $45 million, once the Mexican state assumed responsibility for its bad loan portfolio of $1 billion. Citibank's deal was somewhat soured by news that Confía's owner had been charged with twelve criminal counts and jailed, not to mention the publicity given a U.S. prosecutor's charge that Citibank itself had laundered billions of dollars worth of a Mexican narcotics cartel's proceeds.[50]

In 1997 alone, Mexico was scheduled to pay out a whopping $40 billion on its external debt, most of it to U.S., Japanese, and European private banking and financial market institutions already made nervous by the shaky structures of Latin American, East European, and Asian stock markets, currencies, and banks that they themselves had so enthusiastically helped stimulate through their wild transferring of funds to make quick mega-profits in the "new world order" of free market neoliberalism. This $40 billion debt payment figure, in the absence of debt renegotiation or cancellation, would radically increase in 1999 when certain "grace periods" on Mexico's debt were due to expire.

Once again, as in 1910, foreign (especially U.S.) capital held immense power and influence over Mexico's economic future. In its economic structure and neoliberal state policy dynamic, Mexico, almost a century after its much celebrated "revolution," resembled a giant pool of cheap labor at the disposal of local elites and foreign investors and creditors. In effect, the nation was mortgaged to foreigners. In June of 1997, the director-general of *El Porvenir*, a regional newspaper, lamented: "It is reprehensible that the government reports its economic policies first in Washington or in New York before it does to the [Mexican] people or press."

And once again, even as in the early 1900s, Mexicans of all social classes were responding indignantly to the tremors of earthquakes, rapid economic change, the growing presence of foreigners, and political corruption shaking their daily lives. Through it all, surprising numbers of them were finding grounds for hope.

Chapter 6

Classes in Conflict, 1940 to the Present

Banco Rural is our patrón. *We're the workers and we don't even get a wage or have a labor union.*

—Group of ejidatarios, Michoacán, 1981

In your countries those that own the banks are getting richer with our debt while we are getting poorer and poorer.

—Doña A., owner of a small vegetable shop in Mexico City, and mother of three children, 1987

Now garment work is increasingly located in family workshops. People ask how we arrived at this situation. None other than that is the drama.

—Evangelina Corona, leader of the new "19 de Septiembre" seamstresses' union in Mexico City, 1988 (third anniversary of earthquake)[1]

WHEN SOCIAL CLASSES ARE VIEWED AS DYNAMIC, evolving relationships, not as static entities, capturing a precise and complete picture of classes at any specific moment is difficult if not impossible. Both the nature of a socioeconomic group's relationship to the means of production and the group's consciousness of this relationship change all the time. In the evolution of capitalism, forms of labor are continuously being transformed: from self-employment to wage labor, from simple commodity production to capitalist commodity production, from a society of scattered producers to one organized in corporate groups. Marx characterized this evolution as one "from relations between persons to relations between things," from barter to commercial trade, which he identified as the basis of the "fetishism of commodities" and the "alienation" felt by so many workers. And as capitalism transforms labor for the purpose of extracting surplus value,[2] conflicts between classes take on new, often violent forms.

In the case of Mexico, the primary class struggle between proletariat and bourgeoisie inevitably drew on the energies of intermediate classes and the traditional petty bourgeoisie (owners or possessors of their own means of production, such as artisans and peasants.) It changed those groups in fundamental ways. Most artisans and peasants underwent proletarianization, but a very occasional individual "climbed" into the bourgeoisie. In this sense, class structure was continuously shaped by class struggle, even as class struggle was delimited by economic structure.

This chapter analyzes Mexico's evolving class structure in both the countryside and the cities in terms of such a process of ongoing class formation and transformation. Underlying the period of class struggle from 1940 to the present were changes introduced in capitalist production, a second wave of "modernization" following on that of 1880-1940. Throughout most of this period, the state played a larger and more complex role than it played in the "robber baron" days of the Porfiriato. The state not only regulated labor (and to a far lesser degree capital), but it also helped create classes or class segments. It shaped or conditioned the class structure and affected class attitudes and the class struggle itself. Whether impoverished peasants, urban slum dwellers, unionized workers, low-paid bureaucrats, or influential technocrats, Mexico's social classes and groups grew, declined, prospered, or suffered in relation to the various programs of the capitalist state. In brief, the state acted as an important agent of class formation or transformation.

By 1970, the basic trends of contemporary class formation in Mexico were already established under conditions of the state's consolidation of dependent monopoly capitalism discussed in the preceding chapter. This chapter examines these basic trends: the proletarianization of the peasantry, as well as partial or temporary "re-peasantization"; a growing overlap between different fractions of the large-scale bourgeoisie (also known as the big bourgeoisie); the growth of the intermediate classes, and their increasing internal differentiation; the development of a sizable industrial proletariat, less than a quarter of it unionized (according to government statistics) and most of it low paid; labor exploitation in diverse forms, including proletarianization of the traditional petty bourgeoisie; the fragmentation and atomization of the working class as a whole; and the immiseration of the majority of Mexicans, many of whom regularly migrated to the United States or to Mexico's major cities, which became paved with superhighways and filled with festering slums. The exhaustion of the "stabilizing development" model and its eventual replacement by the "neoliberalism" model, as well as the onset of periodic political and economic crises starting in the late 1960s, contributed to the acceleration of these trends.

Unfortunately, social classes were not recognizable from income-distribution figures. The categories used by statisticians from census data often blurred or obscured class lines. They concealed unemployment or types of employment. Above all, they failed to capture the complexity of economic-survival strategies undertaken by working families, rural villages, ejidos, or urban *colonias* (neighborhoods). In fact, almost everyone in Mexico who could, worked. For most people it was a matter of survival, and even when an entire family worked, it often could barely make ends meet. Without the dollar remittances of family relatives working in the United States, countless families would have been unable to sustain themselves.

In light of the history of Mexico examined in Part I and its bourgeoisie's tradition of taking advantage of large pools of inexpensive labor power, it should come as no surprise that Mexico's major social classes continued to polarize after 1940. Indeed, the major gap in Mexico's social structure continued to be between rich and poor, with growing numbers of intermediate-class families in most decades falling on the poorer side of the divide, even as was the case in 1910. As production, distribution, and exchange became more uniform and centralized during capitalism's development into monopoly capitalism, and as imperialism increasingly integrated its economic stakes with those of the Mexican bourgeoisie and state, a very clear dividing line polarizing the classes emerged. On one side of the line stood the triad of imperialism/state/domestic and foreign bourgeoisies; on the other side gathered much of the lower-paid intermediate classes, and the masses of workers, peasants, and underpaid, underemployed, or unemployed people.

Class consciousness, the composition of class alliances, and social mobilizations were political phenomena that altered from crisis to crisis in Mexican history in quite complicated ways. However, "crisis" in Mexico was not "permanent" any more than Mexico's "Revolution" was. What was permanent, however, was class conflict, whether latent, overt, or shades of both.

This chapter delineates the major trends in class formation in Mexican society after 1940, most of which were established by the time of the 1968 student uprising. It includes some of the changes affecting those trends as a result of the radically different state economic policies adopted first in the 1970s and then in the 1980s and 1990s. Later chapters, using the analysis of Mexico's class structure offered here as backdrop, will examine how the social classes contended, and changed, as a consequence of the political crisis of 1968 and the new economic policies that followed.

Rural Class Structure

Gross differences in the standard of living between the city and the countryside led one historian in 1965 to refer to Mexico's "lopsided revolution."[3] By 1980, in the countryside, schooling averaged only 1.3 years, medical services were minimal, 62 percent of the people lacked safe drinking water, 80 percent of adult workers suffered malnutrition, and 75 percent of the work force received a total annual income far below the equivalent of the legal minimum wage. Two-thirds of the nation's unemployed resided in rural Mexico.

Within the countryside there existed great regional disparities in wealth as well. Ten states, most of them in southern and central Mexico, accounted for 80 percent of the rural unemployment and most of the out-migration.[4] The central-south region (Hidalgo, Oaxaca, Puebla, Querétaro, San Luis Potosí and Tlaxcala) accounted for 60 percent of the minifundios (tiny land parcels), which cultivated mainly corn. In the northwest, on the other hand, large-scale capitalist agriculture was firmly entrenched and a "permanent" rural proletariat existed, supplemented by seasonal migrant labor.

Generalizations about the rural class structure were therefore difficult at best. Even so, post-1940 technification of agriculture did reach all regions. To one degree or another, peasants were dispossessed and they and their land subordinated to capital's needs. In addition, there was widespread ecological destruction, not limited to the northwest. For example, commercial agriculture severely reduced forest reserves in oil-rich Tabasco even before the petroleum boom of the late 1970s and the ecological havoc it wreaked. Chemical fertilizers and pesticides "used up" soils or ravaged several rural areas of Mexico. As a result, some southern and central states such as Oaxaca and Guanajuato contained areas that resembled lunar landscapes.

By 1970, the rural class structure was basically bipolar: a wealthy elite and hoards of poor, mostly landless, peasants. Yet such obvious appearances disguised a more dynamic complexity. Simple formulae that emphasized "de-peasantization" or proletarianization of the rural masses, on the one hand, or the perseverance of communal, folkloric, or other peasant traditions maintaining the peasantry as a single, coherent class, on the other, failed to allow for the shifting patterns of class transformation and intraclass stratification that accompanied the stepped-up tempo of agricultural capitalization after 1940. In any process of capitalist transformation, proletarianization accompanies the continuation of peasant-type farming; that is, a dialectic of dissolution-reproduction of the peasantry emerges, with the long-range trend being one of proletarianization. Capitalism's dominance, together with historical, geographical, or cultural conditions, underlies the specific forms taken by this dialectic.

In terms of income, Mexico's peasants proletarianized but, because they earned too little as paid fieldhands, subsistence farming came to supplement their wages (and not, as sometimes stated, the other way around). In other words, the process of de-peasantization was never completed. Even peasants who migrated frequently to the United States tried to maintain their land parcels in Mexico, which their wives or children continued to farm during their absences.

While in 1950 about 85 percent of Mexico's ejidatarios earned more than half their income from farming, in 1998 hardly any did so. Most engaged in seasonal labor as part of a low-paid proletariat. The vast majority of Mexico's farms *(predios)* did not produce enough even to provide for the farms' owners (or renters). Thus, most rural workers literally could not survive in only one activity, whether it was as a peasant farm owner, renter, sharecropper, or as a proletarian.

The majority of the rural "economically active" population was an irregularly employed rural proletariat. These workers sought wage income where they lived or by following the harvest trail from state to state and crop to crop, from as far south as Chiapas to as far north as Canada. A minority—in 1980 an estimated 12 percent of the rural work force, or 800,000 people—constituted a "permanent" rural proletariat, regularly salaried though underpaid. (More than twice that number of workers were counted in 1980 as occasionally employed fieldhands.) All told, some 2.6 million people in the countryside were classified as "proletariat" by the 1980 census, a number that rose to 3.3 million by 1995 (see Table 14 below). Many of the regularly salaried were employed on small farms or ejido parcels hiring less than five workers. Their employers, because of the low level of technology on small land parcels, sometimes had to take a loss just for having to pay such hired hands. For many small farmers, the only alternative was starvation.

As early as 1980, twelve years before a constitutional amendment removing legal protections for ejidos, 80 percent of Mexico's 28,000 ejidos and Indian communities no longer could support themselves on farming alone, even though "legally" they accounted for 43 percent of cultivable land. Since these peasants were forced to rent out their land parcels or migrate, they, together with similarly desperate small private landholders, actually possessed less than 30 percent of cultivable land—and most of it was un-irrigated, hilly, rocky, high-risk, and not very productive. More than 90 percent of ejidos were non-collective units composed of minuscule individual holdings. There no longer existed sufficient space for the owners' sons to receive parcels; most therefore joined the rural proletariat. This trend worsened in the 1980s' "lost decade of development" and, in light of the 1992 constitutional amendment permitting the sale of all ejidal lands, augured an end to any remnants of viable communal farming in Mexico.

In the view of a knowledgeable seventy-two-year-old peasant leader of an irrigated ejido outside of Morelia in 1997, it was only a matter of time before the entire ejido would be sold off. People on the ejido, most of whom were mestizos, were in debt and could not make enough by farming. Their ejido parcels consisted of from two to four hectares per family, and used modern fertilizers and tractors. The ejido was not as bad off as most. There simply were not enough industries in the region to provide the peasants with jobs. All the ejido's families had several relatives regularly migrating to the United States. (At an assembly at the town's brand new secondary school—built largely by the ejidatarios themselves, and paid for by their dollar remittances—every

Table 14

Social Classes in the Countryside

	1970	1980	1990	1995
Proletariat	2,449,454	2,642,662	2,448,362	3,332,600
percent	48.9	46.4	46.2	55.6
Peasantry	2,334,760	2,843,844	2,784,225	2,479,763
percent	45.7	49.8	52.5	41.4
Bourgeoisie	127,104	214,321	67,527	179,008
percent	2.4	3.7	1.3	3.0
Total	5,103,519	5,700,827	5,300,114	5,991,371

Sources: INEGI, *Censos Generales de Población y Vivienda 1970-1990* and *Conteo de Población y Vivienda 1995*

Note: Non-bourgeois landholding, sharecropping, or tenant elements have been included in the category "peasantry," even though most of them gain over half their income from proletarian labor activities; of prosperous landholders, only capitalist-landlords are included in the bourgeoisie.

student in attendance, when asked if they hoped to emigrate to the United States after completing high school, answered affirmatively.)[5]

Mexico's few remaining ejidos with well-irrigated land—normally for export crops—were as efficient as any of their competitors. In general, however, state agencies like the Banco Rural and other credit institutions ran entire ejidos (and some private small holdings) as state/capitalist enterprises, giving the peasant "owners" part of the difference between the bank's investment and the value of production (which was sometimes negative). Most ejidatarios were forced to seek wage labor. This was because they lacked adequate capital, or the Banco Rural controlled their lands and labor. In addition, the corruption of civil servants, and the emergence of ejidal caciques (local leaders) linked with outside agribusiness and political interests, all contributed to the ejidatarios' poverty.

Those farmers staying on their ejidos often felt like proletarians themselves. As one group of the same mestizo ejidatarios near Morelia, Michoacán, complained in 1981:

> Banco Rural is our patrón [boss]. We're the workers and we don't even get a wage or have a labor union. We feel more exploited by the bank than if we were officially its employees. Our earnings from farming are far less than what we'd get if we were bank employees.[6]

The worst-off peasant and proletarian elements of rural Mexico were the Indians and the women. The census counted Indians as 14 percent of Mexico's

ation, based on the ability to speak one of dozens of indigenous dialects
nguages. Many poor people, however, were considered to be Indian
because of their labor or economic conditions, so that some demographic
estimates of the Indian portion of Mexico's population ranged as high as 30
percent. On the other hand, some prosperous mestizos considered themselves
white, which increased the portion of whites from 1 percent to as much as 15
percent. Once again, class factors determined racial/cultural designation or
perception.

Eighty percent of Mexico's Indians were agricultural workers, and more
than half of these were landless. The land they still held was the worst imaginable and continued to experience encroachment and reduction by outsiders,
especially after oil was discovered on some of it (Veracruz, Tabasco, Chiapas).
In 1975, to cite but one example, Indians from the San Francisco community
of Chiapas told reporters of how soldiers from the Forty-sixth Battalion (with
approval of local authorities) assaulted them, burned their homes, and drove
them from their land—which was then handed over to non-Indians with
political connections.[7]

Until the Zapatista uprising of 1994, most Indians were dominated by a
system of external *caciquismo,* mediated through co-opted community leaders.
Indians also were excluded from the government, although in 1980 the PRI and
the Communist Party each had an Indian deputy in Congress. The Zapatista
revolt caused almost all the nation's Indian linguistic groups to rally to the call
for autonomy for indigenous communities. Prior to the revolt, the INI (National Indian Institute) and the PRI's CNC (National Peasant Confederation),
in spite of Indian resistance, imposed pro-government candidates in elections
for the National Indigenous People's Council. The Council claimed to represent
the Indian population, a third of which knew no Spanish. Only a quarter of
Indian children attended school. Indians repeatedly demanded reforms in what
little education they did receive: more schools, more teachers from the Indians'
own linguistic communities, and an end to teachers beating children who did
not understand or speak Spanish adequately. The Zapatista uprising helped
most of Mexico's Indians move toward nationwide unity and ratchet up all their
demands, especially the call for adequate land and adequate resources to farm
prosperously.

Whether Indian or mestizo, Mexico's women experienced a double exploitation (and triple exploitation in the case of those who worked in production
of capital goods or consumer goods). In the countryside, as well as in urban
slums, women typically cared for a few animals or a small garden plot, made
or sewed clothes, took care of children, prepared meals, cleaned house, and
generally oversaw family subsistence needs—all without pay. Wages paid rural
or urban female or male workers by capitalists supposedly (but not in reality)
covered basic necessities for maintaining workers and their families—the

ongoing reproduction of labor power. Women's unpaid domestic work in the reproduction of labor power, that is, the sustenance of workers and the acculturation and upbringing of future workers, greatly added to the surplus value extracted by capitalists from all workers—precisely because this work by women was not remunerated.

Sometimes, patriarchy reinforced this arrangement by law. For many years Articles 168 through 170 of the Civil Code for the Federal District and Territories permitted a woman to take a paid job only if she continued her legally assigned role of "taking care of the home" and if her husband felt her domestic obligations would still be met. As demands for women's equal rights gained strength, however, and after the PRI lost its congressional majority in the 1997 mid-term elections, the Mexican congress passed legislation for banning spousal rape and started debating other reforms to the patriarchical system, including a bill calling for equal opportunity for women.

Still, good laws were no guarantee that bad practices would cease. In 1997, the Inter-American Development Bank reported on its research into domestic violence and abuse of women in Latin America. It found that Mexico ranked highest, with 70 percent of its women experiencing such mistreatment. Moreover, there was a need for legal, safe abortion, which was prohibited in Mexico except in cases of rape or to save a mother's life. There occurred more than a million abortions a year in Mexico, many of them botched backroom jobs ravaging the lives of thousands of impoverished women.

Among Mexico's women, the most exploited were peasants. Most of them led a cruel life, routinely subjected to beatings by their men, kept to the home whenever feasible, and giving live (or dead) birth every eighteen months or so. In spite of its campaigns for birth control, the government acknowledged that 10.5 percent of Mexican women had no familiarity with contraceptive methods.

Peasant women's work in child rearing, food preparation, farming, handicrafts, and so on, exceeded the labor performed by men. Since so many of their male kin migrated, they were often heads of family without the social rights associated with that role. Many Mexican men, whether rural or urban, were unable or unwilling to conceive of any alternatives for women other than those deriving from patriarchy and capitalism's ongoing reinforcement of it.

To improve their situations, growing numbers of Mexican women began migrating. In 1998 they accounted for an estimated 37 percent of internal migration and more than 20 percent of the post-1965 emigration to the United States. Economist David Barkin concluded that half of 1996's estimated $40 billion worth of migrants' annual remittances in Mexico came from internal migration.[8]

Migration and gainful employment were major factors behind Mexican women's beginning to show more autonomy vis-à-vis male family members. While this contributed somewhat to a breakdown of traditional family structures, that process had already begun during the heyday of male emigration and abuse of women. At the same time, as so many researchers noticed, Mexican women's dedication to their families in the face of economic hardship strengthened the nuclear family and made the household unit central to the class struggle for survival. This development even contributed to men sometimes helping out more around the home—less from adopting new values than from economic necessity.

Naturally, contradictions and ambivalent attitudes among both women and men abounded. The process of family change in Mexico was a dialectical, complex one. While extended kinship systems were becoming a thing of the past and there was evidence of heightened internal family tensions, family unity in the face of economic crisis was also a common occurrence. Moreover, more than a third of household units in Mexico were headed by women.

Thus a sound class analysis of Mexico would have to incorporate gender and take a hard look at "family survival strategies" being generated by household units, including female-headed ones. Multiple types of income-producing work composed the common denominator of these strategies, often with women in the lead. A better understanding of these intra-class trends demanded more extensive overall strategies for political change.

Most of Mexico's rural people suffered the consequences of landlessness, minifundismo (tiny landholdings), and inadequate job opportunities. In the early 1980s, of roughly 6 million rural adult peasants and workers, more than 3 million were permanently landless and had to sell their labor power or remain unemployed. Nearly three-fourths of a million held less than one hectare of land, and an equivalent number held under five hectares.

Less than a fourth of private smallholders made family farming their principal activity. Most of these private smallholders and about 2 million ejidatarios worked their own lands, either for themselves as subsistence parcels or on behalf of people to whom they rented the land. Lesser numbers of colonos, nacionaleros (occupiers of state lands whose status had not been regularized), and avecinados (squatters accepted by the community) also tried to survive in this way. Such "farming" helped supplement income earned seasonally as day laborers or in domestic crafts, petty trade, mining, or other activities.

In effect, then, the common estimate of 5 million landless peasants in the early 1980s was realistic. A minuscule percentage of the rural populace benefited from the impressive production statistics of Mexico's booming agribusiness and neolatifundismo.

While all statistics were subject to error, and while considerable crossing over occurred between non-bourgeois groups in the countryside, the figures in Table 11 reflect both class proportions and the continued proletarianization within the rural class structure. If we break the peasantry down into "rich," "middle," and "poor," then rich peasants constituted about 1 percent of the rural population as a whole, middle peasants about 4 percent, and poor (including pauperized) peasants about 33 percent. If we add the poor peasants and rural proletariat together, as most researchers do, then more than 92 percent of the rural population were proletarians, including unpaid family labor, such as women and their children (who were future proletarians).[9] The poor peasants were often worse off than the landless wage workers and day laborers; they were sharecroppers, tenant farmers, *aparceros* (partners in small plots, private or ejido), and landholders whose wage labor accounted for most of their income and whose wages financed the inputs for their subsistence land parcels.

All of rural society was highly stratified, with each layer tending to exploit the layers immediately below. For example, "middle" peasants were generally at the mercy of the bourgeoisie for credit, supplies, and political and social status, and they in turn exploited less prosperous peasants and ejidatarios, who often became their labor force at planting and harvest time. They usually had a direct and clearly antagonistic relationship with the rural bourgeoisie and less serious conflicts with poor peasants and rural proletarians—with whom they shared a class hatred for bourgeois overlords. Similarly, the tiny number of actually prospering ejidatarios and private small landholders sought control over "middle" peasants and also exploited the more pauperized elements of rural society. And even though less clear and antagonistic, a series of contradictions—of race, gender, language, and regional customs—separated millions of immiserated rural inhabitants, thereby further complicating the class struggle. Moreover, such contradictions sometimes became highly antagonistic, as in the land squabbles among different indigenous peoples. These conflicts even pitted factions of the same linguistic group against one another, as I observed among Michoacán's Tarascas in the 1980s.

Of those peasants who still owned land, whether a tiny parcel of an ejido or a small private plot, nearly 90 percent qualified as impoverished *minifundistas*—down-and-out subsistence farmers unable to produce enough to feed their own families. Big capital's monopolization of land, machinery, credits, and markets determined the conditions of smallholder production. Few peasants were able to prosper even as "kulaks," and the movement of property-possessing rural producers continued to be into subsistence production or the proletariat or both, with only a handful rising into the lower ranks of the rural bourgeoisie. Collective farming traditions persisted in parts of Mexico, especially among Indians, but the collapse of state support for ejido agriculture made it extremely difficult for peasants to take up that option with any hope of improving their lot.

Overall, the process of class transformation in rural Mexico was the immiseration of the masses and their recourse to working a subsistence parcel, hiring themselves out as fieldhands, and using community, ejido, or kinship networks for mutual support. This led sociologists to see most of the rural work force as simultaneously proletarian and peasant. Although there was a continuum from traditional small peasant to full-fledged modern proletarian, many rural laborers engaged in both kinds of activity. Even though income from labor (i.e., proletarian activity) was in the majority of cases a more important component of individual, family, or group survival than subsistence farming or other forms of peasant domestic "self-exploitation" (weaving, etc.), the fact remained that the combination of such activities defined these workers as a class in a manner distinct from either a traditional peasantry or a completely modern proletariat.

Therefore, when the term *peasant* is used here, it incorporates this multiple activity of most rural workers and recognizes that—given the high cost of technical inputs for producing for the modern market and the lack of availability of year-round paid work—they have to emphasize traditional peasant-type demands for land simply to reproduce themselves as a class. As Arturo Warman once observed, "To be 'modern' and propagate grafted fruit trees, use chemical fertilizers, harvest products which were too expensive for themselves to consume, the peasants have had to make themselves more 'traditional.'"[10] In other words, to make ends meet, rural people had to revert to artisan production or subsistence farming—for which they needed adequate raw materials, land, and water.

Re-peasantization thus accompanied de-peasantization. One rural sociologist described the majority of those engaged in such domestic peasant activities as "proletarians disguised as peasants."[11] The reason was that they were part of a larger capitalist context that generated both their exploitation as low-paid farmworkers and their recourse to self-exploitation as subsistence farmers or domestic handicraft producers for the purposes of survival. This double exploitation, as we shall see, extended to the urban subemployed and some of the regularly employed as well. Many factory workers augmented their abysmal wages by weekly gifts of food supplies from relatives in rural areas. In what the French anthropologist Claude Meillassoux called "domestic economies,"[12] the self-production of food, primitive shelter, articles of clothing or furniture, and other necessities by rural and urban workers, especially women, offered up to capital quantities of labor power for which capital never had to pay a wage, or offered pitiful wages to employ when convenient. In Mexico, the high levels of self-sustenance engaged in by workers in general helped fulfill functions that capitalism and its state avoided or barely addressed, particularly the function of social security.

One result of the combined process of proletarianization and re-peasantization was that peasant demands were increasingly being matched by proletarian ones. For example, in May 1978 some 5,000 farm laborers led by a regional peasant federation successfully struck some of Sinaloa's agribusinesses. Similarly, women workers in the booming food-processing industry, most of them from peasant families, started fighting for their proletarian rights in the 1960s, when they won the right to unionize. Then the CTM stepped in to enforce labor discipline. The women renewed their struggle in the early 1980s, launching a wave of strikes at Kellogg's, General Foods, and Coca-Cola against the CTM-TNC alliance. Realizing their struggle was an international one, some of the strikers also made contact with union representatives in the United States.

In one of the first instances of farm workers of the two nations successfully internationalizing their struggles, the CTM's National Union of Farm Workers (SNTOAC) in Sinaloa lent support to a lengthy strike led by the U.S. Midwest-based Farm Labor Organizing Committee (FLOC), composed of mostly Mexican migrant workers from Texas. Just as the Campbell Soup Company was threatening to move its Midwest operations to Sinaloa, the two unions worked out a joint collective bargaining arrangement that helped win the FLOC strike in 1986-1987. FLOC went on to force and win several union elections throughout the Midwest and to affiliate with the AFL-CIO.

Yet Mexican rural workers' proletarian demands were in turn related to their need for productive land. In a case study of the Mezquital Valley of Hidalgo in central Mexico, sociologist Luisa Paré found that 72 percent of those seeking land or water were rural proletarians, as were 68 percent of those demanding wage hikes, steady work, or improved working conditions.[13] Paré found the proletarians' struggle for land to be a rational way of assuring a source of employment or of finding a more fixed source of income. Similar attitudes were encountered by university researchers in 1981 when they interviewed Michoacán peasant families whose male adult members migrated annually to the United States due to lack of sufficient land or jobs.[14]

The fight for productive land, then, was not merely a stubborn persistence of "precapitalist" peasant customs, or of a "simple commodity mode of production" (subsistence farming, artisanry). Rather, it was a reaction to the forces of modern capitalism that uprooted earlier forms of small-farmer or community agriculture, only to recreate them on a new basis. An abundant labor supply recruitable at much less than the national average wage was obviously in capital's interest. Capital—or the state serving capital's goals—used its control over the tools of modern farming and the credit and marketing networks to appropriate the bulk of any surpluses produced by ejidatarios, subsistence farmers, sharecroppers, and tenant farmers. Through a medley of control mechanisms, capital was able both to proletarianize and "re-peasantize" the rural workforce, that is, keep it at capital's beck and call.

Moreover, capital converted peasants and all rural workers, whether waged or regularly employed or not, into "modern" consumers, making it economically impossible for them to revert to "precapitalist" production as such. They now had to buy some of their basic necessities and sell whatever surplus they could generate in a market that, however remote from them, was connected to a national and international process of capital accumulation. Whether buying refined white sugar, soft drinks, the preservative-loaded breads of Pan Bimbo (a subsidiary of International Telephone and Telegraph's Wonder Bread), or packaged tortillas, peasant producers and their impoverished urban relatives were paying more for less quality, when in previous generations they consumed the healthier "panela" (a natural sugar), milk, and ground corn. To do this they needed more money income. Thus the "reproduction" of subsistence-farming peasants and rural proletarians (and, as we shall see, of the urban poor), through multiple economic activities, was imposed by capital's dominance.

"Investment in the Poor"

Representatives of monopoly capital recognized that their development strategies (such as the Green Revolution) ultimately produced hunger and potential revolt among rural producers. Starting in the late 1960s and early 1970s, the World Bank, leader of the cluster of international development enterprises sponsored by monopoly capital, together with the U.S. Agency for International Development (AID), supposedly "changed course." As a solution to the agrarian problems they had helped to generate in the first place, they began advocating the delivery of yet more technical inputs to subsistence farmers in order to "combat poverty." As in the case of the Green Revolution, they chose Mexico as the pilot project. This time, however, instead of dispossessing peasants and incorporating them as free labor into the by now overflowing ranks of the rural and urban proletariat, they aimed to keep them producing on their small parcels as supervised unfree labor.

As World Bank Director of Agriculture and Rural Development Montague Yudelman explained, "The traditional, small-farm sector will have to become the producer of an agricultural surplus rather than the provider of surplus labor, as it has been in the past."[15] In this way, subsistence farmers and domestic handicraft producers were expected to serve as cheap commodity producers for capitalist distribution monopolies, and as key nonwage reproducers of the labor force. Actually, by the World Bank's own testimony, rain-fed, un-irrigated subsistence parcels already were generating about half of Mexico's total agricultural product, while providing food for 87 percent of all peasants.

This new World Bank approach, then, represented an attempt to maintain peasants producing on the land and to obtain their surplus food and handicraft production by controlling the market for distribution, the sale of seeds, fertilizers, insecticides, machinery, and the provision of credit. The goal, in the Bank's words, was "to draw farmers from subsistence to commercial agriculture ... in the form of increased trade in farm produce and in technical inputs and services."[16] The idea was to prevent the "leakage" of technical inputs and resources to large enterprises, the better to build a wealthier class of "family farmers," and to maintain a "dynamic balance" of different types and sizes of agricultural units—which the Bank hoped would mitigate hunger, class polarization, and the danger of revolution. The strategy became known, somewhat cynically, as "investment in the poor."

The commitment of the World Bank, the Mexican government, and other development agencies to "investing in the poor" in rural Mexico became truly mammoth. For awhile, the fresh outpouring of funds did keep peasants tied to the land, as did the Mexican countryside's low wage structure that drove many peasants to "re-peasantize" and a brief period of state populism in the 1970s. There was a momentary leveling off of proletarianization trends for the 1970s and 1980s, as indicated in in Table 14.

Even the least recognized among the poor—women—were encouraged to produce more. As one AID document put it:

> [Women's] contribution to production must be enhanced. . . . The U.S. recognizes that women in developing countries already have skills in agricultural production, processing, and marketing which provide a broad and relevant foundation on which to build. . . . The U.S. . . . [favors]: fostering labor-intensive economic activities to provide more income-earning opportunities; increasing productivity through the introduction of appropriate technology, credit and other inputs; . . . giving people control over their own reproduction.[17]

More than likely, the control over reproduction envisioned by AID was birth control (or sterilization, so often financed by AID) and not control over the economic means of production and reproduction of labor power as such. In order to avoid economic hardship and possible starvation, that is, to control their own lives and family size, poor and working class women in Mexico had increasingly been demanding a range of birth control methods, including the legalization of abortion. However, population control policy by AID and other Western agencies often served the interests of pharmaceutical companies more than those of the women themselves. For example, despite a 1978 Food and Drug Administration ban on Depo-Provera (a synthetic form of the hormone progesterone) for contraceptive use in the United States, AID became a major funder of birth-control injections of Depo-Provera in Mexico and other third world nations. The injection inhibited ovulation for three to six months, but experiments on animals had shown that it could lead to cancer and other deadly side effects, which was why it was banned in the United States. Having few other options, women in Mexico often welcomed Depo-Provera injections, which offered the advantages of long-term effectiveness and not having to depend on unreliable male partners for limiting family size.

In the early 1970s, the World Bank and Mexico's Río Papaloapán Commission launched the first full-scale "investment in the poor" pilot project, known as "PIDER." Assisted by local banks, insurance companies, CONASUPO, provincial elites, and modern agribusinesses, PIDER successfully commercialized a remote area in Oaxaca, Puebla, and Veracruz states by harnessing the energy of the Papaloapán River and the labor of 1.5 million members of hillside peasant families. PIDER established fruit, vegetable, and sugar agro-industries to process crops harvested by peasant labor. A select minority of peasants became prosperous "kulaks," while a network of petty-bourgeois technocrats, merchants, and middlemen expanded. Yet despite PIDER's promises to benefit the poor, the majority of peasants resisted the engineers' pressure to grow new crops and use new technical inputs, not because they were traditional or "backward" but because they soon learned that the consequences were heavy debt, financial loss, and the reduction of their lands. When sabotaging the PIDER plans failed, many peasants withdrew into their previous hillside farming, where at least they knew how to survive. Eventually, most peasants were drawn into the PIDER scheme as laborers or food producers. Immense quantities of cheap foodstuffs were generated, but the peasants were left worse off—having to increase their subsistence farming just to sustain themselves.[18]

Thus, the strategy of "investing in the poor" perpetuated re-peasantization precisely because—in German sociologist Veronika Bennholdt-Thomsen's words—"it is not the lack of market integration, rather its increase, which leads to the immiseration of the peasants and to a retreat to (not persistence in) selfconsumption."[19] The participation of the Mexican government in such schemes tied peasants to state apparatuses, prevented their self-organization, and intensified their division of labor, thereby raising their output and extending the scope of potential internal class conflict.

In the neoliberal 1990s, the World Bank still rhetoricized about "targeting poverty." However, it invested less in programs aimed at reaching the poor than it did before. It advocated privatization of social security systems and the delegation of tasks once conducted by the state to local governments or organizations, including NGOs (non-governmental organizations).

Not coincidentally, the presence of permanent wage laborers in Mexico's countryside was by then concentrated not only in the northwest but also in the supposedly "backward" southern areas that had drawn this new infusion of state and international capital: Puebla, Oaxaca, Campeche, Tabasco, Yucatán, Chiapas, and parts of Veracruz, Morelos, and Guerrero—all falsely reputed to be bogged down in "precapitalist" peasant economies. In the coffee sector, for example, where small or medium-size landholders traditionally handled much of the growing, a state coffee institute had failed to ameliorate the superexploitation suffered by pickers and marginal growers. The institute and a network of TNCs, big coffee exporters, the medium-size agrarian bourgeoisie, some capitalist landlords, and commercial intermediaries had kept the majority of the coffee workers (many of whom were Indian women) in abject poverty. Some 25,000 Tzotzil, Tzeltal, and Mame Indians had harvested the German-owned coffee plantations of Soconusco, Chiapas, while a like number of

Nahuas, Totonacos, and Otomís of Puebla's northern sierra had picked the crop of La Unión on modernized farms of one hundred hectares each.

This sizable labor force was supplemented in the 1970s and 1980s by 30,000 "undocumented" immigrant workers, mostly from Guatemala but also from El Salvador, who were paid a paltry $2 for 13-hour days. While Nestlé and General Foods dominated the domestic market for instant coffee, Folgers (Procter & Gamble), Coca-Cola, and Anderson Clayton accounted for one-sixth of Mexico's huge coffee export trade. (Because of the Brazil frost in the late 1970s, Mexican coffee momentarily gained second place behind oil in exports.)

Nationalization of the tobacco-processing industry in the 1970s likewise did little to alter the exploitation of growers and cutters by commercial and foreign interests, with whom the new state enterprise was in cohoots. Mestizo ejidatario tobacco growers in turn exploited Indian and other migrant fieldhands who did the cutting at harvest time. Similar patterns existed in Yucatán's state-dominated industry of henequen. They also existed in the state-influenced sugar industry of Morelos and other southern and coastal states.

Such forces of state-supported modern capitalism helped convert the Mexican countryside into a scene of immiseration and violent class struggle, heightened by the unscrupulous behavior of state bureaucrats and commercial intermediaries exploiting the peasantry. Not uncommon were cases of a middleman (known as a "coyote") buying corn from a subsistence farmer at a price well below the federal minimum and then, during a time of scarcity, returning to sell it to the same peasant at up to 200 percent above what he first paid for it. The most immiserated were driven to stone-age conditions: women with their children hunting small animals or collecting wild fruits and herbs on mountain slopes, or, when migrating to cities, seeking food in garbage dumps where entire communities built shacks, mingling with the scavenging dogs and rats.

Clearly, the "investment in the poor" strategy for Mexico's countryside failed. In the late 1980s, when it became obvious that neoliberalism had led to massive economic depressions in Latin America ("the lost decade of development"), a new strategy known as "sustainable development" was introduced. As the world's forests disappeared and nuclear and toxic waste disposal problems worsened, a clarion call went out to "develop" third world countries in an environmentally "sustainable" manner. In Rio de Janeiro, Brazil, a world conference on saving the environment took place in 1992—the UN Conference on Environment and Development, or "Earth Summit."

The Union of Concerned Scientists announced on December 12, 1992, that a majority of Nobel Prize scientists and more than 1,500 members of science academies from 68 nations, including the 19 largest economic powers, had issued a "Warning to Humanity" that called for "sustainable development," reduction of poverty, and "sexual equality guaranteeing women control over their own reproductive decisions." Recognizing that "the developed nations are the largest polluters in the world," it called for "a great reduction in violence and war" so that the industrialized world might finance "environmental protection."

All the talk of "sustainable development," quickly echoed by champions of neoliberalism like the World Bank, helped nascent or struggling pro-environ-ment organizations but did nothing to improve the lot of the world's poor. Its rhetoric won over environmental activists more than it actually helped peas-ants, who continued losing their lands, or rural and urban workers, who remained underpaid. In addition, it led to increased access to peasant knowl-edge about local flora and fauna for the benefit of TNCs, including timber, agricultural, and pharmaceutical interests.

Then, in the name of neoliberalism's "privatization" and "free market" schemes, the Mexican state opted to remove constitutional protections for ejidos. The percentage of rural proletarians dramatically increased: from 46.2 percent in 1990 to 55.6 percent in 1995 (Table 14).

In many respects, the poverty, violence, migration, and class warfare in rural Mexico became as intense in the mid-1990s as they had been toward the end of the Porfirio Diáz regime. Peasants continued to mass and invade little used lands in an attempt to ensure their own survival, and the army or the big landholders' hired *pistoleros* (gunmen) continued to drive them back. The Mexican Armed Forces intervened regularly against these peasant movements, often carrying out massacres—and not just in publicized cases like those in contemporary Chiapas or Guerrero.

Caciquismo

A number of peasant movements had a forty- to fifty-year record of ongoing militancy. For example, in 1943 and again in 1953, Rubén Jaramillo, who in his youth had ridden with Zapata, rose in guerrilla war in the south-central state of Morelos. Jaramillo was both an ordained Methodist minister and a member of the Communist Party. With the Bible in his hand and a rifle on his shoulder, he preached revolution. In 1962, after he had met with President Adolfo López Mateos, army soldiers yanked him, his pregnant wife, and their three sons from their home in Xochicalco and massacred them. The land-for-the-tiller move-ment continued in his name and in the late 1960s came to encompass much of the nation. In an effort to reduce post-Jaramillo peasant guerrilla efforts in Morelos, the state placed a sculpted bust of Jaramillo in the center of one of his favorite towns. Commented a disgruntled peasant: "Take a close look at that bust: even in supposedly honoring him, his assassins had to cut off his arms and legs."[20]

For another example, pockets of peasant militants throughout the nation, who since the late 1920s had been known as agraristas, repeatedly rallied to national movements drawing together progressive elements from diverse social classes. In the early 1960s many agraristas joined the nationwide but short-lived Movement for National Liberation (MLN). The MLN represented a vigorous attempt to unite Marxists, disenchanted intellectuals and artists, workers, peasants, and prominent progressive políticos like ex-President Lázaro Cárdenas into a broad-based movement for revitalization of the Mexican Revolution. It fell apart when Cárdenas grew disenchanted with the pro-Fidel Castro leanings of younger militants and the state escalated its dual policy of repression and co-optation. Nevertheless, many ex-MLN peasants continued their struggles locally. In the southwest state of Guerrero, they were led by schoolteacher Genaro Vázquez, from a local peasant family, who formed an armed guerrilla band that remained active after his death in battle, February 2, 1972. (It re-emerged as a powerful force not only in Guerrero but in other states in 1995.)

Since the 1960s, much of the rural class struggle was directed against the traditional mediating process of *caciquismo*. Earlier in the twentieth century, caciques had been used as intermediaries in the introduction or spread of capitalism. After the Revolution, "good" caciques were expected to deliver the benefits associated with agrarian reform. Struggles to replace "bad" caciques with good ones became commonplace, but they were usually in vain. Then leaders of the so-called Northern Dynasty, men like presidents Obregón and Calles, laid the foundations of the national political party (PRI) that brought together warring regional military caudillos and integrated local caciques with the official party (then the PNR) and other organizations of the corporatist state. Although some good caciques emerged, particularly during the Cárdenas presidency (1934-1940), caciquismo and its corruption inexorably persisted as a long-standing Mexican tradition—both in political practice and in most people's daily lives.

Caciques involved themselves in various commercial and financial activities. Whether wealthy regional magnates or simply local bosses with a little more political clout or money than anyone else, they became astute at providing loans and using money as a means of making friends among the people. Only a few rose to prominence by supporting honest leaders instead of corrupt ones. One aging rural cacique told a team of rural sociologists, "Of humble background, I do everything to serve the people." He had held various political offices, including national ones, and was leading a "humble" bourgeois life.[21]

Rather than being the *result* of a lack of popular participation in national politics, caciquismo was its basic *cause*. Marked by populist rhetoric and paternalistic content, caciquismo had always been characterized by a universally recognized streak of violence, capable of being called on at any moment with the help of private armies or the national armed forces. Caciquismo applied control with armed terror, and legitimized control with unarmed (and disarming) spectacle—such as inauguration of a new school, clinic, or road. Caciquismo was also linked to *compadrazgo* (the godfather system) and to religious or cultural ceremonies.

These customs were in turn economically beneficial to merchants and local caciques, as "folklore" becomes "business," not just in the traditional manner of squeezing funds out of the poor to provide for ceremonial rituals, but in the modern mode of national and international tourism. Poor Indians often identified with their rich Indian cacique-exploiters, who used their traditional dances to collect money from tourists, rather than unite with their impoverished mestizo peers. Poor mestizos in turn sometimes supported local mestizo caciques or entrepreneurs selling mestizo wares to tourists. In this and other ways, caciquismo undercut class consciousness.

Caciquismo and its system of bribes, payoffs, and control thus served to disguise or divert the heightened class stratification and conflict within the rural population it buttressed. For instance, in a case study of workers and peasants involved in a regional center of sugar production, sociologist Luisa Paré found that quite complex systems of caciquismo and internal stratification pitted ejidatario producers against proletarian cane cutters, often fellow ejidatarios who were paid directly from credits advanced by the mill or the state.[22]

Caciquismo served to reinforce peasant susceptibility to following state tutelage or to being co-opted. Peasant organizations were easily co-opted once their leaders were, since they typically had a shortage of personnel able quickly to become effective leaders. Because of the organizations' authoritarian paternalistic structures, co-opted leaders could easily bring the memberships with them.

On the other hand, the state lacked sufficient resources to pay off large numbers of co-opted peasants without carrying out genuine and massive agrarian reform, which led to a peasant leadership pattern of rebellion, co-optation, rebellion. For instance, radical peasant leader Jacinto López, a member of the late Lombardo Toledano's Popular Socialist Party (PPS, which ordinarily cooperated with the official political party), was one of the first to organize landless peasants into a mass movement in the 1960s; he was co-opted with a seat in Congress. Then, in 1969, either because of his followers' disillusionment or his own dissatisfaction with wasting time in a do-nothing Congress, López resigned from the PPS to lead an independent agrarian movement. He died shortly thereafter.

A somewhat different course was followed by Alfonso Garzón, who in the early 1960s helped create the Independent Peasant Confederation (CCI), often in opposition to the PRI's CNC "peasant sector" and the state. According to post-Watergate revelations, the FBI cooperated with the Mexican government in harassing CCI. Yet in the 1970s Garzón and the CCI became arms of the state they once opposed, often more useful and effective than the CNC. Garzón too spoke of "serving the people."[23]

As a result, the achievement of immediate reformist goals or longer run radical social change on behalf of peasants and rural workers came to depend, more often than not, on leaders from the non-peasant classes or class fractions. To become leaders, peasants needed either personal charisma or outside resources. The most honest were often jailed or assassinated; others were easily co-opted.

Just in case leadership co-optation did not totally decapitate the peasant struggle, a subtle ideological control became institutionalized: the daily lip service paid to the "law." Since so many abuses in the countryside were in fact illegal, everyone—whether an upwardly mobile good cacique or a down-and-out peasant seeking justice—talked of "carrying out the law," or of making progressive changes "within the law, of course." When the law itself was used as a means of oppression and the legal system appeared as a maze without exit for poor people seeking to better their lives, rural social movements and their leaders became entrapped in the bizarre language and practice of "peaceful, legal protest." In much of rural Mexico, peasants or workers still expressed their faith in the law and deferred to public functionaries with honorific titles like patrón or even the colonial "Don." This manifestation of a paternalistic culture was necessary to daily survival. Sometimes it was also useful for obtaining a local improvement, such as safe drinking water (still unavailable in nearly half of rural Mexico in 1998).

What kept the whole oppressive system working, more or less, was the state's and capital's ultimate recourse to violence. For generations, private armies known as *guardias blancas* had been harassing dissident peasants and workers in rural Mexico. In the 1980s, right-wing paramilitary organizations like "Peasant Torch" (Antorcha Campesina—a virtual death squad) routinely murdered dissident peasants. As class conflict sharpened in the mid-1990s, President Carlos Salinas de Gortari invited Peasant Torch to affiliate formally with the PRI. As already noted, if social movements did mobilize, army massacres often followed.

In spite of so many obstacles, peasants and rural proletarians did recognize and did combat—now subtly, now directly—the oppressive character of capital's dominance and the cacique system. In class terms, the immediate enemy served by caciques was not difficult to spot. The rural bourgeoisie's insolent attitude toward peasants and workers was legendary.

Scarcely having to lift a finger to accumulate capital, the rural bourgeoisie developed as a doubly parasitic class: living off both state subsidies and the cheap labor of the producers, while investing in land and agricultural production, commerce, regional banking, construction, urban real estate, speculative ventures—and conspicuous consumption. In great part it became integrated with urban bankers and industrialists, foreign agribusiness people, state and international credit institutions, exporters-importers, or real estate interests.

Far from being a bunch of lazy latifundistas living off land rent, the leading elements of the rural bourgeoisie were men on the make, accumulating capital on an extended scale. But for their capital and markets they depended on powerful urban forces, mainly domestic and foreign finance capital (i.e., the merger of bank and industrial capital, once defined by Lenin as imperialism). Also, they shared their regulation of the countryside's daily life with a medley of second-level bourgeois and petty-bourgeois groups essential to their own aggrandizement.

Consequently, it was most useful for analytical purposes to view the rural ruling class as a power bloc made up of two broad layers—the large-scale agrarian bourgeoisie and a second-level bourgeoisie—with each layer in turn consisting of three segments. The large-scale agrarian bourgeoisie was made up of capitalist-landlord, agro-commercial, and agro-industrial segments, all of which were ultimately linked to one another through their dependent connections with urban-based finance capital. The second-level bourgeoisie was made up of a medium-scale agrarian segment, a commercial segment, and an agro-political segment, some of whose more successful members graduated into the ranks of the large-scale agrarian bourgeoisie.

The capitalist-landlords based their wealth on the accumulation of capital and land ownership. Though including a few inefficient latifundistas, they were for the most part oriented toward the accumulation of capital on an extended scale, even if often in speculative ventures. Some capitalist-landlords were *nouveau riche* who made it big after the Second World War, while others were descendants of the hacendados of the nineteenth century. A number were former officials of the state bureaucracy. Almost all retained some aspects of the old-fashioned paternalistic populism linking landlords to caciques, state bureaucrats, or commercial intermediaries in a mutually advantageous alliance that demagogically claimed to have the peasantry's best interests at heart. Typical of these landlords were the eighty-five growers who controlled one-fourth of all irrigated land in Sinaloa, as well as those engaged in monopoly-capitalist agriculture in Sonora and other northern states. All had close ties to U.S. agribusiness interests, and some owned distributorships for U.S. farm equipment, automobiles, or insecticides.

The agro-commercial segment of the large-scale agrarian bourgeoisie derived its wealth not from land ownership but from commerce and, occasionally, industry. With state cooperation, this segment controlled a big part of the market for agricultural products and financed much agricultural production.

Large-scale *arrendatarios capitalistas,* who rented land from peasants or from ejidatarios and marketed their produce, were included in the agro-commercial segment. Closely tied to the state and foreign agribusiness, this segment was strong in such leading sectors as the animal-feed industry.

The agro-industrial segment derived its wealth from industry and to some degree from commerce, but not from land ownership. Linked to production either directly or through purchases from members of the agro-commercial bourgeoisie, the agro-industrialists owned the mills, breweries, and food-processing plants. For example, Monterrey's ALFA group and some TNC beer firms controlled the prices, production, and commercialization of barley. Both the agro-industrial and agro-commercial segments of the large-scale agrarian bourgeoisie, more than the capitalist-landlord segment, were concerned with modernizing the overall agro-political structure of the countryside.

The medium-scale agrarian bourgeoisie was the first of three segments of the second-level rural bourgeoisie. It was mainly a product of the agrarian reform. It consisted of small and medium-size independent private farmers, occasional ejidatarios, and those modern *rancheros* (landholders or farmers owning or renting a rancho) who formed the backbone of the relatively self-sufficient period of Mexican agriculture between 1940 and 1960. These farmers were organized into regional political organizations of small proprietors, which in fact incorporated many *neolatifundistas* (big landowners) or their agents.

Representing less than 1 percent of the rural population, the medium-scale agrarian bourgeoisie nonetheless constituted a significant political force in the rural bourgeois power bloc. Although generally a conservative defender of private property, the medium-scale agrarian bourgeoisie did include some neopopulist elements trying to renovate and modernize caciquismo in order to foster their own position. It also included some inefficient elements who were gradually disappearing from the agrarian scene.

The next segment of the second-level rural bourgeoisie was the commercial bourgeoisie, which fed on rural misery at more intermediate and lower levels of production and exchange than those levels dominated by the agro-commercial segment of the large-scale agrarian bourgeoisie. One rural sociologist called this segment the "rural commercial-usury bourgeoisie."[24] Its members included moneylenders; *acaparadores* who bought up indebted peasants' products below their value and resold at a profit; a wide range of intermediaries involved in commerce between agriculture and industry; and merchants trafficking in bottled drinks, furniture, plastics, and similar items in the provincial urban centers that sprang up as a result of the growth of Mexico's internal market. A relatively dispersed group of small capitalists, the rural commercial bourgeoisie had a large network of personal relations among the peasantry and introduced capitalist relations by serving as intermediary between the countryside and big merchant and finance capital or the state. The rural commercial bourgeoisie was thus part of the older system of political and economic corruption, as well as the agent and beneficiary of the explosion in commerce stimulated by modern agribusiness and industrialization.

The final segment of the second-level rural bourgeoisie was the agro-political bourgeoisie. This consisted of the upper ranks of the rural bureaucracy, and incorporated high-level local and federal bureaucrats, congressmen, regional political caciques, officers or heads of military zones, regional presidents of the PRI, presidents of important *municipios* (administrative units of towns or communities), and the like. Some individuals, by means of corruption, had become agrarian capitalists in their own right. Most were quick to seize a share of the economic surplus marketed or appropriated by the state. Because these important officials helped the rural bourgeoisie obtain surplus value from agricultural production, they had to be viewed as part of the bourgeois power bloc and rural ruling class.

As in the case of other rural social classes, the intermediate classes in the countryside were internally differentiated. Only a small portion—for example, some commercial intermediaries, bureaucrats, and caciques—were affluent. These fortunate ones were usually mestizo, not Indian, and had "connections" with foreign or Mexican capitalist employers or government banks and regional political machines. The more acquisitive among them made it into the ranks of the agro-political or rural commercial bourgeoisies. On the other hand, ever larger numbers—from lower-level bureaucrats to small-scale business people to modest farmers to schoolteachers—lived under austere conditions. Even so, just the dream of upward mobility and its occasional fulfillment kept the entire system working to a remarkable degree.

Not surprisingly, political attitudes among these intermediate groups varied. Some individuals adhered to the PRI as an avenue of security or occasional upward mobility. Others supported right-wing, often religious-based, opposition parties. Still others turned to more leftist-oriented anti-state positions, as in the case of many unionized, low-paid schoolteachers who periodically joined regional movements against unrepresentative union leaders and for decent salaries. A minority of the intermediate classes—such as farm administrators or labor recruiters hired by the agribusinesses—even when very poorly paid entered into open class conflict with the rural proletariat.

However complex the evolution of Mexico's rural class structure had been, it generated three transparent problems that were already exploding in the face of the triple alliance forged by the state with the bourgeoisie, TNCs, and global lending agencies. These problems were: (1) widespread unemployment; (2) inadequate food production to meet the minimal nutritional needs of the populace; and (3) lack of truly democratic participation by the masses and the intermediate classes. These problems led to renewed, if unevenly developed, peasant, worker, and intermediate-class insurgencies.

One thing was certain: the rural class struggle had become fundamental to the economic and political crisis gripping contemporary Mexico. It was fueled, and strongly so, by ongoing changes in the world economy. As the recurrent failures of post-Second World War models of "economic development," including "sustainable development" and "neoliberalism," became more devastating in their consequences, it was obvious that there would be more eruptions of political and social protest movements in Mexico's urban factories, schools, and slums, as well as in the countryside. The Zapatista uprising in 1994 and the overwhelming electoral defeat of the PRI in Mexico City in 1997 reflected this evolving class-based reality.

Urban Class Structure

The urban class structure after 1940 continued to be conditioned by Mexico's close economic relationship with the United States. The role of the Mexican state in class formation became more influential, as already evidenced in the discussion of the industrial proletariat in the preceding chapter. The state was also an important factor shaping developments in the urban bourgeoisie and intermediate classes.

By 1970, Mexico's bourgeoisie was in practice neither autonomous, nationalistic, nor progressive—in the sense of trying to achieve the economic development of the nation for the benefit of the majority of its citizens. Known popularly as the "oligarchy," the bourgeoisie was, like the "revolution" it championed, so misdeveloped as to constitute, together with the state, the most effective force for smoothing Mexico's way to continued economic dependence on the United States and to an ever greater maldistribution of income and social benefits.

Leaving aside for the moment the special case of "the narco-bourgeoisie," the modern Mexican bourgeoisie gained its status and power more by means of industrial production, commerce, and banking than by land ownership. It exercised its power inside Mexico through its influential role in select industrial sectors, in the financing and distribution of goods and services, and in the networks of national and regional political power. Single families or clusters of families came to hold national or regional monopolies. Most became loosely grouped into bourgeois fractions or "groups," which had more uniting than separating them. Indeed, the identical surnames of prominent bourgeois families appeared over and over again on several boards of directors of major Mexican firms and of joint enterprises with foreign capitalists.

Despite this overlap, some of the fractions were recognizable by type of economic activity and organizational affiliation. For instance, by state law, industrial capitalists were organized into the Confederation of Chambers of

Industry (CONCAMIN, founded in 1918), and commercial capitalists were grouped into the National Confederation of Chambers of Commerce (CON-CANACO, founded in 1917). As obligatory state-corporatist entities used to assure bourgeois "representation" in state decisionmaking, both CONCAMIN and CONCANACO maintained close ties with the government. They even drew some of their membership from business-minded (or corrupt) políticos who prospered from the informal partnership between state and capital. This corporatist organizational method permitted government bureaucrats to retain a certain autonomy vis-à-vis capital, but also to maintain a direct link to it for the sake of their own accumulation of wealth.

Until the 1980s, the bourgeoisie used CONCAMIN, CONCANACO, and the state bureaucracy to achieve its political aims, rather than to launch its own political party. At the same time, the bourgeoisie always maintained an independent voice through such powerful organizations as the following:

• the Mexican Association of Brokerage Houses (AMCB, the 1990s name for the former Mexican Bankers Association, or ABM, founded in 1928);

• the Employers' Confederation of the Mexican Republic (COPARMEX, founded in 1929), a national business group led by very conservative capitalists from Monterrey and other parts of northern Mexico;

• the Mexican Council of Businessmen (CMHN, founded in 1962), rising during the Salinas presidency to the summit of the bourgeoisie's pyramid of influential organizations, consisting in 1997 of thirty-four wealthy individuals representing the nation's most powerful economic groups;

• the Mexican Association of Insurance Companies (AMIS);

• the Management Coordinating Council (CCE, founded in 1975), the single most united voice of the bourgeoisie until the rise of the CMHN under Salinas, with the majority of its directors routinely coming from the CMHN and nearly half of its interior representation coming from the scarcely 1 percent of all its affiliated firms that belonged to the CMHN, AMIS, and AMCB.

These powerful capitalist organizations were more than "pressure groups" or "autonomous entities." They formed an integral part of the governing bloc. They were connected to the state through their members' circulation in and out of government or proximity to government decisionmaking circles.

For example, until late 1982 the director of the state-dominated Banco de México and the minister of finance routinely delivered the "second" annual state-of-the-nation report to the private bankers' ABM. After the private banks were nationalized during the economic crisis of 1982, members of the CMHN won their campaign for the state to change course to "neoliberal" economic policies—the "privatization" of state enterprises. They went on to purchase the four largest state banks and nearly half of other privatized properties in "sweetheart deals."

"Sweetheart" interchanges occurred throughout the top echelons of government and private capital. Dinner parties in private homes and vacations or weekends at exclusive country clubs and resorts informally sealed the alliance between the state and monopoly capital.

As an example of how things worked we may take a widely publicized dinner party at the home of business mogul and former Inter-American Development Bank director Antonio Ortiz Mena, held in 1993. Present were President Carlos Salinas de Gortari (the host's uncle), thirty of Mexico's wealthiest businessmen (including most of the nation's billionaires), and two top PRI officers. Official reports of the meeting confirmed that the businessmen were asked to contribute moneys to the PRI's 1994 presidential campaign equal to more than ten times the amount raised by Bill Clinton for the 1992 U.S. presidential campaign. Emilio Azcárraga, head of the Televisa company that controlled much of television in Mexico and Spanish-language television in the United States, told the press he would have gladly matched the entire Clinton campaign fund if asked. (Azcárraga died four years later, one of Latin America's richest individuals, although he never joined the CMHN.)

Some of those among the bourgeoisie who in the 1930s had tolerated or encouraged a populist alliance with unionized workers against foreign monopolies, and had begun to develop a viable domestic manufacturing base, were subsequently bought out or partially absorbed by more affluent and technologically better equipped foreign capitalists. Others became big capitalists in their own right, adopting the goals of monopoly capital of any nation.

In 1945, the industrialists' CONCAMIN signed a pact of mutual cooperation with labor's CTM. This helped to maintain low wages and hold strikes to a minimum, as well as to institute a regressive tax system that hurt some of the intermediate classes as well as all of the lower classes while barely touching the wealthy. (Of all Latin American countries, Mexico still had in 1998 one of the lowest tax revenues as a percentage of GDP.)

Until the 1950s, there were two sectors within CONCAMIN representing distinct ideological emphases. Small and medium-size manufacturers, grouped into the National Chamber of Transformation Industries (CANACINTRA, founded in 1941), defended high protective tariffs against foreign competition and benefited from the import-substitution program of the 1940s. Other industrialists, representing larger firms—often "mixed" enterprises with foreign capital—opposed import controls, instead tolerating or encouraging foreign penetration of the economy and handsome profits for those capitalists who cooperated. In the 1990s they did it in the name of "free trade": the North American Free Trade Agreement (NAFTA) and the General Agreement on Tariffs and Trade (GATT).

CANACINTRA and other smaller business people grouped into the CNPP (National Confederation of Small Property) and CNPC (National Confederation of Small Commerce) remain the part of Mexico's bourgeoisie most in need of at least some state intervention in the economy. They also are more likely than other parts of the bourgeoisie to find fault with neoliberalism, especially NAFTA and GATT, since they have greater difficulty competing with monopolies, domestic and foreign.

In practice, since the 1950s, intra-bourgeois ideological differences were dwarfed by a consensus in which nationalistic sentiments were ritualistically expressed while an informal alliance with foreign capital was carried out. One U.S. economist approvingly described this as an "alliance for profits."[25] The differences among Mexico's bourgeois fractions or between them and the state received little publicity except in moments of major crisis, as was the case under Cárdenas in the 1930s, or again in 1982 when the banks were momentarily nationalized, and in the middle and late 1990s when more crises erupted. Even in these instances, however, with the exception of parts of the Monterrey group, the bourgeoisie did not sever its links to the state.

Commentators usually described the Monterrey group as big capital's leading voice of ultra-right conservatism. Its resistance to Cárdenas's reforms and any form of state regulation of capital was legendary. In the early 1960s it opposed President Adolfo López Mateos's nationalization of the foreign-dominated electric companies and campaigned against the state's free school textbook program.

Yet the Monterrey group was by no means a cohesive unit. Its most reactionary wing was led by a secondary group of capitalists, whose most prominent spokesman was Andrés Marcelo Sada. A notorious critic of "socialist" tendencies in the state and a rabid anticommunist, Sada was the director of Celulosa y Derivados, S.A. (CYDSA), a chemical group that included the nation's second largest chemical firm.

Less reactionary but more powerful was the fraction of the Monterrey group called *el gran capital financiero* (big finance capital). The core of this fraction consisted of the brewery group VISA and big steel's ALFA, both linked to SERFIN, one of Mexico's largest financial groups. Though in competition with foreign capital after the Second World War, Monterrey's *gran capital financiero* gradually established links both to TNCs and to state capital. Consequently, its reactionary tendencies became tempered by a sense of economic and political pragmatism.

Although statements continued to be made by Monterrey's bourgeoisie that were critical of state intervention in the economy and espoused ultraconservative values, it should be kept in mind that such propaganda was in the interests of all monopoly capital in the sense that it shifted the terrain of debate enough to the right that any reform, however minor or tokenistic, began to appear too "revolutionary" to tolerate. Like the rest of Mexican monopoly capital, the Monterrey group as a whole, except in times of major crisis, normally did pledge its support—however critical—to the state.

In many ways it was misleading to view the Monterrey group as either nationally predominant or limited in influence to one city. Monterrey's capitalists had spread their investments throughout the nation and abroad (obtaining, for instance, a share of Spanish-language television and specialized parts of glass manufacturing in the United States). They had joint ventures with foreign firms like Coca-Cola, invested heavily in central Mexico, and shared holdings with the "Puebla group" of the bourgeoisie. There existed several other cohesive fractions of the Mexican bourgeoisie that wielded significant power, known by such names as the "central fraction" and the "1940s group."[26] The "Guadalajara group" of capitalists rose to a position of almost equal strength with the Monterrey group during the 1960s.

Yet no bourgeois group or fraction was immune from economic crisis or failure. Monterrey's ALFA group, for example, had to declare many of its enterprises bankrupt in 1982 and undertake a major program of refinancing and reorganization. After that, it prospered partly through increased exports abroad, which accounted for 25 percent of its sales.[27]

A very significant new group in the power complex of contemporary Mexico was a shadowy web of extremely wealthy narco-traffickers, or drug lords, whose organizations were difficult to pinpoint because of the criminal nature of their entrepreneurship. It was said in the 1990s that there existed in Mexico a "narco-press" and even a "narco-state." A February 23, 1997, *New York Times* front page story reported an estimated income for drug dealers in Sonora state alone of $10 billion a year, with 60 percent of it going to government officials as kickbacks.

Given the immense quantities of cash involved in the narco-bourgeoisie's multi-billion dollar trade, and the need to launder it and protect it, there was much speculation and even some evidence that Mexico's drug lords had links to prominent Mexican and U.S. banks (including, as discussed in the final section of the preceding chapter, Citibank) and to Mexican state governments and the federal governments of Mexico and the United States.

Any analysis of intra-bourgeois conflict is made difficult by the numerous contradictions introduced by the phenomenon of the drug trade. For example, NAFTA's opening up of the U.S.-Mexico border to the "free trade of commodities" seemed not only to enrich monopoly capital but also to facilitate the movement of illegal drugs. A damper on state crackdowns on drug lords (other than rampant government corruption) was the simple fact that an untold amount of foreign exchange poured into Mexico's deregulated banks from international narco-trafficking, a significant boost to Mexico's economy. In addition, there were frequent scrambles for quick cash by many of Mexico's most powerful bourgeois elites, who sometimes most easily found it in the narco-circuit of capital, yet had to maintain their image of "honest business-men shocked by the drug trade."

One thing was certain: the "narcotics rush" of the late twentieth century was comparable to the gold and silver rush of the sixteenth century. The amounts of wealth involved relative to other sources of income were remarkably similar, as were some of the military and paramilitary activities associated with the drive to "get a piece of the action." Even the impact of the "newly discovered wealth" on banking and state institutions was comparable. The main difference, of course, was the covert nature of the "narcotics rush," and therefore the more complex maneuvers undertaken by the actors involved, including those mounting a notably ineffective and corrupted "drug war."

While most intra-bourgeois divisions were neither significant nor widely publicized except in times of major crisis, the division between the big bourgeoisie and established businesspeople of the petty bourgeoisie was always recognizable on economic grounds alone. The small simply could not compete with the big. Nevertheless, each needed the other for economic and political reasons.

For example, small and some medium-size capital undertook all kinds of "risky" investments that monopoly capital was reluctant to try until it could be assured of the growth potential of the enterprises involved. Those firms that succeeded were then bought up by monopoly capital, while those that failed did so at the expense of smaller capital alone. Simultaneously, smaller capital depended on big capital and the state for loans, technical assistance, transportation, marketing, and the like.

All capital, big and small, was in fundamental opposition to the disorder, "anarchy," "communism," "rabble-rousing," and rebellious tendencies of the working classes. Thus the state recognized and encouraged regional and national organizations of small and medium-sized business people in much the same manner it did those of big capitalists, even though it granted them fewer concessions.

After the Second World War, Mexico's intermediate classes entered a phase of remarkable growth. By the late 1970s, articles and books on Mexico commonly estimated the size of the "middle classes" as being from 20 to 30 percent of the population. So did many "official" statistics. For example, on a strictly family income basis, according to Table 6 in Chapter 5, we could arrive at the figure of at least 20 percent. About 70 percent of Mexican families in that table qualify as "lower class," while 10 percent qualify as "upper class"—colloquially, the poor and the rich.

All these estimates of the size of the "middles classes," however, were exaggerated. Closer examination of Table 6 suggests that many people in the 20 percent "middle class" group were poorly paid and struggling white-collar and blue-collar workers. Indeed, Table 6 shows that the 20 percent group as a whole suffered a declining percentage of Mexico's total family income since 1977. Some probably fell into outright poverty. Moreover, cleavages exist within classes and lines between classes are often blurred.

Similar problems occur with statistics for people engaged in tertiary labor activity, the so-called services sector, who increased from 19 percent of the "economically active" population in 1940 to 43 percent in 1979, according to the Ministry of Budget and Planning. This figure included many small traders, salespeople, servants, and temporary laborers—a sizable portion of the tertiary labor sector.

This notwithstanding, the growth of the tertiary sector did reflect a real demand for financial and other services generated by capital's rapid growth and centralization. Tertiary labor activity fulfilled important administrative, financial, and related functions associated with the realization (as in commerce or sales) and appropriation (as in banking) of surplus value by capital. In addition, as the late Harry Braverman observed:

> The more productive capitalist industry has become—that is to say, the greater the mass of surplus value it extracts from the productive population—the greater has become the mass of capital seeking its shares in this surplus. And the greater the mass of capital, the greater the mass of unproductive activities which serve only the diversion of this surplus and its distribution among various capitals.[28]

Many intermediate-class people serve capital yet exist in antagonism to it or the state. Their labor power is purchased, and the use values they produce in the performance of necessary administrative or social services is appropriated by either private or public capital.

The growth in service occupations in Mexico after 1940 was accompanied by monopoly capital's gradual destruction of the artisanal basis of production and of the craft sectors of the traditional petty bourgeoisie. Petty-bourgeois merchants and shopkeepers were likewise driven to the margins of viability by big capital's supermarket and department-store chains, as police, tax, and licensing officials regularly harassed them.

Unreliable statistics on the traditional petty bourgeoisie became more and more misleading. For example, the National Chamber of Small Commerce claimed in the late 1970s that there existed 1.25 million small commercial enterprises. Yet many of these were simply minuscule marketplace operations engaged in by the urban poor. As one Chamber president once put it: "He who is without work immediately engages in petty commerce."[29] More often than not, the lives of people in petty commerce were enmeshed in a proletarian reality with a petty-bourgeois appearance.

Among the urban intermediate classes there developed a significant gap in status and income between upper-level bureaucrats, select professionals (doctors, engineers, clergy, etc.), and prosperous small businesspeople on the one hand, and the vast majority on the other. This majority constituted mostly bureaucrats, nurses, paraprofessionals, schoolteachers, clerks, shopkeepers, and struggling small businesspeople. Normally employing servants and living off the redistributed surplus produced by labor, the better-off layers of the intermediate classes came to expect a lifestyle that contrasted sharply with the poverty around them. They tended to blame their declining economic condition on salespeople or peasant producers rather than on the forces of big capital. Economically squeezed, they were ripe for protofascist appeals and authoritarian solutions; right-wing political parties found them good recruiting ground. On the other hand, the left recruited from the intermediate classes as well. Traditionally strong in the schools and universities, where the sons and daughters of the intermediate classes went in large numbers after 1950, the left politicized many students. (By 1972 there were over 300,000 university students and 600,000 pre-university "Preparatoria" students, only 3 percent from peasant background and 7 percent from the working class.)[30] Militants of national and regional unions of university students frequently linked up with elements from radical or independent labor unions and the working class.

As among others of the middle layers of the intermediate classes, only a handful of public school teachers became affluent, while most were reduced to proletarian or even miserable living conditions. Traditionally a respected profession, teaching became a waged trade, and teachers had little voice in the educational process. Much "teaching" activity consisted of supervising overcrowded classrooms, a kind of glorified child-sitting. As agents of the state, teachers were obligated to reproduce the dominant bourgeois ideology and inculcate students with the virtues of *civismo* (good citizenship) and other values that would lead the students to accept their given social position or chance in life. Yet historically teachers had earned their public "image" as defenders of social justice, and to the degree that they learned (from their students) of poor people's complaints or improved the ability of young workers to analyze critically, they became important agents in the struggle to transform society.

This was evidenced in the late 1950s, when the Movement of Revolutionary Teachers arose to infuse democratic life into Latin America's largest teachers' union. Othón Salazar led striking teachers in seizing and holding Mexico's Ministry of Public Education, and for a month the "little giant," as this silver-tongued communist was called, successfully urged the teachers to link their movement to that of railway workers on strike. CTM thugs attacked many of the teachers. Mexico's president finally broke the strike by granting teachers a 17 percent wage hike and slapping Salazar in jail.

But two decades later the teachers launched an even larger movement for democratization of their union, infusing it with some of the feminist outcry emerging among other parts of the intermediate classes, especially university students, 30 percent of whom by then were female. Traditionally barred from union leadership posts, women schoolteachers (who constituted 70 percent of the union) gained up to 10 percent of the new movement's leadership positions—quite an accomplishment in any patriarchical society. The union suffered internal divisions, but its more militant fraction continued to play an important role in the struggle to democratize trade unionism and the Mexican polity right into the 1990s.

Starting in the 1950s, the bourgeoisie began to share a tiny part of its power with a small but growing segment of the intermediate classes: the administrative and technocratic agents of capital and the state. Unlike high-level corporation managers or junior executives, military or police officers, or top state bureaucrats, who usually entered the ranks of the bourgeoisie rather than become a "new managerial elite," these people came from the middle ranks of management, scientific research, technological coordination, and social control. They included a wide range of successful professionals whose labor was purchased not to produce surplus value, but to participate in the overall planning, coordinating, and functioning of capital and the state.

Many of these professionals were trained in Mexican institutions of higher learning, including special business schools, and some were trained in U.S. and foreign universities. Most became a technocracy opposed to labor and enamored of bourgeois and foreign values. They were, by definition, dependent on the productive processes dominated by TNCs. Thus, these technocrats increasingly came to define the continued presence of TNC techniques of distribution, exchange, and education, as being in their own class interests. "Technocracy" rather than "bourgeoisie" was the appropriate term for this grouping because it included people from a number of classes who used positions of power and authority in government to carry out the tasks of administration, education, and control.

The technocracy was reinforced by a form of ideological, or cultural, imitation known as the "cult of technocracy," which exaggerated the importance of "expertise" and called for deference to technocratic solutions at every level of social and political organization. The cult of technocracy, with its corresponding emphasis on TNC-dominated processes of technological change and its mimicking of foreign ways, dominated the highest circles of economic planning and permeated Mexico's higher education system. It reinforced Mexico's historic pattern of economic dependence, as the technocracy was increasingly compared to the "Científicos" ("scientific ones") of Porfirian Mexico (1876-1911).

One result of the technocratic approach was that Mexico's oft-proclaimed quest for an indigenous science and technology was flawed from its inception. The goal was to close the gap between Mexico and a country like the United States. This "closing the gap" approach imposed on Mexico a set of already existing standards of technological efficiency, "models" for economic development, and the accompanying baggage of cultural attitudes and educational biases. The cult of technocracy so elevated and mystified technology as to make independent experimentation virtually impossible. Workers and peasants were excluded from the control over technology and made to feel "unprepared" to tackle technological questions, even at the workshop level of repairing broken parts. Furthermore, the cult of technocracy, and the technocrats who participated in and benefited from it, created a stratum of upper- and middle-level officials and bureaucrats on whom the forces of counterrevolution could rely—especially in situations where the normal supply of consumer goods or replacement parts might become threatened (as happened in Allende's Chile in the early 1970s, for instance).

Mexico's "techno-bureaucracy" constituted a fixed yet fluid layer of the intermediate classes. Its members routinely implemented bourgeois measures of capitalist efficiency, economies of scale, labor discipline, bribery, and corruption. In the 1980s, they became the agents of neoliberalism and its corresponding ideology. As new members entered the techno-bureaucracy's ranks, older members stayed put or moved in other class directions—more often into the bourgeoisie than into the proletariat.

Those who moved into the bourgeoisie accumulated capital for themselves and their friends, mostly through corruption, provision of contracts or favors, and the like. One historic example was the group known as *empresarios del estado,* high-salaried managers and directors in some 1,000 state enterprises before neoliberalism's privatizations of the 1980s and 1990s, from which most of the same individuals again handsomely profited. The best known example consisted of high-level politicians or political appointees (presidents, cabinet members, governors, etc.). These individuals used political power to accumulate funds for investment in the monopoly sectors of the economy and for their extravagantly affluent retirements. Many officials moved easily from one president's government to another's, accumulating capital as they went.

Mexico's presidents, limited to six-year terms and constitutionally barred from reelection, were notorious for making as much money as possible while they could. Some ex-presidents owned hotel chains. Others owned newspaper chains. Still others retired on their wealth, even if self-exiled as in the case of the highly corrupt champion of NAFTA, Carlos Salinas de Gortari. Faced with criminal charges against him and his entourage, Salinas retired to Dublin, Ireland.

This *cuspide* (summit) of the techno-bureaucratic and political pyramid analytically could be described as a "bureaucratic bourgeoisie." But this was not the ruling class: it was only a part of it, and a small part indeed. As part of Mexico's bourgeoisie, and to the extent that it was integrated with Mexican and foreign private capital, it shared the general direction of capitalism and official politics—moved, and strongly so, by the forces of monopoly capital.

This is not to deny the many policy conflicts that representatives of the state and of monopoly capital had to grapple with, including conflicts among themselves. However, such conflicts rarely became antagonistic, since the evolution of the corporatist political system tended to unite, more than to divide, the interests of the state bureaucracy with those of the Mexican bourgeoisie and foreign capital. Only as neoliberalism's failures became evident in the late 1980s did the corporatist system begin to crack, as the PRI underwent a major split that continued to undermine its rule, namely, Cuauhtémoc Cárdenas's 1988 and 1994 campaigns for the presidency and his 1997 election as Mexico City mayor.

Those who argued that Mexico was ruled by a "bureaucratic bourgeoisie" or even a "techno-bureaucracy"—that since the state governed and bureaucrats administered the state, bureaucrats ruled—mistook the form of political governance for the substance of class rule. In form the state was the "strong presidency," but in fact it encompassed all the high executive officials drawn from public and private life. Far from being an "external" force that independently "decided" to support the capital accumulation process, the state was itself a product of class struggle and capitalist economic development.

Bureaucrats did indeed make decisions, but the range of possible decisions they could make was shaped by the class struggle and the power of the ruling class or its dominant fractions, as well as by foreign capitalists. Moreover, even before the advent of neoliberalism, the state shared more and more of its economic enterprises with private capital—one of the reasons these ventures became known as "para-statal" enterprises. The state's momentary takeover of the banks in late 1982 did not alter this pattern, since the state banks continued to service monopoly capital, were staffed by many of the old bank managers, and were later "privatized" as shares were sold back to the "public"—often the previous owners. This was a good example of why it was an idle fancy to argue that the bureaucracy or its "progressive" elements could convert the capitalist state into anything else. Consequently, as proletarians sought their liberation they had to oppose not only the bourgeoisie but the state itself.

True, as history showed, situations could develop in which workers, peasants, or progressive segments of the intermediate classes might benefit from siding with the state. However, these situations would be limited to cases of genuine reform or concrete anti-imperialist actions, as happened under President Lázaro Cárdenas in the 1930s. Mexico's social movements did make demands of the state and periodically found it convenient to ally with forces inside the state to achieve their goals, but the reforms they achieved in this manner rarely had staying power.

Should the struggles of Mexico's working poor, industrial proletariat, and peasants take a quantum leap, however, the corresponding shift in the balance of power within the class struggle would manifest itself within the state. Under such exceptional conditions, we could then, and only then, expect significant change in the behavior of state bureaucrats toward either pole of the underlying labor-capital conflict: they might engineer socialist or other pro-worker, pro-peasant reform measures, or, more likely, they might smash popular mobilizations with military ferocity. There were signs of both tendencies, especially the military one, in the Mexican state of the 1990s, even though a quantum leap in the class struggle had only been augured, not actualized.

It was well known inside Mexico that those few persons within the government who ever advocated genuine revolutionary change were either overruled or gradually co-opted into more "pragmatic" positions of band-aid reformism. Their reforms simply ended by strengthening the system that generated the need for reform in the first place. Under neoliberalism, most genuine reformers found themselves "on the outs"—one reason the PRI experienced several splits starting in the mid-1980s.

The vast majority of public and private bureaucrats, technicians, supervisors, and the like formed part of the intermediate classes. Many of them, in terms of comparative income and nature of work, were undergoing a gradual process of proletarianization. The paradox of gaining a better chance in life through education and access to "white-collar" jobs was that the jobs themselves had become de-skilled and routinized, submitting their practitioners to the despotism of capital in labor processes that more and more resembled a proletarian assembly line. If many of these people were still "middle class" in their values, they increasingly tended to fall on the less affluent side of the polarizing intermediate classes.

Complicating these trends in class formation was Mexico's system of influence-peddling. This system involved techniques such as the following: the *mordida* ("little bite," or bribe); provision of government housing and social security benefits; distribution of seats in Congress and of local offices; promising promotion within the sprawling state bureaucracy; offering dissident intellectuals and professionals lucrative and/or prestigious appointments in government ministries or the education system; and providing favored persons high-status jobs in either the public or private sector with incomes adequate for employing two or more domestic servants and buying expensive consumer goods. The same corrupt system, with its myth of providing for "all the people," penetrated the middle and lower ranks of the intermediate classes and the lower classes, but with far, far smaller payoffs and only limited success.

The political behavior of the intermediate classes strongly affected the outcome of the class struggle at any given stage. Their behavior was characterized by a political ambivalence that corresponded to their "middle" position in the class structure—their relative inability to make it into the ranks of the bourgeoisie and their genuine distress at the gradual proletarianization being imposed on them by the forces of capital. Depending on the intensity and character of the larger bourgeois-proletarian class conflict and according to historical circumstances, a majority of the intermediate classes could consolidate behind one political extreme or another and change quite suddenly.

The expressed values of some in Mexico's intermediate classes, especially among the better paid bureaucrats and professionals, were often mixed between self-proclaimed notions of reform and "helping the downtrodden," and a materialistic daily existence based on consumerism, status through display of wealth, fear of the "rabble," and a personal sense of belonging to the *gente decente* (roughly, "people of decency," meaning wealthy and light-skinned). A significant number of white-collar employees among the intermediate classes internalized the state's and mass media's propaganda of "anticommunism" and "anti-terrorism." Yet the oppressive character of their labor contributed to a divided quality in their "class consciousness" noted by many observers, which helped explain their tendency to leave their offices and join progressive street demonstrations, such as those of the 1968 student movement.

Starting in the 1950s, these ambivalent tendencies among the intermediate classes were manifested in the creation of strong movements against the official political party from both the right and the left. Opposed to the government, they generated contradictions within the state as to the best way to handle the dissent—one reason behind the subsequent attempts to reform the PRI and the eventual breakaway of the Cárdenas faction examined in upcoming chapters.

At the same time, many politically concerned people from the intermediate classes, while sympathetic to the opposition movements, did not join them. They stayed on the sidelines, or expressed their politics through the PRI or other state institutions. Those among the latter who were sympathetic to the right pushed for greater repression of dissent, while those sympathetic to the left advocated reform. Many more refused to go even this far for fear of "rocking the boat" and perhaps worsening their personal economic situation. Growing voter abstention (from 25.8 percent of registered voters in 1952 to 47.5 percent in 1988) and political deviation (only 33.8 percent of eligible voters backed the PRI in 1979, and a majority dealt the PRI a resounding defeat in 1997) reflected the spreading disenchantment.[31]

Officially, the so-called "middle classes" constituted one of the three sectors of the PRI—the "popular" sector, known as the National Confederation of Popular Organizations (CNOP), which also incorporated various organized elements of the urban poor. The largest union in the CNOP was the Federation of State Workers' Unions. For years, the CNOP was stronger than the worker or peasant sectors of the party (the CTM and CNC, respectively), but starting in the 1960s its relative strength tended to diminish. Carlos Salinas de Gortari, a "hands-on" president (1988-1994) who challenged the old guard of the PRI, pretty much circumvented the CNOP.

Nonetheless, as one of the PRI's three sectors the CNOP often played an important role in dealing with Mexico's growing mass of urban poor. As new social movements of discontented elements of both the urban poor and the intermediate classes arose, fell back, and rose again repeatedly from the late 1950s to the late 1990s, the CNOP periodically regained much of its lost strength. For example, under Salinas's "hands-off" successor, President Ernesto Zedillo, the old-guard PRI started bringing the CNOP back to its prior strength. But Zedillo also sped up military intervention against social movements of the rural and urban poor, thus often letting the "stick" of repression supersede the "carrot" of the CNOP's role.

The Proletariat and the Poor

By no means a unified force, Mexico's working classes were fragmented and atomized. The official rate of the working classes' unionization—24 percent of the total labor force—was actually much lower, since so many of the "economically active" were not counted in work-force statistics. These statistics showed a little more than one-third of Mexico's population as "economically active." Many economically active women, children, and aged were never counted. Irregularly employed men often went uncounted as well. Most of the people not counted as "economically active" did work, however. They worked as family labor, or as shepherds, seamstresses, street vendors, carriers, messengers, servants, shoe-shiners, car washers, car watchers, marketplace stall operators, and so on. Thus in reality those earning less than the already inadequate legal minimum wage—officially more than 60 percent of the labor force—constituted a far larger percentage of the population than reported.

In general, the nonunionized segments of the industrial proletariat had a lesser degree of political consciousness than the unionized ones, although they shared a sense of class resentment and even organized at their workplaces from time to time. Indeed, there occurred periodic signs of a new labor militancy among both the unionized and non-unionized members of Mexico's proletariat.

The class struggle in small and medium-size industries, where there were fewer unions, was usually more brutal and personal than that in large industry. The lives of workers and the conditions of the enterprises were more problematic, job security was rare, and there was little opportunity for the worker to achieve more than a token wage increase—usually parallel to inadequate inflation-related adjustments made in the legal minimum wage. Many owners could not compete successfully with the state-favored large enterprises of domestic and foreign monopoly capital. Neoliberalism, NAFTA, and Mexico's currency crises led to the economic failure of large numbers of these smaller industries and the layoffs of hundreds of thousands of their employees.

In urban slum areas there existed many factories that employed fewer than one hundred people, thereby avoiding the constitutional stipulation of housing assistance and other benefits. Case studies revealed that the owners of these factories preferred to hire recent migrants from the same rural region. They often contributed funds to the migrants' hometown churches and became godparents to their children. TNC maquiladoras in the border area also tapped select rural regions. As noted throughout this book, the tradition of godparents (compadrazgo) had many uses, ranging from social cohesion to social control.

Foreign capital was involved in many of these factories, or, if it was not, it soon stepped in to buy out the more successful ones. Political sociologist Susan Eckstein described the two largest such factories she researched, a canning operation and the nation's largest chocolate factory, before and after their sale to U.S.-owned TNCs in 1971. Wherever possible, the foreign firms modernized administration but retained the old hiring patterns and practices of paternalism.[32]

Unable to afford inflated rents, many of the nonunionized urban employed resided near, or in, the slums that housed the unemployed and underemployed. Their homes or apartments were recognizable by their better construction. Their fear of being permanently submerged in abject poverty haunted them. They were torn by two opposing desires: to hold on to the little they had and perhaps improve their lot, or to risk engagement in organized actions against their employers, even against the larger economic and political system itself, in order to change their lives and those of their children. They were open to appeals by radical union organizers or friends. Yet, as in the case of unionizing female maquiladora employees, when they did struggle and achieve victories the most practical way to preserve their gains was to affiliate with the CTM or other corporatist structures, which were always ready to absorb them.

Every decade greater numbers of wage earners moved into and out of the ranks of the unemployed or subemployed, reducing the barriers separating unionized from nonunionized workers. This was particularly true in construction, where the owners liked to rotate their labor force or use new migrant labor in their "crews." Mexico City's labyrinthian subway system was built by a mixture of urban proletarians, impoverished workers, and peasants (some of whom commuted between the city and their subsistence farms weekly).

Similarly, in the nationalized petroleum industry, whose work force grew from approximately 18,000 in 1938 to 150,000 in 1982 and then was reduced by more than half under neoliberalism, more than 70 percent of the workers were hired on a temporary basis, and less than two-thirds of these were unionized. But they were strategically placed, carrying out 60 percent of activities directly related to phases of production (exploration, extraction, refining, petrochemicals). Whether unionized or not, temporary oil workers had to buy their job contracts on a monthly basis from union or private labor contractors. A system of caciquismo flourished in this flesh market, to such an extent that inter-*charro* quarrels over the spoils frequently led to assassinations.

Temporary oil workers sometimes organized and rebelled. For example, they launched angry anti-*charro* street demonstrations in Mexico City in 1967 and 1975. Even some permanently employed, unionized oil workers (among the nation's best-paid proletarians) broke with their tradition of looking down on the temporaries and expressed support for their temporarily employed brethren.

It became fashionable to refer to the urban semiemployed and unemployed as "marginalized." This was misleading, since it implied that they constituted a separate class (or "mass") on the margins of society, removed from the main social and economic processes of capitalist accumulation and class struggle. Far from being marginal, these hungry and overworked millions formed a vast fraction of the working class and were the product of an ongoing process of immiseration, the other side of the coin of capital accumulation. The uprooting of people from the countryside, their separation from the means of production, their crowding into the towns and cities, all constituted a fundamental part of the capitalist mode of production, which fostered the labor pool it needed for its expansion.

Yet as industrial production became more capital-intensive, fewer new migrants to the cities or even long-term urban residents could find stable or adequate wage labor. Instead, they wandered from job to job, working for a pittance as street vendors, lottery ticket sellers, household servants, laundresses, subcontracted seamstresses (and others involved in "industrial homework"), carpenters, irregularly employed factory hands, small-scale workshop employees or owners, and so forth. While technically unemployed or underemployed, most were in fact "overemployed," often working more than one job per person and at least two jobs per adult couple per family. Women took on more and more paid and unpaid work, while children and the aged worked when and where they could.

Through their extended workdays and the so-called independent labor performed in family subsistence activities (self-exploitation, especially among women), impoverished "overemployed" people of the "informal sector" made up from two-thirds to three-fourths of Mexico's working population by the 1980s. They contributed to the capitalists' extraction of surplus value by helping to meet the costs of the reproduction of labor power. Perhaps the most significant commodity they produced and maintained for capital was labor power, but, as we are about to see, they benefited capital in other vital ways too.[33]

The overwhelming majority constituted a subproletariat in a double sense: first, as a relative surplus population or part of the reserve army of labor; second, as a sector that moved in and out of the agrarian, industrial, and service/commercial working classes. In drawing on the labor of this expanding pool of job-hungry workers, whether in Mexico or elsewhere, TNCs internationalized capitalist relations of production, reorganizing the basis of exploitation and conditions of employment and unemployment everywhere, including the more industrialized "home countries" of the TNCs.

As capital and production transcended national boundaries, becoming transnational, labor also became more mobile, crossing national frontiers—but at a slower rate than capital. For monopoly capitalists based in the more industrialized countries this permitted access to a growing reserve army of labor and a higher rate of profit. This in turn had a long-run negative impact on the strength of labor unions and wage rates in the more industrialized nations, which were also undergoing a process of "informalization" of "formal sectors" of the economy (as in the U.S. electronics industry and parts of the automotive industry).

The growth of the "informal sector" and the supposedly "new international division of labor" was an old process deriving from imperialism's creation and distribution of surplus labor on an international scale. National differences in wage levels related in part to the power advantages accruing to imperialist nations over time. From this historical evolution of imperialism there evolved the so-called "new international division of labor" and "need to be competitive in the global market" utilized by TNCs to further their accumulation of capital.

However, the completion of the internationalization of capitalist relations of production was barred by anti-imperialist wars of national liberation, inter-imperialist rivalries, and uneven development patterns and class conflict within capitalist nations. All of these were but forms, or partial expressions, of the contradiction between labor and capital.

Karl Marx characterized a *relative surplus population* as a "condition of existence of the capitalist mode of production." Industrial capitalism, he pointed out, "depends on the constant formation, the greater or less absorption, and the reformation of the industrial reserve army of surplus population, independently of the absolute growth of the population."[34] In this sense, the roots of immiseration of millions of Mexicans had little to do with population growth as such (which in fact had slowed down after 1970) and everything to do with the nature of capitalist production and its penetration into the remotest areas of the countryside.

The relative surplus population could take the floating form (as in modern industrial centers, now employed, now laid off), the latent form (low-paid, subemployed agricultural labor, ready to migrate to town or city), or the pauper form (the unemployed, orphans, poor children, demoralized, mutilated, or sickly workers). Whatever form it took, it grew in rough correspondence to the increase in social wealth, functioning capital, labor productivity, and the absolute mass of the proletariat. In his trenchant way, Marx expressed this dialectical process as follows:

> The same causes which develop the expansive power of capital, develop also the labor power at its disposal . . . the surplus population forms a condition of

capitalist production. . . . The more extensive, finally, the lazarus-layers of the working class, and the industrial reserve army, the greater is official pauperism. This is the absolute general law of capitalist accumulation. . . . The law by which a constantly increasing quantity of means of production, thanks to the advance in the productiveness of social labor, may be set in movement by a progressively diminishing expenditure of human power, this law, in a capitalist society . . . is expressed thus: the higher the productiveness of labor, the greater is the pressure of the laborers on the means of employment, the more precarious, therefore, becomes their condition of existence.[35]

In modern times the antagonistic character of capitalist accumulation—"accumulation of wealth at one pole, accumulation of misery, agony of toil, slavery, ignorance, brutality, mental degradation, at the opposite pole"[36]—generated contradictions that Marx could not foresee. It gave rise to immiseration of millions of people everywhere, especially in imperialist-dominated countries like Mexico with relatively weak bourgeoisies accustomed to relying on undervalued labor. Among the social problems generated by mass misery were disease, crime, drug addiction, and gang warfare. This contributed to the growing tendency of large numbers of the poor to organize themselves, gain political consciousness, and resist or revolt. In turn, considerable expenses were incurred in maintaining a degree of stability and regulating impoverished masses of people, whether through public services, policing, or imprisonment.[37]

Thus, the immiserated masses were both functional and dysfunctional for capitalist accumulation. Increasing amounts of capital and energy had to be channeled out of the accumulation process in order to provide state-run food stores (CONASUPO); minimal health care (IMSS-Coplamar, introduced in the early 1970s and covering 15 percent of Mexico's population but leaving 42 percent without any organized form of obtaining health care); housing; sanitation; and military or police control over ever larger slums.

In late 1998, slums accounted for half the population of the world's largest metropolitan area, greater Mexico City, which contained more than 23 million people, or nearly one-fourth the nation's populace, and to which there arrived 10,000 or more new residents every day. The largest and oldest slum was Netzahualcóyotl (in Nahuatl, "fasting coyote"), commonly known as "Neza." Founded near the international airport in the late 1940s by some 3,000 *ejidatarios*, Neza mushroomed into an unmanageable urban jungle of more than 3 million inhabitants spread over 150 square miles—one of the nation's largest "cities." Only half its residents were employed, and some 80 percent of them worked outside the area. To its north and west on the outskirts of Mexico City was another such *colonia proletaria* of almost equal demographic character, the "Gustavo A. Madero Delegation." Many smaller slums dotted the capital as well.

A study of one such *colonia proletaria* in the early 1980s found that 89 percent of heads of family were proletarians (although only half of them received a stable wage); 10 percent were in the petty bourgeoisie; and a mere 1 percent were "lumpenproletarian."[38] The study found that through their frequent though irregular employment in factories and their living next door to regularly employed proletarians, the *colonia's* residents were picking up a more proletarian class consciousness and were integrating themselves into a larger class culture (not "subclass" or "national" culture, although this also existed). With the worsening of economic conditions for the lower classes since the study, however, there developed signs of increased crime in some of Mexico's slums.

The various jobs undertaken by the immiserated further integrated them with capital's accumulation process, either through their direct production of surplus value or through their role in the circulation, distribution, and servicing of commodities. A good example of their production of surplus value was their widespread operation of sweatshops in the interior of Mexico. In the Federal District alone there were more than 300,000 *maquiladoras de ropa*— workshops that assemble clothing.

In the shoe industry, where they were known as *picas,* there were many more such slum workshops across the nation. These cobbling operations produced more than half the nation's shoes (including several million dollars worth for export), using modern imported machinery as well as imported leather and synthetic materials. The surplus value produced went to the tanners and shoe companies. Hundreds of thousands of other such workshops produced furniture, housing parts, leather goods, various automotive parts or supplies, and so forth, for the profit of capitalists.

In the clothing workshops, the individuals (sewing at home) or the workshop owners (who hire a few laborers to work in their homes) own part of the constant capital, often modern sewing or cutting machinery they have purchased on credit or with their savings. However, they are dependent for raw materials (textiles, pieces, etc.) on the capitalists, who often, like the traditional "jobbers" on New York City's Lower East Side, subcontract the work to them (the so-called "putting-out system"). When the slum workshop "owners" attempt to purchase the raw materials outside the monopolized market, prices are increased beyond their ability to pay, or the purchase is simply denied them.

Case studies have estimated that the rate of surplus-value appropriation by capitalists employing this type of productive labor, most of which is female, is more than double that of large-scale clothing factories hiring regular proletarians.[39] Even the workshop "owner" who exploits the labor of poorer neighbors fails to appropriate a portion of the surplus value thereby produced. In fact, she usually makes more when not having to hire other laborers, since the "wage" paid in self-exploitation is normally half or less of that paid a hired worker (and this is in turn less than half the legal minimum wage). Moreover, workshop owners are often recent rural migrants who have not engaged in this type of activity before—and are easily victimized by capitalists using the "putting-out" system.

Since the number of slum workshops in various industries rose dramatically during the neoliberal era of the 1980s and 1990s—in part because of the working class's feverish attempts to compensate for its inadequate earnings or employment—they could not be viewed as precapitalist modes of production destined to disappear. On the contrary, these workshops were a product and tool of modern capitalist accumulation.[40] Viewed from the capitalist's vantage point, they were profitable because the wages were substandard or nonexistent; there was no problem of labor unions, strikes, or state-enforced labor benefits; and much of the cost of constant capital was paid by the workshop "owners." Moreover, the rate of recuperation of the cost of constant capital was rapid, once the capitalist recuperated the cost of raw materials with the sale of the finished product, but it was low for the workshop "owner," whose overhead and machinery payments were spread over a much longer period.

Slum workshops furthered capital accumulation in less direct ways . Capital benefited politically from the belief of many slum workshop operators that they were not proletarians since they owned part of their own means of production. This was a false belief, however, since in terms of their overall relations of production they were disguised proletarians whose ownership of a humble workshop masked their insertion into a larger capitalist structure that appropriated the fruits of their labor. Similarly, the workers hired by such sweatshop owners often tended to view their immediate *patrones* (bosses) as the "enemy," more than the actual appropriators of their surplus value, the capitalists who resided elsewhere.

The final proof, if any be needed, that the slum workshop "owners" and "their" employees were proletarians and not petty bourgeois was given in a dramatic way immediately after the earthquake of 1985 in Mexico City. With women at their sewing machines still buried in the rubble, trucks sent by the absentee capitalists arrived not to rescue them but to take away the machines. Soldiers prevented volunteers from entering until the machines were carted off in the trucks. Within days, angry seamstresses walking on crutches, followed by other seamstresses who had not been working at the time of the earthquake, conducted a protest march of thousands. They demanded, and soon obtained, the right to unionize.[41]

It is often assumed that most of the immiserated gain their employment in the rapidly expanding services or tertiary sector of the economy, but case studies indicate otherwise. It is true that, for example, one of every five employed women in Mexico City in the 1990s was a domestic servant, and there were untold numbers of girls from eight to fourteen years of age engaged in low-paid household labor. However, a much larger percentage became involved in either productive activities like sweatshop or factory labor or in ostensibly "independent" commercial activities for the purposes of capital accumulation (but not their own). Once again, now as shopkeepers, stall "owners," or street vendors (3 million street vendors in the Federal District alone), a petty-bourgeois appearance masked a proletarian or immiserated reality.[42]

One study of *misceláneas*—one-room stores selling tobacco, soft drinks, cookies, oils, and so forth—found that about one-third of their products were of foreign origin and over two-thirds were delivered direct from the factory; that prices were universal throughout the Federal District (i.e., fixed pricing); and that the average local "merchant" worked fifteen hours a day and earned 45 percent less than the minimum wage.[43] Bribes were routine, and a gangland network of fake health inspectors parasitically fed off the hundreds of thousands of such stores, typically marked by Coca-Cola signs. The state charged a series of small taxes, and the store operator was also obliged to pay dues to the National Confederation of Small Commerce. The millions of immiserated engaged in petty commerce of this or other types were dependent for their "business opportunities" on the Coordinating Federation of Small Industrialists and Merchants, a part of the PRI's "middle-class" CNOP.

A *personalista* network of low-level officials of various state organizations made sure that these store operators and vendors paid them off or appeared at PRI party rallies. Failure to cooperate led to the takeover of a store or a route by the local official, or to his placing another poor person in front of the store or stall, selling one of the products at a lower price. There were less tactful means of enforcement as well.[44] The process was not unlike what we observed in Chapter 5's discussion of the labor bureaucracy's control of the dues, wages, and jobs of those who sought and gained employment in large industry or the TNC maquiladoras.

The immiserated contributed to capital accumulation in the consumption of goods as well. The slums offered a vast, teeming market for capitalists large and small: for the sale of furniture, wood products, school and stationery supplies, soft drinks, liquor, tobacco, processed or packaged foods, construction materials, and sundry domestic articles, almost all of which encompassed significant portions of foreign or Mexican monopoly-capital investment. Slum dwellers, unable to travel elsewhere to obtain commodities at reasonable prices, provided a captive market that paid exorbitant prices for everything from tortillas to rent. Even when some of the urban poor took clothing home to stitch or labor at the slum "domestic workshops," they normally saved neither money nor time. Instead, they sweated, produced, distributed, and ended up buying that which they produced at inflated prices.

At the same time, most "formal sector" workers bought numerous goods and services at a relatively low price from the immiserated masses hawking their wares or skills on neighborhood streets or in the marketplaces. This helped reduce pressure on what the wage could buy, an indirect subsidy to capitalists.

Thus, whether in the production, distribution, sale, or consumption of commodities, the immiserated were scarcely marginalized from the national and international system of capital accumulation. Further, the capitalist mode of production supplanted or "absorbed" noncapitalist modes of production; it did not "preserve," "combine with," or "coexist with" them. It restructured many of their forms of economic activity, in both rural and urban areas, for the purpose of capital accumulation on an extended scale. What looked like "noncapitalist forms" of production and distribution offered up to capital raw materials, certain necessities of life for labor power's reproduction, and even finished products.

In the countryside a de-peasantization process was disguised by peasant production for markets and subsistence, thereby limiting the completion of proletarianization in the modern sense. But in the cities a process of proletarianization and immiseration was often disguised by petty-bourgeois forms of economic activity that more often than not generated surplus value or realized it on behalf of capitalists. Superexploitation of labor developed and created anew these "noncapitalist forms" of production and distribution, thereby helping to combat the declining tendency of the rate of profit inherent in capital-intensive industrial production while also absorbing some of the unemployed and inculcating them with an ideology which anthropologist Sol Tax once called "penny-capitalist."[45] The resultant widespread immiseration of many, which accompanied the transformation of some into a modern industrial work force, denied the benefits of proletarian status (social security, unionization, etc.) to millions while limiting those benefits won in hard-fought battles by the industrial proletariat.

For these and other reasons, monopoly capital repeatedly sought to fortify its relation with village- or neighborhood-based "domestic economies." This was reflected in the World Bank's programs for "investing in the poor," discussed earlier in this chapter. While continuing to fund mega-dam and other environmentally destructive projects in the interests of agribusiness and private capital, the bank simultaneously emphasized financing subsistence farming and "independent" urban neighborhood enterprises.

On September 26, 1977, World Bank President Robert McNamara (former Ford executive and U.S. Secretary of Defense during the Vietnam war) outlined the urban component of this strategy. He said that the bank planned to create and aid independent producers in the development of artisanal operations, domestic workshops, small grocery stores (misceláneas), and so on. Tying as many of the urban poor as possible to international credit systems was one further way to integrate them with monopoly capital, which in turn accumulated new dividends in its realization of surplus value through marketing of artisan products and sales of its own goods in the new stores established.

The Political Potential of the Poor

As illustrated by several social movements among the urban poor and by the 1994 Zapatista uprising in Chiapas, the growing numbers and rage of the immiserated can provoke wide-ranging political consequences. However, of all social movements, those of the immiserated are the least stable, consistent, or predictable. Their political direction often depends on the social movements and political character of other groups in the society, particularly the employed proletariat, the petty bourgeoisie, and sometimes intellectuals who become political activists. Priests advocating liberation theology co-exist with evangelical holy-rollers and mystics in Neza and other *colonias*.

The state uses populism and paternalism to fixate the peasantry and urban poor on owning a parcel of land or a dwelling in order to keep them as dependent as possible on state favors. Many of the immiserated thus have a tendency to support the status quo, and to tolerate or even support capitalist or reactionary values. Eight years of literacy, co-op, and political work in Neza showed Jesuit priest Martín de la Rosa that "the values of bourgeois ideology have been profoundly incorporated into the consciousness of a large portion of the popular classes."[46] His and others' interview data suggest that almost all individuals engaged in petty commerce, as well as many workshop owners, see their situations as determined by larger class, social, and political forces beyond their control, but still tend to mix petty-bourgeois profit-making (or debt-paying) goals with proletarian ones of rebellion against oppression.

Referring to the "irony of organization," political scientist Susan Eckstein concludes that many of the immiserated have shown great will and ability to organize, only to find that their various organizations, through co-optation or government regulations, end up serving to "legitimate a regime, extend a government's realm of administration, and reinforce existing social and economic inequities."[47] When co-optation fails, repression is used: from the burning of squatters' cardboard hovels to the assassination of leaders, including radical priests (as in Torreón and Chihuahua during the 1970s, or in Chiapas later).

Yet co-optation is a tricky business. Francisco de la Cruz, a co-opted leader of Mexico City's oldest and most politically conscious, self-organized, and self-policed *colonia*, "2 de Octubre" (created in 1969 by land invaders), claimed he was arrested in March 1981 because the PRI (which he had joined years earlier) had asked him to become a congressional deputy "in exchange for selling out my people." Most progressives thought he had already sold out, because the "2 de Octubre" colony was becoming rife with corruption he had fostered.

More ominous was what happened on the night of de Ia Cruz's arrest. Thousands of heavily armed police and military groups, many on horseback, stormed the colony in the early dawn hours and razed it to the ground. Sleeping women, children, and old folk were crushed in the melee, then herded off to temporary camps pending "resettlement" of some of them in state-provided housing in another neighborhood. The raid itself was not new—for years the state had sent troops and elite units like the Radio Patrols Battalion of the State of Mexico (BARAPEM) to militant *colonias* to kill, wound, or intimidate their residents, reflecting the intensity of the class war raging in the daily lives of millions of impoverished Mexicans.

But the savagery of the dawn raid on "2 de Octubre" was a clear and symbolic escalation, serving to warn all politicized slum dwellers that they could be next. Shortly after the raid, Nuevo León's governor publicly threatened Monterrey's independent slum-based Land and Liberty Front with a similar action. It is believed by some that a few of the woman organizers in these slums later went to Chiapas to link up with the Zapatistas' revolt there.

More elite police SWAT teams emerged in the 1980s and 1990s, with names like "Zorros" (foxes) and "Jaguares" (jaguars). Several members of the Zorros in November of 1997 were accused of torturing and murdering six youths from the Buenos Aires slum in central Mexico City. Some 360 Zorros then mutinied, leading to a momentary confrontation with army troops before peace was restored. Earlier in 1997, police in Neza were believed to have severely beaten forty-eight people while breaking up a punk music concert. Obviously, life in the slums resembled a boiling cauldron.

Recognition of the potential for political consciousness among the poor does not negate the limitations imposed in a corporatist, controlled, and regimented social formation like Mexico's. Sociologist Diane E. Davis has pointed out that often "Mexico's poor and traditional middle classes" have united "with certain local factions of capital against others" and sided "with local [municipal] state actors against organized industrial workers then in alliance with national state actors."[48] To divide and rule the ever more atomized working classes is, in fact, a major function of the PRI and its corporatist system.

The Mexican government acted to regulate the poor, concentrating them in certain areas, organizing their political behavior through the CNOP sector of the PRI, and channeling their economic activity. It did not enforce tax or labor laws on the sweatshops. It tolerated a high degree of graft, deception, brutality, and police complicity in migratory flows to the cities and especially to the United States. When not driving squatters off the land, it encouraged a mock "petty-bourgeoisification" of the poor by organizing them into petty trade networks, regulating their markets, and introducing land concession schemes and a minimal degree of public services—to confirm them as "respectable home or apartment owners."

The government also sponsored or assisted occasional squatters' "self-help," training, or services programs. For example, "training centers" were established for Indian women who migrated to Mexico City (the so-called Marías). At the centers, the women's homecraft skills were exploited to produce rag dolls, clothes, kitchen accessories, and the like. The women were paid token wages, but if they asked for more they were reminded that they were "students" being taught "skills" by their "professors." Their hand-crafted products were then sold to the residents of luxury suburbs like San Angel and Polanco or, increasingly under NAFTA, exported to the United States.

The immiserated were both central to the capitalist productive process and a critical force in the struggle to replace it with a more democratic, collective, or socialist one. This was clearly recognized not only by the PRI, but also by the imperialists, who poured hundreds of millions of dollars into research projects designed to control or win over the "marginalized," and into armaments for repressive state apparatuses, including the most sophisticated military technology for SWAT teams, crowd control, counter-insurgency, and the maintenance of "internal stability." Globally, despite neoliberalism's pretensions to phase out state intervention and leave everything to the free market, the frenetic pace of national and international accumulation of capital accelerated state intervention. This produced increased repression, militarization of society, and technocratic bureaucratization and organization of social groups. All these tendencies were evident in Mexico.

Yet most "daily life" organizational networks among the immiserated in Mexico were (with growing numbers of exceptions) not politically progressive: petty crime syndicates; male-dominated family systems; overdependence on religious or social institutions like the *compadrazgo* (which did have a positive side in economic survival terms); traditional deference to *el patrón* and related informal patron-client systems; and so on. Almost all these forms of social organization served to block political organizing for progressive change.

From the viewpoint of slum dwellers, whose social movements usually were limited to struggles for public services, jobs, elections of local officials, and the like, to perceive themselves as "marginalized" from society instead of integrated into the larger proletariat involved serious political and human consequences. Similarly, those self-sacrificing organizers who attempted to instigate or support slum political or social movements on the basis of a theory or assumption of "marginalization" were unlikely to achieve more than temporary goals based on charity, self-help, and mutual aid.

More importantly, the struggle against women's oppression in both its patriarchical and capitalist forms was central to any accurate class analysis and potentially successful strategy for political or social change. As we have seen, women constituted the major superexploited group among the immiserated and much of the working class. Making up well over a third of Mexico's workforce in 1998, women subsidized both capitalist firms and household economies—and were central, not marginal, to both (including the TNCs that owned the maquiladora plants). Women's unpaid household work made it easier for employers to pay all workers less, while patriarchical and related gender ideologies and practices made women even more superexploitable.

Of all social movements in human history, those of the urban poor were always the least stable or predictable. Yet their power was manifested repeatedly. Most recently, the urban poor, and especially women, played a central role in several attempted revolutions—Iran, the Philippines, South Africa, Nicaragua, El Salvador, Guatemala, to name a few. Whatever the long-range results of those particular attempts at change, no one could deny their profound national, regional, and international impact.

The role of the immiserated and the women among them was not only that of a "reserve army of labor" but also that of a highly important actvated arm of capital accumulation for domestic and foreign capitalists. Recognizing that role has been proven crucial for the class struggle in Mexico, which took on increasingly significant gender, ethnic, and international characteristics after 1968.

Chapter 7

Oil and Neoliberalism: 1968-1993

When [IMF] stabilization programs, justified by transitory condi-
tions, are perpetuated, greater injustices result than those supposedly
being corrected. Fatally, salaried workers' wages are restricted; capital
centralizes; and the state's room for maneuver is reduced. The state's
capacity to resolve conflicts is annulled, its possibility of governing
canceled.

–President José López Portillo, Third State of the Nation Address,
September 1979

If El Salvador has a revolution, then the Mexican oilfields 150 miles
away will be hit by revolution: we can't permit either.

–State Department officials to Enrique Alvarez Córdoba,
president of Salvadoran Democratic Revolutionary Front, as
reported by Alvarez to group at New York City's Riverside
Church, August 1980[1]

AS THE TWENTIETH CENTURY DRAWS TO A CLOSE, a crisis has emerged in
Mexico's corporatist state. This crisis appears to derive from a colossal foreign
debt and sharp falls in oil prices in 1981, 1986, and 1998.[2] In actuality, however,
Mexico's state crisis is both an economic and a political crisis, with structural
causes dating back to earlier periods.

Economically, the crisis is rooted in the problems described in the preceding
chapters: uneven patterns of capital accumulation because of foreign domination and a weak bourgeoisie's historic reliance on low-paid labor; a corresponding failure to develop either a large, dynamic home market or a vigorous
production of capital and intermediate goods; and the consequent lower levels
of productivity in Mexican capitalism, which made Mexican products less able
to compete with those of foreigners. This inability to compete reinforced the
Mexican bourgeoisie's dependence on cheap labor, creating a vicious circle. It
also contributed to Mexico's growing dependence on foreign capital and the
exhaustion of the "import-substitution industrialization" and "stabilizing-
development" models, followed by the failures of neoliberalism.

This chapter examines the interaction between class struggle, gender, ethnicity, politics, and economics, from the 1968 student uprising through the dozen years of neoliberalism preceding the 1994 Zapatista uprising and implementation of NAFTA. The chapter begins with an examination of the underlying economic causes of the state's crisis and the contradictory nature of the corporatist capitalist state. Then it moves to the first major political expression of the incipient crisis, the 1968 student revolt. Next, the social movements of the 1970s and early 1980s are taken up, including guerrilla activities, peasant organizing, the new labor militancy, protests by the urban poor, and the important roles played by women and Indians in these movements. The corporatist state's use of populism to contain social movements faltered in the face of the mid-1970s recession, the bourgeoisie taking a bigger role in politics through its Management Coordinating Council (CCE), and a CIA destabilization campaign. The state ultimately had to repress the popular insurgencies by armed force.

In a corporatist system regulated by a technocratic-authoritarian state, the governing party was not organizing the class whose interests it generally served—the bourgeoisie's CCE was doing that. Nor were the official trade unions representing the class they supposedly served—the "Democratic Tendency" and independent unions of the new labor militancy were doing that.

The state attempted to polish its tarnished image by introducing "political reform" and "playing the oil card." The rush to expand oil production between 1977 and 1982 helped balloon the public debt, as the state borrowed heavily to pay for much-needed U.S. machinery. Rising debt payments and IMF austerity programs undermined the state's ability to fund programs needed to "cool out" popular unrest. Step by step, U.S. corporate leaders sought to recapture control of Mexico's oil (nationalized from U.S. and British control in 1938).

High interest rates, a fall in oil prices, and inflation triggered Mexico's economic collapse in August 1982. The state accepted an international financial bailout, in exchange for its agreement to "restructure" the economy according to a "neoliberal" model of development. Neoliberal development was based on a market-driven, private sector-led, export-based strategy that opened up the country even more to foreign capital. In September 1982, the state nationalized non-foreign banks, absorbing their bad debts and compensating the owners. Mexico's bankers moved to challenge the PRI's longstanding control over the state but were unsuccessful. In less than a decade, the banks were theirs again, but not the state.

From 1982 to 1994, the foreign-dominated, export-based *maquiladora* program boomed, as the neoliberal model proved remarkably similar to the one engineered a century earlier by the Díaz dictatorship. Succeeding presidents slashed state expenditures on social programs; froze wages; lowered tariffs; "privatized" more than a thousand state enterprises; ended agrarian reform; began privatizing *ejidos*; helped dismantle scores of labor unions; expanded the stock and bond market; and opened the country to foreign speculators. Mexico joined first the General Agreement on Trade and Tariffs (GATT) and later the North American Free Trade Agreement (NAFTA).

Poverty and discontent spread across the land. The government's poor handling of the 1985 Mexico City earthquake emergency further undermined the PRI's legitimacy. Citizens began taking direct action to solve problems the state could not. In the presidential election of 1988 the PRI was humiliated, though unvanquished. PRI candidate Carlos Salinas de Gortari claimed victory despite the public's view that he had received far fewer votes than his opponent Cuauhtémoc Cárdenas, whose pro-democracy faction of the PRI the party had expelled earlier. After the election, Cárdenas founded the Party of the Democratic Revolution (PRD).

The state's corporatism had long served as a kind of historic compromise between the bourgeoisie and the working classes. Neither pole of the class conflict had been strong enough to achieve its hegemonic project alone. However, once the corporatist state committed itself to neoliberalism and rolling back labor unions, it could not as easily pursue its corporatist approach of co-opting dissenters. Instead, it introduced special programs to try to cool out social unrest or "buy" votes at election time.

Because of harsh economic conditions imposed on them by neoliberalism, Mexico's workers, peasants, and poor found it difficult to sustain the momentarily reenergized social movements. At the same time, the class structure became more polarized than at any time since the 1930s.

The Economic Causes of Political Crisis

The political crisis had underlying economic causes rooted in the nature of Mexican capitalism. Neoliberalism failed to address these underlying causes, and in fact made matters worse.

These causes could be traced to the uneven and incomplete industrialization process that the bourgeoisie and the state had carried out during and after the Second World War. In spite of achieving rates of industrialization and economic growth superior to those of most of the rest of Latin America, Mexico never emerged into autonomous sustained economic growth, due to the weaknesses of Mexico's patterns of capital accumulation and the economy's dependence on foreign capital.

Employers in Mexico since late colonial times had relied on abundant supplies of inexpensive labor for their capital accumulation. The most "modern" industrial and dynamic sectors of Mexico's economy continuously were able to attract labor from, and expel it back to, the economy's "traditional" sectors. The immiserated masses provided an immense reserve army of labor. Because of this, monopoly capital, with the state's support, was able to stem wage advances even in the most capitalized industries, and in the face of labor unrest. The bourgeoisie, able to rely on cheap labor, never had to attempt total industrial transformation.

Under capitalism, capital accumulation on an extended scale depends on continuous and growing value transfers from traditional areas of production to the modern industrial sector, development of which in turn depends on vigorously producing the means of production, and an ample home market of adequately paid consumers. Mexico lacked full development of either.

Since 1950, the traditional areas of production (food processing, textiles, etc.) did not transfer value out to, but instead mostly *received* value from the other sectors of the economy, through subsidized prices, low-cost inputs, and the like. The modern industries (metallurgy, industrial manufacturing, etc.) failed to receive value from the traditional sector on a continuous and expanding basis. Only agriculture, forestry, fishing, construction, electricity, transportation, and services continuously transferred value out—to both traditional and modern areas of production. Also, since wages were higher in the modern industrial sector than in the traditional ones, the rate of surplus value, or rate of profit, was less in the modern sector.

Although it is very difficult to measure the rate of profit, economist Abelardo Mariña Flores of Mexico City's Universidad Autónoma Metropolitana-Azcapotzalco has estimated that Mexico's rate of profit fell from 40 percent in 1952 to 25 percent in 1976, 23 percent in 1982, and 20 percent in 1986. It recuperated to 27 percent in 1990, only to drop again to 23 percent in 1992 prior to Mexico's economic collapse of 1994-1995. At first glance, this may seem somewhat surprising. After all, in 1982-1992, the first decade of neoliberalism, capitalists almost doubled their rate of exploitation of variable capital (money paid out as wages to purchase labor power, the ultimate source of all surplus value), slashing real wages by almost half. However, in the same decade, the capitalists' investments in constant capital (non-wage items like machinery) increased by two and a half times. It is, of course, this growth in the organic composition of capital (ratio of constant capital to variable capital) that underlies the structural tendency of the rate of profit to fall in the first place. This was also a time of major peso devaluations, making imported machinery even more costly.

One result of Mexican capitalists' reliance on inexpensive labor and failure to develop the capital goods industry was the lower productivity of Mexican industry vis-à-vis that of the United States. Despite momentary rises in productivity in Mexico, the gap vis-à-vis the United States became especially stark during the era of neoliberalism. In turn, Mexican products were less able to compete with those of foreigners, at home or abroad. This inability to compete, however, only served to reinforce the Mexican bourgeoisie's dependence on cheap labor, the root cause of the nation's weak accumulation pattern in the first place.

The traditional source of this labor supply was the countryside. Not surprisingly, therefore, Mexico's industrial crisis became symbiotically linked to its agrarian crisis. In 1965 the average rural wage was more than a small-parcel farmer could earn through "self-exploitation" (reliance on farming alone)—a major cause of small farmers' abandonment of more than 2 million hectares of rain-fed farmland in the next decade. Much of this land had provided the bulk of food staples for Mexico's provincial centers and big cities. In addition, wholesale food prices failed to keep pace with the peasants' cost of living (agrarian tools, seeds, and other inputs). Consequently, land monopolization and agribusiness expansion dispossessed peasants in ever growing numbers. Peasant emigration to the cities and to the United States accelerated.[3]

A drought in 1979-1980 compounded Mexico's agrarian problem. In 1980, the nation had to import a quarter of its nutritional needs, mostly from the United States. By 1981, Mexico's imports of basic foodstuffs were greater than its agricultural exports. This reduced the state's financial resources. Short of finding other sources of funding, such as taxing big business or increasing other exports, the state had less financial ability to provide public housing, sanitation, or other services for the mushrooming *colonias proletarias*.

In addition, the TNCs quadrupled their investments in Mexico during the 1970s, elevating the level of capital needed for the creation of each new job. Mexican industrialists' productivity problems structurally worsened with their competitive disadvantages vis-à-vis the TNCs. Mexico's self-reproducing pattern of limited capital accumulation deepened. Millions of the unemployed and subemployed were forced to undertake the petty but useful economic activities described at the end of Chapter 6, or equally useful labor performed as migrant workers in the United States. These activities in turn retarded poor people's development of a more organized political or class-conscious response to oppression, thereby helping to perpetuate the cycle of low wages, low social productivity, non-competitiveness of Mexican industry—and imperialism's relative economic hold over Mexico.

As already noted, a huge part of Mexico's economic surplus never filtered down to the masses or even stayed in the country. Using official figures, economist Edur Velasco Arregui concludes that, under neoliberalism, Mexico's transfer of value overseas was equivalent to 15 percent of net internal private investment inside the United States in 1996, a hefty contribution by Mexico to the international restructuring of production.

This international restructuring, sometimes mistakenly called "economic globalization," started in earnest after the general economic crisis in world capitalism touched off by the 1973 recession. Restructuring accompanied the winding down of the Vietnam War and uneven ending of the Cold War. It responded to a typical capitalist crisis of overproduction, with more goods produced chasing fewer outlets for their consumption. Most U.S. and European corporate profit rates peaked in the mid-1960s and began declining after that. So to recuperate their rates of profit and expand their markets, Western corporations sought a bigger world market and lower production costs through TNC investments overseas, free trade agreements, and, especially in the case of U.S. capital, the "lean and mean" worker dismissal policies of neoliberalism and the "runaway plant" strategy of setting up assembly plants in low-cost labor areas like Mexico. By 1994, U.S.-based TNCs employed 40 percent of their personnel in third world nations, and conducted a third of their internal trade with affiliates in those nations.[4]

Corporate moguls also sought new sources of capital through financial speculation and the expansion of stock markets in Asia and Latin America, especially Mexico. This had the effect of creating and then overheating financial bubbles that eventually burst, first in Mexico (1982, 1994-1995) and later in Asia (1997-1998). Because of the resultant worker layoffs and severe IMF-imposed austerity programs of "wage stabilization," "budget balancing," and "privatization," the working people of Mexico and Asia ended up absorbing most of the costs of these debacles.

In Velasco Arregui's felicitous phrasing, under neoliberalism the "transfer of surplus from the periphery to the industrialized center" accelerated. In the case of Mexico, neoliberal policies concentrated investments "in small islands of modernity, enclaves of the globalized economy." This was known as the *maquiladorization* of Mexico. Velasco Arregui has noted that, outside the *maquiladora* sector, industrial expansion in Mexico was limited to capital-intensive areas that provided very few jobs, such as transportation equipment, metallurgical production, and petrochemicals. For every new job created, there were at least ten new young people entering the job market.[5]

Starting in the late 1980s and early 1990s, but especially from 1994 to 1998, the number of *maquiladora* plants in Mexico quintupled to nearly 4,000. TNCs were highly attracted by Mexico's declining wage and union structure and the state's lax enforcement of environmental standards.[6]

Most of the new *maquiladora* plants' productive apparatuses were capital-intensive and high-tech, including the use of robotics in automotive.[7] There was little linkage between the *maquila* sector's production and Mexico's home market, as the top ranks of high-tech knowledge remained in foreign hands and only 1.4 percent of *maquila* inputs were obtained from Mexican companies, down from 2 percent before NAFTA's implementation in 1994.[8]

More than 1,000 *maquiladoras* were set up in Mexico after NAFTA went into effect, a time when the hourly wage differential between the United States and Mexico reached a whopping 12 to 1. The number of Mexicans employed in the *maquila* sector, 75 percent female, rose from about one-half million in 1993 to

1 million by the end of 1998. This was far fewer than the number of people who were losing their jobs because of the shutting down of tens of thousands of Mexican manufacturing plants unable to compete with cheaper imports from Asia and the United States under NAFTA's free trade provisions.

Many Mexican employees in the *maquila* sector were graduates of universities, technical institutes, and high schools. Others had an elementary school education or less. The newer technologies were so automatic and routine in their operations, however, that often employee educational or skill requirements on the assembly lines were minimal. Regardless of prior skill or educational background, Mexican workers often exceeded their U.S. counterparts in the intensity, quality, and productivity of their labor. This reality, along with the downward pressure on wages caused by the superabundance of surplus labor in Mexico, proved a dream come true for the TNCs. By 1990, *maquila* wages were lower than those of East Asia.[9]

In Mexico, Japanese and Korean *maquiladoras* appeared alongside the more numerous U.S. ones; some Mexican capitalists invested in the *maquila* sector as well. From 1994 to 1996, while Mexico's GDP annual growth rate fell from 2 percent to a negative 607 percent, the rate of production increase in the *maquila* sector was skyrocketing 30 percent.[10] Almost all the value added in Mexico through this *maquila* production went abroad. It showed up in export statistics as 40 percent of the dollar value of Mexico's exports, not far behind petroleum products. In reality, however, much of it consisted of sales by TNCs and represented TNC profits.

Under neoliberalism, despite the dramatic drop in real wages and the sharp increase in the upper classes' portion of income in Mexico (see Tables 5 and 6), Mexico's net domestic savings plummeted 13 points from 18.5 percent of GDP in 1981 to 5.4 percent of GDP in 1994—an equivalent of $87 billion *annually*. If all that money was not saved inside Mexico, then where did it go?

Using internationally recognized and meticulously cautious accounting techniques, Velasco Arregui concludes that unequal exchange in international trade siphoned off $30 billion of the "missing" $87 billion a year. Of the $30 billion amount, $10 billion came from a 50 percent decline in Mexico's terms of trade, and $20 billion from TNC "in-house" *maquiladora* transactions using the tricks of "transfer-pricing" explained in Chapter 5. (On terms of trade, see Table 15.) Another $17 billion left Mexico in service payments on the foreign debt and profit remittances and patent or royalty fees to TNCs. An additional $4 billion a year left in the form of "flight capital," or "deposits by Mexican residents in the international banking system."

The equivalent of another $6 billion left Mexico in the form of the portion of wages paid the Mexican workforce that went to family members who emigrated to the United States, minus the emigrants' dollar remittances to Mexico. In effect, this paid for the production of labor power, or reproduction of the workforce, which takes place on a daily and generational basis and involves the unpaid labor of women. Because of the difficulty in estimating the dollar value of this unpaid women's labor, the amount of $6 billion is far lower than the actual dollar value expended on producing the emigrant labor power. The remaining $30 billion, Velasco Arregui concludes, went for the "conspicuous consumption" of Mexico's upper classes and "the high rates of depreciation" of machinery deriving from "the Mexican bourgeoisie's inability to develop technology."

Mexico's continuing post-Second World War trade deficit (except during the first decade of rapid industrialization and the later oil boom) was rooted in the colonial legacy of selling commodities to more industrialized countries relatively cheaply and "in exchange" buying commodities dear. Unequal exchange was thus a product of power relations between people in which the labor of generations of Mexican peasants and workers subsidized the economic development of the more industrialized nations.

Naturally, as Mexico's economy stumbled through periodic peso devaluations and debt renegotiations (1976, 1982, 1989, 1994-1995), the PRI increasingly lost any claims to legitimacy. The political and economic powers that dominated Mexico's destiny kept passing the costs of a misdeveloped capitalism and a mismanaged state down the line to the toiling masses. Meanwhile, by most estimates, narco-trafficking added $30 billion a year to the economy, but it was of little use to the state. Indeed, it increased corruption and crime and possibly contributed to assassinations of top PRI leaders, examined in the next chapter.

The high GNP growth rates and monopoly-capitalist nature of Mexico's "miracle years" of semi-industrialization generated new needs in the economy. These included needs at the state level. In order to assert social control, the state increasingly had to affirm its legitimacy through costly programs of limited social reform; yet its legitimacy as a supposed democracy was undermined by ongoing military/police repression of organized popular protest, as well as by corruption in the state. Such contradictions permeated every major state apparatus.

The legitimacy of the state thus required compromises. But these compromises were always conditioned by the state's role as the agent of monopoly capital and the state's own economic interests within state areas of production (as well as in the subsequent privatization of state companies). This pro-bourgeois, antilabor tendency on the part of Mexico's corporatist state continuously created friction even with class-collaborationist labor leaders like CTM boss Fidel Velázquez and his successors. The *charros,* after all, were more directly connected than the state to the proletariat, and so had to "deliver the goods" to the workers to at least a minimal degree.

As rank-and-file workers in the late 1960s and early 1970s began to organize themselves to demand trade union democracy, the *charros* had to address workers' political demands as well. For example, in mid-1977, Velázquez momentarily withdrew CTM's commitment to a 10 percent ceiling on wage increments and demagogically gave lip service to the need for "greater democracy" inside CTM. This exemplified the way pressures from below were mediated repeatedly within all state apparatuses.

In spite of their receiving favored treatment by the state, the Mexican bourgeoisie were challenged to assert their class hegemony inside the government per se. The foreign bourgeoisie by definition was excluded, since it was not Mexican. Indeed, in its U.S. form, foreign capital and its political and military representatives had constituted the only external enemy Mexico had ever had to take seriously in the twentieth century, as witness the U.S. interventions in the 1906-1941 period laid out earlier in Tables 3 and 4. For its part, the Mexican bourgeoisie had always been too weak vis-à-vis other internal and external forces to manipulate the government as an instrument of *only* its interests. Nonetheless, the most important weapon in the Mexican bourgeoisie's political arsenal was the authoritarian-technocratic state, a state the bourgeoisie influenced but did not, strictly speaking, control.

For these reasons, many of the traditional democratic tasks of earlier bourgeois revolutions, such as the creation of credible free elections, the guarantee of basic civil liberties, and the freedom to organize, had fallen on the shoulders of Mexico's intermediate classes and lower classes. Until the 1980s, democratic demands in Mexico, like other reformist demands, had derived their social force and political impact from the working classes and disaffected members of the intermediate classes. In fact, these were the people who expressed democratic demands, *not* the bourgeoisie, which advocated their suppression or else their diversion into "safe" (*i.e.*, state-regulated) channels. Only to the degree that the class struggle escalated and the old corporatist state model's legitimacy disintegrated did growing numbers of Mexico's bourgeois fractions take up public political activism.

1968 Student Revolt

State policies not only helped dispossess people from their lands, expand a low-wage work force, and control organized labor, but also contributed to the creation of a bloated sector of intermediate classes—in small businesses and the professions, as well as in the ranks of an over-staffed government bureaucracy. Mexico, by producing or importing countless luxury consumer goods instead of increasing output of affordable basic necessities, was satisfying the upwardly mobile yearnings of the expanding intermediate classes. This was part of what some observers called the "Americanization" of Mexico in the post-Second World War period. Students from the regularly employed working class and the intermediate classes found their expectations expanding, but good job opportunities contracting.

Table 15

Debt Repayment and Foreign Trade, 1980-1995 (in Billions of U.S. dollars)

Year	Interest & Amortization	Imports	Exports	Exports as % of Imports
1980	9.9	21.1	18	86
1985	14.3	18.4	26.8	146
1990	14.7	41.6	40.7	98
1993	18.1	65.4	51.9	79.4
1994	20.3	79.4	60.8	76.7
1995	25.8	72.4	79.5	109.8
1996	33.1	89.5	96	107.3

Sources: Poder Ejecutivo Federal, *Informes de Gobierno*; Banco de México, *Indicadores Económicos*.

They found that success in job hunting often depended on having good contacts inside an ever more rigid, ingrown, and "closed" PRI. Each new attempt at democratizing the PRI failed. For example, in the early 1960s, incoming PRI president Carlos Madrazo sought to introduce party democracy by phases, only to be promptly removed from his position. Old PRI officials never forgave him, accusing him of backing the 1968 student uprising; shortly afterward he died mysteriously in a plane crash.

As the secrecy of PRI's internal workings and the certainty of its electoral victories became ever more obvious, growing numbers stayed away from the polls. Mexicans grew cynical about their political institutions and the widespread corruption those institutions encouraged in everyday life.

So bankrupt was the PRI's democratic mythology that growing numbers of dissidents no longer considered entrance into the party a politically viable alternative. Given Madrazo's failure and the advancing rigidity and old age of the political system, much popular protest had to be expressed through direct action in factory, field, and school, as well as in the streets.

As the "economic miracle" revealed itself in the late 1960s and early 1970s to be an economic debacle for the majority of Mexicans, frustrated youth turned to political agitation, even guerrilla warfare, and disgruntled workers introduced a new labor militancy to the nation's politics. The urban and rural poor began organizing themselves independently of the PRI.

This nationwide social eruption was initially sparked not by workers or peasants but by students, long a politically volatile element in Mexican society. As in the rest of Latin America, starting in the 1960s, the hopes for revolutionary— or at least democratic—change raised by the Cuban Revolution stimulated among Mexican youth a new politics of social agitation that elicited fierce state repression. Young people were fired up by the humanist and socialist ideals of Ernesto "Che" Guevara. Simultaneously, a new "theology of liberation" emerged among Mexican Catholic youth, inspired in part by Colombia's guerrilla priest Camilo Torres.

Some of Mexico's young people saw themselves as a part of an international community of youth that marked the late 1960s protest movements. The values they championed were honesty, freedom, and sharing, the opposite of the hypocrisy, authoritarianism, and selfishness they perceived in the PRI's state. Socialized in an inspiring nationalist mythology of Morelos, Juárez, Ricardo Flores Magón, Zapata, and Lázaro Cárdenas, these youth saw their leaders following policies which were diametrically opposed to the professed ideals. They wanted to rescue these ideals "from their 'safe' entombment as statues, names of plazas and boulevards, and neon-lit slogans on walls."[11]

The political ideologies of the 1968 student revolt in Mexico varied from rather traditional reformism to a rich blend of Flores Magonista, Zapatista, Guevarista, Marxist (including Trotskyist and Maoist), and Catholic radicalism that called for a worker-peasant-student alliance. This meant confronting the ruling class and the state directly.

Mexico's government had quickly recognized the Bolivian and Cuban revolutions of 1952 and 1959, claiming that Mexico was the first Latin American country to have had a revolution and so did not need another one. In schools and workplaces the government trumpeted a revolutionary heritage, providing Mexicans with an imagery of their own victories against oppression. *Indigenismo* and acts of celebration of the Indian heritage served to mask the exploitation of the nation's first inhabitants. PRI politicians talked up agrarian reform and "profit-sharing," but did little.

There were at least three other reasons that the state's system of ideological persuasion proved ineffective, especially with students. First, the traditional techniques of co-optation had been exposed and criticized, as had their stop-gap nature. Second, state institutions increasingly were unable to pay off their constituents at a level commensurate with the PRI's populist rhetoric or the public's expectations. Finally, students were in a personally freer situation than were workers or peasants. Conscious of the dangers of co-optation, they were less easily co-opted.

The gigantic democratic movement ignited by Mexico's students in July 1968 actually started out as a minor affair involving military and police repression of some streetfighting between students from a vocational school and a preparatory high school. As the protest against state violence spread, previously quarreling vocational and preparatory school student organizations united with the more leftist student organization of the National University (UNAM) to form the National Strike Council (CNH). Soon, demonstrations of half a million people flowed down the capital's Paseo de Ia Reforma, calling for an end to state violence and the start of democracy.

Portions of the less affluent layers of the intermediate classes joined the mass marches. Along with a disappointing wage increase, government employees were indignant and bitter at the dislocation caused by the state's preparations for the October 1968 Olympic Games. The spectacle of their government spending huge sums of money for the pleasure of foreigners, the price increases, and the government's refusal to allow them to take days off during the forthcoming games only increased their resentment.

Peasants, slum dwellers, and workers, all harboring long-standing grievances, also began to join forces with the student militants, calling for democratization of the PRI's peasant and worker sectors. Fearful of the contagion of the students' democratic demands, the CTM leadership struck a deal with the government whereby they obtained improved wages for CTM members in exchange for not interfering with repression of the student strike. The government of President Gustavo Díaz Ordaz wished to take decisive action before the opening of the Olympic Games. So did the U.S. Central Intelligence Agency (CIA), which had dispatched Philip Agee and other agents to Mexico City to see what they could do.

Ever since the outbreak of the Cold War, but especially after the Cuban Revolution, the CIA had cultivated elements inside Mexico's most important ministry, the Interior Ministry (*Gobernación*). President Díaz Ordaz, himself a former interior minister under the previous president, huddled in August with his interior minister, Luis Echeverría (who had received earlier CIA briefings and would later, in 1970, become president). Together, the two top civilian officials of Mexico decided to call out the army. In violation of the Latin American tradition of university autonomy, soldiers invaded UNAM and took several thousand prisoners (including teachers, staff, and parents of students). CNH went underground. By late September, Mexico City glittered with burning jeeps, overturned buses, and barricades.

Then, on October 2, 1968, unarmed student demonstrators marched into downtown Mexico City's housing project area of the Plaza Tlatelolco. As feeder marches of peasants and workers began to arrive, the army and police opened fire with automatic weapons. People ran to a nearby cathedral for shelter from the bullets, but the doors were locked against them. By the time the smoke cleared, an estimated 500 were dead, 2,500 wounded, and 1,500 on their way to jail. In the next days, students circulated photographs of old women impaled on bayonets and children with their heads blown off. CIA agent Agee was shocked and later quit the agency, declaring that what happened at Plaza Tlatelolco "is happening all over the world to people trying to change the system."[12]

Not since the times of Porfino Díaz had a massacre on such a gruesome scale taken place. Mexico had a second generation of political prisoners to join those from the 1950s, the leaders of the railroad strike described in Chapter 5. The nation's boasted political stability had come to a bloody and tragic end. A new era of crisis for the PRI had begun.

Post-1968 Ferment

President Luis Echeverría (1970-1976) started his administration by promising a "democratic opening" ("*apertura democrática*," a choice of words that publicly recognized the authoritarian character of the state). But on June 10, 1971, when thousands of Mexico's students and workers marched in Mexico City to demand basic political rights and the release of all political prisoners, police and goon squads attacked them, killing 11 and wounding more than 200. Some thirty-five "disappeared" (captured and probably executed).

Frustrated student and peasant militants took up rural guerrilla warfare. Most of it was snuffed out by the military. Between 1969 and 1975 a dozen urban guerrilla groups carried out spectacular actions—airplane hijackings, bank robberies, bombings of buildings, kidnappings, and police ambushes. Military intelligence was given the task of hunting them down, and by 1975 the urban armed struggle was broken.

Both the rural and the urban guerrilla movements, though unsuccessful, momentarily radicalized political struggle, especially among poor peasants and urban slum dwellers. In 1974, for instance, the Land and Liberty Settlement of San Luis Potosí extended its urban land occupations into Tamaulipas, Zacatecas, and Veracruz. Its leader, Eusebio García, was assassinated in 1976, but it continued active after that. In 1975, rural *jornaleros* (day laborers), migrant workers, and peasants founded the Independent Confederation of Farm Workers and Peasants (CIOAC), which worked closely with the Mexican Communist Party.

In the countryside the pace of peasant land takeovers rose dramatically in the mid-1970s. As in the past, the army patrolled the troubled zones. Many mestizo and Indian peasants were "disappeared," tortured, even massacred, especially in impoverished states like Oaxaca, Chiapas, Guerrero, and Hidalgo. On orders from local *caciques,* some 500 Triquis of Oaxaca were murdered in the 1970s, and a similar reign of terror was imposed on the Indian majority of the population of the southern border state of Chiapas. In the late 1970s, more than 200 protesting peasants of the Huasteca disappeared or were assassinated. Throughout Mexico, peasants who refused to join the PRI's CNC were routinely packed off to jail.

The character of peasant demands and tactics varied with the nature of peasant activities. Farmworkers launched new unions and struck for better wages and working conditions. The CTM responded by incorporating *jornaleros* into its ranks. It claimed to have enrolled more than 200,000 of them by 1981. Owners of small farms organized for better and fairer prices for their products.

Besides repossessing their lands by armed force, peasants typically occupied and even dynamited municipal offices, took hostages, went on long marches (as far as Mexico City), and disrupted production. Peasants also mobilized against state authorities to demand the release of political prisoners, the punishment of assassins, the breaking up of paramilitary goon squads, an end to the misuse of public funds, and the removal of *caciques* or venal functionaries.

As new independent peasant organizations emerged in the 1970s, they began to form alliances with other sectors of the population—urban squatters (known in the countryside and cities alike as *paracaidistas* or "parachutists" for their sudden seizing of a piece of land), rank-and-file labor militants, teachers, students, and left-wing political organizations. These alliances often proved shaky, however, because of differences over goals and tactics, as happened in the case of Oaxaca's Worker-Peasant-Student Coalition (COCEO) and Coalition of the Isthmus (COCEI). Even so, COCEO forced out a governor in 1977 and COCEI won municipal elections in Juchitán in the 1980s only to be repeatedly repressed.

To divide or co-opt the independent peasant groups, the Echeverría administration stepped up its demagogic populism. In 1975, it launched the *Pacto de Ocampo*. This agreement brought together under the hegemony of the PRI's CNC several major independent peasant organizations in order to support Echeverría's modest land-distribution program and experiments in "collectivization" of a few *ejidos*. Some of the co-opted peasant organizations remained loyal state supporters into the 1990s.

In 1975, the Coalition of Yaqui and Mayo Valley Ejidos sparked the occupation of lands in northwest Mexico and forced President Echeverría to expropriate a *latifundio* of the daughter of ex-President Calles. Echeverría also returned some of the lands held by Sonoran land-sharks to their original owners. The land handed over did not include that controlled by flourishing agribusinesses. The issuance of restraining orders (writs of *amparo*) against the president's expropriation and a "lockout" by the rural bourgeoisie and much of the Monterrey group further diluted the impact of Echeverría's populist land reform. The next president, José López Portillo (1976-1982), paid handsome indemnities to the affected landlords, declared future land invasions a federal crime, and in general conformed to the bidding of the agrarian bourgeoisie.

The most serious challenge to the PRI and government authority in the 1970s came from the ranks of organized labor, where an independent rank-and-file movement for union democracy emerged among some of the nation's best-paid workers. The proletariat's political consciousness had been expanding as immense numbers of industrial workers experienced the concentration, discipline, and unification in single workplaces imposed by the spread of monopoly capital. After 1968, younger workers were more open to Marxist ideas, solidarity with other sectors in revolt at home and abroad, and radical social change. They found their avenues for improving wages and working conditions blocked by *charro* union leaders allied with employers.

In less than a decade, the Independent Worker Unity (UOI, founded in 1972) gained control over four big autoworker unions and 80 percent of the aviation industry's unionized workers. It also established "workers' commissions" (radical caucuses) in the rail, petroleum, metallurgy, steel, telephone, and electrical workers' unions. But it faced severe repression. For example, a 120-day strike of more than 600 workers at the Spicer auto-axle plant was crushed by army troops and CTM goons; the strikers were fired.[13]

A more numerous though less radical wing of the new labor militancy, the "democratic tendency," gained leverage in several major industrial sectors. It preferred to "work within the system" and respect "*el señor presidente*," vowing to "defend the nation and the presidential institution." The leaders of the "democratic tendency" thereby blurred the class nature of the democratic insurgency, reinforced the rule of the PRI, and slandered progressives and independent labor militants as "antinational" or "communist" deviants who lacked respect for the presidency.

In November 1975, the democratic tendency of the electrical workers' union SUTERM sparked a street demonstration of a quarter of a million people in Mexico City, the largest since 1968. These workers had sympathizers inside the PRI who eventually called themselves by the same name—*tendencia democrática* (later, *corriente democrática,* which included the 1988 anti-PRI presidential candidate Cuauhtémoc Cárdenas).

From 1973 through 1977, the new labor militancy generated about 3,600 strikes and "labor conflicts" involving between 1 and 2 million industrial workers. (Because "illegal" and "nonexistent" strikes were only roughly estimated, figures varied widely.) University students, bank employees, and doctors also went on strike, as did workers in shoe, chemical-pharmaceutical, metallurgical-mining, electrical, rail, and agricultural enterprises.

Women made up large minorities or even majorities in several of the most progressive unions where the new labor insurgency took root, such as the 350,000-strong National Union of Social Security Workers, SNTSS, where women gained positions as union officers. The Authentic Labor Front (FAT, founded in 1960 as a Roman Catholic federation) began fighting for an independent labor unionism with a stronger feminist consciousness. Like male workers, women faced the state's use of armed force and intimidation to break their strikes, such as those launched by militant women at the state telephone company TELMEX in the 1970s and 1980s.

As radical students, teachers, and former guerrillas joined with peasants and workers to marshal wider popular alliances during the Echeverría years, the government unleashed armed goons called "The Hawks" (*los halcones*), who shot down peaceful demonstrators. Armed thugs known as *porros* roamed the hallways of high schools and colleges, beating up political dissidents. Hundreds of people were kidnapped and disappeared. Courageous Mexican intellectuals publicly compared the PRI government's actions to Argentina's 1970s "dirty war," notorious for the bloody elimination of thousands of accused dissidents.

Mexico's paramilitary right-wing goon squads were suspected of being assisted by the CIA, as were other such groups in Latin America. These suspicions were reinforced when, in February 1977, the *New York Times* reported that Echeverría had earlier accepted money from the CIA when serving as Díaz Ordaz's minister of interior.

In 1976, the "democratic tendency" electrical workers brought together the university unions and more than 300 organizations to form the National Front of Labor, Peasant, and Popular Insurgency. The *electricistas* then launched a nationwide strike. On July 16, 1976, "*el señor presidente*" showed his respect for the "democratic tendency" by calling out the army. Troops invaded and occupied all major electrical installations to break the strike. Hundreds of strikers were subsequently fired. A year later, soldiers invaded UNAM to break a major strike by university employees that was attracting thousands of supporters from the rest of the insurgent labor movement. The outlawed Mexican Communist Party (PCM) was influential in the UNAM strike. The state's acts of repression dealt a very severe blow to the new labor militancy.

Speaking a populist language, President Echeverría eventually managed to woo some student and guerrilla dissidents back into the official "revolutionary family," giving them intermediate positions in various social agencies. With other third world presidents, Echeverría lambasted the TNCs and called for a "new international economic order" (approved by the United Nations in 1974). He also attempted to build bridges with Mexican communities in the United States by currying favor with prominent leaders of the Chicano movement.

President Echeverría levied some tokenistic taxes on the rich, funded the collectivization of select *ejidos,* and steered a small part of the nation's trade toward Europe and Japan. But his modest reforms were hampered by the lack of an adequate class base (and thus support) among the masses, a dishonest and inefficient bureaucracy, and a fiscal crisis aggravated by the international recession of 1973-1975 and foreign pressures to reduce the state debt. IMF pressures forced a nearly 100 percent devaluation of the peso in late 1976, practically doubling the real foreign debt (to almost $50 billion), as well as the real costs of imported capital goods—to the detriment of non-monopoly firms and the advantage of the TNCs.

Echeverría's attempts to develop the production goods industry further indebted Mexico. A ninefold rise in production goods imports in the 1970s contributed heavily to a sixfold increase in the public sector foreign debt, a trend that worsened over time. (Table 16 shows figures for imported production goods that underestimate the actual costs since they represent only the

Table 16

Production Goods Imported and Public Foreign Debt, 1980-1995
(In Billions of U.S. dollars)

Year	Capital Goods	Raw Materials	Total Production Goods	Public Sector Foreign Debt
1980	8.8	5.6	14.4	33.8
1985	10.8	4.6	15.4	72.7
1990	24.6	8.5	33.1	77.8
1995	24	12.5	36.5	100.9

Sources: Poder Ejecutivo Federal, *Informes de Gobierno*; Banco de México, *Indicadores del Sector Externo*.

declared value of specific goods and omit various other costs associated with their importation.) The total cost of production goods imports averaged out to a third of the public sector's foreign debt. Just the interest and amortization payments on the same debt averaged from one half to one third of the dollar value of all Mexico's exports (see Table 15). Mexico had to run faster just to stay in place.

Meanwhile, the domestic and foreign bourgeoisies began organizing themselves to increase their flagging, if still dominant, influence over the state. Big businessmen of the Monterrey group were alarmed by Echeverría's "collectivist" rhetoric, as were several U.S.-based TNCs whose executives alerted Washington to the troubles brewing "in our own back yard." The FBI and CIA, as evidenced by documents released later under the Freedom of Information Act, were ordered to destabilize the Echeverría government.

Operating through the office of the legal attaché in the American Embassy, the FBI infiltrated Mexico's ministries of the interior, foreign affairs, national defense, public education, and the attorney general's office. FBI agents sponsored acts of terrorism in order to blame them on Mexico's left and to divide the PRI's opposition. FBI Director J. Edgar Hoover wrote the legal attaché of his "pleasure at the wave of night machine gunnings" and congratulated him for the "detonation of strategic and effective bombs."[14]

The Mexican bourgeoisie closed ranks in 1975 to form the powerful Management Coordinating Council (CCE), further constraining the state's room for maneuver. Declaring the need for big business to participate more openly in the nation's political life, CCE brought together the heads of ABM, CMHN, CONCAMIN, CONCANACO, COPARMEX, and other capitalist groups. The CCE coordinated the major fractions of the big and medium-size bourgeoisie and attempted to augment monopoly capital's already dominant influence on the state.

The "central fraction" (big finance capital based in Mexico City) and the Monterrey group and northern bourgeoisie's right-wing COPARMEX spearheaded CCE's founding. Public statements by two of their leading representatives, Agustín F. Legorreta and Andrés Marcelo Sada respectively, reflected their mission. "Not private enterprise versus the state but private enterprise with the state," said Legorreta, "the mixed economy is the guarantee that Mexico will follow the road of democracy and freedom."[15] "Never again," added Sada, would big business assume "second-class citizen status vis-à-vis the national political environment."[16]

While maintaining the bourgeoisie's formal separation from the state, the CCE sought to assure its supremacy over the summit of the state techno-bureaucracy by *insisting* that the state act as guarantor of the bourgeoisie's interests. The CCE was clearly dominated by the powerful businessmen of the CMHN. The CCE immediately spoke out publicly to court "middle-class voters" and champion the "privatization" of state enterprises. Aware of the destabilization campaign being mounted by the CIA, Sada, and other reactionary forces, however, the Echeverría administration initially bristled at this type of activity. Secretary of Finance José López Portillo publicly attacked the CCE and the forces of "nazi-fascism."[17]

The CCE then played a central role in the politicking around the presidential succession of 1976. It could not choose the next president, but it at least could influence his policies. Echeverría chose López Portillo, who, once inaugurated as president, dropped his populist anti-fascist rhetoric and implemented an IMF-style austerity program and a CCE-approved "alliance for production."

President López Portillo also dutifully appointed prominent bourgeois figures to his administration—men like PEMEX director Jorge Díaz Serrano, an associate in Texas business enterprises with one-time CIA head and future U.S. President George Bush. Furthermore, at the CCE's behest, López Portillo approved a "multiple banking" (i.e., non-specialized banking) law that made it possible for the nation's 243 private banks to consolidate into 63 big ones by 1981.[18] In brief, the formation of the CCE produced a more direct presence of the big bourgeoisie inside the corporatist state, thereby facilitating, even more than before, monopoly capital's expansion.

The sharpened labor-capital conflicts of the 1970s were producing among both the workers and the bourgeoisie a critical questioning of the traditional forms of state populist posturing, *charrismo, caciquismo,* and state bureaucratic management of corporatist institutions. Capitalist groups, united in the CCE, saw that the *charro*/rank-and-file conflict was reducing labor's productivity, while growing numbers of proletarians saw *charrismo* as an obstacle to their advance. The political "class" that traditionally had mediated conflicts between classes could no longer easily control these forces. It found its demagogic populism ("politics of the masses") challenged by both major classes. During the final days of the Echeverría regime, rumors that tanks were moving in the streets of Mexico City in preparation for a military coup were taken seriously—a clear sign of the gravity of the state's incipient crisis.

Without sufficient resources to continue buying off dissidents, President Echeverría and his successor López Portillo caved in to the pressures of Mexico's bourgeoisie, the IMF, the U.S. government, and the PRI's old guard (led by CTM's Velázquez). It militarily crushed the labor and student strikes of 1976-1977. Jail doors clanged shut on Echeverría's "democratic opening," as the state bowed to the old economic order of the IMF—peso devaluations, wage freezes, and more profitable operating conditions for private investment. In 1977 the government granted CTM's Velázquez effective control over the National Housing Institute and the new Workers' Bank in exchange for his promise to cooperate with a 10 percent ceiling (*tope*) on wage hikes imposed by incoming President López Portillo at the behest of the IMF.

The savage acts of repression of 1976-1977 and the state's imposition of *topes* caused all of labor to focus the fight on defending earlier economic gains. This defensive posture of labor meant that the number of strikes dropped.[19] The new labor insurgency continued to gain some recruits, but the *charros,* old and new, used the defensive "economist" labor protests to reassert influence over the democratic tendency. For one thing, the *charros* were able to win certain concessions from employers or the state, which undercut the democratic tendency's strength. On the other hand, a second rank of democratizers, who had held back in the earlier period, came to the fore in some CT unions.

Independent leftist labor organizers began emphasizing more than ever the need for greater solidarity with other sectors of the population. A telling example was the long strike in Monclova (Caohuila), which shook the joint state-private steel complex Altos Hornos de México. Responding to Mexico's unemployment problem, these steelworkers, among the nation's best paid, insisted that there be more job openings. Many of their economic demands were met. In other words, far from behaving like a spoiled "labor aristocracy," some industrial employees voiced a *class* solidarity in the larger struggle to democratize Mexico. Similar tendencies of broadening labor's struggle to include the irregularly employed showed up in 1977 during the sixty-two day strike at General Motors, among a number of other strikes.

From 1980 to 1982, a wave of strikes against wage ceilings (*topes*) broke out in automotive, rubber, mining, oil, steel, metallurgy, electric, textiles, food processing, plastics, the telephone and postal services, airlines, and bus transport. Even doctors, nurses, students, teachers, and baseball players went on strike. Some 3,200 GM workers sustained a 106-day strike against the *topes.* On May Day of 1981, up to 300,000 workers heeded a call by the independents'

UOI. They mounted a noisy street demonstration, chanting anti-*charro*, pro-democracy slogans.

Eventually, after co-optation and repression failed, the delegitimized corporatist state granted wage hikes that approximated the rate of inflation. At the same time, aviation, automotive, and rubber workers discovered that the UOI's leader, a purportedly leftist lawyer, was in cahoots with the government. The state hoped to use this lawyer's "Marxist" credentials to outflank the rest of the new labor insurgency. So the workers launched a movement to cleanse their workplaces of both his followers and the CTM *charros*. UOI eventually regrouped as the aforementioned CIOAC.

The new labor militancy spread to the immiserated masses—many of whom were the last hired and first fired by both big and small industry. For example, temporary workers constructing the Tula oil refinery walked off the job in 1976, and those building the Cactus petrochemical plant in Chiapas sustained a militant strike in 1977. In 1976-1977 there were unusually large numbers of protest actions and strikes in small and medium-size industries as well.

Class/Gender Struggles

Just as the different fractions of the bourgeoisie began uniting via the CCE, so Mexico's social movements of the 1970s sought to "nationalize" their struggle. Peasants founded the Coordinating Center of Independent Revolutionary Peasants in 1977. Within two years, it had expanded into the much larger National Plan of Ayala Coordinating Committee (CNPA), whose rallying cry of "Land to the tiller!" galvanized rural workers throughout the nation.

In the ranks of the nonunionized and irregularly employed segments of the urban proletariat, several organizations sprang up and moved to unify nationally as well. In 1979, the National Network of *Colonias Populares* brought together fourteen large organizations of slum dwellers. The urban social movements, largely female in composition, started building coalitions with the democratic tendency, independent unionists, students, and the peasants' CNPA.[20]

All this was happening at a time when both foreign and Mexican capitalists, in response to the 1973 recession and the new labor militancy, were intensifying their use and exploitation of easily replaceable labor. The industrial productive process was becoming marked by strong fragmentation of the work force; deskilling of work and its division into limited, simple tasks; degradation of labor; "feminization" of the work force; and termination-rotation of workers. By making most industrial production consist of interchangeable tasks performable by anyone, capitalists were contributing to an atomization and decomposition of the working class. The division, dequalification, and rotation of labor helped separate workers economically, socially, and politically.

On the other hand, by attracting (even if temporarily) new elements into the industrial process of work, especially women and rural migrants, the same capitalist industrial restructuralization served to concentrate, in one social setting, thousands of persons whose backgrounds were usually individualized (the home, the village, etc.). The new shared social and work experiences of these recruits to the industrial work force created a social-political base for the organization of a rapidly growing fraction of the working class. For example, in the face of *machismo, charrismo*, and likely job loss, women employees in northern Mexico's *maquiladora* plants began forming some unions in the 1970s. Plant managers there resisted their efforts to organize and constantly rotated the labor force. Some companies, however, adjusted by accepting CTM-controlled unions as a means of keeping order on the shop floor.

Meanwhile, families of the disappeared banded together to demand that the government return more than 800 of their loved ones. They were led by Rosario Ibarra de Piedra, a housewife. The mother of one of Mexico's disappeared political dissidents, Ibarra de Piedra became affectionately known as "La señora" and ran in the next two elections as Mexico's first-ever woman candidate for president in 1982 and 1988, on the ticket of the Revolutionary Workers Party, a Trotskyist group. Subsequent amnesties led to the "discovery" and release of some of these people, as well as a number of political prisoners. At least 200 of the disappeared were reported dead. Some of those remaining were seen in the inner confines of Mexico City's Military Camp No.1, where their incarceration was censured by Amnesty International and other international human rights groups.

The popularity of "La señora" reflected the growing importance of women in politics. In the mid-1970s a Feminist Women's Coalition was formed, and intermediate-class women began publishing feminist magazines like *fem*. Some better off women joined "La señora" in reaching out to oppressed lower class women, particularly the incarcerated and "disappeared." People belonging to left-wing political parties mounted a campaign to legalize abortion, and several activists publicly demanded equal rights for homosexuals.

Upon taking office as president at the end of 1976, López Portillo granted a partial amnesty for political prisoners and made short-lived moves to fight corruption. Seeking, as he put it, "to legalize the fight of the opposition," he reformed the Constitution to make opposition parties part of "the national electoral system." He legalized the Communist Party. In future election campaigns the state would pay for television time for all registered political parties.

López Portillo's "political reform," the first of several by the PRI over the next two decades, increased the portion of minority seats in the Chamber of Deputies to 100, while still reserving 300 for the PRI. The president disingenuously argued that since labor unions already participated in a political party, opposition parties should not be allowed to participate in the unions because that would violate the unions' "freedom of decision."

Mexico's "official" political system in effect consisted of labor unions that were not unions and a ruling political party that was not a party. The unions were political arms of the PRI and the state. The PRI was a small group of top union bureaucrats and the twelve members of the party's national executive committee, plus a few other political bosses of "the revolutionary family." In a corporatist system regulated by a technocratic-authoritarian state, the governing party did not organize the class whose interests it usually served (the bourgeoisie's CCE did that). Nor did the official trade unions genuinely represent the class they nominally served; the democratic tendency and independent unions of the new labor militancy did that.

Under López Portillo's political reform, constitutional amendments, regularly imposed by the PRI throughout its reign in power, sanctioned the permanence of PRI control by speaking of "minority parties" as opposed to "the majority party." Changes in Article 41 of the Constitution made political parties "entities of public interest" that "contribute to the integration of national representation." This raised a danger that if certain contradictions erupted—for example, between the working class and the "national interest" or between public employees and the state—political parties legally might be expected to defend the "public interest" against workers. Similarly, the state's virulent anticommunist (or anti-foreign) campaigns now had a constitutional reinforcement in the notion of "integration of national representation." The constitutional reform also permitted the state to do legally what it had previously done by custom: finance the "entities of public interest," principally the PRI but now also other political parties.

Nonetheless, López Portillo's political reform represented a concession by the state to the mass democratic movements of 1968 and afterward. By acknowledging the existence of left-wing parties, the state recognized for the first time in more than thirty-five years that dissent was legitimate. It also allowed the left to claim a victory in its long struggle to expose the illegitimacy of the prevailing political system and the state's anticommunist justifications of repression. (Why else would it be necessary to institute reform and recognize the Communist Party?) By providing other parties with access to public television, the political reform offered Mexicans a chance to fight for all rights, including a change in electoral boards that would permit democratic competition without built-in definitions of "majority" and "minority," as eventually happened. In sum, the political reform presented progressive forces with new terrain for political struggle while simultaneously relegitimatizing the state.

Until the elections following upon the political reforms of López Portillo and his successors, Mexicans rarely had any chance to vote for left-opposition candidates. Even then there was justified fear that to vote for the left was dangerous since so many leftist activists had disappeared or had been violently repressed. To oppose the PRI, Mexicans traditionally would (safely) vote for the right-wing National Action Party (PAN), the PRI's "loyal opposition."

Mexico's two largest left-wing political parties, the new left PMT (Mexican Workers' Party) and the old left PCM, attempted to take electoral advantage of the political reforms. Emerging out of the student movement of 1968, the PMT started out as a loosely organized group of Marxists and Catholic activists. It had put down roots among workers, peasants, clergy, unemployed, and students in a dozen states, wrapping itself in the populist, nationalist *serape* of the 1917 Constitution.

The PCM was Latin America's oldest Communist party. In an effort to change its Stalinist image, it admitted priests into its ranks, replaced the goal of "dictatorship of the proletariat" with "workers' democratic power," and rebaptized its Marxist-Leninist ideology as "scientific socialism." Most of its members and sympathizers were journalists, scholars, and university students. In the 1979 congressional elections the PCM became the nation's third largest electoral force, garnering 5.4 percent of the vote.[21]

In 1981 the PCM dissolved itself, joining with the PMT and four tiny leftist and liberal parties to form the PSUM (Mexican Unified Socialist Party). Riddled with factionalism, the alliance regrouped in 1986 to 1987 to become the PMS (Mexican Socialist Party). In the 1988 presidential race, it backed Cárdenas. After that, Cárdenas's followers, including most of the PMS and newly arriving dissidents from the PRI, founded the left-of-center Party of the Democratic Revolution (PRD). Previously, PRI dissidents had formed several smaller parties over the years, although most ended up functioning as bought-off "satellites" of the PRI (see Table 17).

The bourgeoisie's CCE critically endorsed López Portillo's "political reform." Most of the bourgeoisie's internal differences were buried now that the CCE was calling the shots.

The main visible line of intra-bourgeois division concerned the best approach to the class threat from below. Some, the so-called radicals, favored an intensification of repression of the burgeoning mass social movements and a return to "basic values" of family, religion, patriotism, work discipline, the free market, and "democratic" elections that big business's candidates could win. Most of the bourgeoisie, including a broad sector of monopoly capital, were known as moderates. They favored some political reform in the hope of isolating the harsher critics and co-opting the softer ones.

Over the next two decades, some moderates in domestic manufacturing turned against the TNCs and NAFTA when they discovered they could not compete with U.S. firms. Also, the bourgeoisie was discovering an opportunity to gain the presidency for themselves through the PAN, which ran for president

Table 17
Mexico's Political Parties

Major parties:

PAN *National Action Party,* founded by Catholic conservatives in 1939 as "sole independent opposition party"; right-populist.

PRD *Party of the Democratic Revolution,* left-of-center party founded after Cárdenas's 1988 "stolen victory"; Cárdenas won 1997 election for mayor of Mexico City, second most powerful elected official. Formed by expelled PRI members led by Cárdenas, with the **PMS** *(Mexican Socialist Party),* a 1987-1988 electoral alliance that backed Cárdenas candidacy and merged with PRD in 1988. The PMS included the **PCM** *(Mexican Communist Party),* founded in 1919, banned in 1929, legalized in 1935, banned again in 1947, re-legalized in 1978. The PCM was dissolved in 1981 when it and a few members of the left-populist **PMT** *(Mexican Workers' Party)* founded the short-lived **PSUM** *(Mexican Unified Socialist Party).* The PMT, much larger than the PCM, was founded in 1974 by new leftists, including Catholic radicals. Most PMT members joined the PRD.

PRI *Institutional Revolutionary Party,* founded in 1929, reorganized in 1938, renamed in 1946; multi-faction ruling party; excluded Cárdenas's "democratic current" from central committee in 1986 (see PARM and PRD) and experienced many defections ever since.

Minor parties:

PARM *Authentic Party of the Mexican Revolution,* founded in 1954 to honor 1917 Revolution; very small; viewed as PRI's shadow or satellite but embraced 1988 Cárdenas candidacy and ran own candidate for president in 1994.

PC *Cardenista Party,* created in mid-1990s; drew off votes from PRD; suspected of being a PRI "satellite."

PDM *Mexican Democratic Party,* founded in 1971 by ultra-rightist Catholics and PAN dissidents.

PPS *Popular Socialist Party,* founded in 1948; a pseudo-left wing "satellite" of PRI; ran own candidates in 1994 elections.

PRT *Revolutionary Workers Party,* Trotskyist, very small; ran first woman presidential candidate in 1982, 1988; in 1997, elected first lesbian to Congress (on PRD ticket).

PST *Socialist Workers Party,* social-democratic, founded in 1973 by new leftists of 1968 and disciples of President Echeverría; "satellite" of PRI; renamed **FCRN** *(Cardenist Front of National Reconstruction)* in 1988 to draw off votes from Cárdenas; became an official party (**PFCRN**) for 1994 elections.

PT *Labor Party,* initially based on urban grassroots defense committees in north, founded in 1990 with PRI support; in 1994, ran charismatic woman presidential candidate Cecilia Soto González, a former ultra-rightist, to draw off votes from PRD.

PVEM *Ecological Green Party of Mexico,* first entered elections in 1994; "satellite" of PRI.

in 1988 a candidate who had once headed COPARMEX and the CCE and had long been considered a PRI ally, Manuel J. Clouthier.

López Portillo's political reform partially achieved its goals in the short run, deflecting or holding back the radicalization of millions of people. But ongoing repression and economic changes played important roles as well. IMF austerity packages and related neoliberal economic policies in the 1980s and 1990s greatly undercut labor's insurgency. Using Mexico's swollen debt as leverage, together with an emergency $1.2 billion loan, the IMF imposed on the incoming López Portillo government restrictive guidelines on the federal budget, trade policies, and wage structure.

López Portillo enforced wage *topes* but let the value of the peso and many market prices "float," leading to galloping inflation. From 1977 to 1980 inflation averaged almost 25 percent a year, wage hikes averaged 14 percent, and worker productivity increases (discounting inflation) averaged 10 percent. In other words, instead of raising wages sufficiently to augment the consumption of the masses and the expansion of the home market, the state and the bourgeoisie opted for the usual limited pattern of capital accumulation: more monopolization and higher prices. By the end of 1982, inflation approached 100 percent.

The state's implementation of IMF recommendations letting prices move ahead of wages—inflation in the name of combating inflation—thus permitted at least a momentary renewal of capital accumulation at the expense of fixed- or low-income groups. A newly introduced value-added tax of 10 percent—in effect a sales tax—further squeezed consumers.

Moreover, in spite of the huge debt, U.S. and other foreign creditors sought to prop up Mexico's economy by pouring in some $3 billion worth of new credits in December 1976 and January 1977. To bail out big private bankers, who had been hurt by the mid-1970s recession, the state's leading financial agencies (Nafinsa, Banco de Mexico, etc.) increased their foreign borrowing. This helped Nafinsa save the private banks, but further jeopardized the state banks, whose dependence on foreign loans undermined the state's autonomy in decisionmaking.

Despite López Portillo's political reform, social protest would not go away. Mexico's poorly paid schoolteachers mobilized for "a living wage." They were members of the National Union of Education Workers (SNTE), which in 1998 had approximately 900,000 members, 70 percent of them female. The SNTE was reputedly Latin America's largest labor union. It composed about 40 percent of the Federation of Public Service Workers' Unions (FSTSE, founded in 1938), which in turn accounted for about a third of CT membership. With their strikes of 1979-1981 and again in the 1980s and 1990s, many of the school teachers tried to keep alive the spirit of the labor militancy of the 1970s.

Blocked by corrupted union leaders, the teachers made their main demand internal trade-union democracy. In the late 1970s and early 1980s they built alliances with other groups in labor and reached out to slum dwellers and peasants. More than one hundred teacher militants were mysteriously killed; many more were hauled off to jail.

Out of the SNTE in poorer states like Chiapas, Oaxaca, and Michoacán emerged the National Coordinating Committee of Education Workers (CNTE), which fought for class independence from both the state and the *charros*. The CNTE had several woman leaders fed up with their second-class status in the SNTE. Bilingual Indian women, mainly from the CNTE, played a pivotal role in keeping the teachers' movement going.

School teachers traditionally enjoyed high levels of respect among Mexico's poor. The CNTE activists showed why. They sparked alliances with peasants and workers in struggle against poverty, *charrismo*, and state violence. In 1982, the CNTE, thirty independent unions, twenty rank-and-file "currents," and grassroots democratic organizations like the peasants' CNPA and the urban poor's National Council of Urban Popular Movements (CONAMUP, formed in 1981) founded the short-lived National Union Coalition (COSINA) to demand an unlimited right to strike, union democracy, and an end to repression and austerity programs. The teachers' insistence on solidarity with workers' and peasants' struggles illustrated how supposedly "middle class" people who were being driven economically toward proletarian living conditions could become an explosive force—especially when the fight began as one against their *own* oppression.[22]

Oil and Debt

Realizing that many citizens were dubious about the PRI's political reform and anti-corruption rhetoric, the PRI also played its oil card. President López Portillo announced in 1977 what the PRI's top bureaucrats had known since 1972: fabulous new oil discoveries in Chiapas and along the Caribbean coast. Development of the new-found oil resources presumably would make all Mexicans prosper. For a while, employment did pick up, at least in those industries affected by oil, helping to defuse the new labor insurgency.

Ironically, it was for political reasons that López Portillo's announcement about the oil bonanza came five years late. Although the PRI inner circle knew that Mexico was the Saudi Arabia of the Caribbean, they also realized that once the bureaucratic pirates broke open the oil treasure chest, the ship of state, despite momentary stabilization, might soon be sacked of its cargo and drift toward the rocks. So they had locked the oil story up in the presidential cabinet and had chosen instead a rhetorical "nationalist" tack of verbally assaulting the TNCs' "looting" of Mexico. But by late 1976 U.S. imperialism and its junior partners in the Mexican bourgeoisie had destabilized the country, pulling out much of their capital in the face of the new labor militancy. Informing the public that he "found the nation on the edge of violence," López Portillo was forced to deal the PRI's trump, the oil card.

Not surprisingly, U.S. President Jimmy Carter came gladhanding down for a visit, the IMF and the World Bank opened their fists with giant loans, and foreign investments flowed back into Mexico. In mid-1981, during a worldwide recession, a group of eighty-two banks in eleven nations extended PEMEX a $4 billion short-term loan to help keep the oil gushing. U.S. banks lent 40 percent of the total. U.S. oil equipment companies experienced a veritable boom, selling PEMEX $2 billion worth of machinery in 1981 alone—an amount equivalent to one-seventh of PEMEX export revenues. In addition, industry in Mexico benefited because it was able to buy PEMEX oil and gas products at one-third their world market value.

For their part, the Mexican people experienced repeated price hikes in hydrocarbon products for their vehicles and homes. López Portillo changed Article 27 of the Constitution to give PEMEX rights over all the land in Mexico. Peasants in Chiapas and elsewhere launched protests against their being dispossessed of lands by PEMEX and against pollution caused by PEMEX enterprises. Grumbled one peasant, "What do we gain from that fabulous wealth if the poor are crying from hunger?"

To assure foreign capital's cooperation in its expensive rush to obtain the equipment and technical know-how required for its sudden expansion of oil production, the Mexican government relaxed its regulatory laws on machinery imports for the petroleum industry and foreign investment in petrochemicals—laws further relaxed under NAFTA's schemes of "a level playing field" for all investors under the rubric of "free competition and trade." Petroleum Law changes in 1959 had already opened the door in secondary petrochemicals to U.S. concerns, and by 1982 there was twice as much capital invested in them as there was in the primary chemical sector. Pharmaceuticals, paints, and synthetic fibers were all U.S.-controlled. The petrochemical industry as a whole was succumbing to foreign capital's domination.

By 1982, Mexico's proven oil reserves were estimated at 72 billion barrels, its probable reserves at 90 to 150 billion, and its potential reserves at 250 billion, not far behind Saudi Arabia. In addition, there existed 200 trillion cubic feet of proven natural gas reserves, and four times that amount of potential gas reserves. In the early 1980s, oil production fluctuated between 1.5 and 3 million barrels a day. Ranking fourth in the world or higher in refining capacity, sales, and oil and petrochemical production, PEMEX extended its exploration and technological development programs into the rest of Latin America, including Cuba, which hoped to obtain most of its oil imports from Mexico.

Officially, the state said it would never send more than half its hydrocarbon exports to any single country, but by 1981 it was sending 80 percent (mostly crude oil) to the United States at prices below those of the largely Middle East-based oil export nations' cartel OPEC. The petro-boom furthered the silent integration of the U.S. and Mexican economies, as Mexico sold "petrobonds" and stock shares of Mexican industry in U.S. money markets. It also opened state bank branches in New York (e.g., Somex, a bank with majority state shares).

Once more in its history Mexico became a monoculture, as petroleum products soon accounted for 75 percent of its export earnings. Over half its GNP derived from oil. In the rush to produce oil for export, the amount of gas lost through flaring was equivalent to enough money to pay the minimum wage for half a million Mexicans in the Federal District.

Most of PEMEX's new investments were financed by foreign loans, leading to its mid-1982 debt of $25 billion (or one third of the nation's foreign debt, another 15 percent of which was owed by the state electricity complex CFE). Of Mexico's total public and private debt in 1980, some 95 percent was in dollars, and more than half of this was owed U.S. lenders. For each dollar loaned Mexico, at least $.96 had to be returned in interest payments on earlier loans.[23]

PEMEX export earnings did not suffice to meet the service payments on Mexico's foreign debt, as PEMEX expansion fueled the vicious circle of technology imports/debt already described. Meanwhile, U.S. officials used their leverage inside the IMF and World Bank in 1979 to defend the U.S. dollar internationally by undertaking tight money policies. Interest rates shot up, and Mexico's interest payments on its debt rose accordingly.

When Margaret Thatcher and Ronald Reagan assumed office, neoliberalism began taking hold—and the world sank into the worst recession since the Great Depression of the 1930s. Therefore, in 1981-1982, Mexico's next occasion for an IMF-imposed austerity program, the state found itself unable to bail out the private banks in the accustomed manner.

In 1981 the petro-bubble began to evaporate, and by the end of the year Mexico had to slash its oil-export prices by more than $8 a barrel, leading to a national outcry. For Mexico, depressed world oil prices meant lost earnings of $10 billion in the first half of 1982.

Behind the oil price slashes were such obvious U.S. pressures as withholding loans and investments and canceling contracts with PEMEX. The oil companies claimed there was a world oil glut. One of the contract-breakers, Exxon, was reputed to be implementing a plan to break up the OPEC cartel by accumulating enough crude supplies for a two-year period, forcing producing nations into a price war.

Mexico's government announced that PEMEX had signed a five-year contract to sell crude oil directly to the U.S. Energy Department for its Strategic Petroleum Reserve (SPR)—the first such direct purchase from a foreign government agency by the U.S. Energy Department. Prices were not made public, but it was pointed out that they could be renegotiated every three months and that Mexico was currently underselling the average OPEC price by more than $3 a barrel. Commented one U.S. Energy Department spokesman: "This is a delightful thing."

Early in his administration, López Portillo had promised the Mexican people that "their" state would never use its oil revenues to service its debt or to pay for corn imports. Yet as early as 1981 Mexico was doing just that. Moreover, it no longer completely controlled the energy resources it owned: its oil, gas, and uranium. Such TNCs as Occidental Petroleum and Dallas's Dresser Industries had Mexican oil-related operations generating tens of millions of dollars worth of sales each year, and foreign creditors held the Damocles sword of the swollen foreign debt over the Mexican state's head.

In the end, the Mexican government's increased borrowing to develop the petroleum industry had only accelerated the "petrolization" and "overheating" of the economy. The result was runaway inflation, widespread corruption, a world oil glut, a growing debt crisis, and by the end of 1981, plummeting crude oil prices.

Burdened by high interest rates on its foreign borrowing and falling oil prices, the Mexican state faced insolvency. Mexico's bargaining position with foreign lenders was not helped by the sight of the world's largest oil spill from the Ixtoc I undersea well in the Bay of Campeche fouling beaches in southern Texas, later acknowledged by a Texas oil firm to have been the fault of the rig it had leased to PEMEX.

Accustomed to access to foreign natural resources and influence in the formation of U.S. foreign policy, U.S. oil companies acted as if Mexico's petroleum, gas, and uranium reserves were—in the long run—their own. Besides having roughly one-third of all U.S. overseas investments, they already accounted for about 65 percent of the world petroleum industry's spending (capital investment), 80 percent of its expenditure on oil exploration, and 50 percent of its fixed assets. The United States accounted for almost a quarter of the world's energy consumption and about 13 percent of energy production. However, the United States had only 2 percent of the world's proven oil reserves.

Over the years, executives, lawyers, and bankers associated with the giant Rockefeller-dominated Standard Oil of New Jersey had headed the CIA, occupied top posts in the U.S. government, and determined many ambassadorial appointments. While the U.S. ambassador to Mexico no longer could arrange military coups as easily as in 1913, or push a button on his desk and in a matter of seconds issue a command to the Mexican president, as one acting ambassador in 1964 related he was able to do,[24] the embassy remained—in countries like Mexico and, prior to its takeover by student insurgents in 1980, Iran—a main conduit for moves that guaranteed continued U.S. dominance.

In the light of this background, it surprised no one that Ambassador Julian Nava described Mexico in 1980 as "a strategic and vital zone for U.S. interests"—standard diplomatic language for an area subject to direct U.S. military intervention. Three years earlier Secretary of Energy James Schlesinger had declared that securing U.S. oil supplies was "a military responsibility." A CIA study entitled "The International Energy Situation: Outlook to 1985" anticipated that Mexico would provide the United States 4.5 million barrels of oil a day before 1985. The commander of the U.S. Armed Forces Southern Command described Mexico as the biggest security threat to the United States for the next ten years. Suspected covert Mexican support for Central American guerrillas became a target of concern for the National Security Council.

The proximity of Mexican oilfields to Guatemala, El Salvador, and Nicaragua became a cornerstone of the rationale for U.S. military intervention in Central America. In speeches defending U.S. military actions against the Nicaraguan Revolution, for which the United States was condemned by the World Court, President Ronald Reagan invoked "the threat" he saw Central American revolutions as posing to "Panama, the canal, and ultimately Mexico." He spoke of "millions of feet people" sweeping across the United States' southern border.[25]

"Mexico and Nicaragua bashing" became a favorite game of the U.S. mass media, foreboding preparation of U.S. public opinion for possible direct U.S. military involvement in either country. A 1980 *Gallery* magazine article described an imaginary U.S. invasion south of the border to secure oil supplies, while a 1982 CBS special portrayed Mexico as reeling on the verge of chaos and incoming president Miguel de la Madrid as a somewhat laughable incompetent. In response to the *Gallery* article, widely excerpted in the Mexican press, the Mexican army vowed "to defend the fatherland"—and proceeded to break up peasant protests against PEMEX's raping of their lands.

Oil was greasing an increased militarization of Mexican society. This met the needs of U.S. imperialists, whose preferred strategy for securing Mexican oil was not direct military intervention (except as a last resort) but rather a combination of economic/diplomatic pressures and courtship of Mexico's military and police apparatuses.

As imperialist pressures on Mexico intensified, the government devalued the peso by 65 percent in February 1982. There followed severe federal budget reductions, applauded by the IMF and international banking community.

Then Mexico's government announced it had uncovered a secret U.S. State Department briefing paper that allegedly (and prophetically) said that Mexico's economic crisis might lead it "to sell more oil and gas to us at better prices." Officials tried to assure Mexicans this would not happen, nor would there be any more devaluations. As happened in 1976, capitalists began withdrawing bundles of money from Mexico (up to $100 million a day). Mexico's public and private foreign debt zipped past $80 billion ($66 billion of it public), the highest per-capita debt in the third world.

In August 1982, Mexico stunned the world by announcing it could not meet its debt payments for the next ninety days. The inevitable financial panic erupted. A two-stage 100 percent devaluation of the peso completed a tenfold decline in its value vis-à-vis the dollar since 1976.

U.S. monopoly capital seized the opportunity to obtain more oil and gas and a stranglehold on the Mexican economy and state. The U.S. government arranged a cash-in-advance billion-dollar oil purchase for its strategic petroleum reserve at a per-barrel figure too low to be announced. As part of a $4.5 billion stand-by IMF credit, Mexico agreed to accept a stabilization program similar to the arrangement made in 1976 to 1977 which, in hindsight, had only deepened the nation's economic and political crisis. The first of several debt renegotiations occurred, and new loans were extended to Mexico.

All told, the U.S.-led international bailout of Mexico in August 1982 totaled $10 billion, in exchange for which the Mexican government practically guaranteed U.S. receipt of the bulk of Mexican oil and gas sales at less than market value for the foreseeable future. For the Mexican public, the message of who would ultimately pay for the bailout had been delivered earlier in August, when the government announced a doubling of prices on tortillas, bread, gas, and electricity.

Mexico was well on its way to becoming the United States' principal oil supplier. Oil imports soon accounted for more than half the value of all U.S. imports from Mexico. OPEC never did recover its dominant leverage over oil prices, as the world's big oil consumers (United States, Western Europe, and Japan) and their oil companies, together with the "independents," gained greater influence over the marketing and pricing of oil. Since PEMEX was one of the "independents," the United States moved to increase its influence and control over the activities of PEMEX. A powerful tool at U.S. disposal continued to be Mexico's (and PEMEX's) swollen debt.

On September 6, 1982, Finance Minister Jesús Silva Herzog, Jr., announced that in 1983 Mexico would pay only the interest on its debt. The truth was that Mexico could not pay even the interest short of doubling its oil production and increasing oil exports to the United States, which it proceeded to do. By the end of 1983, Mexican crude oil exports to the United States approached a million barrels a day, compared with only 100,000 in 1975.

As we have seen, to increase its oil production, Mexico had had to borrow money to pay for imported U.S. machinery. Together with peso devaluations, rising interest rates, and inflation, this had ballooned the foreign debt. After the August 1982 double devaluation of the peso, the pattern continued. By the end of the year, the IMF had to persuade private commercial banks to supplement an IMF $3.92 billion extended fund facility for Mexico with a $5 billion loan.

Once more, Mexico's creditors conditioned the loans on the state's implementation of more wage ceilings and other concessions favoring private capital. López Portillo's successor, President Miguel de la Madrid (1982 to 1988), educated in economics at Harvard, complied. Yet Mexico did not pull out of its recession.

Most evidence pointed to a repeat 1982-type financial crisis on a much larger scale at some later time—which eventually happened, in 1994 to 1995. In light of growing mass poverty, signs of unity among major left-wing parties, and the new, though increasingly repressed and "defensive" labor militancy, a natural question arose: was Mexico on its way to some kind of a social explosion like the one that occurred in Iran in 1979, which also took several years to reach a boiling point?

More than a million of Mexico's regularly employed were laid off in the fall of 1982, as an ever greater percentage of the populace were driven into the ranks of the relative surplus population, from which capital could obtain more cheap labor to exploit for a period before discarding it again. Such was the strategy of monopoly capital to extricate itself from the worldwide recession it had generated in the first place. As the manager of a Fisher-Price Toys plant in Tijuana told the *New York Times* (September 20, 1982): "Essentially, we are buying labor, and the [peso] devaluation is going to make it less expensive to purchase that labor."

Augmented use of a dual labor market incorporating superexploited temporary workers, an increase in the reserve army of labor through massive layoffs, lower real wages—all were basic components of capital's strategy to stem declining profit rates and bring itself out of crisis. It was the core of the neoliberal free market doctrine that became official Mexican policy after 1982, but already was largely in place through the IMF "stabilization" programs and bailout packages.

Mexico's state had the contradictory mission of controlling the labor force through concessions like wage hikes, while fomenting capital accumulation. State subsidies to the private sector added to the state's growing indebtedness and fiscal crisis, thereby eroding state autonomy. The IMF's "stabilization" programs, in López Portillo's words, "annulled" the state's ability to mediate the class struggle and left "its possibility of governing canceled." This was a harbinger of the coming crisis of Mexico's corporatist state.

Only in its still relatively independent foreign policy was the Mexican state's "possibility of governing" not "canceled." In order to maintain the nonintervention doctrine of the Mexican Revolution and cool out leftist opposition, as well as to gain leverage in its international bargaining with the United States, the government protested U.S. intervention in Latin America. It lent moral and small-scale economic support to the new revolutions shaking the continent— from Cuba and Grenada to Nicaragua and El Salvador. In 1980-1981, Mexico defined Central America as its "natural area of influence." Mexican capitalists wished to establish an industrial, technical, and financial presence in the Caribbean Basin, another reason the government was willing to accept new "developmentalist" revolutions there (which appeared as inevitable as Mexico's did in 1910).

While in its foreign relations Mexico made only minuscule economic gains in diversifying its trade and sources of foreign investment (e.g., with Japan), it did gain modest international prominence. Its joint proclamation with France in late 1981, recognizing the pro-guerrilla Democratic Revolutionary Front as a legitimate political force in El Salvador, propelled Mexico onto center stage of international diplomacy. Its position stood in stark contrast to the U.S. government's portrayal of popular forces in the region as part of a massive Soviet-Cuban "Marxist" conspiracy. By courting the largely European Socialist International and Nicaragua's Sandinistas, the Mexican state expanded its room to maneuver in its relations with the United States and somewhat refurbished its faded revolutionary colors at home. Mexico contributed to the final peace settlement in Central America.

Mexico's advocacy of peaceful resolution of conflicts, however, was contradicted by its violent suppression of Guatemalan and Salvadoran refugees fleeing right-wing military and paramilitary death squads. Mexico jailed a few and deported many back to their homelands, where most were killed. The Mexican military policed the nation's southern border and gained a nefarious reputation for its manhandling of refugees, many of whom ended up in wretched refugee camps.

GATT

Mexico was only one of several third world nations facing the 1980s debt crisis. Although the Western media blamed the crisis on poor management by foreign governments, Western banks had made serious management errors. They overextended their loans to third world countries after the 1973 recession, when Western capital was rushing to seize more markets, natural resources, and inexpensive labor power to extricate itself from its crisis of overproduction and the tendency of the rate of profit to fall.

After the August 1982 bankruptcy announcement, López Portillo's administration began falling apart. How would Mexico ever pay either the interest or the principal on its foreign debt? In view of the economy's petrolization, dollarization, and relative decapitalization, and the body politic's shakiness, how could social upheaval be avoided, or at least postponed? Finally, who would foot the bill—and accept the blame—for the country's economic doldrums: top state bureaucrats or private bankers and industrialists, all of whom had grown fat off oil revenues during the boom years?

López Portillo answered most of these questions at the end of his "farewell" state-of-the-nation address, September 1, 1982. After droning on about his administration's "achievements," the president excoriated the industrialized powers of the West, whose high interest rates and unfair treatment of the less industrialized countries had contributed to the rapid rise in third world foreign debt. Then he lashed out at Mexico's private bankers, who, he said, had looted the nation far more than had any colonialist power. Those watching the speech on television could see the leaders of the CCE and ABM (Mexican Bankers' Association) stir from their somnolence. The president accused the bankers of sacking the country of $50 billion and stashing it in U.S. banks and real estate. Then, his voice quivering and his eyes filling with tears, the president woke up every member of Congress with the announcement that he was expropriating the nation's private banks, with compensation for their owners.

In one memorable moment, expected by no one, the state had saved itself and much of Mexican private capital by scapegoating the bankers and scooping up bank deposits, the banks' investments in more than one hundred industries, and outstanding bank debts (estimated at $6 billion). The expropriation brought into state hands half of Mexico's non-foreign bank assets; the state already had the other half and, as we noted earlier, had set them to working for private monopoly capital. After a moment of shocked silence, everyone present at the president's announcement, except for the heads of the CCE and ABM and their friends, stood up and applauded.

The PRI whipped up a euphoria of nationalism, comparing López Portillo's action to Cárdenas's 1938 oil nationalization and to the "moment of glory" of Zapata and Villa. The comparison was spurious: there was no mass movement involved in the bank takeover, even though the left and the new labor militancy had long advocated such a step. The government did not talk of raising wages or putting a million laid-off workers back to work. Rather, it emphasized "sacrifice" and defending "the nation's honor."

On September 3, nearly a million people overflowed Mexico City's Zócalo square to back the president at a state-sponsored rally. All of Mexico's opposition parties, except for the two major right-wing ones, the PAN and the Mexican Democratic Party (PDM), critically supported the takeover of the banks. Some of the left, including many Communists, believed the entire "political class" was *not* subservient to the bourgeoisie and imperialism. They argued that at least some of the "techno-bureaucracy" constituted an "intermediate class" (sometimes called a "governing class") that could be pushed to the left by popular mobilization. Meanwhile, those conducting the popular fight from below for basic economic and political rights disavowed this view and continued their struggle, led by various networks of independent workers, peasants, and slum dwellers. Publications like the monthly magazine *Punto Crítico* championed the independent position of struggle from below.

While the president won public support by blaming the bankers and announcing low-interest credit lines for small and medium-size businesses, what of the *políticos* who had pocketed much of the oil revenue? The private banks possessed information on that question. Had the state nationalized the banks in order to avoid a scandal of bureaucratic thievery? The leftist weekly *Proceso* rose above normal standards of self-censorship and published articles, with photographs, about multimillion-dollar homes acquired or being built by Federal District boss Carlos Hank González and police chief General Arturo Durazo Moreno, as well as by President López Portillo himself.

López Portillo's bank decree was a desperate attempt to patch up the state's economic hemorrhage, steal the thunder of the left, divert the new labor insurgency, and reassert state autonomy. More thoroughgoing Cárdenas-style reforms, whether in the areas of oil, technology, or heavy industry, or against the TNCs altogether, would have forced Mexico into an anti-imperialist posture in practice as well as rhetoric—and where would that have left Mexico's ruling class, without imperialism's support? That is why López Portillo moved against unproductive capital—the private banks—and not against imperialism or industry. The move itself was political, giving the corporatist state more "nationalist" breathing room with which to manipulate the class struggle.

The president's nationalization decree excluded foreign banks. The economic motives behind his action met with the approval of many TNC and U.S. government officials, who feared a default on Mexico's foreign debt (representing 10 percent of the combined debt of the less industrialized countries and Eastern Europe). A Mexican default might ignite a chain reaction of debt payment failures among less industrialized nations and a world financial panic.

About two-thirds of the total third world debt was owed to private banks, and 22 percent of that amount was on the books of just nine U.S. firms (far in excess of the banks' total equity capital). Mexico's debt represented 17.1 percent of U.S. bank loans to third world countries and the Eastern bloc. The three largest U.S. banks—Citibank, Chase Manhattan, and Bank of America—reportedly had an estimated 40 percent of their capital tied up in Mexico. Their executives hailed López Portillo's bank nationalization decree, realizing that the state was absorbing the private banks' bad debts and thereby saving bankers from possible insolvency.

The newly expanded alliance between the state and the CCE and ABM was by no means broken by López Portillo's action, even though it was strained. To smooth matters over with the bankers, López Portillo and his successors named people from the banking community or its friends in the state bureaucracy to manage and administer the now-expanded state banking sector. These were the very people responsible for Mexico's economic crisis in the first place.

Some prominent CCE members talked of an employers' lockout to protest the government's insensitivity to the rights of private property, and they threatened a court suit. The Monterrey group, ABM members, and some other big capitalists, who sought to win over Mexico's discontented intermediate classes, claimed that only "privatization" of the economy, not nationalization, could "save the nation." They stepped up their campaigns against labor unions and for "flexibility" in work conditions and labor relations (i.e., no overtime pay, replacement of workers with part-timers, and similar measures that became common practice under neoliberalism). They advocated public participation of the business community in the nation's political life and joined political parties. Some of these elements were presumably behind the rumors of a military *coup d'état* that prevailed during the final months of López Portillo's *sexenio* (six-year term in office).

Within a year, both the CCE and its right-wing member organization COPARMEX were propagandizing for a radical change in Mexico's political structure. They advocated replacing the three-way process of state decision-making (state/labor/business) with a two-way one (state/business), in which a techno-economic rationality would replace the "inefficiency" and corruption of political corporatism.

Yet even the bankers, through crocodile tears, accepted the state's expropriation of private banks after they saw how popular it was and after the nation's leading justices publicly endorsed the president's action. Also, of course, they were receiving money from the state as compensation for the loss of their banks. Most important of all, López Portillo's successors, backers of the CCE's call for neoliberal economic policies, began selling the new state bank shares back to the former owners and to personal friends. This was especially convenient for the bankers, now that the state had paid off their bad debts. Presidents Salinas and Ernesto Zedillo completed the privatization of the state banks in the 1990s, bailing out their remaining debts at great government expense in the process. So the bankers had the last laugh.[26]

Meanwhile, U.S. economic interests nudged Mexico closer to eliminating its tariff barriers that were protecting domestic manufacturing from foreign competition. They urged Mexico to join the General Agreement on Tariffs and Trade (GATT). Central to U.S. policy formation on Mexico was the Rockefeller family. Early in the López Portillo *sexenio*, banker David Rockefeller and his long-time aide Henry Kissinger had met with leaders of Mexico's principal industrial groups to try to persuade them to have Mexico join GATT. They hoped to "develop" Mexico through GATT in the direction of its "natural" oil-exporting advantages in exchange for increased U.S. exports of capital and other goods and services to Mexico. The goal was to make Mexico an "export platform" like Taiwan or South Korea.

Responding to popular pressures against this scheme, López Portillo announced in early 1980 that Mexico was postponing entry into GATT, but the Rockefeller family kept pushing the idea. Implicit in the 1982 economic bailout of Mexico was Mexico's agreement to join GATT, along with the rest of the Rockefeller and neoliberal agenda: debt-equity swaps, "privatization," and "free market" export-oriented "development." López Portillo's successor, President de la Madrid (1982 to 1988), appointed a leader of the "techno-bureaucracy," Carlos Salinas de Gortari (Harvard Ph.D. in economics and public administration), as his minister of budget and planning. Salinas implemented the economic doctrine of neoliberalism then coming into vogue. It was called "shock therapy" for "an ailing economy."

The de la Madrid government privatized 743 state enterprises, slashed state expenditures to 17 percent of GDP (down from 30 percent in 1981), and reduced real wages by 60 percent. The exchange rate of the peso tumbled to about 2,400 to the dollar, making Mexican labor even cheaper for foreign *maquiladora* owners, who responded by investing another $10 billion (much of it in Japanese yen). Debt-for-equity swaps on the nation's $108 billion foreign debt delivered $4 billion worth of Mexican enterprises to foreigners. The Monterrey group of capitalists also offered their foreign creditors stockholdings in exchange for debt reduction. Except for oil, most big industry consolidated in Mexico's north.

In the midst of Mexico's prolonged recession of the 1980s, public and private employees could not maintain their standard of living. Foreign interest rates remained high, food and rental prices skyrocketed, Mexico's oil revenues periodically declined, and annual GDP growth averaged out as negative during the de la Madrid years. Unimpressed by "shock therapy," wealthy Mexicans reputedly sent $6 to $12 billion a year to overseas banks ("flight capital").

While hard-working Mexicans tightened their belts, Mexico's total net payments to foreign countries from 1982 to 1988 totaled $68 billion. Thus, the foreign "suction pump" kept draining much of the surplus Mexican workers produced. Malnutrition came to affect the *majority* of Mexicans.

By 1986, prices on Mexico's oil exports had dropped to their 1973 levels. A massive propaganda campaign by big business was contrasting the evil of "government and bureaucracy" with the good of "civil society and private enterprise." "Civil society" for Mexico's elite meant "market economy." After the 1985 earthquake, however, when citizens did more in the rescue operations than the state did, most Mexicans began to see "civil society" as citizens taking the place of the state.

All these pressures caused President de la Madrid to agree to tie future Mexican debt payments to the price of oil, abandon altogether the now-tarnished "economic miracle" of "import substitution industrialization," and announce that Mexico would indeed join GATT. In Mexico, corporate agribusiness was pleased, since it wished to expand exports to the United States and thus championed "free trade." A few of Mexico's domestic industries that had grown during the import-substitution years also sought larger markets. Their profit rates, as already noted, had been in decline. Moreover, import substitution industrialization had run out of gas, as the gap between rich and poor simply meant that in Mexico there had never emerged enough consumers capable of purchasing manufactured goods at going prices.

To illustrate Mexico's commitment to "free trade" and big business, the de la Madrid administration slashed tariffs and dropped major regulations over private and foreign capital. It also launched a more tax-free approach than ever for private capital, especially in the *maquiladora* free-trade zones, and offered incentives for export firms. It established a "Pact of Solidarity" between big business and the PRI's labor and peasant sectors. In 1987, the alliance between the PRI elite and big business was consolidated with a wage and price control agreement called an "Economic Solidarity Pact." It froze wages at their 1982 level and put the government in control of future wage increases. It was periodically renewed in the rest of the 1980s and in the 1990s. Technocrats like Salinas centralized state economic agencies, further facilitating the smooth introduction of neoliberalism.[27]

President de la Madrid seemed unable to move as fast as the IMF and the big bourgeoisie wished. Inflation was running at 131 percent in 1987 and the foreign debt stood at $108 billion (76 percent of GNP), when Mexico's stock market crashed. A year later, at the end of the de la Madrid administration, 60 percent of the federal budget was going to service the debt. Flight capital in the 1980s reportedly totaled $84 billion.[28]

The Earthquake

A devastating earthquake rocked Mexico City on September 19, 1985, introducing a new phenomenon of bottom-up collective solidarity in Mexican society that seriously threatened the PRI. The earthquake destroyed a higher percentage of government-built structures than other buildings. People were shocked by the faulty construction on public hospitals and schools. They attributed it to the state's corrupt tradition of extending lucrative contracts to suspect construction firms and "winking" at building code violations.

More importantly, people were indignant that the government did not rush to the aid of the victims of the earthquake and instead blocked civilian volunteers who were running everywhere to help. Civilians, not the army or the state, saved most of the lives of those people buried in the rubble who survived. Mismanaged relief efforts and delays in providing new housing deepened public resentment against the PRI government.

Out of the selfless and collective earthquake rescue experience came a new sense of solidarity among people from different walks of life. One of Mexico's world-renowned writers, journalist Carlos Monsiváis, dubbed it "the birth of civil society."[29] In the effort to rebuild, people began turning to their own collective resources rather than to traditional leaders of either the PRI or the opposition parties.

All of a sudden, politicians had to look over their shoulders at the charging masses, now often led by women. Humble seamstresses, left to die in the earthquake's rubble when sweatshop owners came to rescue sewing machines instead of workers, moved to the forefront of "civil society." Led by an illiterate *compañera* named Evangelina Corona (quoted at the opening of Chapter 6), they formed an independent, anti-CTM national union and called it "19 de Septiembre" in memory of their sixty fallen co-workers.

The seamstresses and countless neighborhood women involved in the rescue and relief work around the earthquake breathed new life into labor militancy and the struggling social movements of the immiserated masses. People demanded answers to the most pressing question: What was the future direction of the nation, now tottering on the ruins of failed economic policies and quake-gutted downtowns and villages?

In 1986 the largest peaceful street demonstrations since 1968 took place. One, a combined effort of the CUD (Unified Quake Victims' Committee) and the powerful independent electrical workers' union SME, turned out 70,000 demonstrators during one of the coldest winters in Mexico City's history. The demonstrators called for "Jobs, Housing, Decent Wages!" Instead of echoing the left's decade-old shouts of "Cancel the Debt!," tired of the debt being blamed for their worsening living conditions, they called for its cancellation *only if the government used it as an excuse for not finding the money to meet their pressing immediate needs.*

On the second anniversary of the earthquake, the Metropolitan Front in Mexico City organized a march of 90,000 people to demand jobs and housing. By 1990, some twenty-five states had highly democratic organizations of the urban poor. Several supported Cárdenas's newly launched Party of the Democratic Revolution (PRD), while Maoist members of major northern groups like the Committee for Popular Defense in Durango and the Frente Popular Tierra y Libertad de Monterrey joined the Labor Party (PT), founded in 1990 with PRI support. All were linked to the National Council of Urban Popular Movements (CONAMUP).

Despite state repression, organizers in the proletarian *colonias* had continued their activities both before and after the earthquake. In many cities spontaneous marches and street barricades had stopped bus fare increases and won other gains.

Ever since its founding in 1981, CONAMUP had made its principal demand a piece of land for a dwelling for every poor family. It had denounced the state's previous housing development plans for the *colonias proletarias* as failing to challenge the interests of the bourgeoisie. The plans were called "speculative and corporate," directed by private banking and real estate interests largely responsible for the urban poor's housing problems in the first place.

As an alternative to this "privatization" of the economy, CONAMUP called for democratic socialism and greater state intervention to assist the entire working class. It pledged to continue the struggle of the immiserated to manage their own lives and to build multiclass coalitions to resist state repression and bring about genuine social change. In some instances it practiced a collective self-help approach exemplifying genuine participatory democracy.[30]

Women were especially active in the movements of the urban poor, constituting 80 percent of those participating. They organized community kitchens, laundries, and child-care centers. They campaigned against rape and battering. With support from women of the intermediate classes, they forced the state to pass progressive legislation on these issues, such as the (rarely enforced) 1990 law against sexual harassment in the workplace. In the process of struggle, they broke many, but by no means all, men's beliefs that a woman's only place was in the home. Roman Catholic liberation theologists and Maoists from the intermediate classes were especially active in both the urban and rural poor peoples' struggles.

Prejudices based on patriarchical and *macho* value systems posed formidable obstacles for women in struggle. Several women were beaten by their menfolk for participating in public life. Not so coincidentally, therefore, most female leaders turned out to be unmarried or without male partners. Yet even some of them adopted a style of authoritarian leadership that echoed male or corporatist styles.

Subsequent research on Mexico's social movements revealed that "few of the women [publicly] spoke and fewer became movement leaders."[31] As a result, women began using slogans like "the woman who shuts up will never be listened to," "we are slaves of the slaves," and "if the woman is not liberated then neither will the man be liberated, nor society as a whole." Women organized a single, unified coordinating committee for earthquake victims which championed "democracy in the city and in the home."[32]

Despite the barriers of traditional gender role definitions, women were being forced by the economic changes in Mexico to do more work inside and outside of the home. Whether impoverished or more or less regularly employed workers, women were performing more labor for money, and they were heading more households. Typically, a regularly employed woman was married with three children and had a secondary education (above the average for male workers).[33]

Perhaps the most notable change in the communities affected by these changes, enhanced by the "*concientización*" (consciousness raising) of the social movements, was the large number of women who broke with old patriarchical ways and determined to save themselves and their families through more direct participation in family decision making, individual choice of "things to do," and even political activity (long a male preserve). Family patriarchs began losing their grip. Yet the resultant change in gender relations was by no means unilinear, being filled with ambivalence, confusion, and contradiction at every turn for women.

In the era of neoliberalism, secular and religious non-governmental organizations (NGOs), some Mexican, some international, tried to fill the vacuum left by the state's reduced role in social programs. The number of NGOs involved in the struggles of the working poor mushroomed in city and countryside alike. The number of NGOs focusing just on women's issues rose to ninety-seven by 1994. Several small feminist, AIDS-support, and gay organizations gained strength with NGO support.[34]

Despite their often good intentions, NGOs had little real power to improve peoples' lives, except for those Mexican individuals who found upward mobility by working at salaried NGO jobs. Critics noted that NGOs served the interests of the World Bank, U.S. imperialism, and national elites by atomizing social movements, placing "outsiders" in command of budgets and planning, and reducing political/economic struggle to the local level where resources remained scarce.[35] NGOs in Mexico undermined the earlier national networking and collectivizing of Mexico's social movements. They also divided movements into competing political camps, as some Mexican NGOs even backed the conservative PAN.

After the electoral show of strength by Cárdenas in 1988 and the opposition's forcing the state to introduce more electoral reforms, Mexico's social movements lost many of their key activists to political party activities—mainly the PRD, but also the PT, PAN, and even the PRI. Urban poor women founded a new pluralistic organization oriented to electoral activity and International Women's Day activities. Known as "*Las Benitas*" (Benita Galeana Women's Coalition), it incorporated several groups, including the large *Asamblea del Barrio* (Neighborhood Assembly) founded after the earthquake to demand housing for the newly homeless and to combat high rents. The best known representative of the Asamblea was "Superbarrio," a humorous and popular masked wrestler who paraded around in a cape like Superman. However, "Las Benitas" had no staying power. It fell apart over internal divisions having to do with political choices in elections and competing types of feminism. Meanwhile, in 1994, intermediate-class women founded Woman Citizens in Struggle for Democracy to focus on women's issues and an equal place for women in the fight for electoral reform and political democracy.

Amazingly, labor's struggle, despite the twin obstacles of state violence and workers' shying away from even "defensive" battles because of the harsh economic conditions brought on by neoliberalism, did not end, although it was curtailed. The bourgeoisie's attack on labor unions was so successful that even the CTM unions lost their leverage in the 1980s and 1990s. Several unions were eliminated; union membership declined by as much as 40 percent among such CTM mainstays as oil, railroad, power, and mine and metal workers; and bilateral isolated contract agreements at the plant level became the norm. The largest corporations also used the increased entry of women into the workforce to weaken collective bargaining agreements by playing the patriarchical card of lower wages for women and rotating younger women in and out of the labor force. Through all these measures, monopoly capital became more able than ever to dictate terms to labor and its union representatives.

Many workers fell prey to the argument that CTM's enforcement of wage ceilings, periodic reduced work weeks from the norm of forty-eight hours, and approval of temporary plant shutdowns or automation were "lesser evils" to more mass layoffs. CTM also imitated the AFL-CIO's policy of wage givebacks to help keep companies competitive.

In order to meet criticisms by the rank-and-file labor movement, in early 1983 the CTM formed a short-lived alliance with the independent unions and the left against the de la Madrid government's alliance with big business. This strategy did not work because the government struck special wage deals with the public workers' FSTSE and PRI-satellite union organizations like the Revolutionary Confederation of Workers and Peasants (CROC). So CTM labor boss Velázquez returned to his old ways of serving employers and the PRI. He backed neoliberalism's privatization that did away with 400,000 union jobs; championed joining GATT and, later, NAFTA; and led calls for expelling Cárdenas's "democratic current" from the PRI, and other pro-democracy currents that followed.

The state played a key role in reducing the unions' power. It revised labor legislation to make strikes more difficult. More seriously, it sent in soldiers, policemen, and CT hired goons to quell strikes by DINA-Renault auto workers (early 1980s), steel workers (1982, 1985), soft drink workers (1982), telephone workers (TELMEX, five times between 1976 and 1987), and electrical workers (1987). Many union activists were assassinated. At Mexico City's Modelo Brewery, workers tried electing their own leaders. They resisted state and CTM repression by striking. Riot police crushed the strike, and 5,200 of the workers were fired. In 1983 the government broke a strike by the independent union of nuclear industry workers [SUTIN] by refusing to negotiate, and reorganized the industry to eliminate the unions.[36]

In 1983-1984, Mexican workers launched two symbolic general strikes and one mass public protest march that brought production and distribution of goods to a partial halt. The government's response was stepped-up repression. Seeking an accounting of 500 disappeared people, "La señora" Ibarra told reporters that in the early 1970s "they captured and 'disappeared' guerrillas.... Now they are repressing whole movements—peasants, students, unionists. They don't want centers of agitation anywhere."

On May Day of 1985, workers set off on their traditional march to the Zócalo, many of them in contingents independent of the official CTM. When they got there, they found the immense plaza ringed by troops. Not even the CTM's "official" march was allowed to enter. It marked a low point in the PRI's ability to control labor through co-optive and corporatist practices.

Another tactic used to roll back the unions, especially those whose workers spawned the 1970s' new labor militancy, was privatization of state firms leading to massive worker layoffs, as in the steel industry (Altos Hornos de México), telephones (TELMEX), aviation (Aéro México and Mexicana), mining (Cananea), fish processing, the Veracurz port authority, the state tobacco company, and state-owned sugar mills. In 1989, President Salinas negotiated a debt reduction of $12 billion and within a year halved the number of remaining state enterprises to less than 400. The IMF rewarded him by declaring Mexico a "preferred debtor nation."

After the 1990 sale of TELMEX ($6 billion annual receipts a year in 1997) to Salinas's friend Carlos Slim, the telephone workers' main fight became one of limiting job losses. Their union leader, Francisco Hernández Juárez, supported the privatization and called for a "new unionism" that would cooperate with management. Salinas then put up for sale the rest of the "nationalized" banking sector and acknowledged secret bilateral talks with the United States on a free trade pact (NAFTA). In 1991 Salinas sold for a song the nation's richest bank, the Banco Nacional de México (Banamex), to his good friend Roberto Hernández and Roberto's business associate Alfredo Harp Helú, in effect making Hernández and Harp Helú overnight billionaires. By the end of his term, Salinas had privatized more than 1,000 state firms.

Even in the cases of privatization, armed force was sometimes used against labor unions. To crush worker resistance to privatization of the huge Cananea Copper Mine in 1989, some 5000 soldiers occupied the mine. The national leadership of the union cooperated in breaking the local union and accepted the firing of 700 workers.

Yet there did occur occasional if short-lived labor victories. In 1987, some 10,500 workers at the Volkswagen plant in Puebla won a fifty-seven-day strike against layoffs and a 72 percent wage hike. Five years later, however, when 14,000 of the workers protested CTM's agreement to the "team" concept (worker-management "teamwork," involving "flexibility" on the part of workers on management's terms, job rotation, few job classifications, etc.), Volkswagen, with government backing, closed the plant, re-opened it with lower wages, and fired the previous workforce.[37]

In 1987, UNAM students conducted demonstrations of 150,000 and more (the university's enrollment stood at 340,000, the hemisphere's largest). They were protesting tuition hikes and demanding a student voice in establishing stricter educational standards. Unlike 1968, this time the government did not send troops. It incorporated students into policy negotiations, and within a year the main student organizations had gained a significant voice in UNAM's policymaking. More than one hundred unions, many sympathetic to the PRD, formed a new labor federation, the United Union Front in Defense of Workers and the Constitution.

In 1989, 500,000 schoolteachers led by the independents' CNTE marched on the nation's capital. Rejecting wages only one-third those of 1980, they participated in wildcat strikes and, despite more murders and beatings, won a raise. They objected to the lack of internal democracy in the official teachers' union SNTE and its paucity of woman leaders. They broke PRI's control over several union locals. President Salinas replaced the seventeen-year *charro* leader of SNTE, a man, with Elba Esther Gordillo, a woman and a PRI loyalist. The CNTE then split as some of its members accepted Gordillo's offer to be represented on the SNTE's national executive board.

In 1987-1990, walkouts against corporatism occurred at the Ford plant and other workplaces. The rank and file demanded the removal of ninety-year-old CTM boss Velázquez. Ford broke the strike at its plant in Cuautitlán outside Mexico City by means of a lockout and massive worker firings. When workers persisted by trying to elect their own CTM leaders, goons fired guns at them, killing one and wounding nine. The workers gained backing from Ford workers in the United States and Canada, leading to a certification vote pitting those favoring a new union against the CTM. The vote was held at gunpoint, however, as 2,000 police surrounded the plant and video cameras recorded each worker's vote. Even so, the CTM only barely won.

Events in Mexico's countryside paralleled what was happening elsewhere in society, but under harsher circumstances of political assassinations, beatings, jailings, and military occupation. The growing seriousness, complexity, and interweaving of issues in Mexico's social movements became especially clear with the overlapping of interests—including ethnic and gender ones—involved in two major actions of 1980-1981 relating to oil and nuclear energy. In January 1981, some 10,000 peasants (mostly Indians) in Chiapas blockaded roads to the Cactus and Reforma oilfields and the Cactus petrochemical plant, which supplied about two-thirds of the natural gas used inside Mexico. Troops arrived, the blockade was lifted, and the state agreed to negotiate peasant claims of damage to crops and livestock caused by pollution from the plant.

Similarly, in the winter of 1980 to 1981, Purépecha Indians, particularly women, of the Santa Fé community along the shores of Michoacán's tourist haven Lake Pátzcuaro (famous for its butterfly fishing nets) resisted the state's efforts to build an experimental nuclear energy center on their land. Purépecha women made contact with Indians of the U.S. southwest more familiar with the devastation caused by uranium tailings and the nuclear industry's assault on their land and lives. They learned that the U.S. nuclear industry was holding back on further construction at home, preferring to "transfer" the risk to Indian lands in Mexico, Canada, and other countries ever since the accident at Three Mile Island, Pennsylvania. Uranium-rich Mexico planned to construct twenty nuclear reactors at a final sale price estimated at more than $65 billion.

The Purépecha women then explained to their communities that the promised new job opportunities would lead only to sickness and death for their people, while the traditional fishing industry might well be destroyed. They were less successful in convincing the otherwise progressive nuclear workers' union SUTIN, which perceived the issue as one of jobs for its members and part of Mexico's "anti-imperialist" effort to achieve energy "independence." But they did win the support of the local tourism magnates, whose own vested self-interests were clearly not nuclear. Eventually, the Purépecha united all the Indian communities along Lake Pátzcuaro's shores and forced the government to declare publicly that no nuclear center would ever be built in the state of Michoacán.

That still left the problem of the construction of two nuclear energy plants at Laguna Verde in Veracruz state. A broad coalition of forces, including the region's Totonaca Indians and the Mothers Group of Veracruz, mounted protest marches of thousands. Although the first Laguna Verde plant went into operation in 1988, the homegrown anti-nuclear movement forced the government to cancel plans for building another dozen nuclear reactors.[38]

These incidents illustrated a growing awareness among Mexican Indians and peasant women of their common plight with Indians and oppressed peoples elsewhere. Eight hundred Indian delegates from as far north as Alaska and as far south as Patagonia attended the Second Meeting of Independent Indian Organizations of Mexico, Central America, and the Caribbean, held in Michoacán in March 1981. Among anti-imperialist resolutions passed were ones of solidarity with the people of El Salvador and a ringing denunciation of the U.S.-based Summer Linguistics Institute, accused of having links to the CIA and of destroying indigenous cultures through its programs of "sterilization of women" and "Bible translation."[39]

Such growing Indian militancy evoked ferocious state repression, which in turn only served to spread class, ethnic, and gender consciousness among the different Indian groups. In 1981, the 6 million-strong Supreme Council of Indian Peoples (founded in 1979) successfully led a popular campaign that frustrated the state's traditional practice of imposing pro-government candidates in elections for the official National Indigenous People's Council, which incorporated eighty-five regional councils and represented 9 million Indians. The Supreme Council's democratic slate of candidates triumphed in all but a few areas and proceeded to demand better lands and more schools. A third of the indigenous population knew no Spanish. Only a quarter of Indian children attended school, and a recurrent Indian demand focused on what little education they did receive: the need for more schools, for an end to teachers beating children who did not understand or speak Spanish adequately, and for more teachers from the Indians' own linguistic communities.

Indians also demanded that they be allowed to participate in the decision-making of the National Indian Institute (INI), a demand finally granted in 1986. Three years later, in Oaxaca state, Indians convened the Forum on Human Rights for Indian Peoples. Out of these meetings came an expanded demand for honoring human rights throughout Mexico and new linkages with NGOs. In 1992, the 500th anniversary of Columbus's arrival to the Americas, Indians mobilized large demonstrations throughout Mexico and Latin America to protest the "celebration of ethnocide" and to demand basic human rights.[40]

Both the Indians' Supreme Council and the peasants' CNPA condemned the 1980 Law of Agrarian Development (LDA) and Mexican Food System (SAM) program that presumably would make the country self-sufficient in food production by 1982. They called them "bureaucratic and authoritarian control measures over rural producers accelerating the development of *latifundia* under a new legal cover."

Financed in part by the World Bank, the new programs conditioned aid to subsistence farmers on their "producing more'" and sharing risks with the state and "small farmers" in the development of agro-industries. LDA permitted the expropriation of "idle" *ejido* or Indian land while allowing "certificates of inviolability" for any "intensively used" cattle land. Combined with an earlier legalization of renting out *ejido* lands, LDA and SAM generated an intensified assault on smallholder and subsistence farming by big capital and the state, although some progressives worked in the programs and helped out in the peasant struggle for democracy. The peasants' continued proletarianization was disguised through their association with the state or "small" farmers.

Anticipating all this, the Agrarian Reform Ministry's Co-op Development director resigned in protest in 1980, pointing out that LDA and SAM would aggravate the peasants' basic problem: their lack of equipment and collective organization to market their own products. But the official peasant organization CNC backed the new approach. Sixty percent of SAM's resources went to irrigated districts—the heartland of *neolatifundismo* and agribusiness. CNC understood well that by tying discontented and desperate subsistence producers to the state, SAM would help undermine the independents' CNPA and the Indians' Supreme Council. CNC also used SAM to claim the credit for the creation of 2,000 clinics serving 10 million rural inhabitants—part of the state's program to stem the decline in health conditions of the agricultural work force.[41]

By the end of 1982 the Mexican government was claiming that the drive to make the nation once more self-sufficient in food production was a success. But, by its own definition of self-sufficiency as dietary self-sufficiency, this was not true. Moreover, according to Banco de México figures, food imports continued apace. For example, while corn imports dropped from 4.2 million tons in 1980 to 2.8 million in 1981, bean imports declined only slightly, soybean imports doubled, and other food imports increased.

The 1982 debt crisis and subsequent emphasis on privatization and neoliberalism ended SAM, as state funding for agriculture and food was slashed by half during the rest of the 1980s. By the mid-1990s, Mexico was importing 35 percent of its basic grains and more powdered milk than any other nation in the world.

The changes brought on by neoliberalism fractured all peasant organizations, including the PRI's CNC. The independent, peasant-led CNPA continued active but faded in importance as its members struggled with individual family survival problems or joined political parties like the PRD and PT. Some joined newer groupings—the National Union of Autonomous Regional Peasant Organizations (UNORCA), the National Union of Agricultural Workers (UNTA), or the Coalition of Democratic Rural and Urban Organizations (CODUC). UNORCA was founded in 1985 by intellectuals with a peasant background, many of whom later joined the Salinas administration. The CNPA's ally COCEI continued winning city council elections in Juchitán, Oaxaca, and in 1989 helped organize the First International Forum on the Human Rights of Indian Peoples.

Salinas and the Technocrats

As already noted, the 1988-1994 Salinas administration accelerated privatizations and neoliberalism and brought Mexico into NAFTA. Salinas's government was run by free market technocrats like himself, mainly former students of Yale's graduate program in economics and members of what were sometimes called Salinas's "Harvard group." They came from upper-class backgrounds (just like Salinas, who at age three accidentally killed the family maid while playing with his father's shotgun). They completed what historian Dan La Botz has called Mexico's "technocratic counter-revolution"[42] inside the state and the economy, happily meeting the wishes of the IMF and foreign capitalists at almost every turn.

The Salinas administration eliminated most parts of the "Mexicanization" law that required 51 percent Mexican ownership in strategic industries. It slashed taxes on corporations and the upper-income bracket, rarely collected in any case. It then imposed a 2 percent asset tax aimed at small and medium-sized businesses and a 15 percent sales tax stinging the general public. Many individuals in the intermediate classes and small businesses lost prior tax breaks. Salinas conferred regularly with the millionaire and billionaire members of the Mexican Council of Businessmen (CMHN). By 1994, government budget cuts had generated a balanced budget and the annual inflation rate was down to 7 percent. Salinas was the darling of Wall Street.

Mexican economists noted that neoliberalism benefited the nation's big businesses, especially those with liquid assets linked to banking, trade, and foreign capital. Social spending cuts hurt the general population, including people in the intermediate classes. Mexico's National Institute of Statistics (INEGI) noted that from mid-1981 to mid-1993, the Mexican "middle class" averaged a 50 percent decline in real wages. INEGI defined a "middle class" wage earner as anyone making between three and eight times the minimum wage—about 6.5 percent of the Mexican population.

Numerous reports by the World Bank and the United Nations noted Mexico's falling behind the average for Latin America in the areas of education and health. Fewer Mexican children completed primary school, while more teenagers dropped out of high school. The number of people living below the official poverty line placed Mexico among Latin America's ten worst cases. Mexicans ate less of almost everything, including tortillas. Infant mortality rate figures, which had declined prior to neoliberalism, began rising.

Neoliberalism's impact was to reduce the number of manufacturing and other jobs in the economy, in order to facilitate capital's saving on wages. Millions of workers were laid off or could not find a regular job, as unemployment and underemployment skyrocketed. The government's low figures for unemployment reflected the unrealistic criterion of calling "employed" anyone who worked, with or without a wage, for one hour a week.

In the face of Mexico's reduced educational opportunities and absence of unemployment compensation, more than two-thirds of Mexico's workforce sought economic survival in the so-called "informal sector" or "underground economy" and undertook individual or family strategies of survival. Urban planning scholar Lourdes Benería called it "*privatization* of the struggle." Women bore an especially heavy share of the burdens caused by neoliberalism's failures, having both to increase domestic work at home and to go to work at a "regular job." Many women packed up the kids and joined the growing migratory flow to the United States.[43]

The Salinas free marketeers eliminated price supports for most basic food products. Under NAFTA rules, it started a fifteen-year phase-out of corn price supports—one of the causes of the 1994 Zapatista uprising in Chiapas. Many *Chiapanecos* were corn farmers. Corn, or maize, was the life-giving foundation of both ancient and contemporary Maya religion and culture.

Prior to NAFTA, Article 27 of the Constitution was reformed to terminate land distribution to peasants and to allow the privatization of *ejidos*, an even more important cause of the Zapatista uprising in a state where nearly a third of the people lived on *ejidos*. Nationallly, a reported 28,000 *ejidos* were put "at risk." They occupied almost nearly half of Mexico's agricultural land, produced more than half of the food supply, and supported more than 3 million families. The reform of Article 27 put the nail in the coffin of the agrarian component of the Mexican Revolution.

Salinas's administration also introduced programs that tried to reassure the peasantry, successfully dividing peasant opposition and neutralizing efforts to break the PRI's stranglehold on the rural vote, such as those of the newly founded Cardenista Democratic Peasant Union (UCD). The most important Salinas program was a vast expansion of the fading and tarnished National Plan for Depressed Areas and the Marginalized (COPLAMAR, created in 1977). Salinas renamed it the National Solidarity Program (PRO-NASOL), thereby co-opting the favorite slogan of the earthquake rescuers, "solidarity." Using more than $12 billion of privatization proceeds and federal and state budgets, PRONASOL created public-works projects in states where the PRI was weak.

The program was meant to project Salinas's philosophy of "social liberalism," which in 1993 became part of the PRI's official ideology along with "nationalism" and "revolution." Several Maoist and Communist intellectuals and activists were co-opted to administer PRONASOL and assure communities that Salinas was "progressive." PRONASOL created 150,000 "solidarity" committees, covering almost all of the nation's municipalities. It actually did reduce poverty among some of the extremely poor. In the process, however, it reinforced authoritarian patterns of clientelism.

Independent peasant organizations like the Independent Confederation of Farm Workers and Peasants (CIOAC) split on Salinas's privatization of *ejidos*, in part because some peasant leaders were co-opted by the PRI or the PRONA-SOL program, and in part because some *ejidatarios* desperately needed the pesos from the sales of their *ejido* parcels. PRONASOL also proved effective in dividing and slowing down the urban social movements by obligating their leaders to sign agreements in exchange for funds or social services. By recruiting the labor of impoverished community people in improvement projects that they themselves recommended and PRONASOL then funded, PRONASOL was able to steal much of the thunder of the insurgent social movements. Also, as Canadian scholar Judith Adler Hellman pointed out, social movements easily lost momentum once some of their rudimentary demands were met—a clinic, a paved road, improved sanitation, safe drinking water, housing assistance, etc.[44]

Not all peasants fell for the various schemes of the Salinas administration. In 1992, some of them launched the "el Barzón" movement as a collective way of saying "no" to their own debts owed to state and private creditors. They carried out several huge mobilizations and even physically attacked bank officers. The new movement soon attracted not only peasants but also small businesses and individual credit card holders. El Barzón membership surpassed 300,000 *before* the 1994-1995 economic collapse, which generated nearly three times as many new recruits to its ranks.[45]

In an attempt to "depoliticize" the resurgent pro-democracy movements and co-opt their leaderships, President Salinas introduced a policy of *concertación* ("coming together"). He asked local food committees run by women's councils to administer some of the state's warehousing and food distribution. He lured the independent electrical workers' union SME back into the CTM. He won over to his neoliberal economic program the formerly militant phone workers and electrical workers, who formed the backbone of a new 200,000-strong Federation of Goods and Services Union.

In January 1989, Salinas had arrested oil labor *charro* Joaquín ("La Quina") Hernández Galicia and dozens of other Petroleum Workers Union officials.[46] La Quina had brought corruption charges against a close friend of Salinas and had been sympathetic to the Cárdenas presidential campaign in 1988. His replacement, another *charro*, laid off 30,000 transient workers at PEMEX, de-unionized 10,000 technical and professional workers, agreed to a more "flexible" contract, and eventually reduced the PEMEX labor force by half—to 124,000 workers.

Salinas followed the removal of La Quina with the arrest of a member of the banking elite's Legorreta family, accused of fraud in the 1987 stock market crash. This was meant to show that Salinas could be tough with big business too. It soon became clear, however, that many elite families, along with foreign capitalists and newcomers close to Salinas and the technocrats dominant in the PRI, would grow rich from picking up shares of privatized state firms at bargain-basement prices.

By the early 1990s, Mexico's economy was at last growing once more. However, at least 44 PRD activists and dozens more peasant and worker leaders had fallen before a hail of "*concertación*" bullets. Fair-minded journalists and progressive lawyers were also gunned down.

The apparent "economic recovery" proved illusory, and in late 1994 the economy went bottom up. At that point, things got worse for a lot of Mexicans, especially women and Indians. Yet Mexico's working people did not back down. In the face of ever harsher economic adversities, many Mexicans kept struggling for both political and economic democracy.

Corporatism: Dead or Alive?

It is appropriate to end this chapter with a brief reflection on corporatism in the mid-1990s, and the crisis of Mexico's corporatist state that exploded on the world stage in 1994-1997. According to many observers, the state's corporatist modes of operation no longer sufficed to resolve problems generated by class conflict because of neoliberalism's draining the state of its resources, or because the PRI's new technocratic leadership consciously chose to dismantle corporatism.

These approaches are somewhat short-sighted, non-historical oversimplifications. After all, as this chapter and earlier ones have shown, the state's resources were already being drained *before* neoliberalism, partly through unequal exchange in trade and the "suction pump" effect of foreign investment. Moreover, the PRI's neoliberal presidential technocrats wished to "dismantle" (that is, weaken) *labor unions*, not the corporatist state that the PRI operated. Indeed, they called on the help of Fidel Velázquez, the head of the PRI's CTM labor union sector, to do this.

The PRI's leading technocrats, their families, and their friends wished to retain the PRI state's ability to support monopoly capital and obtain "their fair share" of the nation's economic surplus generated by labor. To do this under conditions of neoliberalism they needed a strong, centralized state to feather their own nests in the required privatization of state enterprises. The 1990 sale of the state telephone company TELMEX and 1991 sale of the nation's richest bank Banamex to personal friends of the president were only two of many such cases of how privatization worked in practice.

Other observers opine that the importance of corporatism was always exaggerated in the first place. Cognizant of the many regional differences inside an ethnically and geographically diverse nation like Mexico, they believe Mexico's state had always been much less corporatist or centralized than commonly assumed.

This too oversimplifies reality. It should be remembered that when the state sent in the army to crush "land to the tiller" movements, student movements, and workers' strikes *throughout* Mexico, it was able do so with relative impunity because it was a powerful, *centralized* state, not a decentralized one. The same holds true for when the state successfully co-opted local leaders all the way from Baja California in the north to Chiapas in the south, using the methods of corporatism. Actually, to abet neoliberalism, President Salinas *centralized*, not decentralized, state economic agencies.

A historical perspective is helpful here. Corporatism came on the Mexican scene initially as a way of resolving the intense class conflicts expressed during the Revolution and its aftermath, from 1910 to 1940. Corporatism eventually succeeded in its class mediation mission within a capitalist economy, not only under President Cárdenas but more importantly during the Second World War and the following fifteen years or so, when import-substitution had its greatest success and the country became semiindustrialized.

Because the bourgeoisie was accustomed to making most of its profits through the superexploitation of low-wage labor and to not being taxed, the raising of capital and technology in Mexico's uneven economic development was left largely to the foreign (mostly U.S.) investment community. By the mid-1960s and 1970s, and even more so by 1994, Mexico's economy had experienced such profound structural changes brought about by the dominance of domestic and foreign monopoly capital and changes in the world economy that old-style corporatism was no longer so easy to practice.

U.S. creditors and investors, having their own problems with capitalist overproduction, falling profit rates, and insufficient markets, were committed to neoliberalism. This required that the U.S. government have a balanced federal budget where social expenditures came from the available tax revenues. U.S. imperialism imposed this model of neoliberalism on Mexico. In a low-wage, high unemployment economy like Mexico's, with an effective prohibition on the taxing of corporations as a source of state revenue, the funds available for the necessary social costs for the reproduction of the working class on a daily and generational basis were savagely inadequate. The corporatist state did not have the social democratic option of forcing the bourgeoisie through corporate taxes to carry a part of the costs of the working class's reproduction. The decades of structural economic changes, combined with these built-in structural obstacles and the PRI's corrupt ways, gradually eroded both the efficacy of corporatism and the PRI's political legitimacy.

So did the escalating popular assault from below against the forces of sexism and racism. Throughout this chapter we have seen the important role of women and Indians in Mexico's class struggle and yet their relative absence from leadership positions. Mestizo and white males almost always called the shots. This indirectly reflected an often overlooked social and cultural dimension of Mexican corporatism, namely the core values of patriarchy and racism which centralized authority in "the father," "the [white] man," "*el patrón*," and "*el que manda*" ("he who commands," a common Mexican and Latin American saying).

Mexico's "revolutionary family" (the PRI leadership) and its centralized, one-party state headed by a strong "father" *("el señor presidente*," or *presidentialism)* were political expressions of patriarchy. So were the PRI state's institutions, such as its women organizations, the CNC, and the INI—and their condescending, paternalistic handling of women, peasants, and Indians. Patriarchy and racism were deep set historical and cultural patterns that effectively reinforced twentieth-century corporatism and the corresponding lack of democracy in Mexico. Patriarchy, racism, and corporatism were "blood brothers."

The PRI's corporatist state was undoubtedly in crisis. But the crisis was rooted in the structural changes over several decades in the capitalist modes of state-guided economic "development" and "modernization," as well as in the class, ethnic, and gender struggles against oppression that accompanied those changes. Thus, despite the PRI's apologists who claimed that this governmental system never really "ruled," and those who said it was consciously finished off by technocrats, corporatism actually *eroded* in a complex historical process.

Chapter 8

Challenges to the PRI

Democracy is governing by obeying—government of the people, for the people, and by the people.

> —Zapatistas' Fourth Declaration of the Lacandón Jungle,
> January 1, 1996

[Free trade] is about how 4 percent of the world's people can continue to hold 22 percent of the world's wealth.

> —President Bill Clinton, addressing AFL-CIO Convention,
> September 1997

They like the Mexican a lot because he's the hardest working person the United States has. . . . No people work as hard.

> —Immigrant worker from Michoacán

We Are the Seeds of Rebellion and We Shall Bear Fruit

> —Placard carried by Mayan women on International Women's
> Day, March 8, 1998, as they marched up to a military trench
> protecting a helicopter landing strip in Guadalupe Tepeyac,
> Chiapas, and wrecked it.[1]

MORE THAN 2 MILLION MEXICANS LOST THEIR JOBS during the first two years (1994-1996) of the implementation of the North American Free Trade Agreement (NAFTA). One-sixth of the job losses were in the "modern" manufacturing sector, which was unable to compete with the influx of cheaper foreign goods. More than 28,000 Mexican businesses went bankrupt. Banks failed, while consumer debt reached astronomical proportions. The minimum wage plummeted to levels below those of 1981, the last year before the formal introduction of neoliberal economic policy. NAFTA's devastating impact and Mexico's economic collapse of 1994-1995 were products of historical misdevelopment and contemporary neoliberalism.

Despite the economic crisis, pro-democracy activists made amazing advances. The Indians, peasants, and women of Chiapas, who supported the demands of the Zapatista guerrilla uprising of January 1, 1994, became a focal point and source of inspiration. Political and social movements against neo-liberalism and for political democracy radically altered the nation's political landscape. By 1998, the PRI had lost its majority in Congress and discontent among the economically squeezed intermediate classes and peasantry was deepening. Worker agitation, long held in check by the *charrismo* of the official labor confederation CTM after the state's repression of the mid-1970s industrial strikes, had begun anew. In brief, the class struggle had commenced an uneven but notable ascent, not witnessed since the 1968-1977 period (except briefly during the aftermath of the 1985 Mexico City earthquake).

This chapter recounts these developments with some historical background where appropriate. It also examines the highly influential roles of narco-trafficking, the military, the Church, the mass media, and the seasonal emigration of nearly one-fifth of Mexico's workforce to the United States.

The 1988 Election

Throughout the 1980s and much of the 1990s, the central electoral trend in Mexico was one of voter apathy, as shown by turnouts of less than half the eligible voters on every election day. Typically, a 1985 newspaper headline trumpeted "Abstention Wins Again!"

The PRI attempted to reverse this trend and to expand its appeal by bringing more women into a newly created (1984) party national council and by loudly announcing new "internal party reforms." But the traditional hierarchical method of running party affairs from the small national executive committee down—a system known as *dedazo* ("fingering")—continued. So did presidentialism, including the president's *dedazo* of his successor.

None of the PRI's internal machinations mattered much to the general populace. No one bothered to wonder which way the three corporativist sectors of the PRI (labor, peasantry, and "popular") might swing in their use of intra-party power, since the arena in which candidates were selected was not there. Rather, the inner circles of the PRI, its highest state officials, and, indirectly, the bourgeoisie, chose the candidates.

Also, in most instances, the PRI candidates automatically won elections since the PRI controlled the vote-counting procedure. Using state funds, the PRI regularly spent fortunes on its U.S.-style campaigns of electioneering hoopla, particularly through trucking peasants and workers to rallies and purchasing chunks of television time. Given the skyrocketing foreign debt, this use of national revenues was viewed by most Mexicans as a disgraceful waste.

As noted in the preceding chapter, people in the social movements repeatedly had to confront state power. This tended to propel them toward a natural alliance with leftist political parties. However, those parties were prohibited by President José López Portillo's "political reform" from participating in the mass organizations. For the left to achieve any meaningful political power it had to relate to the trade unions, for only in mass organizations could a political base be established. The left, in fact, attempted to do this, but confronted two additional obstacles: an anticommunist hysteria sponsored by the *charros*, and a feisty independent mood among rank-and-file union militants who distrusted any political party.

Though not able to win national elections, much of Mexico's left chose to contest them because they provided space for the left to air its views. This space was a limited bourgeois-democratic one managed by the state. In practice it was more bourgeois than democratic, since individual and collective rights continued to be violated at the levels of freedom of expression and association, juridical protection, and the rights to unionize and strike. By shifting so much energy into electoral and propaganda battles, the left ran the risk of becoming cut off from the struggles of workers and peasants at their workplaces. Indeed, one of the aims of the state's political-reform program was precisely that.

Prior to the elections of 1979 and 1982, Mexicans rarely had any chance to vote for left opposition candidates. Those who sought to cast "protest votes" were forced to settle for the candidates of the always present conservative PAN (National Action Party). PAN became the nation's second largest electoral force in the 1979 congressional elections, with 13 percent of the votes cast. Founded in 1939 by Catholic conservatives to fight the populist reforms of Cárdenas, PAN for years filled its coffers with donations from capitalists favoring laissez-faire economics. Never getting very far as the party of the urban entrepreneurs and great landowners, it began developing in the 1960s a more populist politics attacking corruption in government. In the 1970s a new neopopulist party, the Mexican Democratic Party (PDM), was founded to serve part of PAN's old constituency: the more conservative of the Catholics, those most frightened by the anticlerical tradition of Mexican *políticos*. The fascist Sinarquistas affiliated with the PDM. The PAN drew some electoral strength from the intermediate classes in the big cities and provincial towns. Its new populist rhetoric also whipped up support among religious-oriented peasants, a number of emigrant workers returning from the United States or Canada, and a few regularly employed workers.

In the 1980s and 1990s, some of Mexico's bourgeoisie hedged their bets with both the PRI and the PAN, which continued to perform as the PRI's "loyal opposition." The ultra-right "radicals" and some of the "moderates," discussed in the preceding chapter, sought to use the PAN as their pathway to the presidency. As historian Dan La Botz pointed out, there was a parallel between the technocrats' taking over the PRI and big business's funding and managing the PAN, in the sense that this way "Mexican business had two parties."[2]

Both the left and the right repeatedly objected to the state's electoral frauds. Throughout the 1980s and 1990s, countless city halls were occupied by irate citizens who claimed their votes had either gone uncounted or been falsely credited to the PRI.

In 1982, the PRI, operating secretly as always, announced its presidential candidate, or "*destapado*"—from cock-fight jargon, referring to the unhitching of the band on the cock's feet as he enters the fray. He was Miguel de la Madrid Hurtado, who, like López Portillo, was not a veteran of PRI internal politics but had written López Portillo's Global Development Plan. A Harvard-educated technocrat, de la Madrid soon gathered around him a pre-inauguration "kitchen cabinet" of twenty-four fellow technocrats, sixteen of whom had done their postgraduate studies abroad. Only four politicians were included in this closed group. The selection of de la Madrid represented a blow to the old guard PRI loyalists of the state bureaucracies and the PRI's three corporatist sectors. The old guard's ability to control the inroads into the state being made by the private sector was further diminished.

De la Madrid campaigned on a platform of "moral rebirth" of the nation, echoing the anti-corruption theme of his predecessor, whose administration went on to set new records for venality. As an indication of his own honesty, de la Madrid acknowledged that Mexico did indeed have a number of "disappeared" citizens.

Apparently not persuaded, more than half the nation's potential voters did not vote for him on election day, July 4, 1982. In the official count, more than a million votes were annulled. The PRI "won" with 74 percent. The PAN was granted 14 percent. The Mexican Unified Socialist Party (PSUM), a leftist coalition dominated by the former Communists and a few individuals from the Mexican Workers Party (PMT), garnered 5 percent, and other opposition parties the remainder. The largest leftist party, the PMT, was not part of the PSUM and, unable to obtain registration, boycotted the election even though it allowed individual party members to work with the PSUM.

Since a PRI vote was virtually obligatory on the part of the swollen state bureaucracy and the 70 percent or so of the urban and rural work force it influenced or controlled, these official results surprised no one. Indeed, the next day's headlines in most newspapers, dominated by the state and the bourgeoisie (see section on the mass media below), did not bother to announce the winner. Instead, they tried to deny the continued voter abstentionism, headlining "Apathy Defeated!"

Opposition poll watchers came up with a different tabulation, however. They found that the PAN got 20 to 30 percent of the vote, the PSUM 10 to 15 percent, the Trotstkyists' Revolutionary Workers Party (PRT), which ran the nation's first woman candidate Rosario Ibarra de Piedra ("La señora"), 4 to 8 percent, and the PRI only 40 to 50 percent. Thus, state propaganda to the contrary, voter apathy and anti-PRI sentiment remained a problem that was only partially alleviated by the previous six years of political reform. The international wire services did their usual buzzing about the electorate's supposed endorsement of Mexico's "stable guided democracy."

In 1985's midterm congressional elections, all eight opposition parties together polled more votes than the PRI in Mexico City. The electoral law, however, gave the PRI the city's forty congressional seats. The international press fell silent. Shaken by the huge post-earthquake street demonstrations of late 1985, the state saw fit to announce an additional "political reform" in 1986. It raised the number of opposition seats in Congress to 150 out of 500.

The extent of popular discontent with the government's acceptance of IMF-imposed austerity programs in exchange for stretching out debt-payment schedules was suggested by Congress's unprecedented rejection of the president's budgetary proposals in early 1987. For the first time, the PRI-dominated body did not serve as a rubber stamp for executive policies. Inflation was running at 150 percent in 1987. All this set the stage for an electoral disaster for the PRI in 1988 and a sea change in Mexico's politics.

A former PRI senator and governor of Michoacán, Cuauhtémoc Cárdenas, son of the president who nationalized oil in 1938,[3] announced in 1987 that he would run for president. He brought with him the "democratic current" of PRI leaders expelled a year earlier, including former PRI president (1975-1976) Porfirio Muñoz Lerdo. Lacking a ticket to run on, Cárdenas accepted the invitation to run as the candidate of the almost defunct Authentic Party of the Mexican Revolution (PARM). Except for the PRT, Mexico's leftist parties backed him (see Table 17 in Chapter 7).

In the 1988 presidential campaign, Cárdenas drew immense crowds to his rallies, mainly because of the popularity of his father's name, the organizational skills of his supporters (especially the Communists and PMT's new leftists), and the desire of many Mexicans to get rid of the PRI. Peasants walked, or hopped on buses, to go to Cárdenas's rallies. They wanted to size up the new "Tata" (Nahuatl for father, the affectionate name peasants gave President Lázaro Cárdenas in the 1930s). Cárdenas's rallies dwarfed those for the PRI candidate, another lackluster Ivy League technocrat, Carlos Salinas de Gortari. As it always did at election time, the PRI bought people drinks, gave them time off from work, and trucked or bussed them to its rallies.

Campaigning against what he called the "modern fascism" of the PRI, Cárdenas criticized both the old import-substitution and the new neoliberalism economic strategies for Mexico's economic development. He called for renegotiating the foreign debt and for amending NAFTA to provide "upward harmonization" of Mexican wages to levels like those in Canada and the United States. Cárdenas's phones were tapped by the Federal Police and his campaign manager was murdered, but this did not deter his campaign.

In the election itself, half the registered voters abstained—no surprise there. But a majority of the other half voted *against* the PRI. Naturally, the PRI could not allow a true vote count to become public. So computers conveniently "failed" on election night, and the director of the agency in charge of organizing 1994's national elections admitted that his predecessors had "opted for the system to fail." Results from half the nation's voting booths in 1988 were never made public; many ballots were burned. Protests against the "cybernetic fraud" caused the Army to stand guard over impounded ballot boxes and ballots. The impounded ballots were burned a few years later, consistent with the terms of a congressional majority agreement achieved by the PRI and its "loyal opposition," the PAN.

The official results of the 1988 election were not announced until the PRI's "alchemists" could recast the losing scenario into a winning one. It took several days, despite PRI supporters having been allowed to cast multiple ballots ("*tamales*") in ballot boxes. The PRI finally "won" with 50.4 percent of the vote. Cárdenas received 31 percent. The PAN received 17 percent for Manuel J. Clouthier, a northern businessman close to the PRI who in the past had presided over both the conservative employers organization COPARMEX and Mexican monopoly capital's Management Coordinating Council (CCE).

With less than a quarter of the populace believing he had won fairly, President-elect Salinas announced that the era of the one-party state was "ending." Huge rallies across the nation protested the "stolen election," and several people were killed in confrontations with the police. Talk of a military coup filled the air. The PRI stumbled forward, shaken yet unbowed.

The PRD

In 1989, Cárdenas loyalists organized themselves into the PRD (Party of the Democratic Revolution). Under the banner of an Aztec sun, the PRD incorporated much of the Mexican Socialist Party, a leftist merger of 1987 that had expanded the old Communist-dominated PSUM coalition by incorporating the much larger PMT. Some of the smaller parties that had backed Cárdenas's candidacy began cooperating once again with the PRI. The PRD championed popular causes, new elections to substitute for the fraudulent 1988 ones, and the "abolition of the one-party state and corporatism."

PAN's "critical support" of President Salinas earned it recognition of a gubernatorial win in Baja California in 1989, but PRD electoral victories in Michoacán and Guerrero went unrecognized. Peasants, workers, and students occupied several government municipal offices. Salinas sent in the army to take them back. At least sixty PRI opponents, mostly PRD activists, were gunned down in 1990. A near-repeat occurred in Michoacán's disputed 1992 elections, resulting in six more deaths.

President Salinas introduced complex and cautious electoral reforms. In 1989, one such reform rearranged voting districts favorably for the PRI and guaranteed the president an automatic majority of support in Congress. New grassroots alliances for democracy, including people who had once voted for the PRI, sprang up. Despite being subjected to harassment and occasional acts of violence, they eventually forced the Salinas administration to implement additional electoral reforms that by the end of 1993 removed the guarantee for an automatic PRI congressional majority.

Salinas tried to present himself as a "reformer" committed to "democracy." The U.S. government and mass media applauded his every move, calling him "Mexico's democratic modernizer" and elevating him to an heroic status never before experienced by any president from "south of the border." This was because Salinas trumpeted the virtues of Mexico's becoming part of a new North American trading alliance being negotiated and long sought by U.S.-based TNCs (see NAFTA section below).

Cárdenas characterized the Salinas-U.S. alliance as a virtual political bailout of the PRI's undemocratic system. The Salinas administration, he told reporters in 1990,

> offers the U.S. an implicit deal, of which free-trade is the latest step. Mexico will indiscriminately put in place the type of economic reforms that the U.S. always wanted for Mexico but the U.S. will accept and protect the existing political system. The Mexican people want a friendly and balanced relationship with the U.S., but not at the cost of bailing out Mexico's authoritarian government.

In an interview published in 1991, Salinas, in part unintentionally, conceded Cárdenas's point by saying:

> When you are introducing such a strong economic reform, you must make sure that you build the political consensus around it. If you are at the same time introducing additional drastic political reform, you may end up with no reform at all. And we want to have reform, not a disintegrated country.[4]

In the 1991 congressional and gubernatorial elections, the PRI "won" 62 percent of the vote. Not surprisingly, a similar percentage of the electorate abstained from voting. Several state gubernatorial elections were blatantly "stolen" by the PRI. Opposition parties complained about the coverage of the campaign by state television channels and the private monopoly Televisa, owned by a multimillionaire PRI loyalist. Huge protests against electoral fraud erupted.

San Luis Potosí's defeated but very popular independent candidate for governor, 77-year-old Dr. Salvador Nava, ill with bladder cancer, stood up to the PRI. All major opposition parties had backed his candidacy. Known as "the doctor of the poor," Nava now told his followers to create a citizens' movement for democracy. As a result, a crowd of women occupied the governor's palace. Other Nava supporters followed the ailing doctor on a 265-mile "March for Dignity" from San Luis Potosí to Mexico City. Overnight, "the doctor of the poor" became a national hero, called by some "Mexico's Gandhi."

According to the widely respected conservative historian Enrique Krauze, Dr. Nava said that he would like the pro-democracy movement to be based on Madero's 1910 Plan de San Luis Potosí. When reminded that Madero's plan had called for a revolutionary uprising, Nava responded: "We will do the same: call for a revolution of consciences."[5]

On March 1, 1992, Nava's call was answered by the founding convention of the Citizens Movement for Democracy (MCD). The MCD brought together dozens of civic groups demanding an end to excessive presidential control, one-party rule, poverty, state manipulation of the media, and economic dependence on the United States. It included many Indian groups and countless PRD sympathizers. Shortly thereafter, in his last statement before dying, Dr. Nava urged the MCD to fight on and to raise "international awareness of the violation of human rights and political liberties of the Mexican people."[6]

Other citizens protesting electoral fraud conducted a 680-mile march from the southeastern state of Tabasco. Many MCD activists joined the pro-democracy group Civic Alliance, an NGO (nongovernmental organization) that was organized to watch over polling places in the presidential elections of 1994.

Because of the pressures brought by all the nationwide protests, President Salinas had to nullify several disputed local election results by appointing interim officials or granting the opposition its victories. As a result, by 1993 the conservative PAN held three state governorships. But the PRD was still facing state violence.

Zapatista Uprising

In the early morning of January 1, 1994, the day NAFTA went into effect, the "Zapatista National Liberation Army" (EZLN) made a successful lightning strike in the southern state of Chiapas that stunned the entire world. The EZLN's anti-NAFTA stance and its call for political democracy and economic justice for *all* Mexico struck a responsive chord in the Mexican public. Early opinion polls showed 75 percent of the populace supporting the Zapatistas. The uprising radically altered Mexican politics and caused NAFTA's U.S. corporate sponsors to reconsider Mexico's much touted "stability." Mexican and CIA officials had known about the presence of the EZLN as early as the spring of 1993 but had chosen to keep it top secret so that the U.S. Congress might view Mexico as "politically stable" and approve the NAFTA treaty in the fall.

In the first days of the uprising, the EZLN seized major towns in Chiapas and threatened an advance on neighboring states and Mexico City. In ten days of combat, Mexico's Army and Air Force finally checked the guerrillas' advance and began driving them back toward the hills and ravines of the Chiapas highlands and Lacandón Jungle, from where they had come. There occurred widespread indiscriminate bombing of civilians. Hundreds were killed.

As the combat raged, people in the rest of the nation poured into the streets to show their sympathy for the Zapatistas. Tens of thousands marched in Mexico City and other cities. They chanted anti-government, pro-Zaptista slogans and called for the government to stop its use of military force. They advocated a ceasefire, a negotiated peace, and no retributions against the Zapatistas. Most significantly, workers from several major unions appeared at the rallies to declare their solidarity with the Zapatistas.

As a result of this overwhelming sentiment, the government did not find it politically expedient to use its superior fire power to snuff out the Zapatistas. This would not have been an easy task in any case, because of the hilly and irregular terrain and the solid networks of local support the Zapatistas had built up over ten years, when a small band of former university activists from the pro-democracy movements of the late 1960s and 1970s had founded the EZLN in Chiapas. Also, there were clear signs elsewhere of organized peasant and Indian groups moving aggressively to defend their land claims, from the Huicholes in the western Pacific states of Jalisco and Nayarit and the Yaquis in the northwestern state of Sonora to the Huastecas near the Gulf region of Hidalgo and Veracruz states.

So the government decided it would be prudent for the moment to agree to a ceasefire arranged by Bishop Samuel Ruiz of San Cristóbal de Las Casas. The ceasefire started on January 13, 1994. Bishop Ruiz went on to be named president of the National Mediation Commission (Conai), an independent mediating group of prominent Mexicans founded in December 1994.

After the ceasefire, workers continued launching actions to protest neoliberalism and the Mexican military's occupation of much of Chiapas. On February 14, 1994, university union workers briefly occupied the Mexican stock market. The Zapatista uprising was becoming a rallying point for all of Mexico's citizens to take bold political action.

Who were the 2,000 Zapatista guerrillas? The EZLN called itself "a majority-indigenous army" to reflect the fact that its members were mostly impoverished Indian peasant women, men, and youngsters who spoke several ancient Maya tongues (Chol, Mam, Tzeltal, Tzotzil, and Tojolabal). They wore bandannas over their faces as a way of shielding easy identity by security forces. Their face masks served as a vaccine against *caudillismo* and as a symbol of their being ignored by the rest of society as "the faceless ones." They viewed their struggle as part of the 500-year-old resistance of all indigenous inhabitants of the Americas. A millenarian movement with a modern anti-neoliberalism, pro-democracy agenda, the Zapatistas said they acted to draw world attention to the extreme poverty and mistreatment of more than half of Chiapas's population, the Indians, and of all Mexico's and Latin America's indigenous peoples.

The Zapatistas called for the right to autonomy for Mexico's Indian and peasant villages and municipalities. Of Mexico's population, 30 percent were still predominantly Indian, although many shared the culture of the 60 percent or more who were *mestizo*. Ethnicity remained a social construction related to class position in society—what anthropologists called "situational identities."[7] Nearly 40 percent of Mexico's Indians resided in three southern states: Guerrero, Oaxaca, and Chiapas. Eighty percent of the nation's Indians were agricultural workers, and half of these were landless. The land they still held was the worst imaginable and continued to be taken away from them by outsiders, especially after oil was discovered on much of it. In 1975, to cite one example, Indians from the San Francisco community of Chiapas told of how soldiers from the Forty-sixth Battalion (with the approval of local authorities) assaulted them, burned their homes, and drove them from their land—which was then handed over to non-Indians with political connections.[8]

For generations, most Indians had been dominated by a system of external *caciquismo,* mediated through coopted community leaders. Indians were excluded from the government, although in 1980 the PRI and the Communist Party each had an Indian deputy in Congress. The Zapatistas' dramatic appearance on the scene energized Mexico's indigenous peoples and their already strong social movements throughout Mexico. With greater urgency and militancy than before, they began holding regional, national, and international meetings that unified diverse groups and reinforced the Zapatistas' demands.

The Zapatista revolt was a peasant and ethnically pluralistic revolt, not just an Indian one. By speaking for many peoples involved in diverse economic activities, the Zapatistas reflected recent changes in Chiapas. The state's peasantry had enmeshed itself in multiple economic survival strategies. Large numbers had become proletarianized peasants working the lands of cattle and coffee land barons under conditions of virtual debt peonage. Some had become involved in petty and even large-scale commerce that took them as far north as Mexico City. Traditional Indian handicraft artisanry, especially by women, had found new markets. Others had become migrant workers, following seasonal harvests as far north as Sinaloa or California. A few managed to find temporary work in the construction projects of the expanding oil, petrochemical, hydroelectric, and highway projects of Chiapas and nearby states. As other migrants in turn had trekked from northern and central Mexico to find work, Chiapas's population had become more diversified. Some of the new arrivals had joined down-and-out locals in clearing new lands in the Lacandón jungle, either spontaneously or in government colonization projects. All wanted a piece of land, *ejido* or otherwise, to assure at least a bit of food for their families.

The Zapatistas' main slogan, echoing the Magonistas and Zapatistas of the Mexican Revolution, was "land and freedom" (*tierra y libertad*). Their public pronouncements often used the exact written words of Ricardo Flores Magón and Emiliano Zapata or Zapata's spokespeople. Their main demand was for land, most of which had been taken over by cattle barons and other *latifundistas* whose hired guns had terrorized Chiapas's peasants for decades.

Moreover, the Zapatistas declared that their "revolution" was national, not ethnic, and was against "the bad government" and for democracy. The phrase "the bad government," like much of the EZLN's program, had been a favorite expression of Emiliano Zapata himslf.[9] Internationally, the Zapatistas aspired to help end the "plundering of the world" by the forces of neoliberalism.

The EZLN's spokesman was the self-mocking but inspiring "Subcomandante Marcos," or "the Sup" for short. Marcos had a refreshing sense of humor and an ability to be very concrete about daily life for Mexico's working people. He also had a poetic flare in his use of language. In an August 1992 writing "The Storm and the Prophesy," he spoke of a "clash between two winds. . . . Now the wind from above rules, but the one from below is coming, the storm rises. . . . When the storm subsides, when the rain and the fire leave the earth in peace again, the world will no longer be the world, but something better."[10]

Actual EZLN command rested with the General Command of the Clandestine Indigenous Revolutionary Committee (CCRI), composed of indigenous and peasant representatives of various regional and local assemblies accustomed to the Maya tradition of collective decisionmaking. Several CCRI members were women, as were commanders of EZLN units.

Like everything else, the Zapatista rebellion had to be placed in historical and socioeconomic context. Most Mexicans, living that context every day, although not as harshly as Chiapas's Indians, easily recognized the legitimacy of the EZLN's demands and viewed them as realizable. As already noted, capitalism's post-1960 penetration of the most remote corners of Mexico's countryside, especially its poorest state, Chiapas, had displaced thousands of Indian and mestizo peasants, divided their communities, increased class differentiation, and, despite occasional individual upward mobility, pauperized the peasantry. It had caused people to refashion their strategies for economic survival. Most Chiapas peasant families engaged in wage work or petty commerce of one kind or another. Where capital entered, the clergy—Catholic and evangelical Protestant—followed. Traditional Indian values were maintained yet further modified, or in some cases driven underground.

Social protest movements emerged among Chiapas's peasants and school teachers in the 1970s and 1980s. They were backed by Catholic activists and former student and faculty militants (Maoists and Guevarists, among others) of the repressed student movements of the 1970s. Despite savage repression, Chiapas's protesters held strong for awhile. They demanded land, credits, fertilizers, and tools; an end to police brutality, military massacres, and use of hired guns by cattle, coffee, and timber land barons; elimination of the fraudulent electoral process that made Chiapas the surest state for the PRI; and release of all political prisoners. Many of the protesters' organizations were co-opted by the government. Therefore, the Zapatistas in the 1980s struggled to break the peasant struggle away from the *cacique*-plagued state arena.

State repression of the Chiapas people's peaceful protests and the deepening disruptive impact of neoliberal capitalism were the final elements that led to the Zapatista uprising. In 1990 coffee prices were allowed to float on the world market and soon plummeted. NAFTA threatened the peasants' place in Mexico's corn market, since U.S. agribusiness's mega-farms were up to six times more productive than small Mexican producers on poor or hilly terrain. In 1992 the Salinas administration reformed Article 27 of the 1917 Constitution to allow privatization of indigenous communal lands and peasant *ejidos*. For the first time since the Mexican Revolution, peasants and Indians of Chiapas, most of them reduced to extreme poverty, found themselves with no guarantee of their final means of survival: *land*.

Marcos and the EZLN repeatedly stated that this neoliberal "constitutional reform" was the single most important event that forced them to take up arms. In early 1993, community assemblies, held in parts of Chiapas where people had learned about the guerrillas' presence and had lent them support, issued an ultimatum to the CCRI: launch an offensive in one year's time or the communities would no longer cooperate with the guerrilla command. In other words, many peasants felt that they would die without access to land and felt an armed revolution was the only realistic choice left them.

From interviews published by French sociologist and Latin Americanist Yvon Le Bot in April 1997, we now know that when Marcos and his ten comrades first showed up in Chiapas in the mid-1980s they had thought of the EZLN as *strictly* a defensive army to protect people against possible acts of repression by the Mexican military. Marcos had assumed that sooner or later the Army would invade people's communities in Chiapas and other parts of Mexico as citizens increased their protests against the pauperizing effects of neoliberalism. He told Le Bot that he thought the community assemblies' ultimatum to launch an uprising was both foolish and "suicidal," but that he and the CCRI had no choice but "to obey." This conformed with the bottom-up democratic ideals of the EZLN leadership, which were based on each leader's learning "to command by obeying"—that is, obeying the expressed wishes of the local community assemblies. Marcos conceded to Le Bot that the practice of this kind of democracy was by no means perfect.

The "first uprising" actually occurred without a shot being fired and was an internal one. In March 1993, while preparing for the insurrection, the Zapatistas discussed the need for drafting a set of "revolutionary laws." The women present insisted upon a law for their equality and an end to abuses by their men. As Marcos later pointed out: "The first uprising of the EZLN ... was led by the women Zapatistas. They suffered no losses and they won."[11]

In the "second uprising," the armed revolt of January 1, 1994, the Zapatistas' EZLN "obeyed" the decision of the community assemblies and seized control of Chiapas's most famous city, the historic San Cristóbal de Las Casas, as well as several other major populated areas. A third of the EZLN was composed of women, some of whom commanded entire units. The military genius of the Zapatistas in pulling off such a momentous feat impressed everyone at the time, although it was rarely analyzed or commented upon in the rash of articles and books that followed. Le Bot's 1997 interviews elicited an explanation of the EZLN's mililtary/political strategy, which was successfully implemented in a day or two with few weapons other than shotguns, sticks, stones, the element of surprise, arms seized during the initial attacks on military or police outposts, and, above all, the very useful cooperation of local residents.[12] As Marcos told the press on the first day of the cease-fire: "war is not a matter of weapons . . . but of politics." Added a February communiqué of the CCRI: "it is not only the mouth of a gun that will achieve liberty…other mouths must open and shout so that the powerful tremble."[13]

The Zapatistas said they agreed to a ceasefire and to negotiate with "the bad government" because of the outpouring of support for their cause and for peace by Mexico's citizenry. In the words of the EZLN's June 1994 Second Declaration of the Lacandón Jungle: "another force, superior to any political or military power [had] imposed itself . . . civil society."[14] "Obeying" the commands of Mexico's citizenry, the EZLN switched to a strategy of what became known as "armed non-violence"—patient negotiations. Mexico's major political parties signed an Agreement for Peace, Democracy, and Clean Elections, which later became law. It included such electoral changes as making the Federal Electoral Tribunal less weighted in favor of the PRI.

The 1994 Election

President Salinas named as his peace commissioner a political rival in the PRI, Manuel Camacho Solís, a former Mexico City mayor reputed to be a party "democratizer." Camacho Solís earlier had objected to not being picked over Luis Donaldo Colosio, a PRI technocrat, to succeed Salinas as president, and had said he might have to run for the presidency himself. Left in the background, Colosio tried to energize his presidential campaign by adopting several opposition demands, such as more electoral transparency and more outside observers for the upcoming August elections. Colosio called for a shift in economic policy to improve the lives of the poor and of family farmers.

On March 16, 1994, Colosio and Camacho Solís signed an alliance, and six days later Camacho Solís said he would not run for the presidency. A day after that, an assassin shot and killed Colosio in the midst of a Tijuana campaign rally. Not long afterwards, peace talks between the government and the Zapatistas were suspended. Political tensions in early 1994 were also caused by the kidnapping of two important businessmen and an explosion at a Monterrey bank in northeastern Mexico.

The PRI's old guard *políticos*, or "dinosaurs" as they were called (see below), were widely suspected of having engineered Colosio's assassination. On the other hand, some believed Salinas himself wanted Colosio eliminated for having gone too far with his promises of radical political reform (Salinas had warned in 1991, "introducing additional drastic political reform, you may end up with no reform at all."). The Tijuana police chief conducting the Colosio murder investigation was later assassinated. A former senior aide to the attorney general fled to the United States, calling Mexico a "narco-democracy," and charging that drug lords and top PRI officials were behind Colosio's murder.

Named to succeed Colosio as the PRI's candidate was Yale-educated Ernesto Zedillo Ponce de León, a very conservative budget and planning minister for Salinas who had helped oversee the powerful Pronasol anti-poverty program examined in the preceding chapter. Zedillo also had served briefly as education minister, when he unsuccessfully tried to introduce new history textbooks that favorably portrayed foreign investors, the U.S. government, and dictator Porfirio Díaz. Zedillo selected old-guard PRI boss and wealthy businessman (and reputed drug money launderer) Carlos Hank González to be his campaign manager.

Meanwhile, the Mexican army was busy stationing tens of thousands of troops in Chiapas, undertaking what U.S. military manuals called "low intensity warfare." In mid-June of 1994, the Zapatistas refused to return to the peace table, noting the army's incursions and a lack of adequate provisions for political democracy in the government's thirty-four-point peace program. After that, peace negotiations were periodically renewed and interrupted again.

That August, in one of its first public acts after the cease-fire, the Zapatistas held a National Democratic Convention. Among those present was the nation's champion of "the disappeared" Rosario Ibarra de Piedra. In a symbolic gesture, she was given the convention's giant Mexican flag to take back to the capital and hold in safe keeping. Gaining tremendous leverage from the Zapatista challenge to the state, Mexico's pro-democracy movement won guarantees of transparent voter boxes and the right to have domestic and foreign observer teams in parts of Mexico on election day scheduled for that same month of August.

A wounded and divided PRI tried to focus on winning the 1994 elections. Throughout the Salinas administration, the PRI had undergone intense infighting that pitted the "dinosaurs" against the technocrats, men like Salinas who hypocritically wrapped themselves in the garb of "reform." Seasoned *políticos*, the "dinosaurs" looked warily at Salinas, who had never before run for political office. They proved influential in the expulsion of more than one PRI "democratic current" and the removal of Salinas's supposedly "reformist" appointees to head the party. When Salinas's third "reformer" appointee to head the PRI publicly acknowledged in 1993 "we are neither a virtual single party nor the party of government," he was promptly removed.

The "dinosaurs" were miffed that the last three Mexican presidents had come from outside the PRI's inner circle of *políticos*. They fumed when the 1994 "*destapado*" turned out to be Colosio, one more U.S.-educated technocrat. Colosio had once headed the PRI and had commanded Salinas's Ministry of Social Development (SEDESOL), the notoriously ineffective agency in charge of cleaning up the environmental mess along the U.S. border.

Zedillo, like Salinas, at first drew the wrath of the "dinosaurs," although some respected Zedillo's work for Pronasol, an anti-poverty program he turned into a co-optation vehicle. Most "dinosaurs" fell in line with Zedillo's campaign when he appointed some of them to key positions like campaign manager and PRI secretary of information and propaganda.

A month prior to the August 1994 presidential contest, the left-of-center opposition PRD carried out an internal national election for its party leadership. Andrés Manuel López Obrador was elected party president. A former PRI member, he was close to the nation's social movements. He had defended the Indian communities of Tabasco when their landscapes and communities had been devastated by the rush to produce more oil in the 1970s and after. Duly impressed with the PRD's attempt at democracy and its outcome, the EZLN encouraged its supporters to vote for PRD presidential candidate Cárdenas.

For candidate Zedillo, the PRI went all out to avoid a repeat of its 1988 electoral disaster. It made good use of its still powerful, if reduced, role in organizing and administering elections. A television debate between Zedillo, conservative PAN candidate Diego Fernández de Cevallos, and PRD candidate Cárdenas was won handily by the sharp-tongued Fernández de Cevallos. Cárdenas, who moved to the political center by saying he would *not* nationalize the banks or return to protectionism in trade, promised more economic "reform" with a greater social conscience. He came off as lacking color or punch.

Once the official vote count was announced, Zedillo had barely garnered 50 percent of the votes. The PAN's Fernández de Cevallos finished second, the PRD's Cárdenas third. The PRD charged widespread "fraud," including the "shaving" of 6 million voters (leaving them off the national register and so denying them the vote). Few poll watchers denied that, except in Chiapas and one or two other states, the electoral fraud was not as blatant as it had been in 1988.

Voter turnout was higher than usual, in part because the PRI spent huge sums on buying votes and transporting "its people" to the polls. In classic PRI corporatist fashion, on the eve of the election the government implemented the National Program of Direct Aid to the Countryside (PROCAMPO) to win voter support and supplement Pronasol. PROCAMPO paid some 3.3 million peasant producers $100 a hectare to assure their voting for the PRI. As president, Zedillo continued the anti-poverty programs of Pronasol, moving them under SEDESOL. But even before Zedillo's taking office, another major political assassination rocked Mexico.

In September 1994, José Francisco Ruiz Massieu, the PRI's second highest official, was killed. The official investigation into his murder, like the earlier one into Colosio's, bogged down in frequent alleged cover-ups, the resignations of those appointed to investigate, and mysterious deaths. In February 1995, ex-president Salinas's brother Raúl Salinas de Gortari was arrested and eventually imprisoned for allegedly having paid for the murder of Ruiz Massieu and for illegal enrichment.

The "NAFTA Miracle"

When President Salinas took office in 1988, Mexico was still experiencing "the lost decade of development." Neoliberal economic policies were generating a backlash of massive social discontent. The PRI technocrats felt neoliberalism needed more time to succeed and more, not less, free-trade impetus. So they decided to announce that a new Mexican "economic miracle" was about to occur, this time not through the import-substitution policies of the Second World War and its aftermath but by means of their neoliberal opposite: free trade as embodied in NAFTA.

The secretly negotiated 2,000-page treaty known as NAFTA was sponsored by the most powerful business organizations of Mexico, Canada, and the United States, including the U.S. Business Round Table and its Mexican equivalent, the CCE (whose thirty-seven members reportedly held assets equal to one quarter of Mexico's GDP). NAFTA promised to phase out trade barriers over the next fifteen years on goods wholly or largely originating in any one of NAFTA's three countries. NAFTA's big business sponsors believed this would strengthen their "competitiveness" vis-à-vis the growing economic powers of Japan and the European Economic Community/European Union. They claimed that NAFTA augured a $6 trillion market for 363 million consumers, or one-fifth of world trade, and a corresponding rise in workers' wages and jobs. They called it a "win-win-win" situation for all three countries. Mexico was already reaching out to other Latin American countries to form subsets of NAFTA, and the Bush and Clinton administrations spoke of an eventual hemispheric common market.

Mexico had started lowering its tariffs in the preceding administration of President de la Madrid (1982-1988), who had brought Mexico into the General Agreement on Tariffs and Trade (GATT, later replaced by the World Trade Organization, or WTO, which received power to enforce "free trade," that is, a "level playing field for all"). Salinas reduced Mexico's tariffs much further during the years leading up to the 1994 implementation of NAFTA.

Salinas and the technocrats around him not only saw dollar signs for themselves through their handling of the stepped-up pace of privatization NAFTA entailed ("to level the playing field"). They also thought they could save the PRI by using the "NAFTA miracle" as a sign to the populace that the economy would not only grow again but would generate jobs and consumer goods for all. They used government funds to conduct an expensive publicity campaign along those lines in both Mexico and the United States.

This made Salinas practically a hero in U.S. ruling circles. A leaked memo from U.S. Ambassador John Negroponte in 1991 encouraged support for Salinas because his government was changing the attitude toward Washington "dramatically" and NAFTA offered a unique opportunity for expanding U.S. influence. Negroponte had served as ambassador to Honduras during the military buildup of Nicaragua's contras at Honduran bases in the 1980s.

The Salinas government also lobbied the U.S. Congress to vote for NAFTA, which Congress barely did in November 1993 after some votes were "bought" in back room trading of favors between President Bill Clinton and unconvinced congressmen. Polls showed U.S. public opinion turning against NAFTA at the time.

The pre-NAFTA free trade agreement (FTA) between Canada and the United States had guaranteed U.S. access to Canadian oil and gas by obligating Canada to export to the United States at least the average amount of the previous three years. Even water during times of Canadian shortages had to be sent to the United States. But Canadian big business had backed the FTA because it opened up investment opportunities in low-wage areas of the United States, the same benefit Canadian businesses expected from Mexico's economy opening more widely under NAFTA.

Canadian and other critics of NAFTA pointed out that the FTA had caused Canada to embrace neoliberalism's rolling back of Canada's world-class social welfare programs, viewed by the FTA as "unfair trade subsidies." To these critics, NAFTA represented more of the same. They saw the corporate agenda behind NAFTA as one of saving on wages, with North American wages to move more toward the Mexican level rather than vice-versa ("downward" instead of "upward" harmonization of wages). These critics felt NAFTA would revert Mexico into an "enclave economy" of the United States, and that employers would use the threat to move production to Mexico to prevent North American workers from gaining decent wages.

The NAFTA treaty did, in fact, serve to open up Mexico further to foreign investment and to lock Mexico into keeping the state's hands off foreign investments. In addition, it prohibited Mexico from legislating or decreeing performance standards that might obligate a TNC to transfer technology to the host country or to give preference to domestic suppliers. The NAFTA treaty thus delivered one more setback to Mexico's fading efforts to develop a more vigorous and autonomous production of capital and intermediate goods.

Mexican critics saw the U.S. promotion of Salinas and NAFTA as an attempted political bailout for the PRI. These anti-NAFTA people were joined by critics around the world who saw NAFTA as part of a U.S. grab for Mexico's oil, natural gas, uranium, and other natural resources, including the gene pools of tropical flora and fauna of great use to pharmaceutical companies patenting them as part of their "intellectual property rights." Some said that Mexico's "brain drain" would increase as university graduates in computers and scientific research flocked northward for better paying jobs.

Many worried that NAFTA would be dominated by the United States, where the GDP was eleven times bigger than Canada's and twenty times larger than Mexico's.[15] In 1992, 7 percent of all U.S. exports went to Mexico, adding to Mexico's trade imbalance, a trend that later was accelerated by NAFTA (except for a brief period after Mexico's peso devaluations of 1994-1995). Critics denounced NAFTA as a "big business scam" that would open up Mexico and its immense pool of cheap labor to greater, easier, and guaranteed investments by U.S. and Canada-based TNCs.

NAFTA's Mexican opponents wished to develop Mexico in a way that would not keep its wages low and force more and more people to accept poor, unsafe work conditions or migrate northward just to survive. They built a "new politics" coalition of more than one hundred groups called the Mexican Action Network on Free Trade. It forged links with its principal anti-NAFTA counterparts to the north: the Action Canada Network and the U.S.-based Mobilization on Development, Trade, Labor and the Environment. The three together proposed a Continental Development Pact modeled after the Social Charter of the European Economic Community (EEC), which spent $70 billion to upgrade wage levels in poor EEC nations like Spain and Portugal, and a similar plan put forward by Cárdenas. The United States was the only Western country not to have granted workers' rights like those enshrined in Europe's Social Charter. Mexican Action Network's demands included equal pay for equal work, demilitarization of the U.S.-Mexico border, modification of Mexico's unfair electoral laws to permit fair elections, and the inclusion of non-governmental organizations (NGOs) in all NAFTA negotiations.

In the early 1990s, international solidarity groups like the North American Worker-to-Worker Network, the AFL-CIO-backed Coalition for Justice in the Maquiladoras, and the Mexican Action Network on Free Trade increasingly cooperated to apply pro-labor, pro-environment pressures against NAFTA. Some observers called these grassroots coalitions "citizen diplomats."

Those seeking a compromise solution *within* NAFTA also linked up across borders. For example, the well-financed Environmental Defense Fund, whose support for NAFTA proved critical for NAFTA's winning U.S. congressional approval, built bridges to Mexico's "Group of 100," prominent Mexican intellectuals who advocated NAFTA "with a human face." The Group of 100, like the anti-NAFTA forces already mentioned, wanted Mexican labor's northward migration on the agenda to prevent low Mexican wages from becoming a permanent feature of the North American economic landscape.

Acts of international labor solidarity, though still few, related to NAFTA. On January 8, 1991, a tri-nation solidarity task force, MEXUSCAN, organized a Ford Workers Justice Day for the first anniversary of the murder of a striking worker by a CTM goon at the Ford plant in Cuautitlán. Speakers called for building international labor unity to assure upward harmonization of wages in all three countries, with or without NAFTA. Similarly, the Midwest's FLOC (Farm Labor Organizing Committee) cooperated with Sinaloa's SNTOAC (National Union of Farm Workers) in contract negotiations with Campbell Soup. Their earlier cooperation had prevented Campbell from moving its Michigan operations to Sinaloa.

The AFL-CIO critiqued NAFTA in a 1991 publication entitled "Exploiting Both Sides." But by limiting its cooperation to the CTM, whose aging leader Fidel Velázquez backed NAFTA, and by shunning the leaders of the democratic currents in Mexico's trade unions, the AFL-CIO could find no trust among Mexican workers fighting *charrismo*. Both environmental and labor protection, as well as the issue of Mexican immigrant workers in the United States, were topics excluded from the extremely secretive NAFTA negotiations.

Because of the public outcry by the anti-NAFTA forces, however, the Clinton administration was forced to add *non-binding* side agreements to NAFTA to encourage environmental protection and labor's rights. But there was no White House suggestion of moving toward an EEC-style Social Charter. Both side agreements stated that any remedies must conform to existing national laws in each country rather than to international standards. During NAFTA's first five years (1994-1998), neither of the two side agreements led to any changes or substantive solutions to environmental problems or to the lack of workers' rights in any of the three signatory nations.[16]

NAFTA turned out to be not so much a free trade pact as a looting of Mexico by U.S.-based and, to a lesser extent, Canada-based transnational corporations (TNCs), and an attack on all three nations' workers' wages and rights. Also, from its inception, NAFTA was more about trade wars than about free trade. Its corporate sponsors saw in NAFTA a way of beefing up North American business interests in their competition with the growing challenges posed by the early 1990s' strong economies of Japan, East Asia, and the EEC.[17] Indeed, trade wars escalated after NAFTA and GATT's WTO took full effect. Even *within* free trade pacts, trade war fever heated up, as witness U.S.-Canadian tensions over fairness with regard to lumber, salmon fishing, and cultural industries, or the U.S.-Mexico tuna, avocado, strawberry, tomato, and trucking controversies.[18]

U.S. Vice President Al Gore often compared NAFTA to the Louisiana Purchase, a huge economic windfall for the United States.[19] President Clinton tacitly acknowledged the challenge to U.S. economic hegemony posed by Japan and the EEC when he told an AFL-CIO convention in 1997 that free trade was "about how 4 percent of the world's people can continue to hold 22 percent of the world's wealth." The new economic buzz words of the free trade era were "market reforms" and guarantees of NAFTA-style "intellectual property rights" (IPRs), "investment guarantees," and "non-discriminatory treatment," which meant *all* investors' equal access to *any* economy, including the "services sector" (*e.g.*, banking, insurance, real estate, transportation, and telecommunications).

Mexico was rewarded in 1994 for its role in forming NAFTA by being granted entry into the rich nations' powerful consultative body Organization for Economic Cooperation and Development (OECD) and the Asia-Pacific Economic Cooperation forum (APEC). Using NAFTA as its model, the Clinton administration looked forward to gaining more Latin American support for the proposed Free Trade Area of the Americas (FTAA), as well as the Multilateral Agreement on Investment (MAI) and TransAtlantic Free Trade Agreement (TAFTA). Critics called the MAI a "license to loot" and "NAFTA on steroids" because of its granting every conceivable "right" to TNCs and iron-clad protections for their investments. In May of 1998, thousands of demonstrators formed a human chain outside a meeting of the "G-8" heads of state (Britain, Canada, France, Germany, Italy, Japan, Russia, and the United States) to protest the proposed TAFTA and to call for a cancellation of the third world debt by the year 2000.

After NAFTA went into effect, all three of its member nations experienced an initial decline in real wages for the majority of their work forces. Their shrinking labor unions had to fight mainly defensive battles. Mexico suffered the greatest ill effects of GATT and NAFTA. In 1993-1994, some 40 percent of Mexico's clothes manufacturers shut down because of cheap Chinese and Southeast Asian imports sought by the new U.S. retail stores setting up business in Mexico. The Mexican toy industry all but collapsed, while the leather and footwear sector suffered a reduction by more than half in production and employment. The near collapse of domestic Mexican industry and rising number of workers laid off worsened after the 1994 to 1995 peso devaluation crisis. From 1993 to 1996, Mexico imported more agricultural products than it exported, including quantities of corn for which the market price in Mexico went up, not down as NAFTA advocates had predicted. Major importers in charge of corn marketing included such U.S.-based TNCs as Anderson Clayton, Cargill, and Purina. In the NAFTA era, the role of TNCs increased throughout the most productive and profitable areas of the Mexican countryside, while more small farms failed.

As Edur Velasco Arregui has pointed out, Mexico experienced greater environmental devastation than the United States or Canada. NAFTA facilitated Mexico's becoming a kind of North American dumping ground and waste disposal area. Velasco Arregui estimated that the combined costs of soil erosion, water and air contamination, and depletion of non-renewable resources from 1980 to 1997 came to between 8.5 percent and 15 percent of Mexico's GDP, with workers and poor people suffering the worst effects of pollution and environmental degradation.[20]

NAFTA worked pretty much in the ways the TNCs had hoped for in the first place. About half of the U.S. firms belonging to a U.S. industrial group that had lobbied for NAFTA sent jobs abroad and increased their profits nearly 300 percent by early 1997.[21] U.S. exports to Mexico notably increased, as Mexico passed Japan in 1994 as the second largest U.S. trading partner (behind Canada). The U.S. government claimed a four-year gain in U.S. employment from NAFTA of more than 100,000 jobs because of increased exports. However, it also admitted that 151,256 U.S. jobs were lost because of NAFTA, and that this figure understated the true job drain.

By having NAFTA-guaranteed protections of intellectual property rights and of investment opportunities in *all* of Mexico's economic sectors, U.S. and Canadian banks and corporations were able to economize on the costs at home of maintaining decent wages, safe work conditions, and health benefits for their workers. They also were able to save on the costs of meeting environmental standards north of the Mexican border. Insofar as they moved to Mexico or wrenched concessions from organized labor on the basis of their threat to move, they achieved their goals.

U.S. and Canadian banks and corporations wanted to justify their free-trade policies and so-called "downsizings" on the basis of "the need to compete globally"—a justification used by all the world's TNCs and big banks in a global attack on working people's standards of living everywhere. The "global competition" rationale was even used in drawing Mexico into the web of neoliberalism and free trade by claiming that Mexico was becoming *more* competitive *because* of its low-wage structure. Downward harmonization of wages was indeed the hidden agenda of trade pacts like NAFTA and GATT.

The Privatization of Oil

Ultimately, with specific regard to Mexico, free trade pacts were easing the way to privatization of the constitutionally mandated national oil and natural gas industries. NAFTA transferred some of Mexico's energy sector to U.S. companies through the emphasis on deregulation, privatization, the free flow of goods, and the protection of intellectual property rights. NAFTA especially facilitated U.S. service contracts and sales of equipment and technology in highly lucrative secondary petrochemicals, as well as natural gas. It furthered the opening of Mexico's state oil firm PEMEX to "strategic alliances" with U.S. concerns in petroleum exploration/drilling.

When a 1992 Guadalajara explosion killed more than 180 people, PEMEX was blamed, lending momentum to calls for its privatization. U.S. penetration of the primary petrochemical sector had already become possible because of the Mexican government's agreeing to "technical reclassifications" of primary petrochemical items into "secondary" ones, and changes in corporate law. A 1992 change in corporate law converted PEMEX into a "holding company" with subsidiaries in petrochemicals, gas, refineries, and exploration/drilling. These measures helped avoid the delicate matter of the Constitution's call for national ownership of the oil industry. PEMEX and Shell Oil Company, for example, used the 1992 law to form a "strategic alliance" in oil refining. While President Salinas insisted "the ownership and control of oil remains inalterably in the hands of the Mexicans," civil engineer Heberto Castillo, an authority on the oil question, charged "the government was handing over control of the oil to foreigners and private initiative through a series of subterfuges."[22]

President Ernesto Zedillo (1994-2000), another leader of the "techno-bureaucracy" educated in the United States (Ph.D. in economics, Yale), announced that he intended to privatize sixty-one petrochemical plants. In May 1995, under pressure from foreign creditors that helped bail Mexico out of the 1994 to 1995 financial crisis, Mexico modified Article 27 of the Constitution (a nationalist article that had mandated Mexican ownership of all subsoil resources). According to the modifying law, the state would welcome private capital investment in the transport, storage, and distribution of natural gas, a major resource in the production of primary petrochemicals. Later that year, the government announced it would invite domestic and foreign private capital to invest in natural gas development *and production*, by means of service contracts that would technically respect the Constitution while handing over more control of natural gas resources to foreign capital. With lower prices expected at end-century for petrochemical products because of growing technological efficiency, the competition between Mexican and foreign capital could be expected to intensify not only in the natural gas and petroleum industry but also in other industries, such as textiles, auto parts, footwear, construction, and so on. It was obvious that Mexico's competitive position was weakening.

According to UNAM economist Alejandro Alvarez Béjar and most other observers of the Mexican oil scene, by the late 1990s PEMEX's control was becoming limited to "upstream" areas of extraction of crude oil and natural gas. Marketing and even exploration and drilling were gradually passing into the hands of private capital, national and foreign. "Downstream" production, transport, storage, and distribution of petrochemicals and combustibles like natural gas were also passing to private capital. Since profits from the "value added" component of labor were greater over time from production than from extraction, PEMEX was being excluded from the greater profits that came from the long-term production phase of the oil industry. Moreover, as economist Sidney Weintraub pointed out in 1988, "Mexico's single-minded reliance on oil exports . . . prejudiced the development of a competitive manufacturing sector, all the while depleting a nonrenewable resource."[23]

Mexico ranked a close second or third (with the former Soviet Union and Venezuela) to the Middle East nations and Iran as a source of crude oil reserves. PEMEX produced 3 million barrels a day in 1997, or 5 percent of the world total. The United States accounted for more than half of Mexico's oil exports, or 7 percent of all U.S. oil imports. Mexico was the only nation with a special petroleum deal with the United States: it guaranteed supplying the U.S. Strategic Oil Reserve at low cost.

Because of this deal and huge U.S. loans and technology sales to develop the petroleum industry, as well as concessions to U.S. corporations in the natural gas and petrochemical sectors, Mexico no longer securely controlled the fate of its own hydrocarbon resources. In 1993, PEMEX arranged loans with Citibank that came close to pledging its oil as collateral, a step Mexico was later forced to take publicly in exchange for an economic bailout from its 1994-1995 economic collapse. *Fortune, El Financiero,* and other business publications concluded that market forces would ultimately lead to the complete denationalization of Mexican oil, perhaps by modifying the Mexican Constitution as was done in 1992 in order to privatize *ejidos.*

NAFTA vs. the Environment

As already noted, Mexico's environmental degradation worsened because of NAFTA. Mexico entered the 1990s as one of the world's most "biodiverse" nations, but 98 percent of its tropical forests had already been destroyed and one-third of its land turned into desert in the rush to extract natural resources and implement the Green Revolution. Both NAFTA and GATT contributed to a downward harmonization of conservation standards. Article 106 of the NAFTA treaty prohibited environmental regulations that might be "a disguised restriction on trade."[24]

Mexico's first serious environmental protection code was legislated in 1988, but it lacked enforcement. In 1982, the government had created the Secretariat of Urban Development and Ecology (SEDUE), the equivalent of the U.S. Environmental Protection Agency. Both were grossly underfunded. A decade later, President Salinas shut down SEDUE and created SEDESOL, which included environmental concerns but shipped most programs out to private consulting firms and accomplished little. Presidents Salinas and Zedillo placed economic growth before environment. To attract foreign investment, they undertook legal reforms to relax environmental codes.[25]

For NAFTA, U.S. Trade Representative Carla Hills insisted on the permissive standards of the UN Codex Alimentarius Commission dominated by corporate food and agribusiness interests. The Codex standards had been incorporated into the GATT. On one key issue—the use of the pesticide DDT, banned in the United States—Codex declared that there was nothing wrong with a little DDT on food. Mexico might argue that any prohibition of DDT-tainted food was a trade obstacle. Mexico's fruits and vegetables for export and agricultural workers were still routinely sprayed with insecticides banned in the United States.

While President Salinas engaged in some token plant shutdowns to help win the passing of NAFTA in the U.S. Congress, little was done to clean up Mexico's toxin-belching *maquiladoras*, notoriously polluted cities and river basins, or pesticide-sprayed farm fields. Moreover, funding for environmental programs remained extremely low. Good laws were also ineffective, given the ease and tradition of corporate bribery. Bilateral programs like the Integrated Environmental Plan for the Mexican-U.S. Border Area (IBEP) and the International Boundary and Water Commission (IBWC) were understaffed and ineffective.

According to a 1996 U.S. Government Accounting Office (GAO) report, pollution in U.S.-Mexico border areas increased after NAFTA. Numerous other reports documented the earlier judgment by the American Medical Association that the border zone was "a virtual cesspool and breeding ground for infectious disease." A National Toxics Campaign Fund study concluded in 1991 that *maquiladoras* had been "turning the [U.S.-Mexico] border into a 2,000-mile-long Love Canal." Along both sides of the border, above-average rates of hepatitis, liver cancer, lupus, mercury poisoning, polio, tuberculosis, and cholera were attributed to inadequate sewage systems and *maquiladora* pollution.[26]

General Motors (GM), Mexico's largest employer in manufacturing, and Stepan Chemicals in Matamoros were discovered to be dumping xylene into the environment at several thousand times the supposed "safe" level. On both sides of the Matamoros-Brownsville border there appeared the rare killer brain disease anencephaly (babies born with partial or no brains). Women in many electronics *maquiladoras* continued to handle toxic materials without adequate protection.

Women and their families in the slums surrounding the border area *maquiladora* plants organized innumerable protests against *maquiladora* pollution. Many refused to move from their homes, demanding instead that the polluting companies move or else clean up their act. Several *maquiladora* employees complained that when they protested inside or near the plants they were fired.

The number of small environmental groups in Mexico mushroomed in the 1980s and early 1990s. By the mid-1990s, many had merged into networks like the Pact of Ecological Groups and the Mexican Conservation Federation. Poet-ecologist Homero Aridjis of the Group of 100 complained about outside powers that "take our wood and our oil and bring us toxic wastes." The Group of 100 foresaw the destruction of Chiapas's Lacandón forest within fifteen years because of the increased ranching and military activity there.[27]

Mexico's people, particularly its Indians and women, had initiated environmental protest actions long before NAFTA. They continued their movements in the 1990s. For example, in February 1996, some 10,000 Chontal Indians and peasants of Tabasco blockaded sixty oil wells for ten days to protest PEMEX's destruction of 35,000 acres of their land and to demand compensation. Army troops moved in to restore drilling—and stayed. Around the same time, Nahua Indians occupied the village of Tepoztlán outside the tourist center of Cuernavaca, Morelos, and, despite casualties, governed the town until a large Mexican real estate combine suspended its environmentally destructive construction of a luxury golf course. The press dubbed it "the Golf War."[28]

Alternative Scenarios

While serving monopoly capital's interests, in some ways NAFTA backfired on all three nations' ruling elites. First, the negative results soon became quite clear to everyone. In the United States, for example, the U.S. government acknowledged that its figures on NAFTA-related job losses counted only those workers who were certified to receive NAFTA trade adjustment assistance and that many workers did not bother to apply since some of the job-training programs were failures. Non-government estimates of NAFTA-related job losses went as high as 700,000. The garment, electronics, and car parts areas were the hardest hit. African Americans, Latinos, and women experienced a disproportionate share of job losses and environmental problems associated with NAFTA. A report by the Commerce Department and Department of Labor, two very pro-NAFTA and pro-GATT government agencies, warned that U.S. society was becoming polarized between "haves and have-nots," and that the ongoing wage gap between white and nonwhite workers would likely spell an end to social stability and democracy in the United States unless remedial action were taken.[29]

Moreover, several reports indicated that NAFTA boosted narcotics trafficking because of drug traffickers' purchasing *maquiladoras* or using *maquiladora* warehouses. Customs officials gave favored treatment to *maquiladora* shipments. Increased trade also facilitated increased smuggling. As importantly, NAFTA's liberalization of capital flows greatly facilitated drug money laundering by banks, much in need of quick cash to cover overextended loan portfolios and bad loans.

Public opinion polls in all three nations showed a growing majority anti-NAFTA sentiment. In 1997 the U.S. Congress refused to give President Clinton "fast track authority" for extending NAFTA to the rest of Latin America (minus Cuba) in the proposed FTAA. That November nearly 400 delegates from twenty countries traveled to San Francisco, California, to attend the Western Hemisphere Conference Against NAFTA and Privatizations. The meeting was held to oppose NAFTA and the APEC free-trade agenda, as well as the proposed FTAA and MAI. The conference's final declaration called for strengthening global trade unionism.

A similar international meeting occurred in Santiago, Chile, in April 1998. It billed itself as a "Peoples' Summit." It presented alternatives to the FTAA being discussed at the "Summit of the Americas" by the heads of the hemisphere's countries (minus Cuba's). The unpublicized counter-summit brought together 100 major labor leaders, including those of the AFL-CIO and the Canadian Labor Congress (CLC). Mexico's CTM sent delegates to the "People's Summit," apparently modifying its prior endorsement of NAFTA and trying to catch up with Mexican workers' anti-NAFTA sentiments represented by CTM's newly founded rival, the National Union of Workers. The counter-summit demanded that any future trade agreements be submitted to national plebiscites.

Meanwhile, at the official summit, U.S. free traders let South American officials know they were miffed by the 1995 signing of a pact of cooperation with the EU by the Mercosur common market countries of Argentina, Brazil, Paraguay, and Uruguay. President Clinton tried to assure the other heads of state, all of whom were free trade advocates, that the resistance of the U.S. Congress to "fast track authority" would not negate the U.S. role in creating the FTAA.

Like the counter-summits, several labor, environmental, and women's organizations in Mexico, the United States, and Canada, had long championed "fair trade" instead of "free trade." Some had set up alternative people-to-people trade organizations. They all favored alternative scenarios to NAFTA and FTAA for the Western Hemisphere. A typical alternative scenario included the following:

• replace or rewrite existing free-trade pacts with a continental development program that would insist on job security for all, decent pay, and the upward instead of downward harmonization of wages (by means of raising Mexicans' and other Latin Americans' living standards to U.S. and Canadian levels);

• eliminate tax and tariff policies that helped TNCs move to new locales;

• replace conditional loans to Latin America based on privatization and other corporate goals with unconditional loans geared to bring economic prosperity to everyone, regardless of a nation's economic system;

• include free trade for Cuba and other blockaded nations, instead of using economic blockades to starve out peoples with whose economic or political systems the United States did not agree;[30]

• guarantee all workers' human rights, including the rights of immigrant workers, non-white minorities, and women, and protect the right to unionize freely and to strike;

• improve and enforce environmental protection measures;

• tackle the question of U.S. and European demand for drugs (the main cause of narco-trafficking) and confront corruption in law enforcement forces.

Economic Collapse

Mexico's annual inflation rates of over 100 percent in the late 1980s had dropped to less than 10 percent by 1994. But Mexico's trade imbalance—worsened by the lowering of most remaining trade barriers in anticipation of NAFTA—had ballooned. This had left Mexico with a very perilous current account deficit of about $25 billion by the end of 1993, one that grew in the first nine months of 1994 by nearly $10 billion. Anticipating a crisis, many capitalists began sending their money abroad ("flight capital").

In the first year of NAFTA, the stupendous sum of nearly $100 billion of new direct foreign investment (FDI) gushed into Mexico. Some of it was for buying up privatized infrastructure or establishing *maquiladoras*, but most of it, as in the recent past, consisted of speculative portfolio funds—stocks, bonds, and the like, easily transferable back out of Mexico by the touch of a few computer keys. On any average single day, international currency markets were trading $1 trillion dollars. The same instant transfer was available to the Mexican owners of the repatriated flight capital that had finally returned after Mexico "recovered" from its national bankruptcy crisis of 1982, itself a product of too much reliance on FDI and borrowing from imperial high finance.

All around the world, in the age of free market economies and free trade, portfolio investments were moving way out in front of FDI in new productive facilities.[31] In the case of Mexico, foreign investors were speculating on Mexico and NAFTA. Many of them flicked the exit keys after it became obvious the army could not eliminate the Zapatistas and when the PRI's presidential candidate Colosio was gunned down in March 1994. They withdrew $10 billion in a matter of weeks. The U.S. government loaned Mexico $6 billion to try to stop the economic hemorrhaging. High U.S. interest rates also drew capital out of Mexico.

In 1994, the value of U.S.-held Mexican stocks plummeted by $20 billion, something NAFTA's backers never anticipated. The Mexican government issued some $30 billion in short-term dollar-denominated "*Tesobonos*" to cover the flight of capital, but it soon became obvious it would not be able to meet these obligations in the time most of them would come due (spring of 1995). Mexico's 1993 mega-debt of $110 billion rose sharply because of the new foreign borrowing.

As early as mid-1994, those "in the know" talked privately of a probable devaluation of the greatly overvalued peso, a possible Mexican stock market crash, and a 1980s-style massive "flight of capital." However, the public image of Mexico continued to be the "NAFTA miracle" one, including a strong peso vis-à-vis the dollar. President Salinas did not want to devalue the peso in the midst of a presidential election campaign the PRI desperately needed to win. After the election, he still hesitated, not wanting to risk his probable selection to become president of the WTO.

Delaying the inevitable made Mexico's economic collapse, when it happened, all the greater. The new president, Zedillo, took office on December 1. He then attended the Miami "Summit of the Americas" gathering of the Western Hemisphere's governments' top leaders (minus Cuba's Fidel Castro) to help advance imperialism's free trade, neoliberal agenda. At the "summit," the United States presented Mexico as the perfect model of economic reform and free trade wisdom.

Ten days later, Zedillo went on national television to announce that the peso was being devalued radically. By year's end the peso was a shadow of its former self and capital was gushing out of Mexico faster than ever, although much of it would start returning in 1995 to take advantage of the corresponding collapse of Mexican workers' wages. For example, GM opened up a new plant in Mexico to build 100,000 Chevrolet cars a year.

Recognizing that Mexico's economic collapse was beginning to trigger a world-wide financial panic and imperiling neoliberalism worldwide by the manifest failure of its leading model, President Clinton, without congressional consent, and the IMF and Canada, with the grudging help of Europe, bailed out Mexico with a $52 billion emergency loan package. In exchange, Mexico agreed to submit its budget to IMF oversight and to cut social expenditures sharply. President Clinton justified the U.S. share of the bailout as a matter of "national security." As collateral for the U.S. portion, Mexico had to deposit its oil revenues at the Federal Reserve Bank of New York. Mexico used the U.S. moneys to redeem the Tesobonos, many of which were held by U.S. investors. Since the new loans were for paying off old ones, Mexico found itself deeper in debt than ever before, its oil held hostage by the U.S. government.

Because of the December 1994 and January 1995 fall of the peso to less than half its prior value, Mexico's recently privatized banks were burdened with a lot of worthless debt. At least half the banks failed, while the biggest ones were saved by the Mexican government through a rescue mission that cost $40 billion by mid-1997 and even more later.

Mexico's GDP in 1995 was *minus* 6.9 percent, reflecting a true economic debacle. Between 1993 and 1996, some 2.5 million Mexicans lost their jobs. Wages plummeted as inflation renewed, especially in the costs of basic subsistence goods. *Maquiladora* workers took home only $25 to $35 a week, contributing to the boom in new *maquiladora* plants.

The failure of the perfect Mexican model represented a severe setback for the governing authorities of both Mexico and the United States. The lesson of Mexico seemed obvious: neoliberalism and trade pacts like NAFTA were fatal. Canadian sociologist Wally Seccombe summed up Mexico's 1994-1995 economic collapse this way:

> Multinationals didn't suddenly drain the Mexican economy of liquid capital in the space of a few days. Footloose investors did, the ones who had, a year or two earlier, rushed into Mexico, touting it as a gateway to Latin America. . . . When Wall Street got spooked, however, the story changed overnight. Mexico remained a traditionalist backwater ruled by a corrupt feudal oligarchy whose party bosses were now acting like mafia dons in a struggle for turf, profiting from dope smuggling and putting out contracts on the heads of politicians they disliked. . . . The Mexican people may now tell a world "starved for capital": beware the savings of our Northern neighbors—liquid, restless, roaming the earth in cyberspace searching for higher returns, notoriously short-sighted and prone to move in herds, like a panic-stricken mob running for the exits when someone shouts fire.[32]

Mexico tried to lift itself up by pursuing even more aggressively the very neoliberal, free trade "export platform" strategy that had knocked it down in the first place. The low cost of goods produced in Mexico contributed to a trade surplus in 1995. More than half of the surplus came from *maquiladora* exports. Companies in electronics, automobiles/parts, and machinery/precision instruments accounted for 67 percent of the exports, almost all U.S. intra-firm trade. Foreign investment started returning, 60 percent of it in 1996 in industrial plants, mostly *maquiladoras*. Helping the return of foreign investment President Zedillo announced an early payoff of a $12.5 billion emergency U.S. loan that was part of the 1994-1995 bailout.

According to the Inter-American Development Bank, Mexico's GNP grew 5.1 percent in 1996, but this reflected rises in oil prices and *maquiladora* exports, not an "economic recovery." Expanded exports concealed a stagnant domestic market, where retail sales ran below pre-crisis levels. GNP grew in the same deceptive manner in 1997 and early 1998, before oil prices took another nosedive. Edur Velasco Arregui noted, "Fifteen years after the crisis broke out in 1982, Mexico's per capita output was 12 percent lower in terms of the population's access to goods and services, without taking into account the degradation of the environment."[33]

The FZLN and the EPR

Like the Mexican Revolution's PLM and Magonistas, whose colors of black and red they adopted, the Zapatistas were both nationalist and internationalist. Making good use of the Internet, they organized two well attended conferences called "Intercontinental Meeting for Humanity Against Neoliberalism," first in 1996 in Chiapas and a year later in Madrid, Spain.

U.S. military planners worried about the Zapatistas' successful use of the Internet. In the words of a 1998 book published by the conservative California-based think tank Rand Corporation:

> Netwar—a comprehensive information-oriented approach to social conflict—... will often involve nonstate, paramilitary, and irregular forces. ...
> Indeed, it will likely take networks to fight networks, much as, in an earlier era, it took tanks to fight tanks. ... If the United States does not adjust to smaller units of maneuver, our large field armies, air wings, and naval battlegroups will be vulnerable to the attacks of nimbler foes.[34]

Over the Internet, the Zapatistas described themselves as part of a new "International of Hope." Support groups for the Zapatistas sprang up in Europe, the United States, and Canada. In 1994, U.S. friends of the Zapatistas launched the "National Commission for Democracy in Mexico," a network of thirty community-based groups. Several other local and regional U.S. secular and religious groups doing solidarity work for the Zapatistas also appeared. International support helped the Zapatistas not only politically but economically. In the Lacandón Jungle of eastern Chiapas and surrounding hills and ravines, the Zapatistas began building new schools and clinics, agricultural and marketing cooperatives, and facilities to pipe and store water from streams.

Domestically, from August 1994 through February 1995, the Zapatistas conducted three national democratic conventions to promote the organization of "civil society" through "civic committees of dialogue." Thousands attended the first two held in the Lacandón Jungle. Calling for "a plural, tolerant, inclusive, democratic, just, free, and new society ... in a new nation," the EZLN leadership announced their intent to create a new political force, the FZLN (Zapatista National Liberation Front). They called the FZLN not a political party but "a political force given birth by the civic committees of dialogue" which "does not aspire to take power," which "grows from the base which is its social force," and which "is willing to give direction through obedience."

The third national democratic convention took place in Querétaro state just north of Mexico City. That same week Querétaro also hosted the first National Women's Convention. A few days later, in February 9, 1995, President Zedillo ordered the arrest of top Zapatista leaders. Some 60,000 army soldiers invaded Zapatista-controlled areas of Chiapas, including the Lacandón Jungle. They destroyed people's homes, raped women, sprayed insecticides on the people's food supplies, and killed their animals. The army's invasion effectively sabotaged the peace talks.

Tens of thousands of Mexicans rallied to protest the government's brutal militarization of the conflict. Video coverage showed groups of indigenous women and children throwing stones at the invading tanks and Chrysler Mac-1 Armored Personnel Carriers, while shouting obscenities at the soldiers, calling them traitors to their own people. The scenes, involving hundreds of unarmed women and children standing up alone to the military might of the state, were never made public in the United States, where the mass media prefers poigniant symbolism in easily explained settings such as the often shown photograph of a single young man standing up to a tank in Tiananmen Square in 1989.

Prior to the invasion, the EZLN had controlled much of the eastern third of Chiapas, but afterwards they controlled less. On the other hand, their popular support had spread throughout the state and beyond. Moreover, the army proved unable to capture the EZLN leadership or engage in a showdown battle with Zapatistas troops. This army failure, together with continuing support shown the Zapatistas by Mexico's population at large, led to passage of a "Law for Dialogue, Conciliation and Peace with Dignity in Chiapas" by Congress on March 11, 1995. The law bound the government to freeze its troop deployment and engage in dialogue with the Zapatistas.

In August and September 1995, the Zapatistas and their supporters throughout Mexico organized and carried out a national and international "Plebiscite for Peace and Democracy," calling for "a new international order based on and ruled by democracy, liberty, and justice." The plebiscite was a model of people organizing their own elections and voting overwhelmingly for peace and democracy. This had the effect of forcing the government back to the peace table. In October, the EZLN and the Zedillo government were negotiating peace terms in earnest. The congressional multi-party Mediation and Peacemaking Commission (Cocopa) oversaw the talks.

Throughout the post-1994 period, the government stepped up its two-pronged strategy of military intimidation and dividing peasant communities in Chiapas. Its "low intensity warfare" (protracted repression aimed at wearing down guerrilla resistance and its popular bases of support) included the use of several terrorist paramilitary units. "Campaign Plan Chiapas 94," written by an army general who, with a dozen other Mexican officers, had graduated from the U.S. Army School of the Americas, called for "training and support for self-defense forces or other paramilitary organizations."[35] Mexico's paramilitaries carried out "disappearances," political murders, and small-scale massacres not only in Chiapas but in other states.

Young men of Chiapas, without land to farm, jobs, or money, were easy to recruit to serve in the paramilitaries. The youth received training from members of Mexico's security forces, who in turn stood idly by, or guarded areas, while the paramilitaries carried out their acts of terrorism: 500 killings in 1997 alone, bringing Chiapas's death toll to 1,500 since the 1994 uprising. Colombian sociologist Ricardo Vargas Meza called it the "privatization" of state counterinsurgency.[36] It offered the Mexican government a chance to blame violence on groups it could not control and to assure foreign investors that it would "investigate" human rights violations and bring them under control. It also contributed to the racist myth of Chiapas's violence being a kind of family feud among "Indians" or "savages." Some of Chiapas's paramilitaries were the old "white guards" of the big ranchers and logging barons, and several had the *public* backing of the Chiapas state government.

Still favoring Chiapas's cattle, timber, hydro-power, mining, and natural gas and oil interests, the Mexican government talked about the "economic development" of the region. With support from the World Bank, it announced plans to encourage "sustainable development," including commercial tree plantations and ecotourism. The world-famous Mayan ruins of Palenque, natural rain forest habitats, and petroleum, natural gas, and uranium deposits were all, at least in part, located inside Zapatista-controlled areas of Chiapas. The government undertook a plan to attract more *maquiladoras* to the greater Chiapas region to manufacture mostly textiles. The plan was to create 30,000 new jobs in the states of Chiapas, Quintana Roo, Oaxaca, and Yucatán, with the investment to come largely from the United States and Hong Kong.[37]

In addition, the government began implementing its Program for the Integral Development of the Tehuantepec Isthmus. This program included an industrial complex that already was refining much of Mexico's crude oil and most of its petrochemical products. The ultimate goal of the program was to supersede the outdated and too-narrow Panama Canal, over which Panama was scheduled to gain sovereignty in 2000, with an interoceanic route through the Tehuantepec Isthmus. The new route would be mostly a "land bridge" using the Trans-Isthmus Railroad (under the management of four U.S. companies and one Canadian firm) and new overland highways under construction to link the Coatzacoalcos port and Coatzacoalcos River on the Caribbean side to the Pacific port of Salina Cruz. The Isthmus program threatened the ecological balance of the 4.4 million-acre Chimilapas rain forest, known as Mexico's "oxygen bank." The Isthmus's two million citizens, mostly Indians from six different groups, began organizing against the project.[38]

On January 1, 1996, the second anniversary of their uprising, the Zapatistas issued the Fourth Declaration of the Lacandón Jungle. In it they vowed to "continue to struggle and not rest until the land is our own." The declaration characterized the scandals surrounding the Salinas years of narco-trafficking, political assassinations, and privatization schemes for Social Security as "the democratization of misery." The privatization of state banks and other neoliberal measures represented "the unity between the state party system and money." The declaration concluded that "Government and crime are today synonymous and equivalent."

After several months of sputtering peace talks, in February 1996 the government's representatives signed the Indigenous Rights and Culture Accords in the mountain town of San Andrés Larráinzar, Chiapas (renamed San Andrés Sakam Ch'en). These granted most of the Zapatistas' demands for political and cultural autonomy for Mexico's fifty-six indigenous nations.

On June 28, 1996, masked individuals from a guerrilla force calling itself the Popular Revolutionary Army (EPR) showed up at a public meeting attended by the PRD's Cárdenas and called for the overthrow of the Mexican government. The occasion was the first anniversary of a motorized police massacre of a truckload of peasants from the Peasant Organization of the Southern Sierra (OCSS) near Aguas Blancas, Guerrero State. The massacre had been videotaped and shown on Mexican television, shocking the nation. The police had killed seventeen and wounded twenty-three. The slaughter had come on the heels of a corrupt PRI governor's signing of a $10 million deal with the giant North American timber firm Boise Cascade, a deal the OCSS opposed as a threat to the already damaged environment along the Costa Grande.

People wondered if the EPR would draw popular support and become a new threat to the corrupt state government in Guerrero, the way the EZLN had done in Chiapas, and if it would go on to change Mexican politics as the Zapatistas had done. In August, the EPR carried out well-coordinated attacks on military and police installations in six states in just one day. It also carried out propaganda actions in Chiapas, causing Subcomandante Marcos to dash off a letter to EPR soldiers criticizing their presence in Chiapas for endangering the peace process.[39]

The EPR's main base of operations and peasant support was Guerrero, where it had been organizing clandestinely every since the 1970s when the army had killed guerrilla leaders Lucio Cabañas of the Party of the Poor and Genaro Vásquez Rojas of the Guerrero Civic Alliance. The EPR also had strength in Oaxaca and the tri-state Huasteca area near the Gulf of Mexico. Its political voice was the Popular Democratic Revolutionary Party (PDPR), a merger of 15 organizations including the Clandestine Workers Revolutionary Party and People's Union (PROCUP), a fanatical Maoist group often compared to Peru's Shining Path. The PDPR, like the EPR, had followers mainly in Guerrero but also in a few other states. The Broad Front for the Creation of a National Liberation Movement (FAC-MLN), a coalition of radical poor peoples' organizations and ultra-leftists that had broken away from the Zapatistas' National Democratic Convention, was also close to the EPR.[40]

The same "dirty war" pattern witnessed in Chiapas held true in Guerrero as well, where not only suspected EPR "sympathizers" but also PRD activists were gunned down in large numbers. In fact, human rights violations were even more frequent in Guerrero than in Chiapas. The Army dispatched nearly 40,000 troops to Guerrero. In both Chiapas and Guerrero, and to a degree in their neighboring states, the Mexican government also poured in money and resources to form peasant groups opposed to the guerrillas. These peasants grew dependent on government aid and saw their communities undermined by the prostitution and alcohol that accompanied the presence of army soldiers.

In early 1997 President Zedillo refused to sign or implement the San Andrés accords. He apparently feared possible Indian claims of control over the resources of Chiapas: oil, uranium, timber, and water power. The Zapatistas had often stated their belief in indigenous people's control of resources as opposed to the idea that "the land belongs to those who buy it." Their "sympathizers" had already set up thirty-eight functioning autonomous municipalities in the highlands, canyons, and forests of Chiapas.

In response to President Zedillo's betrayal of the San Andrés accords, dozens more indigenous and peasant communities in Chiapas and other states began establishing self-governing "autonomous municipalities." The conflict between people setting up their own governments and the PRI spread throughout northern Chiapas and the state's central highlands.

Prior to Zedillo's betrayal, in the summer of 1996, the Zapatistas had continued to break free of their military encirclement by hosting a national conference of the debtors' organization El Barzón, which said it had a million members. The EZLN and El Barzón cooperated in forging broader alliances with Mexico's many social movements, NGOs, human rights groups, feminist and gay groups, the PRD and PRT, and countless religious and civil associations. Most of these diverse forces met in Mexico City at the end of the summer in a meeting called "the Convergence."

That fall, an El Barzón emissary met with representatives of the IMF, Wall Street, and the U.S. government, in New York and Washington, D.C. Acting on a Mexican federal circuit court finding that Mexico's ten largest banks had been illegally privatized in 1990, he unsuccessfully tried to persuade the ultimate decisionmakers over Mexico's destiny to help small debtors restructure their debt so that they would not have to close down the Mexican banking system by legally refusing to pay their debts.[41]

The Zapatistas also helped organize a National Indigenous Congress (CNI), which held its first national assembly in October, 1996. Hundreds of delegates representing forty-five ethnic groups in twenty-three states endorsed the San Andrés accords. They proclaimed the full property, political, and human rights of women, including a woman's right to control her own body and the number of children she wished to have. The CNI went on to mobilize thousands of Indians for protest marches on Mexico City and to conduct more national assemblies. It was independent of the EZLN.

On the anniversary of the Mexican Revolution, November 20, 1996, a new guerrilla group announced its existence. Expressing solidarity with both the EZLN and the EPR, the Revolutionary Army of Popular Insurgence (ERPI) said it was based in northern Mexico. Later, military authorities said the ERPI was an EPR splinter group based among Indian communities of Guerrero.

Decline of the PRI

Parallel to these developments, the PRI suffered more setbacks at the ballot box made possible by electoral reforms passed in the summer of 1996. The autonomy of the electoral tribunal was increased, and opposition parties were given more government resources. As a result, in eight state elections held in 1996, the opposition to the PRI garnered 52.3 percent of the official vote count. The PRI also did poorly in municipal elections that year. The end result was that the PRI governed only two of Mexico's twelve largest cities, and the PAN had governors in four of the nation's thirty-one states.

The PRI reacted to these setbacks by scuttling further electoral reforms then before Congress, although it left intact future oversight of elections by an independent electoral board. More high-level defections from the PRI followed. It was widely suspected that some defectors were joining the PRD and the PAN in anticipation of the PRI's possible future loss of power.

At the PRI's seventeenth national assembly in the fall of 1996, the "dinosaurs" tried to save the sinking PRI ship. They marshaled majority votes against neoliberalism, for "revolutionary nationalism," and for rule changes that would prevent another "technocrat" running for president in 2000. However, the PRI rarely followed its own rules.

The PRI's fortunes continued to decline in 1997. Fearing an electoral defeat in the upcoming July elections, the PRI and the Zedillo government launched a smear campaign against the PRD for its alleged cooperation with the "advocates of violence," the EZLN, EPR, and ERPI guerrillas. Some $9 billion in new foreign investment poured in, making Mexico the recipient of more foreign capital than any country after China. This was a sign, said government spokespeople, that foreign capital approved of state policies and that the economy was in a phase of rapid recovery. The bankers' ABM repeatedly warned that a PRD victory would lead to "a massive flight of capital."

The electoral reform of 1996 had allowed 300 of the 500 seats in the Congress's lower house, the Chamber of Deputies, to be decided by direct election. The other 200 seats were to be distributed by a complex system of proportional representation. The PRI had included in the reform a clause it assumed would protect its power, the so-called "governability" clause that assured an absolute majority for any party obtaining 42.2 percent of the vote.

In July 1997, however, the PRI lost its majority control of the Chamber. One-fourth of the Senate was up for election, and the PRI lost decisively there too, taking only twelve seats out of thirty-two. Still, the PRI retained control of the Senate. For the first time, mid-term voter participation overtook voter abstention: of 52 million registered voters, 57 percent cast their ballots. In the congressional vote, the PRI finished with 38 percent, the PAN 27 percent, and the PRD 26 percent. The newly elected Chamber had an unprecedented non-PRI majority, made up of 125 members from the PRD, 122 from the PAN, 8 from the ecology party, PVEM, and 6 from the Labor Party, PT—adding up to 11 more than the PRI's 239. The PAN won 2 of the 5 state government elections. There were signs of large-scale fraud by the PRI in the 3 states it managed to win.

Most importantly, in the first election for a mayor of Mexico City in half a century, the PRD's presidential hopeful Cuauhtémoc Cárdenas won a decisive victory, receiving nearly half the votes in a multi-party race. The PRI received only 25 percent and the PAN 15 percent. Cárdenas's campaign had featured slick TV commercials notably absent from his earlier presidential campaigns. He ran as a neo-populist centrist, advocating increased foreign investment in Mexico, lower taxes, wage hikes, and conversion of the nation's capital into a world financial center. Assuring the U.S. National Security Council that he was a reformist, he had told a gathering of bankers in New York City that he not only favored capitalism, but might follow the extreme neoliberal model of Chile. After the election, the Mexican stock market soared. Leading voices of big business in both Mexico and the United States lauded the nation's step toward democracy.

As mayor, Cárdenas became handicapped by the traditional subordination of security forces and much of the budget to the federal government and the PRI, as well as by capitalists' distrust of leftists in his administration. He inherited a city debt of $1.6 billion, a housing deficit of 1 million units, and worsening air pollution problems. His promised crackdown on corruption was made difficult by the outgoing administration's shredding of records. The nation's PRI-controlled labor unions were strongest in Mexico City, where their leaders vowed to block Cárdenas's efforts at reform. One of Cárdenas's first acts as mayor was to appoint a retired Air Force officer to head the police, despite calls for an end to military control of the city's police force. A few PRD optimists thought that if all Cárdenas did was run a clean government for three years he would still win the presidency in 2000.[42]

The main results of the 1997 election were the PRI defeat and the PRD's emergence as the nation's second most important party. In the end, the PRI still governed Mexico, although not with its accustomed guaranteed monopoly on elected posts. Moreover, the 1997 election showed the PRI that spending huge sums, calling opponents like Cárdenas "traitors," and bullying even non-partisan groups—like the election watchdog coalition Civic Alliance whose computers were stolen—no longer assured the PRI easy electoral victories.

President Zedillo tried to put a good face on the PRI's humiliation at the polls by identifying himself with the pro-democracy "generation of '68." He told the press that democracy "first gained prominence in the national conscience in 1968. . . . We were the young people of that time who took the first steps to reclaim the democracy that Mexico needs and deserves."[43]

The Zapatistas' frequent national convocations and proclamations on equal rights for women and for gays and lesbians had provided especially powerful momentum for feminist and gay/lesbian groups, many of whose members lent critical support to the PRD at election time. A Zapatista initiative led to the formation of the National Women's Convention. Esperanza Brito, editor of *fem* magazine, declared at one convention event honoring the EZLN's Comandante Ramona: "The feminist struggle made common cause with that of the EZLN because it is a revolution that does not betray women." The same might be said for the Zapatistas' treatment of Mexico's gay and lesbian activists. Subcomandante Marcos saluted the 1997 election to Congress of a lesbian PRT member running on the PRD ticket.

The EZLN itself decided not to participate in the 1997 elections because of the government's failure to implement the San Andrés accords and all the political parties' failures to deal adequately with the indigenous peoples. The EZLN ridiculed Cárdenas's promise "to get rid of the sharper edges of neoliberalism" by saying it would "run into a hedgehog whose embrace wounds and kills."[44]

Back in Chiapas, the Zapatistas justifiably distrusted the electoral process. Earlier elections there had been totally fraudulent. In the weeks leading up to the July 1997 elections, army troops began advancing against Zapatista strongholds. PRD campaigners were harassed. Having no choice but to retaliate, the Zapatistas did so—on election day. Their supporters blockaded roads and burned ballot boxes ("saving the PRI from having to burn them," quipped some). From one-third to one-half of Chiapas's polling booths were never even set up. Estimates of absenteeism in Chiapas ranged as high as 80 percent. The "official" Chiapas vote count, believed by few, gave the PRI 49 percent to the PRD's 31 percent.

On September 8, 1997, the largest and longest indigenous peoples' march in Mexican history took place, led by 1,111 EZLN members and joined by 6,000 other Indians from across the nation. The five-day march traversed 750 miles from San Cristóbal de las Casas to Mexico City's Zócalo square, where 200,000 supporters welcomed the exhausted marchers. The crowd cheered the EZLN's call to implement the San Andrés accords and withdraw the Army from Chiapas.

During the week after the march the founding congress of the FZLN took place. It was poorly attended and could not agree on leadership, organizational, or programmatic points. Basing itself on 300 Civilian Dialogue Committees throughout Mexico, the FZLN was diffused, confused, and weak compared to the reformist momentum building behind the PRD and new democratic currents in organized labor.

The EPR and its civilian supporters among the FAC-MLN were also in a relatively weak position. The FAC-MLN had been suffering very severe military and police repression in Guerrero and other states. In May 1997 the army had invaded and occupied several of Guerrero's major indigenous communities where the PRD and FAC-MLN were strong. Attempting to protect themselves against more arrests and murders, some FAC-MLN leaders ran as PRD candidates in the July elections for the Chamber of Deputies; two won.[45]

The Militarization of Society

Mexico's "national security forces," including paramilitaries and police, continued gunning down PRD members: some 300 were killed in 1994-1996 alone. Peasants and teachers sympathetic to the guerrillas in Guerrero and Oaxaca were also under attack. Amnesty International (AI) periodically censured Mexico's security forces for its arresting and torturing peasants (4,500 peasants and Indians reportedly were in jails in 1997).

The Zapatistas had brought world attention to the violations of indigenous women's human rights. In 1996, AI denounced "a growing pattern" of sexual assaults and tortures against women in Mexico, particularly against monolingual, politically active Indians. The Mexican government's own National Commission on Human Rights (CNDH) stated on March 1, 1996, that Mexico was becoming "a police state." The CNDH criticized "the militarization of public security and the stripping of juridical guarantees" that was "leading us to a state of *de facto* suspended individual freedoms." Significant parts of Chiapas, oil-rich Tabasco, Oaxaca, Puebla, Guerrero, and the tri-state Huasteca area (where the EPR was said to have a presence) were occupied by the military. Soldiers were also more visible in towns and cities throughout the nation.

In 1997, the European Union tied trade accords with Mexico to improvement of its abysmal human rights record, while AI described Mexico as experiencing "a human rights crisis." The United Nations Human Rights Commission urged the Mexican government to take steps to end human rights violations, especially disappearances and torture. Even U.S. Secretary of State Madeleine Albright expressed concern about death threats against human rights advocates. The U.S. State Department, while claiming that Mexico "generally" respected human rights, condemned the government's repressive military actions against civilians.[46]

But the worst was yet to come. On December 22, 1997, at the height of the Christmas season, families gathered at a chapel in Acteal, municipality of Chenalhó, Chiapas, just twelve miles north of San Cristóbal de Las Casas. Suddenly, a paramilitary squad opened fire on them. Those not killed fled, and for several hours the gunmen chased them down and slaughtered them with machetes, even cutting fetuses out of pregnant women, a trademark tactic of Guatemala's infamous "Kaibiles." (The Kaibiles were an elite counterinsurgency unit that reportedly had trained fifty high-ranking Mexican officers since the 1994 Zapatista uprising.) Authorities did nothing to stop the massacre that left forty-five dead. Most of the victims were Tzotzil Indians; twenty-one were women and fifteen were children. Most belonged to a pacifist group called "*Las Avejas*" (the bees) that agreed with many of the Zapatistas' goals.

The massacre occurred only four days after the PRI delegation for local peace talks in Chenalhó had informed the National Mediation Commission (Conai) that it was breaking off the talks. The Conai was headed by the widely respected Bishop Samuel Ruiz, whose strong role in the peace process had earned him an attempt on his life the previous October. Part of the PRI's strategy in Chiapas all along had been to drive peasants off their few remaining lands to make them more dependent on PRI handouts. December 1997 was the time of the start of the coffee harvest in a year when coffee was expected to fetch high market prices. After the massacre, few peasants felt safe picking the coffee. They lost their way of making money as a result.

The Mexican government and the Chiapas state government initially denied any involvement in the Acteal massacre and blamed it on local conflicts between Indians. More than forty of the alleged killers, including a former PRI municipal president of Chenalhó, were arrested. Later investigations implicated the state government and revealed that military and police officials had known of the massacre as it took place and had done nothing to stop it. Also, a retired army general and an active duty soldier were implicated in the killings. The EZLN, refusing to be provoked, did not strike back. On January 3, 1998, however, members of a shadowy group called the "Justice Army of the Undefended People" reportedly attacked a police command post in Guerrero as its reply to the Acteal massacre.

Acteal marked an escalation of the government's "dirty war" and an apparent decision to eradicate the civilian social base of *Zapatismo*. Under the guise of searching for the Acteal killers, the Army dispatched an additional 5,000 troops to Chiapas. Soldiers swept through suspected Zapatista towns, further disarming or intimidating Zapatista sympathizers. Homes were broken into, people were beaten, women were assaulted, hundreds were arrested, more paramilitary killings occurred, and the level of state violence notably increased. Thousands of civilians fled to already overcrowded refugee camps. Twenty-seven paramilitaries operated with impunity in as many municipalities. By mid-1998, Mexico's Ministry of National Defense had constructed eight permanent concrete buildings and laid 200 kilometers of highways and roads throughout Chiapas, facilitating troop penetration deep into Zapatista zones.[47]

The Acteal massacre sent Mexico and its friends around the world into a state of shock and outrage. Nearly a quarter of a million people marched in Mexico City. Demonstrations took place in several other countries. The Mexican government chose to blame not only Indians for the violence but also foreigners. In early 1998, it started deporting scores of Europeans, Canadians, and U.S. citizens on human rights missions to Chiapas, including key NGO figures, accusing them of "intervening in Mexico's internal affairs." Foreign observer teams defied this intimidation by arriving in larger numbers than before, many on tourist visas.

The government reiterated its little-believed accusation that the Conai lacked impartiality. Still blaming the Zapatistas for the breakdowns in the peace talks, the government urged the congressional Mediation and Peacemaking Commission (Cocopa) to "modify" Conai's role. President Zedillo tried to upstage the San Andrés accords he had broken by announcing a proposed revision of the Constitution to fortify Indian rights. Critics noted it fell short of the San Andrés accords. The EZLN's Subcomandante Marcos reiterated that peace talks could resume once the government implemented the San Andrés accords, released Zapatista political prisoners, disarmed Chiapas's paramilitaries, and ended the huge military and police presence in Chiapas.

Then, on June 7, 1998, in a twenty-four-hour period, two startling though unrelated events rocked the nation: Bishop Ruiz resigned his presidency of Conai, accusing the government of "abandoning the path of dialogue," and the Army carried out another massacre. Bishop Ruiz protested the "lynching climate" of the government's "aggression" against himself and the diocese of San Cristóbal de las Casas. The government, he claimed, had expelled or arrested several priests and closed or destroyed forty churches in recent years. Conai's members, prominent Mexicans, immediately followed Ruiz's resignation by dissolving Conai because of what they termed the government's "war strategy." The FZLN responded by declaring that the government's celebration of these events showed it still had "not understood that the Zapatistas are not alone and that their demands . . . are national demands, fulfillment of which is the only guarantee for advancing not only in building peace in Chiapas but also in the entire nation's democratic transition."[48]

The June 7 army massacre occurred during a pre-dawn raid on El Charco, Ayutla de los Libres municipality, Guerrero, a Mixteca community in the Pacific coastal hills. Ayutla was governed by the PRD. The army claimed its soldiers had been ambushed by either the EPR or the ERPI. There were no army casualties. In supposed self-defense, soldiers opened fire on a bilingual school filled with sleeping people. The community had allowed the school to be used as an overnight dormitory for about twenty-five civilian visitors from other Indian communities and fifteen visiting guerrillas. The school's occupants surrendered. Witnesses said that at least eight were killed execution-style after being forced to crawl to the community basketball court. The final toll was eleven dead, five wounded, and twenty-two arrested.

A few days later, on June 10, 1998, the government's military escalation ratcheted up another notch. Using helicopters, war planes, bombs, and mortars, 2,000 to 3,000 soldiers, police, and paramilitaries carried out pre-dawn attacks on several pro-Zapatista villages in the predominantly autonomous Tzotzil municipality of El Bosque, Chiapas, near the autonomous municipality of San Andrés Larráinzar, site of the interrupted peace talks. The reported toll was: at least nine killed (including a state policeman); nine wounded; several disappeared; fifty-seven arrested and tortured civilians; one damaged helicopter; a "recovered" town hall building where the autonomous government of San Juan de la Libertad had maintained its offices since 1995; and dozens of homes and grocery and supply co-ops bombed or ransacked. Countless women and children fled to nearby hills and canyons.

Protest demonstrations occurred in Mexico and throughout the world. U.S. solidarity groups demanded that the U.S. government condemn the massacres and cease military aid to Mexico. Secretary of State Albright reacted to this pressure by assuring a congressional hearing that "the Mexican government knows our concern in relation to . . . the massacres" and that "we are pressing" the government "to resolve the situation in Chiapas." Predictably, the Mexican government called Albright's remarks a violation of its non-intervention doctrine.[49]

Peace and democracy seemed more distant than ever. Mexico's society was undergoing a continuous and deepening militarization, and not just in southern Mexico. Heavily armed army patrols were already visible in peaceful remote areas of central Mexico from Mexico City to Michoacán state in early 1997. Troops, and not just police, were stationed on some of the streets of the nation's capital itself.

Drug Scandals

During the 1990s, U.S. authorities repeatedly blamed Mexico for narco-trafficking and drug abuse problems. Mexican officials countered that the problem was centered in the United States, where a large part of the market for drug consumption was located.

According to the U.S. Drug Enforcement Administration (DEA), Mexico in 1997 was the transit-point source of 70 percent of the cocaine and most of the heroin and marijuana entering the United States. Mexican government figures put the figure for narco-production and transit at $41 billion in 1990, more than oil export earnings and about 11 percent of GDP. Drug money laundering along the U.S.-Mexico border was conservatively estimated to amount to at least $30 billion a year, with large banks handling most of it. But the drug flow kept up only so long as U.S. citizens continued spending $50 billion a year on narcotics.[50]

Most significantly, the world's financial markets were heavily involved in the drug trade. According to the United Nations, the trade in narcotics in the mid-1990s accounted for 8 percent of all world trade.[51] The flood of moneys associated with narco-trafficking in the last third of the twentieth century was unparalleled in world history, except for the flood of wealth associated with the Europeans' gold and silver bonanza from Latin America in the middle of the sixteenth century. Both phenomena had transforming impacts on the world's economies and politics. Profits from the U.S. drug trade alone were conservatively valued at $200 billion a year, an amount equivalent to two-thirds of Mexico's GDP. In addition to those sums, the drug moneys "laundered" by U.S. banks helped them to recuperate bad loans, speculate in the world's financial markets, and finance U.S. trade imbalances like the ones with Japan and parts of Asia. Mexico's biggest surviving banks, having teetered on the edge of collapse for years, also relied on narco-funds. Some people believed that the U.S. "anti-drug war" was a hype aimed at preventing profits and laundered funds of the drug trade from leaving the United States.[52]

Shortly after President Salinas left office, scandals broke around his family's and friends' involvement in narco-trafficking. Salinas's elder brother Raúl Salinas de Gortari was found to have placed more than $120 million in foreign bank accounts under a false name, with New York's Citibank transferring much of the money. The Salinas brothers' father was also said to have ties to narco-traffickers. The disgraced ex-president, claiming his innocence, went into exile in Ireland. Raúl Salinas fled authorities but was caught in early 1995 and imprisoned. In November 1995, Paulina Catañón, who later married Raúl, was arrested for trying to get some of the Salinas millions out of Switzerland.

Ex-President Salinas proved a convenient scapegoat in Mexico for other government officials' high crimes related to narco-trafficking. State institutions were so compromised by bribes and profits from narco-trafficking that it seemed appropriate to call Mexico's state a "narco-state." As the press in Mexico and the United States reported more details, it became clear that the corruption involved not just prominent individuals or banks but major branches of both the Mexican and U.S. governments, including their militaries, police, and intelligence-gathering agencies. Powerful federal and local officials in charge of cracking down on drug traffickers had made hundreds of millions of dollars from the drug trade. Much of this corruption had been known about for a very long time, despite government denials.[53]

A Mexican Federal Police commander had informed the DEA and Federal Bureau of Investigation as early as 1991 that drug payoffs were taking place at the highest levels of government. However, as a former high U.S. official told the *New York Times* in 1997, "Back in 1993, it was very unpopular to say anything against Mexico, basically because of NAFTA."[54]

Similar reports had been coming into the CIA's Mexico offices (Latin America's largest CIA complex). However, for many decades the CIA had worked under an arrangement with Mexican governments to ignore corruption in high places in exchange for Mexican cooperation with the CIA's Cold War counter-revolutionary activities in the Caribbean and Central America. Typical was the case of Miguel Nazar Haro, Mexico's former secret police chief (director of federal security) under President López Portillo. In 1982, the CIA asked the Justice Department not to prosecute Nazar Haro in California for involvement in a $30 million car theft ring because he was "its most important source of information in Mexico and Central America." A known protector of drug lords and torturer of Mexican political prisoners, Nazar Haro became President Salinas's director of intelligence of the Mexico City Police. Then, when it was discovered that Nazar Haro had set up a new torture chamber, public outrage forced him to resign and his whereabouts became unknown.

In 1997, the *New York Times* reported that a 1986 directive by President Reagan had authorized the CIA to conduct covert anti-drug operations in Mexico. More seriously, according to one U.S. official, the Reagan directive contained a top secret appendix giving the CIA even more authority inside Mexico. U.S. and Mexican law enforcement officers frequently cooperated in policing the 2,000-mile-long U.S.-Mexican border, but with little effect on the flow of drugs.[55]

In early 1997, only eight days after being described by the U.S. "drug czar," retired General Barry R. McCaffrey, as "an honest public servant who could be trusted," Mexico's newly appointed chief of drug enforcement, General Jesús Gutiérrez Rebollo, was arrested on the charge of having worked for Amado Carrillo Fuentes of the Ciudad Juárez cartel, allegedly Mexico's biggest drug lord. Gutiérrez Rebollo was jailed and later tried, convicted, and sentenced to thirteen years in prison. Secret files from Mexico's Defense Ministry proving military cooperation with narco-traffickers were later leaked to the press, causing the army to acknowledge that drug cartels had infiltrated its ranks, and that in 1997 it had handed over to authorities thirty-four officers and former officers.

On July 2, 1997, Gutiérrez Rebollo claimed he was a "political prisoner" who had "discovered that drug trafficking has reached even to the President's Office" and that the "Tijuana Cartel" had been involved in the assassination of 1994 PRI presidential candidate Colosio. A day later, Carrillo Fuentes died while undergoing plastic surgery at a Mexico City clinic. The surgeons disappeared. The clinic's legal representatives happened to be two leading PAN politicians, including the 1994 PAN presidential candidate. Then, in 1998, unnamed U.S. officials revealed that two of the five doctors who performed the plastic surgery operation on Carrillo Fuentes were living in the United States, one under government protection. Gutiérrez Rebollo's former chief lawyer, who had charged that a web of top Mexican military commanders were linked to the Tijuana and Ciudad Juárez drug cartels, was assassinated.

Also in 1998, U.S. Representative Maxine Waters, head of the Congressional Black Caucus, wrote a much-reported letter to President Clinton. Earlier, Waters had led efforts to have Congress investigate reports that the CIA knew that the US-sponsored Nicaraguan contras were financing their war against the Nicaraguan Revolution by selling crack cocaine in U.S. inner cities during the 1980s. Waters wrote to Clinton that she was concerned about more recent reports that Carrillo Fuentes had laundered hundreds of millions of dollars through Citibank, a part of Citicorp, the United States' second largest bank. Citicorp was attempting an $82 billion merger with the financial giant Travelers Group Inc. Waters asked Clinton and Federal Reserve chair Alan Greenspan to block the merger until there was an investigation into possible Citibank money laundering, including the case of Raúl Salinas.

Five weeks after Waters's letter was reported in the U.S. press, the U.S. government announced a successful three-year undercover sting operation and the arrest of twenty-two Mexican bankers for laundering drug money for the Cali (Colombia) and Ciudad Juárez drug cartels at U.S. branches of Mexico's most powerful banks. The arrested bankers had been lured to Las Vegas and Los Angeles to attend supposed "narco-trafficking insider" meetings and parties. They were mostly mid-level executives, but the banks they helped manage were twelve of Mexico's nineteen largest banks, all of which had been privatized, mostly during the Salinas administration. The U.S. Federal Reserve Board filed civil actions against five of the largest banks involved. Despite all the propaganda about bi-national cooperation in fighting narco-trafficking, the three-year U.S. sting operation was carried out without ever consulting Mexican authorities.

The banks' owners read like a "who's who" among Mexico's billionaires and elite families. They included billionaires Roberto Hernández, Alfredo Harp Helú, Eugenio Garza Lagüera, and Adrián Sada González. Hernández and Harp Helú headed the nation's richest bank, Banco Nacional de México (Banamex), which they had bought for a song in 1991 through an insider deal with President Salinas. Garza Lagüera, head of the Monterrey group's Grupo Visa, presided over Bancomer, Mexico's second richest bank (partly owned by Bank of Montreal). Sada González headed Banca Serfín, the third richest bank (associated with J. P. Morgan, as well as with British capital via Hong Kong and the Shanghai Bank Corporation). Sada also headed Grupo Vitro, Mexico's largest industrial group. Also arrested were executives of the Spanish bank Santander, which, together with Morgan and Citibank, had accounted for four-fifths of the $1.3 billion in profits made by fifteen foreign banks in Mexico in 1995 (an amount equal to 41 percent of bank profits in Mexico that year). Santander, Morgan, and Citibank worked with the largest Mexican companies controlling Mexico's foreign trade, apparently including its drug trade. Banca Confía, sold two weeks earlier to Citibank, had been headed by a man who was accused of defrauding its clients of huge sums of money and had stepped down before Citibank closed the deal. Leading shareholders of Banca Confía were from the elite families Garza Sada, Garza González, Sada Zambrano, and Garza Treviño, among others. Interacciones y Union was headed by the politically powerful Hank family.[56]

The sting operation came at an inauspicious moment for Mexico's banks. They were already in disfavor with Mexicans for laying off thousands of their employees to help offset a problem of bad loans that new accounting information showed to amount to 12 percent of all their loans and not 6.7 percent as originally thought. According to the debtors' movement El Barzón, 30 million citizens were in default or unable to pay their debts—owed mostly to the very banks now caught with their hand in the narco-till. El Barzón and the PRD were critical of the PRI and PAN for having recently passed legislation maintaining the 15 percent sales tax (which provided a third of federal tax revenues), in part to continue the bailout of the banks that reportedly had already cost $48 billion in the past three years.

Some people believed that there were hidden agendas of U.S. imperialism behind the crackdown on Mexican money laundering with no corresponding actions taken against Citibank or other U.S. banks suspected of being involved. As already noted, major U.S. goals to be facilitated by NAFTA included gaining more control over Mexico's financial services such as banking, and using economic pressure to recapture Mexico's oil resources (nationalized in 1938). The sting did not implicate a single U.S. citizen in the bank scandal, even though many U.S. citizens worked at the branch offices of the accused Mexican banks and some of those same banks had links with major U.S. players in high finance.

For years, the U.S. government had used "certification" pronouncements about other nations' cooperation with the anti-drug war as a means of pressuring countries to implement policies the United States favored, such as more privatizations of state enterprises or closer collaboration with the DEA, CIA, and Pentagon. Yet the U.S. government rarely cracked down on the big U.S. drug mafias and went to great lengths to cover up the narco-trafficking connections of Lieutenant Colonel Oliver North's White House basement "contra" operation. A few months before the arrests of the Mexican bankers in 1998, the U.S. government had certified that Mexico's government was "fully cooperating" in the fight against narco-trafficking, despite manifest lack of effective results in the anti-drug war and growing evidence of a far deeper involvement in narco-trafficking on the part of Mexico's military, judges, and bankers. The "certification" of Mexico had occurred because the United States considered it important not to stir up Mexican nationalism at a time when NAFTA was coming under fire and U.S. capital had begun returning to Mexico after Mexico's economic collapse of 1994-1995.

Few believed anymore in the appropriateness of these "certifications." Latin American governments were saying that if they were to continue, then the United States would have to be certified too. U.S. drug czar McCaffrey told the press in early 1998 that the time had come to "bury the certification process as being largely irrelevant" and turn matters over to "a multinational cooperative entity" such as the Organization of American States (OAS).[57]

The U.S. anti-drug war was a manifest failure. Building more prisons and throwing in more military aid to Latin America had not stemmed the flow of narcotics. Studies showed that treatment programs were more cost-effective than overseas "wars," yet little attention was paid to harm reduction programs like safe needle exchanges. Numerous U.S. military officers had stated "off the record" that the anti-drug foreign aid was applied to fight guerrillas more than to fight narco-traffickers. According to the New York-based Americas Watch human rights organization, expansion of the U.S. Border Patrol's authority in the name of combating narco-trafficking helped increase "routine" human rights violations against Mexican immigrants. In June 1998, a letter signed by hundreds of world dignitaries, including former U.S. Secretary of State George P. Shultz, criticized the anti-drug war for "causing more harm than drug abuse itself."[58]

But the U. S. government continued to insist on the need for increasing aid and training for the Mexico's security forces in the name of fighting drugs, a convenient rationale for helping the Mexican government fight the Zapatistas and other guerrilla armies and popular social movements. In late 1997, both governments signed agreements expanding the ability for U.S. "anti-drug" airplanes to operate in Mexico.

Security Forces and U.S. Training

After Mexico's 1940 election of the first civilian president since the writing of the 1917 Constitution, the military was widely viewed as having "returned to the barracks." Official ideology held that the days of army rule had expired with Porfino Díaz. Obviously, however, a lot depended on which *class* of civilians ruled. The Mexican military was the armed fist of the bourgeoisie and acted accordingly. It was not surprising, therefore, that despite the proletarian composition of its general ranks (affluent intermediate-class people avoided the draft), the military routinely carried out its class duty when breaking strikes or killing peasants. Moreover, with a few exceptions, until the 1980s the head of the PRI always had been selected from the army officer corps, and in the 1950s and 1960s almost 20 percent of the presidents' cabinets had consisted of military personnel.

In those times, reduced percentages of Mexico's federal budget going to the army led some scholars to believe that attempted military coups were no longer possible. But actual military spending increased sharply in the late 1970s and the defense budget was doubled in 1981. A well-armed, modernized military establishment was created. Generals began running for office, particularly at the gubernatorial and congressional levels. Talk of a military presidential candidate became acceptable. Rumors of an impending military coup were taken seriously.

Some U.S. policymakers and scholars saw "the military coup [as] part of the democratic process in Latin America,"[59] including Mexico. Many Mexican military officers publicly declared themselves "defenders of the nation," "professional," or "constitutionalist." But that was not so unusual in Latin America among military personnel—such was the case in Chile, for example, prior to the 1973 coup against democratically elected President Salvador Allende. Mexican and U.S. security forces frequently conducted joint operations. The wide range of activities undertaken by U.S. security and intelligence forces in Mexico with the knowledge and cooperation of their counterparts in the Mexican state gave the lie to the Mexican government's claims of independence from the United States.

From 1946 to 1982, U.S. military and police aid to Mexico totaled hundreds of millions of dollars. Then, from 1981 to 1991, U.S. military assistance to Mexico shot up 60 percent, ostensibly as part of the "war on drugs." More than 1,000 army officers were trained in the United States, including nearly half of Mexico's generals. At least four attended the infamous "counterinsurgency" School of the Americas in Panama (since moved to Fort Benning, Georgia), noted for its torture manuals and training of Latin American officers who became their countries' dictators.

Some of Mexico's U.S.-trained officers became part of the elite counterinsurgency "White Brigade" (the Ninth Army Brigade, based in Mexico City's Military Camp No. 1), which was accused by human rights organizations of torture and mass murder of Mexico's hundreds of "disappeared" students, peasants, journalists, political dissidents, and alleged guerrillas. A Mexican army deserter confirmed executions of more than one hundred political prisoners in Camp 1. President Salinas appointed a former White Brigade member to be chief of Mexico City's Federal District judiciary police. The new chief sent a chill down Mexicans' spines by telling the press that his mission was "to persuade the *Cardenista* [PRD] majority in this city not to insist on its rights."

The Mexican Army's and Air Force's presence in Chiapas predated the Zapatista uprising there. For decades, the Mexican military maintained close contacts with the Guatemalan military (reputed to be Latin America's worst violator of human rights) in patrolling the two nations' common border. The

southern zone of Mexico and the northern area of Guatemala became in the
1960s a free-fire military theater of operations for the armed forces of Mexico,
Guatemala, and the United States (including representatives of the Green
Berets, or Rangers) against the Guatemalan guerrilla insurgency. In fact, the
first major Guatemalan guerrilla leader, Yon Sosa, was killed by Mexican
soldiers. The technology of the Vietnam war was introduced there, as well as
the practice of massacring civilian populations. Mexico reportedly helped
provide the napalm from its own napalm factory, along with tanks and other
components from its burgeoning arms industry. Mexico's military and paramilitary forces also utilized this type of counterinsurgency warfare to stamp
out guerrilla bands in various parts of rural Mexico. Mexico's army looked the
other way each time Guatemalan soldiers crossed the border allegedly to hunt
down fleeing guerrillas. In the 1970s and 1980s, the Mexican army beefed up
its forces along the Guatemalan border, in part to crush "social unrest" among
the Guatemalan and Mexican Maya Indians there.

Mexico's military retained a significant degree of autonomy, and represented a political force to be reckoned with. The nation was divided into
thirty-five *zonas militares* which received their orders from the minister of
defense, generally a military man. No state governor could give orders to the
jefe of a military zone, who had significant autonomous power in matters of
"social unrest."

Over the years, extensive institutionalized repression resulted in the buildup
of a complex power bloc of repressive forces, including a 175,000-member
military (1998) and 400,000 local police, 26,121 state judicial police, and about
7,000 federal police (1998, or 1 police officer for every 224 inhabitants). There
also existed numerous intelligence-gathering agencies linked to different
branches of the government, paramilitary units, goon squads, and more. These
forces were rarely well-coordinated, until the United States began to declare
publicly in the 1970s that Mexico was a "vital piece" of its national security
doctrine.[60]

President José López Portillo (1976 to 1982) added to the military's basic
Heróico Colegio Militar and Escuela Superior de Guerra (Superior War College, which graduated most of Mexico's future top officers) the National
Defense College, with a master's degree program in "national security." It
undertook an exchange program with such U.S. military schools as West Point.
When asked by journalists how he defined "national security," Minister of
Defense General Félix Galván López answered "social, economic, and political
equilibrium"—thereby confirming the military's central role in Mexican politics and in controlling "social unrest." Galván was the first cabinet member to
be informed by President López Portillo of the decision to nationalize Mexico's
private banks in 1982 and to be asked to support it.[61]

As in most of Latin America, so in Mexico: the U.S.-led "war against drugs" was one of counterinsurgency against popular social movements or guerrillas, as well as against poor peasants dependent on growing crops like marijuana for their livelihood. In fact, Mexico had a long history of this kind of "anti-drug" counterinsurgency. During the mid-1970s, the DEA helped train Mexican police and often served as a cover for CIA agents. From 1973 to 1977 the Mexican police received $47 million from the DEA, much of it to purchase hardware for use against political dissidents. In the Sierra Madre of the northern states of Sinaloa and Durango, for example, 7,000 soldiers aided by 226 DEA advisers fought a "special war" against Indians and peasant land occupiers under the pretext of destroying marijuana fields. Herbicides of a type used in the Vietnam war were used to kill food plants, causing starvation among the Indian population.[62]

In the first month after the 1994 Zapatista uprising, General Gordon Sullivan, commander of the U.S. Army, twice visited Mexico's Secretary of Defense to arrange the sale of "non-lethal" equipment and a near doubling of U.S. funding of Mexico's share of the U.S.-created International Military Education and Training Program. U.S. military "advisers" were spotted in Chiapas, a state noted more for corn and coffee than marijuana fields.

U.S. military aid to Mexico then skyrocketed in the name of "fighting narco-trafficking," when the real targets were guerrillas and their peasant supporters. In 1997, the U.S. government publicly acknowledged the truth of what on-the-scene observers had long since reported: U.S.-supplied helicopters were being used in attacks on people in the guerrilla zones of Chiapas and Guerrero.[63]

The United States spent more money on Mexico's military than on any other Latin American military. Thousands of Mexican soldiers and officers were trained at Fort Bragg and other U.S. military bases. A January 1996 issue of the Fort Bragg magazine *Special Warfare* noted that a "particularly heavy emphasis is being placed on those forces that will be located in the states of Chiapas and Guerrero."[64] The United States also increased the number of DEA, CIA, and other agents operating inside Mexico, while beefing up its military and National Guard presence along the U.S.-Mexico border. In 1997, U.S. Navy, Coast Guard, and Customs ships were reported as entering Mexican waters "in hot pursuit" of narco-traffickers.[65]

By 1998, according to the *Washington Post*, Mexicans made up "the largest group of foreign soldiers receiving U.S. military instruction."[66] They were being trained at the rate of more than 1,000 a year at several U.S. sites, including the School of the Americas at Fort Benning, Georgia. More than 400 Mexican officers and 3,200 Mexican soldiers were trained in the 1996-1998 period at Fort Bragg, North Carolina, by the U.S. Seventh Special Forces Group, the elite counterinsurgency branch that gave many Green Berets jobs after the end of the Vietnam war in 1975. Based on U.S. government reports, the *Post* described the Fort Bragg officer graduates as the "backbone" of Mexico's new elite Airmobile Special Forces Group (GAFE), "trained to conduct low-intensity covert operations." One GAFE unit was later accused of torturing twenty-nine youths, killing one. The Pentagon acknowledged that some members of the unit had been trained at Fort Bragg. In the 1980s, much publicity had been given to a CIA training manual that included terrorist and torture techniques for use by the contras against the Nicaraguan Revolution.[67]

It was not as if U.S. officials did not know about the human rights abuses practiced by their trainees. In 1997 Amnesty International (AI) had issued a blistering critique of the Mexican security forces for "increasing human rights violations, including torture, disappearances, and non-juridical executions . . . and letting those responsible be immune from punishment." AI also had condemned the "systematic transfer of Huey helicopters to Mexico's armed forces." U.S. aid did include seventy-three Huey UH-1H helicopters and four C-26 surveillance airplanes.

A key part of U.S. counterinsurgency doctrine had long been the creation of special paramilitary groups like the ones active in states where the Zapatistas and EPR operated, or those committing widely publicized massacres of civilians in Colombia. A Mexican Defense Ministry document entitled "Campaign Plan Chiapas 94" was leaked to the Mexico City weekly *Proceso* in 1998, shortly after the Acteal massacre. Reportedly written by a Mexican general who had studied at the U.S. Army's School of the Americas, the document stated that "the strategic-operational objective" in Chiapas was to "win the civilian population's support." It called for "secretly organizing sectors of the civilian population . . . who will be employed under orders in support of our operations." This included "advising and supporting self-defense forces and other paramilitary organizations. . . . In cases where self-defense forces do not exist, it is necessary to create them."[68]

All this reflected a growing militarization of U.S. policy and Mexican daily life. As a Mexican researcher at Harvard noted in 1997, policymaking officials of the U.S. State and Treasury Departments increasingly had to attend meetings on Mexico at the Pentagon or the National Security Council.[69]

In the name of "national security," President López Portillo and his successors had cobbled together a more streamlined, centralized repressive state apparatus. In 1995, a new law established the National Public Security Council with the participation of the Armed Forces in police work. The law became known as "the law of national security," meaning security against internal threats such as those posed by guerrillas. In practice, the targets of the military and police extended to trade-union democrats, PRD militants, and all political forces to their left.

President Zedillo in the mid-1990s capped the "national security" centralization of state power with a plan to create a National Security Council (COSENA) that would oversee all government agencies involved with the criminal justice and military defense systems and be under the command of the president. The Mexican presidency already operated a National Security Cabinet that Salinas had set up.

Under these federal umbrellas, elite military and police units such as the "Zorros" ("Foxes") and similar "antiterrorist" squads enjoyed a large degree of operational autonomy that often terrorized the civilian populace. For example, in 1998 it was discovered that a special operations unit formed to capture alleged kidnappers in the states of Morelos and Mexico was actually part of the kidnapping gangs. (Mexico ranked second to Colombia for annual number of kidnappings—1,900 in 1996—and few kidnappers were ever caught.)[70]

Early in 1997, eleven retired military officers endorsed the PRD, a rare event in Mexican history since all officers were socialized to obey the president and uphold the PRI system. Most military officers came from the lower intermediate classes and were snubbed by the nation's wealthy elites. Some of them were nationalistic and were not so easily wooed by U.S. aid and training manuals. In May 1998, some officers reportedly complained of their U.S. counterparts' planning to use infrared heat detection devises in Chiapas—the technique shipped to Bolivia in the 1960s to follow, corner, capture, and murder the world's most famous guerrilla, Ernesto "Che" Guevara.[71]

Most of the officers with nationalist sentiments were reaching retirement age. They seemed unable to control their colleagues' human rights abuses and narco-trafficking. It was becoming very lucrative to be in the military, an attractive place to make money because of all the drug-related corruption. The same held true for the other security forces and the paramilitaries.

Whether the power of nationalist officers would continue to decline or experience a rebound depended in part on the influence of the nation's social movements and the evolution of the contending political parties. In any case, few scholars or journalists were privy to the inner consultations of Mexico's officer corps.

The Church

A force for repression far more subtle and ideological than Mexico's security forces was the Roman Catholic Church. Some 90 percent of Mexicans were said to be nominally Catholic. However, during and after the Cold War numerous Protestant, Pentecostal, and Evangelical groups, some with the support of the CIA and other U.S. government forces, made major inroads into the Church's quasi-monopoly on Christian believers. Most regular attendants of Church services were women, and their numbers began to decline.

From a nineteenth-century liberal's point of view, Church-state relations became obscenely harmonious, especially in the 1960s and after. Both Church and state propagandized against "the evils" of communism and terrorism. To be sure, minor tensions remained, as when the Church criticized free school textbooks or the state's birth-control program. On the other hand, private Catholic education flourished and both the Church and state mounted campaigns to defend the "virtues" of motherhood and family life. Church and state alike rejected leftist and feminist proposals for the legalization of abortion.

Catholic conservative businessmen backed the PAN and PDM, as well as right-wing forces inside the PRI. They wanted the state to repress those "revolutionary" clerics who advocated and practiced liberation theology, a popular trend making inroads throughout Latin America. Tehuantepec Bishop Arturo Lona Reyes stated in April 1981 that "violence becomes legitimate defense" in the face of anti-peasant repression and widespread hunger. He added, "both the government and the Church are carrying people to a new revolution."[72] A growing number of socially committed priests and nuns worked alongside progressive organizations of workers, peasants, slum dwellers, and students to provide assistance to the deprived and to organize politically for radical social change. Some clergy of other faiths, especially Protestants associated with the World Council of Churchs, also became political activists.

To assuage right-wing opposition and gain support for his conservative neoliberal economic policies, President Salinas de-fanged the Constitution of its anticlericalism, restoring the Catholic Church's legal status and giving it access to television. In 1992, new laws gave clergy the right to vote and churches the right to own property and run their own schools without state interference. Mexico restored full diplomatic relations with the Vatican. A Papal Nuncio arrived and mounted a full-scale offensive against members of the clergy who favored liberation theology. In the fall of 1993, he made public a scheduled transfer back to the Vatican of Samuel Ruiz, Bishop of San Cristóbal de Las Casas, Chiapas.

The Zapatista uprising, however, put Ruiz at center stage of Mexico's peace process and left the Papal Nuncio with momentarily diminished influence. Tens of thousands of Chiapas's Indians loved Bishop Ruiz. After interviewing the bishop in 1994, prominent conservative historian Enrique Krauze described him as a "prophet like Las Casas," who practiced "the charity of truth" and hoped to save the Indians "not in another life but in this one." Ruiz, a pacifist, told Krauze, "Of course we have something to do with the [Zapatista] rebellion, because by means of Christian meditation we urged the Indians to recover dignity."[73]

Aware of these challenges and the failures of neoliberalism, Mexico's Catholic Church issued a statement on the eve of the Zapatista uprising that declared increasing unemployment to be a "moral disorder" and criticized government policies that abandoned people to "the whims of the free market."[107] This was startling because the Vatican had long since abandoned such radical pronouncements. However, Mexico's harvest of poverty demanded a response.

The 1993 parking lot killing of Cardinal Juan Jesús Posadas Ocampo in Guadalajara was officially attributed to crossfire between narcotics thugs, although some suspected the slaying was carried out by President Salinas's "narco henchmen."[74] Cardinal Posadas was not a liberationist. Other clergy, who *were* liberationists, received frequent death threats. In June 1995 an attempt was made on the life of Tehuantepec's Bishop Lona Reyes, by then president of the Tepeyac Human Rights Committee. In the fall of 1997, as already noted, Bishop Ruiz escaped an assassination attempt.

Clearly, Mexico's Catholic Church was as divided as Mexican society. On balance, though, it remained a repressive and conservative force. In 1998, Mexico's Archbishop Norberto Rivera Carrera had the final word—for the moment, at least. He publicly censured "feminists, homosexuals, third-worldists, pacifists, liberationists, and malcontents of whatever kind."[75] A growing and powerful right-wing movement backed by the Church and conservative politicians was pushing extreme versions of "family values." Using the PAN's and the Church's access to television, the movement was calling for sexual abstinence, condemning condom use, criticizing people with AIDS, championing patriarchal values, and generally echoing the sentiments of the Archbishop.[76]

Mass Media

More powerful than the Church in influencing public opinion were the mass communications media.[77] Technically Mexico had a "free press," but the media had always been tied to wealthy and conservative financial groups loyal to the PRI and PAN. Foreign and domestic private interests called the tune. Madison Avenue advertising firms did a booming business for monopoly capital by use of the media. Whether through radio, television, records, tapes, books, tabloids, magazines, or *fotonovelas* (short, easy-to-read soap operas combining posed photos with cartoon "word balloons"), Mexicans for the most part were a captive audience for the messages of both political and sexual repression. In this inhospitable atmosphere, less conservative political parties and forces had to try to communicate their alternatives for the nation's future.

All printed communications media, including book publishing firms, were subject to the whims of the state monopoly on paper supplies, Productora e Importadora de Papel, S.A. (PIPSA).[78] The state retained mass media licensing and related prerogatives, which it used from time to time to pull in the reins of independent-minded voices. The Echeverría administration (1970-1976), for instance, dissolved the staff of the nation's most prestigious daily newspaper, *Excélsior,* in order to bring it under the control of the government. News journalists and even some authors of books routinely practiced self-censorship. Not surprisingly, surveys conducted during the 1990s showed that among Mexicans who followed election campaigns via television, most believed the coverage was very pro-PRI. Responding to some journalists' complaints of not being allowed access to their spokespeople, the Zapatistas' EZLN declared that it would deal only with "the honest press."

As only 2 percent of Mexico's population read books, and lesser numbers consulted the leftist press, the main media of communication were television and radio. In 1945, CBS and NBC integrated their radio interests into Radio Programas de Mexico; later they focused on television programming and technology sales. The state operated an occasional radio station, mainly with cultural programs like Radio Educación, founded in the 1970s. In general, radio was controlled by wealthy capitalists, who made sure radio stations spread a highly commercial and conservative message.

As for television, from its inception in 1955 it was a quasi-monopoly in the hands of private capital, although there were a few state-run channels. For years the biggest private monopoly in television was Televisa, subsidized by the government and owned by a multi-millionaire PRI loyalist. Shortly before his death in 1997, Mexico's second largest private network, TV Azteca, also conservative in slant, began cutting into Televisa's market share. TV Azteca was privatized in 1993. *Forbes* magazine listed both Azteca owner Ricardo Salinas and Televisa owner Emilio Azcárraga Jean among the world's wealthiest individuals. Salinas was no relation to the ex-president, although he admitted in 1996 to having exchanged money with Raúl Salinas. He had to defend himself publicly, since it was common knowledge that many journalists were routinely bought off by Mexico's drug cartels, hence the term "narco-press."[79]

There were dozens of smaller commercial television stations. Besides owning controlling interests in various publishing houses and in the new Rufino Tamayo Museum of International Art, Monterrey's ALFA group held considerable economic shares of major networks. Soap operas (*telenovelas*) enjoyed high ratings, though reports about the real-life scandals of the Salinas years momentarily replaced them in popularity. TV Azteca ran a popular soap called "Nada Personal" ("Nothing Personal") that portrayed Mexico's ruling políticos as unfeeling and malevolent.

Independent journalism in Mexico was a risky business. Death squads, suspected of having links to the military or the police, assassinated thirty-six journalists in the 1980s. The murderer of journalist Manuel Buendia turned out to be the person covering it up, the director of the National Security Police. Death squads continued targeting journalists in the 1990s. In June 1990, international political columnist Jorge Castañeda and his assistant, Mariana Rodríguez, received death threats, causing an international outcry. Seven years later, the conservative Inter-American Press Society declared Mexico the country it was most concerned about in 1997, because of the abuses of journalists and lack of press freedom there.

Despite all the obstacles, Mexico could boast of several internationally recognized and highly informative newspapers, magazines, and publishers, including many of those cited in this work's notes. The Mexico City daily newspaper *La Jornada* was widely read nationally and internationally, including its Internet edition. "Siglo XXI" was considered by many to be the world's best publisher of works in Spanish, including several translated works of authors from outside Mexico.

On a far more modest scale, there also flourished an innovative "alternative media." The eight-page, pro-labor newspaper *Corre la voz* ("Spread the Word"), for example, contained readable and excellent analyses of major political and economic developments and was sold in Mexico City's subway system and elsewhere by workers on strike who kept the profits. Its 1997 circulation ranged from 60,000 to 100,000. The capital's "Canal 6 de Julio" produced video cassettes on neoliberalism, massacres, and guerrilla insurgencies that were exemplary reportage.

Labor Reawakens

In the mid-1990s, Mexico's almost dormant labor movement began reawakening, sparked by the Zapatista uprising and later by the PRD's electoral triumphs.

Much worker activism resulted from the deteriorating work conditions and rapid rate of job losses caused by neoliberalism. Workers simply felt they had little more to lose. Mexico's real income per capita in 1998 was less than in 1960.[80] Industrial workers, long among the world's lowest paid, were experiencing drastic shrinkages in real wages and the world's third highest rate of workplace accidents. The situation was made worse in late 1997 by the government's inadequate hike in the minimum wage to an equivalent of $3.20 (U.S.) a day, leaving most workers with their lowest purchasing power since 1935.

The death at ninety-seven of PRI labor czar Fidel Velázquez further weakened the PRI-dominated umbrella Congress of Labor (CT) and its major organization, the CTM. Velázquez's death on June 21, 1997, facilitated the departure of six major unions from the CT in August that a few months later joined other unions in launching a sizable rival organization, the National Union of Workers (UNT). Another loyal PRI *charro*, 76-year-old Leonardo Rodríguez Alcaine, succeeded Velázquez as CTM head.

Acts of defiance by disgruntled workers in the mid-1990s ran up against some of the same obstacles that the new labor militancy had confronted in the 1970s. As noted in Chapter 5, Mexico's Labor Law made strikes almost impossible. Moreover, the often used *requisa* law, Mexico's equivalent of the U.S. Taft-Hartley Act, allowed the state to take over strike-plagued industries considered vital to the national interest. In the state of Nuevo León, seat of the bourgeoisie's conservative Monterrey Group, any strike was automatically declared by the state government "an act of treason." The Monterrey-based, inaccurately named National Federation of Independent Unions (FNSI) loyally served company interests. It claimed to have 280,000 members in the northern states of Nuevo León, Coahuila, and Chihuahua. Meanwhile, CTM goons continued beating up on workers seeking truly democratic or independent unions.

Bus drivers ran into all kinds of problems when they organized an independent union, the Route 100 Bus Drivers Union (SUTAUR), to fight against privatization of the Route 100 Bus Line in Mexico City. The government arrested SUTAUR's leaders and froze union assets. Four SUTAUR members were assassinated. But with help from support groups in seventy nations and a 1995 AFL-CIO convention resolution endorsing their struggle, the union won a partial victory. It signed an agreement with the city administration. When government job promises were broken, the union set up three cooperative city bus routes. In May 1998, a judge sentenced twelve SUTAUR leaders to nine years in prison.

After the 1994-1995 economic collapse, labor actions began to occur a bit more frequently. They started out as "food riots." Peasants robbed freight trains of beans and corn in Veracruz and other states. In mid-1996, nearly 10,000 workers, led by Mixtec and Triqui migrant farmworkers, demonstrated for their human rights in San Quintín, Baja California. They occupied the town, set up barricades, and raided food stores. Later, in the relatively rich northern state of Nuevo León, people used propane gas tanks to block a train and stole its cargo of grain. Members of the 120,000-strong union of government workers of Mexico City occupied union headquarters to demand union democracy and better health services for the city's 4 million citizens experiencing extreme poverty.

In 1997-1998, Indians and peasants increasingly took up blocking highways to demand promised food deliveries, or to protest other government failures. Public health and Ministry of Agriculture workers engaged in work stoppages and public demonstrations against austerity measures. Doctors in Ciudad Juárez stopped work for two hours to protest the gangland-style killing of four colleagues. Thousands of retired people and widows engaged in acts of civil disobedience to protest the privatization of the Mexican Institute of Social Security (IMSS) and their inadequate pensions and related benefits. Oil union workers at various locals conducted simultaneous protests demanding a secret ballot in union elections. Some 400 sugar workers seized a sugar refinery in Morelos to protest the new private owners' threats of layoffs. The CTM-affiliated but remarkably democratic Mexican Electrical Workers Union (SME, 36,000 members) held huge rallies that put off the planned privatization of public electric companies, although development of privately financed co-generation plants and non-union subcontracting continued.

Occupations of buildings, sit-ins, and other means of civil disobedience became everyday occurrences. On May 5, 1997, many groups that were blocked from marching to the U.S. Embassy to protest President Clinton's visit sat down in streets and on sidewalks. They were angry about U.S. imperialist policies and the Mexican government's starting the visit on a nationalist holiday (honoring the military victory against the French at Puebla). Some of the most important and daring labor actions took place in foreign-owned factories and *maquiladora* plants and received support from major U.S. and Canadian trade unions.

Once again, women were in the forefront of the struggle for reform. Women made up 35 percent or more of the labor force in the formal sector of the economy, and a majority in the informal sector, where most Mexicans worked. School teachers launched major strikes and protest actions in several states. Many leaders of these actions belonged to the independent teachers' union caucus CNTE, composing about 20 percent of the membership of the huge educational workers' union SNTE. Allied with the Zapatistas' FZLN, the CNTE worked closely with the debtors' El Barzón movement, the urban poor's CONAMUP, and the May First Inter-union Coalition. As already noted, Indian and peasant women were prominent in the leaderships of many, though by no means all, rural struggles, particularly in Chiapas. A movement among Mexico's estimated 1.2 million female domestic workers also started up, seeking improved wages and working conditions.

Women had a strong presence in the leadership and membership of the PRD, for which Mexico's women voted in large numbers. Senator Rosa Albina Garavito Elías, a former guerrilla, was one of the PRD's main leaders. Women were also prominent in pro-democracy political coalitions like the Civic Alliance. Women's role in Mexico's many human rights organizations was legend. The new reform-minded umbrella labor organization UNT was made possible in great part by women's militancy in city, countryside, and community. Women made up majorities in the major UNT unions.

One UNT organization was the Authentic Labor Front (FAT, founded in 1960), which had long championed an independent labor unionism. The majority of its 50,000 members were women. They came from independent unions, cooperatives, farmworker organizations, and urban community groups. The FAT played a key role in several internationalist, labor, democracy, and anti-NAFTA struggles, sparked in part by feminist union leaders like Bertha Luján, one of its three national officers. The FAT championed labor legislation to serve women workers' needs, such as affordable child care, personal security, maternity and family leaves, and public transportation. FAT's organizers and others documented the abuse of women at the *maquiladoras*, including frequent rapes, exposure to toxic materials, lack of equal pay or promotions, degrading screenings for pregnancy, and forced resignations of pregnant women. These practices violated Mexico's Constitution and Labor Law prohibiting gender discrimination, and later a NAFTA labor side agreement hearing on the matter came down on the side of the FAT.

On March 8, 1998, Mexico's women networks commemorated International Women's Day by organizing a two-day meeting in Congress with female politicians. Their earlier movements had brought the female portion of Congress up to nearly 20 percent. The meeting resolved to demand stricter enforcement of the 1990 law against sexual harassment and to enact a new law to rule out pregnancy screenings and firings and put the burden of proof on those employers who fired pregnant women. It also raised daycare and other demands. It called for affirmative action in decision-making positions in unions and the workplace. There were differences, however, on decriminalizing abortion and on some labor rights issues. The women applauded the new Law against Domestic Violence working its way through Congress. A rally of sixty women's organizations was held at the capital's Zócalo square, under the banner "Without women's rights, there are no human rights."[81]

An important new labor reform organization pre-dating the UNT was "the Foro," or National Trade Union Forum, so named after a February 1995 labor forum conducted by a group of official, semi-official, and independent trade unionists. Emerging from that forum, the Foro said it opposed corporativism and *charrismo*. The Foro fought the privatization of the Social Security system then taking place. Privatization was causing the layoff of some of the 350,000-strong workforce in the health care system overseen by the IMSS. In addition, privatization of IMSS was leaving 11 million workers with inadequate pensions, health care, and workers' disability coverage.

Although the Foro opposed IMF-inspired austerity measures in 1995, in 1997 it signed the neoliberal economic pact between labor, business, and the government. The Foro's telephone workers union (TELMEX) favored "modernization" schemes like "flexibility contracts" and labor pacts with business. The Foro's electrical workers' union SME stood fast against such neoliberal measures. Among PRI leaders involved with the Foro was one of its three founders, Elba Esther Gordillo, the SNTE president appointed by Salinas who later moved over to take charge of the PRI's "popular" sector, the National Confederation of Popular Organizations.

A labor and community coalition more radical than the Foro was the May First Inter-union Coalition, or "Intersindical," founded in March 1995 to organize an opposition May Day demonstration as an alternative to the traditional CTM homage to "el señor presidente" in front of the pr Zócalo. The bus drivers' SUTAUR and its ally, the leftist Independent Proletarian Movement, were among the main founders of the Intersindical.

Unlike parts of the Foro, the Intersindical did not wish to work within the confines of the neoliberal agenda. It sought to go beyond defensive battles of unionized workers by calling for an independent project involving all Mexicans. Composed of various Marxist, anarchist, and populist currents, the Intersindical included many activists from the FAT and other unions, the debtors' El Barzón movement, the indigenous peoples' CNI, segments of the urban and rural poor people's movements, and various pro-democracy trade unionists and factions of leftist parties.

The government canceled the 1995 May Day because it feared a possible eruption of protest among rank-and-file workers, who since 1981 had often mounted militant protest marches on May Day. The Intersindical went ahead with its own May Day parade in 1995, incorporating nearly half a million workers. The same pattern of no official May Day continued until 1998. Each May Day, the Intersindical and the Foro organized their own separate May Day marches. The 1997 marches involved at least 250,000 angry yet confident anti-*charro* working people of all ages.

The Intersindical formed an alliance with the Zapatistas' EZLN and FZLN. In the fall of 1996, it cosponsored with the EZLN a "National Consultation on Work and Trade Union Freedom." Unlike the PRD, which felt democracy could be won through elections, the Intersindical believed a civic insurgency was necessary for the creation of a genuine democracy. It put its faith in the FZLN, mass mobilizations, and the ongoing fight for internal democracy in the labor unions and other mass organizations.

The long anticipated CTM split occurred after its 40-year leader Velázquez died in mid-1997. That November, UNT held its founding convention. Breaking away from the *charros'* CTM and CT, the UNT said it represented 1.5 million workers in 200 workers' and peasants' organizations. The peasant groups were noted for their having larger Indian and female memberships than those of the past, and for having created several co-ops and collectively owned farms to combat the ongoing privatization of the countryside.

The UNT's creation tended to divide and marginalize other labor organizations like the Foro and the Intersindical. For example, the ex-head of the teachers' SNTE, Elba Esther Gordillo, played a major role in keeping the SNTE and other Foro unions inside the official CT. The electrical workers' SME also stayed out of the UNT. On the other hand, the FAT's Benedicto Martínez Orozco, a founder of the Union of Metal and Allied Industry Workers (1991, STIMAHCS), became one of the UNT's seven vice-presidents.

The UNT called for democratization of the Mexican state; an end to corporativism in the trade union movement; a new economic policy (in 1998 it did not endorse the neoliberal economic pact between labor, business, and the government); support for Chiapas's rebellious Indian communities; and greater female representation in union leadership. The UNT had three presidents. All were male. Ironically, each of them came from a large union noted for its militant female membership. And all three of UNT's presidents came from the three unions that constituted the UNT's major force. The presidents and their unions were: TELMEX union leader Francisco Hernández Juárez; Antonio Rosado García, the head of the 350,000-strong National Union of Social Security Workers (SNTSS), long criticized for his lack of democratic practice; and Agustín Rodríguez Fuentes, leader of the 100,000-strong Union of Workers of the National Autonomous University (STUNAM). The first two men were members of the PRI, while the third sympathized with the PRD.

Hernández Juárez was arguably the main founder of both the Foro and the UNT. He favored an anti-*charro* "new unionism" that would still cooperate with management and the forces of neoliberalism. He had backed TELMEX's privatization and had been the major force behind the creation of the Federation of Unions of Goods and Services (FESEBES) that voiced this "new unionism." Although he denied it, his "new unionism" resembled the "new labor culture" notion being pushed by the CT, the CTM, the World Bank, and the world's TNCs.

In 1998, Hernández Juárez agreed to meet with CTM leaders to work out an agreement on revisions in the Labor Law being debated in Congress that conceivably might create a compromise endorsing both the "new unionism" and more union autonomy from corporativism—what some analysts speculated might become a kind of employer-friendly neo-corporativism. Regardless of what happened with the Labor Law, it was clear that the UNT had the potential of playing the kind of role in a new reformist presidency by someone like the PRD's Cárdenas that Vicente Lombardo Toledano's CGOCM had played for President Lázaro Cárdenas in the 1930s (see Chapter 4).

The FAT held its eleventh national convention at the end of November 1997. It was conducted more democratically than the UNT's convention. The FAT had an informal alliance with the PRD. It emphasized a new "globalization from below" of labor, peasant, and social movements. It had been practicing this already through the Mexican Action Network on Free Trade. The FAT also moved women more to the forefront of its leadership, creating a Women's Organization.

Labor historian and trade unionist Dan La Botz pointed out the critical role of women in organized labor's reawakening:

> All Mexican workers, and all workers in Canada and the United States—for we are now all part of the same labor movement—owe a debt of gratitude to the Mexican women. Had there been no women's movement, there could have been no new labor reform movement. The rising of the women has also been the rising of the working class, has been the rising of us all.[82]

Mexico experienced only thirty-nine officially recognized strikes in 1997, but 1998 started off with a bang. In January, 150 farmworkers destroyed buildings and equipment at a packing plant in the northwestern state of Sinaloa to protest CTM union dues checkoffs and to demand transportation and medical care benefits. In February, 2,000 auto workers at Diesel Nacional (DINA) won a one-day strike that resulted in an unusually high 24.5 percent wage increase. Food processing employees, truck drivers, and other industrial workers also struck during the first five months of 1998. In May, workers picketed the Mar Bran frozen food plants in Irapuato, Guanajuato, to protest the company's inadequate profit sharing, low wages, long hours, and bad work conditions. The Texas-based company responded by firing twenty-two workers who were demanding an independent union.

A three-week wildcat strike was launched by members of the Mexican Railroad Workers Union (STFRM) in mid-February against privatization of rail lines and the worker layoffs and abuses that followed. A grassroots movement for more union democracy had objected to the way STFRM leader Víctor Flores Morales had gained power in the early 1990s after his rivals died or were killed. It disputed his re-election at the November 1997 STFRM convention. Most of all, rank-and-file dissidents objected to the way Flores Morales had gone along with the sale of some of Mexico railroads to foreigners and the new "flexible" contracts that were contributing to the layoffs of tens of thousands.

The wildcat strike was started by 3,700 rail workers in Empalme, Sonora, against the private Mexican Railways (FERROMEX, a conglomerate of Mexican capitalists and foreign companies like the U.S. rail giant Union Pacific). Strikers quickly drew the support of the Broad Front of Social Organizations founded by Yaqui Indian groups. Families of strikers and strike supporters blocked highways, as all overland traffic ground to a halt. Major factories throughout the nation were affected by resultant non-delivery of supplies. From 2,000 to 3,000 women and children walked through Empalme, beating empty pots and pans to symbolize hunger caused by unemployment. The strike fueled other labor struggles against privatization, and Flores Morales had little choice but to support it. FERROMEX eventually ended the strike by agreeing to preserve some of the jobs of those affected by privatization.[83]

The CT found itself divided, in debt, and losing members to the UNT. So early in 1998 it decided to take up some of the banners being waved by the anti-CT reformers. It talked of opposing NAFTA and said it would resume the annual May Day celebration. Its major group, the CTM, vowed to organize peasants (many of whom were flocking to the UNT) and to unionize more *maquiladora* workers. Unfortunately for the CT, in April, an opposition senator, among others, discovered several government documents proving beyond any doubt the PRI government's ongoing use of labor spies, double agents, and hired killers to undermine labor militancy. In fact, people seeking jobs as hired goons still were visible every day at the arbitration board building where labor disputes were presumably being peacefully settled.[84]

In the midst of these problems for official labor, Flores Morales joined with CTM boss Rodríguez Alcaine to carry out a CT leadership coup. The two men deposed the CT president who had reformist tendencies and hailed from the huge public employees union FSTSE which, like the CTM, accounted for about a third of CT membership. They replaced him with a more conservative person identified with the Foro group dominated by SNTE leaders. Several CT member unions quit in disgust. The PRI satellite Revolutionary Confederation of Workers and Peasants (CROC), which made up about 7 percent of CT's membership, said it would not recognize the new president whom it called a "goon" (*golpeador*). The electricians' SME announced it would soon withdraw from the CT.[85]

On May Day, the CT did not conduct a march but it did hold a 35-minute morning rally of hundreds of thousands of workers who had been threatened with loss of a day's pay or worse if they did not attend. President Zedillo addressed the silent workers at the Zócalo rally and quickly left. Then separate enthusiastic marches organized by the Intersindical and the UNT arrived on the scene, equaling or outnumbering the CT's dispersed, discontented throng. The Intersindical's march was joined by nearly 100,000 workers, while the UNT's drew hundreds of thousands. Times were changing.[86]

In early June 1998, two more significant strikes occurred. The 1,200-strong National Independent Union of Workers of the Metal and Mechanical Transformation Industry won a five-day strike for a large pay hike at the former national steel plant in Ciudad Sahagún, Hidalgo. The 1,033-strong Airline Flight Attendants Union of Aéromexico won a partial victory in a six-day strike against Aéromexico airlines. Women's organizations and many other unions backed the strike, that also received support letters from flight attendants of 170 other nations. The strike succeeded in bringing 300 Aéromexico "confidential" or management employees into the union but won only a modest pay hike.

"Border Wars"

Historically, whenever economic hard times occurred in the United States, capitalists have tried to divert the blame for unemployment onto immigrants, scapegoating them for "taking American jobs." The recessions of the mid-1970s, early 1980s, and early 1990s were no different. The U.S. mass media and public officials whipped up a "brown scare" against the largest and most vulnerable immigrant group, the Mexicans. The "brown scare" campaign added Central Americans in the 1980s. By the 1990s, all Latino immigrants were targeted. By then, their numbers made them the equivalent of the fifth largest Latin American nation. Of an estimated 5 million "undocumented" immigrants in the United States in late 1996, some 2.7 million (54 percent) were Mexican; 40 percent of all the "undocumented" or "illegal aliens" resided in California.[87]

During the new wave of U.S. nativism or immigrant-bashing, U.S. politicians liked to garner votes by warning of an invasion of "illegal aliens" and what President Reagan called "feet people." The 2000-mile-long U.S. border with Mexico became a veritable war zone. In the name of combating narco-trafficking and stemming the flow of "illegals," the U.S. government militarized the border in a domestic version of the "low intensity conflict" doctrine it was implementing in foreign areas of "instability" or attempted social revolution (e.g., Nicaragua and El Salvador in the 1980s).

Reports of shootings of immigrants by the U.S. Border Patrol and the white supremacist Ku Klux Klan became common. Law enforcement clubbings of two defenseless immigrants in California, one a woman, were shown on national television. Suspected "illegals" detained by the Immigration and Naturalization Service (INS, or what Latino immigrants called "la migra") were often beaten; some were raped. San Diego television stations ran special news reports on white suburban teenagers shooting at Mexicans "for sport." Numerous "illegal" Haitian and Central American political refugees, including children, fleeing dictatorships or U.S.-backed counterrevolutionary wars in their home countries, as well as some undocumented Mexican immigrants, were thrown into "detention centers." Mainstream journalists and human rights observers likened the holding pens to concentration camps. Occasionally, Border Patrol officers fired their guns into Mexico's national territory, drawing loud complaints from a Mexican government otherwise unable or unwilling to do anything about the conditions that were driving its citizens toward "el norte."

In 1997, a U.S. Marine patrol backing up federal agents in an anti-drug operation shot in the back and killed a Texan teenager of Mexican ancestry. A year later, Amnesty International (AI) issued a damning report on human rights violations by the Border Patrol, noting that the agency had acknowledged its abuse problem by creating an advisory panel four years earlier but had in no way improved its record. Rather, the AI report concluded, "There is a perception that INS officers act with impunity" and agents often give "cruel, inhuman or degrading treatment" to those people they detain. AI's report was echoed by the U.S. human rights organization Americas Watch, which for years had condemned what it called the INS's "frontier justice."[88]

According to the Tijuana-based Binational Center of Human Rights, 1,500 Mexicans died in the dangerous migratory passage during the first eleven months of 1997. But the nature of economic life in both countries added to the flow of Mexican labor northward, either to the maquiladora zones or to the United States and Canada. As already noted, 27 percent of Mexico's workforce in the mid-1990s were either unemployed workers or working in "el norte." In addition, as political repression in Mexico increased, so did the number of Mexicans seeking refuge in the United States or Canada. In a six-month period in 1996 to 1997, U.S. officials received 13,313 applications by Mexicans for political asylum.[89]

Several basic facts flew in the face of the negative stereotypes being circulated in the United States about Mexican and other Latino immigrants. The immigrants were *not* "a drain on U.S. taxpayers." They were never eligible for welfare (unless present for more than five years). They never drew much on U.S. tax dollars and always paid far more into the system than they took out. A 1994 study by the conservative think tank Rand Corporation found that the annual taxes paid by immigrants totaled $25 to $30 billion *more* than the costs of services they received. Indeed, Social Security payments contributed by immigrant workers accounted for a significant chunk of that system's trust fund—up to $80 billion a year in the 1980s by some estimates. A 1984 Ford Foundation report noted: "As more whites reach Social Security age, their support will depend on Social Security taxes paid by an increasingly Hispanic and black workforce."[90]

The 1996 U.S. welfare reform applied more than 40 percent of federal budget reductions to *legal* immigrants who had previously qualified for welfare, a group that represented only 5 percent of those actually receiving welfare benefits. According to the Urban Institute, the welfare reform pushed 1.1 million additional children and 1.5 million more adults into extreme poverty, most of whom were immigrants. (Women and children also bore the brunt of the 1990s repeals of "affirmative action" civil rights decrees.) In violation of a 1971 Supreme Court decision that had invoked the "equal protection" clause of the Fourteenth Amendment of the U.S. Constitution to prohibit states from denying immigrants welfare benefits, the welfare reform eliminated benefits for *all* legal residents who were not yet citizens. The major benefits denied were Supplemental Security Income (SSI), food stamps, and Medicaid. This hit Latinos particularly hard since, according to the U.S. Census Bureau, nearly a third of all Latinos residing in the United States were not U.S. citizens. Seventy-one percent of the "legal" Latino population (excluding Puerto Ricans) was of Mexican ancestry (18 out of 25.3 million).

More than ever, Mexican and other immigrants were losing the benefits for which they had paid taxes, experiencing a cruel and heartless form of "taxation without representation." Employers benefited since the welfare reform left workers more willing to work for substandard wages and unlikely to unionize or protest, for fear of being fired with no unemployment or other welfare compensation.

In the case of education, Mexico paid for the cost of educating immigrant workers who *then* headed north and contributed to the U.S. economy. Counting *only* the undocumented workers, in the early 1990s this saved just one state,

California, $3.2 billion in the annual costs of educating the workforce. The same undocumented immigrants contributed roughly 7 percent of California's Gross State Product. The taxes deducted from the "undocumented" immigrants' paychecks helped fund their children's attending public schools. Yet in 1994 California voters passed Proposition 187 which barred noncitizens (including "legal" immigrants) from attending public schools and prohibited "illegals" from obtaining public health services (except for emergency care). Four years later California's electorate passed Proposition 227, mandating the end of bilingual education. Both propositions were unconstitutional and became tied up in the courts.

By the 1970s, Mexican immigrants on average were neither the least educated nor the poorest of Mexico's population.[91] The main causes of their emigrating were not poor schools or poverty. The main causes were a lack of decent paying jobs at home and, more importantly, U.S. employers' increasing demand for Mexican immigrant labor after the mid-1970s recession. Facing a crisis of overproduction and declining rates of profit, U.S. capital attempted to restructure the U.S. economy in a way that would not only send jobs to low-cost areas like the *maquiladora* zones of Mexico and Central America, but also would reduce domestic costs of production by saving on wages through the increased use of immigrant labor. Knowing little or no English, immigrants were less likely than U.S. workers to unionize or protest unfair treatment. Moreover, demographic trends indicated future shortages of labor. According to the U.S. Census Bureau, some 7 million fewer workers would be entering the labor force in 1996 than in 1981. As *Business Week* (June 23, 1980) noted, "The U.S. will need immigrants to buttress the labor supply if the economy is to grow."

Corporations were attempting to improve profitability and labor's productivity by increased mechanization, cost-cutting layoffs, and recourse to more easily disciplined and low-wage immigrant workers in the course of rotating the work force. The technological revolution of computers, telecommunications, and robotics had already begun to reduce the need for mainline U.S. factory workers. Meanwhile, high-tech firms were finding highly motivated, hard-working, low-wage employees in the pool of immigrants, who were finding employment in modernized production systems like those in California's Silicon Valley. There, up to 70 percent of electronics and computer chip production work consisted of semi-skilled, low paying, non-unionized operative jobs, taken up largely by Mexican women and other immigrant workers. They worked long hours, some taking the work home where they were "often responsible for their own overhead, such as machinery and electricity."[92] Modern capital's aim, wrote urban sociologist Manuel Castells, was to activate a "twenty-first-century technology with a nineteenth-century proletariat"—in other words, high-tech, low-wage "restructuring."[93]

Although high-tech industries were increasing the number of their employees, this was not the sector of the U.S. economy creating the most new jobs. That sector was services (80 percent of all U.S. employment in 1997), particularly the restaurant, health, sanitation, retail trade, and personal services, much of which depended heavily on immigrant labor and had low rates of unionization. Labor-intensive manufacturing sectors like garments and food processing also drew heavily on immigrant labor. A rapidly growing number of Mexican immigrants were entering industry proper or its subcontracted workshops, whether in automotive parts, electronics, or other assembly work.

Since the "silent integration" of the two nations' economies, the U.S.-Mexican border had become a legal fiction. The border served to justify the deportation of "unwanted illegals," such as those who attempted to unionize; 10 percent or less of immigrants joined unions. Just the threat of deportation helped discipline Mexican immigrant labor. The border also assured that the Mexican working class, through its export of human capital, subsidized the U.S. economy, since the United States did not have to bear the costs of raising and educating the temporary immigrant workers. The immigrant was encouraged to come alone and to remit home small amounts of money (by U.S. standards) for the subsistence of his or her family. Sixty percent or more of Mexican immigrant workers' wages were spent in the United States. Meanwhile, U.S. cities and businesses along the border received the bulk of the spending money of *maquiladora* and other employees in Mexico who did their shopping "across the border."

Above all, the legal fiction of the border reinforced the argument that the cause of U.S. unemployment was in main part the immigrants' "taking American jobs." In fact, unemployment rates were lower in areas receiving large numbers of immigrants.[94] Nativism reinforced racism and prevented U.S. workers from seeing their "common enemy," unscrupulous employers. The fact was that few Mexican immigrants displaced U.S. workers because they responded to a labor market with rules that were unacceptable to most U.S. citizens. There was one group that did lose jobs to immigrants, however. This group was African Americans in domestic services and parts of construction, proving the validity of that old American folk song about racism: "If you're white, you're right/ If you're brown, stick aroun'/ but if you're black, get back." This, of course, was not the immigrants' fault but that of anti-black racist employers and institutionalized racism which oppressed both African Americans and Latinos.

The border served as a barrier, not only to working class unity in the United States, but to international class unity. It separated workers in the United States from their sisters and brothers in Mexico, while capital had far more freedom and means than labor to move across international frontiers and collaborate with its class partners.

While most of the discussion of Mexican immigrants focused on the "unskilled," a growing number of them were trained professionals—an estimated 20,000 in 1981. That number increased with each successive economic crisis in Mexico, as well-educated intermediate-class people headed north. The drain of income and skills caused by this out-migration contributed to Mexico's failure to develop more prosperously. Mexico suffered extreme shortages in all areas of skilled labor, from engineers to skilled and semi-skilled operatives. Moreover, most Mexican immigrants were employed in Mexico prior to their emigration. Despite a U.S. emphasis on preferred immigration status for skilled workers in the Immigration Act of 1990, the American Manufacturers Association and U.S. Chamber of Commerce alleged in 1998 there were not enough skilled U.S. workers in fields like information technology, medical services, and academic research, a claim refuted by the U.S. Congress's General Accounting Office. The AFL-CIO pointed out that high-tech firms were intent on reducing labor costs by hiring inexpensive foreign workers.

The old profile of male farmworkers composing the bulk of Mexican immigrants in the U.S. labor force was no longer applicable. Less than 15 percent of Mexican immigrants were employed in agriculture. As more Mexican women entered Mexico's labor force, only to be laid off after a few years, they too began to migrate northward, some bringing their children, many coming from the *maquiladora* zones. By the mid-1990s, at least a third of Mexican immigrants were female. Employers increasingly recruited them because they often had higher levels of education, and yet could be hired for lower wages than men. Interviews conducted in 1997 with Mexican and Central American immigrant women revealed that almost all of them had experienced sexual assault during the migratory passage; those spared were usually the ones who had located "protective" *coyotes* (smugglers) in their home towns or had raised the money to fly.[95]

Mexican immigrants were the pivot of the economy of the Southwest, the U.S. region experiencing the most economic vigor since the 1970s. As the *Wall Street Journal* headlined on May 7, 1985: "Illegal Immigrants are Backbone of Economy in States of Southwest—They Make Computer Parts, Package Arthritis Pills, Cook, Clean, and Babysit—Prisoners in the Bunkhouse." The same pro-business newspaper earlier observed that "Legal or not, the present wave of Western Hemisphere immigrants is already enriching and contributing to North American society... illegals may well be providing the margin of survival for entire sectors of the economy."[96]

That is why so many employers supported the Immigration Reform and Control Act of 1986 (IRCA) with its provision for 350,000 or more "guest workers" from Mexico, a labor law disguised as an immigration reform law. They realized the new law would help them stabilize and guarantee the flow of Mexican labor in much the way the old *bracero* program of 1942-1964 had done. Low-cost immigrant labor could, as it had done before, help depress the average wages of Americans, provide scabs against strikes, and generate higher profits. IRCA's employer sanction provisions were not seen as a real threat, since they had never been enforced in the past and, in fact, would help employers control the immigrants even more.

IRCA's guest-worker program reinstituted a system of contract labor outlawed in 1886 and again in 1964. It neutralized Supreme Court decisions giving all workers, including the undocumented, the right to strike and to unionize, and all their families the right to attend school. It rode roughshod over federal court rulings preventing INS raids (*redadas*) at workplaces and neighborhoods. Factory and workplace raids rose dramatically in the 1990s, at a rate that paralleled sharp budgetary increases for the INS and Border Patrol.[97]

U.S. employers obtained the same profit-boosting and union-busting results from the unilateral IRCA that they had enjoyed under the old bilateral *bracero* program. For example, IRCA had the effect of making "illegal" the Mexican undocumented immigrants' 40,000-strong American Federation of Workers. In addition, IRCA threatened all U.S. workers by requiring an identification system for getting a job and mandating future employment identification cards.

Moreover, employers had all these new powers without having to worry about any constraining input of the Mexican government, which now had no say whatsoever in the recruitment of "contract labor" from its own citizenry. Mexico's government was in too weak a position to issue a serious complaint in any case. Besides, it benefited from the social "escape valve" of emigration, and the dollars migrant workers sent home—Mexico's third largest legal source of income after oil and *maquiladora* exports.

IRCA required an increased budget for the Border Patrol, which was already being militarized. Under President Jimmy Carter, the Border Patrol had started to receive training in counterinsurgency techniques, and work had begun on construction of spiked steel-wire fencing many feet high along the U.S.-Mexico border. Mexican immigrants dubbed it "the tortilla curtain." Presidents Reagan, Bush, and Clinton continued the fence building and hiked the Border Patrol budget ever higher, while continuing the Border Patrol's militarization and doing nothing about its human rights abuses.

Additional changes in U.S. immigration law after IRCA further threatened millions of Mexicans and other Latin Americans with instant deportation. The 1996 immigration law removed federal courts' jurisdiction for most appeal claims by immigrants, leaving them deportable at the whim of INS and Border Patrol agents. This was in violation of international treaties governing human rights as well as political refugees. The minimum income required for sponsoring immigrants was hiked past the ability of most Latinos to pay. Like IRCA, the new laws reversed earlier family preference standards and broke up

Mexican and Latino families on a massive scale; two thirds of all U.S. Latinos were immigrants or the children of immigrants.

They also reintroduced McCarthyism by allowing denial of admission to anarchists, communists, and anyone supporting "a revolutionary organization." Finally, they continued a phasing out of the "guest worker program" of IRCA, although agribusiness fought for its preservation. In any case, there were other laws available for importing needed workers.

Claims that NAFTA would reduce Mexican immigration to the United States proved bogus. NAFTA offered up an even more abundant supply of cheap Mexican labor, whether exploited in Mexican *maquiladoras* or as immigrants to the United States. More Mexicans than ever before headed "*al norte*," especially as *ejidos*, small commercial businesses, and small and medium size industries failed in Mexico. NAFTA fueled the raging fires of nativism, despite the fact that some of the loudest immigrant-bashers, such as California Governor Pete Wilson, continued to urge guaranteeing a permanent supply of immigrant laborers to keep industries like textiles, agriculture, and janitorial services going.

Nativism had the effect of intensifying racism against Chicanos and other Latinos. While petty bourgeois and some better-paid Chicano proletarians no longer had as much in common with Mexico's immigrants as they once did, they nonetheless were subject to stop-and-search raids by INS and Border Patrol agents at their workplaces, in their cars, on buses, at schools, or on city sidewalks. In one year, for example, according to INS statistics, 95 percent of all "illegal" immigrants deported were "Mexican," of whom 35 percent were not legally deportable in the first place; most were forced to sign "voluntary" departure forms.[98]

Between the two poles "Chicano" and "Mexican immigrant" there stretched a long continuum built of kinship ties, relative length of immigrant residency in the Chicano community, similarities of work and life situations, and cultural values. The fact was that Chicanos were aware and proud of their Mexican roots and had long been in the forefront of the defense of the human rights of Mexican immigrants. Where divisions most strongly occurred was along *class* lines—for example, some petty-bourgeois bureaucrats, certain employers, and labor foremen *versus* Mexican *and* Chicano workers.

A new militancy among U.S. citizens of Mexican descent followed in the wake of the civil rights movement of the 1960s and early 1970s. By the 1980s, a combination of repression and government cutbacks on social programs had taken most of the steam out of the Chicano movement. The United Farm Workers (UFW), founded by Cesar Chavez and Dolores Huerta, had seen its membership drop from a peak of 50,000 to just over 20,000. However, the decade saw a new wave of protest marches against the draft and U.S.

intervention in Central America; the most notable development was the emergence of Latinos as leaders, and large numbers of Chicano participants.

Increasingly, the dynamic of Latin American migration and internationalization of U.S. capital and class conflict was generating a transnational community of human rights and labor activists. The U.S.-Mexico border area was particularly representative of the new transnational exchanges and culture that was developing.[99] Neither the U.S. nor the Mexican government knew how to handle this incipient human eradication of the "legal fiction" by the very people who had been most abused by it.

By the mid-1990s, all of Mexico's contending classes and groups began to sense (however gradually) that the one change that might reverse the pattern of repression and militarization was a strengthening of the mass social movements and an internationalization of labor's struggle to match monopoly capital's global reach. Activists in U.S. and Canadian labor and social movements also began to realize that the success of their struggles hinged on the same variables, as they watched "their" capitalists seek more easily exploitable labor power by moving production offshore and by relying more heavily on immigrant labor. Immigrant-bashing in the United States, as in other major industrialized nations, reflected capital's attempt to divide and rule workers and to tighten labor discipline. Human rights activists too, like labor organizers, were recognizing that they had to link their causes to larger international ones like the fights against NAFTA, GATT, and MAI.

To succeed in these struggles, however, labor and human rights activists had to catch up with other new workplace realities, especially the increasingly important roles of women and immigrants. Thus, not only internationalizing labor's struggle but also "feminizing" and (in the United States) "Latinizing" it would prove crucial to its progress. Concretely, this meant organizing the unorganized.[100]

Starting in the 1970s, before IRCA and other immigration laws were passed to block their efforts, the unorganized, many of them undocumented Mexicans, were organizing the most militant labor actions in the United States. While the AFL-CIO's top leadership was backing IRCA and calling for "give-backs" to keep U.S. industry "competitive," Mexican immigrants were organizing themselves and others into independent unions in the Southwest, Northwest, Midwest, New Jersey, and Florida. Many of them were farmworkers; others worked at subcontracted industrial workshops, shipyards, and high-tech assembly lines. Most later joined the independent International Coordinating Committee (ICC) which in 1982 changed its name to the American Federation of Workers (AFW). Membership in the AFW grew to more than 40,000 mostly "undocumented" workers before IRCA gave it the *coup de grâce*.[101]

Back then, the number of immigrant workers was already approaching 10 percent of the U.S. labor force. The biggest group came from Mexico. In urban areas like Los Angeles-San Diego and rural ones like Maricopa County, Arizona, the Mexicans conducted militant strikes. One of their biggest victories was sparked by women in a coalition effort with other groups, the twenty-one-month-long strike against Farah Clothing Company in Texas and New Mexico border towns in 1973 to 1974.

In 1980, the ICC convened in Mexico City an international conference that passed a thirteen-article Bill of Rights for the Undocumented Worker, emphasizing international human rights and fair treatment of labor. The Bill of Rights was endorsed by Mexico's umbrella CT, which set aside a "resistance fund" for the undocumented.

Several international conferences followed, starting with a National Chicano Immigration Conference that brought together Latino organizations in an effort to abolish contract labor and the Border Patrol. The United Electrical, Radio & Machine Workers of America (UE) had long been involved in organizing immigrant workers. UE's work was supplemented in the early 1980s by stepped-up organizing drives conducted by locals of the Teamsters, the International Ladies' Garment Workers Union (ILGWU), and the United Auto Workers (UAW), among others.

These and earlier experiences had taught a growing number of U.S. and Mexican workers about the need to show solidarity across borders. Starting in the 1970s, U.S. and Mexican workers increasingly expressed mutual support for each other's strikes in the textile, electronic, agriculture, mining, and automotive sectors. The UE and Mexico's FAT sparked unprecedented internationalist endeavors at uniting North American and Mexican workers.

A key, but difficult, sector of labor that clearly needed international solidarity was the *maquiladora* workers in Mexico. In the late 1970s, some 250 women at Tijuana's Solidev Mexicana electronics plant organized their own union, the first independent *maquiladora* union ever organized. Members of Tijuana's Center of Migration Studies and Information contacted UE activists across the border, who mobilized support for Solidev's courageous women. Eventually the women won a contract that resulted in the rehiring of fired workers and impressively high wages. But in 1983 the parent company, Solitron Devices Corporation, shut down its Solidev operation. During the reactionary period of neoliberalism, such audacious organizing and internationalist efforts continued, though on a much diminished level. They helped, however, to keep the dim flame of labor internationalism burning.

Then, in the 1990s, as NAFTA moved to center stage, the flame of international labor solidarity flared up again. The FAT drew support from Canadian and U.S. Honeywell workers in protesting the company's arbitrary and illegal dismissal of employees at its Chihuahua *maquiladora*. The Mexican workers were fired because they had decided to form an independent union and join the FAT affiliate Union of Metal and Allied Industry Workers (STIMAHCS, founded in 1991). A similar experience occurred in the case of FAT's organizing endeavors at Ciudad Juárez's GE plant, responsible for producing small motors that used to be made in Decatur, Illinois, prior to GE's closing the Decatur plant in 1989. In 1993, workers at the Boston-based Carlysle Plastics *maquiladora* in Tijuana won backing from U.S. workers across the border in their fight for an independent union. In June 1997, some 400 workers at GM's six *maquiladora* plants in Reynosa carried out a partially successful wildcat strike, helped by the support of the AFL-CIO-backed Coalition for Justice in the Maquiladoras.

The AFL-CIO, under a new reform leadership since 1995 was no longer as pro-TNC in Latin America as in the past. It gladly helped fund the Coalition for Justice in the Maquiladoras, which continued exposing polluters on "chemical row" in Matamoros and protesting firings and police brutality incidents like those against Sony employees in Nuevo Laredo. Other cross-border coalitions took shape.

Two major NAFTA-related labor struggles gained international attention in 1997 to 1998: the Han Young and ITAPSA-Echlin *maquiladora* workers' fights to form independent unions. In June 1997, workers at Han Young *maquiladora* in Tijuana began to organize an independent union. The plant produced truck and trailer chassis for Hyundai Precision America in San Diego, part of the powerful South Korean TNC Hyundai. Despite firings, physical attacks, and arrests of union militants, the workers won two consecutive fall elections to join the FAT's STIMAHCS. Under pressure from the San Diego-based Maquiladora Workers' Support Committee and major U.S. and Canadian trade unions, the Mexican government finally recognized the union.

In April 1998, the U.S. Labor Department's National Administrative Office (NAO), the new hearing body established under NAFTA, handed down a decision in FAT's favor in an earlier complaint filed against Hyundai by nine major unions and human rights organizations of Mexico, Canada, and the United States, including the UAW and the U.S. based tri-national Maquiladora Health & Safety Support Network. Mexico's government responded that the opinion went beyond the terms of NAFTA; in any case, the side-agreement did not allow for such rulings to be binding.

A month later, forty welders of the Han Young *maquiladora* went on strike to protest management's refusal to negotiate a new contract. It was the first legal strike in history by an independent *maquiladora* union. A new company manager began offering union militants $1,200 to leave. Few accepted the offer, so the manager began firing them.[102] The local labor board ordered a third election at the plant and once again the independents, despite more intimidation, won the vote. Then, on June 3, 1998, hundreds of tactical police violently attacked pickets and brought replacement workers into the plant. State authorities issued arrest warrants for the main union leader and the union's attorney. Rallies for the Han Young workers quickly spread from Mexico City to other parts of the world. Protesters mobilized by the Cross-Border Labor Organizing Coalition (CBLOC) shut down the Hyundai Corporation docks at the Port of Portland (Oregon) for twenty-four hours. The Han Young struggle has continued.

In the summer of 1997, some 300 workers at the ITAPSA-Echlin plant outside Mexico City tried to free themselves from their CTM "protection contract" by organizing an independent union to become part of STIMAHCS. While being exposed to asbestos and toxic chemical solvents, the workers produced disc brakes for export to the United States and Canada. They earned an average of six dollars per day, or less than half of what the government estimated to be the cost of the daily "basic basket of goods." Female workers faced harassment, and were told they would be raped if they backed the organizing drive. As in the Han Young case, the parent company was a powerful foreign TNC, the Connecticut-based auto parts manufacturer Echlin Inc., the world's fourth largest auto parts producer, with 1997 sales worth $3.6 billion and eight plants in Mexico.

Once more, international solidarity proved helpful. In 1996 to 1997, the UE had sparked the formation by unions from all three NAFTA nations of a tri-national Echlin Workers' Alliance, to coordinate collective bargaining within the international Echlin chain. In the spring of 1998, upon hearing of the illegal acts carried out at the ITAPSA-Echlin plant, major labor organizations like the AFL-CIO, Teamsters, and UAW, the Canadian Labour Congress (CLC) and Canadian Auto Workers (CAW), and Mexico's UNT joined with the UE and FAT to file a complaint with the NAO under the NAFTA side-agreement. The CAW and UAW had worked closely with unions in Mexico for some time, as in the case of the already mentioned Ford strike in Cuautitlán. Part of the 1998 complaint before NAO dealt with Echlin's firing of fifty-two pro-STIMAHCS union activists, followed by its use of 170 thugs carrying guns and steel pipes to intimidate workers on the day a union election was held for workers to decide whether to stay in the CTM or have STIMAHCS represent them; not surprisingly, CTM "won."[103] On July 31, the NAO found in the unions' favor and encouraged the U.S. and Mexican governments to undertake ministerial consultations.

By 1998, even the CTM was sufficiently aware of its lack of credibility among *maquiladora* employees to decide to call strikes. In January it struck two Ciudad Juárez plants employing more than 3,000 workers. Both plants decided to close down.[104]

Also in January, the CTM got in over its head with a three-day strike movement it launched at ten *maquiladoras* in Matamoros in northeastern Mexico. Some 13,000 workers, or about a fourth of those employed by the city's one hundred *maquiladora* plants, struck at six GM plants and Lucen Technologies, Sunbeam, and other plants. Workers at nearby plants engaged in stoppages to show their support. The UAW lent support to the huge Matamoros *maquiladora* walkout. The affected TNCs obtained the backing of the Interior Ministry (Gobernación) and the national CTM to impose a settlement.[105]

The *maquiladora* strikes and independent union organizing endeavors were critically important to the future of all workers in the Americas and indeed the world. After all, Mexico's *maquiladora* zones had long been portrayed as a model of supposed TNC benevolence. Yet *maquiladora* workers were superexploited and, in the case of their women employees, sexually abused. The value of *maquiladora* exports, according to Mexico's Ministry of Commerce, accounted for 42.5 percent of Mexican exports (1997). If wages and work safety conditions could be improved in the *maquiladoras*, then social justice would be served, TNCs would be dealt a body blow, and impetus would be given to other labor movements.

Throughout the 1990s, there took place numerous international meetings of workers from the United States, Mexico, and Canada. They were organized by groups like the Transnational Information Exchange (TIE), a global, industrially based network of workers from different nations; the Detroit-based monthly publication *Labor Notes*; the tri-national Mujer a Mujer; and the Maquila Women Workers' Network. The Transportation Trades Department of the AFL-CIO sent a message of solidarity to Mexico's striking railroad workers in March 1998. The FAT-UE alliance continued bringing together unions within the same company no matter where the unions were located.

Both the UNT and FAT labor conventions of November 1997 were attended by visiting observers sent by the major trade union organizations of the United States and Canada. They were sympathetic to the UNT's new reformism, in part because of the policy differences they had experienced with the CT and CTM over NAFTA.

There was an additional reason for the AFL-CIO's sending its representatives to Mexico's reformist labor conventions. In late 1995, in the first democratic election ever allowed, AFL-CIO members had voted in a reform slate. The newly elected president was John J. Sweeney, the long-time president of the 1.1 million-member Service Employees International Union (SEIU). A Latina, Linda Chavez-Thompson of the American Federation of County, State, and Municipal Employees (AFCSME), became AFL-CIO executive vice president. Women, African Americans, and Latinos had become a majority of what once had been a predominantly white male organization. They proved key to the reform slate's victory. SEIU's locals had sparked the predominantly Latino immigrant "Justice for Janitors" 1990 unionizing victory in California that had helped place Sweeney in the AFL-CIO limelight. Not surprisingly, Sweeney called for organizing the unorganized, but he shared the "new unionism" views of the UNT's Hernández Juárez, often speaking of a labor-business partnership aimed at increasing productivity and "competitiveness."[106]

Latinos, African Americans, and women were also strong constituencies behind the Teamsters for a Democratic Union (TDU) rank-and-file movement that helped elect reform candidates to the Teamsters executive board in 1991, including an African American and the board's first woman and first Latino. In 1996, Latino votes for Teamster reform president Ron Carey arguably made the difference in his re-election by a slim 16,000-vote margin.

Women, African Americans, and Latinos were some of the most dedicated strikers during the victorious 1997 Teamsters strike against the United Parcel Service (UPS).[107] Latinos were also active in the UAW strike of 1998, although it was mostly white and African American workers in Flint, Michigan, who started the strike.[108]

The analysis offered throughout this book leads to the logical conclusion that labor's struggle in any one of the three NAFTA nations would likely benefit from efforts to internationalize, Latinize (in the U.S. case), and feminize it. Starting in the 1970s, as we have seen, such efforts in fact began, and by the mid-1990s they were assuming not only an augmented urgency but also greater breadth and depth.

Indeed, strikes in the United States in the 1990s by Latino and Mexican immigrant workers and Latino citizens (especially women within those groups) reflected the international, feminine, and Latino dimensions of modern labor. Whether farmworkers, walnut workers, fish-packing workers, janitors, carpenters, drywallers, hotel employees, waterfront crews, public school teacher assistants, or other low-wage workers, Latinos were generating a militant unionism not seen in the United States in a long time. The UFW was also coming to life again, launching widely supported organizing drives among 20,000 strawberry workers in California and 5,000 apple pickers in Washington State. In Los Angeles, the Domestic Workers Association and the Day Workers Association were bringing together superexploited Mexicans, Central Americans, and Asians.

There was another reason why "Latinizing" and feminizing the labor struggle, at least in the United States, was becoming possible, and that was, ironically, the historical neglect by organized labor of precisely those segments of the workforce. This neglect meant that Latinos and women had to "do it for themselves," so to speak. As a result, internationalism and class consciousness among Latinas and Latinos was proportionatey strong.

This was illustrated by the success of the unprecedented march of October 12, 1996, "Día de la Raza" (the Latinos' name for Columbus Day), on the nation's capital, organized over the course of three years. From 30,000 to 75,000 Latino and other immigrants and their supporters marched that day to call for human rights, not just for immigrants but *all* workers. Major Hispanic civil rights organizations doubted the march would amount to anything and so had ignored it until the last minute when they asked organizers to allow their leaders to speak at the rally. Permission was granted.

The grassroots organizing for the march was initiated by the mostly Mexican and Central American immigrant communities of California and their Latino supporters, including One Stop Immigration's José Jacques Medina, who earlier had been a Mexican immigrant worker who helped found the ICC and AFW. Drawing support from UE and other labor unions, they launched the Coordinadora de la Movilización Nacional por los Derechos Civiles (Coordinating Committee of the National Mobilization for Civil Rights), which became known as Coordinadora '96. The Coordinadora's slogan was "Bill of Rights, Jobs, and Justice for All." Its initial call insisted that "democratic and economic rights must be affirmed nationally and internationally by workers themselves." Its list of demands included a minimum wage of seven dollars an hour, various specifics on women's rights, expansion of health services, regularization of the status of undocumented workers, speeding up of citizenship for legal immigrants, and world peace.

A third or more of the marchers were immigrants from countries other than Latin America. Some Irish carried the flag of the Saint Patrick's Battalion, recalling the time when large numbers of Irish and other immigrant draftees left "the aggressor's ranks" to fight on the Mexican side in the U.S.-Mexico War. The huge and militant demonstration was a wake-up call for many people in the United States who still did not understand what was happening with "all these aliens."[109]

While the percentage of the U.S. workforce in unions continued to drop (to about 14 percent), the number of Latino union members grew by 12 percent from 1992 to 1996. Women made up a third of union membership, African Americans a fifth, and Latinos at least a tenth. In terms of percentage of sub-group population, Latinos were as well-represented as whites—and there was a higher percentage of Latina women in unions than of white women. By AFL-CIO estimates, Latinas were entering the labor force at twice the rate of all other U.S. women. According to the U.S. Census Bureau, by the year 2000 Mexican American youth would be the second largest group among new members of the workforce. By 2050, Latinos would make up 25 percent of the U.S. population.[110]

The AFL-CIO still did not pay adequate attention to these new trends and possibilities. Its long racist and sexist heritage was difficult to shake. In Mexico, similar problems existed with regard to women and Indians in the workforce. However, when it came to immigrant workers in the United States, it was easy for Mexico's trade unionists to support them, at least rhetorically. In 1997, for example, Mexico's CT called for a continental labor alliance to defend migrant workers.

Though less economically endowed than U.S. unions, Mexican unions could also practice international solidarity. In 1998, they jumped on the NAFTA side-agreement bandwagon when the UNT, FAT, and STIMAHCS filed a case charging Washington employers with intimidation and deportation threats against apple workers attempting to unionize.

As the crisis in capital accumulation continued, and as monopoly capital tightened its grip over people's lives in Mexico, the United States, and Canada, working and progressive people would increasingly have to forge international networks of unity and struggle if a better future for them were to dawn. Labor Notes editor Kim Moody noted the value of forging a new international "social-movement unionism" based on some of the experiences in countries like Mexico, Brazil, South Africa, and South Korea. This type of unionism works closely with movements of the urban poor, part-time workers, and the unemployed. Within the European Union too there were signs of social-movement unionism relating to part-timers and the unemployed.

Political Prospects

While most Mexican workers and peasants continued to focus on the struggle to survive, the mass media is already fixating on the politics surrounding preparations for the presidential elections scheduled for the year 2000. In early 1998, the PRD's Cárdenas was running ahead in the polls. The PRD is a multi-factioned party with considerable internal democracy, yet it remains precariously dependent on a single individual with a famous name. Its treasury for mounting a successful campaign is paltry compared with either the PRI or the PAN. Cárdenas is courting big business more than ever.

The PAN, long close to big business's Monterrey Group and COPARMEX, remains a conservative party championing Catholic Church causes and neoliberalism. It has strong regional bases in the northern and some north-central states, the Yucatán, and numerous wealthy suburbs. To expand nationally, it has tempered its "loyal opposition" type of alliance with the PRI to cooperate on some issues with the PRD. For example, it has helped elect PRD leader Muñoz Lerdo speaker of the House. Also, the PAN uses populist rhetoric to seek support in the UNT, whose main leader, Hernández Juárez, promotes the "new unionism." A leading candidate for the PAN presidential nomination is Guanajuato's neopopulist Governor Vicente Fox, an independent and charismatic businessman. He announced in May 1998, however, that he would withdraw if polls continued to show the PRD's Cárdenas as the front-runner.

Meanwhile, President Zedillo told a New York meeting of news media executives in June 1998 that the PRI would abandon the "*dedazo*" tradition of the president's naming his successor, and instead would conduct an "open election" for selecting the PRI's presidential candidate. The PRI's "dinosaurs," however, are determined to return to old ways, with no more technocrats calling the party's shots. Some "dinosaurs" hope to become president. For example, Puebla governor Manuel Bartlett, who once oversaw Mexico's secret police, hopes to gain the PRI's presidential nomination under party rules that mandate ten years in the party and at least one electoral victory to become a candidate. (Only two of Zedillo's ministers met that criterion, but party rules were routinely ignored by top PRI bureaucrats.) The PRI is more wracked with internal divisions than ever, including ones pitting pro-Salinas elements against pro-Zedillo ones—and pro-Colosio members against both! Many high leaders of the PRI have already left the party, including Manuel Camacho Solís, the frustrated presidential aspirant of 1994 who in February 1998 announced he was forming the Party of the Democratic Center.

A wild card in the next presidential election is the emigrant community. An estimated 6 million Mexicans of voting age reside in the United States, most of whom have already voted with their feet and are anti-PRI. One of 1996's political reforms permits them to vote for the first time in 2000. However, it requires a National Citizens Registry which, because of PRI stalling tactics, will probably not be ready in time.

Another unpredictable element is the large number of younger Mexicans who will have their first or second chance to vote in 2000 (half the population is under twenty-five years of age). They are a diverse lot, ranging from spoiled offspring of traditional elites to student rebels very active in the FZLN. Most students who are politically active back the PRD. "*Los porros*" (armed thugs) are reappearing on campuses and at schools, causing students to launch marches against "*el neoporrismo.*" A growing number of impoverished working class youth are into gangs, punk, graffiti, and other forms of rebellion, sometimes with a political edge of admiration for the great Mexican revolutionaries Ricardo Flores Magón and Emiliano Zapata.

Mexico's economic crisis is having multiple political and social effects. Crime is a growing problem. The ruling class, like the PRI, seems to be fragmenting. The social movements are taking many different forms, including fresh focuses on the rights of indigenous peoples and women. The petty bourgeoisie, including most of the El Barzón debtors' movement, is being pauperized. The intermediate classes are growing disenchanted with the PRI. Civic organizations and NGOs are more numerous and active than ever. The guerrilla movements, though encircled by the government's "dirty war," are, at least in the case of the Zapatistas, drawing moral and even material support from people all over the world.

Given the many forms of political activism spreading across the land, Mexico can be said to be in a state of semi-insurrection. The Mexican state is in full crisis. Large chunks of the nation are occupied by its security forces, which have direct ties with U.S. security forces. Mexico's economy is being held hostage by the United States and the foreign investment and banking communities. Lurking in the shadowy wings are powerful military forces, domestic and foreign. And still Mexicans hope. . . .

CONCLUSION

Mexico's Hope

Without democracy there can be neither freedom, nor justice, nor dignity, and without dignity there is nothing.

—Communiqué from the CCRI-CG of the EZLN, from the mountains of the Mexican Southeast, February 26, 1994[1]

AS WE HAVE SEEN, MEXICO'S ECONOMY, from pre-colonial and colonial times, was marked by its low-wage structure and strong centralized states. The colonial state oversaw the economy's insertion into the world market. After independence, domestic elites extended these trends during the continuous development of capitalism in the nineteenth and twentieth centuries, in their own interest and in that of foreign, increasingly U.S., investors.

Throughout history, Mexico's low-wage basis of capital accumulation resulted in a limited development of the production of capital and intermediate goods, slowing economic growth compared with the pace being set by emerging imperialist powers. The home market also did not grow as vigorously as it might have done had wages been lifted above subsistence levels for all workers. Because of the relative weakness of the domestic elites vis-à-vis foreign capitalists and states, and the elites' own reliance on strong, undemocratic states, Mexico's class struggles for improved economic conditions or political democracy always fell heavily upon the shoulders of the peasantry and the working and intermediate classes. This was true from the indigenous wars against foreign subjugation, to the Wars of Independence against Spain in the 1810s and the national liberation war against France in the 1860s, as well as the Mexican Revolution and the social movements and pro-democracy struggles of the 1930s and post-1950s period.

Mexico's emergent, expanding low-paid industrial proletariat was always relatively weak in its ability to determine the outcome of historic class struggles. Consequently, other forces in society often proved decisive in moments of radical political or economic change—Indians, women, peasants, students, and intellectuals.

Since the 1940s consolidation of a corporatist state under the political hegemony of the PRI, Mexico's class struggle generally evolved in the context of working peoples' fights against the PRI's corporatist mechanisms of control.

Weakening the PRI was central to achieving the popular demands of their class struggle.

The weak nature of Mexico's bourgeoisie meant that it relied on a strong state that could control the proletariat, peasantry, and combative intermediate-class elements through corporatism or repression. What made the corporatist state strong and effective for the bourgeoisie was the PRI's hegemonic single-party control. Therefore, the parts of the bourgeoisie that supported the conservative "loyal opposition" National Action Party (PAN) had to be careful not to create a crisis of the state by challenging the PRI too much. Similarly, when the popular classes challenged the PRI they were, in effect, challenging the bourgeoisie's main mechanism of control.

Should Mexico's contemporary movements for democracy actually achieve the dismantling of the corporatist state and its replacement by a people's government respectful of pluralism, the battle for economic democracy would still have to be fought. Here, the lessons of Mexico's historical experiences under foreign-dominated capitalism were clear. Neither the Díaz-era Científicos' "liberalism" nor the modern-day technocrats' neoliberalism of oil-based monoculture and so-called export-led growth dependent on foreign investment could provide economic well-being for the citizenry.

Never intending to deal with the underlying low-wage basis of Mexico's incomplete industrialization, but rather hoping to take advantage of it, Mexico's contemporary architects of neoliberalism are constructing a dollar-studded castle of sand. Sweeping the sand northward are the currents of modern monopoly capital's neoliberal strategy of pauperizing Mexican workers to stem declining corporate profit rates and restructure production internationally in the "global economy." Mexico's manufacturing activity, like its agriculture and hydrocarbon industry, is more completely export-oriented and foreign-dominated than at any time since the Díaz dictatorship eighty years ago. Mexico's encounter with its earlier politics and history is coming full circle.

Mexico's neoliberal architects are mortgaging the nation and its labor supply to foreigners. On an unprecedented scale, Mexico is transferring value to the United States, not only in natural resources and labor's value added at points of production, but also in the literal removal of nearly a fifth of its economically active population to the United States ("immigrant labor"). Mexico could be compared to a giant pool of inexpensive labor power at the disposal of foreign elites and creditors—a key link in imperialism's chain, but, as the Zapatista uprising and economic collapse of 1994-1995 revealed, a "weak link."

Neoliberalism and NAFTA have accelerated the "petrolization" and "maquiladorization" of the economy, creating a divided Mexico. On the one hand, there are a few gems of of prosperity, especially in the northern states. On the other hand, layers upon layers of poverty are encrusting these gems, especially in the southern and south-central states.

Given this economic concentration and polarization, another economic collapse may already be taking shape. The U.S. Federal Reserve Bank reported in mid-1998 that $33.6 billion of personal and corporate Mexican capital is stashed in U.S. banks (flight capital), more than Mexico's current foreign reserves and more than the amount in December 1994 when Mexico's last economic collapse occurred.[2] Furthermore, huge foreign debt payments coming due in the 1998-2000 period will deprive Mexico of funds needed for productive domestic investment.[3] The state is already spending an amount equal to 12 percent of the 1997 GDP on covering bad loans by the private banking sector. In rating banks in sixty-one countries in 1997, Moody's Investors Service rated Mexico's banks as the most likely to "need outside rescue" (along with those in Pakistan, Romania, and Tunisia).[4] All of this leaves Mexico more vulnerable than ever to U.S. pressure. But it also leaves the imperial chain subject to a major break.

The peso again seems overvalued. Inflation is on the rise, with prices racing far ahead of wages, leaving 75 percent of families unable to afford "the basket of basic goods."[5] Per capita GDP production is declining and terms of exchange in foreign trade continue to be unequal at a time when Mexico is importing expensive capital goods more than ever.[6] With Mexico's labor supply growing by more than 1 million new entrants each year and its mass poverty worsening, even the new president of domestic monopoly capital's Management Coordinating Council (CCE) is saying that Mexico has to give top priority to creating a million new jobs a year in order to "assure society that we are not going to fall again into recurrent crises."[7] But private firms are laying off more workers than they are hiring, and the few remaining state enterprises employ less than 7 percent of the work force. Other voices of Mexican monopoly capital, recalling the devastating consequences of delaying the peso devaluation in 1994, urge prompt "fiscal adjustment" even at the price of not creating enough jobs.[8]

A drought in early 1998 and a shaky Mexican stock market do not augur durability for the highly touted but misnamed "economic recovery." Guerrilla insurgencies, electoral challenges by the PRI's opposition, and an increased U.S. military presence along the U.S.-Mexico border do not testify to "stability." Of gravest economic concern is the "free fall" in crude oil prices to their lowest level in two decades, leading to more federal budget cutbacks in social programs.[9]

Yet the architects of Mexico's castle burrow their heads deeper into the sand. They have announced more privatization and foreign borrowing plans. They say that the already semi-privatized state oil firm PEMEX, through its sales (worth $29 billion in 1996) and more capital investment (which doubled in 1995 to 1997), will raise daily production from 3 million to 3.7 million barrels by the year 2000. This entails more foreign loans and a possible overheating of the economy, as happened in the years leading up to the 1982 economic collapse.[10]

Moreover, if the development of production of the means of production—capital and intermediate goods—remains dependent on the "good will" of TNCs, this can only accelerate the accumulation of capital abroad and further tie Mexico's subordinated, semi-industrialized economy to imperialism and its lending institutions. Mexico in the 1990s imports 90 percent of its machinery and intermediate capital goods. During the first six years of the 1990s, the cost of high-technology imports from the United States more than doubled to $28 billion (nearly 10 percent of GDP). Mexico's R&D spending in 1991 to 1992 was a mere 0.3 percent of GDP, or less than an eighth of what the United States spent, and R&D expenditures dropped further after the economic collapse of 1994 to 1995.[11]

By contrast, left-of-center economists in Mexico like Carlos Perzabal believe Mexico needs to break the deepening cycle of dependence on foreign industrial technology imports, and reassert state intervention in the economy to emphasize domestic development of the capital goods industry and the home market.[12] Certainly state intervention to prevent the outflow of flight capital and bank/drug money would help make the state solvent again. So would corporate and income taxes on the upper 5 percent income bracket, heretofore rarely attempted or effectively carried out. Domestic savings would skyrocket instead of disappear.[13]

All that money could then be plowed back into the development of technology resources, improvements in infrastructure and outdated factories, construction of schools and hospitals, and provision of jobs and housing for all. Raising the minimum wage to levels well above the rate of inflation would facilitate breaking the historic pattern of low-wage-based capital accumulation and stimulate expansion of the home market for locally produced goods and services. Oil export earnings and moneys saved from debt relief could also help in this. According to economist David Barkin, a food self-sufficiency program based on autonomous local development could create 3 million new jobs in three years or less, while a safe drinking water program would add another 3.4 million jobs.[14]

To succeed, such an approach would have to break the integrated blocs of power represented by the triumvirate of private capital/foreign capital/state. It would entail re-nationalizing oil, asserting a democratic state's control over other commanding heights of the economy, and bringing into convergence the uses of the nation's natural resources, labor power, community needs, economic needs, and industrial productive capacity (two-thirds of which is not being used fully).[15] It would certainly entail renegotiating NAFTA and the relationship with the United States. Above all, this approach would require popular support among Mexico's citizenry, obtainable only through genuine democratic participation, from the grassroots on up, through every level of a new state. And, as the late Dr. Salvador Nava kept insisting, it would also require a heightened support from human and labor rights activists of the world, starting with those in the United States and Canada.

One thing is clear. The U.S. government views Mexico as critical to U.S. "national security."[16] Mexico has three attractive commodities in abundance: oil, natural gas, and cheap labor. Any attempt by Mexico's already "economically challenged" state to change course would meet imperialist resistance. In 1998, a proposed amendment to the charter of the International Monetary Fund (IMF) went so far as to allow the IMF to examine a country's "openness" and criticize any country restricting foreign investment, whether in industry, services, or stock and bond markets. Mexico's economic sand castle was already "open." Yet, in the face of the U.S. Congress's growing disenchantment with NAFTA and other neoliberal linchpins, there is no longer any assurance that the U.S. government or the IMF will be politically and financially able to "rescue" lesser economies like Mexico or Indonesia, much less major powers like Japan.

As important as Mexican oil and natural gas are to the U.S. economy, Mexican immigrant labor is even more so. Yet U.S. nativism and new immigration laws threaten mass deportations of Mexicans, causing alarm in Mexico. In an address to the Mexican people during a state visit in 1997, President Clinton said those who break the laws "must face the consequences."[16]

Actually, reducing Mexican immigration even modestly is an impossibility so long as its *causes* remain in place. Those causes are U.S. employers' demand for inexpensive Mexican labor and the lack of decent wages in Mexico. If the migratory flow were to be even modestly reduced by means of radically stronger police measures against undocumented immigrants, reduced quotas for legal immigrants, and denial of hospital care and schooling for immigrants per recent California referenda, then several things would happen that would only worsen matters. The border would be further militarized; there would be growing numbers of beggar children not allowed to go to school; and rates of contagious diseases in poverty-stricken areas would continue to rise.

In reality, the border can *never* be sealed against the migratory flow, even by throwing in the entire U.S. military and building a 2,000-mile long concrete wall. For U.S. employers, curtailing Mexican immigration would sabotage the economy of the Southwest and many newly vitalized urban centers, like Chicago and New York, that depend heavily on immigrant labor. U.S. workers would not benefit, since keeping immigrants out would make Mexico even more of a low-wage reservation for U.S. businesses ("runaway shops"). Nor would the Mexican government look kindly on the consequent loss of dollar remittances or the removal of an important safety valve for social unrest. Capital would lose its prime scapegoat for the job problems in the United States.

Meanwhile, Mexico's legislature has passed a law making it possible for Mexicans in the United States who choose U.S. citizenship to remain Mexican citizens too if they wish. "Dual citizenship" allows one to maintain full citizen rights in both countries, including freedom of travel, freedom of land or other ownership, freedom to take a new job in the other country, and voting rights. However, the United States has refused to recognize Mexicans' dual citizenship, even though the United States has bilateral agreements for dual citizenship with 134 other nations, including fellow NAFTA member Canada. Suspecting racism, Mexicans ask: why Canada but not Mexico?

A sensible U.S. policy to resolve immigration issues would confront their causes, including Mexico's low-wage structure. This would entail a foreign policy that insists upon harmonizing wages upward instead of downward. It would mean revising the 1986 IRCA and subsequent immigration laws to grant "amnesty" to currently employed "illegals" and to equalize political refugee provisions consonant with the U.S. Refugee Act of 1980 that obligated the United States to use UN criteria for defining a political refugee. It would also mean extending the "dual citizenship" arrangement to Mexico. Instead of throwing billions of dollars into a cat-and-mouse game of chasing Mexican immigrants, a sane policy would disband the border patrol and use the moneys saved to provide for legalization services and language instruction programs, as well as a cultural subsidy to celebrate the thriving transnational, bilingual society developing along the "legal fiction" of the U.S.-Mexico border.

Instead, the U.S. government pursues a wasteful and violent immigration policy that draws the censure of human rights groups around the world. So much for the exaggerated myth of "welcoming immigrants to the land of freedom."

The same could be said about U.S. drug policy. It too is wasteful and violent, especially to innocent victims of police raids in the United States, and to peasants in Mexico and much of the rest of Latin America with no other means of survival. Greater coordination between the two nations' security forces is an unrealistic solution, since that has already been attempted without success due to the corruption of both nations' security forces and large banks' reliance on billions of dollars of "laundered" funds. Greater changes are needed in both the United States and Mexico if the drug problem is to be realistically addressed, starting with adequate drug-rehabilitation programs for the addicted, and changes in Mexican agriculture to permit peasant to make a living from from the production of corn and other crops.

Just as the "legal fiction" of the border provides multiple benefits to security forces and to employers seeking cheap labor, so the phony "drug war" helps perpetuate the U.S. "military-industrial complex" that President Dwight

Eisenhower warned of in the late 1950s. The U.S. economy, like other powerful capitalist economies in history, has never prospered for long without receiving a state subsidy for production of war materials and economic windfalls "won" by domination or conquest. This is the true sense in which Mexico is being defined as a U.S. "national security" problem—not as a threat of invasion, but as a potential loss of capital revenue. Caspar Weinberger, the U.S. Secretary of Defense during the 1980s "low intensity war" in Central America, wrote a book in 1997 that envisioned a possible U.S. invasion of Mexico in the year 2003 to overthrow a "narco-government" there. How convenient, except for the fact that 1998 was not 1848.[18]

As already noted, U.S. imperialism's preferred strategy for securing Mexican oil and natural gas is not some unrealistic, concocted war, but a combination of economic/diplomatic pressure and training of Mexico's national security forces to put down citizen protests against denationalization, and to break up protests by peasants against the rape of their lands by oil, natural gas, petro-chemical, and construction companies. Most of Mexico's hydrocarbon exports are already going to the United States, and Mexico is gradually surrendering its national patrimony through alliances between PEMEX and foreign firms.

On the political front, Mexico is experiencing a crisis of the one-party authoritarian-technocratic state that makes government even less able to meet the needs of the masses. Although privatization schemes have brought billions of dollars into state coffers, thereby preventing complete state collapse, most of the new moneys are returning to the private sector through state subsidies and debt repayments, or to individuals and private firms through corruption. Constrained state budgets in the face of rising popular demands leaves the state even weaker.

In spite of frequent differences of opinion within the Mexican state, it maintains a harmonious relationship with imperialism, which only serves to aggravate the crisis of the state. Why? Because the state, like foreign capital, has to struggle to show its national legitimacy, to prove to a skeptical public its Mexican and independent character rather than its IMF-dictated and dependent character. This is one more reason why the Mexican government emphasizes its "independent" foreign policy, such as its advocacy of readmitting Cuba to the Organization of American States.

Whether the PRI's humiliating defeat in the 1997 election will lead to further democratization in Mexico or to more "dirty war" remains to be seen. Guerrillas, though encircled, still represent a threat to the survival of the PRI state. In the case of the Zapatistas, they retain a kind of moral advantage, or at least leverage, nationally and internationally, which helps hold back the Zedillo government's militarization of the nation. Even so, shadowy death squads, goon squads, and paramilitaries remain very active, intimidating or selectively killing journalists, pro-human rights and pro-labor lawyers like those associated with the Mexican National Democratic Lawyers' Association, PRD militants, prominent clergy and intellectuals critical of the PRI, and student, teacher, peasant, Indian, or worker dissidents.

The PRI still holds the reigns of power, including its elaborate patronage system that many people depend on for their jobs. Corruption is as rife as ever, and recent presidents have centralized power and militarized society to an alarming extent. At the same time, the PRI leadership's divisions, its failures to solve economic problems, and the rising protests of Mexico's social movements have forced the PRI governments to agree to political reforms. Initially, the PRI had hoped that reforms would turn the tide of discontent into electoral channels where it might be more easily contained. The pro-democracy groups and opposition parties, however, have used the reforms to gain control of numerous local and state governments and to eliminate the PRI majority in Congress.

With the PRI—and therefore the corporatist state—losing public credibility, and Mexicans taking to the streets to demand their basic rights, talk of a military coup has become more common. Many observers note, however, that the PRI has survived tough times before and might well weather even this latest storm.

A number of Mexicans look ahead to a new century with a hope that they might yet win a political and economic democracy. Why? One obvious reason is that the crisis of the single-party state is in their interests, since that state has long contributed to their oppression. As a result of the growing popular distrust of the existing state, Mexico's toiling masses, led only partly by regularly employed industrial workers and mostly by the more oppressed (women and Indians), seem to be following a strategy of fighting for greater control over economic production at factory, mill, and field. They seem more interested in building workplace and community/neighborhood power or autonomy than in gaining control over the bankrupt state. Much of their fight against the state is directed to the same end: local control.

Despite state repression, the popular social movements have forced open some democratic space in Mexican politics. Under new laws making it obligatory to vote, Mexicans are beginning to vote more often, and fewer are opting for the PRI. People who most regularly vote are the better-off elements of the intermediate classes, and those peasants and workers bribed by the PRI.

As elections become more honestly conducted, new opportunities arise, along with new problems. For example, the left-of-center PRD cannot afford the high costs of electioneering that the PRI and the PAN can. Also, anti-PRI political parties may siphon off the talents and energies of social movements, leading to internal divisions within movements and a reduction of their influence. This is the logic behind the Zapatistas' declaration that they do not want the FZLN to be a political party or to take state power. They see the existing state as so corrupt that involvement in it necessarily will corrupt and weaken the movements.

Another problem is that attempts at democratization, even though opening up space for political representation, tend to provoke even greater state repression and militarization of society. This is one more reason why the pro-democracy movements do not expect democratic transformation "from above" but realize they will have to construct it "from below."

Ultimately, the only check against state repression is the strengthening of the mass social movements and the internationalizing of labor's struggle to match monopoly capital's internationalization. And therein too lies the hope, since there are clear signs of growing international labor support networks, especially in the NAFTA context, with increasing solidarity between unions of the three countries. Also, the hope matches the lessons of Mexico's political and economic history.

It was, after all, working peoples' mass social movements that had sparked the great watershed revolutions of Mexican history, first against Spanish colonialism, then against French military occupation, and finally against the Díaz "liberal" dictatorship. It was peasant guerrillas like Emiliano Zapata and revolutionary internationalists like Ricardo Flores Magón who formulated the programs and practices of direct local democracy that gave rise to the most progressive clauses of the Mexican Revolution's Constitution of 1917. In several of their communiqués, today's Zapatistas seem aware of the dangers of being "tricked" or "betrayed" again, as happened to their forerunners in 1911 when Zapata's troops handed in their arms, or in 1915 when the urban workers' movement split from the peasant movement to form the Red Battalions, or in 1919 when Zapata was assassinated.

Mexico's Indians and women remain central to any successful political transformation. Mexico's diverse Indian peoples (Mayans, Mixtecs, Purépecha, Zapotecs, etc.) are engaged in both a class struggle within a modern capitalist economy and a cultural one within a racist society. Their class struggle is reflected in the fights by peasants and rural workers to have a piece of land and decent working conditions; or in struggles by workers to obtain better wages and work conditions; or in demands connected to petty bourgeois crafts and commercial enterprises; or in demands of migrant workers. Their cultural demands center around the issue of land ownership and usage and the closely related issue of collective decisionmaking, or democracy. This is the basis for the National Indigenous Congress's endorsement of the Zapatistas' program in 1996. For the indigenous peoples, land is not a commodity to be bought and sold. Their demand for "autonomy" means not only local self-governance according to traditional (culturally specific) ways, but also control over the lands, rivers, and elements of nature they long have respected and understood in ways that run counter to capitalism's easy exploitation of these resources.

Culture is particularly harmonized with the class struggle as land becomes the only means of survival for so many rural people, of whatever ethnicity, in a superexploitative setting.

Because of patriarchy and related gender ideologies, capital has had an added ability to superexploit women, which is one reason behind women's increased participation in both the formal and informal sectors of Mexico's economy. Capital has always found in women a non-waged source of production of labor power that subsidizes capital in production of capital and consumer goods by reducing the costs of labor power. In addition, however, capital increasingly taps a vast pool of inexpensive, non-unionized, and sometimes skilled female labor power for production of capital and consumer goods. More women everywhere are becoming heads of families and major family "breadwinners." [19]

In the words of the head of the Inter-American Development Bank's development program for women, "Investing in women offers policymakers the highest economic and social returns at the lowest cost." [20] Mexico's "maquiladorization" owes in great part to patriarchy's making possible the *maquiladoras'* superexploitation of a largely female workforce. The same logic lies behind several U.S. high-tech industries' increased use of Mexican and other immigrant women workers, as in California's Silicon Valley. [21]

Mexico's women too, like its Indian peoples, have had a dual struggle to conduct, one based on class and another based on specific gender demands. And, like Indian women, working women of all racial and ethnic groups are increasingly unifying around both class and gender demands. Moreover, "family survival strategies" consisting of multiple types of income-producing work are becoming the dominant form of economic struggle for Mexico's immiserated masses, with women often in the lead.

Increasingly, Indians and women are in the forefront of all Mexico's social movements for political and economic change. A lack of a gendered and racial/ethnic class analysis and *praxis* could lead, however, to a failure to match the reality of heightened female and indigenous peoples' initiative and participation in social change and revolutionary processes with sufficient commitment to having a female and Indian leadership and a serious implementation of reforms meeting their specific needs and rights. Only when the working poor, the working class, and concerned organizers and intellectuals recognize the role of the immiserated masses and the women and Indians among them as not only that of a "reserve army of labor," but also as a highly important activated arm of capital accumulation for domestic and foreign capitalists, can Mexico's burgeoning mass social movements and union organizing drives among poor workers be linked in the fundamental dynamic of class struggle, the one pitting capitalist owners against urban and rural proletarians.

Many people in organized labor recognize the need to internationalize labor's struggles and to incorporate feminist demands. They, like human rights activists, realize that their struggles must relate to larger issues like NAFTA, GATT, and the MAI (Multilateral Agreement on Investment), as well as to specific union organizing drives like those among Mexico's *maquiladoras* or California's strawberry workers. Labor union confederations like Mexico's newly created National Union of Workers (UNT) and its member organization the Authentic Labor Front (FAT), or the United States' AFL-CIO and its member organization the United Farm Workers (UFW), now recognize the need to "organize the unorganized"—mainly female and migrant workers, many of whom had already started organizing themselves in both countries prior to the 1990s.

And this too gives many Mexicans cause for hope.

However, in their struggle for democratic space, economic improvement, and state transformation, Mexicans face bigger guns (U.S.-supplied) and slicker politicians than ever. To succeed, they will have to confront and build upon the lessons of their history, of which they continue to be very active agents. They will also need to insist on international solidarity, the key element of which is the rising current of international worker, feminist, and human rights solidarity already putting Mexico back into the limelight, as NAFTA or other agendas of modern monopoly capital have done in the recent past. Inexorably, the destinies of working people, not just of Mexico but of all the Americas—indeed, the world—are becoming mutually dependent on the successes or failures of national struggles for workers' rights and genuine pluralistic democracies within their different yet interrelated countries. For that reason, Mexico's hope is the hope of the world.

Notes

Introduction: Modern Mexico's Encounter with History

1. The "new international division of labor" refers to low-wage labor forces in the third world (or "South") providing raw materials, agricultural products, and assembled parts (sometimes complete units, such as automobiles in Mexico) for the more industrialized nations of "the North." Employers in the North in turn grow wealthier, while reducing the average wage levels of their own work forces through "runaway plants" (to the third world) and the importation of cheap immigrant labor.

2. In the 1980s, Western "modernization" theoreticians recast their ideas as "neoliberalism" and "privatization." Neoliberalism was an economic ideology that argued for free enterprise capitalist development through the privatization of state industries, reduced social spending, and "free market" solutions to social problems. The 1980s witnessed Latin America's "lost decade" of economic depression; the economies and life standards of East Europeans in the 1990s took a nosedive under neoliberal policies.

3. Subcomandante Marcos, *Shadows of Tender Fury: The Letters and Communiqués of Subcomandante Marcos and the Zapatista Army of National Liberation,* (New York: Monthly Review Press, 1995), 137-39.

Chapter 1: Invasion, Colonization, and the Beginnings of Mexican Capitalism

1. Karl Marx, *Capital* I (New York: International Publishers, 1967), 751. Chapters 26 and 31-33 of Part 1 of *Capital* explain the role of "original accumulation" in the birth of the capitalist era. Its role in earlier noncapitalist class systems is explored by Alexander V. Chayanov, "Sobre la teoría de los sistemas económicos no capitalistas," *Cuadernos Politicos* 5 (June-September 1975): 15-31; John Clammer, ed., *The New Economic Anthropology* (London: Macmillan, 1978); and Maurice Godelier, *Perspectives in Marxist Anthropology* (New York: Cambridge University Press, 1977).

2. Traditionally, scholars often called the production of labor power "reproduction," easily confused with "reproduction of the species." This naturalizing of a *socially constructed relationship* has been challenged in recent feminist analysis. On women in pre-capitalist economic production, see Stephanie Coontz and Peta Henderson, "Property Forms, Political Power, and Female Labour in the Origins of Class and State Societies," in *Women's Work, Men's Property: The Origins of Gender and Class,* ed. Stephanie Coontz and Peta Henderson (London: Verso, 1986), 108-55. On women in pre-colonial and colonial Mexico, see Susan Schroeder, Stephanie Wood, and Robert Haskett, eds., *Indian Women of Early Mexico* (Norman: University of Oklahoma Press, 1997).

4. Archeological findings in the mid-1990s still under analysis suggest an even longer period for human existence in the Americas. For earlier estimates, see Alex D. Krieger, "Early Man in the New World," in *Prehistoric Man in the New World,* eds. Jesse D. Jennings and Edward Norbeck (Chicago: University of Chicago Press, 1964).

5. See Robert S. MacNeish, "The Origins of American Agriculture," *Antiquity* no. 154 (June 1965); and "The Origins of New World Civilization," *Scientific American* (November 1964), and William Sanders and Barbara Price, *Mesoamerica* (New York: Random House, 1968).

6. The Olmecs' society flourished in both the highlands and lowlands of Mexico from about 800 to 400 B.C. They and their successors used signs and mathematical symbols. Many scholars attribute the first full-fledged appearance of the state in Mexico to the Olmec period. Monte Albán civilization (ca. 250 B.C.-A.D. 900), centered in the Valley of Oaxaca southeast of Mexico City, was characterized by intensive agriculture based on irrigation and terraces, high population density, long-distance trade (in obsidian, for example), and production of both cotton and cochineal (later to become important Mexican exports to Spain and Europe). On the Maya, see Robert M. Carmack, Janine Gasco, and Gary H. Gossen, eds., *The Legacy of MesoAmerica: History and Culture of a Native American Civilization* (Upper Sadle River, N.J.: Prentice Hall, 1996). On Teotihuacán, see Rebecca Storey, *Life and Death in the Ancient City of Teotihuacan: A Modern Paleodemographic Synthesis* (Tuscaloosa, AL, 1992).

7. The Maya could accurately chart the course of planets such as Venus without a telescope, and they could calculate the exact dates of solar eclipses. They had a chronology and calendar that defined the 365-day solar year more accurately than was done a thousand years later under Pope Gregory in 1582. In mathematics, they mastered the positional notation system unknown to the Greeks and Romans. They used a vigesimal system and the figure zero. (Europeans did not become acquainted with the figure zero until A.D. 1202, when the Arabs introduced it from India.)

8. See Gordon Willey, "The Structure of Ancient Maya Society, Evidence from the Southern Lowlands," in *Ancient Mesoamerican Selected Readings*, ed. John A, Grahame (Stanford: Stanford University Press, 1966).

9. See Georges Baudot, *Utopie et histoire au Mexique: Les premiers chroniqueurs de la civilisation mexicaine, 1520-1569* (Toulouse: Ed. Edouard Privat, 1976); and Robert Ricard, *The Spiritual Conquest of Mexico* (Berkeley: University of California Press, 1966).

10. See Pedro Carrasco and Johanna Broda, eds., *Economía política e ideología en el México prehispánico* (Mexico City: Nueva Imagen, 1978); and Pedro Carrasco et al., *Estratificación social en la Mesoamérica prehispánica* (Mexico City: INAH, 1976).

11. See Hernando Cortés, *Cartas de relación de la conquista de la Nueva España escritas al Emperador Carlos V, y otros documentos relativos a la conquista, años de 1519-1527*, ed. Charles Gibson, Josef Stummvoll, and Frans Unterkircher (Graz, 1960); and Bernal Díaz del Castillo, *Discovery and Conquest of Mexico, 1517-1521* (New York: Farrar, Strauss, and Cudahy, 1956).

12. Henry F. Dobyns, "Estimating Aboriginal American Population," *Current Anthropology* 7 (1966): 395-449. Statistics fluctuate widely in this difficult area, but experts agree that Tenochtitlán contained about 300,000 people, making it larger than Madrid or Rome.

13. A highly durable and self-reproductive grain that grows in a variety of climates and does not require irrigation, maize was a crucial factor in the transition to sedentary agriculture, village and community development, and class-stratified societies. To this day, it accounts for nearly 75 percent of the daily energy intake of most of Mesoamerica's peoples.

14. Cited in Andre Gunder Frank, *Latin America: Underdevelopment or Revolution?* New York: Monthly Review Press, 1969, Indians (and African slaves) were brought *to* the northern silver mines—so the bishop presumably had in mind Indian labor power and not just the mere presence of Indians.

15. Most non-Mexican (and some Mexican) historians ever since have emphasized these "moral" concerns of the Crown, and yet dismissed as hopelessly "biased" the research conducted by Las Casas. See, for example, Lewis Hanke, *The Spanish Struggle for Justice in the Conquest of America* (Boston: Little, Brown and Company, 1965). Las Casas interpreted the Conquest as a product of bloody power and pillage in his *Historia de las Indias*, 2 vols. (Madrid, 1957) and *Very Short Account*

of the Destruction of the Indies (1552). See also Cockcroft, "Prescott and His Sources: A Critical Appraisal," Hispanic American Historical Review 48, no. 1 (February 1968): 59-74.

16. See Segundo Montes, El compadrazgo (San Salvador: Uca Editores, 1979). For regional case studies confirming continuity of pre-Columbian social practices, consult James Lockhart, The Nahuas after the Conquest: A Social and Cultural History of the Indians of Central America, Sixteenth through Eighteenth Centuries (Stanford, CA: Stanford University Press, 1992); Ida Altman and James Lockhart, eds., Provinces of Early Mexico: Varieties of Spanish-American Regional Evolution (Los Angeles: UCLA Latin American Center Publications, 1976); Hugo G. Nutini, Ritual Kinship: Ideological and Structural Integration of the Compadrazgo System in Rural Tlaxcala, vol. 2 (Princeton, N.J.: Princeton University Press, 1984).

17. Eric R. Wolf, Sons of the Shaking Earth (Chicago: University of Chicago Press, 1959), 200.

18. J. I. Israel, Race, Class and Politics in Colonial Mexico (London: Oxford University Press, 1975), 39. Indians sometimes fared better on haciendas, to which some retreated. See François Chevalier, Land and Society in Colonial Mexico (Berkeley: University of California Press, 1963), chapter 8.

19. The word cacique comes from the Arawak "kassiquan" ("to have or maintain a house"). The Spaniards imported this term from the Caribbean to apply to coopted Indian authorities, although not all caciques were coopted. On cacicas, see June Nash, "Aztec Women: The Transition from Status to Class in Empire and Colony," in Women and Colonization: Anthropological Perspectives, ed. Maria Etienne and Eleanor Leacock (New York: Praeger, 1980), 134-48, and Steve J. Stern, The Secret History of Gender: Women, Men, and Power in Late Colonial Mexico (Chapel Hill: The University of North Carolina Press, 1995).

20. On the institutional role and actual practices of the Inquisition, the ecclesiastical tribunals, and state juridical organs, consult Michel Foucault, Vigilar y castigar, 4th ed. (Mexico City: Siglo XXI, 1980). Father Zumárraga was the first Inquisitor and aimed his persecutions at both unruly colonists and at Indians following non-Christian ways or otherwise resisting the clergy's demands, especially in the instances of land-grabbing, tribute-exacting former Indian nobles. Punishment of this latter "sin" was one of the causes of the Mixton Rebellion of 1541.

21. For example, cacao was a major export crop in early colonial Mexico, but by the mid-seventeenth century Spain had shifted its trade quotas and investment opportunities to Venezuela, thereby contributing to the demise of cacao as a money-earner for Mexican merchants and producers, and its ascent to the position of leading export of Venezuela. Venezuela then exported most of its cacao to Mexico, where it was a basic component of the daily diet.

22. Other variations included the persistence of agricultural repartimiento in parts of Oaxaca and Guadalajara until the eighteenth century. In most of Oaxaca, on the other hand, Indians retained much of their own land in plots two or three times the size (per family) of the plots they hold today. In Yucatán, private encomiendas were not abolished until 1786, and Indians were also subjected to labor drafts by Crown officials. In New Spain's northeastern frontier area of mixed agriculture (cattle and food), free labor was supplemented by a system called congrega, in which landowners captured nomadic Indians who attacked them and brought them back to work their farms as prisoners of war. In central New Spain, where the majority of the population lived, agrarian estates were almost all worked by free labor.

23. Marx, Capital I: 753-54. Thus, even if in a certain sense, as Randall argues, "the acquisition of Mexico was not economically profitable for Spain," it was certainly so for other Europeans. The costs of empire always reduce and increasingly tend to undermine the gains—yet one can only speculate how Spain might have fared without Mexican silver. See Laura Randall, A Comparative History of Latin America, 1500-1914 (Ann Arbor: 1977), volume on Mexico, 113.

24. Adam Smith, An Inquiry into the Nature and Causes of the Wealth of Nations (New York: Random House, 1937), 204-207, cited in James D. Cockcroft, Andre Gunder Frank, and Dale L. Johnson, Dependence and Underdevelopment: Latin America's Political Economy (New York: Anchor, 1972), 21.

25. Cited in John Lynch, *Spain under the Hapsburgs* (London: Oxford Basil Blackwell, 1964), vol. 1, 141.

26. A typical annual report of Royal Treasury income in New Spain in the late eighteenth century shows more than 11 million pesos collected, 72 percent of which went to Spain and most of the remainder to the colonial bureaucracy in Mexico.

27. P. J. Bakewell, *Silver Mining and Society in Colonial Mexico: Zacatecas, 1546-1700* (Cambridge: Cambridge University Press, 1971), 223-35; Richard Boyer, "Mexico in the Seventeenth Century: Transition of a Colonial Society," *Hispanic American Historical Review* 57, no. 3 (1977): 455-78; D. A. Brading, *Miners and Merchants in Bourbon Mexico, 1763-1810* (Cambridge: Cambridge University Press, 1971), 8-l2; Israel, *Race, Class, and Politics*, 30-33; and Lynch, *Spain*, vol.2, l99-200. These and other works effectively revise the Borah argument that epidemics led to the mid-seventeenth century mining decline, and the Chaunu thesis of Mexico's failure as a market. See Woodrow Borah, *New Spain's Century of Depression* (Berkeley: University of California Press, 1951), 5-54; and Pierre Chaunu and Huguette Chaunu, *Seville et l'Atlantique, 1504-1650* (Paris, 1955-59), vol. VIII.

28. Spain did not respond to British attempts to sell it machinery for building drainage canals and similar tools for "mine modernization." See Brading, *Miners;* Walter Howe, *The Mining Guild of New Spain and Its Tribunal General, 1770-1821* (New York: Greenwood Press, 1968); and Robert W. Randall, *Real del Monte: A British Mining Venture in Mexico* (Austin: University of Texas Press, 1972).

29. Doris M. Ladd, *The Mexican Nobility at Independence 1780-1826* (Austin: University of Texas Press, 1976), 34-36. See also Lindley, Richard, "Kinship and Credit in the Structure of Guadalajara's Oligarchy, 1800-1830," University of Texas, 1976, and Louisa Schell Hoberman, "Merchants in Seventeenth-Century Mexico City," *Hispanic American Historical Review* 57, no.3 (1977): 479-503.

30. Peter Singelmann, "Peripheral Capitalist Development and the Persistence of Peasant Production: the Contradictions of an Incomplete Transition," paper presented at the Fifth World Congress of Rural Sociology, Mexico City, 7-12 August 1980.

31. For more, see Susan Deans-Smith, *Bureaucrats, Planters, and Workers: The Making of the Tobacco Monopoly in Bourbon Mexico* (Austin: University of Texas Press, 1992).

32. Jeffrey Bortz, "Wage Determination in Mexico," unpublished manuscript (1981) and "Industrial Wages in Mexico City, 1939-1975," UCLA, 1982.

33. Cited in Frank, *Latin America*, 235-36.

34. José María Quiroz, "Memoria de estatuto. Idea de la riqueza que daba la masa circulante de Nueva España a sus naturales producciones," in *Colección de documentos para Ia historia del comercio exterior de México* (Mexico City, 1959).

35. Ladd, *The Mexican Nobility*, 50-51.

36. Enrique Semo, *Historia mexicana: economía y lucha de clases* (Mexico City: Era, 1978), 83-87, 163-69; Friedrich Katz, "Labor Conditions in XIX Century Mexican Haciendas," *Hispanic American Historical Review*, 54, no. 1 (February 1974): 1-47; and John H. Coatsworth, "Obstacles to Economic Growth in Nineteenth-Century Mexico," *The American Historical Review*, 83, no.1 (February 1978): 87-88.

37. For more, see Jean Franco, *Plotting Women: Gender and Representation in Mexico* (New York: Columbia University Press, 1989) and Stern, *The Secret History*, 312-14.

38. Ruth Behar, "Sexual Witchcraft, Colonialism, and Women's Powers: Views from the Mexican Inquisition," in *Sexuality and Marriage in Colonial Latin America*, ed. Asunción Lavrin, 178-206 (Lincoln: University of Nebraska Press, 1989); Stern, *The Secret History*, 318-19.

37. The term "intermediate-class" is used in place of the more common the term "middle-class." See the early pages of Chapter 2.

38. To cite but one example: "They had known grinding poverty under the old regime, and were

finding it perpetuated and sometimes increased under the new one; but it seemed less painful now because the Franciscans, after their gentle founder, made of poverty a virtue." See R. C. Padden, *The Hummingbird and the Hawk: Conquest and Sovereignty in the Valley of Mexico, 1503-1541* (Columbus: Ohio State University Press, 1967), 241. Description of lower class revolts in the following pages is intended to offset the main literature on colonial Mexico in its overemphasis on Indian, African, and *casta* adaptation to class domination, acculturation, etc.—not because such did not occur, but because in dwelling on these elements the literature underemphasizes or glosses over the basic class contradiction (and corresponding repression) engendering such adaptation. Moreover, adaptation was a two-way process, with most colonists and their descendants adopting aspects of Indian culture.

39. See Peter Gerhard, "A Black Conquistador in Mexico," *Hispanic American Historical Review* 58, no. 3 (1978): 451-59.

40. For example, in 1611, some 1,500 blacks rioted in Mexico City at the burial of a black woman said to have been flogged to death by her master. A plot was alleged, and in 1612 the authorities tortured or killed the leaders of the black brotherhoods, lynched about thirty-five other men and women in the central plaza, and displayed their severed heads on pikes. In 1665 there were various outbreaks by blacks and mulattos in Mexico City, all of which were suppressed with the aid of the Inquisition. For more on blacks and mulattos, consult Gonzalo Aguirre Beltrán, *La población negra de México, 1519-1810: Estudio etnohistórico* (Mexico City: Fuente Cultural, 1946); Patrick J. Carroll, *Blacks in Colonial Veracruz: Race, Ethnicity, and Regional Development* (Austin: University of Texas Press, 1991); and Colin Palmer, *Slaves of the White God: Blacks in Mexico, 1570-1650* (Cambridge, MA.: Harvard University Press, 1976).

41. Cited in Stanley J. Stein and Barbara H. Stein, *The Colonial Heritage of Latin America* (New York: Oxford University Press, 1970), 57.

42. For the class character of these *tumultos*, consult Chester Guthrie, "Riots in Seventeenth-Century Mexico City: A Study in Social History with Special Emphasis on the Lower Classes," Ph.D. diss., University of California-Berkeley, 1937; and N. J. Stowe, "The Tumulto of 1624: Turmoil at Mexico City," Ph.D. diss., University of Southern California, 1970.

43. Archivo General de Indias (Seville), section i, Patronato real 224. Later *visitadores* (e.g., Pedro de Quiroga and Juan de Palafox y Mendoza) verified widespread class conflict and hatred "in all classes of society" for Spanish colonialism. A minor incident touched off the 1624 *tumulto*, which almost all groups joined. As wealthy whites locked their gates or boarded up their windows, the *castas*, blacks, Indians, and poor whites left their squalid quarters, took to the streets, and rioted in a crowd 30,000 strong. Open warfare ensued: angry mobs ransacked the palace, hauled down royal banners, and forced the viceroy to flee for his life. Only after militia opened fire on the crowd did the *tumulto* subside.

Chapter 2: Independence and Civil War, 1770-1880

1. For full text of this reply, dated 19 February 1848, see Moisés Gonzáles Navarro, *Raza y tierra: la guerra de castas y el henequén* (Mexico City: Colegio de México, 1970), 309-10.

2. Ponciano Arriaga, *Voto particular del C. Ponciano Arriaga sobre el derecho de propiedad* (San Luis Potosí: Impresa "Al Libro de Caja," 1959).

3. The term "Mexico" is used throughout this chapter, whether referring to the independent nation of Mexico or the colony of "New Spain" prior to Mexico's winning independence in 1822.

4. While this chapter's analysis of Mexico's nineteenth-century political economy is my own, I wish to thank historians Gilberto Arguello and Barbara A. Tenenbaum for their helpful suggestions and informed insights.

5. Cited in R. W. Van Alstyne, *The Rising American Empire* (New York: Oxford University Press, 1960), 81.

6. Enrique Florescano, *Precios del maíz y crisis agrícolas en México (1708-1810)* (Mexico City: Colegio de México, 1969), xvi-xvii, *passim*. Florescano attributes the sharp rise in population in the last third of the century in part to the earlier good harvests of the mid-1750s and of 1762 to 1770. But it seems just as likely that peasants and workers, suffering such extreme hardships, resorted to having more children for the purposes of subsistence production and economic survival. Everywhere there began to appear tiny cultivated parcels, as people sought to cope with food shortages and inflation.

7. Cited in Enrique Semo, *Historia mexicana: economía y lucha de clases* (Mexico City: Era, 1978), 204.

8. Doris M. Ladd, *The Mexican Nobility at Independence, 1780-1826* (Austin: University of Texas Press, 1976), 29, 52.

9. Cited in R. A. Humphreys and John Lynch, *The Origins of the Latin American Revolutions, 1808-1826* (New York: Alfred A. Knopf, 1966), 27. On tensions between *criollos* and *peninsulares*, consult Hugh M. Hammill, Jr., *The Hidalgo Revolt: Prelude to Mexican Independence* (Gainesville: University of Florida Press, 1966); Salvador de Madariaga, *The Fall of the Spanish American Empire* (New York: Collier, 1963); and H. G. Ward, *Mexico in 1827* (London: Henry Colburn, 1828), vol. 1.

10. Cited in Florescano, *Precios*, 191.

11. On the role of the Spanish army in Mexico, see Christon I. Archer, *The Army in Bourbon Mexico, 1716-1810* (Albuquerque: University of New Mexico Press, 1977) and Lyle McAllister, *The "Fuero Militar" in New Spain, 1764-1800* (Gainesville: University of Florida Press, 1957).

12. Alexander von Humboldt, *Ensayo político sobre el Reino de la Nueva Espana* (Mexico City: Ed. Porrúa, 1966), 452.

13. Karl Marx, *Capital* III (New York: International Publishers, 1967), 123.

14. Karl Marx, *Grundrisse* (New York: Vintage, 1973), 60.

15. There are various versions of Hidalgo's exact words, but this is the one used most frequently.

16. Cited in Humphreys and Lynch, *Origins*, 263.

17. Carlos María de Bustamante, *Cuadro histórico*, vol. 2, 610-11, and José María Luis Mora, *México y sus revoluciones*, vol. 3, 33, 362, all cited in Ladd, *The Mexican Nobility*, 114.

18. Ladd, *The Mexican Nobility*, and the author's conversations with Gilberto Arguello.

19. See the insightful works of John H. Coatsworth, such as "Obstacles to Economic Growth in Nineteenth-Century Mexico," *American Historical Review* 83, no. 1 (February 1978): 80-100, and *Growth against Development: The Economic Impact of Railroads in Porfirian Mexico* (DeKalb: Northern Illinois University Press, 1981). For good overviews of obstacles to Mexico's and Latin America's "catching up" economically with the world's more industrialized nations, see E. Bradford Burns, *The Poverty of Progress: Latin America in the Nineteenth Century* (Berkeley: University of California Press, 1983); Stuart Voss, *Latin America's Middle Age: From Imperial Reform to World Depression* (Chapel Hill: University of North Carolina Press, 1999).

20. Cited in James D. Cockcroft, Andre Gunder Frank, and Dale L. Johnson, *Dependence and Underdevelopment: Latin America's Political Economy* (New York: Anchor, 1972), 30.

21. Mariano Otero, *Obras* (Mexico City: Ed. Porrúa, 1967), vol. 1, 178.

22. Barbara A. Tenenbaum, "Merchants, Money, and Mischief: The British in Mexico, 1821-1862," *The Americas* (January 1979): 335.

23. Cited in Lewis Hanke, ed., *History of Latin American Civilization: Sources and Interpretations* (Boston: Little, Brown, 1967), 25. As late as 1981, Mexican Freemasonry still claimed 1.7 million members, twenty-six of thirty-one state governors, and eight holders of Cabinet posts.

24. Quoted in Gilberto López y Rivas, *The Chicanos* (New York: Monthly Review Press, 1973), 17.

25. Added the pro-war *New York Herald*, "It is a part of our destiny to civilize that beautiful country." Quoted in James D. Cockcroft and Hedda Garza, *Amazing Lost Stories of Our Multicultural*

History (Danbury, CT: Franklin Watts, 1999), Chapter 1 ("Heroes or Traitors?"). It should be remembered that during the decades leading up to the U.S.-Mexico War of 1846 to 1848, the United States had already been championing this racist "civilizing" mission when it was exterminating Native Americans and forcibly expelling them to areas west of the Mississippi River.

26. The full text of this letter, dated February 19, 1848, is reproduced in Gonzáles Navarro, *Raza y tierra*, 309-10.

27. For all quotations and descriptions of incidents, see Rodolfo Acuña, *Occupied America: A History of Chicanos* (New York: HarperCollins, 1988), 13-16; James D. Cockcroft, *Latin America: History, Politics, and U.S. Policy* (Chicago: Nelson-Hall Publishers, 1996), p. 89; Cockcroft and Garza, *Amazing Lost Stories*, Chapter 1; Hedda Garza, *Latinas: Hispanic Women in the United States* (Danbury, CT: Franklin Watts, 1994), 23-24; Carey McWilliams, *North from Mexico* (New York: Greenwood Press, 1968), 102.

28. Robert Ryal Miller, *Shamrock and Sword: The Saint Patrick's Battalion in the U.S.-Mexican War* (Norman: University of Oklahoma Press, 1989), 31 (Taylor quote) and 155-56 (song quote). For more on the Saint Patrick's Battalion, see Cockcroft and Garza, *Amazing Lost Stories*, and the documentary video by Mark Day, *The San Patricios* (Day Communications). On the U.S.-Mexico War and important Texas and California background, consult Acuña, *Occupied America*, and Garza, *Latinas*, 22-27.

29. Quoted in *New York Times*, 6 May 1997. For more details on the origins of the treaty and its historical impact to the present, see Richard Griswold del Castillo, *The Treaty of Guadalupe Hidalgo: A Legacy of Conflict* (Norman: University of Oklahoma Press), 1990.

30. See Acuña, *Occupied America*, and Griswold del Castillo, *The Treaty*.

31. For an account of Juárez and his times, see D. Ross Gandy, *Benito Juárez: The Making of Modern Mexico* (Springfield, N.J.: Enslow Publishers, Inc., 1998).

32. Cited in Alonso Aguilar, *Dialéctica de la economía mexicana* (Mexico City: Nuestro Tiempo, 1968), 188.

33. Arriaga, *Voto particular*. Actually, the breaking up of communal lands had begun in earnest after Mexico gained independence—it reached its apex with the Liberal Reform. Also, sometimes an economic crisis would make peasants willing to divide up an ejido and work or sell their private parcels, as happened in 1896 in the Totonac community of Veracruz after a drop in vanilla prices and some failed rebellions. See Roger Bartra, *Estructuras agrarias y clases sociales* (Mexico City: Era, 1976); Emilio Kouri, "The Business of the Land: Agrarian Tenure and Enterprise in Papantla, Mexico, 1800-1910." Ph.D. dissertation, Harvard, 1996.

34. Otero, *Obras*, 162.

35. Arriaga, *Voto particular*.

36. Gandy, *Benito Juárez*, drawing on Ralph Roeder, *Juárez and his Mexico: A Biographical History* (New York: Viking, 1947), 572.

37. Gandy, *Benito Juárez*, drawing on Ivie E. Cadenhead, Jr., *"Bentito" Juárez* (New York: Viking, 1947), 113.

38. The author is grateful to Ross Gandy for pointing this out.

39. Gandy, *Benito Juárez*, drawing on Florencia Zamarripa, ed., *Los apuntes para mis hijos de Benito Juárez* (Mexico City: Centro Mexicano de Estudios Culturales, 1968), 7.

40. For more on Mexico's emerging proletarian movements, see James D. Cockcroft, *Intellectual Precursors of the Mexican Revolution 1900-1913* (Austin: University of Texas Press, 1968). and John M. Hart, *Anarchism & the Mexican Working Class, 1860-1931* (Austin: University of Texas Press, 1978).

41. Hart, *Anarchism*, 41.

Chapter 3: From Dictatorship to Revolution, 1880-1920

1. In the name of objectivity the occasional U.S. scholar has played down the significance of Mexico's emergent industrial proletariat or the influence of the PLM's 1906 to 1908 strikes and revolts in undermining the Díaz regime. Mexican scholars, however, have generally agreed on their pivotal importance. See, for example, the unanimity on this point among the different interpretations of the Revolution offered in Héctor Aguilar Camín (ed.), *Interpretaciones de la revolución mexicana* (Mexico City: Nueva Imagen, 1979). The standard monograph on the PLM is James D. Cockcroft, *Intellectual Precursors of the Mexican Revolution 1900-1913* (Austin: University of Texas Press, 1968).

2. For analyses of economic changes during the Porfiriato, see John H. Coatsworth, *Growth against Development: The Economic Impact of Railroads in Porfirian Mexico* (DeKalb: Northern Illinois University Press, 1981); Stephen H. Haber, *Industry and Underdevelopment: The Industrialization of Mexico, 1890-1940* (Stanford: Stanford University Press, 1989); and Francisco Valdés Ugalde, *Autonomía y legitimidad: los empresarios, la política y el estado en México* (Mexico City: Siglo XXI, 1997), 72-94. See also the early chapters of Cockcroft, *Intellectual Precursors*.

3. Cited in Josefina Vázquez de Knauth, *Nacionalismo y educación en México* (Mexico City: Colegio de México, 1970), 55. For more on education, including the role of school teachers in the Mexican Revolution of 1910 and after, see Mary Kay Vaughan, *The State, Education, and Social Classes in Mexico, 1880-1928* (DeKalb: Northern Illinois University Press, 1982).

4. Matías Romero, quoted in Charles C. Cumberland, *Mexico: The Struggle for Modernity* (New York: Oxford University Press, 1968), 196.

5. All foreign investments in 1900 to 1910 tripled the total for 1876 to 1900. For more, see articles by Fernando Rosenzweig and Luis Nicholas D'Owler in the multivolume history edited by Daniel Cosío Villegas, *Historia moderna de México* (Mexico City: Hermes, 1956-1974). On the influential role of Doheny in Mexican and U.S. history, see Dan La Botz, *Edward L. Doheny: Petroleum, Power, and Politics in the United States and Mexico* (New York: Praeger, 1991).

6. See John Womack, Jr., *Zapata and the Mexican Revolution* (New York: Alfred A. Knopf, 1969), 39-50; Arturo Warman, *. . . y venimos a contradecir* (Mexico City: Ediciones de Ia Casa Chata, 1976), 73-74; and next note.

7. Jorge Basurto, *El proletariado industrial en México, 1850-1930* (Mexico City: UNAM, 1975), 25-27. By 1900, many more laborers were acting as free wage labor unfettered by intermediate or noncapitalist forms of labor discipline such as slavery, serfdom, debt-peonage, piecework, share-cropping, etc. This marked an important step in the transition to capital accumulation on an extended scale, a transition strongly underway during the Porfiriato. See Domenico E. Sindico, "Modernization in XIX Century Sugar Haciendas: The Case of Morelos (From Formal to Real Subjection of Labor to Capital)," *Latin American Perspectives* 7, no. 4 (Fall 1980): 83-99.

8. See Frans J. Schryer, "A Ranchero Economy in Northwestern Hidalgo, 1880-1920," *Hispanic American Historical Review* 59, no. 3 (1979); and "The Role of the Rancheros of Central Mexico in the Mexican Revolution," *Canadian Journal of Latin American Studies* 4, no. 7 (1979).

9. Cited in Andre Gunder Frank, *Latin America: Underdevelopment or Revolution* (New York: Monthly Review Press, 1969), 238.

10. The reporter was John Kenneth Turner, and the quotation is from Francie R. Chassen-López, "'Cheaper Than Machines': Women and Agriculture in Porfirian Oaxaca, 1880-1911," in Heather Fowler-Salamini and Mary Kay Vaughan (eds.), *Women of the Mexican Countryside, 1850-1990* (Tucson: The University of Arizona Press, 1994), 41. See also Teresa Meade, "Gender: 1821-1910," in *Encyclopedia of Mexico: History, Society and Culture*, ed. Michael S. Werner (Chicago: Fitzroy Dearborn, 1997); Margaret Towner, "Monopoly Capitalism and Women's Work During the Porfiriato," *Latin American Perspectives* 4, no. 1-2 (1977): 90-105; and Vivian Vallens, *Working Women in Mexico During the Porfiriato, 1880-1910* (San Francisco: R&E Research Associates, 1978).

11. U.S. Consul in Veracruz William W. Canada, quoted in Cockcroft, *Intellectual*, 140.

12. For more on "Saint Teresa," see Hedda Garza, *Latinas: Hispanic Women in the United States* (Danbury, CT: Franklin Watts, 1994), 40-41, and Paul Vanderwood, "Santa Teresa: Mexico's Joan of Arc," in Judith Ewell and William H. Beezley (eds.), *The Human Tradition in Latin America: The Nineteenth Century* (Wilmington, DE: Scholarly Resources, 1989), 215-32.

13. For more on the PLM and this period, see Cockcroft, *Intellectual;* Juan Gómez Quiñones, *Sembradores, Ricardo Flores Magón y el Partido Liberal Mexicano: A Eulogy and Critique* (Los Angeles: Chicano Studies Research Center, UCLA, 1977); John M. Hart, *Anarchism and the Mexican Working Class, 1860-1931* (Austin: University of Texas Press, 1978); W. Dirk Raat, *Revoltosos: Mexico's Rebels in the United States, 1903-1923* (College Station: Texas A&M University Press, 1981).

14. *El Estandarte* of San Luis Potosí, quoted in Cockcroft, *Intellectual*, 141.

15. Cited in Garza, *Latinas*, 45.

16. *Regeneración*, 24 September 1910, cited in ibid., 44.

17. Cited in ibid., 48.

18. *New York Times*, 10 May 1911, cited in ibid., 45.

19. Garza, *Latinas*, 45-50; Dan Georgakas, *Solidarity Forever: The IWW Reconsidered* (Chicago: Lakeview Press, 1985), 30-53; Juan Gómez-Quiñones and Luis Leobardo Arroyo, *Orígenes del movimiento obrero chicano* (Mexico City: Ediciones Era, 1978), 77-78, passim. For Mexicans' absolutely pivotal roles in U.S. struggles for social justice and democratic rights, largely omitted from standard history books by non-Latino "scholars," see James D. Cockcroft, *The Hispanic Struggle for Social Justice* (Danbury, CT: Franklin Watts, 1994), *Latinos in the Struggle for Equal Education* (1995), *Latinos in the Making of the United States* (1995).

20. In San Luis Potosí, for example, of about twenty elite families, thirteen were active in industry, and two of these industrialists were governors for all but six years of the Porfiriato (during which time a *hacendado* held office). See Cockcroft, *Intellectual*, 27; Friedrich Katz, *La guerra secreta en México*, 2 vols. (Mexico City: Era, 1982), vol. 1, 24, cited in Valdés Ugalde, *Autonomía*, 91.

21. For more on the background to the Mexican Revolution and/or the events that marked it form 1910 to 1917, see Rodney D. Anderson, *Outcasts in Their Own Land: Mexican Industrial Workers, 1906-1911* (DeKalb: Northern Illinois University Press, 1976); Anita Brenner, *The Wind That Swept Mexico* (Austin: University of Texas Press, 1971); Coatsworth, *Growth;* Cockcroft, *Intellectual;* Adolfo Gilly, *La revolución interrumpida* (Mexico City: Ediciones "El Caballito," 1973); Francois-Javier Guerra, *México: del antiguo régimen a la revolutión*, 2 vols. (Mexico City: Fondo de Cultura Económico, 1988); John M. Hart, *Anarchism*, and *Revolutionary Mexico: The Coming and Process of the Mexican Revolution* (Berkeley: University of California Press, 1987); Friedrich Katz, *La guerra secreta; The Life and Times of Pancho Villa* (Stanford: Stanford University Press, 1998); and *Francisco Villa: Su vida y sus tiempos* (Mexico City: Ediciones Era, 1998); Alan Knight, *The Mexican Revolution*, 2 vols. (Cambridge: Cambridge University Press, 1986); and several other sources cited throughout this chapter.

22. Hart, *Revolutionary Mexico*, 245.

23. Cockcroft, *Intellectual*, 159.

24. *Regeneración*, 3 September and 8 October 1910, cited in ibid., 175.

25. Ibid., 181-82.

26. The phrase is from Gilly, *La revolución interrumpida*. For more on Zapata, see Womack, *Zapata*.

27. See Hart, *Revolutionary Mexico*.

28. Cited in Antonio Díaz Soto y Gama, *La revolución agraria del sur y Emiliano Zapata, su caudillo* (1960), 133.

29. The author is grateful to Michoacán *ejidatarios*, some of whom lived on *haciendas* until 1935, for

explaining from their own life histories the lack of participation by acasillados and what actually happened.

30. For more, see Fowler-Salamini and Vaughan, *Women;* Garza, *Latinas,* 44-48; María Herrera-Sobek, *The Mexican Corrido: A Feminist Analysis* (Bloomington: Indiana University Press, 1990); Elizabeth Salas, *Soldaderas in the Mexican Military: Myth and History* (Austin: University of Texas Press, 1990); and Shirlene Soto, *Emergence of the Modern Mexican Woman. Her Participation in Revolution and Struggle for Equality, 1910-1940* (Denver: Arden Press, 1990).

31. See Katz, *La guerra secreta.*

32. Quoted in Jesús Silva Herzog, *Breve historia de Ia Revolución Mexicana* (Mexico City: Fondo de Cultura Económica, 1947), vol. 1, 34-35.

33. Alvaro Obregón, *Discursos* (Mexico City: Biblioteca de Ia Dirección General de Educación Militar, 1932), vol. 1, 279.

34. Salvador Alvarado, *La reconstrucción de México: Un mensaje a los pueblos de América* (Mexico City: J. Ballesca y Cia., 1919), vol. 3, 91-94.

35. For evidence of this, see Katz, *Life and Times.* For more on the Villistas, see Katz, ibid., and *La guerra secreta;* and John Reed's personal observations when traveling with Villa, in John Reed, *Insurgent Mexico* (New York: International Publishers, 1969).

36. U.S. Department of State, *Papers Relating to the Foreign Relations* (Washington, D.C.: Government Printing Office, 1914), 444.

37. See Michael G. Meyer, "The Arms of the Ypiranga," *Hispanic American Historical Review* 50, no. 3 (August 1970): 543-56.

38. U.S. Department of State, *Papers* (1914), 510.

39. Edith O'Shaughnessy, *A Diplomat's Wife in Mexico* (New York: Harper, 1916), 290.

40. Quoted in Gregg Andrews, *Shoulder to Shoulder? The American Federation of Labor, the United States, and the Mexican Revolution 1910-1924* (Berkeley: University of California Press, 1991), 33.

41. Quoted in Robert E Quirk, *The Mexican Revolution, 1914-1951: The Convention of Aguascalientes* (New York: The Citadel Press, 1963), 109-11.

42. Ibid., 135-38.

43. See Rosendo Salazar, *La Casa del Obrero Mundial* (Mexico City: Costa-Amic, 1963), as well as other works by Salazar, especially, with Jose G. Escobedo, *Las pugnas de Ia gleba, 1907-1922* (Mexico City, 1922), 2 vols; see vol.1, 157-60.

44. See Hart, *Revolutionary Mexico,* 242-43 (photo caption).

45. Arnaldo Córdova, "Mexico: Revolución burguesa y política de masas," in Aguilar Camín (ed.) *Interpretaciones,* 55-89.

46. Cited in Robert F. Smith, *The United States and Revolutionary Nationalism in Mexico, 1916-1932* (Chicago: University of Chicago Press, 1972), 576.

47. Ibid., 580-81.

48. Cited in Ferdinand Lundberg and Lyle Stuart, *The Rich and the Super-rich* (New York: Bantam, 1969), 890; and Scott Nearing and Joseph Freeman, *Dollar Diplomacy* (New York: Monthly Review Press, 1969), 273.

49. Womack, *Zapata,* 300-17, 346-51.

50. Katz, *Life and Times.*

51. See Gilly, *La revolucion,* and some of the views offered in Aguilar Camín (ed.), *Interpretaciones.*

Chapter 4: Corporatism and Cárdenas

1. There is a vast theoretical literature on the state. For good primers, see Colin Hay, *Re-stating Social and Political Change* (Bristol, PA: Open University Press, 1996) and Martin Oppenheimer, *The State in Modern Society* (Atlantic Highlands, N.J.: Humanities Press, 1999). On the Mexican

state in particular, there is a growing literature too lengthy to list here without showing undue favoritism. However, the footnotes throughout this book mention several of the works.

2. Antonio Gramsci, *Selections from the Prison Notebooks* (New York: International Publishers, 1971).

3. "Corporatism" is employed here to describe a political system that relies for its legitimacy and perpetuation on a politics of masses, where the capitalist state provides modest concessions to popular movements and ties their mass organizations to its tutelage and where those resisting such incorporation are usually repressed by state force. The official party serves as an administrative committee of the affairs of the mass organizations in the matters of national and local elections. Various authors have employed the concept "corporatism" to Mexico's political system. For a summary, see Arnaldo Córdova, "El desafío de la izquierda mexicana," *Nexos* 18 (June 1979): 3-15.

4. See Frank R. Brandenburg, *The Making of Modern Mexico* (Englewood Cliffs: Prentice-Hall, 1964).

5. Jean Meyer, *Historia de la Revolución mexicana 1924-1928: estado y sociedad con Calles,* Vol. 11 (Mexico City: El Colegio de México, 1977), p. 308, cited in Francisco Valdés Ugalde, *Autonomía y legitimidad: los empresarios, la política y el estado en México* (Mexico City: Siglo XXI, 1997), 116.

6. Valdés Ugalde, 116.

7. For this and other examples, see Nora Hamilton, *The Limits of State Autonomy: Post-Revolutionary Mexico* (Princeton: Princeton University Press, 1982). For more on the evolution of Mexico's bourgeoisie after 1920, see Roderic A. Camp, *Mexico's Leaders: Their Education and Recruitment* (Tucson: University of Arizona Press, 1980).

8. Friedrich Engels, letter to Danielson, June 18, 1892, cited in Hal Draper, *Karl Marx's Theory of Revolution: State and Bureaucracy* (New York: Monthly Review Press, 1977), 585.

9. Valdés Ugalde, *Autonomía,* 109, citing Lorenzo Meyer, *Los grupos de presión en el México revolucionario, 1910-1940* (Mexico City: Secretaría de Relaciones Exteriores, Colección del Archivo Histórico Diplomático Mexicano, 1973).

10. John Child, *Unequal Alliance: The Inter-American Military System, 1938-1978* (Boulder: Westview Press, 1980), 13 (based on U.S. War Department, War Plans Division, "General Mexican War Plan," Entry 282, RG 165 and Entry 365, RG 407, U.S. National Archives). Such military contingency planning probably continues today. In Caspar Weinberger, *The Next War* (New York: Regnery, 1997), the former U.S. secretary of defense sketches a scenario of a 2003 invasion of Mexico to overthrow a narco-government and block the flow of refugees into the United States. For more on U.S. interventionism to protect "its" oil, see Jonathan C. Brown, *Oil and Revolution in Mexico* (Berkeley: University of California Press, 1993); Brown and Alan Knight (eds.), *The Mexican Petroleum Industry in the Twentieth Century* (Austin: University of Texas Press, 1992); and Linda B. Hall, *Oil, Banks, and Politics: the United States and Postrevolutionary Mexico, 1917-1924* (Austin: University of Texas Press, 1995); and Lorenzo Meyer, *México y Estados Unidos en el conflicto petrolero (1917-1942)* (Mexico City: El Colegio de México, 1968).

11. Quoted in Gregg Andrews, *Shoulder to Shoulder? The American Federation of Labor, the United States, and the Mexican Revolution 1910-1924* (Berkeley: University of California Press, 1991), 195. For more on the anarchists, other leftists, and interaction between various U.S. and Mexican labor organizations in this period as well as subsequent years, see Juan Gómez-Quiñones, *Mexican American Labor, 1790-1990* (Albuquerque: University of New Mexico Press, 1994); John M. Hart, *Anarchism & the Mexican Working Class, 1860-1931* (Austin: University of Texas Press, 1978); Donald C. Hodges, *Mexican Anarchism after the Revolution* (Austin: University of Texas Press, 1995); and Daniel La Botz, "Slackers, Wobblies and Radicals: The Impact of American Exiles and Migrants on the Mexican Labor Movement and State: 1917-1927," Ph.D. dissertation, University of Cincinnati, 1998.

12. Quoted in Meyer, *México y Estados Unidos,* 87.

13. Quoted in Robert F. Smith, "The Morrow Mission and the International Commission of Bankers on Mexico: The Interaction of Finance Diplomacy and the New Mexican Elite," *Journal of Latin American Studies* 1, no. 2 (November 1969): 150.

14. Cited in James W. Wilkie, *The Mexican Revolution: Federal Expenditure and Social Change since 1910* (Berkeley: University of California Press, 1967), 62.

15. The Cristero Revolt was a complex affair, mixing agrarian protest with anticommunism, anti-government rebellion, and the redemptive qualities of the Virgin of Guadalupe. The Catholic Church, although divided between progressives and conservatives, backed it. See David C. Bailey, *Viva Cristo Rey! The Cristero Rebellion and the Church-State Conflict in Mexico* (Austin: University of Texas Press, 1974).

16. *Futuro,* May 1934: 54-61.

17. Archivo de Ia Secretaría de Relaciones Exteriores 41-26-139, IV/241 (73) (03)/1, Jan.27, 1932.

18. Cited in Wayne A. Cornelius, Jr., "Nation-Building, Participation, and Distribution: The Politics of Social Reform under Cárdenas," in Development Episodes in Comparative Politics: Crisis, Choice, and Change, ed. Gabriel A. Almond and Scott C. Flanagan (Boston: Little, Brown and Company, 1973), 84.

19. Cited in Arnaldo Córdova, *La ideología de la revolución mexicana* (Mexico City: Era, 1973), 235.

20. See Gramsci, *Selections from the Prison Notebooks.* Such a hegemonic project normally takes form in times of crisis, often during a transition from one stage of economic development to another; also, during a period of political transition (itself related to economic change). In the course of a given crisis, a particular class or class fraction (often the ascendant one) attempts to carry through the transition and the class goals it seeks through ideological combat, alliance-building, and other forms of political struggle. The aim of the project is to gain dominance over the state and its ideological apparatuses, to transform the state in corresponding ways, to subordinate or defeat rival projects and the class interests behind them—in sum, to alter the balance of power in society as a whole.

21. Haber, *Industry.*

22. Wilkie, *The Mexican Revolution,* 265.

23. Cited in Joe C. Ashby, *Organized Labor and the Mexican Revolution under Lázaro Cárdenas* (Chapel Hill: University of North Carolina Press, 1967), 27.

24. Ibid., 273.

25. The full text of this historic speech may be found in Lázaro Cárdenas, *Palabras y documentos Públicos de Lázaro Cárdenas, 1928-1940,* vol. 2 (Mexico City: Siglo XXI, 1978).

26. Cárdenas told a delegation of bankers and industrialists that even in the most extreme cases of uncooperative behavior by big business, "the most that could happen would be that certain branches would be withdrawn from the sphere of private interest to become social service." Cited in Ashby, *Organized Labor,* 37. What is "withdrawn," of course, can always be returned.

27. Lyle C. Brown, "General Lázaro Cárdenas and Mexican Presidential Politics, 1933-1940: A Study in the Acquisition and Manipulation of Political Power," Ph.D. diss., University of Texas, 1964, 211.

28. Jesús Silva Herzog, *El petróleo mexicano* (Mexico City, 1941), 5; personal interview, 1964.

29. Cited in Albert L. Michaels, "The Crisis of Cardenismo," *Journal of Latin American Studies* 2 (May 1970): 70.

30. Nora L. Hamilton, "The State and Class Conflict: Mexico during the Cárdenas Period," in *Classes, Class Conflict, and the State,* ed. Maurice Zeitlin (Cambridge: Winthrop Publishers, Inc., 1980), 358.

31. Cited in Michaels, *Crisis,* 57.

32. See Ernesto Laclau, *Politics and Ideology in Marxist Theory* (London: New Left Books, 1977), 184.

Chapter 5: The State, Foreign Capital, and Monopoly Capital

1. All quoted statements widely reported in the press except for migrant worker's, whose statement comes from James D. Cockcroft, unpublished field notes, 1981.

2. In general, more industrialized countries' sales of technology to less-industrialized developing countries (LDCs) derive from the historic tendency of capital to expand more rapidly in Department I, production of the means of production, than in Department II, production of articles of consumption. Earlier in the history of more industrialized countries, Department I's high organic composition of capital (ratio of constant capital, or instruments and raw materials of production, to variable capital, or labor power—the only source of surplus value and profit) had been balanced by a lower organic composition in Department II, allowing for an acceptable generalized rate of profit. (Growth in the organic composition of capital generates the tendency of the rate of profit to fall.) As more and more workers became unionized in countries like the United States, capitalists introduced more machines into Department II production, causing the organic composition of capital to rise there too, and putting more pressure on capitalists to find other areas to reestablish the accustomed pattern of rates of profit. They found those areas in LDCs undertaking industrialization, at first in those countries' Department II of production and eventually in their Department I as well.

3. TNCs are corporations that have their base in one country but draw much of their income, raw materials, and operating capital from several other countries, through ownership of foreign subsidiaries, joint ventures with foreign governments or investors, and a host of other means. The compelling force behind the rise of TNCs is the need for corporations to grow and maintain their profitability, as well as to gain control over as much of the world's resources and capital as possible. *The TNC, a logical outgrowth of monopoly capital that has outgrown nations, constitutes the economic heart of modern imperialism.* The term "transnational" is preferable to "multinational" because it is a less ideological and more accurate concept, combining the control aspects implicit in "national" with the global aspects of "trans."

4. Marcela Lagarde, "El indigenismo, un proceso ideológico" (Tesis de Licenciatura, Escuela Nacional de Antropología e Historia, 1974), 79; Ricardo Pozas and Isabel H. de Pozas, *Los indios en las clases sociales de México* (Mexico City: Siglo XXI, 1971), 99-100.

5. There is an abundant literature on Mexican and Latin American *machismo*, most of which overlooks its roots in European patriarchy. For more on this point, see Hedda Garza, *Latinas: Hispanic Women in the United States* (Danbury, CT: Franklin Watts, 1994), 14-16. The other side of Mexican *machismo* was *marianismo*, or the exaggerated worship of the "Mary" figure, as in the case of the Virgin of Guadalupe, as somehow the ultimate representation of the good and pure (and in the Virgin's case, savior of suffering humanity). Under patriarchy, Mexico's women were expected, to one degree or another, to "measure up" to this demanding ideal.

6. For a pioneering feminist work behind this reconceptualization, see Wally Seccombe, *A Millennium of Family Change: Feudalism to Capitalism in Northwestern Europe* (New York: Verso, 1992) and *Weathering the Storm: Working-class Families from the Industrial revolution to the Fertility Decline* (New York: Verso, 1993).

7. Cited by Professor Peter F. Bell of State University of New York-Purchase in his unpublished paper "Thailand's Economic Miracle: Built on the Backs of Women" (1997), 4, 10. See also Ann K. Nauman and Mireille Hutchison, "The Integration of Women into the Mexican Labor Force Since NAFTA," *American Behavioral Scientist* 40, no. 7 (June/July 1997): 950-56.

8. Such is the criterion of the Mexican Census Bureau. However, there are some rural towns with slightly more than 2,500 residents that resemble "big city" areas in no way whatsoever.

9. Mexico's industrialization achievements were made possible by its not becoming bogged down in a colonial or neocolonial "enclave economy," which characterized most of its production and trade from the Spanish Conquest to the 1938 nationalization of oil. During those earlier times,

Mexico had produced mainly mineral and agricultural goods for export and imported manufactured goods and raw materials for production, which often occurred in foreign-controlled "enclaves." The Revolution and Cárdenas's reforms, however, had sufficiently loosened foreign controls over the economy to permit the Mexican bourgeoisie and state to begin to assert some influence over key parts of the economy, especially in energy, minerals, tourism, light industry, and economic infrastructure.

10. Roger Bartra, "Peasants and Political Power in Mexico: A Theoretical Model," *Latin American Perspectives* 2, no. 2 (Summer 1975).

11. Rodolfo Stavenhagen et al., *Neolatifundismo y explotación de Emiliano Zapata a Anderson Clayton & Co.* (Mexcio City: Nuestro Tiempo, 1968), 19, 30-31, 75-78, 86-87.

12. Jeffrey Bortz, "Industrial Wages in Mexico City, 1939-1975" (Ph.D. dissertation, History Department, UCLA, 1982); Jeffrey Bortz et al., *La estructura de salarios en México* (Mexico City: Universidad Autónoma Metropolitana Azcapotzalco, 1985); Bortz and Ricardo Pascoe P., "Salario y clase obrera en Ia acumulación de capital en México," *Coyoacán* 1, no. 2 (January-March 1978): 79-93; Pablo Gonzáles Casanova, *La democracia en México* (Mexico City: Siglo XXI, 1965); and Ifigenia M. de Navarrete, "Income Distribution in Mexico," in *Mexico's Recent Economic Growth*, ed. Enrique Pérez López et al. (Austin: University of Texas Press, 1967), 13-72.

13. *Le Monde diplomatique* (Mexican edition), 2 June 1997, citing a January 1997 policy paper by political scientist Edward J. Williams for the Center for Strategic and International Studies.

14. Dan La Botz, "Inside Mexico's Massive Crisis," *Against the Current,* November/December 1996; *Democracy in Mexico: Peasant Rebellion and Political Reform* (Boston: South End Press, 1995), 119, citing *Multinational Monitor,* November 1994.

15. This felicitous phrase was borrowed from Dan LaBotz's obituary of the late CTM leader Fidel Velázquez in *Mexican Labor News and Analysis* no. 121 (22 June 1997), located at 103144.2651@compuserve.com.

16. *Business Trends,* 1972, 1977; John Warnock, *The Other Mexico: The North American Triangle Completed* (Montréal: Black Rose Books, 1995), 84-86.

17. Karl Marx, *Capital* I (New York: International Publishers, 1967), 599.

18. On women in the *maquiladora* industry see: José Antonio Alonso Herrero, *Mujeres maquiladoras y microindustria doméstica* (Mexico City: Fontamara, 1991); Devon G. Peña, *The Terror of the Machine: Technology, Work, Gender, and Ecology on the U.S.-Mexico Border* (Austin: University of Texas Press, 1997); and Susan Tiano, *Patriarchy on the Line: Labor, Gender, and Ideology in the Mexican Maquila Industry* (Philadelphia: Temple University Press, 1994).

19. *Dollars and Sense,* May/June 1997, 21; *El Nuevo Topo* (San Francisco) no. 10 (Spring 1998).

20. Many Mexicans loaned their names to front for foreign investors *(prestanombres),* disguising foreign penetration and takeover of the economy. Corruption, bribery, and economic pressure applied by foreign investors and creditors further diluted the effect of "Mexicanization."

21. Cited in NACLA, *Mexico 1968* (New York: NACLA, 1968).

22. U.S. investors accounted for more than 70 percent of the foreign direct investment, while those of England, West Germany, Switzerland, Japan, and France made up most of the rest.

23. As the World Bank's 1993 annual report pointed out, most of the new foreign capital entering Mexico in the early 1990s was "hot money" for the stock and bond markets. Foreign direct investment in productive companies actually dropped for awhile. See Chapter 8, however, for the huge upsurge in foreign maquiladora activity under neoliberalism, especially after the implementation of NAFTA.

24. *Financial Times,* 3 February 1969.

25. Y. U. A. Sergeyev and N. Yu Strugatshya, "Scientific and Technical Development, the Monopolies and the Patent System," reprinted from Russian research journal *SSHA: Ekonomik, Politika, Ideologiya* in *Idea* 15, no.2 (Summer 1971); and UNCTAD, *Transfer of Technology* (New York: UN

Conference on Trade and Development Secretariat, Junta del Acuerdo de Cartegena, TD/1O7, 29 December 1971).

26. See Fernando Fajnzylber and Trinidad Martínez Tarrago, *Las empresas transnacionales: expansión a nivel mundial y proyección en la industria mexicana* (Mexico City: FCE, 1976).

27. Business International Corporation, "Nationalism in Latin America" (September 1970), 21, 29.

28. "Technical Cooperation with Iran," Report to the Agency for International Development, 11 April 1972, 9.

29. Vandana Shiva, *Biopiracy: The Plunder of Nature and Knowledge* (Boston: South End Press, 1997), 79, 81, 122.

30. Quoted in Richard S. Newfarmer and W. F. Mueller, *Multinational Corporations in Brazil and Mexico: Structural Sources of Economic and Noneconomic Power* (Washington, D.C.: Report to the Subcommittee on Multinational Corporations of the Committee on Foreign Relations, U.S. Senate, August 1975), 17.

31. Gary Gereffi, "Drug Firms and Dependency in Mexico: the Case of the Steroid Hormone Industry" (Yale University & Harvard University Center for International Affairs, mimeo, 1977).

32. Fajnzylber and Martínez Tarrago, *Las empresas;* Bernardo Sepúlveda and Antonio Chumacero, *La inversión extranjera en México* (Mexico City: FCE, 1973).

33. Mauricio Schoijet and Richard Worthington, "Globalization of Science and Repression of Scientists in Mexico," *Science, Technology, & Human Values* 18, no. 2 (Spring 1993): 209-30. On TNC beneficiaries of CONACYT's neoliberal policies, see Schoijet, *La ciencia mexicana en la crisis* (Mexico City: Editorial Nuestro Tiempo, 1991), 117-18.

34. Quoted in *La Jornada,* 9 June 1997.

35. John W. Barchfield, "The Structure of Power and the Deformation of Agrarian Reform in Mexico," *Revista del México Agrario* 14 (1981).

36. James D. Cockcroft, unpublished field notes, 1963.

37. *Dallas Morning News,* 30 April 1980.

38. James D. Cockcroft, unpublished field notes, 1981.

39. Ernest Feder, *Imperialismo fresa* (Mexico City: Ed. Campesina, 1978).

40. In June of 1997, the U.S. and Canadian governments announced a ten-year technical and economic plan of assistance to eliminate the use of DDT in Mexico. On child labor and child prostitution, see *Mexican Labor News and Analysis* II, no. 23 (16 December 1997) and III, no. 4 (16 February 1998).

41. See Tom Barry, Harry Browne, and Beth Sims, *The Great Divide: The Challenge of U.S.-Mexico Relations in the 1990s* (New York: Grove Atlantic, 1994), 387.

42. See Cynthia Hewitt de Alcántara, *La modernización de la agricultura mexicana, 1940-1970* (Mexico City: Siglo XXI, 1978), 300-301.

43. See Alonso Aguilar and Fernando Carmona, *México: riqueza y miseria* (Mexico City: Nuestro Tiempo, 1967), 65.

44. Cited in Alonso Aguilar, "La burgesía no sólo manda, gobierna," *Estrategia* 28 (July-August 1979): 2-32.

45. Banco de México, annual reports; and Carlos Perzabal, *Acumulación capitalista dependiente y subordinada: el caso de México (1940-1978)* (Mexico City: Siglo XXI, 1979), 128.

46. For example, a paper from Nafinsa-Unida, "A Strategy to Develop Capital Goods in Mexico" (Mexico City: Nacional Financiera, 1977).

47. The 1994 figures are from Dan La Botz's review of María Cristina Bayón, *El sindicalismo automotriz frente a un nuevo escenario: una perspectiva desde los liderazgos* (Mexico City: FLACSO and Juan Pablos Editor, 1997), in *Mexican Labor News and Analysis* II, no. 23 (16 December 1997), and La Botz, *Democracy,* 118.

48. In 1910, agriculture accounted for 67 percent of economic activity and only 24 percent of production, while mining and manufacturing accounted for 15 percent of the employed and 23 percent of production.

49. Carlos Marichal, "The Rapid Rise of the Neobanqueros: Mexico's New Financial Elite," *NACLA Report on the Americas* XXX, no. 6 (May/June 1997): 28.

50. *New York Times*, 21 November 1997.

Chapter 6: Classes in Conflict, 1940-1999

1. The first quotation is from James D. Cockcroft, unpublished field notes, 1981. The second is from Lourdes Benería and Shelley Feldman (eds.), *Unequal Burden: Economic Crises, Persistent Poverty, and Women's Work* (Boulder: Westview Press, 1992), 83. The third is from the Mexico City daily *La Jornada*, 19 September 1988, cited in José Antonio Alonso, *Mujeres, maquiladoras, y microindustria doméstica* (Mexico City: Distribuciones Fontamara, 1991), 11.

2. Surplus value is surplus labor, that is, the value of the total product of the employed workforce beyond the equivalent of the socially necessary labor time (including women's unpaid household work) requisite for the maintenance of the workers and their families.

3. Moisés González Navarro, "México: The Lopsided Revolution," in *Obstacles to Change in Latin America*, ed. Claudio Veliz (London: Oxford University Press, 1965), 206-29.

4. México, Michoacán, Hidalgo, Guanajuato, Chihuahua, Sinaloa, Tlaxcala, Jalisco, Oaxaca, and Chiapas. Most of the rest of out-migration flowed from Durango, Veracruz, and Zacatecas.

5. James D. Cockcroft, unpublished field notes, 1997.

6. Cockcroft, unpublished field notes, 1981.

7. *Excélsior*, 15 July 1975, as summarized by Philip Russell, Mexico in Transition (Austin, TX: Colorado River Press, 1977), 112.

8. David Barkin, panel discussion at a convention of the Latin American Studies Association held in Guadalajara, Mexico, 1997.

9. Women and children went uncounted in most statistical compilations, even though case studies showed them making up half the labor force on northern Mexico's fruit and vegetable farms. See John Warnock, *The Other Mexico: The North American Triangle Completed* (Montreal: Black Rose Books, 1995), 205.

10. Arturo Warman, *y venimos a contradecir: los campesinos de Morelos y el estado nacional* (Mexico City: Ediciones de Ia Casa Chata, 1976), 15.

11. See Luisa Paré, *El proletariado agrícola en México* (Mexico City: Siglo XXI, 1977).

12. Claude Meillassoux, *Mujeres, graneros y capitales* (Mexico City: Siglo XXI, 1977).

13. Paré, *El proletariado*.

14. See Cockcroft (with UAM-Azcapotzalco Migration Research Team), *Trabajadores de Michoacán: historia de un pueblo migrante* (imisac Ediciones "Contraste," 1982).

15. Cited in Cheryl Payer, "The World Bank and the Small Farmer," *Monthly Review* 32, no. 6 (November 1980): 35.

16. Ibid.

17. AID, U.S. Delegation, World Conference on Agrarian Reform and Rural Development, Rome, 12-21 July 1979, "Integration of Women in Development" (mimeo), 24 May 1979.

18. Hannes Lorenzen, "Investment in the Poor: A World Bank Project in Mexico," Rome Declaration Group, Gartenhofstrasse 27, Zurich, 1980, mimeo; and John W. Barchfield, "The Structure of Power and the Deformation of Agrarian Reform in Mexico," *Revista del México Agrario* 14 (1981). See also "Rhetoric and Reality: The World Bank's New Concern for the Poor," *NACLA Report on the Americas* 29 no. 6 (May/June 1996).

19. Veronika Bennholdt-Thomsen, "Investition in die Armen. Zur Entwicklungsstrategie der Weltbank," *Lateinamerika, Analysen und Berichte* no. 4 (1980).

20. James D. Cockcroft, unpublished field notes, 1973.

21. 1 Roger Bartra et al., *Caciquismo y poder político en el México rural* (Mexico City: Siglo XXI, 1975).

22. See Paré, *El proletariado*.

23. See Bo Anderson and James D. Cockcroft, "Control and Cooptation in Mexican Politics," *International Journal of Comparative Sociology* VII, no. 1 (March 1966), 11-28. Reprinted in various books, this article and its sequel by Cockcroft, "Coercion and Ideology in Mexican Politics," appear in James D. Cockcroft, André Gunder Frank, and Dale L. Johnson, *Dependence and Underdevelopment: Latin America's Political Economy* (New York: Doubleday-Anchor, 1972), 219-68. Both articles draw on interviews I conducted with Garzón.

24. Armando Bartra, "Sobre las clases sociales en el campo mexicano," *Cuadernos Agrarios* no. 1 (1976).

25. Clark W. Reynolds, *The Mexican Economy: Twentieth-Century Structure and Growth* (New Haven: Yale University Press, 1970).

26. The central fraction, which was based in Mexico City, was primarily big finance capital, a fusion of banking and industrial capital with some elements of commercial capital, and had considerable political clout through its strong financial role in public and private economic activities. It was the single most important voice in financial capital's ABM, which traditionally had been linked to the state's main development bank Nafinsa and to the Banco de México, two of whose long-time chief advisers had been the heads of the largest private banks—Banco Nacional de México and Banco de Comercio, each of which had ties to foreign capital (see Chapter 5). It included the Mining and Mercantile Bank group, a group of capitalists independent of foreign capital with roots in the breweries and department stores of the Díaz period, who were in turn linked to Banco de Comercio (a fusion of several banks and much of the chemical industry). The "1940s group," so named because most of its members became industrialists and financiers with the assistance of the post-1940 state industrialization programs, was the fraction of the big bourgeoisie that had the strongest links to the state bureaucracy. It is difficult to distinguish between the bureaucrats and private entrepreneurs in this group. Ex-president Alemán, former Obregón cabinet member Aarón Sáenz, and 1981 Federal District *jefe* (boss or mayor) Carlos Hank González had not only used their high state positions to accumulate capital but had also invested it in such powerful financial groups as those of Carlos Trouyet (banking, manganese, steel, cellulose, cement, paper) or Bruno Pagliali (steel, aluminum, real estate, finance). Members of the "1940s group" were also very influential in CONCAMIN and CONCANACO.

27. *The Economist*, 6 December 1997.

28. Harry Braverman, *Labor and Monopoly Capital* (New York: Monthly Review Press, 1974), 415.

29. Cited in *Uno Más Uno*, 14 November 1979.

30. Carlos Alberto Torres, oral commentary at the Thirteenth Congress of Latin American Sociologists, Panama, 22 November 1979.

31. Sometimes the younger, more educated people were more apt to voice their discontent. For example, graduating university students, 15 to 30 percent of whom were not able to find immediate employment by 1970, flooded the ranks of the state bureaucracy where they helped organize and expand the Federation of Workers Serving the States and Municipalities (110,000 members in 1979) as a combative alternative to the "official" Federation of State Workers' Unions founded in 1938.

32. See Susan Eckstein, *The Poverty of Revolution: The State and the Urban Poor in Mexico* (Princeton: Princeton University Press, 1977).

33. The Mexican Social Security Institute (IMSS) reported in 1995 that 25 million Mexicans out

of the 38 million "economically active population" lacked fixed employment and were working in the "informal" sector (*La Jornada*, 12 July 1996).

34. Marx, *Capital* I (New York: International Publishers, 1967), 633. This is the seed for Marx's polemic against Malthus, treated for the Mexican case by Luis A. Serrón, *Scarcity, Exploitation, and Poverty: Malthus and Marx in Mexico* (Norman: University of Oklahoma Press, 1980).

35. Marx, *Capital* I, 644-45. It is not true that Marx called the various forms of surplus population the "dangerous classes," a colloquial term he applied only to vagabonds, criminals, and prostitutes—and then in quotation marks. Nor did he ever suggest that the most downtrodden, the so-called lumpenproletariat, could serve only reactionary causes. He recognized in the suffering of the surplus population the same degradation of work that increasingly alienates all the proletariat as capitalism develops.

36. Ibid.

37. The Radio Patrols Battalion of the State of Mexico (BARAPEM), an elite paramilitary assault squad, was founded to drive out "land invaders" in greater Mexico City. Its violent attacks led to a campaign in the early 1980s among the poor by leftist-influenced political coalitions to have it dissolved. In the mid-1990s, units of the Mexican military and highly specialized, well-armed police squads patrolled much of Mexico City, offering an intimidating but costly show of force. (In 1997 the United States ranked first in the world for the number of prisoners per capita, reflecting the fact that immiseration was not limited to third world nations.)

38. See Pedro Moctezuma and Bernardo Navarro, "Clase obrera, ejército industrial de reserva y movimientos sociales urbanos de las clases dominados en México: 1970-1976," *Teoría y Política* 1, no. 2 (October-December 1980): 53-72.

39. Jorge Alonso et al., *Lucha urbana y acumulación de capital* (Mexico City: Editorial de Ia de Casa Chata, 1980); José Antonio Alonso, *Mujeres*, and his *Las costureras domésticas de Netzahualcóyotl* (Puebla: Universidad Autónoma de Puebla, 1981), and *Sexo, trabajo y marginalidad urbana* (Mexico City: Editorial Edicol, 1981); and Cristina Padilla, "Maquiladoras de Santa Cecilia: marginadas o asalariadas?" Tesis de Licenciatura, Universidad Ibero-Americana, 1978.

40. Famed Mexican economic historian Sergio de la Peña long ago pointed out that the capitalist mode of production "wherever it spreads, absorbs other modes of production" rather than coexisting with them. See de la Peña, "Accumulación originaria y el fin de los modos de producción no-capitalistas en América Latina," *Historia y Sociedad* no. 5 (Spring 1975): 65-73.

41. For interviews with some of the seamstresses involved, see José Antonio Alonso, *Mujeres*. See also Silvia Tirado, "Weaving Dreams, Constructing Realities: the Nineteenth of September National Union of Garment Workers in Mexico," in *Dignity and Daily Bread: New Forms of Organizing Among Poor Women in the Third World and the First*, ed. Sheila Rowbatham and Swatsi Mitter (New York: Routledge, 1994).

42. Jorge Alonso et al., *Lucha urbana*, 245.

43. Ibid.

44. See Eckstein, *Poverty*.

45. Sol Tax, *Penny Capitalism* (Chicago: University of Chicago Press, 1963).

46. See Martín de la Rosa, *Promoción popular y lucha de clases: análisis de un caso, Netzahualcóyotl* (Mexico City: Taller de Impresiones Populares, 1979), 139.

47. Eckstein, *Poverty*, 101, 107.

48. Davis, *Urban Leviathan*, 312-13.

Chapter 7: Oil and Neoliberalism, 1968-1993

1. James D. Cockcroft, unpublished field notes, 1980. Three months later, ultra-rightist forces kidnapped Alvarez and other Front leaders from a press conference in San Salvador and assassinated them.

2. The 1981 drop in oil prices contributed to the debt crisis of 1982; the 1986 drop precipitated the Mexican stock market crash of 1987; and the 1998 drop further undermined the state's solvency.

3. The number of landless workers doubled in the 1970s, and continued rising after that. In addition, day labor became harder and less well paid. The average number of workdays per year for rural wage earners dropped from 90 in 1970 to 65 in 1980.

4. Richard B. Du Boff, "Globalization & Wages: the Down Escalator," *Dollars and Sense* no. 213 (September/October 1997): 36-40.

5. Edur Velasco Arregui, "Industrial Restructuring in Mexico during the 1980s," in Ricardo Grinspun and Maxwell A. Cameron (eds.), *The Political Economy of North American Free Trade* (Montreal: McGill-Queen's University Press, 1993), 163-75.

6. For more on this, see Daniel La Botz, "Manufacturing Poverty: The Maquiladorization of Mexico," *International Journal of Health Services* 24, no. 3 (1994): 403-08.

7. For more on this, see Harley Shaiken, *Mexico in the Global Economy: High Technology and Work Organization in Export Industries* (San Diego: University of California Center for U.S.-Mexican Studies, 1990), and "Advanced Manufacturing and Mexico: A New International Division of Labor?" *Latin American Research Review* 29, no. 2 (1994): 39-71.

8. Dan La Botz, "Inside Mexico's Massive Crisis," *Against the Current* (November/December 1996); Enrique Duseel Peters, "From Export-Oriented to Import-Oriented Industrialization: Changes in Mexico's Manufacturing Sector, 1988-1994," in *Neoliberalism Revisited: Economic Restructuring and Mexico's Political Future*, ed. Gerardo Otero (Boulder: Westview Press, 1996), 63-83.

9. Du Boff, "Globalization": 40; Shaiken, "Advanced": 51-55. Shaiken adds that low-wage un-skilled employees in Mexico's hi-tech auto plants can also make "larger profits . . . attainable on more sophisticated autos because they require more hours of labor" (67).

10. Noted by economist Paul Cooney in presentation at the New York Marxist School, Brecht Forum, 2 March 1998.

11. NACLA, *Mexico 1968* (New York: NACLA, 1968).

12. Philip Agee, *Inside the Company: CIA Diary* (London: Penguin Books, 1975), 554, cited in John Ross, *The Annexation of Mexico* (Monroe, ME: Common Courage Press, 1998), 122.

13. For details, see Raúl Trejo Delarbre, *Este puño si se ve* (Mexico City: Ediciones El Caballito, 1987), 23-58.

14. *NACLA Report on the Americas,* January/February 1978. See also the following issues of the same journal: July/August 1976; January 1977; March 1977; July/August 1977; September/October 1977; January/February 1978; March/April 1978; May/June 1978; and September/October 1978. The author gratefully acknowledges the assistance of the late Professor Sheldon Liss of the University of Akron's History Department for compilation of much of this material. The *New York Times* reported on 22 November 1977 that the FBI "conducted extensive operations in Mexico to undermine Communist groups there that it said might filter across the border." More than a hundred pages of material released under the Freedom of Information Act are available for consulatation at the FBI headquarters in Washington. For more commentary on the FBI and CIA in Mexico and Latin America, see Cockcroft, "Che Guevara and the FBI," *Monthly Review* 49, no. 11 (April 1998), a review of Michael Ratner and Michael Steven Smith, *Che Guevara and the FBI: The U.S. Political Police Dossier on the Latin American Revolutionary* (Melbourne and New York: Ocean Press, 1997). See also John Ross, *The Annexation of Mexico* (Monroe, ME: Common Courage Press, 1998).

15. ABM, *Informe del congreso directivo a la convénción anual* (1973).

16. *Uno Más Uno,* 11 March 1978.

17. *El Día,* 17 May 1975.

18. The top four banks, holding 70 percent of private bank assets, augmented their profits more

than tenfold during the same period. For more, see Francisco Valdés Ugalde, *Autonomía y legitimidad: los empresarios, la política y el estado en México* (Mexico City: Siglo XXI, 1997), 198.

19. Labor militants conducted some 300 strikes in 1977 and mounted 80 public demonstrations in Mexico City—numbers far lower than those for the preceding years.

20. Important urban movements were Mexico City's Union of Popular Colonies; Monterrey's Land and Liberty Popular Front (50 neighborhoods); Durango's Popular Front (20 communities); the Popular Defense Committee of Chihuahua (300,000 slum dwellers, whose leader was assassinated in 1981); and, in Mexico's northeast, the Coalition of Independent Organizations for the Defense of Popular Economy, founded in 1978. They incorporated slum dwellers, workers, peasants, students, and housewives.

21. The much larger PMT had been denied electoral registration. For an excellent history of the Communist Party, see Barry Carr, *Marxism and Communism in Twentieth Century Mexico* (Lincoln: University of Nebraska, 1992).

22. The author thanks members of the teachers' strike movement, particularly Juana María Gandy, for their generous help in providing information on their struggle. For more on the teachers' movement, see Maria Lorena Cook, *Organizing Dissent: Unions, the State, and the Democratic Teachers' Movement in Mexico* (University Park: Pennsylvania State University Press, 1996).

23. Banco de México, annual reports.

24. James D. Cockcroft, unpublished field notes, 1964.

25. President Ronald Reagan to National Association of Manufacturers, 10 March 1983.

26. For the whole story, see Sylvia Maxfield, *Governing Capital: International Finance and Mexican Politics* (Ithaca: Cornell University Press, 1990), 142-64. One Standard and Poor analyst reportedly put the states's costs of the Salinas-Zedillo bailout of the state banks being privatized at a whopping $47 billion, or about 13 percent of Mexico's 1995 GDP.

27. Miguel Angel Centeno, *Democracy within Reason: Technocratic Revolution in Mexico,* 2nd ed (University Park: Pennsylvania State University Press, 1997).

28. *New York Times,* 5 June 1989; *Wall Street Journal,* 25 September 1989.

29. His articles of the time are collected in Carlos Monsiváis, *Entrada libre: Crónicas de la sociedad que se organiza* (Mexico City: Ediciones Era, 1987).

30. See Lynn Stephen, "Democracy for Whom? Women's Grassroots Political Activism in the 1990s, Mexico City and Chiapas" in *Neoliberalism Revisited: Economic Restructuring and Mexico's Political Future,* ed. Gerardo Otero (Boulder: Westview Press, 1996), 167-86.

31. Alejandra Massolo, "La otra cara de la luna: género y democracia en los movimientos urbano populares," in Jorge Alonso and Juan Manuel Ramírez Sáliz (eds.), *La democracia de los de abajo en México* (Mexico City: UNAM Centro de Investigaciones Interdisciplinarias en Humanidades, 1997), 190, citing Gisela Espinosa, "Mujeres del movimiento urbano popular, 1983-1985," in Alejandra Massolo (ed.), *Mujeres y ciudades* (Mexico City: El üologeio de México PIEM, 1992).

32. Massolo, in Alonso and Ramírez Sáliz, *La democracia,* 192-93.

33. See Richard Roman and Edur Velasco Arregui, "Zapatismo and the Workers Movement in Mexico at the End of the Century," *Monthly Review* 49, no. 3 (July/August 1997): 98-116.

34. The best analytical overview on gay and lesbian movements for Mexico and other third world countries remains Peter Drucker, " 'In the Tropics There is No Sin': Sexuality and Gay-Lesbian Movements in the Third World," *New Left Review* no. 218 (July/August 1996).

35. See, for example, James Petras, "Imperialism and NGOs in Latin America," *Monthly Review* 49, no. 7 (December 1997): 10-27.

36. See Antonio Gershenson, *México: sindicalismo y poder la experiencia nuclear* (Mexico City: Ediciones El Caballito, 1987).

37. See Dan La Botz, "The Team in Mexico," in *Working Smart: A Union Guide to Participation*

Programs and Reengineering, ed. Mike Parker and Jane Slaughter (Detroit: Labor Notes, 1994), and Yolanda Montiel, *Proceso de trabajo, acción sindical y nueva tecnologías en Volkswagen de México* (Mexico City: Colección de Miguel Othón de Mendizabal (CIESAS) and SEP, 1991).

38. James D. Cockcroft, unpublished field notes, 1981, and Hugo García Michel, *Más allá de Laguna Verde* (Mexico City: Editorial Posada, 1988).

39. Cockcroft, ibid.

40. A good background piece is "Mexico's New Indian Movement," *Interhemispheric Resource Center Bulletin* no. 45 (December 1996).

41. For more on SAM, see Jonathan Fox, *The Politics of Food in Mexico: State Power and Social Mobilization* (Ithaca: Cornell University Press, 1992).

42. See La Botz, *Democracy in Mexico: Peasant Rebellion and Political Reform* (Boston: South End Press, 1995), 101-19, which includes excellent background on Salinas and his coterie.

43. Lourdes Benería and Shelley Feldman (eds.), *Unequal Burden: Economic Crises, Persistent Poverty, and Women's Work* (Boulder: Westview Press, 1992), 97.

44. Judith Adler Hellman, "Mexican Popular Movements, Clientelism, and the Process of Democratization," *Latin American Perspectives* 21, (Spring 1994): 124-42.

45. See Alva Senzek, "The Entrepreneurs Who Became Radicals," *NACLA Report on the Americas* 30, no. 4 (January/February 1997): 28-29; Gabriel Torres, "El derecho de 'barzonear' y sus efectos políticos," in Alonso and Ramírez Sáliz, *La democracia,* 265-91.

46. La Quina got out of jail in December, 1997. He told reporters he was leaving politics.

Chapter 8: Challenges to the PRI

1. President Clinton's statement went mostly unreported, but I found it in Kim Moody, "Up Against the Polyester Ceiling: The 'New' AFL-CIO Organizes—Itself!" *New Politics* VI (New Series), no. 4 (Winter 1998): 7. For the quotation from the Maya women's placard, see *Mexican Labor News Analysis* 3, Special Issue on International Women's Day (March 1998). The Michoacán immigrant worker's statement is from James D. Cockcroft, unpublished field notes, 1982.

2. Dan La Botz, *Democracy in Mexico: Peasant Rebellion and Political Reform* (Boston: South End Press, 1995), 62.

3. As a four-year-old boy, Cárdenas contributed the contents of his piggy bank as part of the national campaign to help compensate the nationalized oil companies. As a young man, he joined his father's short-lived breakaway movement from the PRI, the early 1960s Movement for National Liberation (MLN). For more on Cárdenas's background and the people and ideologies that he gathered around him, see La Botz, *Democracy,* 83-99; and Adolph Gilly, *El cardinismo, una utopia mexicana* (Mexico City: Cal y Arena, 1994).

4. Salinas quote from *New Perspectives Quarterly* 8, no. 1 (1991), cited by Joseph L. Klesner, "Political Change in Mexico: Institutions and Identity," *Latin American Research Review* 32, no. 2 (1997): 185. The Cárdenas quote was widely reported in the press.

5. See Enrique Krauze, *La presidencia imperial: Ascenso y caída del sistema político mexicano (1940-1996),* (Mexico City: Tusquets Editores, 1997), 430.

6. See La Botz, *Democracy,* 135.

7. For example, an Indian could feel an Indian identity in her or his home state, yet feel "Mexican" in Los Angeles, California, while others might view the Indian as a mestizo in some settings, even as they might view an impoverished mestizo peasant as an Indian.

8. *Excélsior,* 15 July 1975, as summarized in Philip Russell, *Mexico in Transition* (Austin, TX: Colorado River Press, 1977), 112.

9. See, for example, a statement by Zapata read at the 1914 Aguascalientes Convention quoted in Subcomandante Marcos, *Shadows of Tender Fury: The Letters and Communiqués of Subcomandante*

Marcos and the Zapatista Army of National Liberation (New York: Monthly Review Press, 1995), 229. A most revealing book in Spanish is the set of interviews with EZLN leaders conducted by French Latin Americanist and sociologist Yvon Le Bot, with Maurice Najman, *Subcomandante Marcos: El sueño zapatista. Entrevistas con el Subcomandante Marcos, el mayor Moisés y el comandante Tacho, del Ejército Zapatista de Liberación Nacional* (Mexico City: Plaza & Janés, 1997). Perhaps the most authoritative and up-to-date account on the Zapatistas, as well as on their negotiations with the government, is Héctor Díaz-Polanco, *La rebelión zapatista y la autonomía* (Mexico City: Siglo XXI, 1997). The most recent compilation of Zapatista women's perspectives, put together by a dozen women's groups, is Sara Lovera and Nellys Palomo (ed.), *Las Alzadas* (Mexico City: Centro de Información de la Mujer and Convergencia Socialista, Agrupación Política Nacional, 1997). To obtain Zapatista communiques and related items on the World Wide Web, consult http://www.actlab.utexas.edu/zapatistas/index.html. Good videos include Saul Landau's "Sixth Sun" (PBS documenatry) and Thierry Zéno's "Ya Basta! The Battle Cry of the Faceless" (New York: Icaraus Films).

10. See Marcos, *Shadows*, 50-51.

11. Ibid., 98.

12. See especially Le Bot, *Subcomandante Marcos*, 206-28.

13. Marcos, *Shadows*, 72, 123.

14. Ibid., 230.

15. Harvard researcher Juan Enriquez, in a lecture at CUNY Bildner Center, New York City, 20 March 1998, placed the size of Mexico's economy in perspective by noting that its roughly $300 billion GDP was only a bit more than half that of Fidelity Mutual Fund.

16. The North American Development Bank, created to help clean up the environmental mess along the U.S.-Mexican border, approved only four loans in three years. Cases about violations of workers' rights received attention but resulted in no direct remedies.

17. The United States had long complained about the high tariffs of its rivals in the world market. It claimed it had slashed its tariffs to 6 percent, far lower than the tariffs of other industrial powers. According to the World Bank, however, U.S. use of non-tariff barriers (anti-dumping duties, quotas on imports, etc.) to offset the influx of manufactured exports from Japan and East Asia made U.S. tariffs, in effect, not 6 percent but 23 percent. See John Warnock, *The Other Mexico* (Montreal: Black Rose Books, 1997), 3, citing World Bank, *World Development Report* (Washington, D.C.: World Bank, 1993). Any doubt about how regional "free trade" blocs serve to enforce protectionism against other blocs should be buried by the breakdown in trade talks between the United States and Japan in early 1994. Moreover, the free trade framework agreements signed by the United States with Chile and other Latin American countries were aimed at assuring favorable investment conditions for U.S.-based TNCs and—through "local content" clauses similar to those in NAFTA—at placing Japanese and European companies at a disadvantage in the U.S. "backyard." The "free trade wars" were, in effect, undemocratic since they tended to be carried out by small circles of elites, without input from working people whose wages and living standards the elites were so willing to sacrifice in order to "make the nation competitive."

18. See *Multinational Monitor*, November 1997.

19. Noted in James Petras, "Latin America: The Resurgence of the Left," *New Left Review* no. 223 (May/June 1997): 39.

20. See Edur Velasco Arregui, "Commentary on Statistical Tables: Neoliberalism, The Long Wave in Mexico, and the Economic Integration of North America" (unpublished ms.).

21. Statistics of U.S. Labor Department and *Forbes*, cited by U.S. House Minority Whip David E. Bonior in *New York Times*, 13 July 1997.

22. An essay by Castillo on this topic was included in José Luis Manzo Yepez and Rosa Albina

Garavito Elías, *La Petroquímica Mexicana: Industria estratégica o subordinada?* (Mexico City: Instituto de Estudios de la Revolución Democrática and Editorial Nuestro Tiempo, 1995).

23. The Weintraub quote is from Peter S. Cleaves and Charles J. Stephens, "Businessmen and Economic Policy in Mexico," *Latin American Research Review* 26, no. 2 (1991): 187-202, reviewing Sidney Weintraub, "Mexican Trade Policy and the North American Community," (Washington, D.C.: Center for Strategic and International Studies, 1988).

24. Inappropriate livestock and mining production since 1970 caused Mexico to account for one-fourth of Latin America's tropical rain forest loss. Environmental protection hinged on how dispute resolution cases were handled. Only governemnts, not environmental or other citizen groups, were allowed by NAFTA's terms to initiate a dispute. For more on the environment and NAFTA, see Joel Simon, *Endangered Mexico* (San Francisco: Sierra Club Books, 1997).

25. Salinas claimed that adequate funding for the enforcement of environmental regulations could be budgeted only after the national debt problem was overcome, the economy was in a sustained growth phase, and the budget deficit and trade imbalance were corrected. Zedillo acted on the same premises.

26. A random survey of U.S. factories in Mexico conducted in 1992 by the U.S. government's General Accounting Office found that all violated Mexico's environmental laws. Arizona had hepatitis rates 20 times the U.S. national average; El Paso County, Texas, had tuberculosis rates twice the national average. On 12 July 1997, ABC News reported outbreaks of cholera, typhoid, and polio in California's Imperial Valley. Pesticides from the Valley's megafarms and pollutants from the poor sewage system of Mexicali, Baja California, had flowed into the New River which ran in both countries. The New River was more polluted than before NAFTA, when complaints were already being made.

27. Aridjis quote cited in *NACLA Report on the Americas* 30, no. 4 (January/February 1997): 30; Lacandón forest crisis described in NewsPak no. 105 (27 January-9 February 1997), Human Rights Documentation Exchange, P.O. Box 2327, Austin, TX 78768.

28. See David V. Carruthers, "Indigenous ecology and the politics of linkage in Mexican social movements," *Third World Quarterly* 17, no. 5 (December 1996): 1007-1028; John Ross, "Zapata's Children: Defending the Land and Human Rights in the Countryside," *NACLA Report on the Americas* 30, no. 4 (January/February 1997): 30-35.

29. *New York Times,* 3 June 1994. Conclusions about U.S. industries and ethnic and gender makeup of employees most negatively affected by NAFTA were based on data compiled by the U.S. Labor Department and widely reported in the press.

30. Canada, Mexico, and the European Union (EU) passed legislation making it illegal for their citizens to comply with the U.S. Helms-Burton Act that had tightened the economic blockade of Cuba by preventing firms that sold or traded goods to Cuba from trading with the United States.

31. See Wally Seccombe, "Labour's Capital Circulating in Cyberspace," *Socialist Register* 1999 (Suffolk: Merlin Press, 1999).

32. Ibid.

33. See Velasco Arregui, "Commentary."

34. John Arquilla and David Ronfeldt, *In Athena's Camp: Preparing for Conflict in the Information Age* (Santa Monica, CA: Rand, 1998), 6, 16, and 18 of pre-publication version.

35. Cited in *NACLA Report on the Americas* 31, no. 5 (March/April 1998): 12.

36. Ibid.: 6; *Mexican Labor News Analysis* 3, no. 2 (16 January 1998).

37. *La Jornada,* 11 December 1996, as reported in *Mexican Labor News Analysis,* 16 December 1996.

38. Marcos, "Siete piezas sueltas del rompecabezas mundial," *Le Monde diplomatique,* June 1997: 20, citing Ana Esther Ceceña, "El Istmo de Tehuantepec: Frontera de la Soberanía Nacional," *La Jornada del Campo,* 28 May 1997; *Multinational Monitor,* November 1997: 6-7; Nancy Nusser,

"Mexico May Build Overland Route to River Canal," latinolink.com/biz/1005bist.htm; Ross, "Zapata's Children."

39. For the full text, see *La Jornada*, 4 September 1996, and, in English, *International Viewpoint*, September 1996. In November, the EPR carried out more raids in three states, including an attack on a military barracks on the outskirts of Mexico City *(New York Times*, 2 November 1996).

40. For more on the EPR, see Georgina Gatsiopolous, "The EPR: Mexico's Other Guerrillas," *NACLA Report on the Americas* 30, no. 4 (January/February 1997): 33.

41. Ibid.: 14-15, 27.

42. Mexico City experienced only twenty-seven days in 1997 where the air quality was "good." See *Mexican Labor News Analysis* 2, no. 22 (5 December 1997) and 3, no. 4 (16 February 1998).

43. See *Mexican Labor News Analysis* 3, no. 1 (2 January 1998); *New York Times*, 9 July 1997; Scott Sherman, "Mexico's Morning After," *The Nation*, 28 July/4 August 1997: 20-23.

44. The Brito quotation is from "Mexico's New Indian Movement," *Interhemispheric Resource Center Bulletin* no. 45 (December 1996): 6. The EZLN quote is from *Weekly News Update on the Americas* no. 388 (6 July 1997).

45. *Mexican Labor News Analysis* 3, no. 1 (2 January 1997); *Weekly News Update on the Americas* no. 383 (1 June 1997).

46. *Mexico NewsPak* no. 105 (27 January-9 February 1997), citing press reports. See also *The Nation*, 22 December 1997: 4, and various notes below. As early as 14 June 1990, the U.S.-based Americas Watch condemned Mexico's "policy of impunity" for human rights abusers. A year later Amnesty International reported: "Torture remains endemic in Mexico." For more, see Human Rights Watch/Americas, *Implausible Deniability: State Responsibility for Rural Violence in Mexico* (New York: 1997).

47. *La Jornada*, 15 June 1998. For more, see Peter Gellert, "Mexican Government Launches Offensive Against Zapatistas," *Mexican Labor News Analysis*, 2 April 1998, and other issues from 1998.

48. The FZLN declaration, sent out on the Internet, echoed the Conai members' resignation statement that "a just and honorable peace will not be possible without respect for the collective rights of the Indian peoples and a significant advance in reform of the state and the transition to democracy." See *La Jornada*, 8 June 1998, and *New York Times*, 9 June 1998.

49. *Weekly News Update on the Americas* no. 438 (21 June 1998), translating from *La Jornada*, 17 and 20 June 1998.

50. The U.S. drug consumption figure was provided by U.S. drug czar Gen. Barry McCaffrey (see *Wall Street Journal*, 7 May 1997); the laundering figure was given out by a member of a U.S. House banking subcommittee. See *The Nation*, 30 September 1996: 6. The Mexican government's 1990 figure came from the Mexican National Program for Drug Control. See Warnock, *Other*, 232.

51. Reported on "All Things Considered," National Public Radio, 26 June 1997.

52. See Marcos, *Shadows*, 13; Petras, "Latin America": 46; and Cockcroft, *Latin America: History, Politics, and U.S. Policy* (Chicago: Nelson-Hall Publishers, 1996), which lists several top-rate sources on the narco-trafficking issue.

53. See *New York Times*, 11 July 1997; *Weekly News Update on the Americas* no. 436 (7 June 1998).

54. Ibid., as well as press coverage at the time of the incidents.

55. Ibid.

56. *La Jornada*, 19 May 1998; Carlos A. Heredia, "Downward Mobility: Mexican Workers After NAFTA," *NACLA Report on the Americas* 30, no. 3 (November/December 1996): 35; personal e-mail communiqué from UNAM economist Alejandro Alvarez Béjar, 3 March 1998.

57. *Wall Street Journal*, 28 February 1998. On the Oliver North operation, see Cockcroft, *Latin America*.

58. As reported by the *New York Times*, 9 June 1998. See also Eva Bertram and Kenneth Sharpe,

"War Ends, Drugs Win," *The Nation,* 6 January 1997: 11-14. On numerous occasions, Americas Watch censured the Border Patrol's "routine" physical and verbal abuses of the immigrants, including several cases that led to death or permanent disablement. See *New York Times,* 31 May 1992; *Washington Post,* 14 May 1993.

59. See John J. Johnson, *The Military and Society in Latin America* (Stanford, CA.: Stanford University Press, 1964).

60. A particularly insightful review of the U.S. and Mexican "national security" doctrines and their interrelationship is an article to be translated and published in 1998 or 1999 by *Latin American Perspectives* entitled "Las estrategias político-militares del estado mexicano y del Ejército Zapatista de Liberación Nacional: Seguridad Nacional versus Soberanía Nacional." The figures for the police are from the Mexico City daily *El Nacional,* 5 January 1998, cited in *Mexican Labor News Analysis* 3, no. 2 (16 January 1998).

61. See Roderic A. Camp, Generals in the Palacio: The Military in Modern Mexico (New York: Oxford University Press, 1992), 32.

62. See *NACLA Report on the Americas,* January/February 1978.

63. On U.S. government's public acknowledgment, see *New York Times,* 4 June 1997; *La Jornada,* June 18, 1997.

64. Cited in *Weekly News Update on the Americas* no. 422 (1 March 1998).

65. Ibid., no. 406 (9 November 1997).

66. *Washington Post,* 26 February 1988.

67. For more on the CIA manual, see Cockcroft, *Latin America,* 221. On the GAFE unit accused of torture, see *Weekly News Update on the Americas* no. 427 (6 April 1998). The GAFE training was a special program with no congressional oversight and received $28 million in government funding in 1997. The trainees received instruction in "helicopter assault tactics, explosives, rural and urban warfare, and operational intelligence gathering and planning." They then returned to Mexico to train "rapid reaction groups" there. By early 1998, some forty-two of these hundred-man units were deployed by the Mexican Army.

68. Quoted in *Weekly News Update on the Americas* no. 414 (5 January 1998).

69. Juan Enriquez, "Dealing with Mexico," *New York Times,* 9 November 1997.

70. For Latin America's kidnapping statistics, see *Latin American Weekly Report,* 15 July 1997.

71. *Washington Post,* 31 May 1998.

72. Quoted in *Proceso,* 6 April 1981. For excellent presentations of the different, conflicting tendencies within the Mexican Church from different perspectives, consult Roderic A. Camp, *Crossing Swords: Politics and Religion in Mexico* (New York: Oxford University Press, 1997).

73. See Krauze, *La presidencia,* 434.

74. Cited in Warnock, *Other,* 185.

75. See Luis González Meza, *Un asesino en la presidencia* (Mexico City: Editorial Gonzáles Meza, 1996).

76. *La Jornada,* 27 April 1998. See also *The Economist,* 6 December 1997.

77. For more, see Marta Lamas, "Scenes from a Mexican Battlefield," *NACLA Report on the Americas* 31, no. 4 (January/February 1998): 17-21. The author thanks Geoffrey Fox for advising on some useful sources on the mass media in Mexico.

78. In 1981, for instance, the leftist publishing house Nueva Imagen had to halve its publication programs because PIPSA withheld paper and the government impounded imported paper at the port of Veracruz.

79. *Latin American Weekly Report,* 29 July 1997. The author thanks Ross Gandy for calling attention to the "narco-press," which consisted mainly of articles and reports serving drug cartel interests (e.g., defending a governor or a general in cahootswith narco-traffickers).

80. Harvard researcher Juan Enriquez, lecture at CUNY Bildner Center, New York City, 20 March 1998.

81. Male supervisors in some *maquiladoras* routinely inspected female employees' sanitary napkins to verify that they were menstruating. In 1997, the FAT and other labor and human rights groups joined Mexico's National Association of Democratic Lawyers to file a "Sex Discrimination in Mexico's Maquiladora Sector" petition before the U.S. Labor Department's National Administrative Office (NAO) under the NAFTA side-agreement on labor. In January 1998, the NAO found in the petitioners' favor and called for ministerial consultations.

82. *Mexican Labor News Analysis* 3, Special Issue: International Women's Day (March 1998). Much of the information on women in this section is elaborated there.

83. Dan La Botz, "The Story Behind the Mexican Rail Workers' Wildcat," *Labor Notes*, May 1998: 8-9; *Mexican Labor News Analysis* 2, no. 21 (16 November 1997) and 3, no. 6 (16 March 1998).

84. *Mexican Labor News Analysis* 3, no. 9 (2 May 1998).

85. Ibid.; *La Jornada*, 14 April 1998. On CT's membership estimates, see Warnock, *Other*, 117.

86. Ibid.; *New York Times*, 2 May 1998.

87. These figures were from the INS, which counted as "undocumented" only those persons who had remained in the country "illegally" for more than twelve months. See Jorge del Pinal and Audrey Singer, "Generations of Diversity: Latinos in the United States," *Population Bulletin* 52, no. 3 (October 1997), 20-23.

88. *New York Times*, 31 July 1997 and 21 May 1998. Americas Watch regularly censured the U.S. Justice Department for failing to seriously investigate hundreds of well-documented complaints against the Border Patrol. Its 1997 report said INS policies allowed the arrest of minors without access to legal assistance and created conditions conducive to the Border Patrol's shootings, beatings, and sexual assaults on people suspected of immigrating illegally. See *La Jornada*, 5 December 1997.

89. See *Excelsior*, 19 June 1997.

90. Ford Foundation, *Hispanics: Challenges and Opportunities*, New York, June 1984, 20. For more on the immigrants' contributions to the economy, see Gregory DeFreitas, *Inequality at Work* (New York: Oxford University Press, 1991), 209-31, 248-51.

91. Impoverished Mexicans lacked sufficient funds to pay the *polleros* (labor smugglers, also called *coyotes*) and related costs of the trip to the United States. The composite educational level of Mexican immigrants surpassed the national average (seventh grade), a little-noticed but significant part of the "brain drain" from Mexico to the United States. For more data on educational costs in Mexico and California and immigrants' contributions to California's economy, see *NACLA Report on the Americas*, November/December 1995. See also James D. Cockcroft, *Latinos in the Struggle for Equal Education* (Danbury, Ct.: Franklin Watts, 1995).

92. Donna Van Houten Kelly, "Women Workers, Multinational Assembly Lines and Informal Work: Liberation or Marginalization" (unpublished paper for my "Societies in Transition" course, Center for Distance Learning, SUNY-Empire State College, 1996), 1. Kelly's paper drew heavily on Karen J. Hossfeld, "Their Logic Against Them: Contradictions in Sex, Race and Class in Silicon Valley," in *Women Workers and Global Restructuring*, ed. Kathryn Ward (Ithaca: ILR Press, 1990).

93. Manuel Castells, *La teoría de las crisis económicas y las transformaciones del capitalismo* (Mexico City: Siglo XXI, 1978), 15.

94. According to the U.S. Labor Department, in the eight Southwest and Midwest labor market areas that experienced the greatest increase in Mexican illegal immigrant workers from 1968 to 1977, the unemployment rate was lower than the national average. Nor was it true that certain jobs were inherently bad or low-wage, while others were good or high-wage. The "good" jobs became that way because of labor's organizing and fighting to improve them. According to researcher Timothy C. Brown of Stanford University's Hoover Institution, Mexican shoppers "spent $22

billion in the United States, paid $1.7 billion in taxes, and generated 400,000 jobs but received no services" in 1995. See Timothy C. Brown, "The Fourth Member of NAFTA: The U.S.-Mexico Border," in Paul Rich and Guillermo De Los Reyes (eds.), *NAFTA Revisited: Expectations and Realities, Annals of the American Academy of Political and Social Science* 550 (Thousand Oaks, CA: Sage Periodicals Press, 1997), 105.

95. Sample interviews conducted in 1997 appear in Sara Poggio, "Traveling in the Dark"; appendix in Cockcroft, *Outlaws in the Promised Land: The Politics of Immigration* (Albuquerque: University of New Mexico Press, 1999).

96. *Wall Street Journal,* 18 June 1976.

97. On 1997-1998 escalation in INS raids and campaigns to stop them, see *Immigration New Briefs,* (a monthly supplement to *Weekly News Update on the Americas),* May 1998, and the New York-based Coalition for Human Rights of Immigrants web site (http://home.earthlink.net/ -dbwilson/chri).

98. The INS data were submitted by INS to the U.S. Select Commission on Immigration in the early 1980s. The pattern remained the same in the 1990s.

99. For more on this, see Frank Bonilla (ed.), *Borderless Borders: U.S. Latinos, Latin Americans, and the Politics of Interdependence* (Philadelphia: Temple University Press, 1998).

100. For a concise summary of the theoretical points behind the analysis in this section, see James D. Cockcroft, "Gendered Class Analysis: Internationalizing, Feminizing, and Latinizing Labor's Struggle in the Americas," *Latin American Perspectives* 25, no. 6 (November 1998): 42-46.

101. In early 1982, ICC's main affiliates—the International Brotherhood of General Workers, the Arizona Farm Workers Union, the Texas Farm Workers Union, and the Florida Farm Workers Union—merged to form the AFW. Some of the leaders of the farm workers unions had grown disenchanted with Chavez's and de la Huerta's UFW. Chavez had long opposed organizing undocumented Mexican immigrants.

102. *Mexican Labor News Analysis* provided continuing comprehensive reports on the Han Young workers' struggle. See also David Bacon, "Testing NAFTA's Labor Side Agreement," *NACLA Report on the Americas* 31, no. 6 (May/June 1998): 6-9; issues of *Weekly News Update on the Americas,* e.g. no. 434 (24 May 1998).

103. See issues of *Mexican Labor News Analysis,* e.g. 2, no. 23 (16 December 1997) 3, no. 2 (16 January 1998), and 3, no. 5 (2 March 1998).

104. *La Jornada,* 23 and 24 January 1998. Two more CTM work stoppages occurred in maquiladora plants in June. See *Mexican Labor News Analysis* 3, no. 12 (16 June 1998).

105. See *Mexican Labor News Analysis* 3, no. 3 (2 February 1998) and no. 7 (2 April 1998).

106. See Marc Cooper, "Class.War@ Silicon.Valley Disposable Workers in the New Economy," *The Nation,* 27 May 1996: 11-16; Hector Figueroa, "The Growing Force of Latino Labor," *NACLA Report on the Americas* 30, no. 3 (November/December 1996): 19-24; Kim Moody, "American Labor: A Movement Again?" *Monthly Review* 49, no. 3 (July-August 1997), 71, "The Dynamics of Change in American Labor," in *The Transformation of U.S. Unionism: Voices, Visions and Strategies from the Grassroots,* ed. Ray Tillman and Michael S. Cummings (Boulder: Lynne Rienner, 1998).

107. In 1996, there were 100,000 Spanish-surnamed members in the 1.4 million-member Teamsters organization. On the Teamsters' rank-and-file movement for democracy, See Julio Cesar Guerrero, "Latino Activism Could Change the Teamsters," *Labor Notes,* May 1997: 3; Phill Kwik, "The Teamsters Victory: A Successful Strategy for Revitalizing the Labor Movement," *New Politics* 4, no. 1 (Summer 1992): 155-66; Dan La Botz, *Rank and File Rebellion: Teamsters for a Democratic Union* (New York: Verso Books, 1990). On the UPS strike and its aftermath, see various issues of *Labor Notes* (1997-1998).

108. For more, see the *Christian Science Monitor,* 24 June 1998; Kim Moody, "On the Line in Flint," *The Nation,* 13 July 1998: 6.

109. For more on the immigrants' march on Washington, see *Hispanic*, December 1996. The author thanks all those anonymous people involved in organizing the march who granted interviews and provided mimeographed publications of Coordinadora '96. Thanks also to Mario Nelson of the Social Justice Center, Albany, New York, for his help.

110. Cockcroft, *Hispanic*, 130, and *Latinos*, 161; del Pinal and Singer, "Generations"; Figueroa, "The Growing Force"; Nicolás Kanellos (ed.), *The Hispanic-American Almanac* (Detroit: Gale Research Inc., 1993), 334; Edwin Melendez, Clara Rodriguez, and Janis Barry Figueroa (eds.), *Hispanics in the Labor Force: Issues and Policies* (New York: Plenum Press, 1991); *Mexican Labor News Analysis* 3, no. 10 (16 May 1998); Moody, "American Labor," and "Membership Still Slipping, But Some Organizing Tactics Work," *Labor Notes*, March 1998: 11-14. According to Jack Otero of the Labor Council for Latin American Advancement, Latinos made up "more than ten percent of all union members." See Juan Gómez Quiñones, *Mexican American Labor, 1790-1990* (Albuquerque: University of New Mexico Press, 1994), 231.

Conclusion: Mexico's Hope

1. Subcomandante Marcos, *Shadows of Tender Fury: The Letters and Communiqués of Subcomandante Marcos and the Zapatista Army of National Liberation* (New York: Monthly Review Press, 1995), 152.

2. *La Jornada*, 4 July 1998 (drawing data from an article in the June 1998 issue of the *Federal Reserve Bulletin*).

3. For details, see Carlos Marichal, "The Vicious Cycles of Mexican Debt," *NACLA Report on the Americas XXXI*, no. 3 (November-December 1997): 25-31.

4. *Wall Street Journal*, 7 May 1997.

5. Inflation was 16.7 percent on the cost of the market basket of basic goods in 1997. According to Mexico City's Workers University (Universidad Obrera), prices rose 177 percent while wages fell 36 percent between the December 1994 devaluation of the peso and August 1997 (noted in *Mexican Labor News Analysis*, 15 September 1997). The real minimum wage was back down to its mid-1930s level in 1998.

6. See Edur Velasco Arregui, "Commentary on Statistical Tables: Neoliberalism, The Long Wave in Mexico, and the Economic Integration of North America" (unpublished ms.), Charts 1 and 2.

7. CCE president Eduardo Bours Castelo, who also was reported as saying that a costly political transition was preferable to perpetuating the corruption of the past. See *La Jornada*, 16 June 1997 and 29 June 1998.

8. See *La Jornada*, 15 April 1998.

9. This takes into account inflation. From the fall of 1997 to the spring of 1998, the per barrel price of crude fell $8 to under $13 *(New York Times*, 21 May 1998). According to the Banco de México, Mexico had more than $30 billion in foreign reserves in April 1998, but that was $10 billion less than the interest payments on the debt in 1997. The Asian economic crisis increased the flight of capital out of Mexico and helped drive prices down on the Mexican stock exchange. A retiring Finance Minister warned of more cutbacks on milk, tortilla, and school breakfast subsidies and "the risk of social conflicts because of public discontent" *(La Jornada*, 8 May 1998). For more, see *La Jornada*, 30 October 1997, 15 April 1998; *Mexican Labor News Analysis* 3, no. 4 (16 February 1998); *New York Times*, 25 March 1998.

10. The PEMEX statistics and plans were reported in *The Economist*, 6 December 1997. On the other hand, the possibility of falling oil prices threatened to force PEMEX to agree to lower its production in agreements worked out with other oil producing countries in order to send oil prices back up.

11. The Mexican government funded 68 percent of R&D, while private industry financed the rest. Academic expenditure on developing technology was practically nil (0.06 percent of GDP). See

UNESCO, *World Science Report,* 1996. In the spring of 1998, CONACYT announced a 10 percent reduction in scholarships because of falling oil export prices. For more, see *La Jornada,* 26 March and 8 May 1998.

12. The Latin American Economic System (SELA), a UN body, warned in late 1993 that the monopolization of technological transformation by twelve industries involving more than 1,000 competing TNCs threatened to leave Mexico and the rest of Latin America behind. Some 40,000 TNCs dominated the international economy, accounting for two-thirds of global trade.

13. See Velasco Arregui, "Commentary."

14. David Barkin, commentary on a panel at the Twentieth International Congress of the Latin American Studies Association, Guadalajara, Mexico, 1997. See also DavidBarkin, *Distorted Development: Mexico in the World Economy* (Boulder: Westview Press, 1990.

15. For more on this idea of bringing into convergence a society's diverse resources, peoples, capacities, and needs, see Clive Yolande Thomas, *The Poor and the Powerless: Economic Policy and Change in the Caribbean* (New York: Monthly Review Press, 1988). It should be noted that no country ever gained economic prosperity through laissez-faire economics or neoliberalism. All the early industrial powers benefited from strong state interventions on behalf of capital, including protectionist tariffs and state subsidies for overseas expansion. The newly industrializing countries of East Asia generally used state intervention as the basis for their economic development strategy. The world's fastest growing economy of the 1990s, China, also retained a key role for state economic intervention.

16. See John Saxe-Fernández, "El gas natural mexicano: Su integración vertical a Estados Unidos y la Seguridad Nacional." *El Cotidiano* Año 12, no. 71 (septiembre 1995): 31-42; The White House, "National Security Strategy of the United States" (Washington, D.C.: U.S. Government Printing Office, March 1990).

17. *New York Times,* 8 May 1997.

18. Caspar Weinberger, *The Next War* (New York: Regnery, 1997).

19. See Helen I. Safa, *The Myth of the Male Breadwinner: Women and Industrialization in the Caribbean* (Boulder: Westview Press, 1995).

20. Mayra Buvinic, "Women in Poverty: A New Global Underclass," *Foreign Policy,* Fall 1997: 38-39. This represents a late 1990s version of a more feminized investment in the poor strategy initiated by the World Bank thirty years earlier. This version made women a focus of the World Bank's new "Social Investment Funds" (SIFs) strategy. SIFs were temporary measures that sought to mitigate neoliberalism's devastating impact on poor people's lives without touching the underlying structural causes of poverty. For more, see Michael Lipton and Jacques van der Gaag, *Including the Poor* (Washington, D.C.: World Bank, 1994); *NACLA Report on the Americas* 29, no. 6 (May/June 1996). Not surprisingly, a 1997 two-volume history critical of the World Bank (published by the Brookings Institution with Bank authorization) received little attention in the press. See *The Nation,* 23 March 1998: 4-5.

21. In interviewing Silicon Valley's immigrant women workers, Karen Hossfeld found that they had not only "numeric strength, but also a wealth of creativity, insight, and experience that could be a shot in the arm to the stagnating [U.S.] national labor movement." Hossfeld wrote that they "struck me as potentially effective labor and community organizers and rank-and-file leaders. Yet almost none of them were interested in collective organizing, because of time limitations and family constraints and because of their lack of confidence in labor unions, the feminist movement, and community organizations." See Karen J. Hossfeld, "Their Logic Against Them: Contradictions in Sex, Race and Class in Silicon Valley," in *Women Workers and Global Restructuring,* ed. Kathryn Ward (Ithaca: ILR Press, 1990), 176-77.

RELATED WEBSITES

- Fourth World Documentation Project: Indigenous Peoples Information for the Online Community *<http://www.halcyon.com/FWDP/fwdp.html>*
- Guide to sites and resources on Latinos in U.S. and U.S.-Mexico border issues *<http://lib.nmsu.edu/subject/bord/latino.html>*
- Instituto Nacional de Estadística Geográfica e Informática (INEGI), Mexico's official statistical agency *<http://ags.inegi.gob.mx>*
- Inter-American Development Bank, for data on Mexico and other countries *<http://www.iadb.org>*
- Interhemispheric Resource Center background and update materials *<http://www.zianet.com/ircl>*
- Interpress Latin America Wire news stories arranged by country and subject *<http://worldnews.net/interpress/iphome.html>*
- IPL Trade Directory for business information on 50,000 companies in Mexico and Central America *<http://www.ipl.com.gt>*
- Latin American history book reviews and links to other sites covering history *<http://www.h-net.msu.edu/~latam>*
- Latin America Working Group, National Council of Churches information newsletter *Legislative Update* with materials on U.S. policy formation *<www.igc.apc.org/lawg>*
- Library of Congress, with abstracts and bibliographical information on variety of Latin America topics *<http://www.lcweb2.loc.gov/hlas/hlashome.html>*
- *Mexican Labor News Analysis*, excellent source for news and social statistics about Mexico with background explanations *<03144.2651@compuserve.com>*
- Mexican Online News, for access to online newspapers, magazines, and commercial and academic publications *<http://eng.usf.edu/~palomare/newspapers.html>*
- *NACLA Report on the Americas*, 475 Riverside Drive, Suite 454, NY, NY 10115, widely respected source for analytical materials, including U.S. policy *<http://www.nacla.org>*
- NACLA updates on Mexico *<http://www.igc.org/nacla/mexico.html>*
- NAFTA-related materials *<http://NAFTA.net>*
- North American Institute data on trade, environment, socio-cultural issues involving Canada, United States, Mexico *<http://www.santafe.edu/~naminet>*
- North American Integration and Development Center at UCLA tracking NAFTA, investment projects, etc. *<http://naid.sppsr.ucla.edu>*

- Premier social sciences organization of Latin America databases and books from 100 affiliated research centers of 19 Latin American countries <http://www.webcom.com/~clacso>
- PROFMEX information on Mexico in English and Spanish <http://profmexis.sar.net/>
- UN Economic Commission for Latin America social statistics, highly reliable <http://www.eclac.cl>
- University of Texas LANIC gateway to materials on Mexico and other Latin America-related topics and sub-topics <http://www.lanic.utexas.edu>
- University of Texas U.S.-Mexican Policy Studies Program policy reports and papers on current affairs <http://www.utexas.edu/depts/lbj-school/usmex.html>
- U.S.-based National Commission for Democracy in Mexico, for documents of Zapatista EZLN and other Mexican organizations <http://www.igc.apc.org/ncdm/>
- *Weekly News Update on the Americas*, excellent publication covering news on Mexico and other countries—from Nicaragua Solidarity Network of Greater New York, 339 Lafayette St., NY, NY 10012 <home.earthlink.net/~dbwilson/wnuhome.html>
- World Bank publications, e.g., economic reports on Mexico, environmental data sheets, etc. <http://www.worldbank.org>

Index

415